Social Media and the New Academic Environment:

Pedagogical Challenges

Bogdan Pătruţ
Vasile Alecsandri University of Bacău, Romania

Monica Pătruţ
Vasile Alecsandri University of Bacău, Romania

Camelia Cmeciu
Danubius University of Galaţi, Romania

Information Science
REFERENCE

Managing Director:	Lindsay Johnston
Editorial Director:	Joel Gamon
Book Production Manager:	Jennifer Yoder
Publishing Systems Analyst:	Adrienne Freeland
Development Editor:	Myla Merkel
Assistant Acquisitions Editor:	Kayla Wolfe
Typesetter:	Henry Ulrich
Cover Design:	Nick Newcomer

Published in the United States of America by
Information Science Reference (an imprint of IGI Global)
701 E. Chocolate Avenue
Hershey PA 17033
Tel: 717-533-8845
Fax: 717-533-8661
E-mail: cust@igi-global.com
Web site: http://www.igi-global.com

Library of Congress Cataloging-in-Publication Data

Social media and the new academic environment: pedagogical challenges / Bogdan Patrut, Monica Patrut and Camelia Cmeciu, editors.
    pages cm
 Includes bibliographical references and index.
 Summary: "This book provides relevant theoretical frameworks and the latest research on social media challenges in the educational context"--Provided by publisher.
 ISBN 978-1-4666-2851-9 (hbk.) -- ISBN 978-1-4666-2852-6 (ebk.) -- ISBN 978-1-4666-2853-3 (print & perpetual access)
1. Social media. 2. Communication in education. 3. Education--Social aspects. I. Patrut, Bogdan, 1969- II. Patrut, Monica, 1972- III. Cmeciu, Camelia, 1975-
 HM742.S628193 2013
 302.23'1--dc23
                        2012032523

British Cataloguing in Publication Data
A Cataloguing in Publication record for this book is available from the British Library.

All work contributed to this book is new, previously-unpublished material. The views expressed in this book are those of the authors, but not necessarily of the publisher.

Table of Contents

Section 1
Pedagogical Challenges of Social Media in Academia

Section 4
The Impact of Social Media Technologies on the Academic Environment

Detailed Table of Contents

Section 1
Pedagogical Challenges of Social Media in Academia

Chapter 1

> *Charlotte Holland, Dublin City University, Ireland*
> *Miriam Judge, Dublin City University, Ireland*

Higher education' institutions are promoting the integration of online technologies in teaching and learning as an attempt to provide flexible modes of delivery, to diversify the profile of students accessing higher education and to facilitate the development of life-long learning skills. The availability of personal digital devices, such as wireless laptops and mobile phones, and campus-wide Internet connectivity has the potential to enhance or detract from learning in higher education. This chapter explores the trend towards online learning in higher education, examining the potential of and current practices in the integration of Information and Communication Technologies, focusing on the use of Web 2.0 technologies in teaching and learning, and presenting some of the challenges that arise in the integration of online technologies and implementation of Learning 2.0 in higher education.

Chapter 2

> *Derek E. Baird, Facebook for Educators, USA*
> *Mercedes Fisher, Milwaukee Area Technical College, USA*

Investigating the social structure that works in online courses helps us design for and facilitate student collaboration. The integration of social technologies, and collaborative activities into the course design has a positive influence on student retention in online courses. In this chapter, the authors present an exploratory study of computer mediated groups which utilized this collaborative based model to participate in online and/or blended learning courses. Participants were put into groups and observed as they constructed new knowledge using both online dialogue (synchronous and asynchronous), and social media technologies (blogs, Facebook, Twitter, wiki) as tools to support and facilitate their learning in the program.

This chapter addresses the topic of Facebook use in education, with focus on the learning issues concerning the student-faculty relations and communication on this Social Network. Its main purpose is to reveal academics' general and particular attitudes towards the use of Facebook with instructional aim. Therefore, it presents a generous theoretical perspective on the emerging phenomenon of social networks integration on education, in the United States mainly. Further on, it puts side by side these views with the findings of a particular, empirical study conducted by the authors. A survey applied to a sample of Facebook users from "Alexadru Ioan Cuza" University from Iaşi, Romania (N=160) revealed that the academics partially agreed that the use of Facebook is suitable for educational exchanges. Whilst the literature suggested that students have more positive attitudes than faculty towards the use of Facebook in education, this present study doesn't support this view.

In this chapter, the focus falls on integrating mobile learning, digital storytelling, and social media into vocational learning practices. The literature review introduces the development of mobile learning and digital storytelling and presents ways in which these concepts can piggyback the interactive features of social media. A case study during which participating students used mobile phones and videos with a mobile social video application (MoViE) to design and produce representative digital stories based on local tourism attractions is also presented. Twenty-five students participated in the internet inquiry about student attitudes towards the use of social media as part of their vocational expertise and their learning experiences with mobile devices and MoViE. This chapter illustrates the benefits as well as the shortcomings of the used learning concept in order to produce more concrete knowledge of the use of mobile devices and social video applications in learning.

Section 2
Social Media as a Means for Current Education

The purpose of this study is to examine the impact social media has on the development of communities of practice and social development in distance education courses. This study evaluates the effectiveness of the integration of social media tools including Ning in Education (an educational social networking tool), Twitter, and WordPress into three distance education courses in instructional technology. The social media tools are examined to identify the educational and pedagogical benefits each tool affords. Utilizing a mixed-method methodology, student data was collected through a series of three online surveys coupled with student interviews. The pre-/post- data collected as part of this study provides empirically based findings indicating that social media technologies can help support online communities of practice as well as the development of social presence. Data analyzed from student interviews provides data triangulation in addition to a richer and deeper understanding of the pedagogical affordances social media tools provide.

Chapter 6

Bogdan Pătruț, Vasile Alecsandri University of Bacău, Romania
Monica Pătruț, Vasile Alecsandri University of Bacău, Romania
Camelia Cmeciu, Danubius University of Galați, Romania

Schools and universities are not the only providers of knowledge any longer. Other types of organizations have become aware that a solid public-serving reason should lie beyond the firm-serving motive. "Doing well by doing good" has been the syntagm that prevails nowadays in the organizational discourse focused on corporate social responsibility (CSR) campaigns. This chapter has a twofold aim: to highlight two paradigmatic shifts (CSR 1.0 → CSR 2.0 & formal education → non-formal education), and to provide an analysis of the Web 2.0 practices and items ad of the verbal and visual framing devices used in a CSR 2.0 campaign on non-formal financial education. Social media have provided the applications to put into practice the concept of edutainment specific to non-formal education since educators get a multifold identity, being, at the same time generators and receivers of knowledge.

Chapter 7

Ana Adi, Bournemouth University, UK

Beyond influencing the ways we communicate and we do business, social media is currently challenging traditional higher education in many respects: from the way in which courses are delivered and students interact with each other and with their lecturers to the content that the courses cover. In particular, the emergence of the social media specialist working in marketing-communications, creative industries or journalism, and their use of ever-changing content management and analytics tools require adaptation of courses to the constant changes in industry. Starting from two case studies of teaching social media auditing and analytics as part of courses taught in Belgium and Bahrain, this chapter aims to present a model exercise for marketing and public relations classrooms covering these topics. The discussion of the challenges of teaching social media audit and analytics emphasizes the need of more and constant collaboration between academia and industry as well as the need to ensure that students have a high level of media literacy before they embark on such a career route.

Section 3
National Practices of Social Media in Higher Education

Chapter 8

Violeta Maria Şerbu, The Bucharest Academy of Economic Studies, Romania

This chapter aims to explore some critical functions that social media is playing for the internal processes included in an alternative higher education model – The Alternative University, developed in Romania, since 2007. This case study highlights challenges and opportunities associated with using this new communication as well as information technologies in order to generate effective learning environments.

The collaborative and student-centered traits of higher education models using social media for learning activities are mainly treated in our study. Functions such as connecting people, sharing knowledge, collaboratively generating knowledge, community building, management platform, accumulation and construction of knowledge, knowledge assessment, raising learning motivation, personal branding, or networking are identified as important assets of social media for their use in a higher education setting.

Mihai Deac, Babeş-Bolyai University of Cluj-Napoca, Romania
Ioan Hosu, Babeş-Bolyai University of Cluj-Napoca, Romania

There has been much research dedicated to the use of blogs in higher education, but a great deal of its enthusiasm is based on data that have the potential to be distorted by social desirability. The current chapter attempts a more balanced look at the use of educational blogs, taking into account the shortcomings, as well as the benefits of their proliferation amongst students. The authors write from the perspective of the blog users. Although their feedback is mostly positive, user behavior is also affected by fear of peer appraisal, lack of engagement, lack of trust or unwillingness to share knowledge or to debate. In order to support this argumentation, the authors use traffic data from the educational blog "blogdeseminar", survey data from a convenience sample of Romanian students, and qualitative data from 11 interviews.

Chapter 10

María-Jesús Díaz-González, University of A-Coruña, Spain
Natalia Quintas Froufe, University of A-Coruña, Spain
Almudena González del Valle Brena, International University of Rioja (UNIR), Spain
Francesc Pumarola, Expert in Internet issues, Spain

There have been many contributions to scientific literature which have helped develop a theoretical framework in the field of education and Information Technologies. The contributions have come from the educational sciences and from the communication processes and collaboration perspectives. The purpose of this chapter is to make a contribution within the specific scope of university teaching and social media. In order to achieve this objective, a case study methodology was chosen to analyze the use and implementations of social media networks in Spanish Schools of Communication. The parameters used were chosen out of the same social media nature (potential use). The success of social media presence at Schools of Communications must follow an initial plan and a further control and supervision of the plan. The relationship of social media with the university community depends greatly upon the specific community manager's profile and commitment.

Sónia Pedro Sebastião, Technical University of Lisbon, Portugal
& Center for Administration and Public Policies, Portugal

The chapter relates several of the difficulties associated with public relations as an academic subject. Bearing these obstacles in mind, a public relations academic program has been defined, along with, a teaching strategy using web-based social media (blog and facebook profile) to communicate with students. The main purposes of the research are: to understand how university students see public relations as a subject and to ascertain their attitude toward the importance of using web-based communication tools in the assessment of public relations disciplines. The results have shown that students understand that the use of web-social media is important to their academic life and to their relationship with the teacher. Nevertheless, it is also recognized that the use of technological tools must be followed by motivation, interest in the subject of public relations and in general academic work.

Chapter 12

This chapter discussed a research conducted in a university setting which involved 405 undergraduate students. The aim of this research is to determine the relationships between social media and personality traits particularly in identifying the profile of social media adoption among students in Malaysia, including duration, frequency of use, purpose, and person/s that introduced the social media, and determining the relationships between social media and personality traits.

Chapter 13

In recent years, cross-national Web-based teaching projects have become very popular in many fields. During such projects, participants from different countries work together on collaborative tasks. Communications among project participants take place over the Internet, including via social media. In this chapter, the authors report the results of social media use in one such project, which brought together students from the United States and Ukraine. A pre and post project survey taken by the participants demonstrate the main opportunities and challenges afforded by social media to educators. The reporting and analysis of the survey results are preceded by a review of relevant literature, which contextualizes findings.

Chapter 14

Through the lens of an archival theoretical framework, this chapter examines the digital outputs of the use of social media applications by students, faculty and educational institutions, and discusses the need to control and manage their creation, use, maintenance and preservation. The authors draw on a case study that explores the identification, arrangement, description and preservation of students' records produced in an eLearning environment in Singapore and is used as a starting point to highlight and discuss the implications that the use of social media in education can have for the management and preservation of educational institutions' records as evidence of their activity and of students' learning, to fulfill legal and accountability requirements. The authors also discuss how the use of social media by educators in the classroom environment facilitates the creation of records that raise issues of intellectual property and copyright, ownership, and privacy: issues that can further impact their maintenance and preservation.

Section 4
The Impact of Social Media Technologies on the Academic Environment

Chapter 15

Martin Ebner, Graz University of Technology, Austria

In the last few years, microblogging has become a phenomenon of our daily lives. Communicating, sharing media files, as well as acting on digital social communities platforms using mobile devices assist our everyday activities in a complete new way. Therefore, it is very reasonable that academic environments are influenced arbitrarily too. In this publication different settings for the use of microblogging are pointed out – for teaching and learning as well as for further scientific purposes such as professional conferences. It can be summarized that there are different possibilities to use microblogging in an academic context; each of them are new advantages for the academic life. The publication gives a short overview and a first insight into the various ways to use microblogging.

Chapter 16

Gabriela Grosseck, West University of Timisoara, Romania

Carmen Holotescu, Politehnica University of Timisoara/Timsoft, Romania

Bogdan Pătruţ, Vasile Alecsandri University of Bacău, Romania

The Web, as a socio-technical environment, comprises various means of interactions, as well as the social practices related to their use. In the online landscape, structured on four axes of interactions (communication, collaboration, creation, and curation), microblogging is seen as a new social media revolution. Even if this social media instrument has come into use only relatively recently (the first platforms appeared six years ago, in 2006), more and more educators, practitioners, and researchers worldwide are actively involved in finding, testing, and sharing educational uses for microblogging. This chapter introduces the phenomenon of microblogging and presents the most relevant options for educators. The chapter has a descriptive character, and it is structured into two large parts that provide a general-to-specific approach of both theoretical and practical aspects related to the microblogging phenomenon and the impact of microblogs in the educational space.

Chapter 17

Antonella Esposito, University of Milan, Italy

This chapter reports selected findings from a small-scale, exploratory study aiming to provide a snapshot of actual modes of uptake of new digital tools for research purposes. The study consists in an interview project, carried out in a large Italian university and constituted by semi-structured interviews to 14 senior, young, and Doctoral researchers, working in humanities, social sciences, medicine and physics subject areas. Whereas the most popular attitude is a pragmatic and efficiency-driven approach in selecting and using old and new tools, a few isolated profiles of 'digital scholars' emerge, championing the construction of their digital identity along with networked modes of knowledge production and distribution, despite the lack of legitimation of their own research context.

The fixity of knowledge, the accumulation of fix elements of knowledge no longer meets the requirements of nowadays society. The capacity of change, adaptation and constant updating of these elements
according to individual needs, but also to the needs of the various contexts the knowledge must be used,
is a prerequisite of social integration for the graduate. Education stepped into the era of deep reforms
based on new concepts: student-centered learning, informal education, personal learning environment,
stating that to teach means to model and to demonstrate; to learn means to practice and to consider. The
information technology provides to the new student with the learning environemnt he/she needs in the
new context, connects him/her rapidly to the up-to-date information and to the rest of the world. Finding
new ways of recreating student community on the background of the change of the student structure, the
profile of the new student, their interests and individual learning habits on the one hand and the main
challenges of the workforce training/retraining for the current and future information society is the main
concern of this chapter. Due to the spectacular extension of the Internet use, the blog is a solution for the
development of the student community, for social interaction and serves as an alternative or extension
of classroom discourse.

This chapter discusses the impact of using social media resources and new emerging technologies in
teaching and learning processes. The authors are focused in Spanish architecture-education framework,
by analyzing three case studies, carried out by students finishing architecture and building degrees. Students interaction with this resources is assessed, as well as their derived academic results, and the degree
of satisfaction from students and teachers using these resources and technologies. To conduct the study,
authors worked with Web based freeware applications, such as Dropbox, blogging systems, Moodle,
YouTube, Wikipedia, and Google Maps. Mobile devices, such as Smartphones and tablets PCs, were
used to test QR-Codes (Quick Response Codes) and Augmented Reality technology based applications
as Junaio and Ar-Media Plugin.

Chapter 20

This study explores personal and public implications of intense social media dependency. Twenty-five
college students took part in a ten-hour detoxification intervention to experience a day of face-to-face
interaction without access to social media. Qualitative, triangulation research strategies were used in this
empirical study to correlate participants' self-reported experiences with direct observation by trained

moderators. The primary concerns of the study were to discover if digital social-media use inhibits college students' social and intellectual development, potentially limiting their participation in a public, postmodern culture. Their social-media dependency is shown to be inhibiting, but with revocable negative effects, suggesting a continuum of pathological use that educators can help mitigate in the new academic environment of the millennial generation.

Foreword

The book "Social Media and the New Academic Environment: Pedagogical Challenges" is devoted to those really dramatic changes in educational environment, which are caused by the phenomenon of social media. We are all witnesses of the increasing impact of social media upon our studying the surrounding world and, of course and especially – on higher education. It is fully understood that teachers and educational researchers cannot overlook the great popularity of social web technologies, and their increasing professional interest is fully justified. No doubt, many interesting papers on this topic have been submitted to the IGI Global.

Collecting the high quality papers in one book (this book) provides a considerable value for our readers. Firstly, these papers together present a good state-of-the-art picture of the current research on social media affecting academic environment. Secondly, the papers present different points of view on the future development of the educational environment under "pressure" of social media.

The set of papers included in this book is exactly as diverse as we would like the introduction to this research direction to manifest. But of course, the most important and prospective is the fact that the popular social technologies currently explored in some educational environments - such as blogs, wikis, and social tagging - are addressed by more than one paper in this book.

Today it is the time to recognize that Information Technology (IT) is more a social phenomenon rather than a technological one. This recognition appears to be significant for people's everyday social life, and of course for education in particular.

Obviously, education as the most sensitive and updatable sphere of human life requires deep studies of the new phenomenon of integration of social media into it. Due to the rapid development in the field of social media, such studies require wide vision and high qualification of researchers.

The book you read is the one, which demonstrates both the wide vision and the high qualification of the authors. It comprises a variety of points of view on the problem, it gives analysis of the present condition of social media in formal and informal education, and it foresees future tendencies and includes some real cases.

In a nutshell, the research works presented in the book can be briefly divided into two types: (a) integration of social media into the existing academic environment; (b) moving to a new social academic environment which would be originally integrated with social media.

Researches of both of the types are very important for teachers and scientists from the theoretical and practical points of view.

More specifically, the book comprises works distributed in four sections.

Issues concerning the new social pedagogy are covered by a group of four papers under the title "Pedagogical Challenges of Social Media in Academia". These papers deal with: (a) collaboration between faculty and students on the basis of Facebook; (b) mobile learning for vocational education; (c) social design and (d) "learning-2.0" in high school.

The section "Social Media as a Means for Current Education" is devoted to the papers that deal with integration of the social media into the recent (existing) educational environment. They study actual problems we feel today in the educational field, for example: impact of social media on the development of communities, changes in corporate social responsibility focused on informal education when moving to the Web 2.0, adaptation of social media based courses to the constant changes in industry.

A number of case studies of integration and using the social media in educational institutes are presented in section "National Practices of Social Media in Higher Education". They show examples and results of educational use of social media in different countries: Romania, Spain, Portugal, Malaysia, Ukraine, USA, and Singapore – countries with different educational systems and cultural traditions. The case studies are no doubt of a great interest for practitioners and scientists in the educational field.

A new academic social educational environment that is replacing the traditional learning environment is the focus of the section entitled "The Impact of Social Media Technologies on the Academic Environment". The papers from this section mostly speak about social media technologies such as: educational blogging, intensive data communication and Augmented Reality. I would like to emphasize however, that there might be many other possibilities, which may be seen as combinations or developments of the described ones.

The above notes a number of reasons to read the presented material, since it has everything to inspire specialists. And I am sure, some new surprising aspects and versions of the modern educational environments are expected to appear after the presented book becomes familiar to the practitioners and scientists in the field.

Further, it is my opinion that the publishing of this book is a significant step in presenting the subject "social media in education" as a serious academic discipline, which requires intensive study in the coming years.

Ilya Levin
Head of the Department of Mathematics, Science and Technology Education, School of Education,
*   Tel Aviv University, Israel*

Preface

The book "Social Media and the New Academic Environment: Pedagogical Challenges" addresses all those who want to know, to continue and enrich the research on the implications of social media in higher education. Based on the idea that social media radically transforms the environment in which university students and professors interact, in the teaching-learning process, but also in the field of scientific research, this book aims at presenting the latest achievements, studies, discoveries, national practices related to social media use in the academic environment.

This work provides researchers, teachers, students, Master's, and Doctoral candidates, as well as developers of technological solutions in social media, with working tools and analyses of the impact of social networks, microblogging, and other instruments upon the modern academic environment. Using Web 2.0 technologies, higher education enjoys unprecedented pedagogical challenges. The way students communicate with each other or with their teachers, how they learn, and the way in which contents are provided to learners are undergoing significant transformations due to the Web 2.0.

Are we witnessing today a new pedagogical paradigm? Can we talk about Pedagogy 2.0 or is it all just an embellishment of the traditional educational paradigms? Do social media have real implications in the educational field, or are they just a set of tools meant to entertain the participants? Are there any clear cases of successful use of social media in higher education? If yes, then what are the results? These are just some of the questions that contemporary researchers try to answer. These researchers approach the educational aspects of social media from various perspectives, depending on their experience, as well as their training and field of expertise. This work is a collection of papers written by a group of senior and young researchers, from various parts of the world, belonging to various cultures and educational environments. The general conclusion is that social media can have an impact upon the educational academic environment, and this phenomenon is worthy of further research.

The book is structured in four sections. The first section approaches pedagogical challenges of social media in academia. Chapter 1, authored by Charlotte Holland and Miriam Judge from Dublin City University, Ireland, deals with Future Learning Spaces, specifically with The Potential and Practice of Learning 2.0 in Higher Education. How Social Design Influences Student Retention and Self-Motivation in Online Learning Environments is the topic of Chapter 2, written by the American Professors Derek Baird and Mercedes Fisher.

Chapter 3 (L. Șoitu & L. Păuleț-Crainiceanu) addresses the topic of Facebook use in education, with focus on the learning issues concerning the student-faculty relations and communication on this Social Network. In Chapter 4, the focus falls on integrating mobile learning, digital storytelling and social media into vocational learning practices. A case study during which participating students used mobile phones and videos with a mobile social video application (MoViE) to design and produce representative digital stories based on local tourism attractions is also presented. The study belongs to the Finnish researchers Miikka Eriksson and Hanna Vuojärvi from the University of Lapland, and Pauliina Tuomi, from Tampere University of Technology.

The second section of the book is entitled *Social Media as a Means for Current Education*. The purpose of the study from Chapter 5 (L Holcomb & M. Krüger-Ross) was to examine the impact social media have on the development of communities, of practice and social development in distance education courses. This study evaluated the effectiveness of the integration of social media tools including Ning in Education (an educational social networking tool), Twitter, and WordPress into three distance education courses in instructional technology.

Chapter 6, authored by the editors of this book (Bogdan Pătruţ, Monica-Paulina Pătruţ, and Camelia-Mihaela Cmeciu), is entitled *Framing Non-Formal Education through CSR 2.0*. This chapter has a two-fold aim: to highlight two paradigmatic shifts (CSR 1.0 → CSR 2.0 & formal education → non-formal education); to provide an analysis of the Web 2.0 practices and items and of the verbal and visual framing devices used in a CSR 2.0 campaign on non-formal financial education. Chapter 7 approaches Social Media Audit and Analytics. It presents exercises for marketing and public relations courses, based on the experience of Ana Adi from Bournemouth University, UK.

The third section of the book is called *National Practices of Social Media in Higher Education*. Chapter 8 presents a case study on the functions of Social Media in Higher Education, providing an interesting case study (Alternative University) written by the young researcher Violeta Maria Şerbu.

The focus of Chapter 9 (M. Deac and I. Hosu) is upon the *Users' Perspective on Academic Blogging*. It includes a case-study on a Romanian group of students. Chapter 10 is the work of researchers María-Jesús Díaz-González and Natalia Quintas Froufe from the University of A-Coruña, Spain, Almudena González del Valle Brena (Bureau Veritas Business School, Spain) and Francesc Pumarola, expert in Internet issues. Chapter 10 is entitled *Uses and Implementation of Social Media at University* and consists of a case study of the Schools of Communication in Spain. The success of social media presence at Schools of Communication must follow an initial plan and a further control and supervision of the plan. The relationship of social media with the university community depends greatly upon the specific community manager's profile and commitment.

Chapter 11 (Sónia Pedro Sebastião) presents a Portuguese illustration on web use in public relations education. The main purposes of the research are: to understand how university students see public relations as a subject and to ascertain their attitude toward the importance of using web-based communication tools in the assessment of public relations disciplines. Chapter 12 is a study conducted in Malaysia on social media usage among university students. The aim of this research, conducted by Doctor Norsiah Abdul Hamid and her collaborators, is to determine the relationships between social media and personality traits particularly in identifying the profile of social media adoption among students in Malaysia, including duration, frequency of use, purpose, and person/s that introduced the social media, and determining the relationships between social media and personality traits.

The title of chapter 13 is *Social Media and other Web 2.0 Technologies as Communication Channels in a Cross-Cultural, Web-Based Professional Communication Project*. This chapter is a report of the results of social media use in one such project, which brought together students from the United States and Ukraine. Pavel Zemliansky from the University of Central Florida and Olena Goroshko from The National Technical University: Kharkiv Polytechnic Institute, Ukraine, are the authors of this interesting chapter.

Professors Luciana Duranti and Elizabeth Shaffer (University of British Columbia, Canada) are the authors of Chapter 14, that aims at answering the question *Are There Any to Manage the Learning Records:? If so, How?* The authors draw on a case study that explores the identification, arrangement, description and preservation of students' records produced in an eLearning environment in Singapore and is used as a starting point to highlight and discuss the implications that the use of social media in education can have for the management and preservation of educational institutions' records as evidence of their activity and of students' learning, to fulfill legal and accountability requirements.

The last section, *The Impact of Social Media Technologies on the Academic Environment* includes the last 5 chapters. Chapter 15, *The Influence of Twitter on the Academic Environment* focuses on microblogging as a phenomenon of our daily lives. Martin Ebner, from Graz University of Technology, gives a short overview and some challenging insights into the various ways of using microblogging.

Chapter 16 (Gabriela Grosseck, Carmen Holotescu, and Bogdan Pătruț) introduces the phenomenon of microblogging and presents the most relevant options for educators. The chapter has a descriptive character, and is structured into two large parts that provide a general-to-specific approach of both theoretical and practical aspects related to the microblogging phenomenon and the impact of microblogs in the educational space.

Chapter 17 reports selected findings from a small-scale, exploratory study, aiming to provide a 'snapshot' of actual modes of uptaking new digital tools for research purposes. The study consists in an interview project, carried out in a large Italian university and constituted by semi-structured interviews to 14 senior, young and doctoral researchers, working in the fields of Humanities, Social Sciences, Medicine and Physics. The chapter is written by Antonella Esposito, University of Milan.

Chapter 18 (R. Vasilescu et al.) deals with the topic of *Digital Literacy for Effective Communication in the New Academic Environment: The Educational Blogs*. In Chapter 19, the researchers Ernest Redondo, Isidro Navarro, Albert Sánchez, and David Fonseca, from Barcelona, discuss the impact of using social media resources and new emerging technologies in teaching and learning processes. It focuses on Spanish architecture-education framework, by analyzing three case studies, conducted by students finishing architecture and building degrees. Students' interaction with these resources is assessed, as well as their derived academic results, and the degree of satisfaction from students and teachers using these resources and technologies.

Chapter 20, written by Professor Theresa Renee White (California State University, Northridge) focuses on Digital Social Media Detox (DSMD). This study explores personal and public implications of intense social media dependency. Twenty-five college students took part in a ten-hour detoxification intervention to experience a day of face-to-face interaction without access to social media. Qualitative triangulation research strategies were used in this empirical study to correlate participants' self-reported experiences with direct observation by trained moderators. The primary concerns of the study were to discover if digital social-media use inhibits college students' social and intellectual development, potentially limiting their participation in a public, postmodern culture. Their social-media dependency is shown to be inhibiting, but with revocable negative effects, suggesting a continuum of pathological use that educators can help mitigate in the new academic environment of the millennial generation.

We are convinced of the usefulness of this book and we look forward to any kind of feedback from readers.

Bogdan Pătruț
Vasile Alecsandri University of Bacău, Romania

Monica Pătruț
Vasile Alecsandri University of Bacău, Romania

Camelia Cmeciu
Danubius University of Galați, Romania

August, 14, 2012

Acknowledgment

We wish to personally thank all the authors of this book and, also, the following people for their contributions in reviewing the chapters and other help in creating this book:

- Adrian Adăscăliței (Gh. Asachi Tehnical University of Iasi, Romania);
- Adrian Runceanu (Constantin Brâncuși University of Targu Jiu, Romania);
- Anca Velicu (Institute of Sociology, Romanian Academy. Romania);
- Andrei Gaitanaru (National School of Political Studies and Public Administration, Romania);
- Andrei Kojukhov (Tel-Aviv University, Israel);
- Angelica Hobjila (Alexandru Ioan Cuza University of Iasi, Romania);
- Anita Grigoriu (Spiru Haret University, Romania);
- Anita Howarth (Kingston University London, UK);
- Anna Heudorfer (University of Augsburg, Germany);
- Aránzazu Román San Miguel University of Seville, Spain);
- Aurora-Adina Ignat (Ștefan cel Mare University of Suceava, Romania);
- Aykut Arikan (Yeditepe University, Istanbul, Turkey)
- Bianca Marina Mitu (University of Westminster, UK & University of Bucharest, Romania);
- Bogdan Nadolu (West University of Timisoara, Romania);
- Can Bilgili (Yeditepe University, Istanbul, Turkey);
- Christina Gasser Scotte (University of Wyoming, USA);
- Cosmin Herman (Moodle, Romania);
- Cristiana Cătălina Cicei (National School of Political Studies & Public Administration, Romania);
- David Mathew (University of Bedfordshire, UK);
- Domenico Consoli (University of Urbino, Italia);
- Dorin Bocu (Transilvania University of Brașov, Romania);
- Elena-Mădălina Vătămănescu (National School of Political Studies & Public Administration, Romania);
- Ersin Erkan (Yeditepe University, Istanbul, Turkey);
- Gabriela Oana Olaru (Yeditepe University, Turkey);
- Gemma Martínez Fernández (The University of the Basque Country, Spain)
- Georgeta Drulă (University of Bucharest, Romania);
- Hüseyin Kınay (Fatih University, Turkey);
- Ilya Levin (Tel-Aviv University, Israel);
- Ioana Boghian (Vasile Alecsandri University of Bacau, Romania);

- Ioan-Lucian Popa (Vasile Alecsandri University of Bacau, Romania).
- Iulian Furdu (Vasile Alecsandri University of Bacau, Romania);
- Katherine Landau (Harmony Science Academy, Texas, USA);
- Liliana Mata (Vasile Alecsandri University of Bacau, Romania);
- Liliana Ursache (Ferdinand I National College, Bacau, Romania);
- Mar Camacho (Universitat Rovira i Virgili, Spain);
- Maree Gruppetta (University of Newcastle, Australia);
- Terry Mason (University of Western Sydney, Australia);
- Maria Lazăr (Alexandru Ioan Cuza University of Iasi, Romania);
- Marie-Luise Gross (SAP AG / University of Vienna, Austria);
- Marin Vlada (University of Bucharest, Romania);
- Marius Călin Popoiu (University of Medicine & Pharmacy Victor Babes Timisoara, Romania);
- Matthew J. Kruger-Ross (North Carolina State University, USA);
- Mădălina Manolache (Europe Direct Bacău Information Centre, Romania);
- Myla Merkel (IGI Global, USA);
- Narelle Lemon (RMIT University, Australia);
- Nicoleta Laura Popa (Alexandru Ioan Cuza University of Iasi, Romania);
- Osman Tolga Arıcak (Fatih University, Turkey);
- Otilia Clipa (Ştefan cel Mare University of Suceava, Romania);
- P. Sol Hart (American University, USA);
- Parvaneh Khosravizadeh (Sharif University of Technology, Tehran, Iran);
- Raluca Moise (University of Bucharest, Romania);
- Răzvan Bocu (Transilvania University of Braşov, Romania);
- Rick Kenney (Florida Gulf Coast University, USA);
- Rocío Alcántara López (University of Seville, Spain);
- Sandra Hofhues (Hamburg University of Applied Sciences, Germany),
- Sara Konnerth (Lucian Blaga University of Sibiu, Romania);
- Scott Talan (American University, USA);
- Sinem Siyahhan (Arizona State University, USA);
- Taşkın Tanrıkulu (Fatih University, Turkey);
- Theodosios Tsiakis (Alexadrian Technological Educational Institute of Thessaloniki, Greece);
- Timea Kabai (Ioan Slavici National College, Romania);
- Ufuk Ozgul (Yeditepe University, Istanbul, Turkey);
- Valentina Marinescu (University of Bucharest, Romania);
- Vladimir-Aurelian Enăchescu (Academy of Economic Studies, Romania).

Section 1
Pedagogical Challenges of Social Media in Academia

Chapter 1
Future Learning Spaces:
The Potential and Practice of Learning 2.0 in Higher Education

Charlotte Holland
Dublin City University, Ireland

Miriam Judge
Dublin City University, Ireland

ABSTRACT

Higher education institutions are promoting the integration of online technologies in teaching and learning as an attempt to provide flexible modes of delivery, to diversify the profile of students accessing higher education and to facilitate the development of life-long learning skills. The availability of personal digital devices, such as wireless laptops and mobile phones, and campus-wide Internet connectivity has the potential to enhance or detract from learning in higher education. This chapter explores the trend towards online learning in higher education, examining the potential of and current practices in the integration of Information and Communication Technologies, focusing on the use of Web 2.0 technologies in teaching and learning, and presenting some of the challenges that arise in the integration of online technologies and implementation of Learning 2.0 in higher education.

INTRODUCTION

ICT are key enablers for creating future learning spaces, although they are not the sole drivers. (Punie & Ala-Mutka, 2007, p.213)

The traditional notion of what constitutes learning spaces in higher education evokes images of lecture halls, chalkboards and lecture-dominated instruction for many. Teaching and learning processes and practices in higher education are evolving from this didactical institutional model towards a student-centered, active learning model. According to Ituma (2011), this shift towards a student-centered learning model is being facilitated by the integration of online learning in higher education' institutions.

Punie & Ala-Mutka (2007) present a vision of future learning spaces that integrate Information and Communication Technologies (ICTs) to enable

DOI: 10.4018/978-1-4666-2851-9.ch001

personal digital spaces for learners and educators, to connect the community of learners and to enable individual and collective knowledge construction and transformation. ICTs are critical in providing access to multiple perspectives, facilities to promote reflexivity, opportunities to rate, recommend or certify contributions from members of the learning community, and to motivate learners. They also can support the inclusion of learners of all ages with varying abilities, learning styles and learning preferences, as well as those from socio-economic disadvantaged backgrounds or with special needs. Online technologies in particular are perceived as a means to reduce costs whilst providing greater access and flexibility in the service of education.

Higher education institutions are promoting the integration of online technologies in teaching and learning in an attempt to provide flexible modes of delivery, to diversify the profile of students accessing higher education and to facilitate the development of life-long learning skills. This chapter explores the trend towards online learning in higher education, examining the potential of and current practices in the integration of ICTs. It focuses on the use of Web 2.0 technologies in teaching and learning, and presents some of the challenges that arise in integrating online technologies and implementing Learning 2.0 in higher education.

Trends in Online Education in Higher Education

Graetz (2006) commented that "campuses can expect the boundaries between virtual and brick-and-mortar learning environments to continue to blur" (p.72). The availability of personal digital devices, such as wireless laptops and mobile phones, and campus-wide Internet connectivity has the potential to enhance or detract from learning in higher education. In a report on the future of online teaching and learning in higher education, Kim & Bonk (2006) reported that

"online learning environments are now facing a "perfect e-storm," linking pedagogy, technology and learner needs" (p.22). The quality of learning and the creation of a meaningful learning experience must be central to the deployment of online technologies in higher education. Social media applications widely available on the Internet need to be carefully harnessed within face-to-face and online settings to engage learners individually and collaboratively in meaningful learning experiences and processes in higher education.

Courses within higher education are now delivered primarily in one or more of three modes, namely, face-to-face, blended and/ or online. The Sloan Report (Allen & Seaman, 2011, p.7) summarises each of these modes as follows:

- Face-to-face course delivery where up to 29% of the course may be delivered online. Thus, either no online technology is used in the delivery or communication of the course or web-based technologies (such as course management systems) are used as a basic repository for the course material.
- Blended course delivery where between 30-79% of the course learning is offered online, with the remainder being offered face-to-face. Blended learning offers a high degree of online engagement, through facilities such as discussion forums.
- Online course delivery offers a more immersed online experience, with at least 80% of the course content provided. Typically there is little or no face-to-face interaction.

Within institutions of Higher Education, there is varying levels of acceptance of the value and legitimacy of online education among management, staff and students. However, the move towards online education is very high in the United States. According to the Sloan 2011 Online Education Report (Allen & Seaman, 2011, p.8), online education is increasingly being rated by chief academic leaders as critical to the long-term strategy of institutions engaged in Higher Education in the United States (US). Furthermore, the number of students in the US taking at least one online course has increased from circa 1.9 million in 2003 to over 6 million in 2010. This represents 31% of the overall total enrolment of students in degree granting institutions (Allen & Seaman, 2011 p. 11).

The trend towards online education is less visible within the European Union. Redecker, Ala-Mutka & Punie (2010) noted in a review of the Eurostat 2008 & 2009 data that typically only 5% of Europeans used the Internet to engage in an online course. An average of 31% of Europeans aged between 16 and 74 search the internet for information related to learning. Other data from Eurostat, highlighted by Redecker et al. (2010), provide evidence that Web 2.0 technologies are increasingly being used to create or share online content through tools such as file-sharing, email, chat and/ or discussion forums.

An investigation into the role of technology in shaping learning in higher education by the Economist Intelligence Unit (ECI) in 2008, noted that technology would continue to have an impact in higher education, particularly in relation to changing teaching methodologies, and that online learning provision would continue to increase. It also highlighted that the integration of mobile technologies within higher education would bring the challenges of "plagiarism, cheating and distractibility" (ECI, 2008, p.4). Graetz (2006) also raised the issue of learners becoming distracted by social media, such as e-mail, instant messaging, or social networking sites like Facebook, within face-to-face lectures. He commented that learners may use lecture time to respond to or personalize their social media profiles or posts and re-engage with the face-to-face lecture only when motivated by information about their assignments for example.

In this respect social media and networking technologies present a challenge for educators as such tools can be considered a form of distraction or a form of motivation in higher education. If viewed as a form of distraction, then policies and other types of controls (disconnection or blocking of Internet access) that limit their use would need to be implemented. However, if viewed as a form of motivation, then educators must re-think the use and integration of social media and social networking technologies in face-to-face and online environments so as to facilitate greater learner autonomy, increased collaboration and more active student engagement with online learning opportunities.

Web 2.0 Technologies

Information and Communications Technologies (ICTs) are technologies used to store, transmit, create, transform and communicate information. In the 1990s, millions of hyperlinked web-pages, which became known as the World Wide Web, were launched using Web 1.0 internet technology. Often referred to as the 'read only' web, internet users at that time mainly used the web to browse and download information from web-pages uploaded by various providers. At the turn of the 21st century, a suite of Internet applications, more commonly referred to as Web 2.0 technologies or social media was released. This expanded the web's capability and allowed users to individually and collaboratively edit, communicate, create, rate and upload online content. Neil Selwyn (2008) notes that Web 2.0 or the read/write web as it is often called, advances on Web 1.0 technologies by facilitating: "'interactive' rather than 'broadcast' forms of exchange, in which information is shared 'many-to-many' rather than being transmitted from one to many" (p.4). Web 2.0 technologies are thus social media that enable the widespread uploading of individual user content, leading to new forms of collaboration and participation in the sharing and tagging of this content.

Web 2.0 technologies allow users greater autonomy to individually and/or collectively upload, edit and annotate (categorise, label and rate) online content in a participatory manner on a massive scale – allowing users "to share and rate, mash-up and re-mix, friend and trend" (Selwyn, 2012, p.1). The utilization of these technologies in learning can bring many benefits for learners including: expression of learners' voice, exposure to multiple perspectives, and the ability to access, share and contribute to the collective classification and rating of information and knowledge. Thus, Web 2.0 technologies can be perceived as increasing the voice and presence of the individual user and enhancing the expression of collective 'intelligence' in the online setting.

Web 2.0 technologies essentially have facilitated the decentralization of web communication, content creation and publication. Web 2.0 activities have been categorised by Crook et al (2008 pp.9-15) to include: Media Sharing, Media Manipulation, Mash-ups, Discussion arenas, Online games and Virtual worlds, Social networking, Blogging, Social bookmarking, Online surveys, Rating systems, Collaborative editing, Wikis and Syndication. Furthermore, Crook et al (ibid) identified activities commonly undertaken by users within these categories, which have been outlined as follows:

- **Media Sharing and Manipulation:** Users upload or download digital media, such as videos, music, images, audio, slideshows and sketches. Commonly used web applications such as You-tube, Flickr, Slideshare and Sketchful support media sharing. Users can also edit, combine or mash-up various media files (including Podcasts) using web applications such as Splashup, Toondoo, Gifup, Voice thread, Makeinternettv or Popfly.
- **Discussion Arenas:** Discussions can take place in real-time using Instant Messaging Services or online applications like Skype, or can take place offline using forums where users post or respond to contributions.
- **Online Games and Virtual Worlds:** Users can interact with other users in online games or participate in immersed are-

nas within virtual worlds such as Second Life. In some cases, users create their own online persona in the form of an avatar.
- **Social Networking:** There are web applications that facilitate social interaction and sharing of media between members of a special interest group or friends. Some common examples of social networking sites include LinkedIn (Business oriented sharing of CVs), Facebook (Connecting Family/ Friends), MySpace (Oriented towards media sharing).
- **Blogging:** This is a web application that supports journal or diary writing, which can be made public or private. Twitter is an example of a micro-blog in that it allows users to 'tweet short messages (up to 140 characters) about a particular topic. Others like Tumblr allow for sharing of multimedia blogs.
- **Social Bookmarking:** This is a web application that allows users to comment or annotate text, images or other forms of media available online, and then share this information with other users. This personal tagging or 'folksonomy' can be facilitated through web applications such as Diigo and Del.icio.us.
- **Online Surveys:** These are web applications such as Surveymonkey that allow for the deployment of surveys across a wide range of users, and the collation of the results in various forms.
- **Rating Systems:** These are web applications that allow users to vote or rate items, (such as news articles that are prioritized for publication using Digg) or on services from professionals (such as Teachers using ratemyteacher).
- **Collaborative Editing:** These are web applications like Googledocs that allow multiple users to design, develop, edit and publish digital content.

- **Wikis:** These are web applications that allow open access to users to create, edit and publish pages. Wikipedia is the most well-known wiki.
- **Syndication:** Real Simple Syndication is a facility that updates users on changes or updates to website content in regular news feeds.

New Literacies, Connectivism, and ICT-Enabled Learning in Higher Education

We are living in a networked society, increasingly being facilitated by Internet or web-based technologies. The Internet has revolutionised communication between human beings – it connects people and allows for transfer and transformation of knowledge. Educators within this ICT-enabled networked society should recognise that collective learning and collective intelligence is highly valued, that access to this knowledge or intelligence is more open, and that space and time boundaries imposed in traditional formal educational structures have been removed (Cornu, 2007). Furthermore, educators and learners need to be made aware that inclusive decision-making and communication is critical to effectively harness this medium in order to foster creative, interactive and democratic learning spaces within the ICT-enabled networked society.

There is no doubt that being able to access and use information and communication technologies are critical to functioning in a post-modern world. The notion of literacy has been expanded beyond the three R's – Reading, Writing and Arithmetic – to include technological or 'digital' literacy. Lankshear, Gee, Knobel and Searle (1997, p.141) perceive 'technological literacies' as social practices in which texts are constructed, communicated, shared and transformed through the use of technologies. This multi-dimensional concept of literacy is no longer solely aligned with an ability to read, understand or produce 'print'based text, graphs or diagrams. Instead, literacy is assessed and valued on the ability to individually and collaboratively search, interact with, create and critique web-based and print materials within multiple and diverse contexts. It is therefore important that educators and learners in higher education have acquired the necessary literacies and skills to interact with new technologies and can utilise them to create and engage in meaningful learning experiences that enable social praxis.

Siemens (2005, p.8) presents a theory of learning for the digital age called "connectivism" based on a "collective-centered" rather than a 'learner-centered' learning. He argues that "know-how and know-what are being supplemented with know-where" i.e. the ability to find the knowledge needed. According to Simoes and Borges-Gouveia (2008) this emerging theory differs from that of classical 'connectivism' in that it perceives knowledge as being distributed dynamically through networks of people and appliances (database/ community/ network), rather than solely being distributed within an individual's brain. Punie & Ala-Mutka (2007, p.212) note that "knowing where knowledge is located and who has access to various kinds of knowledge and why, is becoming more important in this networked society." They also highlight that to capitalize on Web 2.0 technologies within the knowledge economy, digital competence, and thus digital literacies, must include development of "social skills and 'relationship capital'. Thus, there is a need for new pedagogies (or the refinement of existing pedagogies at the very least) that allow for the meaningful development and integration of new literacies required for ICT-enabled learning environments within higher education.

ICTs can be used to "extend human capacity to perceive, understand and communicate" (Paas, 2008, p.4). For educators in higher education, it also creates new challenges in terms of developing: new pedagogies (particularly in fostering individual and collective intelligence); new teaching and learning approaches (particularly focused on individual, cooperative and collaborative learning opportunities); new resources through the manipulation or creation of digital materials; new tools for learning through the use of interactive, multi-media self-assessment tools for example; and new skills in the management of time and space within a virtual teaching and learning environment.

Learning 2.0: Web 2.0-Enabled Pedagogy in Higher Education

Learning is a social process involving learners and their peers, teachers, family and the community actively engaging in the construction and transformation of information and knowledge. ICTs, particularly Web 2.0 technologies, have the potential to connect these partners in the learning process in a dynamic, flexible and interactive manner allowing for the social construction of knowledge and the transformation of learning for the individual learner. Punie & Ala-Mutka (2007, p.191) referring to the integration of ICTs in education comment: "Learning spaces are not instructorless computer-generated spaces without interaction and community building." The role of the educational practitioner needs to move, as outlined by King (1993), from being 'sage on the stage' (a dispenser of information and primary source of knowledge) to 'guide on the side' (a facilitator of knowledge construction and transformation). This role of facilitator requires that educational practitioners are familiar and comfortable with the use and creation of inclusive ICT-enabled learning environments that meet the learning needs and preferences of individual learners.

Learning is a 'process of becoming' for the individual learner. This 'process of becoming' has admittedly been poorly mediated in the past with the deployment of didactic teaching methodologies and an emphasis on a body of knowledge that had to be 'learnt' as the dominant form of educational strategy. However, in the 20th century more enlightened approaches to teaching and learning, promoted by educationalists such as Dewey, Mezirow and Friere, have embodied the need for participatory, democratic, collaborative, active and transformative approaches in teaching and learning. Web 2.0 technologies can be effectively harnessed to support these constructivist and transformative learning environments; enabling collaborative engagement in authentic learning situations, reflective practice and sharing of learners' knowledge and experience.

Redecker et al., (2010, p.8) suggest that the integration of Web 2.0 in teaching and learning, heretofore referred to as Learning 2.0, can lead to innovation in four different dimensions: Content, Creation, Connecting and Collaboration. Learners can access a diversity of learning content using social media technologies, offering multiple perspectives and content in multiple formats (such as audio, video, simulation, animation). This access, according to Redecker et al (2010), contributes to equity and inclusion within the learning environment. Learners can create digital content using social media, which can be shared by the community of learners. Learners can connect and thus communicate in a seamless manner with peers, teachers, experts and other members of the learning community using social media technologies. Learners can collaborate with peers and other members of the learning community, through the use of social annotation applications, wikis and other tools. More broadly, Learning 2.0 allows for more interactive, dynamic, empowering, participatory, individualized and collaborative learning opportunities. Learning 2.0 can be used to enhance the learning experience, by empowering teachers and learners to "discover new ways of actively and creatively developing their individual competences" (Redecker et al, 2010, p.9). It can support lifelong learning and promote equity and active citizenship among those who have been traditionally marginalized in society.

Web 2.0 technologies therefore can play a pivotal role in providing collaboration, access to and communication of information and knowledge in the field of higher education. Garrison, Anderson and Archer (2000) point out the need for a cognitive presence, a social presence and a teaching presence in facilitating a cognitive experience in an online setting. Learners in higher education need to examine individual perspectives, generational and inter-generational perspectives, interdisciplinary perspectives, inter-cultural perspectives and historical perspectives. The opportunities to gain access to multiple perspectives, to provide personalised accounts, reflections and peer review are many and varied on the Internet with the development of Web 2.0 facilities such as: Social networking sites (Facebook, Myspace etc.), Weblogs or blogs (online diaries), Podcasts (audio-clips or testimonies), Wikis (websites that allows users to collectively create and edit content), Instant Messaging services (such as MSN), Real Simple Syndication or RSS (transmitting and updating information feeds such as news), and Twitter (short information feeds).

Furthermore, as Garrison et al. (2000) previously highlighted, there needs to be a teaching presence within the online learning environment; educators need to actively facilitate the process of learning through moderation of learning content, teaching and learning strategies and social interaction. The challenges in providing online support and online moderation include low levels of digital literacy among participants, poor online communication strategies and the lack of social cues that would be present in a face-to-face setting. In a study of approaches in e-moderation within a higher education setting, Vlachopoulas and Cowan (2010) found that e-moderators adopted six different types of interventions when mediating online interaction. These were labeled as follows: One-track mind, Top of the list, Going the second mile, Critical friend, Balancing priorities and Rescuing. One-track mind involved the e-moderator prompting the participants to work towards meeting the learning outcomes; Top of the list involved the moderator encouraging the participant to prioritise what needed to be done.

Going the second mile involved the e-moderator encouraging specific learners to extend their learning beyond the task being undertaken. Critical friend involved the moderator developing a collegial relationship with learners. Balancing priorities involved the e-moderator re-directing learners towards an important aspect of the task that has not been attended or poorly addressed. Rescuing involves the e-moderator encouraging learners to reconsider work that is of a low standard or insufficiently addresses the intended learning outcomes. The identification of these approaches highlights the complexities inherent in e-moderation and point to the need for specialized training for those who intend to tutor within an online context.

Web 2.0 Technologies in Higher Education: A Review of Research

There is a dearth of large-scale, longitudinal studies focusing on the integration of multiple social media tools in Higher Education and as argued by Meyer (2010) and Crook et al (2008) there is a need for more empirical studies on the educational use, adoption and effectiveness of Web 2.0 in higher education. A recent review of the literature on social media in higher education by Davis III, Deil-Amen, Rios-Aguilar, & González Canché (2012, p.24) further highlighted the lack of research on the impact of social media technologies on student achievement and attainment outcomes. However a number of individual studies in different jurisdictions provide some insight into how and to what effect social networking tools are being deployed higher education.

Crook et al. (2008, p.51) reported overall a low integration of Web 2.0 technologies in Higher Education in the United Kingdom. However, where social media have been successfully integrated (usually by linking online engagement with assessment), blogs and wikis and to a lesser extent Podcasts have been utilized the most. In the United States a study by Cassidy et al. (2011) on popular internet and communication technology usage among undergraduate students across the library service at a US University, revealed a high degree of interest in technologies, such as Mobile phones, Podcasts, Chat and/or Instant Messaging. However a low percentage of students indicated use of or interest in library services utilizing Twitter, RSS feeds or Second Life. Nonetheless a higher than expected number of students requested the integration of Facebook and Youtube videos within the Library service. In their review of the educational use of social annotation tools in higher education. Novak, Razzouk & Johnson (2012), reported that the use of collaborative web applications or social annotation tools which allow students to collaboratively review and comment on readings and other resources is still limited. Nonetheless, the use of Web 2.0 applications, like Delicious.com, that allows for the social tagging and bookmarking of learning resources has been shown to be effective in small scale studies, such as that undertaken by Farwell & Waters (2010).

In a study of emerging web technologies in higher education, Saeed, Yang and Sinnappan (2009, p.106) found there were correlations between Web 2.0 technology preferences and various learner styles. The findings indicated that those with a 'sensor' style of learning (tend to be more careful and detailed) prefer to rely on email rather than instant messaging, blogging or using wikis; those with an 'intuitor' style of learning (like to discover for themselves) preferred blogging to using email or course management systems; those with a 'visual' style of learning (stimulated by images, diagrams, flowcharts, photo graphs, animation) preferred vodcasts; those with a 'sequential' style of learning (like to follow a logical sequence) preferred podcasts (audio recordings of lectures). Saeed et al. (2009) also found that participants preferred to use both synchronous and asynchronous forms of communication. When the read/write web first emerged tools such as wikis, blogs and podcasts caught the imagination of innovative educators and as the read/write web

evolved the communication potential of social networking tools such as facebook, myspace and twitter began to register on the academic radar. The remainder of this section will discuss key research findings on the deployment of these web 2.0 tools in higher education.

Wikis, Blogs, and Podcasts

Wikis have been reported as the social media tools of choice in many institutions (Crook et al, 2008). A study comparing wikis with online forums, undertaken within the Open University in the United Kingdom by Kear, Woodthorpe, Robertson & Hutchison (2010), found that students and tutors valued the collaborative capabilities of wikis but highlighted usability and sociability issues. They found that wikis (at that point in time) were more difficult and slower to use than forums, and that collaborative tools, like wikis, needed to 'be robust and responsive, and to exhibit good usability' (Kear et al, 2010, p.223). Kear et al.'s (2010) study also highlighted students' concerns in relation to editing each others' work within the wiki, which align with Allwardt's (2011, p.602) findings of a lack of 'meaningful peer critiques' of contributions within wikis. Kear et al. (2010) further pointed to the need for a 'cultural shift' in the mindset of students to understand the roles, norms and etiquette of wiki engagement, particularly with regard to ownership of contributions and sociability. A case study by Ruyters, Douglas & Law (2011) highlighted issues with collaborative editing within wikis, and identified the need for team protocols to be developed in editing and annotating content within wikis. A study undertaken by De Wever, Van Keer, Schellens & Valcke (2011) in Belgium, examining the use of peer assessment of the collaborative processes within wikis, found that 'peer assessment in a wiki environment is reliable and feasible' (p.206). Therefore, wikis can also be reliably utilized to support collaboration and peer assessment, and have the potential to reduce the work-load of tutors, particularly with regards to the assessment of large groups of students in higher education.

Blogs are increasingly being used in higher education, however much of the research on the integration of blogs in higher education tends to be small-scale and/ or localized to a specific context. In one such small-scale study on students' perceptions on the effectiveness of blogs for learning in higher education by Halic, Lee, Paulus & Spence (2010), the majority of participants reported that their blogging experience was positive and furthermore felt that engagement in blogging enhanced their overall learning. Interestingly, this study showed that participants' perceptions of learning within blogs aligned with 'sense of community' and 'levels of computer experience' – if the *sense of community* and *level of computer experience* were higher, perceptions of learning were also higher, and vice versa. This study also found that participants 'did not particularly value the comments of their peers' (Halic et al., 2010, p.211). This perhaps raises concerns regarding the mindset of those engaging in online blogging activities, whether they are sufficiently prepared for the collaborative nature, dynamic roles, norms and etiquette of engagement in blogging environments. A further case study that utilised blogs as one of several social media within a legal education course, (Ruyters, Douglas & Law, 2011), found that blogging encouraged participants to engage in peer and self-reflection and to identify the key learning experiences. A case study on blog-based learning based within a higher education institution in Korea (Kang, Bonk & Kim, 2011), found that blogging can be used to facilitate a social-constructivist learning environment, thereby enabling a community of practice while preserving the 'unique networked individuality' (p.227) of students and instructors. With regards to the latter, Kang et al. (2011) write of the blogger's identity being revealed through the decoration of blogs with 'diverse design elements and structures according to the blogger's taste and interests; thereby reflecting the blogger's personality or

concerns' (p.231). The authors furthermore refer to the role of blogging in self-disclosure, which in turn affords opportunities for peers to express attitudes, perceptions and empathetic feelings. This is critical for meaningful social interaction and in ultimately developing a *sense of community* among participants within the blogosphere.

Podcasts are audio files distributed digitally containing music and speech. A variant of podcasting known as vodcasting refers to the podcasting of video material. According to McGarr (2009) podcasting in higher education typically falls into three catgories, substitutional, supplementary and creative. The most used and probably the least imaginative use of podcasts is the substitutional or "coursecasting" (King & Gura, 2007, p. 181) format where audio recordings of lectures in full are made available to students. Used in this way podcasts merely replicate the traditional face to face lecture and understandably have created fears among academics that widespread use could lead to a decline in class attendance. While some studies have suggested the effects on lecture attendance is negligible (Copley, 2007; Maag, 2006; Mayer, 2006) other studies have questioned the validity of such findings based on contextual concerns (Holbrook, 2011), with other studies reporting declines in class attendance (Nworie and Haughton, 2008; Williams and Fardon, 2007; Lane, 2006). Nonetheless from the student perspective podcasting of traditional lectures appear to offer a number of benefits including flexibility, convenience and enhanced learning opportunities. The latter is particularly interesting in that it seems to suggest that even students who don't use podcasting as a substitute for attending lectures, view them as a valuable resource in terms of improved note taking, for reviewing difficult course concepts and for examination preparation. One consistent finding across most research studies is that contrary to expectations that podcasting would support mobile learning with students downloading podcasts to their personal mp3 players to use while on the go, most students accessed lecture podcasts from computers (Knight, 2010: Evans, 2008; Lee and Chan, 2007). This suggests that they use podcasting in a more formal, sombre and traditional study context.

Rather than using podcasts to merely transmit recorded lectures some lecturers have used podcasting in a more imaginative way to provide supplementary course materials such as short (10-15 minute) lecture summaries, discussions based on key course themes, role playing, fieldwork and practice based exercises particularly in language learning. Knight (2010) in her study of the use of exercise podcasts for speech and language therapy students found them beneficial for training students in phonetic transcription skills. Instead of replicating material already used in class, Knight (2010, p. 271) "created a series of podcast exercises which provided students with the opportunity to practice a wide range of transcription and listening skills required for university assessments and clinical practice". This gave them the opportunity to practice what they had learned in class with a variety of new material to enhance their skill competence. Her research revealed that the majority of students (69%) repeatedly listened to the same podcasts even though she had designed them to be only used once and that all students (100%) felt that they were both "very useful" for their learning and that they preferred podcasts of exercises to lecture podcasts. Her study also revealed that although she provided students with a .pdf file containing model answers to the podcast exercises, 93% of students reported waiting until they had listened to the podcasts before consulting the answer sheet. With no prompting from her on this issue it seemed that students' behaviour closely mirrored in-class behaviours where traditionally students completed the exercises and then checked the answers.

While Knight's research was based on students self reported benefits and did not include any hard evidence of the actual impact of supplementary podcasting on student outcomes a study by Siciliano, Jenks, Dana and Talbert (2011) indicates a distinct improvement in learning outcomes with supplementary podcasting. Their study was designed to investigate the impact of podcasting on horticultural and landscape architecture students enrolled on a study abroad course on the English Garden. Using an experimental design involving two groups, three gardens based on a high, medium and low complexity rating were chosen for the study. All students attended introductory lectures prior to conducting their field research and were given a course reading pack comprising 2-3 pages for each of the gardens to be visited. One group of students (Group A) were also given audio podcasts narratives for each of the three garden types during the first week of lectures. Although these podcasts contained the same material as that covered in class and textbook readings, the narratives were constructed in the form of garden tours to be used by students during live visits to the sites. In the aftermath of the live visits students were subjected to both written and oral examinations. The written examination which consisted of quizzes to test students' knowledge of historical and garden design techniques revealed no significant differences between the two groups. However the oral examinations which tested students' depth of understanding in relation to garden design philosophies, garden symbolism and horticultural richness, revealed a significant difference in Group A's depth of learning when it came to the gardens rated as being in the intermediate and higher level complexity bracket. No reported difference was apparent between the two groups when it came to the garden rated at a low level of complexity.

While the research evidence indicates that most podcasts are produced by lecturers and teachers, a small number of studies highlight instances where instructors have sought to use podcasts in a more creative way through the use of student generated podcasts. From business students (Frydenberg, 2006) to multimedia students (Lazzari, 2008) to pre-service teacher education (King & Gura, 2007; Forbes, 2011) various disciplines have used student created podcasts to encourage collaborative learning, group work, critical thinking, metacognition, authentic learning and reflective practice. This is a welcome development particularly in the field of pre service teacher education as it provides hands on opportunities to explore the potential of educational technology for learning while building teacher competence in the use and adoption of new technologies in the classroom.

Social Networking Tools

Specific studies on the use of social networking tools in higher education reveal some interesting trends. For example in a mixed methods study across four universities in the UK, Jones, Blackey, Fitzgibbon & Chew (2010) found that more than 70% of respondents rarely used social media for learning purposes even though most students made extensive use of and enjoyed engaging with educational technology. It would seem that students are reluctant to use social media for learning as they value their private space and wish to keep their 'work' (sic academic) life separate from their social life.

Similar findings were reported by Madge, Meek, Wellens & Hooley (2009) who used an online survey to examine how first year undergraduates in their institution used Facebook for social integration into university life and for academic purposes. They found that while Facebook acted as an important 'social glue' in helping students adjust to university life, students thought that the use of Facebook was more important for social reasons rather than for formal teaching purposes. Although students in this study used Facebook for informal learning activities such as collaborating on group projects they were less than enthusiastic about the idea of academic staff using Facebook to contact them. This is consistent with findings from outside the purely educational realm where it has been reported that while among young people "social networks and SMS are the preferred method of communication among peers, email is how you communicate with elders in formal situations" (Kirkpatrick 2009, cited in Hayes, Ruschman & Walker 2009, p. 110).

The distinction between students' use of Facebook for informal rather than formal learning is also highlighted by Selwyn (2009). In an in-depth qualitative study exploring the use of the Facebook 'wall' activity of almost a thousand undergraduate students he found that most educational postings, which in themselves were limited, compared to the volume of social and personal postings, tended to be confined to the exchange of practical and academic information. Students used Facebook to exchange information in relation to the more mundane aspects of academic life such as clarifying the location and time of lectures and seminars, the timing of assessments and guidelines around exam and coursework assignments. Although students occasionally offered peer guidance and assistance to students struggling with assignments, such instances were rare with most students "unwilling to offer extensive assistance to each other" (Selwyn, 2009, p. 167). Selwyn contends that students primarily use Facebook for meaning making activities in relation to understanding what it means to be a student and the culture of undergraduate life. As such he sees Facebook as primarily an instrument for identity performance, which is firmly rooted in the 'identity politics' of student life. The traditional and often anti-intellectual discourse around student and university life which once took place in the offline world of private student to student conversations is now being played out in a more public online forum through social networking systems like Facebook. On this basis Selwyn cautions against attempts by faculty and university authorities to appropriate this space for "educationally 'appropriate' or 'valid' uses" (Selwyn, 2009, p. 172). Understood in this context it is easy to appreciate why students as reported above in other studies were not keen to have lecturers invade their Facebook space.

Nonetheless some US studies have reported positive findings from faculty use of social networking tools like Facebook and Twitter in terms of student engagement and student teacher relations. While a comparative study by Robyler, McDaniel, Webb, Herman & Witty (2010) on student and faculty use of Facebook revealed that it was seldom used for instructional purposes, their research revealed that students were more open to it being used in an instructional context than their teachers.

The relationship between teachers' use of Facebook and Twitter and teachers' credibility was investigated in two interesting studies. Previous research (Nussbaum, Comadena & Holladay, 1987; McCroskey, 1992; Myers and Bryant, 2004) conducted in the offline space have shown that a teacher's capacity for self-disclosure i.e. the ability to reveal personal information about oneself positively impacts a teacher's credibility rating. This in turn influences student learning outcomes and motivation (McCroskey, Valencic & Richmond 2004; Frymier and Thompson 1992). Mazar, Murphy & Simonds (2009) investigated how different levels of self-disclosure in Facebook affects a teacher's credibility. Using an experimental design they tested how students reacted to high, medium and low levels of teacher's self disclosure. Adding to the well documented body of evidence from the offline world, as cited above, on the relationship between self-disclosure and teacher credibility they found similar results in relation to computer mediated self-disclosure as the teacher exhibiting a high level of self-disclosure in Facebook in their experiment appeared more credible to students than the teacher exhibiting low self-disclosure levels. Nonetheless they advise that teachers should adopt a cautious approach to how they use an SNS like Facebook, not only because they believe a teachers use of self-disclosure online must be consistent with their offline teaching style, but also because of the potential which this medium affords to violate professional distance in student teacher relationships as well as the openness of the Facebook environment which could negatively affect a teachers credibility if students posted defamatory messages on users' Facebook websites.

In a related study Johnson (2011) investigated the effects of Twitter posts on students perception of instructor credibility. Again using an experimental design Johnson constructed three scenarios involving (1) an instructor using Twitter to disclose only personal information; (2) an instructor disclosing only scholarly information and (3) an instructor disclosing both personal and scholarly information. One hundred and twenty undergraduates, aged between 18 and 23 divided into three groups of 40 participated in the study. Using McCroskey and Teven's (1999) tried and tested method of measuring teacher credibility along the three dimensions of competence, trustworthiness and caring, participants were asked to rate their teachers once they had read their tweets. Results indicated that there was a significant difference in the impact of social versus scholarly tweets on students' perceptions of instructor credibility, with no significant differences between the other groups. Instructors using Twitter for social posts were perceived by students to be more credible than those posting scholarly tweets. However this study also revealed that students were divided on the issue of the appropriateness of teachers having social networking accounts with 53% thinking it was a good idea compared to 47% who felt it was a bad idea. Among the latter group concerns abounded in relation to professional boundaries between students and instructors, a diminution of student respect for instructors and the posting of inappropriate information. The research also revealed a correlation, albeit a weak one, between age and whether or not students believed it appropriate for their teachers to use Twitter. The older the student the less likely they were to deem it appropriate.

Dunlap and Lowenthal (2009) report favorable feedback from their use on Twitter in distance education. They believe that the advantages of Twitter in online learning far outweigh any reported drawbacks. They argue that the added value of Twitter resides in its ability to enhance social presence between student and faculty and student to student, a crucially important ingredient for enhancing student engagement and therefore retention in online learning; in its synchronous communication protocol which facilitates just in time communication; in its ease of use compared to the cumbersome and multi-step process involved in accessing the average Learning Management System where communications is typically asynchronous in nature and therefore off-putting for many busy professionals engaged in distance learning; and in its suitability as a platform for the development of personal learning networks.

On this latter point they make an interesting observation regarding Twitter's educational suitability compared to Facebook. Drawing on the work of social media researchers who differentiate between friendship driven and interest driven social media sites, Twitter they argue encourages more interest driven participation because it is a "less bounded and more open networking tool" (Dunlap & Lowenthal, 2009, p. 5) than Facebook. Consequently Twitter appears a more natural home for the establishment of Communities of Practice and personal learning networks compared to Facebook whose raisons d'être is largely friendship driven. Furthermore by using Twitter rather than Facebook for instructional purposes they felt they were respecting the privacy of students' personal online space because as has been indicated in other studies, their students too liked to keep their professional/academic life separate from the personal.

The cumbersome nature of many learning management systems has also acted as a spur for other educationalists to use more everyday social networking tools. Frustrated by their efforts to encourage chemistry students to engage with the communications and collaboration features of WEB CT such as the bulletin board and chat facilities, Schroder and Greenbowe (2009) turned to Facebook as an alternative space for student communications and interaction. Although less than half (41%) of the undergraduate students enrolled on their organic chemistry actually joined the facebook group they established, they found

students much more willing to interact and engage. Although this was not a scientific study the authors noted that the number of postings on facebook was much higher than the equivalent postings in WebCT and that the topics raised by students in their facebook postings were more complex and attracted a greater number replies from fellow students. They also noted that although facebook postings ebbed and flowed in accordance with tasks on hand, the facebook discussions continued throughout the semester, whereas discussions on WebCT ceased after the first few weeks of term.

Similarly, in a study of the use of a dedicated social networking facility called Connect, by students and staff in a higher education institution in the UK, Oradini & Saunders (2008) found that half the students would have preferred the use of existing social networking technologies (such as Facebook) while others preferred to keep their personal social networking activity separate from academic activity by using dedicated facilities like Connect. They also found that students have difficulty maintaining online communities and that there was a need for tutor interaction to mediate and promote meaningful participation within the learning communities. Finally, they found that students wanted integrated systems; thus the social networking system needed to be embedded within the learning management system.

The ease of use, intuitive interface and popularity of Facebook were instrumental in McCarthy's (2010) decision to use Facebook rather than a standard learning management system to support blended learning on a first year elective course in design in the university of Adelaide. Although most of the students were local, a fifth was international. McCarthy's main aim was to enhance the experience of first year by immersing students into university culture through social and academic interaction between peers. Beginning with a pilot project in 2008, McCarthy continued the project with a follow on cohort in 2009 incorporating some key findings from the initial pilot. The 2008 study revealed that participation in online activities was greater in the early part of the semester as students were less distracted by other course tasks such as assignment deadlines etc. It also revealed that blended really does mean blended in the sense that there must be a clear connect between the objectives of the online learning space (Facebook) and what's taking place in the physical learning space (classroom) to produce sustainable peer interaction. Therefore in 2009 he frontloaded the Facebook assessment process, compressing it into an intensive six week programme and redesigned the learning activities to ensure coherence between the virtual and physical environments. The 2009 data showed a large increase in both social and academic interaction between local students and in academic interaction between local and international students. In this study facebook proved to be a successful tool in helping the more introverted student interact with their peers, a task which shy first years in particular often find daunting. It also broke down the cultural and communication barriers which frequently exist between local and international students based around second language skills, social inhibitions and critiquing and feedback mores. This resulted in more open, richer and intense academic debates in the physical classroom towards the end of the semester.

Challenges in Use of Web 2.0 Technologies in Higher Education

Punie et al. (2007, p.216) note that technology-enabled learning spaces are "a challenging vision of personalized learning paths with an increased role of social connections." The success of online learning in higher education is reliant on high-speed networks, a willingness to engage in the online environment by staff and students alike and increasingly on high quality educational resources. Typical challenges to the inclusion of Web 2.0 technologies in teaching and learning environments include limited access to or use of the technologies, low digital skills, low digital literacy, low level of funding available to build

the infrastructure, uncertainty as to the value or relevance of the technology within particular disciplines, safety and privacy concerns, attitudinal or dispositional stance against the integration of technology in education and/ or poor pedagogic knowledge on how to effectively integrate technology in teaching and learning. Other challenges include the differing levels of access to social media and/or the Internet, and the ineffective use of social media from a learning perspective by learners. These challenges are, according to Selwyn (2012, p.5), impacted by inequalities along the lines of socio-economic status, social class, disability, race, gender, geography, age and educational background.

The rapid advancement of ICTs has purportedly brought with it an increasing digital divide within and among countries and has resulted in disparities in access to and the quality of education. The 'digital divide' refers to those have access to and/ or can use information and communications technologies, and those who don't. Prensky (2001) offers another perspective on the digital divide, suggesting that there exists a second divide between those who have grown up with technologies and those who have not. He posits that the generation of learners born after 1980, who have grown up immersed in technology, are familiar with and reliant on ICTs, and has called this group the 'digital natives'. This generation are said to be reliant on ICTs for communication, collaboration and accessing information, to possess sophisticated technological skills and also learn differently (different learning styles than previous generations of learners). According to Tapscott & Williams (2007, p.52), these learners also have a "desire for choice, convenience, customization, and control", as cited in Selwyn, 2012. The generation born before 1980, known as the 'digital immigrants', are purported to lack technological skills and also lack proficiency in accessing or using information and communication technologies. The issue for higher education is that most educators fall within the category of the digital immigrant. The resultant effect is a disjoint between the technological skills and learning styles of learners (digital natives) and those of their educators (digital immigrants), which is alleged to be creating dissonance among learners (as noted by Bennett, Maton & Kervin, 2008, p.777). The issue according to Prensky (2001) for education at all levels (including higher education) is that the system currently is not able to facilitate the learning of these digital natives, and that education must change to address the needs of this new generation.

It is important to note that Bennett et al. (2008) challenged the assumptions about digital natives and digital immigrants and found in their review of research in this field that there existed a significant proportion of learners who had limited use of technology and poor technological skills. They highlighted the danger of assuming that 'digital natives' were a homogenous group. They also pointed out that the call for change within the educational system to address the needs of the digital native is a form of "moral panic" (Bennett et al., 2008, p.782) – meeting the needs of the digital native is being portrayed as an imperative, where lack of immediate action will result in the widespread disillusionment and disaffection amongst learners and within the educational system. They believe that this classification of digital natives and digital immigrants has resulted in unnecessary and unproven divisions between generations of learners. Whether a divide between these generations exists or not, the reality is that within higher education there is significant variation in the use and meaningful application of technology in educational practice that must be addressed.

A separate but related issue to that of the digital native is the manner in which Web 2.0 technologies are perceived and valued by learners in everyday life, as opposed to within the learning environment. This tension between how social media are perceived, used and valued in everyday life, which Hosein, Ramanau & Jones (2010) refer to as living technologies, and how social media are

used and valued within learning environments, which Hosein et al. (ibid) refer to as learning technologies, is a critical factor in whether learners meaningfully engage with social media in learning contexts. Learners may be reluctant to use personalised social media (such as their personal Facebook account) within educational contexts; perceiving the integration of personal technologies in the learning environment as an intrusion into their private domain. Furthermore, social media infusion that results in high-level engagement but lower-order learning cannot be allowed to propagate. The key to overcoming this tension is in understanding learners motivation, the creation of authentic learning activities and acceptance that the focus of any learning activity or intervention must be on how it enables learning as a 'process of becoming'. Finally, the value and sustainability of social media infusion within the learning environment must be constantly evaluated.

Other barriers include safety and privacy concerns around the use of social media in higher education. Formal educational engagement is no longer 'confined to the lecture-hall' or directed within the conventional higher education institutional norms and structures. According to the British Educational Communications and Technology Agency, BECTA, (2006) the UK government is promoting the notion of integrated online learning which will allow learning to take place any-time, anywhere, customised to support individual learning styles, needs and pace. It is envisaged that technologies will be harnessed in an interdisciplinary manner within teaching and learning to facilitate this form of personalised learning. The integration of online technologies in education in particular, presents a number of challenges in terms of e-Safety. According to British Educational Communications and Technology Agency, BECTA, (2006), risks associated with using the Internet and digital technologies can be categorised under four categories: Content, Contact, Commerce and Culture. These e-Safety issues include access to age-inappropriate, inaccurate and illegal material, inappropriate contact in the form of grooming of minors, inappropriate commercial advertising or financial scams, illegal downloading of media and cyberbullying.

A fifth e-Safety concern more relevant in the context of higher education would be the 'openness' and 'informality' that Web 2.0 technologies can facilitate, which may result in breaches of Intellectual Property and copyright and in exposure to litigation of educators and learners. Crook et al. (2008, p.56) advised that: "it might be better to talk less of 'Web 2.0 technology' and consider instead 'Web 2.0 mentality'". Web 2.0 technologies reflect changes in attitudes and practices in society and vice versa. Web 2.0 technologies have the potential to enhance participation and facilitate a degree of 'openness' that was hitherto unheard of. Learners can, with relative ease, share and make public their thoughts, opinions and perceptions of the learning content and the learning medium. This use of Web 2.0 technologies to freely and publicly share learners' informal thinking mirrors the informality and participatory mood evident within wider societal and cultural practices. This is particularly evident among the younger population who publicly release personal information about themselves and their lifestyles on social networking sites, such as Facebook or MySpace. There is a real need for those investigating the integration of Web 2.0 technologies in higher education and elsewhere to identify the ethical and other risks to learners and the wider societal and / or cultural impacts in the use of particular Web 2.0 technologies in education.

Another key challenge in engaging in online learning is time management. Allan (2007) highlights the need for careful consideration of the time involved in networked learning, and the need for online learners to modify their personal time management 'clock' in line with the requirements of online learning. She cautions against engaging online learners in activities that involve learners simply collating information from different sources, characterised as 'fast time' by Eriksen (2001), as opposed to allowing them opportunities to reflect or engage in the individual and collective transformation of new ideas and knowledge, characterized as 'slow time' by Eriksen (2001).

The final challenge in implementing online learning is in evaluating whether learners' degree of engagement or performance in learning has been enhanced or not through the use of the online medium. A meta-analysis of online learning studies by the US Department of Education (2010, pp. 18-19) found that blended learning opportunities had stronger learning outcomes than face-to-face instruction alone. However, purely online courses were found to be as effective as face-to-face courses. It also identified the need to "incorporate mechanisms that promote student reflection on their level of understanding" (2010, p.48). In a study of the use of blended online learning in a single module in a higher education context, Turner, Robinson, Lee & Soutar (2009) found that student learning was significantly improved through the integration of technology, particularly in terms of increasing the pass rate for those foundational students at risk of not progressing in higher education. They also emphasized the need for the alignment of the integration of technology with the aims of the module, and identified that there was a risk of strategic learning approaches (particularly in terms of reduced attendance in face-to-face classes) being adopted. They recommended the retention of face-to-face contact in recognition of the individual preferences of learners for this mode of contact.

Furthermore, a study of online learning approaches of undergraduates by Knight (2010) found that online learners who accessed web-based resources consistently throughout the module performed much higher than those learners who engaged with online resources at the start or end of the module. The author further notes that those that accessed online resources consistently throughout the module were also found to have engaged in complex levels of interaction with the online resources i.e. learners were accessing the online content in different order and different ways. In a review of the literature on blended learning in higher education, Harris, Connolly & Feeney (2009) found that evaluation of blended learning interventions should examine: Learning outcomes, Participants learning styles and preferences, Motivation, Clarity of goals and content, Degree of interaction, Perceived value and satisfaction, effectiveness, Appropriate support, workload and assessment, Access to resources, usability and design, How the blend of learning worked, Confidence logs if possible and Evidence of meta-cognition.

Finally, in a review of the research conducted on the application of technology in support of collaborative learning in higher education, Resta and Laferriere (2007, p. 77) conclude that more research is needed on the presage variables (student characteristics and technologies that enhance or constrain collaborative learning), process variables (structuring of tasks, problems, mediation, student engagement, scaffolding in enabling online interaction) and the product variables (learning outcomes, higher-order thinking, critical thinking and knowledge transformation). Therefore, these variables need to be incorporated in future evaluations on the effectiveness of online courses.

CRITICAL PERSPECTIVES AND FUTURE RESEARCH DIRECTIONS

This review of the literature on the use of social media in higher education suggests that early web 2.0 tools such as wikis, blogs and podcasts, are the social media tools of choice within higher education institutions. As social networking tools, such as Facebook and Twitter have become the communication tool of choice in popular culture, educators have also begun to investigate how these tools can be used in higher education. However, it must be noted here that there is a paucity of research on how and in what contexts social media tools are being used within institutions particularly in terms

of delineating between its usage for instructional purposes vis-à-vis its usage for administration, marketing and other purposes. Trends emergent from this review of the literature include:

- Blogs are being increasingly used in higher education because they can enhance and deepen learning. They have been shown to be effective in supporting self-disclosure, which is critical in developing a sense of community. Interestingly, Facebook has also been shown to be successful in facilitating self-disclosure for both instructors and students, although the disclosure by instructors has not always been perceived by students as a positive development. The development of a 'sense of community' and 'levels of computer experience pre-engagement' within blogs is directly aligned to participants' perceptions of learning - a higher 'sense of community' or 'levels of computer experience' correlates to higher perceptions of learning among participants.

- Wikis have been successfully used for engagement in collaborative learning and in peer assessment in higher education. Some concerns have been identified around the usability of wiki platforms and sociability-related issues, such as expectations of wiki participants to critically review each others' contributions within the wiki environment. Similar concerns regarding critiquing the work of peers has emerged from a review of research on blogs and wikis. This perhaps highlights the need for a cultural shift in the mindset of social media users to ensure that there is a sound basis of trust, a spirit of openness and collaboration, and an understanding of the roles, norms and etiquette within learning environments enabled through social media. In effect, there is a need for development of new literacies among educators and students in higher education, such as those highlighted by

Lee & Young (2011, pp.28-29) of: *multi-tasking, distributed cognition, collective intelligence, judgement, networking and negotiation*, so that they can critically engage in and contribute to Learning 2.0.

- Podcasting, although less widely used than Blogs and Wikis has been utilized in higher education in a variety of ways to support the curriculum and a variety of learning objectives. "Coursecasting" i.e. the direct recording of face to face lectures in full continues to be the most common use of podcasting. This has its downsides not only because it can lead to a decrease in class attendance but also because it is modeled on a transmissive or behaviourist view of the learning process which encourages passive student behaviour. Consequently some commentators have been quite critical of coursecasting referring to is as the *"artless use of technology"* (King and Gura, 2007, p.181). However this view is not necessarily shared by students as a number of studies have shown that they find lecture podcasts a valuable tool for course review, notetaking and exam revision purposes. A less mundane and more imaginative use of podcasts is their utilization for the provision of supplementary course materials. This has proved to be particularly effective for language learning and field trip exercises, where podcasts have been used to provide complementary yet distinctively different information and exercises from that utilized in class. However some studies have revealed that supplementary podcasts which merely provide summaries of class lectures and activities can actually lead to less student engagement with course materials as they over rely on this source of information at the expense of studying core texts. Although used to a lesser extent than substitutional (sic. coursecasting) or supplementary podcasting, some research studies have demonstrate how podcasts can be used in a more creative way with students rather than course tutors producing podcasting materials. It is argued (Lee, McLouglin & Chan, 2008) that this use adds most value to the learning process as it supports a constructivist rather than a behaviourist model of learning with students becoming active knowledge producers rather than passive knowledge consumers.

- Facebook has been shown to be effective in developing social interaction, acting as a 'social glue' between participants. However, it has also been shown to be more 'friendship' driven that 'interests' driven, which poses challenges, such as e-moderation, for educators within higher education focused on its use in enabling participants to realise particular learning outcomes.

- Twitter has been shown to be effective in enhancing the social presence of participants and contributors, and in enabling self-disclosure. It has evolved as a more 'interests' driven medium, and as such has the potential to better support the development of a sense of community, communities of practice and/ or personalised learning networks.

CONCLUSION

The integration of social media in higher education requires institutional change. According to Redecker et al. (2010, p.11), this requires educational institutions to "reevaluate their role in society as knowledge providers". Resistance to re-envisioning the purpose of higher education (particularly with regards to the inclusion of ICT & Web 2.0 technologies as key enablers within the knowledge society) may prove to be the key challenge to implementing the necessary changes for Learning 2.0 within the structures and practices in higher education.

Overcoming such resistance will not be easy. Despite substantial investment in ICT in education in OECD countries since the 1990's, the impact of digital technologies on teaching and learning has been disappointing overall, leading the OECD to conclude in its 2005 report that ICT in higher education had more impact on administrative services than on teaching (Balasubramanian et al., 2009). A view also endorsed by Laurillard (2006) who argues that in addition to administration, ICT in higher education is also being used effectively to support traditional teaching practices.

Such conclusions are not unusual. From its earliest inception ICT has often been viewed as a catalyst for change, a type of 'trojan horse' (Papert, 1997; Hodas 1993; Newman 1992) through which fundamental education change can be delivered. Unfortunately as Starr (1996, p. 51) reminds us "the history of education in the twentieth century is littered with mistaken forecasts of technological revolutions in education". In this context, as the early decades of the twenty first century unfold, we should be mindful of Hodas' (1996, p.210) argument that one of the great ironies of the computer is that is "unusually polyvalent in that it can both support and subvert the symbolic, organisational and normative dimensions of school [sic. education] practice". This means that ICT can be used either to support and reinforce traditional pedagogic practices or transform them.

By its very nature, and in the right hands, Web 2.0 technology has the capacity to transform existing pedagogic practices in higher education by creating a teaching and learning environment that supports participation, interactivity, communication and the development of learning communities where students can share and co-construct knowledge with each other and their instructors. The question for us as third level educators is – can we rise to this challenge or will Web 2.0 follow in the footsteps of previous technological innovations

and live out its days as a representational medium (Hamilton & Freenberg, 2005) designed mainly to increase the efficient delivery of a traditional, largely unchanged pedagogy? Were this to happen, the future learning space in Higher Education would indeed look bleak.

REFERENCES

Allan, B. (2007). Time to learn? E-learners' experience of time in virtual communities. *Journal of Management Learning, 38*(5), 557–572. doi:10.1177/1350507607083207

Allen, I. E., & Seaman, J. (2011). *Going the distance: Online education in the United States, 2011. Sloan Online Survey Series.* United States: Babson Survey Research Group.

Allwardt, D. E. (2011). Teaching note. Writing with wikis: A cautionary tale of technology in the classroom. *Journal of Social Work Education, 47*(3), 597–605. doi:10.5175/JSWE.2011.200900126

Balasubramanian, K., Clarke-Okah, W., Daniel, J., Ferreira, F., Kanwar, A., & Kwan, A. … West, P. (2009). *ICT's for higher education: Background paper from the Commonwealth of Learning.* Paris, France: UNESCO Retrieved June 5, 2012, from http://unesdoc.unesco.org/images/0018/001832/183207e.pdf

BECTA. (2006). *Safeguarding children in a digital world. Developing a strategic approach to e-safety.* BECTA Publication. Retrieved February 13, 2008, from http://publications.becta.org.uk/download.cfm?resID=25933

Bennett, S., Maton, K., & Kervin, L. (2008). The 'digital natives' debate: A critical review of the evidence. *British Journal of Educational Technology, 39*(5), 775–786. doi:10.1111/j.1467-8535.2007.00793.x

Cassidy, E. D., Britsch, J., Griffin, G., Manolovitz, T., Shen, L., & Turney, L. (2011). Higher education and emerging technologies: student usage, preferences and lessons for library services. *Higher Education and Emerging Technologies, 50*(4), 380–391.

Copley, J. (2007). Audio and video podcasts of lecture for campus-based students: Production and evaluation of student use. *Innovations in Education and Teaching International, 44*(4), 387. doi:10.1080/14703290701602805

Cornu, B. (2007). *Being a teacher in the knowledge society.* Presentation. European, Distance and E-Learning Network (EDEN). Conference, Stockholm 2007. Retrieved February 10, 2011, from http://www.eden-online.org/contents/conferences/OCRCs/Poitiers/Keynotes/Cornu.ppt

Crook, C., Cummings, J., Fisher, T., Graber, R., Harrison, C., & Lewin, C. … Sharples, M. (2008). *Web 2.0 technologies for learning: The current landscape – Opportunities, challenges and tensions.* BECTA Publication. Retrieved January 15, 2011, from http://dera.ioe.ac.uk/1474/1/becta_2008_web2_currentlandscape_litrev.pdf

Davis, C. H. F., III, Deil-Amen, R., Rios-Aguilar, C., & Gonzalez Canche, M. S. (2012). *Social media in higher education: A literature review and research directions.* The Center for the Study of Higher Education. Printed by University of Arizona and Claremont Graduate University. Retrieved June 5, 2012, from http://works.bepress.com/cgi/viewcontent.cgi?article=1003&context=hfdavis

De Wever, B., Van Keer, H., Schellens, T., & Valcke, M. (2011). Assessing collaboration in a wiki: The reliability of university students' peer assessment. *Journal of Internet and Higher Education, 14*, 201–206. doi:10.1016/j.iheduc.2011.07.003

Dunlap, J. C., & Lowental, P. (2009). Horton hears a Tweet. *EDUCAUSE Quarterly Magazine, 32*(4). Retrieved June 5, 2012, from http://www.educause.edu/EDUCAUSE+Quarterly/EDUCAUSEQuarterlyMagazineVolum/HortonHearsaTweet/192955

Economist Intelligence Unit (ECI). (2008). *The future of higher education: How technology will shape learning.* A Report from the Economist Intelligence Unit, London.

Eriksen, T. H. (2001). *Tyranny of the moment: Fast and slow time in the information age.* London, UK: Pluto.

Evans, C. (2008). The effectiveness of m-learning in the form of podcast revision lectures in higher education. *Computers & Education, 50*, 491–498. doi:10.1016/j.compedu.2007.09.016

Farwell, T. M., & Waters, R. D. (2010). Exploring the use of social bookmarking technology in education: An analysis of students' experiences using course-specific Delicious.com account. *Journal of Online Learning and Teaching, 6*(2), 398–408.

Forbes, D. (2011). Beyond lecture capture: Student-generated podcasts in teacher education. *Waikato Journal of Education, 16*(1), 51–63.

Frydenberg, M. (2006). Principles and pedagogy: The two P's of podcasting in the information technology classroom. In *Proceedings of the Information Systems Education Conference 2006,* Vol. 23 (Dallas).

Frymier, A., & Thompson, C. (1992). Perceived teacher affinity- seeking in relation to perceived credibility. *Communication Education, 41*(4), 388–399. doi:10.1080/03634529209378900

Garrison, D. R., Anderson, T., & Archer, W. (2000). Critical inquiry in a text-based environment: Computer conferencing in higher education. *The Internet and Higher Education, 2*(2-3), 87–105. doi:10.1016/S1096-7516(00)00016-6

Graetz, K. A. (2006). The psychology of learning environments. In Oblinger, D. G. (Ed.), *Learning spaces* (pp. 6.1–6.14). Educause.

Halic, O., Lee, D., Paulus, T., & Spence, M. (2010). To blog or not to blog: Student perceptions of blog effectiveness for learning in a college-level course. *Journal of Internet and Higher Education*, *13*, 206–213. doi:10.1016/j.iheduc.2010.04.001

Hamilton, E., & Freenberg, A. (2005). The technical codes of online education. *E-Learning and Digital Media*, *2*(2), 104-121. Retrieved June 5, 2012, from http://dx.doi.org/10.2304/elea.2005.2.2.1

Harris, P., Connolly, J. F., & Feeney, L. (2009). Blended learning: Overview and recommendation for successful implementation. *Industrial and Commercial Training*, *4*(3), 155–163. doi:10.1108/00197850910950961

Hayes, T., Ruschman, D., & Walker, M. (2009). Social networking as an admission tool: A case study in success. *Journal of Marketing for Higher Education*, *19*(2), 109–124. doi:10.1080/08841240903423042

Hodas, S. (1993). *Implementation of the K-12NREN: Equity, access, and a Trojan horse*. ERIC Document ED, 358829.

Hodas, S. (1996). Technology refusal and the organisational culture of schools. In King, R. (Ed.), *Computerization and controversy* (2nd ed., pp. 197–217). doi:10.1016/B978-0-12-415040-9.50106-8

Holbrook, J. (2011). Making the decision to provide enhanced podcasts to post-secondary science students. *Journal of Science Education and Technology*, *20*, 233–345. doi:10.1007/s10956-010-9248-1

Hosein, A., Ramanau, R., & Jones, C. (2010). Learning and living technologies. *Learning, Media and Technology*, *35*(4), 403–418. doi:10.1080/17439884.2010.529913

Huntsberger, M., & Stavitsky, A. (2006). The new "podagogy": Incorporating podcasting into journalism education. *Journalism and Mass Communication Educator*, *61*(4), 397–410. doi:10.1177/107769580606100405

Ituma, A. (2011). An evaluation of students' perception and engagement with e-learning components in a campus-based university. *Active Learning in Higher Education*, *12*(1), 57–68. doi:10.1177/1469787410387722

Johnson, K. A. (2011). The effect of Twitter posts on students' perceptions of instructor credibility. *Learning, Media and Technology*, *36*(1), 21–38. doi:10.1080/17439884.2010.534798

Jones, N., Blackey, H., Fitzgibbon, K., & Chew, E. (2010). Get out of MySpace! *Computers & Education*, *54*, 776–782. doi:10.1016/j.compedu.2009.07.008

Kang, I., Bonk, C. J., & Kim, M.-C. (2011). A case study of blog-based learning in Korea: Technology becomes pedagogy. *Journal of Internet and Higher Education*, *14*, 227–235. doi:10.1016/j.iheduc.2011.05.002

Kear, K., Woodthorpe, J., Robertson, S., & Hutchison, M. (2010). From forums to wikis: Perspectives on tools for collaboration. *Journal of Internet and Higher Education*, *13*, 218–225. doi:10.1016/j.iheduc.2010.05.004

Kim, D., & King, P. (2011). Implementing podcasts and blogs with ESOL teacher candidates' preparation: Interpretations and implications. *International Forum of Teaching and Studies*, *7*(2), 5-19).

Kim, K., & Bonk, C. J. (2006). The future of online teaching and learning in Higher education: The survey says…. *EDUCAUSE Quarterly*, *29*(4), 22–30.

King, A. (1993). From sage on the stage to guide on the side. *College Teaching*, *41*(1), 30–35. doi:10.1080/87567555.1993.9926781

King, K., & Gura, M. (2007). *Podcasting for teachers: Using a new technology to revolutionize teaching and learning.* Charlotte, NC: Information Age Publishing.

Knight, J. (2010). Distinguishing the learning approaches adopted by undergraduates in their use of online resources. *Journal of Active Learning in Higher Education, 11*(1), 67–78. doi:10.1177/1469787409355873

Knight, R. A. (2010). Sounds for study: Speech and language therapy students' use and perception of exercise podcasts for phonetics. *International Journal of Teaching and Learning in Higher Education, 22*(3), 269–276.

Lane, C. (2006). *Podcasting at the UW: An evaluation of current use.* Retrieved June 5 from www.washington.edu/lst/research/papers/2006/podcasting_report.pdf

Lankshear, C., Gee, J. P., Knobel, M., & Searle, C. (1997). *Changing literacies.* Buckingham, UK: Open University Press.

Laurillard, D. (2006). E-learning in higher education. In Ashwin, P. (Ed.), *Changing higher education: The development of learning and teaching* (pp. 71–84). London, UK: Routledge Falmer.

Lazzari, M. (2008). Creative use of podcasting in higher education and its effect on competitive agency. *Computers & Education, 52*(1), 27–34. doi:10.1016/j.compedu.2008.06.002

Lee, J., & Young, C. (2011). Building wikis and blogs: Pre-service teacher experiences with web-based collaborative technologies in an interdisciplinary methods course. *Journal of Technology, Humanities. Education and Narrative, 8,* 8–37.

Lee, M., & Chan, A. (2007). Pervasive, lifestyle-integrated mobile learning for distance learners: An analysis and unexpected results from a podcasting study. *Open Learning: The Journal of Open and Distance Learning, 22*(3), 201–218.

Lee, M., McLoughlin, C., & Chan, A. (2008). Talk the talk: Learner-generated podcasts as catalysts for knowledge creation. *British Journal of Educational Technology, 39*(3), 501–521. doi:10.1111/j.1467-8535.2007.00746.x

Maag, M. (2006). Podcasting and mp3 players: Emerging education technologies. *Computers, Informatics, Nursing, 24*(1), 9–12. doi:10.1097/00024665-200601000-00005

Madge, C., Meek, J., Wellens, J., & Hooley, T. (2009). Facebook, social integration and informal learning at university: 'It is more for socialising and talking to friends about work than for actually doing work'. *Learning, Media and Technology, 34*(2), 141–155. doi:10.1080/17439880902923606

Mayer, J. P. (2006). *Legal education podcasting project – End of semester survey results.* Retrieved June 5, 2012, from http:// caliopolis.classcaster.org/blog/legal_education_podcasting_project/2006/07/05/leppsurvey

Mazar, J. P., Murphy, R. E., & Simonds, J. (2009). The effects of teacher self disclosure via Facebook on teacher credibility. *Learning, Media and Technology, 34*(2), 175–183. doi:10.1080/17439880902923655

McCarthy, J. (2010). Blended learning environments: Using social networking sites to enhance the first year experience. *Australasian Journal of Educational Technology, 26*(6), 729–740.

McCroskey, J. C. (1992). *An introduction to communication in the classroom.* Edina, MN: Burgess International Group.

McCroskey, J. C., & Teven, J. J. (1999). Goodwill: A reexamination of the construct and its measurement. *Communication Monographs, 66,* 90–103. doi:10.1080/03637759909376464

McCroskey, J. C., Valencic, K. M., & Richmond, V. P. (2004). Toward a general model of instructional communication. *Communication Quarterly, 52,* 197–210. doi:10.1080/01463370409370192

McGarr, O. (2009). A review of podcasting in higher education: Its influence on the traditional lecture. *Australasian Journal of Educational Technology, 25*(3), 309–321.

Meyer, K. A. (2010). Web 2.0 Research. Introduction to the special issue. *Journal of Internet and Higher Education, 13*(4), 177–178. doi:10.1016/j.iheduc.2010.07.004

Myers, S., & Bryant, L. (2004). College Students' perception of how instructors convey credibility. *Qualitative Research Reports in Communication, 5*, 22–27.

Newman, D. (1992). Technology as support for school structure and school restructuring. *Phi Delta Kappan, 74*(4), 308–315.

Novak, E., Razzouk, R., & Johnson, T. E. (2012). The educational use of social annotation tools in higher education: A literature review. *The Internet and Higher Education, 15*(1), 39–49. doi:10.1016/j.iheduc.2011.09.002

Nussbaum, J. F., Comadena, M. E., & Holladay, S. J. (1987). Classroom verbal behaviors of highly effective teachers. *Journal of Thought, 22*, 73–80.

Nworie, J., & Haughton, N. (2008). Good intentions and unanticipated effects: The unintended consequences of the application of technology in teaching and learning environments. *TechTrends, 52*(5), 52–58. doi:10.1007/s11528-008-0197-y

Oradini, F., & Saunders, G. (2008). *The use of social networking by students and staff in higher education.* iLearning Forum, European Institute of E-Learning, Paris, France. Retrieved on February 29, 2012, from http://www.eife-l.org/publications/proceedings/ilf08/contributions/improving-quality-of-learning-with-technologies/Oradini_Saunders.pdf

Paas, L. (2008). *How information and communications technologies can support education for sustainable development current uses and trends.* Canada: International Institute for Sustainable Development. Retrieved February 10, 2011, from http://www.iisd.org/pdf/2008/ict_education_sd_trends.pdf

Papert, S. (1997). Why school reform is impossible. *Journal of the Learning Sciences, 6*(4), 417–427. doi:10.1207/s15327809jls0604_5

Prensky, M. (2001). Digital natives, digital immigrants: Part 1. *On the Horizon, 9*(5), 1-6. Retrieved February 10, 2011, from http://www.emeraldinsight.com/journals.htm?articleid=1532742

Punie, Y., & Ala-Mutka, K. (2007). Future learning spaces: New ways of learning and new digital spaces to learn. *Digital Kompetanse, 2*(4), 210–225.

Redecker, C., Ala-Mutka, K., & Punie, Y. (2010). *Learning 2.0 – The impact of social media on learning in Europe.* Luxembourg: European Commission Joint Research Centre. Retrieved February 20, 2012, from http://ftp.jrc.es/EURdoc/JRC56958.pdf

Resta, P., & Laferriere, T. (2007). Technology in support of collaborative learning. *Educational Psychology Review, 19*(1), 65–83. doi:10.1007/s10648-007-9042-7

Robyler, M. D., McDaniel, M., Webb, M., Herman, J., & Witty, J. (2010). Findings on Facebook in higher education: A comparison of college faculty and student uses and perceptions of social networking sites. *The Internet and Higher Education, 13*, 134–140. doi:10.1016/j.iheduc.2010.03.002

Ruyters, M., Douglas, K., & Law, S. F. (2011). Blended learning using role-plays, wikis and blogs. *Journal of Learning Design, 4*(4), 45–55.

Saeed, N., Yang, Y., & Sinnappan, S. (2009). Emerging Web technologies in higher education: A case of incorporating blogs, podcasts and social bookmarks in a web programming course based on students learning styles and technology preferences. *Journal of Educational Technology & Society*, *12*(4), 98–109.

Schroeder, J., & Greenbowe, T. (2009). The chemistry of Facebook: Using social networking to create an online community for the organic chemistry laboratory. *Innovate Journal of Online Education, 5*(4). Retrieved June 5, 2012, from http://innovateonline.info/pdf/vol5_issue4/The_Chemistry_of_Facebook-_Using_Social_Networking_to_Create_an_Online_Community_for_the_Organic_Chemistry_Laboratory.pdf

Selwyn, N. (2008). *Education 2.0? Designing the web for teaching and learning. A commentary by the technology enhanced learning phase of the teaching and learning research programme.* London, UK: TLRO-TEL Institute of Education.

Selwyn, N. (2009). Faceworking: Exploring students' education-related use of Facebook. *Learning, Media and Technology, 34*(2), 157–174. doi:10.1080/17439880902923622

Selwyn, N. (2012). *Social media in higher education. The Europa World of Learning 2012.* Routledge.

Siciliano, P., Jenks, M., Dana, M., & Talbert, B. (2011). The impact of audio technology on undergraduate instruction in a study abroad course on English gardens. *NACTA Journal, 55*(1), 46–53.

Siemens, G. (2005). Connectivism: A learning theory for the digital age. *International Journal of Instructional Technology & Distance Learning, 2*(1). Retrieved February 10, 2011, from http://www.itdl.org/Journal/Jan_05/article01.htm

Simoes, l., & Borges Gouveia, L. (2008). Web 2.0 and higher education: Pedagogical implications. IN *Proceedings of the 4ᵗʰ International Barcelona Conference on Higher Education Vol. 2 Knowledge technologies for social transformation.* Barcelona, Spain: GUNI. Retrieved February 13, 2012, from Http://www.guni-rmies.net

Starr, P. (1996). Computing our way to educational reform. *The American Prospect, 27*, 50–59.

Tapscott, D., & Williams, A. (2007). *Wikinomics.* New York, NY: Atlantic.

Turner, C. S. M., Robinson, D., Lee, M., & Soutar, A. (2009). Using technology to direct learning in higher education. The way forward? *Journal of Active Learning in Higher Education, 10*(1).

US Department of Education. (2010). *Evaluation of evidence-based practices in online learning: A meta-analysis and review of online learning studies.* Retrieved January 13, 2012, from http://www.ed.gov/about/offices/list/opepd/ppss/reports.html

Vlachopoulas, P., & Cowan, J. (2010). Choices of approaches in e-moderation: Conclusions from a grounded theory study. *Journal of Active Learning in Higher Education, 11*(3), 213–224. doi:10.1177/1469787410379684

Williams, J., & Fardon, M. (2007). Perpetual connectivity: Lecture recordings and portable media players. In R. J. Atkinson & C. McBeath (Eds.), *Proceedings of ASCILITE,* (pp. 1084-1092).

KEY TERMS AND DEFINITIONS

Asynchronous Communication: In online environments asynchronous communication refers to a form of delayed communication where the sender and receiver do not communicate in real time. Examples of asynchronous communication include email, blogging, discussion forums and mobile phone text messaging.

Blended Learning: The combination of traditional classroom teaching with online learning.

Connectivism and ICT Enabled Learning: A theory of learning for the digital age based on the notion that knowledge is distributed dynamically through networks comprising both people and technologies.

Digital Divide: Inequality of access to information and communication technologies (ICT's) between groups both within societies and across countries based on socioeconomic and demographic divisions.

E-Learning 2.0: The integration of Web 2.0 technologies in particular social media tools in online learning.

Emoderation: The process of managing online communication and group work within an online learning environment.

Learning Communities: Learning communities are groups of people, usually sharing common interests, who create and acquire new knowledge through working together.

Personalised Learning: A student centered approach to learning to ensure optimal student performance based on individual needs and abilities.

Synchronous Communication: In online environments synchronous communication refers to direct communication where both parties i.e. sender and receiver communicate in real time. Examples of synchronous communication include chat rooms, instant messaging and Skype.

Chapter 2
How Social Design Influences Student Retention and Self-Motivation in Online Learning Environments

Derek E. Baird
Facebook for Educators, USA

Mercedes Fisher
Milwaukee Area Technical College, USA

ABSTRACT

Investigating the social structure that works in online courses helps us design for and facilitate student collaboration. The integration of social technologies, and collaborative activities into the course design has a positive influence on student retention in online courses. In this chapter, the authors present an exploratory study of computer-mediated groups that utilized this collaborative-based model to participate in online and/or blended learning courses. Participants were put into groups and observed as they constructed new knowledge using both online dialogue (synchronous and asynchronous), and social media technologies (blogs, Facebook, Twitter, wiki) as tools to support and facilitate their learning in the program.

1. INTRODUCTION

In this chapter, we describe our approach to utilizing current and emerging social media to support Millennial learners, facilitate the formation of learning communities, foster student engagement, reflection, and enhance the overall learning experience for students in synchronous and asynchronous learning environments.

The proliferation of old and new media, including the Internet and other emerging digital (and mobile) technologies, has changed the way

DOI: 10.4018/978-1-4666-2851-9.ch002

students communicate, interact, and learn. The pedagogy of teaching and learning online is based on authentic learning activities, observation, collaboration, intrinsic motivation, and self-organizing social systems.

In many cases, students spend as much (or more) time, receive more feedback, and interact with peers more in an online environment than they do with their teachers in the classroom.

While traditional approaches in the past preferred learners to act "under order", a new look at the learner as constructing his or her knowledge has resulted in a change of theoretical concepts. It is our contention that current research on the topic of online course design has focused, for the most part, solely on the instructor's perspective.

While we see the value and place for this type of research, we also feel that the perspective of distance learning from the student's perspective can also yield some valuable insights for online course design. In addition, design principles for learner self-regulation and social support in online courses will be explored and examined in terms of trying different structures for presenting online content and learning.

The data included in this paper is intended as a directional means to help instructors and course designers identify social and participatory media resources and other emerging technologies that will enhance the delivery of instruction while meeting the needs of today's digital learning styles.

1.1 Growth of Online Learning

In the past decade, online learning programs have gone from being summarily dismissed by traditional institutions of education to a widely accepted and booming industry (Nagel, 2011).

Due to the rapid expansion of distance learning programs educators need to re-evaluate traditional pedagogical strategies and find ways to integrate a new generation of emerging social media technologies in a manner which supports and fosters student motivation and self-confidence in online learning environments.

A recent report conducted by US-based Instructional Technology Council that looked at the impact of online learning at community colleges (ITC Council, 2010) and provides some key insights on the growth of online learning:

- Online student services remain a priority on most campuses.
- Growth in the use of blended/hybrid and web-assisted/web-enhanced/web-facilitated classes continues.
- The completion rate gap between distance learning and face-to-face students has significantly narrowed. Completion rates jumped to a reported 72%, just below the 76% rate for face-to-face classes.
- Online education administrators continue to address the need for course quality and design, faculty training and improving student readiness and retention. Due to financial restraints, many online programs are challenged by a lack of adequately trained staff and resources to be successful.
- Older, non-traditional students are attracted to online classes and degree programs since they fit into their busy schedules to offer a solution for career advancement and/or change.

As colleges continue to navigate the costs associated with maintaining traditional educational structures online learning programs--often more cost-effective than campus-based courses--will continue to grow in popularity.

This shift in student population and teaching models will require administrators to effectively address the need for faculty training to teach online courses and provide them with the tools and resources needed to improve student learning, self-regulation and retention.

1.2 How Digital Media Contributes to Student Retention in Online Learning

Seymour Papert (1993) asserts that learning "is grounded in the idea that people learn by actively constructing new knowledge, rather than having information 'poured' into their heads."

Moreover, he asserts that people learn with particular effectiveness when they are engaged in "constructing personally meaningful artifacts" using participatory media tools like blogs, iPod, podcasting/audio blogs, wiki, social networking sites (Facebook, Twitter), and other forms of user-generated content (UGC). Content sharing tools provide students' the opportunity to socialize around the context of the content, produce cultural artifacts and learn from peer-generated commentary.

The use of participatory media elements in a situated context provides both the structure and building blocks for interaction to take place. The end result is an environment that combines social media, web-based information resources, and communities to provide a more diverse, active, and engaging learning experience.

So what is the definition of "participatory learning?" While this field of study still in its very early stages, Dr. James Bosco, a Professor Emeritus in the Department of Educational Studies at Western Michigan University, has developed a list of the key attributes of participatory learning and offers a definition of what is happening in best practice situations (Bosco, 2010).

In a participatory learning environment the learner:

- Is intrinsically motivated to learn and engaged in the learning process.
- Actively pursues a personal, rather than imposed, agenda for learning based on their own needs, interests, capabilities, and goals.
- Makes abundant and effective use of Collaboration and involvement in learning communities.

- Produces and shares products that play a critical role in the learning process for themselves and other learners.
- Encounters learning in tasks that have meaning and relevance for the learner by connecting the learning to their own frame of reference and to "real world" physical, social, and cultural contexts.
- Constructs their knowledge and competencies experientially through authentic engagements with objects, persons, ideas and other cultural artifacts rather than through didactic instruction.

This opportunity to be engaged socially is generating new content in and of itself. These experiences become integrated into today's use of mobile devices in the everyday lives of the students for whom we design courses. As a result, the learning is embedded in and transferable to other contexts for the student.

Recent studies (O'Connor, 2012) on user experience and online course design have shown that the integration of web-based communities and collaborative assignments into the course design has a positive influence on learning and student retention, this is especially true when teaching Millennial students (Table 1).

Moreover, there are many correlations between student motivation, interaction, and an information-rich environment. The name "Web 2.0", "participatory media" or "social media" may change, but the trend is well underway: students expect to create both the context and content for a personalized learning experience.

2. DESIGNING SOCIAL LEARNING COURSES TO FOSTER STUDENT MOTIVATION

From a cognitive and metacognitive perspective learners control and actively influence their learning activities and understanding. The motivational element determines why and to what extent self-

Table 1. Millennial digital learning attributes

Interactive	Interactive, engaging content and course material that motivates them to learn through challenging pedagogy, conceptual review, and feedback. Students expect to find, use, and "mash up" various types of web-based media: audio, video, multimedia, edutainment and/or educational gaming/simulation.
Student Centered	Shifts the learning responsibility to the student, and emphasizes teacher-guided instruction and modeling. Customized, ability to use interactive and social media tools, and ability to self-direct how they learn.
Situated	Reconcile classroom use of social media with how technology is being used outside of the classroom. Use of technology is tied to both authentic (learning) activity and intrinsic motivation.
Collaborative	Learning is a social activity, and students learn best through observation, collaboration, and intrinsic motivation and from self-organizing social systems comprised of peers. This can take place in either a virtual or in-person environment.
On-Demand	Ability to multitask and handle multiple streams of information and juggle both short and long term goals. Access content via different media platforms, including mobile, computer, or other handheld (portable) computer device.
Authentic	Active and meaningful activities based on real-world learning models. Industry driven problems and situations are the focus and require reflective elements, multiple perspectives and collaborative processes for relevant applicable responses from today's student.

(Baird, 2006)

regulating options are taken. Student motivation in online courses is driven by a need to achieve internal personal goals, as well as a need to meet the expectations of their peers (Bereiter, Scardamalia 1991, 1994).

To what extent the learner participates in the online learning community is largely determined by the structure of the course and its ability to provide the learner with projects and activities that will allow them to fulfill their dual identity as an individual and member within a learning community.

Therefore, learners not only need to know what steps to take in order to be successful in the online learning process, but must also discover and tap into their internal motivation to be a successful learner.

Online course design should include the use of technologies and activities which foster "modeling-mirroring" (Hung 2002) opportunities which allow learners to build interest, relevance and motivation to participate in the community, as well as construct their learning experience in the course.

This creates a symbiotic process wherein the course design piques their interest in the subject while still allowing the learner the freedom/leeway to construct knowledge necessary to meet their individual/immediate needs.

This self-interest creates the motivation to actively participate in the learning process and collaborate within the learning community. Another side benefit of the specific notion of student self-regulation through peer support is the possible relief of instructor load in online teaching.

Another key factor to weave into the course design that will promote self-regulation and motivation is to allow students opportunities to maintain their individual creativity and autonomy in the types of projects and assignments (Arnaud, 2000).

These types of projects are important because they allow students to work on activities and assignments that they find intellectually stimulating and relevant thereby making them an active architect of their learning process. To be clear, the course designer must have a rubric or project parameters in mind, but there is enough leeway to allow students to feel as though they have choices in terms of topic and relevance.

2.1 Role of the Online Instructor

The online course moderator must manage a carefully balanced mix of activities and projects that will foster social motivation, while at the same time provide students with access to the information and knowledge that motivated them to initially join the program.

We have used the following methods to help student self-regulation: incremental deadlines, student guided discussions, blueprints, communities outside the classroom, cohorts, small group projects, peer evaluations, blogs, student created rubrics, media and self-reflection activities. These strategies also help the instructor support self-regulation, while at the same time fostering the socialization process of the online student within the context of group and individual learning environment.

While the moderator is available to assist students it's also important that students are given a wide breadth of parameters to explore their interests. "If people have the sense of autonomy, they are more likely to be motivated by things that are personally important to them, and less likely to be motivated by externally imposed rewards or threats. Intrinsic motivation is a key to self-regulated learning, because it persists beyond the immediate circumstances and enables the individual to be truly self-motivated (Sharp, Pocklington, Weindling 2002)."

Moreover, we view the course as a learning roadmap, and the moderator as a guide, offering suggestions and supporting students as they construct the knowledge they are seeking to meet their intrinsic needs. As Seufert points out "a key task for the moderator is to reduce the amount of communication between the participants and the moderator and instead to stimulate the communication between participants (Seufert 2002)."

Another important design factor that will contribute towards increased student self-regulation and motivation is to provide them with opportunities to share their newly acquired knowledge with their classmates. In this manner students are supported and reassured about their acquisition of new knowledge by assuming the teachers role and leading group discussions in the synchronous led piece of the course (Arnaud 2001).

In short, learners not only need to know the right steps to be successful in the learning process but must also discover and tap into their own motivation and feel confident in their own understanding to be a successful online learner. The aforementioned methods allow course moderators to create a learning environment that provides students the freedom to construct new knowledge, while at the same time providing them the support needed.

2.2 Social Media, Student Motivation, and Retention

In most schools or higher learning environments, theory and practice must be encapsulated in the online learning, otherwise students will not have the opportunity to practice and learn from peers. In businesses, the support mechanism is strong and the pressure to apply ideas is inherent because of job expectations. There is no guarantee that the self-regulation works; the human elements of having poor instructors, not knowing or having online learning skills are roadblocks.

We suspect the difference lies in the opportunities for participants to rapidly apply new knowledge in the business setting, whereas in the traditional classroom there are limited opportunities for 'real world' applications of new skills and information. The online classroom, however, provides a platform wherein the benefits of both worlds can be blended into an effective model to acquire and then immediately apply new information into the student's workplace.

The ability of students to find immediate relevance in their coursework motivates them to delve further and sustain their level of participation in the course (See Table 2). Students will gain a better understanding of the course materials when they can link what they are learning with what they are doing. Differentiated learning styles, in conjunction with the life experience a student brings to the online classroom, must also be taken into consideration (Kelly, 2003).

One must then identify what types of accountability will manifest a sense of motivation and ownership. For example, we have students identify posts they made to the asynchronous threaded course discussion, which they feel moved the class forward by contributing to understanding.

In this way, by making judgments about their own task matching in a course, students have a direct ownership of their participation (Hadwin, Winne 2001). This ownership, along with other markers for success such as intention to complete the course, early submission of work, degree of interaction in the course and course relevance all are related to motivation in the course, drives the student to modify their behavior for success (Table 2).

To what extent the learner participates in the online learning community is largely determined by the structure of the course and its ability to provide the learner with projects and activities which will allow them to fulfill their dual identity as an individual and member of within a learning community (Fisher, 2004).

Table 2. Course design, participatory media, and student motivation

How does the online course allow for more self-regulated learning/motivation?	Curriculum activities must provide immediacy and relevance Social collaboration activities Use of newsgroups, wiki's (collaborative website), blogs, instant messaging, streaming audio/video, and other participatory media technologies **Example:** Students will form small groups and then read book as a group, discuss online at least twice, and develop a web-based activity and/or artifact to share with their peers.
Which design elements encourage self-regulation and social support?	Student led discussions **Example:** Students are allowed to choose a topic of relevance to them and then lead their peers in a discussion. These TI times are often creative and unique. Not only do they provide an opportunity for social learning, but also serve as an opportunity to learn more about the student's presenting. In addition, students prepare web-based presentation materials that they can project on the online whiteboard in the classroom. Providing opportunities for autonomy, creativity Group projects/collaboration Immediate relevancy of projects **Example:** Students create a learning blueprint wherein they self-select a type of technology to learn more about and then exhibit their findings in a web-based portfolio. Students are then required to use their selected technology in some capacity, and also teach it to another person. Utilizing various social software technologies (online discussion boards, blogs, IM), students will solicit assistance and/or collaborative feedback from members of their course cohort. Many students used this technology piece as an important part of their Action Research Project (ARP) because it had such immediate importance and relevance in their own practice.
How do instructors deal with individual differences between learners?	Allow for opportunities for autonomy and creativity
What motivates self-regulation in online courses?	Projects meet intrinsic needs of students Relevance of projects, readings; need to fill knowledge deficits User-centered design, social networks, web-based collaborative tools Support and feedback from peers **Example:** Group projects allow students to find others in their cohort with the same interests and form clusters of "critical friends" that help each other overcome both technology and curriculum issues.

2.3 Leveraging Social Media to Support Learning

Raised in the "always-on" world of interactive media, the Internet, and social media technologies, students today have different expectations and learning styles than previous generations. The ubiquitous use mobile technologies gives students an unprecedented opportunity to use tools like Facebook or Twitter to create self-organizing learning communities or Personal Learning Networks (PLN) that are available for 'on-demand' learning opportunities (Fisher & Baird, 2006).

While many educators feel that email is a good way to reach students, research from ComScore (Mashable, 2011) shows that young adults are moving away from the use of email. Instead they are using social networking sites like, Facebook to communicate.

The use of social technologies, such as a blog, Twitter or Facebook, provides students with an opportunity to self-regulate their understanding (or lack of) of the current course topic with their peers (Phillips, Baird & Fogg, 2011). Moreover, as students utilize these social technologies to share their thought processes with their peers, they are able to help each other work through cognitive roadblocks, while also building a collaborative peer support system.

When the curriculum is designed to leverage self-directed online learning, students can learn more than what is taught in class because they are able to create meaning for themselves as well as learn from the cross-pollination of ideas, life experience and opinions that exist in online learning environments (Baird & Fisher, 2010).

Critics of online learning environments claim that because a cohort of peers may not know each other very well, it may create a learning environment that makes it awkward and difficult for students to exchange ideas and collaborate.

However, research conducted by Facebook (Bakshy, et al., 2012) on the role of information sharing in online social networking environments, found that it is the "more abundant weak ties who are responsible for the propagation of novel information."

It is important to assemble cohorts that strike a balance between students who have 'weak' and 'strong' ties. Doing so prevents students from remaining in an information silo and exposes them to new and more diverse information sources. When students with strong ties work together, they tend to exchange similar types of data, information and sources. In doing so, it prevents them from the opportunity to be open to exposures to new and differing sources of information.

As a result the conversational dialogues that emerge online are more interdisciplinary, authentic, and situated learning experiences for the cohort. The ability to discuss relevant issues fuels their interest in the subject matter, which in turn, motivates them to continue in the course.

In fact, when carefully integrated into online courses these web-based classrooms can support a new level of social exchange and interaction that will, in turn, promote and foster student motivation. These sophisticated social software platforms will empower students and instructors to interact with each other to exchange ideas and multiple perspectives (Richardson & Swan, 2011).

Understanding and incorporating opportunities for social interaction and information sharing into your coursework will increase student motivation and enhance learning, while better meeting the needs of today's students and their digital learning styles.

We have seen the benefits in quality since we have required students to post in a public forum, such as Facebook Groups, Twitter (or other microblogging platforms), or LMS. For example, posting dialogue in a Facebook Group helps students feel known and simultaneously builds a sense of community and accountability with the other members of the cohort. Many times these postings take the form of conversational writing; however, it's a little more coherent than speaking in class since students have time to reflect, research, and ponder before they post.

2.4 How Technological Challenges Affect Student Motivation

While social technology is a wonderful tool, nothing can be more frustrating to the online student than having their learning hit a roadblock. Unresolved technical problems and lack of support can quickly drain student momentum and lead to drop out rates. Therefore, it's vital that online courses provide avenues to assist students with technical issues so they can continue their learning process (Levin, Araheh, Lenhart & Rainie, 2002)179.

Most technology related problems encountered during the lifespan of an online course program will be resolved through peer-to-peer technical support. Kawachi (2003) describes one aspect of motivation as the personal motivation that one has when they become a technology expert within their group. This is both intrinsic in that it will make the student feel more empowered and extrinsic because they are recognized by the group.

In this manner, the more technologically advanced students are helping less advanced students with issues of technical support that in turn, motivates and stimulates interest in completing the course (Newton /Ledgerwood 2001).

Online learners have unique needs and issues that need to be understood and supported by the university (Newton/Ledgerwood 2001). The key is to have support mechanisms in place to minimize the impact of technical challenges on student motivation and retention in online learning environments.

2.5 Peer Support

Due to the rapid adoption of social media students are becoming more involved in supporting their learning through the use of social networks and online communities. These learning communities are formed around issues of identity and shared values; they are not place-based (Palloff, Pratt, 1999).

Recognizing and supporting the importance that students are placing on peer-to-peer support will allow higher education educators with the opportunity to design more self-determined learning opportunities for students.

As students are involved in the process of collaboration they begin to form social bonds that, as they deepen, motivate the learner to establish an identity within the group through active participation and contributions to their learning community.

When social technologies are integrated into the course design, the collaborative aspects of the projects undertaken in the course allow students to interact with other members of the class, identify who has a particular skill or expertise they want to acquire, and then provides opportunities for them to model and scaffold this knowledge from their peers.

In the earlier stages, opportunities are given for the students to quantify their knowledge and skills and view that of the other students in order to help them identify their place as well as other students with specific expertise (See Table 3).

Through this process learners become motivated on an individual level as well as fostering a sense of accountability to the group to continue to participate. The learner in an online course is constructing a base of knowledge on both and individual and group level. As their personal understanding of the subject deepens learners are motivated to contribute to the collective understanding and receive positive feedback from the group.

As students make connections with other members of the class and begin engaging with the course curriculum, it creates a powerful learning experience that propels them deeper into the subject, fostering their motivation to continue the process of learning.

Group discussion is an important component within an online class as well. Rovai (Rovai 2003) examined the effects that the discussion element

Table 3. Roles of online students

Roles	Task	Procedure	Group Value
Organizer	Provides an ordered way of examining information	Presents outlines, overviews, or summary of all information	Lead thinker
Facilitator	Moderates, keeps on task	Assures all work is done and/or all participants have opportunity	Inclusive
Strategist	Decides the best way to proceed on a task	Organization	Detail
Analyst	Looks for meaning within the content	Realizes potential of content to practical application	Analytical
Supporter	Provides overall support for an individual or group	Looks for ways to help members or groups	Helpful
Summarizer	Highlights significant points; restates conclusion	Reviews material looking for important concepts	Gives the overall big picture
Narrator	Generally relates information in order	Provides group with a reminder of order	Keeps group focused on goal
Elaborator	Relates discussion with prior learned concepts or knowledge	Presents previous information as a comparative measure	Application or expansion
Researcher	Supplies outside resources to comparative information	Goes looking for other information with which to compare discussion	Inclusiveness
Antagonist	Supplies contrasting ideas	Looks for opposing viewpoints and presents in a relative way	Opposing viewpoint

(Fisher, Coleman, Sparks, & Plett, 2006)

had on the sense of community and found that when discussions were a graded component, there were significantly more discussions per student and that there were also higher levels of interaction.

In addition, as students collaborate on projects and in course discussion boards they begin to formulate social codes which will both support and regulate the participation, behavior, and depth of learning that occurs in the online classroom. The observance of these self-determined social codes legitimizes participation in the learning community (Seufert, 2002). Conversely, students who choose not to abide by this group determined social codes will most likely be censured (or have their level of participation severely limited) by the group, thereby making it more likely that they will not complete the course.

The continuing support of the social network plays a key role in the success of the online course and student retention. Social motivation though is not the best indication of learning, even if the student enjoys this aspect; it does not compensate or make up for the need of actual information. The information and the knowledge that is constructed by the learner is the intrinsic motivation that the student is looking for in order to become a successful learner.

2.6 Student Non-Participation

Occasionally the instructor will experience a student who seems uninterested or unwilling to engage in either the synchronous or asynchronous pieces of the course. One area where the online and traditional teachers face similar challenges is how to draw the isolated learner into a class rooted in constructivist-based principles. This is a rather traditional problem and it applies to all socially situated learning environments, not just the online variety.

It is important that the instructor work with the student to identify the root causes and/or external factors that are impacting active participation in the learning community. There are many possible factors which may be contributing to a student's lack of participation in the learning community including: a sense of isolation from the group, medical, job or family related issues, and learning disabilities. Only when the reasons for not participating are clearly identified can the instructor effectively help re-engage the student into the community of the course.

One of the initial actions an instructor might explore is to ask themselves how would they resolve or correct the situation in a traditional setting, and then seek technological avenues that emulate and/or support that approach. A good first approach is to privately email the student and invite them to engage in the process and explain how the learning community is dependent on what they have to bring to the process as much as the learner will gain from what the other members of the group will share.

Additionally, the instructor could invite the student to share any situations in their personal or working life that may be preventing their full participation in group. At this point the instructor will be able to assess if this is a temporary situation that will be resolved in the short term and will not hamper further participation. If the situation is more serious, the instructor can then work with the student to make other arrangements to complete the course. Finally, it's important to encourage the student to continue to check in with the instructor as events develop.

It is common that groups that engage in active online dialogue and activities will develop strong self-regulatory habits. In many cases, the group itself will seek out the learner who is not participating and actively seek to draw them back into the learning community.

While the reasons for continued non-participation are varied, one common reason may be a sense of not feeling accepted or isolated from the group. This could be a reaction from others in group who feel as though they are openly sharing and contributing to the dialogue and that other students are not honoring the social contract

of reciprocity. This situation can be corrected if the isolated student can be encouraged to make a renewed effort to actively participate in the discussion.

Most importantly, when confronted with a student who seemingly lacks interest in the course, it is vital that the instructor realize that the student's lack of motivation may not necessarily be rooted in a lack of desire and actively works with the student to find avenues to guide them back into full participation. This type of self-regulatory activity cannot be overlooked or ignored and may even be modeled by the instructor if they do not naturally occur or are initiated by the members of the learning community.

2.7 The Myth of the Digital Native

If we over-estimate their skills we underestimate the support they need and misunderstand their practices. – Dr. Sonia Livingstone

Over the last decade there has been lots of debate, in both the press and educational circles, about the technological prowess of "digital natives." We've heard a lot about what's exciting in educational technology, but the reality is that teachers still see a lot of students struggling to use technology (Livingstone, 2010).

During her keynote at the 2010 Digital Media Learning Conference, Dr. Sonia Livingstone, London School of Economics, shared the following examples from her research and interviews with both parents and children on the difficulties "digital natives" face using technology:

- **Example:** Going to a Web site–can take a half hour, require parents to help find what they are looking for on the web, or the child will simply give up.
- **Example:** Parents thought their child was very savvy, but something about the style of her use didn't reveal her struggles. "Megan" is confident, but one can ob-

serve her many struggles while she uses technology.

- **Example:** 17-year-old, quoted: "With books it's a lot easier to research. I can't really use the internet for studying." Another, "Every time I try to look for something, I can never find it. It keeps coming up with things that are completely irrelevant."
- **Example:** Teens often didn't know how to change their privacy settings, unsure about what to click to manage this task. (Nervousness about unintended consequences: stranger danger, parental anxiety, viruses, crashed computers, unwanted advertising, etc.)

When it comes to youth and digital media we tend to be conservative in the type of content we give young people and far more aggressive when approaching them with digital media tools. It's important to remember that, just because we include digital media, it doesn't mean youth know how to use these technologies effectively.

3. CONCLUSION

We discuss the need for a new pedagogy for online education and how the needs of the online student differ from the traditional student. In Section 3 we discussed how student participation is tied to course design and how it must satisfy their dual identity as both a member of the learning community and their individual (intrinsic) learning goals. In addition, we discussed the role of the online instructor as a guide, peer support and the formation of social codes, the cross pollination of ideas and opinions by their peers and the 'legitimization" via active participation in the group dialogue.

We shared how we integrated the ideas of course design in section two into our courses. We discussed the use of the digital portfolio, book group and group reflection activities as a means to fuel student interest, motivation and self-regulation in the online learning environment.

We outlined how social media technologies support learning through social and textual exchange of ideas and problem solving activities. Additionally, technology that allows for online exchange allows students, instructors and universities to provide technical support for the online student so they can avoid technical challenges along their learning journey.

Moreover, we explored how the coursework and assignments were designed to allow students to place new knowledge into a contextual or situated framework. The projects were multi-faceted in nature in that they required students to develop technical and collaborative skills, while reflecting and engaging in the coursework to meet their intrinsic goals.

In addition, we illustrated how the projects, coursework and social software technologies utilized in the program are designed to provide opportunities for social and collaborative learning. As students work together they are also building social bonds that support both their satisfaction and retention in the course.

In light of these socio-cultural changes, educators need to find ways to dovetail the curriculum with digital learning styles by designing curriculum which integrates opportunities for student's to use social media to collaborate and interact with their peers, as well as customize, create, and publish their own content as a means to achieve both short and long term learning goals.

The success of the online learning programs hinges on the ability of the instructors to ingrate social technologies into their course design that foster social support, provide technical support, expose students to a cross-section of ideas and design courses which allow students to explore, share and develop their intrinsic learning goals.

As online learning continues to expand and new instructors deepen their understanding of the online learning environment they will be able to focus on students learning and supporting their needs in this environment.

In the end, successful web-based learning comes when instructors and designers recognize first the importance of cultivating relationships, and then carefully balance the symbiotic relationship between social technologies, community, and constructivist learning as a means to provide engaging learning experiences for students to achieve their full potential.

REFERENCES

Arnaud, M. (2000). *How to improve group interactions in open and distance learning configurations*. [Electronic Version]. International Federation of Information Processing Conference. Retrieved October 3, 2003, from http://www.ifip.or.at/con2000/iceut2000/iceut02-01.pdf

Baird, D. (2006). Learning 2.0: Digital, social and always-on. *Barking Robot*. Retrieved June 3, 2010 from http://www.debaird.net/blendededunet/2006/04/learning_styles.html

Baird, D., & Fisher, M. (2010). Social media, Gen Y and digital learning styles. In Dasgupta, S. (Ed.), *Social computing: Concepts, methodologies, tools and applications*. Hershey, PA: IGI Global Publishing.

Bakshy, E., Marlow, C., Rosenn, I., & Adamic, L. (2012). The role of social networks in information diffusion. *Facebook, Inc.* Retrieved January 15, 2012 from http://www.scribd.com/facebook/d/78445521-Role-of-Social-Networks-in-Information-Diffusion

Bosco, J. (2010). *Participatory learning in schools: Square peg, round hole*. 2010 Digital Media Learning Conference. Retrieved March 5, 2010, from http://www.scribd.com/doc/33297174/Participatory-Learning-in-Schools-Square-Peg-Round-Hole

Fisher, M. (2004). *Designing courses and teaching on the Web: A "how to" guide to proven, innovative strategies*. Lanham, MD: Rowman & Littlefield Publishing Group.

Fisher, M., & Baird, D. (2006). Making mobile learning work: Utilizing mobile technology for collaboration, assessment and reflection in higher education. *Journal of Educational Technology Systems*, *35*(1), 3–30. doi:10.2190/4T10-RX04-113N-8858

Fisher, M., Coleman, P., Sparks, P., & Plett, C. (2006). Designing community learning in web-based environments. In Khan, B. H. (Ed.), *Flexible learning in an information society*. Hershey, PA: Information Science Publishing. doi:10.4018/978-1-59904-325-8.ch004

Hadwin, A. F., & Philip, H. (2001). CoNoteS2: A software tool for promoting self-regulation. *Educational Research and Evaluation*, *7*(2-3), 313–334. doi:10.1076/edre.7.2.313.3868

Hung, D. (2002). Forging links between communities of practice and schools through online learning communities: Implications for appropriating and negotiating knowledge. *International Journal on E-Learning*, (April-June): 2002.

Instructional Technology Council. (2010). *Distance education survey results: Tracking the impact of elearning at community colleges*. Instructional Technology Council. Retrieved May 1, 2010 from http://www.scribd.com/doc/31893631/Trends-in-eLearning-Tracking-the-Impact-of-eLearning-at-Community-Colleges

Kawachi, P. (2003). Initiating intrinsic motivation in online education: Review of the current state of the art. *Interactive Learning Environments*, *11*(1), 59–81. doi:10.1076/ilee.11.1.59.13685

Kelly, D. (2003). *Adult learners: Characteristics, theories, motivations, learning environment*. Retrieved October 4, 2003, from www.dit.ie/DIT/lifelong/adult/adlearn_chars.pdf

Ledgerwood, N. (2001). Evolving support for online learning: An action research model. In M. Wallace, A. Ellis, & D. Newton (Eds.), *Moving Online II Conference*, Gold Coast, Australia, 2 - 4 September, Southern Cross University, (pp. 18-29).

Levin, D., Araheh, S., Lenhart, A., & Rainie, L. (2002). *The digital disconnect: The widening gap between internet-savvy students and their schools*. Retrieved January 5, 2006, from http://www.pewinternet.org/report_display.asp?r=67

Livingstone, S. (2010). *Youthful participation: What have we learned, what shall we ask next?* Paper presented at the 2010 Digital Media and Learning Conference. Retrieved March 5, 2010, from http://www.scribd.com/doc/27906764/Sonia-Livingstone-2010-Digital-Media-and-Learning-Conference-Keynote

Mashable. (2011). *ComScore says you don't got mail: Web email usage declines, 59% among teens*. Retrieved November 2, 2011, from http://techcrunch.com/2011/02/07/comscore-says-you-dont-got-mail-web-email-usage-declines-59-among-teens/

Nagel, D. (2011). Online learning set for explosive growth as traditional classrooms decline. *Campus Technology*. Retrieved May 20, 2012, from http://campustechnology.com/articles/2011/01/26/online-learning-set-for-explosive-growth-as-traditional-classrooms-decline.aspx

O'Connor, E. (2012). A survival guide from an early adopter: How Web 2.0 and the right attitude can enable learning and expansive course design. *Journal of Educational Technology Systems, 40*(2).

Palloff, R., & Pratt, K. (1999). *Building learning communities in cyberspace: Effective strategies for the online classroom*. San Francisco, CA: Jossey-bass.

Papert, S. (1993). *The children's machine: Rethinking school in the age of the computer*. New York, NY: Basic Books, Inc.

Phillips-Fogg, L., Baird, D., & Fogg, B. J. (2011). *Facebook for educators*. Retrieved May 15, 2011, from http://facebookforeducators.org/educators-guide

Richardson, J., & Swan, K. (2011). *Examining social presence in online courses in relation to students' perceived learning and satisfaction*. Retrieved May 23, 2012, from http://hdl.handle.net/2142/18713

Rovai, A. P. (2003). Strategies for grading online discussion: Effects on discussions and classroom community in internet-based university courses. *Journal of Computing in Higher Education, 15*(1), 89–107. doi:10.1007/BF02940854

Rovai, A. P. (2004). A constructivist approach to online college learning. *The Internet and Higher Education, 7*(2), 79–93. doi:10.1016/j.iheduc.2003.10.002

Scardamalia, M., & Bereiter, C. (1991). Higher levels of agency for children in knowledge-building: A challenge for the design of new knowledge media. *Journal of the Learning Sciences, 1*(1), 37–68. doi:10.1207/s15327809jls0101_3

Scardamalia, M., & Bereiter, C. (1994). Computer support for knowledge-building communities. *Journal of the Learning Sciences, 3*(3), 265–283. doi:10.1207/s15327809jls0303_3

Seufert, S. (2002, May). *Design and management of online learning communities*. 2002 European Academy of Management Conference.

Sharp, C., Pocklington, K., & Weindling, D. (2002). Study support and the development of the self-regulated learner. *Educational Research, 44*(1), 29–41. doi:10.1080/00131880110107333

Wallace, L. (1996). Changes in the demographics and motivations of distance education students. *Journal of Distance Education, 11*(1), 1-31. Retrieved December 2, 2003, from http://cade.athabascau.ca/vol11.1/wallace.html

KEY TERMS AND DEFINITIONS

Blog: A blog, short for 'weblog' is a self-publishing platform where the author shares opinions, educational resources, rich media or syllabus materials.

Social Networking: A term used to describe online communities of shared practice (twitter, Facebook, Google+, ORKUT).

Social Software/Social Media: Social software enables people to connect or collaborate through computer-mediated communication (wiki, blog, podcast, social networking) and form online communities.

Social Design: Term used to describe the strategic integration of social media and networking technologies into the face-to-face and/or online curriculum to encourage the exchange of ideas, knowledge and build community between students.

Web 2.0: Web 2.0 generally refers to a second generation of services available on the web that allow people collaborate and share information online.

Wiki: A collaborative web environment where any user can contribute information, knowledge or embed rich media such as video, audio, or widgets.

Chapter 3
Student–Faculty Communication on Facebook:
Prospective Learning Enhancement and Boundaries

Laurenţiu Şoitu
Alexandru Ioan Cuza University of Iaşi, Romania

Laura Păuleţ-Crăiniceanu
Alexandru Ioan Cuza University of Iaşi, Romania

ABSTRACT

This chapter addresses the topic of Facebook use in education, with focus on the learning issues concerning the student-faculty relations and communication on this social network. Its main purpose is to reveal academics' general and particular attitudes towards the use of Facebook with instructional aim. Therefore, it presents a generous theoretical perspective on the emerging phenomenon of Social Networks integration on education, in the United States mainly. Further on, it puts side by side these views with the findings of a particular, empirical study conducted by the authors. A survey applied to a sample of Facebook users from "Alexadru Ioan Cuza" University of Iaşi, Romania (N=160) revealed that the academics partially agreed that the use of Facebook is suitable for educational exchanges. Whilst the literature suggested that students have more positive attitudes than faculty towards the use of Facebook in education, this present study does not support this view.

DOI: 10.4018/978-1-4666-2851-9.ch003

INTRODUCTION

Facebook, a Legitimate Learning Environment?

Facebook, the biggest Social Network in the world (Facebook, 2011), used mainly as a virtual space for social relations enhancement and as a valuable marketing tool, recently began to take shape as an educational platform. This phenomenon can be witnessed above all in the United State of America, where the adoption rate of the new technologies in colleges is higher, but also in European countries, where the young adults are deeply emerged into the online environment. Nevertheless, the practice of teaching college students on Facebook is quite new and recusant in the academic environment. While Facebook is not being used for traditional and direct teaching, it is becoming more of an informal education network. Consequently, several debates surrounding its legitimacy as being or not an appropriate medium for learning and for a healthy development of the teacher-student relationship are undergoing. Enthusiasts have praised Facebook for its potential of being a space equipped with communication tools that suit the collaborative and constructivist approach towards the educational act. The skeptics expressed their unease referring to the lack of borders between private and public, personal and institutional communication in this unregulated environment. Selwyn (2009) argued that "whilst growing numbers of educators celebrate the potential of social networking to (re)engage learners with their studies, others fear that such applications compromise and disrupt young people's engagement with 'traditional' education provision" (p. 157). It is recognized that some of the qualities of social networking may clash with current pedagogical paradigms, as Selwyn (2009) highlighted. Educationalists hope that social networking promotes exchanges between learners that are related to formal educational objectives, but social networks

as Facebook are also distinguished for providing channels for informal and unstructured learning.

Moreover, the communication practices on Facebook between students and faculty vary from one course to another, one university to another, one country to another. While some instructors only use dedicated closed groups or official pages to stay in touch with their students, others accept friend request from their students, allowing them to see their profile and to share different type of contents with them.

The scholars in the fields of Education, Sociology, Media Communications and Information Technology are just beginning to direct their research interests on this matter. Ellison, Steinfield, and Lampe (2007) state that "Facebook constitutes a rich site for researchers interested in the affordance of social networks due to its heavy usage patterns and technological capabilities that bridge online and offline connection. We believe that Facebook represents an understudied offline to online trend..." (p. 2).

Yet, research on the use of Facebook for educational purposes has been limited. Most of this literature has focused on the unprofessional content of students' Facebook profiles and the need to provide students with social media guidelines (Karl & Peluchette, 2011). The authors of the present study found various content analyses of wall posts of students, quantitative and qualitative analyses of surveys applied to students, in depth interviews or exploratory studies regarding teachers' and students' attitudes towards Facebook. Nonetheless, these studies, especially undertaken in the United States of America, haven't been able to provide reliable findings in order to settle on a positive or a negative impact of Facebook usage as a learning tool in universities or to address the issue of teacher-students Facebook mediated communication. Nor they suggested directions towards an operational learning model that could complement the traditional teaching methods and other e-Learning practices. Therefore, further exploration of the boundaries and prospective of student-teacher communication on Facebook should be carried out, while Facebook could be education's opportunity to re-engage students as Selwyn (2009) pointed out.

How do Romanian Students Connect with their Faculty on Facebook?

In Romania, Facebook has grown as the leading Social Network in students' preferences within the last two or three years and it is argued in formal and informal debates that it is still not effectively used as a learning platform. Some universities have Facebook pages, but they use them more as a marketing promotion tools than as an educational one. Yet, many Romanian students and teachers have Facebook personal accounts and are members of various discussion groups where they exchange academic information. Based on nonsystematic observation procedures, it has been witnessed that in Romania teachers and students use to connect on Facebook through friendship and subscription procedures.

The purpose of this study is to reveal the degree to which teachers and students perceive Facebook as a truly educational platform and which are their attitudes towards carrying out learning activities on Facebook. The means and the practices required are also questioned.

Chapter Purpose, Design, and Objectives

In this broad, least investigated context of "educational Facebook", this present study has four main objectives:

O1: To disclose academics general and particular attitudes towards the use of Facebook in educational purposes;

O2: To conceal the extent to which academics use Facebook as an education tool and at what comfort rate;

O3: To reveal is there are significant differences between faculty and students regarding general and particular attitudes towards Facebook.

O4: To highlight which are the advantages and disadvantages of Facebook interaction as perceived by academics.

In order to meet these objectives, the authors have conducted a mixed, theoretical and empirical research on this matter. Therefore, the first part of this chapter consists of a relevant international literature review. The purpose is to highlight the directions and results in the research field of Learning and Technology, concerning the teacher-student relation on Facebook advantages, drawbacks, considered boundaries and prospective learning enhancement or consequences. The second part is meant to be an exploratory study in which the authors will reveal and discuss upon the results of a survey applied to students and faculty members (N=160) from the "Alexandru Ioan Cuza" University of Iași, Romania. The main focus of the survey was to reveal the attitude towards teacher-student communication on Facebook of three different categories of academics, based on different dimensions. Results of the closed questions are interpreted based on an SPSS conducted statistical analysis. Also, the authors carried out a qualitative analysis in order to construe a broader perspective on the matter, based on answers the subject offered in the open questions fields.

BACKGROUND AND THEORETICAL FRAMEWORK

Universities Open the Gates towards Facebook Frenzy: Stats and Facts

World seems obsessed with Facebook. According to the last study published by Facebook (2011) with over 500 million users, Facebook is now used by 1 in every 13 people on earth, with over

250 million of them (over 50%) who log in every day. The most fervent users are the young adults aged between 18-25 years, consisting in a 35 per cent of the total population of Facebook users.

In the interest of our study, we must take into account that since its launch, in 2004, Facebook has been associated with college students and with the academic environment. According to Hirschorn (2007), "Facebook was started by Mark Zuckerberg, 23, while he was a student at Harvard in 2004. The general concept was to digitize the legendary (Harvard) freshman-year 'facebook,' and allow students not only to gawk at one another's photos but also to flirt, network, [and] interact" (p. 154). At first, Facebook.com was limited to college students at Harvard with a university email address (Boyd & Ellison, 2008, p. 218). It was after it opened up to all college students when the Facebook phenomenon began to take scale. As Boyd and Ellison (2008) said, "as Facebook began supporting other schools, those users were also required to have university email addresses associated with those institutions, a requirement that kept the site relatively closed and contributed to users' perceptions of the site as an intimate, private community" (p. 218). This was changed in 2005, when Facebook opened its doors to people outside the university network (Boyd & Ellison, 2008, p. 218). As Roblyer et al. (2010) appreciated "now has a diverse community of users at all levels of education and areas of society, including companies and universities". In other words, although now it has multiple uses, the Facebook phenomenon has its roots in the college environment. And now it seems to return, much more powerful and well equipped to its origins.

While it provides personalized and interactive services based on users' interest and activities on the web, "Facebook is one of the most popular SNSs for college students and was by far the one website that helped 'tip' SNSs into the mainstream culture" (Roblyer et al., 2010). According to an infographic published in October 2011 by OnlinePhd.org, in 2011 Facebook reached 800 million

users, with students spending 100 minutes per day on this network, and visiting the network site 6 times daily.

Another aspect depicted in the infographic material referred to the fact that even the educators are on Facebook. 82% of the American universities have pages to communicate with prospective students. And, the most important aspect for this present research, it is factual evidence that students connect with their professors on Facebook: while 40% of faculty have students as friends, 60% of the students have faculty as friends. Regarding the students activity on Facebook, it seems that the less engaged students in the educational realm spend more time playing games, posting photos and checking friends' profiles. According to the same infographic, 20% of the students who use Facebook while studying, get lower grades that the ones that do not complement these activities. In comparison, the more engaged and active ones who spend time creating and sharing events, are more likely to stay in college.

All these things considered, Facebook plays a significant role as communication tool in the present, especially for students. The proportions of the phenomenon entitle researchers in the related fields to undergo research related to the inquiry of Facebook being or not a suitable platform for learning.

Facebook Use in Academic Field

Phillips et al. (2011) acknowledged in a study entitled "Facebook for educators" that "the proliferation of digital, social and mobile technologies has created a culture in which youth participate more in creating and sharing content, profoundly changing the way students communicate, interact, and learn. In many cases students spend as much (or more) time online in an informal learning environment-interacting with peers and receiving feedback than they do with their teachers in the traditional classroom" (p. 3).

The use of Facebook among academia was studied with predilection in the broader context of e-Learning, constructivist learning and Social Networks (SNSs) educational employment. The majority of the studies were conducted on the United States of America and Anglo-Saxon environment, where the social media and new media technologies have had for some time a great rate of penetration and a more wide spread use than in other countries. In the US, Facebook is also officially used as a college e-Learning platform on which students and teachers interact, exchanging course materials and offering feedback. According to Muñoz (2009), since its 2004 inception, virtually all colleges in the United States (and growing internationally) have designated college networks within the site. The adoption rates of Facebook in universities and colleges are remarkable; 85% of college students that have a college network within Facebook have adopted it (Arrington, 2005). Karlin (2007) reported that "almost 60% of students who use social networking talk about education online, and more than 50% talk about specific school work" (p. 7).

Roblyer et al. (2010) designed a study to gather preliminary evidence of the current adoption of SNSs such as Facebook by students and faculty, and to determine their willingness to segue their use of these tools from the social arena to the instructional one. The reason behind their study is the fact that "SNSs such as Facebook are one of the latest examples of communications technologies that have been widely-adopted by students and, consequently, have the potential to become a valuable resource to support their educational communications and collaborations with faculty" (p. 134). Selwyn (2007) argued that since it's beginning, Facebook has quickly become the social network site of choice by college students and an integral part of the "behind the scenes" college experience. But as Mazer, Murphy, and Simonds (2007) highlighted "This [Facebook] network is increasingly being used not only by students but also by [college] faculty. According to a Facebook spokesperson, approximately 297,000 Facebook members identify themselves as faculty or staff." (p. 3)

It seems like professors have found Facebook to be a useful communication tool (Bollman & Wright, 2008; Soder, 2009) and that administrators and college faculty have taken a more positive approach and are using Facebook to build connections with students (Heiberger & Harper, 2008). Sturgeon and Walker (2009) revealed that several faculty members claimed to have created a Facebook account to assuage their own children or families, but they have since recognized the academic benefits, with over 50% of them mentioning that Facebook has the potential to be a useful academic tool. As the authors highlight, the idea that Facebook provides an open line of communication between faculty and students was mentioned by over 90% of the interviewed faculty members. Over 50% of faculty members believe that Facebook gives both faculty and students the opportunity to know each other better, in a more personal way. These personal connections are possible, according to one interviewee, when faculty members can "see the kinds of activities their students are involved in, they can use that information to make connections, helping people to be drawn into the course a little better".

Yet, there is one other aspect of Facebook academic exploitation: the one that relates to the administrative use. Facebook, as well as other SNSs, like LinkedIn and Twitter, have been used to open the communication lines between students and universities by informing them of college events and other collegiate activities. "The most prevalent use of SNSs in the university community is creating profiles and groups to communicate events with users. Colleges are also using SNSs for university marketing campaigns", believe Roblyer et al. (2010, p. 137). What is more, Facebook seems to be perceived as "an excellent mechanism for communicating with our students because it allows us to go where they already are; it is an environment that students are already comfortable with" (Mack et al., 2007, p. 4).

Prospective Learning Enhancement on Facebook: Pros and Cons

The use of social networking is a controversial element of the digital education landscape. Despite the numerous functions Facebook has which academia could exploit, Roblyer et al. (2010) highlighted that faculty members have a track record of prohibiting classroom uses of technologies that are frequently used by students. Nevertheless, same authors appreciate that Facebook has some features that could appeal to faculty members and be adopted if it proves to facilitate communication with students. For example, teachers may perceive it as akin to e-mail technology on which they already highly rely on for communication with students. On other campuses, faculty members have created Facebook groups for their classes to facilitate communication. (Sacks, 2009; Wolfe, 2009). Roblyer et al. (2010) consider that "a second aspect is the social one. Faculty who see teaching as establishing a relationship with students may view Facebook-like technologies as an efficient, even business-like way to accomplish that connection […] many educational institutions seem to be sold on the idea of communicating with students in this way. They have their own Facebook pages and actively seek to link with those of their students. This modeling may help persuade educators that SNSs of this kind are a practical solution to teachers' need to keep in close contact with students." (p. 135)

Another attribute of Facebook that could have an instructional value is the aperture towards social interaction. In modern education, interaction is considered to be an essential aspect. "The social and interactive nature of SNSs presents the intriguing possibility that by enhancing social interactions with and among students through the use of an SNS such as Facebook, instructors can increase the overall quality of engagement in a given instructional setting and, thus, create a more effective learning environment. SNSs

also provide easily-measured evidence of both student and instructor interaction" Roblyer et al. (2010, p. 137) say. Same authors cite Roblyer and Wiencke (2003) who list five different types of interactions that can contribute to the overall quality and potential impact of an online course: socially-designed interaction, instructionally-designed interaction, interactivity affordances of technology, student engagement, and instructor engagement. All these features can be found using Facebook means of interaction, such as discussion groups, multimedia sharing tools, chat options, dedicated applications and others.

Perceiving Facebook as a highly-interactive instructional communication field, from her own experience as a higher education instructor, Schwartz (2009) believes that this SNS can provide an opportunity for pedagogical mentoring. Citing Fletcher and Ragins' work on "relational mentoring" in The Handbook of Mentoring at Work: Theory, Research and Practice said that "growth in relationships happen when both people experience…increased energy and well-being, potential to take action, increased knowledge of self and other, a boost to self-esteem, and an interest in more connection" (p. B13). And this could happen on Facebook. As Selwyn (2009) emphasizes, the prominence of SNSs in the lives of learners of all ages has prompted great enthusiasm amongst some educators. It has been claimed, for example, that social networking applications share many of the desirable qualities of good 'official' education technologies – permitting peer feedback and matching the social contexts of learning such as the school, university or local community (Mason, 2006). It has been also suggested that social networking offers the opportunity to re-engage individuals with learning and education, promoting a "critical thinking in learners" about their learning, which is one of "the traditional objectives' of education" (Bugeja, 2006, p. 1). Going further on, Ziegler (2007) mentioned that SNSs have "the capacity to radically change the educational system… to better motivate students as engaged learners rather than learners who are primarily passive observers of the educational process" (p. 69).

Demski (2009) believed that "a secured social networking site allows schools to incorporate the technology into academics while preparing students to the perils of online communities" (p. 1). Demski stated that web 2.0 is not just a passing trend; it is an "activity that has embedded itself into the way work gets done" (p. 2). This has encouraged some educationalists to explore the potential of social networking to augment 'conventional' interactions and dialogue between students and teachers. Some have welcomed the capacity of social networking services to offer educators a forum for 'easy networking and positive networking with students' (Lemeul, 2006, p. 1). According to Pascarella and Terrenzini (1991), some of the most effective faculty members are those that create an informal relationship with their students. And Facebook is a network that suits that type of interaction. Phillips et al. (2011) suggest that Facebook can provide students with the opportunity to effectively present their ideas, lead online discussions, and collaborate. In addition, Facebook can help educators to tap into the digital learning styles of students. "For example, it can facilitate student-to-student collaboration and provide innovative ways for you to involve students in your subject matter" (p. 3). They also say that Facebook can be a powerful tool to help educators connect with their colleagues, share educational content, and enhance communication among teachers and students.

According to Towner, VanHorn, and Parker (2007), there are a plethora of positive reasons to integrate Facebook into the classroom. First, Facebook is a cost-effective teaching resource. Second, the network is already set-up and functioning and most students are already using it. Third, it can be placed in the category of internet based learning. Moreover, same authors argue that "The benefits of Facebook's networking and social communication capabilities can greatly enhance the learning experience of both the teacher and the student by tapping into a greater number of learning styles, providing recommended relief from the traditional lecture format, and by building a top the community already established by the students themselves". (p. 13) Same position take Muñoz and Towner (2009) saying "it is our conjecture that the benefits of Facebook's networking and social communication capabilities can benefit both the instructor and the student by tapping into a greater number of learning styles, providing an alternative to the traditional lecture format, creating an online classroom community and increasing teacher-student and student-student interaction". (p. 9)

There are different means to integrate Facebook in the learning activity. Muñoz and Towner (2009) discuss four "Levels of Integration" for Facebook in education; profile page (the teacher uses for communication with students), group page for a class (students can find classmates, communicate with each other and the teacher, post discussions and the professor can sent announcements and remind students about events), replacing/duplicating webcourse functions on Facebook (discussions and instant messaging, posting information about websites and additional links), and integration of Facebook applications (applications can expand the functionality of Facebook for a class but both the teacher and students must download these).

Despite the trend positioning of social networking as exciting educational tools, some critics think they may distract learners from their studies (Cassidy, 2006). Among concerns that have been raised are the heightened disengagement, alienation and disconnection of learners from education and to the detrimental effect that social networking tools may have on "traditional" skills and literacy (Brabazon, 2007). Other says that SNSs could contribute to the intellectual and scholarly de-powering of a 'Google generation' of learners incapable of independent critical thought.

Teaching on Facebook is (De)Pending

Just one pilot study pertaining to Grosseck, Bran and Tiru (2011 investigated how Romanian college students perceived the use of Facebook social network for academic purpose and if they integrated it in their learning and training activities. The results showed that for most of the subjects, Facebook represents a much more natural learning environment than the real one. 57% said that they prefer to receive assignments via messages or posted on the class group. Around 30% of the students have stated that the Facebook is an environment in which they feel comfortable and in which they feel motivated to research, discover, create and fulfill school assignments. 16,7% of the subjects appreciated that their teacher should adapt to this highly personal medium of interaction.

Sturgeon and Walker (2009) highlight that students appear to be more willing to communicate with their instructors if they already know them through the use of Facebook. This relationship might suggest that the in-class interaction between student and instructor is enriched based merely on the use of a social network. According to the same study, there were more than twice as many students that agreed on the matter of Facebook working as a platform that could help facilitate the opening of communication lines. In turn, there were more faculties that disagreed on this matter than there were students; however it was a thin margin.

Other American studies have supported the notion of using social network sites in education. For example, two-thirds of students surveyed in one study were "comfortable" with faculty on Facebook (Hewitt & Forte, 2006) and another study found that 39% of college students surveyed wanted regular on-line discussions with faculty (Fischman, 2008). Waldeck, Kearney, and Plax (2001) found that students are more likely to communicate online with teachers who utilize immediacy behaviors (e.g., use students'

first names, 'emoticons' to convey emotion) in email messages. O'Sullivan et al. (2004) found that students who viewed an instructor's website with high levels of mediated immediacy, including forms of self-disclosure, reported high levels of motivation and affective learning, indicating positive attitudes toward the course and the teacher.

Mazer et al. (2007) say that "Students may perceive a teacher's use of Facebook as an attempt to foster positive relationships with his or her students, which may have positive effects on important student outcomes ... (However), teachers may violate student expectations of proper behaviors and run the risk of harming their credibility if they utilize Facebook. Despite this potential consequence, teachers may enhance their credibility among students by signifying an understanding of contemporary student culture." (pp. 3-4). The results of their study revealed that those who viewed the high-self disclosure Facebook page, had higher levels of anticipated motivation and learning than those in the group of students who viewed the low teacher self-disclosure page. The study also showed that students who viewed the high self-disclosure page perceived the classroom climate more favorably than those who did not. It is also important to note that, "the amount of teacher self-disclosure did not appear to affect how participant perceived the appropriateness of the teacher's use of Facebook" (p. 11). The students were also asked if they thought that the teacher having a Facebook page was inappropriate. One third of the students found teacher having a Facebook profile somewhat inappropriate and another third somewhat appropriate. In the discussion section Mazer et al. (2007) draw attention that "certain forms of face-to-face self-disclosure can have disastrous effects on teacher credibility; however, the nature of computer-mediated communication allows teachers to determine how they appear on Facebook. In other words, teachers can strategically reveal pictures, quotes, and personal information that present them as competent and trustworthy instructors who have the students' best interests in mind" (p. 13).

Yet, there are concerns related to privacy and anxiety in interacting with professors in this environment (Hewitt & Forte, 2006). Others believe that Facebook does not serve an academic purpose (Charnigo & Barnet-Ellis, 2007). Some opinions highlight that faculty should simply avoid to "educationally appropriate" these "backstage" social spaces (Selwyn, 2007). In fact, the expression, "creepy treehouse" was meant to explain educators' use of online social spaces like Facebook (Young, 2008). Mazer, Murphy & Simonds (2007) draw the attention to one potential hazard, the one of losing control over the content. While teachers may post information on Facebook as an attempt to make interpersonal or academic connections with students, their Facebook student-friends can post discrediting or defamatory messages on their 'Wall'. Same authors say that despite this potential consequence, teachers may enhance their credibility among students by signifying an understanding of the contemporary student culture. The question is not what to present in a digital form, but how to develop the conventions for serious communication and use it in the context of the desired learning environment believes Liestol (2007).

A study conducted by Hewitt and Forte (2006) revealed that contact on Facebook had no impact on students' ratings of professors and that students are skeptical about faculty use of Facebook as an educational platform. "We found it striking that one third of the students we surveyed did not believe that faculty should be present on the Facebook at all. Some raised concerns about identity management and privacy issues." (p. 1) Furthermore, according to their study, many of the surveyed students indicated that the student/faculty relationship should remain professional and should not be familiar or sociable. Nonetheless, two thirds of the students surveyed reported that they are comfortable with faculty on the site. Positive comments tended to focus on the alternate communication channels afforded by the site and on the potential for students to get to know professors better.

Teacher in Class, Friend on Facebook: Privacy Issues

The issue of teachers becoming friends with students is among the most controversial one regarding the use of Facebook as an educational platform. Sturgeon and Walker (2009) reveal that nearly 75% of the interviewed faculty members' concerns are about the balance between being a teacher and being a friend to their students. There was a general consensus that faculty do not want to be viewed by students as equals, and the line that differentiates faculty and students seems to fade with the incoming of social networking. While more students feel a connection with their instructors because of Facebook, the faculty responses did not suggest that the connectedness was felt in both directions. As the authors further on highlighted, students want to have relationships with their professors and to know them as real people, not as people who are always kept at arms-distance. However, faculty members do not put as much weight into the use of Facebook for relationship purposes as students do, they say.

The majority of college faculty members believe that sending friend requests to students crosses too many boundaries (Haynesworth, 2009; Young, 2009). Another faculty concern is the unequal power distribution between faculty and students. Sacks (2009) and Haynesworth (2009) reported that faculty members believe that extending friend requests to students would put students in an awkward position. Students may have negative reactions receiving friend requests from their professor but, at the same time, they may feel powerless to refuse such requests (Karl & Peluchette, 2011). It also seems that students are reluctant too, while they don't want their content to be seen by their instructors. Cain et al. (2009) found that the majority of pharmacy students they surveyed (60.7%) did not want faculty members to friend them on Facebook. Other studies revealed that student felt that their personal life should be kept separate from their classroom life.

Karl and Peluchette (2011) concluded that students were most suspicious of friend requests from their worst professor or an unknown professor and were most irritated by requests from their worst professor. And although most students indicated that they would accept such a request from an unknown professor, they would have uncertainties about doing so and they would ignore a friend request from their worst professor. "By ignoring the friend request from the worst professor, students limit that faculty member's access to their personal information and do not appear to be concerned about any potential consequences to their grade" (p. 220). Moreover, the study revealed that receiving friend requests from these faculty sources was less appreciated by students because in both of these cases the relationship between the two parties was either less established or less positive.

While these studies indicate students are in most of the cases comfortable with receiving friend requests on Facebook from their teachers, faculty should be cautious about this practice. Lipka (2009) considers that it may be appropriate to accept a friend request from a student, but it is not appropriate for faculty to initiate such requests to students. Likewise, Schwartz (2010), cited by Karl and Peluchette (2011) argued for the importance of faculty being open to new technologies but also setting boundaries. Instead of following her colleagues' policy of not interacting with students on Facebook, she takes a passive stance by accepting students' friend invitations but not initiating them and only responding to student posts directed to her. She has found that students appreciate the accessibility and respect her boundaries.

Because Facebook involves making aspects of the individual student's private life public, privacy is a serious concern. Students may feel uncomfortable with their 'private' matters on

Facebook being visible to teachers. Whatsoever, on Facebook, it is clear the notions of 'friend' and 'privacy' are altered. As Fahey (1995) has proposed, instead of one public/private boundary, "it may be more accurate to speak of a more complex re-structuring in a series of zones of privacy" (p. 688). But, according to The Communication Privacy Management Theory, cited by Mazer et al. (2007) it is required that students and teachers should be given some guidelines to using sites like Facebook. The theory emphasizes the use boundaries in order to distinguish between public relationships and private information. The authors recommend teachers to establish in the classroom context, the type of public relationships with their students and manage their disclosure of private information. Also, they suggest that teachers must determine what to conceal in order avoiding negative ramifications.

Because of these 'dangers', Read and Young (2006) discussed upon what steps schools administrators should take to ensure the privacy and safety of students. In the United States there are certain policies regarding Facebook use. Some universities addressed students to not have Facebook or to keep their profiles private. Yet, Facebook, as it was argued has the potential to become a valuable tool for education. That is why Mazer et al. (2007) offered some suggestions to teachers who plan on using Facebook in their curriculum. Facebook should be used as a teaching tool and appropriate material should be posted on the page. The say it is important to include photos and links and some background information but it should be kept strictly professional. Professors should make sure not to talk about students and staff via Facebook. Professors should set their profile to "open" and tell students that they can add as a friend but teachers should not add students. Professors should make sure to tell students that they will not be viewing their profile page, and setting their page to "limited" insures that they will not see anything the student does not want them to see. According to Muñoz & Towner (2009) it is important to make sure that students know joining Facebook is an option and should not be forced into it.

Phillips et al. (2011) present some official guideline for educators. The authors of the 'manual' "Facebook for educators" suggest teachers to create groups that are "closed," not "open". This keeps the content of the group private, available only to members of the group and helps protect the privacy of the students. While Facebook group is used to complement what is taught in the classroom, authors recommend educators to provide students with on-demand learning opportunities. With a use of Facebook page (that has collaborative features, including notes and comments) a teacher could extend teaching beyond the classroom. For example, they can continue a discussion that started in the classroom. Teachers are advised not to send or accept friend request from their students. For their professional development they can use "like" the Facebook Pages that relate to their subject matter or the professional association and conferences they attend. They could also use Facebook groups to connect to other members of faculty and to share documents with the use of dedicated applications.

All in all, Facebook role as an educational platform is questionable and yet open-ended. It presents inherent strengths, weaknesses and it offers both opportunities and threats to education. The optimists say that "It will not be easy but by following some recommendations and using Facebook and other technologies teachers and students can learn and collaborate together" (Couillard, 2009).

EMPIRICAL STUDY

Research Questions

Taking into account the controversial literature on Facebook use in colleges and the lack of scientific literature in Romania on this matter, the purpose of the empirical study is to disclose which are the communication borders and the learning enhancement potential regarding academic communication on Facebook on the groundwork of general and particular attitudes Romanian college instructors, graduates and undergraduates have. The present study is based on a survey distributed to members of the oldest institution of higher education in Romania, "Alexandru Ioan Cuza" University of Iasi, which already use Facebook as an educational tool. In brief, it is meant to measure the attitude towards Facebook use in college, to reveal the advantages and the disadvantages perceived by the academics, and to reveal which features of Facebook are the ones used for educational purposes. The authors are interested if there are significant differences regarding the use of Facebook between undergraduates, graduates and teachers concerning the educational use of Facebook.

Consequently, the empirical part of this paper will address the following research questions:

RQ1: What is the general attitude of academics towards Facebook use?
RQ2: Are there significant differences between faculty, graduate students and undergraduates regarding their general attitude towards the use of Facebook according to their field of activity?
RQ3: What position do academics think that the university should take regarding the educational use of Facebook?
RQ4: Do academics perceive Facebook as a complementary educational space?
RQ5: What are the issues concerning faculty-students interaction on Facebook?
RQ6: What is academics attitude towards privacy issues on Facebook?
RQ7: What do academics think about educational value of information on Facebook?
RQ8: Which are the accepted Facebook means that academics use in educational purposes?
RQ9: What contents faculty should make public to students?

RQ10: Which type of educational communication style do academics have on Facebook?

RQ11: What are the advantages and drawbacks of using Facebook as an instructional tool?

Study Procedures and Data Sources

To deal with these questions, data were gathered via an online survey administered to the academics at "Alexandru Ioan Cuza" University of Iasi (UAIC). UAIC was chosen because is the oldest university in Romania and the only public university of Iasi which has an active Facebook page used both for endorsement and for interaction with students and teachers[1]. Before this survey, a prior enquiry has been conducted. It was meant to determine if there are UAIC academics that use Facebook as an educational tool. To the brief pool distributed by the authors via UAIC's official page, 276 academics responded with "yes". Consequently, the authors decided to address a survey to the academics that already use Facebook in order to measures their attitudes and perceptions on the topic of this network's usage in education.

In this idea, the link of the survey on which the present study is based was distributed online to academics from all 15 faculties. The questionnaire was delivered via UAIC's Official Facebook Page, via UAIC faculties Facebook dedicated groups, via Yahoo groups and e-mail to all UAIC members that use one of these means of online communication. The 160 academics that completed the survey represent a convenience sample of the university's academic population.

The survey consisted in 20 mandatory fields with different types of items. Out of these fields, four demanded background information on these respondents: sex, age, academic activity field and academic position. Also, the respondents were requested to specify why they created their Facebook account and how often do they access it. Other items were meant to question the type of means and interactions preferred on Facebook. Four of the items were open ones and requested

respondents: to list three advantages and three disadvantages of teacher-student communication on Facebook; to list other e-Learning platforms which they use in faculty; to consider why Facebook isn't adopted in Romania as an educational platform at a large scale.

Last but not least, the most important item of the questionnaire (item_11) encompassed 22 positive and negative affirmations to address the general attitude towards Facebook use. The instrument is composed of five dimensions designated to measure:

D1: Attitudes towards university's position concerning Facebook use;

D2: Attitudes towards Facebook as a complementary educational space;

D3: Attitudes towards the issue of faculty-students interaction on Facebook;

D4: Attitudes towards privacy issues on Facebook;

D5: Attitudes towards the educational value of information on Facebook.

Respondents had to rate every affirmation on a four point scale: total agreement (1), partial agreement (2), partial disagreement (3) and total disagreement (4). In order not to induce the respondents a positive or a negative attitude, some affirmations were inverted.

Data Analysis Procedures

The closed items of the survey were statistically analyzed in SPSS. Before applying more advanced procedures, reliability of item_11 as a research instrument, which was built to measure the general attitude towards Facebook use, was tested. Before the reliability test, the negative items were recoded into positive ones. An α-Crombach coefficient of .834 (>.7) indicated that the instrument is a valid one for measurement and no item had to be deleted. For item 11, all sub items were computed in order to perform a general analysis on the attitude. Also particular analyses on specific dimensions and items were performed. Due to the ordinal nature of data from the survey responses, various nonparametric analyses were conducted to address the research questions of interest. The multiple response items were submitted to specific analysis procedures. The open items of the survey were submitted to a qualitative content analysis. Researchers manually coded the content and defined the thematic categories. By undergoing all this types of analyses the authors intend to provide a broader view of the general subject of this study.

RESULTS

Composition of Respondents' Sample

The analysis of frequencies revealed that out of the sample of respondents (N=160) 113 were females and 47 males; 35 respondents came from sciences, 62 from humanities and 63 from social sciences. 77 were undergraduates, 52 graduates and 31 faculty members. Further on, a Crosstab analysis between the academic activity field of the respondents and their academic position. Table 1 presents the observed frequencies for each of the nine cells resulted from our cross tabulation. Out of

the total of 77 undergraduates, 16,9% came from science, 51,9% from humanities and 31,2% from social sciences. Out of the total of 52 graduates, 11,5% came from sciences, 32,7% from humanities and 55,8% social sciences. Out of the 31 faculty members, 51,6% came from sciences, 16,1% from humanities and 32% from social sciences. The Pearson Chi-Square comparison revealed that the two nominal variables associate, consequently there is a significant statistic interdependency between the two variables. This analysis reveals us that from out convenient sample, the undergraduate Facebook users are likely to come mainly from humanities, the graduates from humanities and the faculty from sciences. Consequently, the use of Facebook may be conditioned by the combined effect of the two nominal variables.

More than half of the respondents have their Facebook account from two to four years and 30.6% from one year. Just 8.8% have recently created Facebook accounts (less than six months) and only 3.1% have their account from more than four years. 28.8% created their Facebook account with a leisure purpose, 23.8% to stay informed, 20.6% for entertainment and 17.5 for networking. Others created the account for personal branding, chat and dating. 45.0% said they access Facebook more than three times a day, 14.4% two or three

*Table 1. Subjects' academic position * subjects' academic field crosstabulation*

			Subjects' academic field			
			Sciences	Humanities	Social Sciences	Total
Subjects' academic position	Undergraduate	Count	13	40	24	77
		% within Subjects' academic position	16.9%	51.9%	31.2%	100.0%
	Graduate	Count	6	17	29	52
		% within Subjects' academic position	11.5%	32.7%	55.8%	100.0%
	Faculty	Count	16	5	10	31
		% within Subjects' academic position	51.6%	16.1%	32.3%	100.0%
Total		Count	35	62	63	160
		% within Subjects' academic position	21.9%	38.8%	39.4%	100.0%

Figure 1. General attitude towards Facebook use in college

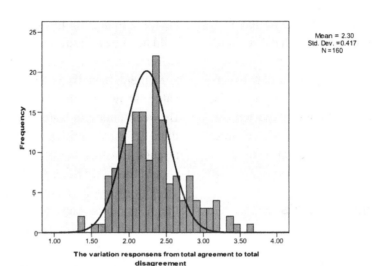

times a day and the rest more seldom. It can be said that, from our respondents sample, the ones that now use Facebook as an educational tool, have been users for more than two years and access two or three times a day their Facebook account. Nonparametric Spearman correlation analysis revealed that there is a correlation between the time when account was created and the access rate of Facebook account, but that this correlation is weak.

The General Attitude towards Facebook Use

In order to address research questions RQ1 a frequency test was performed. To measure subjects' general attitude towards Facebook a computed score of items was calculated. Results indicate that attitudes towards the use of Facebook do not follow a normal distribution, and the curves extends to the right which means that extreme responses are more inclined towards agreement, than disagreement. The distribution curve flatter than a normal distribution, with values dispersed around a higher average range, indicate that probability of

extreme values is less than for a normal distribution (see Figure 1). In other words, the academics tend to partially agree and partially disagree with the use of Facebook, with predominant tendency inclined towards agreement. The tendency towards extremes is weak and it traduces in total agreement towards the use of Facebook. While we would have expected more extreme attitudes, as other studies have revealed, the analysis showed that academics have mild positive attitudes towards the integration of Facebook in their instructional activities.

Because the distribution curve of our dependent variable (item_11) the attitude towards the use of Facebook) is not normal, a Kruskal-Wallis H nonparametric test were conducted to address RQ2. A first test was conducted around the grouping variable subjects' academic position. Results indicated that between undergraduates, graduates and faculty there isn't any significant difference related to the attitude towards the use of Facebook. The second test was conducted around the grouping variable subjects' academic field of activity. Results indicated that between academics from sciences, humanities and social sciences there isn't any significant difference related to the attitude towards the use of Facebook. These results are unanticipated while we had expected that graduates and undergraduates to have a more positive attitude towards Facebook than faculty. Also, the lack of significant differences between subjects pertaining to different activity fields is unexpected, while we would have expected the ones in sciences and social sciences to have more positive attitudes towards the integration of technology than the ones is humanities.

Particular Attitudes towards Facebook Use

Frequency analysis applied for each dimension (see Table 2) and sub item of item_11 revealed the following results for each dimension that the instrument encompasses.

Further on, Kruskal-Wallis H and A Mann-Whitney U test were performed in order to see if there are significant differences between undergraduates, graduates and faculty concerning particular attitudes regarding the use of Facebook. Also, more detailed descriptive analyses were conducted (see Table 3).

To address RQ3, several analyses on item11_D1 were conducted. Results indicated that the academics tend to partially agree and partially disagree with the use of Facebook, with pre-

dominant tendency inclined towards partial agreement. In other words, the respondents appreciated that in general the university should have a mild positive attitude towards Facebook use. The extreme responses are more inclined towards agreement, than disagreement, however the indicators show that they are unlikely to manifest. Between undergraduates, graduates and faculty there isn't any significant difference related to the attitude towards the position that a University should have regarding the use of Facebook.

A more detailed analysis on each item revealed that respondents had a general moderate positive attitude regarding the fact that university should encourage the use of Facebook for its inherent benefits. These results are consistent with the idea that Facebook opens an arena towards more connectedness and communication between students and faculty. This contradicts the idea that academics are reluctant to the integration of Facebook in education. Yet, academics have divided opinions if communication between faculty and students should take place only on dedicated platforms.

Facebook as a Complementary Educational Space

In order to answer to RQ4, several analyses of the computed item11_D2 were performed. Results indicate that academics tend to partially agree and

Table 2. Frequencies analysis of the dimensions measuring the five dimensions of attitude towards Facebook use

		item11_D1	item11_D2	item11_D3	item11_D4	item11_D5
N	Valid	160	160	160	160	160
	Missing	0	0	0	0	0
Mean		2.1833	2.2703	2.0641	2.1453	2.8875
Median		2.1667	2.2500	2.0000	2.0000	2.7500
Std. Deviation		.47148	.62443	.61060	.66910	.45194
Variance		.222	.390	.373	.448	.204
Skewness		.393	.485	.564	.299	.119
Std. Error of Skewness		.192	.192	.192	.192	.192
Kurtosis		.075	-.070	.054	-.415	-.662
Std. Error of Kurtosis		.381	.381	.381	.381	.381

Table 3. Frequencies analysis of the dimensions measuring the five dimensions of attitude towards Facebook use

		Statements	Total agreement	Partial agreement	Partial disagreement	Total disagreement
D1	(1)	On Facebook I feel I can talk more easily with faculty / students	13.10%	59.40%	18.80%	8.80%
	(2)	On Facebook I feel more close to faculty/ students	13.10%	54.40%	9.40%	23.10%
	(8)	Faculty is not open enough to Facebook communication	19.40%	46.90%	25.00%	8.80%
	(17)	Romanian universities should encourage faculty and students communication on Facebook	16.90%	47.50%	23.80%	11.90%
	(20)	University should prohibit the of Facebook for faculty	80.60%	13.80%	5.00%	0.60%
	(21)	The communication between students and faculty should take place only on platforms and special groups, created and approved by the university	29.40%	30.00%	26.90%	13.80%
D2	(4)	Traditional communication in college is no longer sufficient and effective	35.00%	34.40%	15.60%	15.00%
	(9)	Facebook communication between students and faculty complements the activities in halls	28.80%	46.30%	20.60%	4.40%
	(12)	Facebook is not a suitable environment for instructional communication	15.60%	28.80%	38.10%	17.50%
	(19)	Facebook has become a complementary education field	11.30%	41.90%	28.10%	18.80%
D3	(3)	Faculty should not interact with students on Facebook	9.40%	19.40%	33.10%	38.10%
	(15)	Facebook feedback from students/ faculty motivates both students and faculty to perform better in halls	20.00%	53.80%	20.60%	5.60%
	(7)	It is adequate for faculty to be friends with students on Facebook	49.40%	30.00%	14.40%	6.30%
	(14)	Faculty teacher that has a Facebook account is more popular and valued by students	22.50%	48.80%	18.10%	10.60%
D4	(10)	Faculty that post personal information on Facebook diminishes their authority	8.10%	16.90%	31.30%	43.80%
	(13)	Information posted on Facebook can affect my academic public image	13.10%	32.50%	33.80%	20.60%
	(16)	Facebook interactions affect and diminishes credibility of academics	9.40%	26.30%	39.40%	25.00%
	(5)	I don't think that my Facebook profile should be open to faculty/ students	8.10%	26.30%	33.80%	31.90%
D5	(6)	Academic tasks received/ sent via Facebook are preferred to the traditional ones	5.00%	21.90%	32.50%	40.60%
	(11)	Information circulating on Facebook does not have an educational value	4.40%	27.50%	46.90%	21.40%
	(18)	Students learn with greater contentment on Facebook	10.60%	36.90%	31.90%	20.60%
	(22)	Students must be careful with words they use when interacting with faculty on Facebook	76.90%	16.90%	4.40%	1.90%

University's Position Concerning Facebook Use

partially disagree with the fact that Facebook is a valid complementary educational environment, with predominant tendency inclined towards mild agreement. In other words, the respondents appreciated that in general Facebook should be perceived as a trustful educational space. Yet, although the mean is around partial agreement, there are extreme values that indicate that some academics totally agree with that fact that Facebook has become a complementary educational space. Between undergraduates, graduates and faculty there isn't any significant difference related to the attitude that concerns perceiving Facebook as an appropriate educational environment.

The general tendency is that respondents partially agreed with the idea that Facebook can complement the educational activities from college halls. The results suggested that the integration of new means of education is a preoccupation for academics from our sample population. Also it seems like academics are aware of Facebook's potential to complement traditional teaching activities.

The Issue of Faculty-Students Interaction on Facebook

In approach to RQ5, a number of tests of the computed item11_D3 were carried out. Results indicated that academics tend to partially agree with the fact that faculty should interact with students on Facebook. Respondents' attitudes on the issue proved to be moderate ones, with insignificant number of academics inclined towards extreme attitudes. Between undergraduates, graduates and faculty there isn't any significant difference related to the attitude they have related to the faculty-students interaction on Facebook.

Nonetheless, there are significant differences between undergraduates and faculty regarding the adequacy of being friends with faculty/ students on Facebook. Faculty, in comparison with the undergraduates perceives that is more adequate to have a friendship relation on Facebook. This comes as a surprise, while we would have expected faculty to be more cautious on the issue of getting friends on Facebook with students.

All in all, results indicate that both faculty and students agree that the interaction between faculty and students on Facebook is appropriate. Respondents supported the idea that Facebook is a space of where self-disclosure should promote self-knowledge between the academics. Academics appreciated that they agree with idea of getting friend with faculty/ students on Facebook. This confirms the results of the nonsystematic observations which were a premise for this current study. However, it opposes to the emerging policies some universities in the United States have adopted and experts proposed – not to friend faculty/ students on Facebook.

Privacy Issues on Facebook

To answer RQ6, several analyses of the computed item11_D4 were conducted. Results indicate that academics tend to partially agree with the fact that they should not have privacy concerns on Facebook. Moreover, a tendency for extreme positive attitudes towards the unrestricted use of Facebook was manifested. Between undergraduates, graduates and faculty there isn't any significant difference related to the issue of privacy on Facebook. This comes as unexpected, while previous studies reflected that faculty has more concerns regarding the privacy issues on Facebook than students.

Nevertheless, authors found that there are specific significant differences between undergraduates and graduates regarding their perception that Facebook affects credibility of academics. Graduates believe more than undergraduates that Facebook interactions could diminish credibility of academics. It would have been expected to be significant differences between undergraduates and faculty, but there is not the case. There are also significant differences between undergraduates, graduates and faculty regarding their opinion on the issue of having a public profile on Facebook. The significant differences are between faculty and undergraduates, with faculty considering more

than undergraduates that their Facebook profile should be public for students. These results could be explained by the fact that undergraduates may have more things they would want their faculty not to see, than faculty has, which shouldn't be public for the students.

Further specific analysis suggested that the self-disclosure on Facebook is welcomed from faculty and it is not perceived as a risk to diminish the authority of the teachers, although academics are partially aware of the possibilities of unrestricted self disclosure.

All analyses considered, some aspects related to the privacy of interactions on Facebook are viewed differently by the groups formed according to the academic field. Yet, academics don't seem to worry about the privacy issues on Facebook.

The Educational Value of Information on Facebook

In order to respond to RQ7, some analyses on the computed item11_D5 were carried out. Results indicated that academics tend mainly to partially disagree and partially agree with the fact that the information on Facebook has educational value. Tendencies towards extreme responses didn't manifest. It can be said that respondents attitude towards the issue is a moderate one, being more inclined towards the moderate disagreement. Yet, between undergraduates, graduates and faculty there isn't any significant difference related to their perception of the educational value that information has on Facebook. Yet, there are significant differences between undergraduates, graduates and faculty regarding the fact that students should be careful with the language when addressing their faculty. The significant differences were found between undergraduates and faculty. The means revealed that in comparison with faculty, graduates and undergraduates think less about the fact they should be careful with the language used on Facebook.

All in all, respondents believe that students could learn with more contentment on Facebook, even though tasks on Facebook are not preferred by academics. Nonetheless, information circulating on Facebook is perceived as valuable from an educational point of view.

How do Academics Interact on Facebook?

To address RQ8, Multiple Responses analysis tests of frequencies were conducted on two items.

Most Used Interaction Means

An initial test revealed 88 academics from our respondents' sample, representing 28.8% from our total sample, use Facebook closed groups in educational purposes. 20.6% (63 respondents) said that they use the official pages on Facebook to interact with students and faculty. 19.6% (60 respondents) connect with academics via friend request procedures and 13.1% (40 respondents) via page subscription procedures. 18.0% communicate with faculty and students via closed Facebook groups. The Crosstab (see Table 4) between the variable 'mean of interaction' and 'subjects' academic status' revealed that most members of faculty and most undergraduates use closed groups for educational purposes. Faculty use with predilection open groups and students interact on Facebook with their faculty and colleagues via official pages. Graduates equally use friend request procedures and closed groups to connect with university. The other means are less used. The results indicate that although academics connect with each other by friend request procedures, they use for educational communication mainly the closed groups and official pages.

Table 4. Interaction means*academic status crosstabulation

| | | | Respondents' academic status | | | |
			student	graduates	faculty	Total
$interaction_mean^a	Friend Request	Count	25	25	10	60
		% within $interaction_mean$	41.7%	41.7%	16.7%	
		% within status	32.5%	48.1%	32.3%	
		% of Total	15.6%	15.6%	6.3%	37.5%
	Page Subscription	Count	17	16	7	40
		% within $interaction_mean$	42.5%	40.0%	17.5%	
		% within status	22.1%	30.8%	22.6%	
		% of Total	10.6%	10.0%	4.4%	25.0%
	Closed Groups	Count	49	25	14	88
		% within $interaction_mean$	55.7%	28.4%	15.9%	
		% within status	63.6%	48.1%	45.2%	
		% of Total	30.6%	15.6%	8.8%	55.0%
	Open Groups	Count	21	23	11	55
		% within $interaction_mean$	38.2%	41.8%	20.0%	
		% within status	27.3%	44.2%	35.5%	
		% of Total	13.1%	14.4%	6.9%	34.4%
	Official Pages	Count	39	15	9	63
		% within $interaction_mean$	61.9%	23.8%	14.3%	
		% within status	50.6%	28.8%	29.0%	
		% of Total	24.4%	9.4%	5.6%	39.4%
Total		Count	77	52	31	160
		% of Total	48.1%	32.5%	19.4%	100.0%

Note: Percentages and totals are based on respondents.

a. Dichotomy group tabulated at value 1.

The Least Used Facebook Services

Most of the academics (109 subjects) appreciated that the least used Facebook services by the university are the dedicated educational application. 68 respondents appreciated that the discussion groups are the least used ones and 66 that the communication on official pages is the least used one. This result is consistent with the idea that academics are not aware of all the possibilities Facebook offers for educational purposes. Yet, it is surprising that respondents also think that groups and official pages are least used, while admitting that they mainly use those means in educational purposes. A Crosstab analysis revealed that the results don't differ within the group defined by academic status. That means that undergraduates, graduates and faculty have similar perceptions regarding the least used Facebook services in university.

What Students Shouldn't
See on a Faculty's 'Wall'

In order to respond to RQ9 Multiple Responses analysis tests of frequencies were conducted on several items.

Most of the respondents appreciated that faculty should not post on Facebook private pictures that could be seen by students. Also, many considered that neither the marital status nor sexual orientation should be found on a faculty wall. Almost half of the academics responded that on a teacher wall shouldn't be found information that is unrelated to education. 56 persons responded that the comments of people who are not from n academic environment should not be public on faculty's profile page. Just 15.6% from the respondents disagreed with the idea that faculty could have their preferences and activities open to public access. Nine respondents appreciated that from a faculty's profile should be absent all kind of posts and ten said that all comments should be private.

A Crosstab analysis (see Table 5) revealed that the majority of the faculty members think that sexual orientation and marital status of the teachers shouldn't be public information for students. Just 39% of the total number of graduates responded the same. Almost all faculty members said that private pictures shouldn't be public for students. A majority of the undergraduates had the same opinion. The other crosstabs further revealed a more reserved approach towards Facebook self-disclosure from teachers, than from graduates and undergraduates.

Most of the academics appreciated that on a faculty's wall the professional status and the academic position should be public to students. Likewise, a majority said that faculty should post links towards educational resources. 98 believed that pictures from academic reunions and conferences are welcomed on a faculty's profile. 106 also agreed that the on a faculty's profile should be found the institutions where they studies. 90 appreciated that faculty's work places should be public to students. Just 12 respondents thought that marital status and sexual orientation of a faculty should be public to students, and 48 said that a faculty should have a profile picture. 12 subjects responded on this item with 'others'. These responses reflect that academics welcome a complete profile from faculty to be seen by students, while this profile contains relevant instructional information for students and information that recommends faculty as a professional in this field of activity. A Crosstab analysis revealed that the results don't differ within the group defined by academic status. That means that undergraduates, graduates and faculty have similar perceptions regarding the information that should be found on a faculty wall.

The Relational Education
Type on Facebook

In order to respond to RQ11 various analysis procedures were performed. Out of the sample of respondents, 41.9% said that they have formal

*Table 5. $inform_NO*status crosstabulation*

			Subjects's academic status			
			undergraduate	graduate	faculty	Total
Informations on a faculty's wall that shouldn't be public for students[a]	Sexual orientation or marital status	Count	30	26	25	81
		% within $inform_NO	37.0%	32.1%	30.9%	
		% within Status	39.0%	50.0%	80.6%	
		% of Total	18.8%	16.3%	15.6%	50.6%
	Activities and preferences	Count	11	7	7	25
		% within $inform_NO	44.0%	28.0%	28.0%	
		% within Status	14.3%	13.5%	22.6%	
		% of Total	6.9%	4.4%	4.4%	15.6%
	Private pictures	Count	46	36	30	112
		% within $inform_NO	41.1%	32.1%	26.8%	
		% within Status	59.7%	69.2%	96.8%	
		% of Total	28.8%	22.5%	18.8%	70.0%
	Wall posts which lack educational content	Count	32	15	21	68
		% within $inform_NO	47.1%	22.1%	30.9%	
		% within Status	41.6%	28.8%	67.7%	
		% of Total	20.0%	9.4%	13.1%	42.5%
	All wall posts	Count	2	1	6	9
		% within $inform_NO	22.2%	11.1%	66.7%	
		% within Status	2.6%	1.9%	19.4%	
		% of Total	1.3%	.6%	3.8%	5.6%
	Non-academic comments	Count	17	18	21	56
		% within $inform_NO	30.4%	32.1%	37.5%	
		% within Status	22.1%	34.6%	67.7%	
		% of Total	10.6%	11.3%	13.1%	35.0%
	All comments	Count	4	2	4	10
		% within $inform_NO	40.0%	20.0%	40.0%	
		% within Status	5.2%	3.8%	12.9%	
		% of Total	2.5%	1.3%	2.5%	6.3%
	Others	Count	10	8	1	19
		% within $inform_NO	52.6%	42.1%	5.3%	
		% within Status	13.0%	15.4%	3.2%	
		% of Total	6.3%	5.0%	.6%	11.9%
Total		Count	77	52	31	160
		% of Total	48.1%	32.5%	19.4%	100.0%

Note: Percentages and totals are based on respondents.

a. Dichotomy group tabulated at value 1.

educational relation with their students/ faculty. 36.3% admitted to have an informal relation and 21.9% a nonformal one. From the total of 77 undergraduates, 33 claimed to have a formal, 29 an informal and 15 a nonformal educational relation on Facebook. From the total of 52 graduate respondents, 24 reported a formal relation, 17 an informal one and 11 a nonformal one. Most of the teachers (12 subjects) reported an informal relationship on Facebook with their students, ten a formal one and nine a nonformal one. The Chi-Square test on this variable $\chi^2(2)=10.212$, $p=.006$ (<0.5) indicated that in our sample there is a shaped opinion regarding the types of relation developed on Facebook.

Test revealed that there are no significant differences between undergraduates, graduates and faculty concerning the type of educational relation. Yet, there are significant differences between the academics that have a formal relation on Facebook and the ones that have a nonformal or an informal relation. Also significant differences were found between the subjects that have a formal relation on Facebook and one that have an informal one. Because the mean rank is higher for formal type of educational relation that for informal type of educational relation means that those who have a formal educational relation would have a more positive attitude towards Facebook. The results are unexpected, while we have anticipated a more positive attitude from those who have more 're-laxed' interactions on Facebook.

Should We be on Facebook?

In order to address the last research question, RQ12, a qualitative content analysis was under-taken. Four open items were analyzed. One of them required respondents to list three advantages of Facebook, another three advantages. The other two required to list other e-Learning platforms which they use in faculty; to consider why Face-book isn't adopted in Romania as an educational platform at a large scale.

Advantages and Drawbacks of Facebook Use

On the item which required to list the advantages, the respondents (N=160) listed 243 answers. 26 respondents said there were no advantages in using Facebook as an educational tool and eight refused to answer. The 209 valid answers were grouped according to the five dimensions deter-mined by authors to measure the attitude towards Facebook. They were submitted to a qualitative analysis. Same method was used for the disad-vantages which were listed. From the total of 147 answers, 22 said there were no disadvantages and eight refused to respond. The remained 117 were analyzed (see Table 6). The authors will discuss upon the most frequent answers.

Respondents' answers regarding the advan-tages of Facebook use were grouped under the categories of *D2* and *D3*. This indicated that most

respondents correlated the advantages of Facebook with the issues of student-faculty interaction and with the emergence of this social network as an alternative educational space. Under D2 category, most responses reflected that on Facebook the information travels faster, and that the communi-cation is more efficient. Ten said that education content can be shared much easily. Nine respon-dents said that accessibility is one important ad-vantage and eight that it offers more opening towards the educational act. Under *D3* category, most answered that they perceived as an advantage the relative closeness that establishes between faculty and students on Facebook. Other people said that Facebook is a friendly environment where they can communicate without anxiety and that a major advantage of Facebook is the bidirec-tional communication and the feedback that can be received in real time. All in all, academics praised Facebook for the easiness of sharing in-formation and the interactional potential that could generate more open communication between students and faculty.

Respondents' answers regarding the disad-vantages of Facebook use were grouped under all the categories. Under *D1* following respondents' answers were listed: non-compliance of behavior; lack of Internet access for everyone; lack of cred-ibility and confidence; student's lack of involve-ment in real academic life. Within *D2*, respondents raised the issues of subjectivity; the frivolity of the communication; the substitution of direct commu-nication. Under D3, the following concerns were raised: the diminishment of teacher's authority, the excessive familiarity and permissiveness, the wrong interpretations, losing the respect for faculty, frivolity, alienation of teacher-student relationship. Under *D4* most occurrences referred to the open access to personal data and to the convergence between public and private spaces, and the others to inappropriate comments and to the exposure of informatics attacks, three to false identity and one to self-censorship. Within the last

Table 6. Advantages and drawbacks of Facebook use as an educational tool

Attitudes towards	Advantages	Occ	Disadvantages	Occ
D1			Non-compliance of behavior	7
university's position			Lack of Internet access for everyone	4
concerning Facebook			Lack of credibility and confidence	4
use			Student's lack of involvement in real academic	4
			Wasting faculty's time	2
			Additional expenses	2
			Computer dependency	1
			The inability to measure practical skills	2
	Totals			26
D2	The information travels faster	20	Subjectivity	9
Facebook as a	Communication is more efficient	15	Substitution of direct communication	3
complementary	Education content can be shared much easily	10	Frivolity of the communication	2
educational space	Accessibility	9		
	It offers more opening towards the educational act	8		
	Simulative effect on motivation and involvement	8		
	Optimal use of each person's time	7		
	More Information	7		
	Receptivity towards each user needs	5		
	Oopen to debates	3		
	Promptitude	3		
	The possibility to share courses and links	3		
	Totals	98		14
D3	Closeness established between faculty and students	17	Diminishment of teacher's authority	15
the issue of faculty-	Communication without anxiety	14	Excessive familiarity and permissiveness	12
students interaction on	Feedback, in real time	13	Wrong interpretations	8
Facebook	Encouraging the mutual knowing	13	Losing the respect for faculty	7
	Encouraging the interaction	10	Frivolity	5
	The freedom of expression	8	Alienation of teacher-student relationship	3
	Relationship more open to communication	8		
	Convenience	7		
	The permissive nature of the environment	5		
	Mutual trust	5		
	Group interaction	4		
	Respect	4		
	The availability of the faculty	3		
	Totals	111		50
D4			Convergence between public and private spaces	9
privacy issues on			Inappropriate comments	4
Facebook			Exposure of informatics attacks	3
			False identity	3
	Totals			19
D5			Information's distortion	5
the educational value of			Chaos of messages	3
information on Facebook				
	Totals			8
	Grand totals	209		117

category *D5*, eight occurrences were listed, out of which five referred to information's distortion and three to the chaos of messages. All in all, most concerns of the respondents related to the relational dimension. Academics expressed their worry that on Facebook the excessive permissiveness could harm teacher's academic image and that the communication between faculty and teacher could be affected by non-compliance behaviors.

To conclude, although the academics believe that on Facebook there is interactional potential that could generate more open communication between students and faculty, their concerns regard the possible deviations that a permissive medium suites. The analysis revealed that the dimension to which advantages and drawbacks pertain is the one concerning the relational aspect between faculty and students on Facebook.

Facebook, an Educational Tool that Fails to be Recognized in Romania

192 different answers were listed on the item which requested respondents to consider why Facebook isn't adopted in Romania as an educational platform at a large scale. 13 replied with "I

don't respond", 11 admitted they do not have a given opinion. Out of the remained 168 answers, eighteen conjured the traditionalist and conservative public/ mentality of Romanians. Thirteen answers mentioned that Facebook is perceived more like a social network than an educational platform in Romania. Other addressed the issue of the systemic reluctance to progress/ new. Many responses grouped around the idea that Romanian academics are not well informed and not aware of the educational benefits Facebook has. Eleventh respondents raised the issue of distrust that will be adopted as a method of education because of it provides too much freedom for academics. Other answers grouped around the idea that in our country there is in general slow growth of markets and delayed adoptions of technologies. Eight academics raised the issue of the lack of funds and resources and also to the lack of a specific legislation. Another eight persons said that Facebook is not yet as popular as an educational space. Some said that academics might want to avoid having official interactions online. Others stated that Facebook might be regarded as excluding traditional education.

Among the other reasons which were alleged from one to five times stand: the existence of other means of sharing online information; a general distrust of users; lack of internet connection; the fear of new: students' frivolity; closed society; the fear of losing respect and of making educational compromises; the existence of other priorities in the Romanian educational system; lack of interest; lack of sociability; the fact that the most of the faculty is old aged; the fear of losing privacy; faculty's reluctance in posting information; too much unequal exposure; the lack of online learning courses; prejudices; skepticism poverty; setting the wrong priorities.

It can be said that the main reasons why academics perceive that Facebook isn't enough recognized as an educational tool group around

the conservative mentality and to reluctance. Yet, in question are not the privacy concerns. The lack of funds or the delayed adoption rates of the technologies are issues for academics, even though Facebook is a free resource. The matter of official acknowledgment of Facebook as a trustworthy environment seems also to be a concern. Another reason for the low adoption rates of Facebook in educational purpose might be the fact that academics use other E-learning platforms. This is not the case as results suggested. From the open responses is obvious that respondents don't actually use alternative learning platforms. They relate to the use of e-mail or the access of Internet Pages as they would be educational platforms. We can conclude that, for our sample of respondents the use of e-Learning platforms is limited.

Conclusions of the Empirical Study

According to the results of our empirical study, the academics from our respondents sample have demonstrated moderated positive general attitudes towards Facebook use as an educational tool and were less inclined towards extreme responses. As the results revealed, respondents of the survey were less inclined towards extreme responses. This indicated that academics haven't a strong position on the issue of educational Facebook issues. Most of them have Facebook for two or three years and access Facebook more than two times a day and they partially trust this medium of communication.

The main finding of this study is that between undergraduates, graduates and faculty there are no significant differences regarding their attitudes towards Facebook. While we have expected faculty to be more reluctant, this is not the case as revealed by this particular study. The educational field type (science, social science, humanities) didn't influence the respondent's views on the topic either.

They also manifested particular positive attitudes. Many agreed to some extent that Facebook has become a complementary educational field. Academics believe that the use of Facebook is welcomed and they consider that university's officials should support the use of Facebook in education. The content analysis performed on open answers showed that the academics reflect on the issues of possible positive or negative. They take into consideration the effects Facebook interactions could have on the relations between students and faculty. Although academics recognize the potential of Facebook towards a more open relationship between faculty and students, they fear of the non-compliant behavior of some users.

At the moment, most academics interact on Facebook closed group or keep in touch with faculty and university on official pages. However, the academics do no perceive as inappropriate for students to be friends with their faculty on Facebook, or to connect with them by page subscriptions procedures. Respondents thought that dedicated applications were the least used means for Facebook educational communication.

The statistic analysis results reflected that most of the academics do not have privacy related concerns neither do they fear that their credibility would be affected by Facebook interactions. Nevertheless, the content analyses of perceived advantages and disadvantages have disclosed some worries of the kind. The educational style practiced by faculty, graduates and undergraduates is most of the times formal, but a consistent number of respondents said they do have informal relations with other academics on Facebook. Yet, academics perceive that Facebook profiles of faculty and students who have educational related interactions should limit their profile visibility if they have private pictures or information. They appreciate that content shared on Facebook could have informational value, but don't think that tasks on Facebook are more constructive that those in halls.

GENERAL CONCLUSION, DISCUSSIONS, AND FUTURE RESEARCH DIRECTIONS

Nowadays, students and faculty members are caught in the middle of the convergence between public and private, between online and offline media, between formal and informal, between eagerness and reluctance in the academic field. Both of them need to try to adjust to each other more than ever, towards a collaborative approach to learning. Nevertheless, they should know that it is important to set their own operational boundaries on this unregulated environment called Facebook. Consequently, the design of this chapter allowed authors to offer an extensive view on the issue of the use of Facebook in educational purposes. This approach was preferred to a narrower one due to the multipurpose nature of this medium of communication and the lack of a consistent literature on the matter. Thereby, it revealed Facebook's potential of shaping the new academic environment with some new challenges.

The chapter focused on the issue of student-faculty interaction on Facebook. While the theoretical approach listed the most recent studies conducted mainly in the Anglo-Saxon environment, the empirical one centered on practice at the oldest Romanian university in the country. The results of the study conducted by the authors revealed that, within out sample from "Alexandru Ioan Cuza" University, most academics had moderate positive attitudes towards the Facebook use as a learning platform, highlighting the advantages and drawbacks. Surprisingly, the results didn't show any difference between undergraduates, graduates and faculty concerning the use of Facebook. Although these results could be influenced by the limited sample of faculty members, the statistic procedures revealed that the results were relevant. Nevertheless, the authors suggest that future researches should take into account an equal number of respondents from within the academic status category and to conduct their study on a larger sample.

Future researches should undergo more specific studies on Facebook use, with the purpose of measuring the levels of integration of Facebook or the type of interaction conducted in education. Furthermore, we believe that a longitudinal study will be a suitable approach to measure the growth in relationship of students and faculty that interact on Facebook and their impact on halls environment, motivation rates and affective learning. And, because most of the studies were designed to analyze the content students put on their 'walls', some future papers should examine the information on faculty's wall and their specific interactions.

In conclusion, Facebook isn't yet a lawful education platform, but researchers, faculty and students are just beginning to learn what its benefits and shortcomings are.

REFERENCES

Arrington, M. (2005, September 7). 85% of college students use Facebook. *TechCrunch*. Retrieved January 22, 2012, from http://www.techcrunch.com/2005/09/07/85-of-college-students-use-facebook/

Bollman, M., & Wright, J. (2008). Professors and students come Facebook to Facebook. *Lee Clarion*. Retrieved February 3, 2012, from http://www.leeclarion.com/life/2008/09/17/professors-and-students-come-facebook-to-facebook/

Boyd, D. M., & Ellison, N. B. (2008). Social network sites: Definition, history, and scholarship. *Journal of Computer-Mediated Communication*, *13*(1), 11.

Brabazon, T. (2007). *The university of Google*. Aldershot, UK: Ashgate.

Bugeja, M. (2006). Facing the Facebook. *The Chronicle of Higher Education*, *52*(21), C1–C4.

Cain, J., Scott, D. R., & Akers, P. (2009). Pharmacy students' Facebook activity and opinions regarding accountability and e-professionalism. *American Journal of Pharmaceutical Education*, *73*(6), 1–6. doi:10.5688/aj7306104

Cassidy, J. (2006). Me media. *New Yorker (New York, N.Y.)*, *82*(13), 50–59.

Charnigo, L., & Barnett-Ellis, P. (2007). Checking out Facebook.com: The impact of a digital trend on academic libraries. *Information Technology and Libraries*, *26*(1), 23–34.

Couillard, C. (2009). *Facebook: The pros and cons of use in education*. Unpublished doctoral dissertation, University of Wisconsin-Stout, US.

Demski, J. (2009). Facebook training wheels. *The Journal*, *36*(4), 24–28.

Ellison, N. B., Steinfield, C., & Lampe, C. (2007). The benefits of Facebook "friends:" Social capital and college students' use of online social network sites. *Journal of Computer-Mediated Communication, 12*(3), 1. Retrieved January 30, 2012, from http://jcmc.indiana.edu/vol12/issue4/ellison.html

Fahey, T. (1995). Privacy and the family. *Sociology*, *29*, 687–703. doi:10.1177/0038038595029004008

Fischman, J. (2008, October 13). Dear Professor, students want to chat with you. *The Chronicle of Higher Education*. Retrieved January 24, 2012, from http://chronicle.com/wiredcampus/article/3384/dear-professor-students-want-to-chat-with-you

Fletcher, J. K., & Ragins, B. R. (in press). Stone center relational theory: A window on relational mentoring. In Ragins, B. R., & Kram, K. E. (Eds.), *The handbook of mentoring: Theory, research, and practice*. Thousand Oaks, CA: Sage. doi:10.4135/9781412976619.n15

Grosseck, G., Bran, R., & Tiru, L. (2011). Dear teacher, what should I write on my wall? A case study on academic uses of Facebook. *The 3rd World Conference on Educational Sciences*, 2011, February 03-07, Vol. 15, (pp. 1425-1430). Istanbul, Turkey: Bahcesehir University.

Haynesworth, L. (2009). Faculty with Facebook wary of friending students. *The Daily Princetonian*. Retrieved January 23, 2012, from http://www.dailyprincetonian.com/2009/02/18/22793/

Heiberger, G., & Harper, R. (2008). Have you facebooked Astin lately? Using technology to increase student involvement. *New Directions for Student Services*, *124*, 19–35. doi:10.1002/ss.293

Hewitt, A., & Forte, A. (2006, November). *Crossing boundaries: Identity management and student/faculty relationships on the Facebook*. Paper presented at the Computer Supported Cooperative Work Conference, Banff, Alberta, Canada. Retrieved February 9, 2012, from http://basie.exp.sis.pitt.edu/710/1/CrossingBoundariesIdentityManagementandStudentFacultyRelationshipsontheFacebook(14).pdf

Hirschorn, M. (2007). About Facebook. *Byliner: The Atlantic*. Retrieved February 9, 2012, from http://byliner.com/michael-hirschorn/stories/about-facebook

Ito, M., Horst, H., Bittanti, M., Boyd, D., Herr-Stephenson, R., Lange, P., & Robinson, L. (2008). *Living and learning with new media*. Chicago, IL: MacArthur Foundation.

Karl, K. A., & Peluchette, J. V. (2011). "Friending" professors, parents and bosses: A Facebook connection conundrum. *Journal of Education for Business*, *86*(4), 214–222. doi:10.1080/08832323.2010.507638

Karlin, S. (2007). Examining how youths interact online. *School Board News*, *73*(4), 6–9.

Lampe, C., Ellison, N., & Steinfeld, C. (2007). A familiar Face(book): Profile elements as signals in an online social network. *Proceedings of Conference on Human Factors in Computing Systems* (pp. 435-444). New York, NY: ACM Press.

Lemeul, J. (2006). Why I registered on Facebook. *The Chronicle of Higher Education*, *53*(2), C1.

Lipka, S. (2007, December 8). For professors, "friending" can be fraught. *The Chronicle of Higher Education*, *54*(15).

Mack, D., Behler, A., Roberts, B., & Rimland, E. (2007). Reaching students with Facebook: Data and best practices. *Electronic Journal of Academic and Special Librarianship*, *8*(2).

Madge, C., Meek, J., Wellens, J., & Hooley, T. (2009). Facebook, social integration and informal learning at university: 'It is more for socializing and talking to friends about work than for actually doing work'. *Learning, Media and Technology*, *34*(2), 141–155. doi:10.1080/17439880902923606

Mason, R. (2006). Learning technologies for adult continuing education. *Studies in Continuing Education*, *28*(2), 121–133. doi:10.1080/01580370600751039

Mazer, J. P., Murphy, R. E., & Simonds, C. J. (2007). *I'll see you on "Facebook": The effects of computer-mediated teacher self-disclosure on student motivation, affective learning, and classroom climate*, *56*(1), 1-17. London, UK: Routledge.

Muñoz, C. L., & Towner, T. L. (2009). *Opening Facebook: How to use Facebook in the college classroom*. Paper presented at the Society for Information Technology and Teacher Education Conference, Charleston, South Carolina, USA.

O'Sullivan, P. B., Hunt, S. K., & Lippert, L. R. (2004). Mediated immediacy: A language of affiliation in a technological age. *Journal of Language and Social Psychology*, *23*, 464–490. doi:10.1177/0261927X04269588

Pascarella, E. T., & Terenzini, P. T. (1991). *How college affects students: Findings and insights from twenty years of research.* San Francisco, CA: Jossey-Bass.

Peluchette, J., & Karl, K. (2010). Examining students' intended image on facebook: "What were they thinking?! *Journal of Education for Business*, *85*, 30–37. doi:10.1080/08832320903217606

Phillips, F. L., Baird, D. E., & Fogg, B. J. (2011). *Facebook for educators.* Retrieved January 25, 2012, from http://facebookforeducators.org/educators-guide.

Read, B., & Young, J. R. (2006, August 4). Facebook and other social-networking sites raise questions for administrators. *The Chronicle of Higher Education*, *52*(48), 37.

Roblyer, M. D., McDaniel, M., Webb, M., Herman, H., & Witty, J. V. (2010). Findings on Facebook in higher education: A comparison of college faculty and student uses and perceptions of social networking sites. *The Internet and Higher Education*, *13*, 134–140. doi:10.1016/j.iheduc.2010.03.002

Roblyer, M. D., & Wiencke, W. R. (2003). *Validation and uses of a rubric to assess and encourage interaction in distance learning.* Paper presented at the annual meeting of the American Educational Research Association, Chicago.

Sacks, I. (2009). Student, professor Facebook friendships bring communication, risks. *The Maneater.* Retrieved January 14, 2012, from http://www.themaneater.com/stories/2009/2/23/student-professor-facebook-friendships-bring-commu/

Schwartz, H. (2009). Facebook: The new classroom commons? *The Chronicle of Higher Education*, 1–5.

Selwyn, N. (2007, November). *'Screw Blackboard... do it on Facebook!': An investigation of students' educational use of Facebook.* Paper presented at the 'Poke 1.0 - Facebook social research symposium', University of London, UK. Retrieved January 13, 2012, from http://www.scribd.com/doc/513958/Facebook-seminar-paper-Selwyn

Selwyn, N. (2009). Faceworking: Exploring students' education-related use of Facebook. *Learning, Media and Technology*, *34*(2), 157–174. doi:10.1080/17439880902923622

Soder, C. (2009). Social media extend search for prospective students; Universities build relationships, canvass recruits with Facebook, other online tools. *Crain's Cleveland Business*, 0012.

Sturgeon, C. M., & Walker, C. (2009). *Faculty on Facebook: Confirm or deny?* The 14th Annual Instructional Technology Conference. Middle Tennessee State University Murfreesboro, Tennessee, US.

Towner, T., VanHorn, A., & Parker, S. (2007). Facebook: Classroom tool for a classroom community? *Midwestern Political Science Association Conference*, (pp. 1-18). Retrieved January 28, 2012, from http://citation.allacademic.com/meta/p_mla_apa_research_citation/1/9/7/1/3/pages197133/p197133-1.php

Waldeck, J. H., Kearney, P., & Plax, T. G. (2001). Teacher email message strategies and students' willingness to communicate online. *Journal of Applied Communication Research*, *29*, 5470. doi:10.1080/00909880128099

West, A., Lewis, J., & Currie, P. (2009). Students' Facebook 'friends': public and private spheres. *Journal of Youth Studies*, *12*(6), 615–627. doi:10.1080/13676260902960752

Wolfe, K. (2009). *Facebook: Not just for students. What started as a college networking site now has university faculty jumping on the bandwagon.* Retrieved January 13, 2012, from http://www.mndaily.com/2009/02/25/facebook-not-just-students

Young, J. (2008, August 18). When professors create social networks for classes, some students see a "creepy treehouse". *The Chronicle of Higher Education.* Retrieved January 10, 2012, from http://chronicle.com/wiredcampus/article/3251/when-professors-create-social-networks-for-classes-some-students-see-a-creepy-treehouse

Ziegler, S. (2007). The (mis)education of Generation M. *Learning, Media and Technology, 32*(1), 69–81. doi:10.1080/17439880601141302

KEY TERMS AND DEFINITIONS

Attitudes of Academics Towards Facebook: Used to describe the extent to which student and faculty are willing to integrate Facebook communication in the educational process and to highlight prospective learning enhancements and boundaries of Facebook use in academic field.

Facebook Services: Facebook applications and features which facilitate online communication.

Facebook: The biggest Social Network in the world which it began being used as a complementary educational space.

Faculty-Students Interaction on Facebook/ Teacher-Student Facebook Mediated Communication: Mechanism which describes the contact which establishes on the Facebook platform, in various forms, between students and faculty.

Informal Learning Environment: Used to describe those platforms that facilitate an informal communication between academics and students.

Learning Communication Technologies: Tools, devices, applications or programs which can be used for enhancing students-faculty communication on the Internet.

ENDNOTES

[1] The official Facebook page of UAIC had on 25th of February 2012, last time the authors accessed it, 13.509 likes from Facebook users (university and non university personnel) and 598 refers in Facebook user posts.

Chapter 4
Integrating Mobile Learning, Digital Storytelling and Social Media in Vocational Learning

Miikka Eriksson
University of Lapland, Finland

Pauliina Tuomi
Tampere University of Technology, Finland

Hanna Vuojärvi
University of Lapland, Finland

ABSTRACT

In this chapter, the focus falls on integrating mobile learning, digital storytelling, and social media into vocational learning practices. The literature review introduces the development of mobile learning and digital storytelling and presents ways in which these concepts can piggyback the interactive features of social media. A case study during which participating students used mobile phones and videos with a mobile social video application (MoViE) to design and produce representative digital stories based on local tourism attractions is also presented. Twenty-five students participated in the internet inquiry about student attitudes towards the use of social media as part of their vocational expertise and their learning experiences with mobile devices and MoViE. This chapter illustrates the benefits as well as the shortcomings of the used learning concept in order to produce more concrete knowledge of the use of mobile devices and social video applications in learning.

INTRODUCTION

Today, mobile technologies like cell phones or laptop computers are widespread. Mobile manufacturer Ericsson estimates that there were half a billion mobile broadband subscribers in 2010

and that this figure will reach close to five billion by 2016 (according to Johnson, Smith, Levine, & Haywood, 2011). A considerable proportion of cell phones is already multifunctional smartphones that enable communication in several ways, information seeking on the Internet and e.g. video

DOI: 10.4018/978-1-4666-2851-9.ch004

capturing and sharing through social networks. As the number of active mobile accounts continues to grow rapidly, the supporting infrastructure will also continue to expand – including remote areas (Johnson et al., 2011). Mobile devices are increasingly becoming capable tools for learning with their ubiquity, mobility and the wide range of things one can do with them. In addition, because of their popularity among students, schools do not always have to buy or maintain mobile devices to take advantage of their functionalities.

As mobile devices are increasingly common and ubiquitous, mobile media is also finding its way into discussions about modern education. Although, according to Mwanza-Simwami (2007), mobile learning has become somewhat of a trend, learning with mobile devices is still a relatively new research area, and more work is therefore needed to understand the benefits and effects of using mobile technologies to support learning. It is therefore important to discuss the characteristics of learning with technology and to build theoretical concepts and frameworks that support the design and implementation of applications that are pedagogically meaningful for learning. Social media and Web 2.0 technologies provide mobile learners dimensions that enable frequent, multifunctional, and synchronous or asynchronous interactions even between distant partners, providing the base to increase the conversational and collaborative characteristics of learning. These technologies also enable easy production and sharing of digital videos which education and learners can benefit in many ways (e.g. Hakkarainen, 2007).

In this chapter we review the literature related to the development of mobile learning and digital storytelling and introduce the possibilities these two concepts or methods can offer when combined with the features of social media. In addition, we introduce a case study where students used mobile phones and a mobile social video application, MoViE, to create digital stories as part of their vocational education. The questionnaire used for data collection also included questions about students' social media use and their attitudes towards social media as part of their vocational expertise. We will use the case study as an example to illustrate the possibilities but also the complications related to the use of technologies in education. The case study aimed to answer the following research questions:

1. *How students perceive using social media as part of their vocational expertise?*
2. *How did students experience the use of mobile camera phones and MoViE to create digital stories for the purpose of learning?*

In practice, the study was conducted during a teaching experiment that was arranged as a part of vocational tourism and audiovisual communication (AVC) studies. The participants included 14 tourism and 20 media students from two vocational colleges. The data was collected by means of an Internet-based questionnaire and contains both qualitative and quantitative data. A detailed description of the teaching experiment, participants, data and analysis methods is presented in the methods section of this chapter.

BACKGROUND

The theoretical background of our study is based on the concepts of mobile learning and digital storytelling. We will consider the integration of these two concepts together with the features and possibilities social media provides for learning. We will also contemplate how these concepts relate to the concept of meaningful learning and elaborate on the possibilities and shortcomings of mobile learning based on our own experiences during the case study.

A Short History of Mobile Learning

Mobile devices allow flexible learning according to times and places. One can, however, argue about which tools actually are truly mobile. We certainly think that, for example, laptops allow one to effectively study anytime and in various locations - the restrictions are mainly related to battery life and partly to the availability of wireless network connections. They are excellent for writing and several other tasks for which you need big screens, computing power and a physical keyboard of decent size. However, laptops still are so large that a backpack or similar is mostly needed to feasibly carry them around. For the abovementioned reasons mobile learning is usually related to handheld devices which are easy to move around, fit into your pocket and also provide multiple functionalities. Therefore, in this chapter, mobile devices are considered mainly as handhelds like mobile camera phones, smartphones, or personal digital assistants (PDA). Tablets are borderline cases as they are lightweight and handheld but don't fit into one's pocket and consequently need some sort of bag to easily carry them around.

The first notable trials on mobile learning were already conducted in a few schools in the 1980s with early handheld devices (Kukulska-Hulme, Sharples, Milrad, Arnedillo-Sánches, & Vavoula, 2009). These experiments were conducted in classroom environments and a broader perspective on mobile learning did not arise until the mid-1990s. To fully capitalize on the handheld mobility factor Klopfer, Squire, and Jenkins (2002) were looking for several features of handhelds that are now practically a standard e.g. in modern smartphones:

- **Portability:** Real mobility of the device at hand
- **Social Interactivity:** Ability to exchange data and collaborate with other people face-to-face
- **Context Sensitivity:** Ability to collect data independently of time and place
- **Connectivity:** Ability to connect to networks
- **Individuality:** Ability to provide individual paths of investigation

It might be because of the somewhat restricted functionalities of the early mobile devices that originally the perspectives of mobile learning were so technology centred. Quinn (2000), for example, defined mobile learning as "elearning through mobile computational devices". Some authors like Fagerberg and Rekkedal (2004) contended that mobile learning was just a new expression for distance education, which had always been independent of time and place. However, they acknowledged that the introduction of online education first excluded students without access to computers and at least confined students to a fixed place and sometimes at fixed times.

Simonson, Smaldino, Albright and Zvacek (2003) indicated a shift from traditional education in formal classroom settings with instructor-led teaching towards education where students are considered active and central actors in their learning processes and where social interactions and collaboration are promoted and facilitated by instructors. To make these processes a part of educational practices does not necessarily involve any technologies as long as instructors and learners share the same learning facilities. However, the shift to learners outside classrooms and the need for time- and place-independent learning possibilities has produced the need to provide tools to support the processes of collaboration and interaction.

Along with the development of mobile devices getting smaller, lighter, ubiquitous, and more powerful and therefore providing more possibilities to access learning materials as well as to produce learning objects by learners themselves, the focus of mobile learning has shifted from a technology perspective to a wider context of learning as a part of an increasingly mobile lifestyle (Sharples, Milrad, Arnedillo Sánchez, & Vavoula, 2009). O'Malley et al. (2003) defined mobile learning as "any sort of learning that happens when the learner is not at a fixed, predetermined location, or learning that happens when the learner takes advantage of the learning opportunities offered by mobile technologies" (p. 6). Sharples, Taylor and Vavoula (2007), instead, introduced a perspective that tries to shift the focus of investigation from the learner or technology to the communicative interaction between these two to advance knowledge. They defined mobile learning as "the processes of coming to know through conversations across multiple contexts among people and personal interactive technologies" (p. 225). This definition emphasizes the importance of conversation as the driving force of learning (e.g. Pask, 1976). Pimmer, Pachler and Attwell (2010), although basing their perception on a similar understanding as Sharples et al. (2007), defined mobile learning as "the processes of coming to know, and of being able to operate successfully in, and across, new and ever changing contexts with and through the use of mobile devices" (p. 2). Instead, this definition emphasizes more the importance of learning how to cope in ever faster developing society – stressing the importance of learning through participation in cultural and social practices.

Mobility in mobile learning can have different "forms" as learners move, not just from one place to another, but also from one context or technology to another. Sharples et al. (2009) actually describe five types of mobility. Physical mobility describes the actual shifting from one place to another. Technological mobility affords flexibility in terms of times and places - when and where the technology is actually usable. The more mobile and usable technology is, the more are the opportunities for its use. Most often learning is also mobile in social space as learners operate among various social groups even during an ordinary school day. At last, learning is also dispersed in conceptual space and time. Dispersion in conceptual space indicates the shift from one topic or theme to another and dispersion over time refers to the cumulative process of learning that continues from one learning episode to another. The last three viewpoints reveal that this approach to learning is tightly connected to the socio-cultural tradition in education (Säljö, 2004; Vygotsky,

1978). Learning is a phenomenon that cannot be isolated from the activity, culture, context, and environment in which it takes place.

Pimmer et al. (2010) views learning in an ecological environment of agency, practices and structures. Agency describes one's capacity to act in the world and is e.g. about learners' competencies in media use, the capacity to engage the mobile tools, and the capacity to construct one's own life-world and use media for meaning making (Pachler, Cook, & Bachmair, 2010). Practices can be viewed as one's engagement with particular settings. Cultural practices affect the routines users engage with in their everyday lives – e.g. the use of mobile devices for socializing, networking and even learning are all affected by the social norms and practices that affect the acceptability of these functions. "Traditional regulations of public and private spaces are being renegotiated" (Pimmer et al. 2010, p. 4). Instead, social and technological structures govern the learners' possibilities to use their devices. Students increasingly are living in a society of individualized risks, individualized mobile mass communication and complex technological infrastructure and their learning is largely governed by both curricular frames and institutional approaches towards the use of new resources for learning (Pachler et al., 2010).

When properly used, a multitude of technologies can have an important role in learning processes as a mediator of thoughts, interactions, and activity and as a tool and a mindware (Säljö, 2010). Mindware is understood as a technology that is thoroughly integrated into practices such as teaching and learning. However, even sophisticated technologies do not facilitate or improve learning in a linear sense. The impact of technology on learning depends on several variables, such as student engagement, group participation, frequency of interaction, feedback, and connections to real-world contexts. Mobile devices make possible active multi-locational learning through formal or informal processes of training, support, collaboration and conversation (e.g. Caballe,

Xhafa, & Barolli, 2010). Although mobile learning has substantial potential to increase mobility outside classrooms, it also provides instructors and learners with the possibility of enhancing collaborative learning processes and increasing social interactions through a wide range of communication tools. These processes are still in their infancy – at least when it comes to formal education.

Experiences of Mobile Learning

Kukulska-Hulme et al. (2011) studied the way in which mature higher education students make use of handheld devices in connection with learning, social interaction, entertainment and work. Concerning learning, the most prominent benefits or uses of mobile devices were contact with other students, immediate access to information, reading e-books, listening to podcasts and scheduling studies. Video production and taking photos were not included in the learning category. Instead, these functions were categorized by students as belonging to the entertainment category. Despite these responses students were still using their mobile devices to capture their ideas and experiences in digital mode. In addition, mobile devices were used for social interaction with friends and family and, as regards work, to make appointments and create reminders. Inquiries about innovative uses of mobile devices elicited, for example, combining a walk or run with listening to podcasts, and instant documentation of whiteboard notes. Mobile devices also benefitted field trips which become more fruitful and challenging. Other significant benefits offered by mobile devices were their use in groups or communities to enable spontaneous communication, flexibility, speed, support, experience of sharing and also coping with changing arrangements.

Sharples (2010) argued that: "The main barriers to developing these new modes of mobile learning are not technical but social." (p. 4) He continues by writing: "We have little understand-ing of context and learning outside the classroom and even less about how this can be supported through new mobile technologies." (p.4) Some research on mobile learning has, however, also been conducted outside classrooms. It can promote learning "in the wild" in several areas like biology or environmental studies (Rogers et al., 2005; Chen, Kao, & Sheu, 2005) and even mathematics (Knox et al., 2010; Wijers & Jonker, 2010). One example of a well- thought-of project that has been continued even after the project itself ended is the Case Forest project (Vartiainen & Enkenberg, 2011). During this project students studied in small groups, partly in school and partly in the chosen cultural or natural environments, and gathered different materials on their way: video, audio, pictures and expert interviews. The only mobile tools the students used were digital cameras and recorders. This example shows that mobile learning can be based on very affordable tools that were supported by classroom activities involving e.g. the use of Wiki and Image gallery software which can be used with basic desktop computers.

The problems and/or disadvantages reported by mobile learners include the most evident ones such as small screen size, slow writing and costs (e.g. Motiwalla, 2007; Kukulska-Hulme et al., 2011). There are, however, also other ergonomic, technical and social issues that affect the usability of these devices. Students mentioned e.g. difficulties with scanning when reading, noisy and restrictive environments, poor sound quality, inequality of access, and said that the feeling of "physical togetherness" was missing (Kukulska-Hulme et al., 2011). Universities have also experienced problems in assuring the sustainability of their mobile learning projects beyond pilot phase (Kukulska-Hulme & Traxler, 2005). If mobile learning would be based on students' own mobile devices, carrier costs and the equality between students might be problems. However, not all mobile learning has to involve the use of wireless data for information exchange as the mobile devices can be used e.g. just for gathering information in the form of digital photos or videos (e.g. Vartiainen & Enkenberg, 2011). The data gathered can be transferred through cables inside classrooms later and the processing of the information can then be conducted with proper computers and big screens.

Students also seem to indicate that the increased complexity of the teaching process also increases dissatisfaction with it (Lindquist et al., 2007). The best experiences with mobile learning have been with devices providing enough computing power, adequate input mechanisms and a large display area. It should also be remembered that quite a large part of the research on mobile learning has been implemented with mobile tools that are totally outdated at the moment, and that the most recent top-of-the-line smartphones (or tablets) already provide decent computing power and much larger displays than the earlier cell phones, smartphones or PDAs. However, the problem with many of the latest mobile devices might be the absence of physical keyboards that may make writing tasks even more challenging than before - at least for those who are new to the onscreen keyboards.

Mobile learning should also be based on rational grounds and reasoning. These small mobile devices should never, in our opinion, be thought to be the only computing devices learners use. However, a device with a small display and low computing power might be better than not having access to a computer, the Internet or social networks at all – e.g. in the case of developing countries with low resources but, in many cases, adequate mobile networks. We also do not see much sense in using small mobile devices for long periods inside classrooms if devices with larger displays and better usability are also available. For example, the possibility of using a decent keyboard and several applications, like a web browser and word processing software at the same time, is a considerable advantage when processing the data collected from the field. A large part of the mobile learning concept is that learners are on the move

and changing contexts – that's where the mobile concept is at its strongest. You cannot use your laptop in the forest or in the streets of a city but it is easy to use your smartphone there to collect digital notes in whatever mode or shape the device enables you to do so.

Previous research in the field of mobile learning focuses primarily on isolated technology solutions (Lopes & Ribeiro, 2010; Shiratuddin & Zaibon, 2010) or on the work practice and development process of the whole mobile learning initiative (Wingkvist & Ericsson, 2010; Caballe et al., 2010; Liaw, Hatala, & Huang, 2010). The case study within this chapter, on the other hand, tackles questions concerning students' attitudes towards mobile learning, and presents the results of integrating mobile phones into learning practices in two different, but partially overlapping, areas of vocational education.

Digital Storytelling

According to the literary review of Alaa Sadik (2008), within the last 10 years, digital cameras, editing software, authoring tools and electronic media outlets have encouraged teachers to utilize many more approaches and tools than before to help students construct their own knowledge and ideas and to present and share them more effectively (Standley, 2003). One of these approaches to multimedia production is digital storytelling or the production of digital videos. According to Meadows (2003), digital storytelling is the social practice of telling stories that takes advantage of digital cameras, non-linear authoring tools and computers to create short multimedia stories. The Digital Storytelling Association (2002), according to Sadik (2008), described digital storytelling as:

The modern expression of the ancient art of storytelling. [...] Stories have been adapted to each successive medium that has emerged, from the circle of the campfire to the silver screen, and now the computer screen (p. 490).

Robin and Pierson (2005) believe that digital storytelling has captured the imagination of both students and teachers and the act of crafting meaningful stories has elevated the experience for both groups. Compared to conventional storytelling, digital storytelling audiences are viewed not only as listeners but also as learners who can interact and shape the story (Dorner, Grimm, & Abawi, 2002).

Storytelling is the original form of teaching (Pedersen, 1995). It is a simple but still powerful method that may help students understand their sometimes complex and unordered experiences by crafting story lines (Bruner, 1990; Gils, 2005). The idea of digital storytelling originates from the digital storytelling movement in the late 1980s when the Center for Digital Storytelling (CDS) was founded in Berkeley, California (Robin, 2008). Since the early 1990s, CDS has helped people create and share their personal narratives. Digital storytelling can be defined in several ways, but in general, they all revolve around the idea of combining the art of telling stories with a variety of digital multimedia, such as images, audio, and video. As is the case with traditional storytelling, digital stories also revolve around a chosen theme and usually contain a particular viewpoint. Stories can be just a few minutes long and have a variety of uses like the telling of personal tales, recounting historical events, or as a means to inform or instruct on a certain topic (Robin, 2005).

Stories (not just the digital ones) can be used in education in a number of ways. They can be used at the beginning of a lesson to help engage students in learning (Burmark, 2004; Ormrod, 2004), as a bridge between previous knowledge and new information or knowledge (Ausubel, 1978), as exemplars of concepts or principles being taught by direct instruction, as problem cases to be solved by students, and as advice to students, helping them learn to solve problems (Jonassen & Hernandez-Serrano, 2002). The process of creating digital stories can bring out the creative talents of students as they begin to search information from libraries and the Internet for rich and deep content, analyse and synthesize the found content, and finally tell stories of their own (Robin, 2005). Students who participate in the production of digital stories may develop enhanced communications skills as they learn to organize their ideas, ask questions, express opinions, and construct narratives. They may also benefit as they learn to create stories for other people, and present their ideas and knowledge in a new way – different from the more traditional essays or presentations.

When digital stories are published on social media sites, students may easily share their work and gain valuable experience in both receiving critique of their own work as well as critiquing other students' work, which can promote emotional intelligence and social learning (Robin, 2005). Digital storytelling may appeal to students with diverse learning styles and might also foster collaboration when students are given the possibility to work in groups. It can provide value in enhancing the student experience through personal ownership and accomplishment. Barrett (2006) suggests that digital storytelling supports the convergence of four student-centred learning strategies: student engagement, reflection for deep learning, project-based learning, and the effective integration of technology into instruction. Robin (2005) suggested that educators at all levels and in most subjects can use digital storytelling to support their students' learning by motivating them to organize and express their ideas and knowledge in an individual and meaningful way.

Gils (2005) suggested several advantages of using digital storytelling in education:

1. To provide more variation;
2. To personalize the learning experience;
3. To make an explanation or the practicing of certain topics more compelling;
4. To create real life situations in an easy and cheaper way; and

5. To enhance the involvement of students in the process of learning. Tsou, Wang and Tzeng (2006) found that the integration of digital storytelling into the language curriculum is a creative language learning technique that may improve students' level of learning in reading, writing, speaking and listening.

Sadik (2008) studied the use of meaningful technology, digital storytelling in this case, in engaging students with learning. Sadik states that although research emphasizes the importance of integrating technology into the curriculum, the use of technology can only be effective if teachers themselves are able to use technology in the classroom in a meaningful way. His study aimed to assist teachers in developing their teaching and learning through the application of a certain digital technology. Students produced their own digital stories while being introduced to desktop production and editing tools. Afterwards, students presented, published and shared their own stories with their peers. Student-produced stories revealed that students managed to produce stories that met many of the pedagogical and technical attributes of digital stories. Despite the problems observed and reported by teachers, digital storytelling was still perceived as a method that could increase students' understanding of curricular content and teachers were willing to transform their teaching to include this method. Like Sadik, other researchers also indicate that the effectiveness of technology integration into education is largely dependent on its ability to engage students in learning (Dexter, Anderson, & Becker, 1999) and that the key to using educational technology is to utilize meaningful activities that engage students to construct their knowledge in ways not available before (Trilling & Hood, 1999).

According to Hakkarainen's (2007) thesis about the concept of meaningful learning through the integrated use of digital videos, there are several positive impacts to be found in using digital videos as a part of learning. Hakkarainen went

through a number of case studies and listed the positive outcomes found in previous research. In the light of the study presented in this chapter, the most central of those are enhanced motivation and enjoyment, engagement with the subject matter (e.g. Jonassen, 2000; Schuck & Kearney, 2004; Kearney & Schuck, 2006), provision of creative possibilities for expression (e.g. Jonassen, 2000; Counts, 2004), projection of students' own personalities (Schuck & Kearney, 2004), enhancement of communication and presentation skills, supporting the development of domain specific conceptual knowledge and skills (Schuck & Kearney, 2004), an increase in self-directed studying activities, and an improvement in teamwork skills (Schuck & Kearney, 2004; Kearney & Schuck, 2006).

However, digital storytelling does present some challenges to students and educators, which is something the case study presented in this chapter also emphasizes. Robin (2005) highlighted possible problem areas that should be considered. Respect for copyright and the intellectual property of others is an important issue as it is always tempting for students of all ages to use the Internet to find images, music and other material for inclusion in their digital stories. Educators should also be aware that digital storytelling can be very time consuming. Teachers who wish to include digital storytelling in their teaching practices should also be aware that it may take students several attempts at creating digital stories before they demonstrate technological proficiency and an understanding of their selected topic. As with all new instructional methods, students will need time to learn what is expected of them as they begin using digital storytelling. A useful option for educators is to use peer reviews and reflections where students and teachers together have an opportunity to discuss student work and the learning process. There is no doubt that more needs to be learnt about digital storytelling as a teaching and learning tool. Barrett (2005) suggests that if digital storytelling is to become an accepted practice in today's schools, it will be necessary to collect more data about its impact on student learning, motivation and engagement as well as teaching practices and strategies. This is also the intention of our study.

Combining Social Media with Mobile Digital Storytelling

The United States' National Research Council (1999) concluded that effective learning should be learner, knowledge, assessment, and community centred and therefore broadly matching the social-constructivist approach as well as the elements of mobile learning. Both view learning as an active process of knowledge building (Sharples, Taylor, & Vavoula, 2005). The latest definitions of mobile learning also stress the importance of conversation and participation in cultural and social practices as the driving forces of learning (Sharples et al., 2007; Pimmer et al., 2010). These elements of learning suggest a close relationship with the features of social media which is built on three main elements (Ahlqvist, Bäck, Heinonen, & Halonen, 2010): content, communities and Web 2.0 technologies. Content in social media is user created and may appear in various different forms like photos, videos or information. Communities and interaction, whether being a discussion or an exchange of media content, between users are the basis of social media. Web 2.0 technologies, at least when supported by mobile technologies, make possible the almost time- and location-independent content creation, sharing and diverse discussions. Many social media applications support users to actively participate, e.g. in creating content, evaluating content, annotating content with tags, and creating social networks with other users who share similar interests (Lerman, 2008).

YouTube statistics (http://www.youtube.com/t/press_statistics) offer some views on how extensively people are contributing to one of the most popular social network sites in the world. For example, in February 2012, about 48 hours of video were uploaded onto Youtube every minute

and over three billion videos were viewed every day. This video-based format has become the location of choice to present personal views, productions, commercials and even political agendas. It can, therefore, be argued that now already a large population of people with access to digital video recording technologies and the Internet enjoys producing videos and even posting them for public reviews and discussions. It is also probable that more and more of the videos submitted to social media sites are shot with smartphones. Preece and Shneiderman (2009) well conveyed the transition in the relation between mobile devices and social media: "The purpose of mobile devices such as cell phones has expanded beyond person-to-person communication to become the facilitator of the rich social web" (p. 14).

Preece and Shneiderman (2009) presented the four-stage Reader to Leader model that describes how users start to familiarize themselves with social media by first becoming readers, or maybe viewers in the case of videos, then contributors, collaborators or even leaders. When attending to these social media sites, user is introduced to the informal learning opportunities built into the trajectory of his or her community membership. Clough (2010) fitted this model and the framework for assessing meaningful learning with technology, adapted from Jonassen, Howland, Moore and Marra (2003) to categorize the related informal learning opportunities. Practically active participation at all stages of community membership, except the reader where the user is not contributing to the community, realize all the attributes in Jonassen et al. (2003) framework, namely active, intentional, authentic, constructive, and cooperative characteristics of learning. Meaningful learning itself is a concept that originated from Ausubel's (1963) work on cognition and learning. It emphasizes students' ability to relate new concepts, information and their linkages to their previous experiences and knowledge. Jonassen (1995) argued that engagement in meaningful learning should be the basis of any pedagogically significant use of technology.

Since Jonassen's (1995) first thoughts on technology supported meaningful learning, several researchers have pursued the achievement of meaningful learning by using different forms of ICTs (e.g. Karppinen, 2005; Hakkarainen, Saarelainen, & Ruokamo, 2007; Rick & Weber, 2010; Vuojärvi, Eriksson & Ruokamo, In Press). Hakkarainen et al. (2007) extended the concept of meaningful learning by adding some extra characteristics (e.g. contextual, individual, emotionally involving, multiple perspectives oriented, critical, experiential and creative) that should be considered when aspiring to meaningful learning in technology-mediated environments (Model for Teaching and Meaningful Learning = TML). In their study they found that designing and producing digital videos as well as solving the digital video supported cases facilitated especially the active and contextual aspects of students' learning but also positively affected their emotional involvement in the learning process.

Vuojärvi et al. (In Press) adapted the TML model in the context of mobile learning to create the model for "meaningful work-based mobile learning". They added two more characteristics, situated and authentic, to better represent the possibilities mobile learning provides but also condensed the model by integrating characteristics that are conceptually close to each other. The setting where this model was first tested included students' apprenticeship periods in tourism companies in Finland. Students were expected to keep weblog-based learning diaries during their apprenticeship period as this was supposed to be the main means for them to reflect their learning as well as their instructor's tool to follow their learning and to keep in touch with the students when needed. Despite having laptops for this task, some students reported they were not able to update their blogs as the place where they worked lacked the needed Internet connections. Some said that they were too tired to write after the very long days in

the field, but they also indicated that most of them had several breaks during the workday which they spent just waiting for customers – these breaks could also be used for blogging. One solution to these problems could be the use of smartphones which can easily be carried around, and which will enable them to connect to the widespread 3G networks and the social media sites, to write notes and even short blog posts, and which will provide the possibility of immortalizing some moments of their apprenticeships in the mode of pictures or videos.

If we think about the possibilities that the settings of the pilot, described in the next section, enable in vocational education, we can see that the possibilities are limitless. Two groups of students from two separate areas of the educational scene with partly overlapping interests provide the possibility of fruitful collaboration, sharing ideas and professional knowledge, learning how to comment on others' work and how to develop one's own work based on the comments made by others. Digital storytelling provides students with an interesting new way of representing their ideas even if they are not that good writers or are uneasy about presenting their work in front of an audience. Mobile devices make it easy to take learning outside the classroom where the real world exists and where these future professionals will actually have to work after graduating. Suitable social media applications enable collaboration, discussions, sharing, commenting, editing and so on even with distant partners. It is a package that is just waiting to be piggybacked.

METHODS AND DATA SOURCES

Digital videos are rather new tools for learning; therefore, most video-sharing services are not designed to be learning applications. The Mobile Video Experience (MoViE), developed at the Tampere University of Technology, however, is designed particularly to be used in learning, especially with mobile devices such as smartphones. MoViE is a social media service that enables users to create video stories using their mobile devices. MoViE supports private group creation, user-generated tags, tag spaces, geotags, the remixing of clips, and moderation. Therefore, students using MoViE can take videos with their smartphones, upload the videos wirelessly to MoViE and even edit and remix their and other students' shared videos with their mobile devices. MoViE was developed to address the collaborative and creative demands of learning, and it offers several novel ways to utilize videos for educational purposes (Kiili, Multisilta, Suominen, & Ketamo, 2010). Digital storytelling is a good way to bring variety into classroom learning as well as to create a continuum between different learning contexts. Mobile videos can be used both for data collection and for showing results. Previous research results on MoViE have revealed that it is quite suitable for learning purposes, at least in elementary and middle school grades (Tuomi & Multisilta, 2010, 2012). Both studies were conducted to study educational mobile video blogging. The first study and testing were conducted in fall 2009 and MoViE was used to teach biology and cultural geography to 7th to 9th graders. The second study was conducted with 5th graders in 2010. Overall, the younger students' perceptions were far more positive than teenagers' responses. The 5th graders were more open to new technology and less critical about completing assignments given during the pilot courses. This probably has a lot to do with the fact that it might be a bit more challenging to get students aged fifteen excited about something compared to students aged about ten.

The participants of this case study were 14 tourism students and 20 AVC students from two vocational colleges in Finland. Before starting the MoViE teaching experiment, the tourism students (N=14) were interviewed by the researchers in order to ascertain their general wishes concerning their upcoming studies. The interviews revealed students' need and willingness to study indepen-

dently/co-operationally in groups. The students requested more responsibilities and freedom. They also wanted studying to be more challenging - a factor that surfaced in almost all their responses. Accordingly, the course at hand and its specific tasks were organized based on students' wishes.

The students' were tasked with creating videos focusing on three topics: 1) Local food - possible specialties, 2) Culture tradition and history - happenings, living legends, local stories and people, and 3) Nature. Tourism students were free to choose the topics of their videos themselves within the set limits. For AVC students, tourism teachers at their institution selected a list of topics from which students could choose. The students were instructed to choose topics that are not exploited very much in local tourism. Videos were to be planned, shot and edited in groups of three or four students. For tourism students the aim of the course was clearly to learn more about local tourism products related to the topics above – producing digital stories with mobile tools and MoViE was just a way to present the results of their learning easily. For AVC students the aim was more to practice their ability to create interesting digital stories on given subjects (tailor-made work) with challenging, non-professional tools. It was considered important for both groups to learn how to give and receive both positive and negative feedback and to develop their work further.

The course started with one-day training on how to use MoViE application. All 34 students, their teachers and three researchers were present at the training. The designers of the MoViE application provided technical assistance by phone when needed. Tourism students were also given a short introduction to the basics of video photography and the production of videos. After the training, students had three weeks to write screenplays, share them with other students to get feedback, shoot and edit the videos and share them through MoViE. The feedback phase before continuing with shooting videos was organized so that the AVC students could provide feedback to tourism students and vice versa. It was thought that AVC students could consider tourism students' screenplays from the point of view of their media expertise (e.g. technical advice for filming, screenplay structure) and tourism students could consider the interest value of the topics (e.g., content, details that should be emphasized) the AVC students had chosen for their videos from a tourism professionals' point of view.

After the course, data was collected by means of an Internet-based questionnaire. The inquiry contained 38 questions related to MoViE and its usage, as well as students' learning experiences and attitudes towards smartphones and mobile learning. To make the interpretation of these results easier and more reliable, we also collected student opinions on the use of social media both as a learning tool and as a tool or media to publish self-created material to illustrate professional knowhow. Most of the questions were open-ended, which enabled respondents to speak freely on the topic and comment on the questions. In addition, some questions in multiple-choice format (based on the 1-5 *Likert scale*) were included. Twenty-five of the 34 students who participated in the course (74%) responded to the survey. Of the respondents, 16 were female and 9 male, the average age being 18.4 years. Given that the quantitative data is narrow, the qualitative material – open questions – was handled as the main substance. Students' answers to open-ended questions were themed with regard to research questions presented before (Gray, 2004).

RESULTS AND DISCUSSION

In this study our goal was twofold. First, we wanted to explore students' attitudes towards the use of social media as part of their vocational expertise. Second, we wanted to gather student experiences of using mobile camera phones and MoViE, a mobile video social media platform, to create digital stories with a learning purpose.

In addition to examining how students experienced the use of mobile camera phones and MoViE, it was considered important to know how these students had previously used social media, how they perceived publishing self-created material (pictures, videos) on the Internet and what kind of role students thought social media plays in their future professions. This knowledge was considered important for at least two reasons. First, students' attitudes towards and experiences of social media may affect the way in which they perceive the use of social media applications like MoViE. Second, social media is a significant tool for both advertising and informing customers in the tourism industry, as it already constitutes a significant part of the search engine results when searching for information on tourist destinations (Xiang & Gretzel, 2010). Since a large number of tourism companies e.g. in Finland is quite small, many jobs in this industry include a large spectrum of tasks of which e.g. the use of social media to promote business might well be one. For AVC professionals the production of videos or pictures for advertising purposes in social media is a part of their job. Therefore, both tourism and AVC students are quite probably going to use social media tools in their future professions.

To answer the first research question we asked students about their social media habits and attitudes towards the vocational use of social media. The results show that all the respondents had a Facebook account and 80% also had an account on at least one other social media site. At least 84% of respondents had used social media sites for publishing pictures and 44% had either published their own videos or had at least taken part in producing videos later published on social media sites (mainly Facebook, Vimeo and Youtube). Forty per cent indicated that they enjoy publishing material they have created while only 8% prefer not to do so. They were also asked whether it has an impact if material is published with one's name or not. The answers reflect that students seem to take care of their privacy settings in social media, and carefully consider what kind of material they submit to these sites with their names on it. Some students also indicated that it is not just about privacy or their personal reputations, but also their professional reputations — a kind of a digital business card that is updated every time new content is published online.

[...]when you have something really good, you probably like to add your name when publishing. — Male (tourism)

Yes, it has an impact (publishing content with one's own name), it brings reliability in many ways if you are able to publish material as yourself. — Female (AVC)

You don't want to publish just any rubbish if it has your name on it. — Male (AVC)

I don't want to publish any badly produced material. Everything that has my signature on it, must also show my skills. — Male (tourism)

In accordance with these thoughts, over half (64%) of respondents acknowledges that social media and its tools will be an essential part of their vocational expertise in future. No one argues and only 36% are unsure. To use social media publicly as a part of their vocational expertise is accepted by a majority (56%) of the students. Only 12% are uneasy about the thought that social media would play an important role in building their career in future. The attitudes towards the use of social media for professional purposes in both groups were very much alike, which is why they have not been elaborated on in more detail. All the students, despite their background education, had similar ideas concerning the publication of identifiable content, and they all share quite similar opinions of how important it is for their future careers to publish quality material online.

Our second research question concerned students' experiences with learning with mobile camera phones and MoViE application. According to the results, vocational students (average age 18.4 years) did not respond as positively as younger students in previous studies (Tuomi & Multisilta, 2010, 2012). Our participants were more cautious and also more aware and critical of the quality of the recorded video material as well as the malfunctions in using MoViE.

MoViE as an application is generally very easy to learn since it was developed for use with mobile devices and, therefore, smaller screens. Seventy-six per cent of the students stated that they were able to learn MoViE quickly and 45% thought that MoViE was easy to use. Despite the easiness of use MoViE inspired only 8% of students to learn and perform given tasks. Quite surprisingly, only 20% thought that the presence of others and the reliance on co-operation was a positive factor. The comments on using MoViE were in accordance with the above results. Although there were also some positive comments, many thought that MoViE was a bit boring and the web page too plain.

MoViE was boring. Making videos was actually fun, the phone was practical and easy to use. — Female (tourism)

It was a nice experience and it was fun to be able to record videos with a phone. — Female (AVC)

I think MoViE looked even too plain. [...] On the other hand it was practical and clear to use with a phone. — Male (tourism)

Especially the editing possibilities of MoViE received criticism as currently it is only possible to edit sections of the timeline to cut something irrelevant out of the video or to mix sections of two or more videos. The editing is then based on cutting and adding the material by choosing the timespan one wishes to edit. This is a really simple way of editing but when done on mobile phones, it is, however, a new feature and quite unique.

The students were expecting a wider range of editing tools to use, for example voice and image libraries, and possibilities to add artistic features to their movies. The common effects of fading and dissolving were missed and overall editing as an extra value of MoViE was not positively perceived.

I don't consider MoViE that practical or good. With modern high-end phones one can edit videos and submit to Youtube. The functions (of MoViE) were totally inadequate. — Male (AVC)

MoViE did not provide a lot of editing possibilities – maybe that's why it was a bit boring. — Female (tourism)

As mentioned earlier, quite a large number (44%) of the respondents had published their own video material on the Internet (Vimeo or Youtube) even before this pilot. Many tourism students and all the AVC students were already used to better quality cameras with significantly better video quality and usability than what the quite basic camera phones used could offer.

As I am used to record videos with semi-professional SLR equipment – recording with a phone camera feels like clowning around. Male (tourism)

A phone is a handy piece of equipment, but the quality (of the picture) is hardly professional. Female (AVC)

The video recordings produced low quality results and the voice was also bad ... Female (AVC)

In addition to the low quality of videos the phones produced, students also complained about the small size of the screen and the slowness of the Internet connection which made uploading videos onto MoViE quite hard.

[...] uploading raw material (from the phone) was slow — Male (tourism)

Similar comments were found in several answers. This was not surprising as the used phones were not any high-end smartphones with large screens but quite plain camera phones with internet access. All comments, however, were not that negative as some students could also see the benefits these mobile devices could offer – despite the quality issues with the phones used this time.

It works well. It's always with you and you can do anything anywhere. — Female (tourism)

Smartphones are especially well suited to producing content for social media sites! Publishing becomes easier and independent of place. The picture quality should, however, be better [...] — Female (AVC)

It's getting better (smartphones). For example, Nokia has handed over their N8 smartphones for snowboarders and those that video record snowboarding. As I've watched some of those (videos) I have to say that it works quite well when you can use it!" — Male (tourism)

The largely negative experiences with the equipment used did obviously affect students' motivation right from the start of the pilot. This frustration was also seen in the comments made about the given assignment.

Challenging, frustrating. Video recording with a phone is damn inconvenient. The technical characteristics just simply constrain recording a lot. Male (tourism)

Boring, because it wasn't possible to bring out (because of the equipment) the things we really wanted to be seen. — Female (AVC)

However, the technical problems were not the only problems during the pilot. Some students also complained that they were not able to invest enough time in the assignment as they had a lot of other projects on the side. However, these thoughts were most probably related to the lack of motivation rather than the lack of time as all students reported quite a small amount of time was used to complete the assignment.

Recording took about two hours. Editing took about the same amount of time. — Male (tourism)

During the school day, in small prearranged groups and it took about 5 hours. — Female (AVC)

The methods and instruction during the course were quite informal, although it was easy to notice from students' answers that the AVC students' learning was instructed a bit more. The fact that learning was not strictly scheduled was evident particularly from tourism students' responses.

We planned the videos in school time and did the filming of the videos in our free time. — Female (tourism)

All the planning was done in our group while driving. — Male (tourism)

Most AVC students confronted the task and the formal component of the content by searching the Internet for appropriate information. Instead, quite a substantial portion of tourism students did not actually do any ground work on the matter since they chose topics with which they were already familiar—quite the opposite of what they were urged to do. This is one of the reasons why many students said they had learnt nothing new.

All the information needed was gathered from the internet. — Female (AVC)

My local knowledge was enough. — Male (tourism)

In addition, tourism students' video manuscripts were very simple—mostly just airy-fairy descriptions of their topic and a few sentences about their actual filming plans e.g. filming location. Students of AVC had a slightly more professional attitude towards planning and filming the videos as their video screenplays and filming plans were far more precise. They included precise descriptions of the tools used, filming locations, possible interviewees, angle of view for the camera, etc. This probably has a lot to do with their background as students of AVC but probably also their instructor's background and the amount of instruction during the process.

SOLUTIONS AND RECOMMENDATIONS

As stated in the previous section, there were a few problem areas worth noticing in order to enhance the use of social media and mobile technology in future education. The problems encountered can roughly be divided into: 1) dissatisfaction with the capacity of the phones used for video recording, 2) editing possibilities of MoViE (and camera phones) were not satisfactory, 3) slow transfer of video files from mobile phones to MoViE, and 4) motivation-related issues. It is probable that most of the abovementioned problems are at least partly related to the fact that most participating students had previous experience of video recording and editing with more advanced equipment. Dissatisfaction and frustration with the used technology had an inevitable impact on the whole study since the camera phones and MoViE played a large part in it. Along with some technical problems this naturally led to negative experiences throughout the study as students did not devote their full effort to the task given. However, mobile learning does not require wireless data transfer or the use of camera phones. The same tasks can be performed using professional equipment if such tools are available and editing can be done with better editing tools and more powerful computers, big screens and keyboards – something some of the students did also in this case study. Mobile devices like smartphones could still be great tools to support collaboration, communication and commenting through social media outside classrooms.

According to the students, MoViE was technically very easy to learn but at the same time they did criticize the technical difficulties and errors encountered while using MoViE. For younger students simple applications are probably a great solution but for more advanced students, as in this case, it would have been more meaningful to have an application with more advanced editing capabilities instead of simply having an easy and simple interface. The youngest students (Tuomi & Multisilta, 2012) appreciated the easiness of MoViE. The students of this study found MoViE more or less boring and inadequate from their point of view. They could not see any sense in producing technically low quality videos with mobile phones and MoViE when they knew they could do much better with the right equipment. The learning perspective of the experiment was clearly left in the background. This emphasizes the importance of setting a technical level suitable to the students' age and background. It is clearly one of the most important factors when motivating the students to actually engage in learning.

The promotion of digital literacy aims at preparing students for 21st century multi-media society and it starts by enabling instructors to encounter their students (Simanowski, 2009). The instructor needs to know what the actual skills of the students are - who really needs assistance and who has enough knowledge to perform the assigned tasks self-directed. It is recommended that before similar try-outs with MoViE, the background of the participating students be explored thoroughly so

that their level of knowledge and technical skills is taken into account when planning the course and its tasks. The applications and technologies used should be well considered to match the students' age, skills and demands.

Eventually, only 12% of respondents felt that MoViE was well suited to learning, and 68% thought that it did not suit the intended purpose. It is clear that the technologies used and the course itself did not motivate these students during the try-out, which is seen in the fairly large amount of negative responses of the inquiry. It was still quite surprising that the comments mostly focused on the low quality of the videos and the inadequate editing possibilities of MoVie even though there was no intention of evaluating the picture quality or even the structure of the videos. Students could not see the use of these devices simply as a part of learning where the process of information searching, screenplay writing, commenting, and the content of the final videos is so much more important than the technical quality of the videos.

CONCLUSION AND FUTURE RESEARCH DIRECTIONS

This chapter introduces the concepts of mobile learning and digital storytelling and how the use of social media can promote the adaption of both concepts. The case study dealt with two interesting themes. First, the questionnaire results indicate how a group of young Finnish students perceive content creation for social media as a part of their vocational expertise and as a public platform to express their talent. Second, the study provided important data on how important it is to know one's students to be able to plan courses and to select or let students select the appropriate tools for the given tasks.

The attitudes towards the use of social media for professional purposes were very much alike in both groups. All the students, despite their education, seemed to be very careful about the material they submit to social media sites and had similar ideas concerning the publication of identifiable content. Many students indicated how important it is for their future career and their professional reputation to publish good quality material online. They seem to share the idea of a kind of a digital business card that is updated constantly as new content is published online. Because of the small number of respondents and the fact that they represented only two areas of vocational education, the results concerning attitudes towards social media are not straightforwardly generalizable. These students had quite a tight and somewhat professional attitude towards the use of social media and it is probable that they have given these things a bit more thought than others in their age group. These attitudes should, however, be further studied on a much larger scale.

This study gave us beneficial knowledge of and information on the suitability of mobile technologies for learning and what things should be taken into account when planning technology mediated education. Many experiments with technologies might give a slightly false image of their benefits as they usually involve the testing of the latest technologies – which in many cases provide an additional boost for learning. In this study the used phones were not the latest top-of-the-line models and the WOW effect was therefore lacking. This study also differed from the previous and more successful experiments with MoViE where the target groups were significantly younger. The requirements from the vocational students, when it comes to the meaningfulness of technology use, were far more demanding than they had been with younger students. After the try-out it was clear that MoViE or the used camera phones could not please the students on a vocational level as a functional tool or as an inspiring feature to learn something new. The technology must meet the age and background level of the students. On the other hand, the content of the course must

also meet the students' level of intelligence and skills in order to carry out a successful try-out and learning experience. The clear majority of the vocational students, in both groups, felt that they did not learn through the experiment and that the technologies used did not motivate them. It is clear that in addition to the dissatisfaction with the technologies, the given assignments were not motivating enough or the purpose of the course was not conveyed to students clearly enough. The results concerning satisfaction or dissatisfaction with the used technology can probably be generalized to apply also to large range of students and for different technologies. To really engage students in learning, the suitability of technologies for each group of students should always be carefully considered whenever planning technology mediated education.

Despite the negative experiences with the equipment, we still encourage the use of mobile phones in future research, especially in everyday education, as they are tools many students frequently use in their lives already. Mobile devices and smartphones in particular enable a large variety of applications that can be used to collect data, communicate and collaborate independently of time, place and even distance. If it is possible to use student-owned devices there is also no need to waste a lot of time on getting familiarized with technology. That time can be used for learning. Most importantly, mobile devices allow students to leave the classroom and easily collect real data from the real world and experience things they cannot experience inside classrooms. Whether it is possible to use wireless data transfer, online communication or the latest smartphones or tablets is not on the list of priorities – just an ordinary digital camera will provide students with the possibility of obtaining some digital material (if that is pursued) that can be further processed with stationary computers.

REFERENCES

Ahlqvist, T., Bäck, A., Heinonen, S., & Halonen, M. (2010). Road-mapping the societal transformation potential of social media. *Foresight, 12*(5), 3–26. doi:10.1108/14636681011075687

Ausubel, D. (1963). *The psychology of meaningful verbal learning*. New York, NY: Grune and Stratton.

Ausubel, D. P. (1978). In defense of advance organizers: A reply to the critics. *Review of Educational Research, 48*, 251–257.

Barrett, H. (2005). *Digital storytelling research design*. Retrieved March 14, 2012, from http://electronicportfolios.com/digistory/ResearchDesign.pdf

Barrett, H. (2006). Researching and evaluating digital storytelling as a deep learning tool. In C. Crawford, et al. (Eds.), *Proceedings of Society for Information Technology and Teacher Education International Conference 2006* (pp. 647–654). Chesapeake, VA: AACE.

Bruner, J. (1990). *Acts of meaning*. Cambridge, MA: Harvard University Press.

Burmark, L. (2004, May/June). Visual presentations that prompt, flash & transform. *Media and Methods, 40*(6), 4–5.

Caballe, S., Xhafa, F., & Barolli, L. (2010). Using mobile devices to support online collaborative learning. *Mobile Information Systems - Mobile and Wireless Networks, 6*(1), 27–47.

Chen, Y.-S., Kao, T.-C., & Sheu, J.-P. (2005). Realizing outdoor independent learning with a butterfly-watching mobile learning system. *Journal of Educational Computing Research, 33*(4), 395–417. doi:10.2190/0PAB-HRN9-PJ9K-DY0C

Clough, G. (2010). Informal learning with mobile and social technologies: Framework for analysis. In E. Brown (Ed.), *Education in the wild: Contextual and location-based mobile learning in action* (pp. 4–6). A report from the STELLAR Alpine Rendez-Vous workshop series. Retrieved March 7, 2012, from http://www.lsri.nottingham.ac.uk/ejb/preprints/ARV_Education_in_the_wild.pdf

Dexter, S., Anderson, R., & Becker, H. (1999). Teachers' views of computers as catalysts for changes in their teaching practice. *Journal of Research on Computing in Education, 31*(3), 221–239.

Dorner, R., Grimm, P., & Abawi, D. (2002). Synergies between interactive training simulations and digital storytelling: A component-based framework. *Computers & Graphics, 26*, 45–55. doi:10.1016/S0097-8493(01)00177-7

Fagerberg, T., & Rekkedal, T. (2004). Enhancing the flexibility of distance education – Designing and trying out a learning environment for mobile distance learners. In T. Rekkedal, A. Dye, T. Fagerberg, S. Bredal, B. Midtsveen, & J. Russel (Eds.), *Design, Development and Evaluation of Mobile Learning at NKI Distance Education 2000-2005* (pp. 173–183). Bekkestua, Norway: NKI Forlaget. Retrieved March 6, 2012, from http://www.dye.no/articles/mlearning/m_Learning_2000_2005.pdf#page=173

Gils, F. (2005). *Potential applications of digital storytelling in education*. 3rd Twente Student Conference on IT, University of Twente, Faculty of Electrical Engineering, Mathematics and Computer Science, Enschede.

Gray, D. E. (2004). *Doing research in the real world*. Los Angeles, CA: Sage.

Hakkarainen, P. (2007). *Promoting meaningful learning through the integrated use of digital videos*. Doctoral dissertation, University of Lapland. Acta Universitatis Lapponiensis 121. Rovaniemi, Finland: University of Lapland, Faculty of Education.

Hakkarainen, P., Saarelainen, T., & Ruokamo, H. (2007). Towards meaningful learning through digital video supported, case based teaching. *Australasian Journal of Educational Technology*, *23*(1), 87–109.

Johnson, L., Smith, R., Levine, A., & Haywood, K. (2011). *The 2011 horizon report*. Austin, TX: The New Media Consortium. Retrieved February 16, 2012, from http://net.educause.edu/ir/library/pdf/HR2011.pdf

Jonassen, D. H. (1995). Supporting communities of learners with technology: A vision for integrating technology with learning in schools. *Educational Technology*, *35*(4), 60–63.

Jonassen, D. H. (2000). *Computers as mindtools for schools. Engaging critical thinking*. New Jersey: Prentice-Hall.

Jonassen, D. H., & Hernandez-Serrano, J. (2002). Case-based reasoning and instructional design: Using stories to support problem solving. *Educational Technology Research and Development*, *50*(2), 65–77. doi:10.1007/BF02504994

Jonassen, D. H., Howland, J. L., Moore, J. L., & Marra, R. M. (2003). *Learning to solve problems with technology: A constructivist perspective*. Upper Saddle River, NJ: Merrill Prentice Hall.

Karppinen, P. (2005). Meaningful learning with digital and online videos: Theoretical perspectives. *AACE Journal on Information Technology in Education*, *13*(3), 233–250.

Kearney, M., & Schuck, S. (2006). Spotlight on authentic learning: Student developed digital video projects. *Australasian Journal of Educational Technology*, *22*(2), 189–208.

Kiili, K., Multisilta, J., Suominen, M., & Ketamo, H. (2010). Learning experiences on mobile social media. *International Journal of Mobile Learning and Organisation*, *4*(4), 346–359. doi:10.1504/IJMLO.2010.037533

Klopfer, E., Squire, K., & Jenkins, H. (2002). Environmental detectives: PDAs as a window into a virtual simulated world. *Proceedings of the IEEE International Workshop on Wireless and Mobile Technologies in Education*. IEEE. Retrieved March 6, 2012, from http://140.115.126.240/mediawiki/images/9/93/Environment_Detective.pdf

Knox, S., Sharpe, G., Oldham, E., Weber, S., Soloway, E., & Jennings, K. (2010). Towards the use of smartphones for the contextualized teaching of mathematics. In E. Brown (Ed.), *Education in the wild: contextual and location-based mobile learning in action* (pp. 13–16). A report from the STELLAR Alpine Rendez-Vous workshop series. Retrieved March 7, 2012, from http://www.lsri.nottingham.ac.uk/ejb/preprints/ARV_Education_in_the_wild.pdf

Kukulska-Hulme, A., Pettit, J., Bradley, L., Carvalho, A. A., Herrington, A., Kennedy, D. M., & Walker, A. (2011). Mature students using mobile devices in life and learning. *International Journal of Mobile and Blended Learning*, *3*(1), 18–52. doi:10.4018/jmbl.2011010102

Kukulska-Hulme, A., Sharples, M., Milrad, M., Arnedillo-Sánchez, I., & Vavoula, G. (2009). Innovation in mobile learning: A European perspective. *International Journal of Mobile and Blended Learning*, *1*(1), 13–35. doi:10.4018/jmbl.2009010102

Kukulska-Hulme, A., Sharples, M., Milrad, M., Arnedillo-Sánchez, I., & Vavoula, G. (2010). The genesis and development of mobile learning in Europe. In Parsons, D. (Ed.), *Combining e-learning and m-learning: New applications of blended educational resources* (pp. 151–177). Hershey, PA: Information Science Reference (an imprint of IGI Global). doi:10.4018/978-1-60960-481-3.ch010

Kukulska-Hulme, A., & Traxler, J. (2005). *Mobile learning: A handbook for educators and trainers*. London, UK: Routledge.

Lerman, K. (2008). *Social browsing & information filtering in social media*. Retrieved March 6, 2012, from http://arxiv.org/abs/0710.5697

Liaw, S. S., Hatala, M., & Huang, H. M. (2010). Investigating acceptance toward mobile learning to assist individual knowledge management: Based on activity theory approach. *Computers & Education*, *54*(2), 446–454. doi:10.1016/j.compedu.2009.08.029

Lindquist, D., Denning, T., Kelly, M., Malani, R., Griswold, W. G., & Simon, B. (2007). Exploring the potential of mobile phones for active learning in the classroom. *ACM SIGCSE Bulletin, Session: Emerging Instructional Technologies, 39*(1). Retrieved March 6, 2012, from http://cseweb.ucsd.edu/~wgg/Abstracts/fp142-lindquist.pdf

Lopes, L., & Ribeiro, B. (2010). GPUMLib: An efficient open-source GPU machine learning library. *International Journal of Computer Information Systems and Industrial Management Applications*, *3*, 355–362.

Meadows, D. (2003). Digital storytelling: Research-based practice in new media. *Visual Communication*, *2*(2), 189–193. doi:10.1177/1470357203002002004

Motiwalla, L. F. (2007). Mobile learning: A framework and evaluation. *Computers & Education*, *49*(3), 581–596. doi:10.1016/j.compedu.2005.10.011

Mwanza-Simwami, D. (2007). Concepts and methods for investigating learner activities with mobile devices: An activity theory perspective. In I. Arnedillo-Sánchez, M. Sharples, G. Vavoula G. (Eds.), *Beyond Mobile Learning Workshop* (pp. 24–25). Trinity College Dublin Press.

National Research Council. (1999). *How people learn: Brain, mind, experience, and school*. Washington, DC: National Academy Press.

O'Malley, C., Vavoula, G., Glew, J. P., Taylor, J., Sharples, M., & Lefrere, P. (2003). *Guidelines for learning/teaching/tutoring in a mobile environment*. Mobilearn Project. Open University. Retrieved February 17, 2012, from http://www.mobilearn.org/download/results/guidelines.pdf

Ormrod, J. E. (2004). *Human learning* (4th ed.). Upper Saddle River, NJ: Pearson Educational Inc.

Pachler, N., Cook, J., & Bachmair, B. (2010). Appropriation of mobile cultural resources for learning. *International Journal of Mobile and Blended Learning*, *2*(1), 1–21. doi:10.4018/jmbl.2010010101

Pask, A. G. S. (1976). *Conversation theory: Applications in education and epistemology*. Amsterdam, The Netherlands: Elsevier.

Pedersen, M. E. (1995). Storytelling and the art of teaching. *FORUM, 33*(1), 2–5. Retrieved March 14, 2012, from http://eca.state.gov/forum/vols/vol33/no1/P2.htm

Pimmer, C., Pachler, N., & Attwell, G. (2010). Towards work-based mobile learning: What can we learn from the fields of work-based learning and mobile learning. *International Journal of Mobile and Blended Learning*, *2*(4), 1–18. doi:10.4018/jmbl.2010100101

Preece, J., & Shneiderman, B. (2009). The reader-to-leader framework: Motivating technology-mediated social participation. *Transactions on Human-Computer Interaction, 1*(1), 13–32.

Quinn, C. (2000). mLearning: Mobile, wireless, in your pocket learning. *LineZine, Fall 2000.* Retrieved February 16, 2012, from http://www.linezine.com/2.1/features/cqmmwiyp.htm

Rick, S., & Weber, R. A. (2010). Meaningful learning and transfer of learning in games played repeatedly without feedback. *Games and Economic Behavior, 68*(2), 716–730. doi:10.1016/j.geb.2009.10.004

Robin, B., & Pierson, M. (2005). *A multilevel approach to using digital storytelling in the classroom.* Digital Storytelling Workshop, SITE 2005, University of Houston. http://www.coe.uh.edu/digital-storytelling/course/SITE2005.

Robin, B. R. (2005). *The educational uses of digital storytelling.* Retrieved March 13, 2012, from http://faculty.coe.uh.edu/brobin/homepage/Educational-Uses-DS.pdf

Robin, B. R. (2008). Digital storytelling: A powerful technology tool for the 21st century classroom. *Theory into Practice, 47*(3), 220–228. doi:10.1080/00405840802153916

Rogers, Y., Price, S., Randell, C., Stanton-Fraser, D., Weal, M., & Fitzpatrick, G. (2005). Ubi-learning: Integrating outdoor and indoor learning experiences. *Communications of the ACM, 48*(1), 55–59. doi:10.1145/1039539.1039570

Sadik, A. (2008). Digital storytelling: A meaningful technology-integrated approach for engaged student learning. *Educational Technology Research and Development, 56*(4), 487–506. doi:10.1007/s11423-008-9091-8

Säljö, R. (2004). Learning and technologies, people and tools in co-ordinated activities. *International Journal of Educational Research, 41*(6), 489–494. doi:10.1016/j.ijer.2005.08.013

Säljö, R. (2010). Digital tools and challenges to institutional traditions of learning: Technologies, social memory and the performative nature of learning. *Journal of Computer Assisted Learning, 26*(1), 53–64. doi:10.1111/j.1365-2729.2009.00341.x

Schuck, S., & Kearney, M. (2004). *Students in the director's seat. Teaching and learning across the school curriculum with student-generated video.* Faculty of Education, University of Technology, Sydney. Retrieved from http://www.ed-dev.uts.edu.au/teachered/research/dvproject/home.html

Sharples, M. (2010). Foreword. In E. Brown (Ed.), *Education in the wild: Contextual and location-based mobile learning in action* (pp. 4–6). A report from the STELLAR Alpine Rendez-Vous workshop series. Retrieved March 7, 2012, from http://www.lsri.nottingham.ac.uk/ejb/preprints/ARV_Education_in_the_wild.pdf

Sharples, M., Milrad, M., Arnedillo Sánchez, I., & Vavoula, G. (2009). Mobile learning: Small devices, big issues. In Balacheff, N., Ludvigsen, S., de Jong, T., Lazonder, A., & Barnes, S. (Eds.), *Technology enhanced learning: Principles and products* (pp. 233–249). Berlin, Germany: Springer.

Sharples, M., Taylor, J., & Vavoula, G. (2005). Towards a theory of mobile learning. *Proceedings of mLearn 2005 Conference*, Cape Town, South Africa.

Sharples, M., Taylor, J., & Vavoula, G. (2007). A theory of learning for the mobile age. In Andrews, R., & Haythornthwaite, C. (Eds.), *The SAGE handbook of e-learning research* (pp. 221–224). London, UK: Sage. doi:10.4135/9781848607859.n10

Shiratuddin, N., & Zaibon, S.-B. (2010). Mobile game-based learning with local content and appealing characters. *International Journal of Mobile Learning and Organisation, 4*(1), 55–82. doi:10.1504/IJMLO.2010.029954

Simanowski, R. (2009). Teaching digital literature didactic and institutional aspects. In Simanowski, R., Schäfer, J., & Gendolla, P. (Eds.), *Reading moving letters: Digital literature in research and teaching: A handbook* (pp. 15–28). Bielefeld, Germany: Transcript Verlag.

Simonson, M., Smaldino, S., Albright, M., & Zvacek, S. (2003). *Teaching and learning at a distance*. Upper Saddle River, NJ: Prentice Hall.

Standley, M. (2003). *Digital storytelling using new technology and the power of stories to help our students learn—and teach*. Cable in the Classroom. Retrieved from http://www.ciconline.org/home.

Trilling, B., & Hood, P. (1999). Learning, technology, and education reform in the knowledge age or we're wired, webbed, and windowed, now what? *Educational Technology*, *39*(3), 5–18.

Tsou, W., Wang, W., & Tzeng, Y. (2006). Applying a multimedia storytelling website in foreign language learning. *Computers & Education*, *47*, 17–28. doi:10.1016/j.compedu.2004.08.013

Tuomi, P., & Multisilta, J. (2010). MoViE: Experiences and attitudes—Learning with a mobile social video application. *Digital Culture & Education*, *2*(2), 127–151.

Tuomi, P., & Multisilta, J. (2012). Comparative study on use of mobile videos in elementary and middle school. *International Journal of Computer Information Systems and Industrial Management Applications*, *4*, 255–266. http://www.mirlabs.org/ijcisim/regular_papers_2012/Paper28.pdf Retrieved March 6, 2012

Vartiainen, H., & Enkenberg, J. (2011). Enlargement of educational innovation: An instructional model of the case forest pedagogy. In H. Ruokamo, M. Eriksson, L. Pekkala, H. Vuojärvi (Eds.), *Social media in the middle of nowhere – Proceedings of the NBE 2011 Conference* (pp. 76–86). Rovaniemi, Finland: Lapland University Press.

Vuojärvi, H., Eriksson, M. J., & Ruokamo, H. (in press). Designing pedagogical models for tourism education: Focus on work-based mobile learning. *International Journal of Mobile and Blended Learning*.

Vygotsky, S. L. (1978). *Mind in society*. Cambridge: Harvard University Press.

Wijers, M., & Jonker, V. (2010). MobileMath: A location-aware game for mathematics. In E. Brown (Ed.), *Education in the wild: Contextual and location-based mobile learning in action* (pp. 20–22). A report from the STELLAR Alpine Rendez-Vous workshop series. Retrieved March 7, 2012, from http://www.lsri.nottingham.ac.uk/ejb/preprints/ARV_Education_in_the_wild.pdf

Wingkvist, A., & Ericsson, M. (2010). Extracting and expressing experience with mobile learning: Lessons learned. *International Journal of Mobile Learning and Organisation*, *4*(4), 428–439. doi:10.1504/IJMLO.2010.037538

Xiang, Z., & Gretzel, U. (2010). Role of social media in online travel information search. *Tourism Management*, *31*(2), 179–188. doi:10.1016/j.tourman.2009.02.016

KEY TERMS AND DEFINITIONS

Digital Storytelling: Digital storytelling is the social practice of telling stories that takes advantage of digital cameras, non-linear authoring tools and computers to create short multimedia stories.

Mobile Devices: In most cases the term is related to handheld devices (e.g. smartphones and personal digital assistants) which are easy to move around, fit into one's pocket and also provide multiple functionalities.

Mobile Learning: Emphasizes the importance of conversation as the driving force of learning and the importance of learning through participation in cultural and social practices – mobile devices can make these processes independent of time and place.

Mobile Social Video Application: Mobile social video applications enable any participant to upload their videos, recorded with mobile devices, wirelessly to the particular Web 2.0 application, share the videos with other users, and enable users to create video stories using their mobile devices.

Social Media: Social media is built on three main elements: content created by users, interaction between users, and Web 2.0 technologies.

Web 2.0 Technologies: Enable the almost time- and location-independent content creation, sharing and diverse discussions.

Section 2
Social Media as a Means for Current Education

Chapter 5
Enhancing Social Presence and Communities of Practice in Distance Education Courses through Social Media

Lori B. Holcomb
North Carolina State University, USA

Matthew Krüger-Ross
Simon Fraser University, Canada

ABSTRACT

The purpose of this study was to examine the impact social media has on the development of communities of practice and social development in distance education courses. This study evaluated the effectiveness of the integration of social media tools including Ning in Education (an educational social networking tool), Twitter, and WordPress into three distance education courses in instructional technology. The social media tools were examined to identify the educational and pedagogical benefits each tool affords. Utilizing a mixed-method methodology, student data was collected through a series of three online surveys coupled with student interviews. The pre-/post- data collected as part of this study provides empirically based findings indicating that social media technologies can help support online communities of practice as well as the development of social presence. Data analyzed from student interviews provides data triangulation in addition to a richer and deeper understanding of the pedagogical affordances social media tools provide.

INTRODUCTION

The influx of technology into education is continually redefining teaching and learning. With new technologies emerging at a rapid rate, educators are continuously seeking ways to leverage how to best incorporate these new tools into their educational practices in order to further support and enhance learning (Krüger-Ross & Holcomb, 2011). Among the fastest growing technologies is the use of social media (Lenhart, Purcell, Smith, & Zickuhr, 2010). Social media tools, such as

DOI: 10.4018/978-1-4666-2851-9.ch005

blogging, Twitter, and social networks sites, are growing in both popularity and demand inside and outside of the educational context. In 2010, it was reported that 73% of wired teenagers and 47% of online adults use social networking sites (Lenhart et al, 2010). Additionally, over one third of online adults utilize Twitter, while 24% of young adults reported being active bloggers. Similarly, distance education is also expanding at an unprecedented rate. The 9.7% growth rate in the number of college and university students enrolled in at least one online class reported by Allen and Seaman (2007) significantly exceeded the 1.5% growth rate in the overall higher education student population during the same period (Brady, Holcomb, & Smith, 2010). Given the rising popularity of social media and distance education, it seems logical to merge these areas with the goal of improving teaching and learning in the online environment. Research has shown that distance education courses are more successful when students are able to develop and engage within a community of practice (Barab & Duffy, 2000; Brady et al., 2010) while also fostering high levels of social presence (Anderson, 2005). Through the creation of a community of practice, students are able to engage with one another and work collaboratively towards a set of shared goals. However, developing a community of practice in an online course can be exceedingly difficult due to differences in time and location (Brook & Oliver, 2003). The use of social networking tools has the ability and potential to aid in the development of communities of practice within the online environment. By nature of their design and functionality, social networking sites have the ability to connect and build community in a socially and educationally constructed network. As noted by the Educause Learning Initiative (2007), social networks have the ability to "facilitate a strong sense of community among students" and encourage "personal interactions that can lead to the creation of new knowledge and collec-

tive intelligence" (p. 2). The following chapter provides empirically based research findings on how social media technologies can help support online communities of practice as well as the development of social presence. Data analyzed from student observations and interviews provides data triangulation in addition to a richer and deeper understanding of the pedagogical affordances social media tools provide.

REVIEW OF THE LITERATURE

Social Media

The nature of web-based communication and community has changed radically in the past few years. At the forefront of this evolution is the prolific integration of social media tools and technologies. Often classified as a subset of Web 2.0 or web-based technologies, social media tools have transformed the way we communicate and interact. Web 2.0, a term coined by Tim Berners-Lee in 2006, is frequently misrepresented and misunderstood (Krüger-Ross & Holcomb, 2011). Rather than representing an entirely new kind or type of technology, Web 2.0 is used to describe a way of interacting with the Internet and web-based technologies that reposition and challenge the traditional roles of "content producer" and "recipient." The focus for social media is how media are being used to communicate, share, and maintain social connections between individuals, groups, and organizations. Kaplan and Haenlein (2010) define social media as "a group of Internet-based applications that build on the ideological and technological foundations of Web 2.0, and that allow the creation and exchange of User Generated Content" (2010, p. 61). With its growing emergence, the impact of social media is now reported regularly, chronicling the influence of new media and a variety of other technologies on any number of users (e.g. teens, youth, older adults) by the Pew Internet & American Life Center. For example, Lenhart & Fox (2006) report that 8% (12 million) of American users regularly update their own blog and 39% (54 million) regularly read and consult blogs. The growth of social media technologies and their usage has resulted in shifts within field ranging from education (Thomas & Brown, 2011), business (Li & Bernoff, 2011) and politics (Lilleker & Jackson, 2008). With social media expanding across numerous fields, there are several ways to define and categorize the tools and technologies that encompass social media. One definition provided by Kaplan and Haenlin (2010) defines social media as any technology that is web-based and supports the creation and sharing of user-generated content. The following sections will highlight specific social media technologies that have become prevalent for scholarly communication, collaboration, and instruction.

Adhering to the aforementioned definition, blogs, microblogs, wikis, and social networking sites are among the most often-referenced social media technologies. From an educational standpoint, these tools all enable the creation and exchange of user-generated content. Blogs and micoblogs (i.e. Twitter) enable users to connect, share, and engage in reflective practice. For example, blogs allow learners to create content, share it with others, receive comments, integrate multimedia, and incorporate RSS feeds. Furthermore, blogs, wikis, social networking sites, and video sharing sites enable students to post their contributions, view and analyze the work of peers, and engage in a dialogue through posting reviews and comments. These affordances of social software facilitate a participatory culture amongst students (Jenkins, 2006). Blogs and microblogs allow students to gather resources, share the resources with others, and facilitate active participation of each user. These tools support and encourage individuals to learn together while retaining individual control over their identity (Anderson, 2004). Research found that blogging within online courses can help support students'

sense of community (Halic, Lee, Paulus, & Spence, 2010; Farwell & Krüger-Ross, 2012). Similarly, the integration of social networking sites in education has also transformed learning (Brady et al., 2010). According to boyd and Ellison (2007), social network sites (i.e. Facebook, Google+) are web-based tools that allow users to develop a public or semi-public profile, electronically communicate with other users with whom they share a connection, and view and comment on their list of communications with other members of the group. Social networking sites have dramatically altered the way individuals communicate on the Internet (Holcomb, Brady, & Smith, 2010). Research on the use of social network sites in education has found that students who regularly use social networking sites indicate that enhanced technology skills, creativity, receptivity to new and diverse views, and communication skills were among the most important educational benefits (University of Minnesota, 2008).

In addition to having a profound impact on learning, social media technologies have also affected educational scholarship as researchers strive to explore the educational advantages social media technologies afford. For example, social networking sites, such as Ning in Education, have been explored as a means to enhance social presence and communities of practice in distance education (Brady et al., 2010). Twitter has also been examined as an avenue to continue conversations that begin in the classroom and continue beyond the physical classroom walls (Krüger-Ross, Farwell, & Waters, 2012). Given the primarily asynchronous activities that dominate distance education (National Center for Education Statistics, 1999; 2008), social media technologies may provide instructors and students with opportunities for greater connection, social presence and sense of community. Enabled by ubiquitously accessible communication platforms, social media has substantially changed the way organizations, communities, and individuals communicate within the educational context.

Distance Education

Distance education as a primary means of instruction is expanding significantly at the college and university level (Allen & Seaman, 2007). This growth includes the number and types of individuals learning outside traditional classrooms, the range and variety of providers, and the range and effectiveness of new technologies serving as delivery tools for learning. With the demand for distance education increasing, reports indicate that the number of undergraduate students enrolled in a distance education course has grown from 8% in the 1999-2000 school year to 20% in 2007-2008 (National Center for Educational Statistics, 2008). In fact, according to Sloan (2010), "there is no compelling evidence that the continued robust growth in online enrollments is at its end" (p. 4). While evolving from correspondence courses, distance learning continues to be a predominantly asynchronous activity (National Center for Education Statistics, 1999; 2008). Common distance education activities include discussion boards (Vrasidas & Stock-McIssac, 1999), consulting course websites, and uploading course assignments (Conrad & Donaldson, 2004), each of which is inherently asynchronous. Researchers and developers of professional development continue to recommend the use of asynchronous instruction for online learning (Palloff & Pratt, 2001). However, with the growth of the Internet and social media, synchronous opportunities are now available for online instructors and students (Walker, 2007). Specifically, instructors are now looking to Web 2.0 and social media technologies to help facilitate traditionally asynchronous activities as synchronous learning opportunities (Maloney, 2007). Researchers and instructors are also striving to identify how Web 2.0 technologies cab be utilized to support interactive and engaging learning in the online environment (Collis & Moonen, 2008).

The increase in the methods of interacting with students outside the traditional classroom have led some scholars to propose that higher education is nearing a learning revolution. For example, Keengwe & Kidd (2010) proposed that distance education began to shift away from static, individualistic, and limited web-based education in 1995 to a more comprehensive e-learning approach in 2005 by more fully embracing such activities as video and audio conferencing made available by newer technologies. They further argue that the age of social networking and mobile learning are shaping educational technology and how traditional and online instructors deliver their course material (2010). Distance education, as a field, has continued to grow and support online learning research not only in the realms of social networks and mobile learning, but also virtual worlds, ubiquitous learning, and location-based technologies (Searson, Dawley, Field, Owens, & Penny, 2011)

However, there are challenges to success in distance education. Research has shown that one of the major obstacles to successful learning in the online environment is social in nature. Students who feel isolated and disconnected in distance education courses have been found to endure more struggles and challenges (Pigliapoco & Bogliolo, 2008; Song et al., 2004; Tello, 2007; Vonderwell, 2003; Woods, 2002). More recent research is also exploring the connection between social constructs and students' lack of success and higher percentage of dropout rates (Lee & Choi, 2010). Social media technologies, with their focus on connectivity and collaboration, can be used to support students' sense of social presence. The following section examines research regarding communities of practice and social presence, both of which have been demonstrated to be key to student success in online learning (Kirschner & Lai, 2007).

THEORETICAL BACKGROUND

Communities of Practice

Communities of practice grew from the seminal research of Lave and Wegner (Lave & Wegner, 1991; Wegner, 1998). While the definition of a community of practice continues to evolve (Cox, 2005), Kirschner and Lai (2007) note that a community of practice may be best understood as a "process in which social learning occurs because the people who participate in this process have a common interest in some subject or problem and are willing to collaborate with others having this same interest over an extended period" (p. 128). Additionally, Wenger defines a community as "a way of talking about the social configurations in which our enterprises are defined as worth while pursuing and our participation is recognizable as competence" (Wenger 1998, p. 4). The concept of learning through communities of practice views learning as social participation in the process of being active participants. More specifically, a key concept of communities of practice is community knowledge, in which the sum of the community knowledge is greater than the sum of the individual knowledge. This results in a symbiotic relationship, where the collective knowledge of the group advances, while simultaneously advancing the knowledge of the individual (Bielaczyc and Collins, 1999). Research provides evidence that strong feelings of community may not only increase persistence in courses, but may also increase the exchange of information, availability of support, commitment to group goals, cooperation among members, and satisfaction with group efforts (Bruffee, 1993; Dede, 1996; Wellman, 1999). Walker (2008) found that students who are a part of the online classroom community are more successful than students who are not. In particular, communities of practice have been found to support the successful completion of distance education courses (Barab & Duffy, 2000; Brady et al., 2010).

In distance education courses, sound instructional practice includes, but is not limited to, supporting and fostering the development of communities of practice (Salmon, 2005). Students need a venue to connect and actively engage with other students, who they often have never met in person (Brady et al., 2010). As noted by Dunlap & Lowenthal (2009), students see social interaction and connection as a foundational attribute of online courses. However, due to the geographic and physical boundaries associated with distance education, developing a community of practice in an online course is inherently difficult. In the online environment, communities of practices are organized around an activity and are formed as a need arises (Squire & Johnson, 2000). The Internet also becomes the shared "physical" space for the community. As a result, distance education courses need to utilize technologies that allow students to connect, collaborate, and interact with other members of the course, all of which are important components for building a community of practice. Likewise, students must also be provided with technologies that enable them to apply their learning to authentic educational contexts while also engaging in collaborative efforts (Correia & Davis, 2008). Integrating social media technologies that promote engagement, collaboration, and authentic learning have the possibility to support the generation of communities of practice in distance education courses (Brady et al., 2010; Walker, 2008). Given the challenges associated with fostering a community of practice in the online environment, social media tools have the potential to play a central role in the development of communities of practice.

Social Presence

Among the many factors that promote a sense of community in online courses, social presence has been found to be one of the most significant (Cobb, 2009; Gunawardena & Zittle, 1997). Oztok and Brett (2011) frame their review of the history of social presence research within the social constructivist perspective. "Social constructivism reminds us that learning is essentially a social activity, that meaning is constructed through communication, collaborative activity, and interactions with others. It highlights the role of social interactions in meaning making ... [and] knowledge construction" (Swan, 2005, p. 5). Given the known barriers to success in distance education, research demonstrating the influence of social presence is promising (Bai, 2003; Dawson, 2006). Previous research has shown that social presence is an essential component of education and learning (Garrison, Anderson, & Archer, 2000), can be a predictor of students' perceived learning (Richardson & Swan, 2003), and is crucial toward establishing a critical community of practice (Fabro & Garrison, 1998). DeSchryver, Mishra, Koehler, & Francis(2009) found that a mutually beneficial relationship exists between social presence and participation in online activities in distance education courses. In particular, students in distance education courses with higher social presence were found to be more involved and engaged in course discussions (Cobb, 2009). Similarly, Bai (2003) indicates that social presence leads to reduced feelings of isolation and detachment while simultaneously encouraging student interaction and participation in online courses.

However, the limited or nonexistent face-to-face interaction of distance education courses can make building a community of practice and fostering students' sense of social presence online challenging (Dawson, 2006). If course participants share few common interests or have a minimal commitment to each other, interactions may be limited and often diminish over time (Selwyn, 2000). Given these challenges, it is important to investigate how social media tools can foster and support communities of practice and social presence. Social media technologies may well be the "killer app" (Anderson, 2005) for nurturing social presence in distance learning. Existing research demonstrates that social presence is important

for teaching and learning (Garrison, Anderson, & Archer, 2000) and can be linked to students' perceived learning (Swan, 2005). Brady et al. (2010) note that the use of social networks has shown to enhance social presence and therefore communities of practice. Within social media, blogs (Nardi, Schiano, & Gumbrecht, 2004) and Twitter (Dunlap & Lowenthal, 2009) have been shown to be useful in developing students' social presence. While additional research is needed in order to more fully understand the experience of the individual within an online community, consideration of social presence has become an important aspect of online learning (Oztok & Brett, 2011).

METHODOLOGY

This study used both quantitative and qualitative research methodologies to examine the impact of social media tools in distance education courses. The following research questions were used to guide this study:

1. Does the integration of social media tools impact social presence for online learners?
2. Does the integration of social media tools support the development of communities of practice?
3. What are the educational advantages and disadvantages to utilizing social media tools in distance education?

Participants

This research study used a convenience sample. A total of 55 students agreed to participate in the research study, however only 45 students fully completed all of the required data components. All participants in this study were enrolled in one of two graduate-level instructional technology distance education courses. The two instructional technology courses were fully asynchronous and focused on web design and development and the integration of emerging technologies in education, respectfully. Both instructional technology courses utilized the following social media tools throughout the course of the semester: Twitter, Wordpress (or other blogging platforms), the educational social networking site, Ning in Education, and Google+. These tools were used both for the delivery of instruction and completion of assignments.

The sample varied in demographic and academic characteristics (see Table 1). The vast majority of participants surveyed had prior experience with online learning, with 82% (n=37) of the participants having completed at least one online course prior to the study. All but four of the students (91%) were currently enrolled in a graduate, degree-granting program. Of the students surveyed, 49% (n=22) were enrolled in Instructional Technology graduate program; 20% (n=11) were enrolled in an Adult and Higher Education graduate program; 18% (n=8) were listed as post-baccalaureate students; and the remaining 6 students (13%) were enrolled in a Curriculum and Instruction graduate program. Nearly all of the students (80%) surveyed were seeking a Master's degree (either M.Ed or M.S.) versus a doctoral degree (5%). The sample consisted of 31 females (69%) and the average age of the participants was 32.4 years. A little more than half (56%) of the students surveyed were currently employed in an educational faculty position. With regards to the use of social media, 82% (n=37) had a Facebook account, 44% (n=20) used Twitter, and 13% (n=6) maintained an active blog prior to the study. Of those students who used social media, only 16% (n=7) had used social media for instructional purposes.

Data Collection

Several instruments were used to collect data about student demographics and attitudes, including a pre- post-survey and an open-ended question-

naire. Over the course of a traditional, 16-week semester, students were asked to complete three online surveys and one open-ended questionnaire. Additionally, ten students were randomly selected and interviewed regarding their experiences using social media in distance education.

The first survey students completed at the start of the semester was the *Technology Background and Demographics Survey* that was comprised of 16 items relating to student demographics and general technology competency. Only the demographic data was pulled from this survey for the purpose of this study (e.g. educational background, prior distance education experience). Students were also asked to complete the *pre-, post-Social Media in Distance Education Surveys* at the start and conclusion of the semester (see Appendix A). Comprised of 26 items, the pre-, post-surveys asked students to rate their level of agreement on a five-point Likert-scale ranging from Strongly Disagree to Strongly Agree. Likert-scale questions addressed four key themes, identified by a survey of previous research (e.g., DeSchryver et al., 2009; McCann 2009; Wheeler, Yeomans, & Wheeler, 2008): communication; collaboration; reflection & comprehension, and social presence. In addition, the survey included six open-ended questions asking about the benefits and drawbacks of using social media tools in distance education. Prior to administration, two external evaluators systematically reviewed and evaluated the surveys for content validity. During this process items were reworked, removed, or added to the survey.

Student interviews were conducted at the completion of the semester. Ten students were randomly selected to participate in the interview process. In order to be eligible to be interviewed, students had to fully complete the *Technology Background and Demographics Survey,* the *pre-, post-Social Media in Distance Education Surveys,* and the open-ended questionnaire. The intent of the interviews was to elicit feedback and recommendations from students regarding the use of social media tools in distance education courses.

Table 1. Student demographics

Gender			
Female		Male	
31(69%)		17(31%)	
Prior Online Experience			
Yes		No	
37(82%)		10(18%)	
Enrolled in a Graduate, Degree-granting Program			
Yes		No	
42(93%)		3(7%)	
Graduate Program			
Instructional Technology	Adult & Higher Education	Post-baccalaureate	Curriculum & Instruction
22(49%)	11(20%)	8(18%)	6(13%)
Degree Program			
Master's	Doctoral		Post-baccalaureate
36(80%)	5(11%)		4(9%)
Social Media Tools			
Facebook	Twitter		Blogging
37(82%)	20(44%)		7(13%)
Prior Use of Social Media for Instructional Purposes			
Yes		No	
7(15%)		38(84%)	

The interviews were conducted electronically using virtual meeting software such as Google+ or Elluminate Live due to geographical constraints. Student interviews consisted of ten questions (see Appendix B) and lasted approximately thirty minutes.

Results

A principle components analysis (PCA), with varimax rotation, was run on the 26 items in the *Social Media in Distance Education Survey*. One factor emerged, accounting for 49.63% of the total variance. However, based on design and prior research (Brady et al., 2010), the Social *Media in Distance Education Survey* was forced into four composite scores: communication, collaboration, reflection & comprehension, and social presence. The first composite score, communication, was comprised of 7 items and had .74 and $\alpha = .86$ respectfully. The second composite score, collaboration, was comprised of 6 items and had reliability measures of $\alpha = .90$ and $\alpha = .80$ while the third composite score, reflection & comprehension had reliability measures of $\alpha = .94$ and $\alpha = .91$. The final composite score, social presence, had reliability measures of $\alpha = .92$ and $\alpha = .75$ respectfully. Each of the composite scores proved to have good reliability estimates for affective instruments, as defined by Gable and Wolf

(1993). Individual scale scores were then computed for each participant using the arithmetic average of the individual items in each factor, respectively, as suggested by Gable and Wolfe (1993), Hopkins, Stanley, and Hopkins (1990) and Worthen, Borg and White (1993).

To address the research questions, a series of paired-sample t-tests were conducted to compare the pre- and post-attitude measures for each of the four composite measures. There were significant differences for communication (M=2.57, SD=.83; M=2.94, SD=.98; t(44)=-2.027, p=.049), collaboration (M=3.16, SD=1.06; M=4.01, SD=.60; t(44)=-5.179, p=.000); reflection& comprehensions (M=3.17, SD=1.01, SD=4.27, SD=.49; t(44)=-6.676, p=.000), and social presence (M=3.89, SD=.85, M=4.60, SD=.35; t(44)=-5.915, p=.000). See Table 2 for complete results.

To analyze the open-ended questions and interview data, an independent rater read through all of the responses to indicate themes that were present in the responses. The themes were reviewed and placed into categories. Responses were then reexamined and rated for the presence or absence of each theme. Three themes emerged for the use of social media in distance education courses: learning/pedagogy; collaboration; and communication.

Numerous students throughout the study echoed the educational benefits of social media tools. The majority of students (84%) indicated that the use of social media tools, such as Twitter, social networking sites, and blogging, enhanced their learning experience in an online course. Students reported that various social media tools allowed for "greater reflection;" "more in-depth discussions;" and "access to more resources and information." Similarly, students expressed that the use of social media tools in an online class aided in comprehension of course material. In the words of one student, "Ning and Twitter allowed for me to ask questions and get answers in a timely manner. Being able to get feedback so quickly helped clear up any confusion and check my understanding of key topics." One student shared that Twitter enabled her to maintain engagement in the course through her mobile device. "I was able to be a part of the course even when I was not a computer because of my phone." Additionally, more than half of the students surveyed (62%) indicated that the use of social media tools allowed for them to be more active in their learning. More specifically, students shared that Ning in Education, Twitter, and blogging enabled them to "actively engage with classmates;" "reflect on the viewpoints of others;" and "extend learning beyond the course."

Students identified the use Twitter, Ning in Education, and Google+ as significant factors for increasing collaboration. Nearly all students (93%) stated that the use of Google+ facilitated collaboration and enabled group work to be "seamless" in an online environment. While most students used Ning in Education as the main venue for group work, 44% of students preferred using Google+ for collaboration. As stated by one student, "Google+ is great for collaboration because you can communicate by video and text as the same time. The video chat makes it feel like we are all working together in the same room, which is something I never would have expected in an online class." Twitter also allowed for students to "touch base"

Table 2. Paired-sample t-test results

	Mean	Std. Deviation	Std. Error Mean	t	df	Sig.
Communication	-.371	1.229	.183	-2.027	44	.049*
Collaboration	-.852	1.103	.164	-5.179	44	.000**
Comprehension & Reflection	-1.012	1.107	.165	-6.676	44	.000**
Social Presence	-.719	.815	.121	5.915	44	.000**

* Statistically significant, p < .05

** Statistically significant, p < .01

and quickly respond to their peers. When asked what was the best means for communicating with peers, 85% of students indicated that email was still the most frequent form of communication. One student explained, "Initial contact with groups members was always done first by email. We would then decide as a group how we went to continue to talk and work together." So while email provided the means for initial contact, students went on to identify that they preferred to use Google+ (60%) or the discussion board feature within Ning in Education (33%). Students identified the following features as important components for selecting which technology to use for collaborative efforts: ability to meet synchronously; ability to use video; ability to communicate via multiple media (video, audio, text); and ability to document and record information. "When I work with my group members I want to be able to see them and talk to them live. For me, this makes group work more successful." Several students also mentioned access and availability of the technology as being important factors as well: "so many technology tools are very expensive and I do not have access to them at my school. It's great when we are able to use a free software for course work." The array of social media tools (i.e. Twitter, Ning in Education) allowed for students to effectively communicate and collaborate with peers in an online setting.

Increased collaboration was not the only benefit of using social media tools. An overwhelming number of students (93%) indicated that the use of social media tools greatly increased communication for an online course. "Using multiple tools for communication made it easy to stay up-to-date and current with course requirements and expectations." Another students shared, "I was worried that communication was going to be one of the biggest challenges in an online class. But because of Twitter and Ning, I was surprised with how easy it was to communicate with both individuals and the entire class." Students also felt that Google+ made it easy to communicate with the entire course synchronously. "One of the things I like

the best about face-to-face classes is being able to connect with classmates and put a name with a face. With Google+ we were able to meet as a class and see one another virtually." The student went on to expand that for him, it was important to engage in synchronous communication while also being able to see whom he was speaking. When asked what the biggest factors for successful communication in an online course, students identified the following criteria: clarity, response time, and personal connection. Nearly half (44%) of the students surveys indicated that written text can often times be ambiguous and difficult to interpret. "Sometimes it is unclear what some is trying to say via email. I prefer being able to speak or see the person so that I am not left wondering or confused by their message." By utilizing social media tools, such as Google+, students are able to communicate directly and establish a personal connection with their peers. Likewise, the use of social networking sites affords students the opportunity to develop personal relationships. The integration of social tools in an online course afforded the students the opportunity and venue to effectively communicate with their peers.

Yet despite the numerous educational benefits identified by students, there were some drawbacks relating to the use of social media tools. In terms of the disadvantages associated with the use of Ning in Education, time emerged as the major theme. While some identified Ning in Education as allowing more time to reflect (40%), other students identified the amount of time required to stay current in the social network as a significant obstacle. One student stated, "It takes time to sit down and view the information . . .and respond." This thought was echoed across social media tools with statements regarding the delay in responses to postings and comments, such as, "getting a response to a question/comment may not be immediate." Nearly one third of students indicated that at some point in the semester they were frustrated with Twitter due to an unexpected response delay. One student stated, "I was frustrated with Twitter when it took more than a day and two messages before I received a response to my question. I was expecting the response to be immediate. I should have just used emailed." Other students (29%) indicated that a lack of familiarity with a specific technology prevented them from using the tool on a regular basis. Likewise, 9% of the students surveyed expressed they would rather not use Twitter, Google+, or blogging as a means for communicating and collaborating. And handful of students also indicated they did not wish to be a part of social network, even if it was educational in nature.

When asked to provide feedback and recommendations about the use of social media, students were mostly positive. In addition to highlighting the previously mentioned educational benefits, students also felt that the use of social media tools provided them with skills necessary for the 21st century workforce. "By having us using social media tools to communicate and collaborate, we gained valuable experience with 21st century skills." Another student shared, "these tools are important for the future and in order to keep up, we need to know how to use them." However, students did acknowledge some drawbacks and limitations while also offering recommendations for how to better utilize social media technologies. More than half of the students interviewed commented that there were times when they were not sure if they were using the technology correctly. This could be due in part to the fact that students did not receive extensive training on how to use the various technologies. While resources and tutorials were provided, no class time was dedicated to training how to use the various tools. A few students indicated that they felt comfortable using the array of social media technologies while others expressed a sense of unease and uncertainty towards the technologies. One student stated, "I often wondered if there was more to the technology than I knew. I mean, were there other capabilities for this technology that I did not know about? And if so, how would that

have changed my experience in class?" Similarly, a second student commented, "I knew the jist of Ning because it was kind of like Facebook but I was not too sure about Twitter. I was confused about tweeting and direct messaging classmates and never knew which one I should do or why." In addition to the lack of formal training, numerous students expressed the desire for a set of guidelines to follow with regard to using social media tools for learning. "I think it would have been helpful if we created a set of guidelines on how to use Twitter and Ning and the other tools so that everyone was on the same page. For example, knowing what tools to use and when would be helpful. I also think it would be helpful if the class agreed on an acceptable use policy." These comments indicate there was a level of uncertainty and a need for greater structure. The final recommendation that emerged from the student questionnaire and interviews was the desire to not have the use of the social media tools required. This recommendation is particularly interesting, as students were only required to use a specific technology to completed particular assignments. Beyond those assignments, students were able to select and use the various social media tools as frequently or infrequently as they wished. Despite this a few students indicated that they "only used the tools because I had to."

Solutions and Recommendations

Findings from this study signify that the use of social media tools in distance education courses promotes the development of communities of practice and fosters social presence. More specifically, results from the study indicate that students felt they were able to achieve a sense of identity in the online environment while also establishing personal connections with their peers. No longer feeling as if they were "just a name," students commented that they believed the use of Ning in Education allowed for them to establish a personal identity, while other tools, such as Twitter, afforded them the venue to have a voice. In particular, profile pages within Ning in Education enabled students to share personal information in addition to their educational and professional backgrounds. This helped to add an element of familiarity amongst students to the course. This is particularly promising, as social presence has been found to be an indicator of success in distance education courses (Cobb, 2009; Gunawardena & Zittle, 1997). Feelings of isolation and disconnect are not uncommon in the online environment (Russo & Benson, 2005) so it is encouraging that these results suggest that students are able to connect and form personal relationships with their peers. This in turn, can have a positive impact on the development of a community of practice. Significant findings (p=.000) from this study suggest that the integration of social media tools into distance education courses can aid in the development and support of social presence and the formation of communities of practice.

While the majority of the findings from this study were supportive of the use of social media tools in distance education, some results did suggest that social media tools alone are not enough to foster and support social presence and communities of practice. While there was a significant difference on pre- and post-measures for communication (p=.049), some students indicated that they felt forced to use the social media technologies and were therefore resistant to its use. One student shared, "if I was not required to use Twitter, I wouldn't. I prefer to stick with email." It is also possible that a majority of the students in this study did not know all of the capabilities and functionalities of the various social media tools. To ensure proliferation of tools such as Twitter and Google+, educators and students may require ongoing training, support, and active involvement in both the new technologies and communities they maintain (Kienle & Ritterskamp, 2007). This echoes numerous technology integration studies that highlight the importance of training

and support (Brinkerhoff, 2006; Hew & Brush, 2006; Lawless & Pellegrino, 2007).

Just as it can be especially difficult to establish a community of practice in distance education (Brook & Oliver, 2003; Selwyn, 2000), communities of practice cannot be forced, even in media that lend themselves to high levels of engagement. In addition to needing time to feel comfortable using a social networking site for educational purposes, students may need more than a semester to feel that they are a part of the community of practice available in that environment (Brady et al., 2010). Liedka (1999) points out that communities of practice are not formed; rather they evolve and disband out of necessity of the members. Therefore, communities of practice develop over time (Squire & Johnson, 2000). Educators need to identify ways in which they can provide the structure and support that allows the development of communities of practice within the span of a semester. This may include reaching out to and connecting with students prior to the start of the semester.

LIMITATIONS

Findings from this study are also only generalizable to those who share similar traits with the participants involved in the study as this study utilized a convenience sample. As a whole, the students used in this study are not representative of all students because of the limited domain knowledge studied. The majority of students enrolled in the courses were either enrolled in an Instructional Technology program or were highly interested in the topics covered in the courses that comprised this study. These findings can only be generalized to students enrolled in graduate level distance education courses that are comparable in scope and structure to the courses utilized in this study.

FUTURE RESEARCH DIRECTIONS

Ozkan and McKenzie (2008) contend that educators need to engage students with a more 21st century approach to teaching and social media technologies can provide such a venue. Tools such as social networking sites, Twitter, Google+, and blogs provide viable alternatives for distance education courses. The incorporation of social media tools into distance education courses may have an impact on the higher educational community. Based on findings from this study and students' responses, it is evident that they are calling for the incorporation of social media tools into distance education. As both distance education and social media technologies continue to grow, it is becoming increasingly more important to examine how two domains can be combined most effectively to enhance student learning in an online environment. Future research needs to explore the attributes that best enable the development of communities of practice in an online environment. Having a stronger understanding of how communities of practiced are established in the online environment could enable educators to provide necessary structure and support. Likewise, future research needs to explore time constraints and the development of communities of practice. Prior research has indicated that students may require more than a semester to form a community of practice (Brady et al., 2010). Given the important role communities of practice can have in distance education (Barab & Duffy, 2000; Brady et al., 2010; Walker, 2008), future research needs to explore if it possible through the integration of social media tools and technologies to compress the amount of time it takes to develop a community.

Additionally, while researchers agree that social presence is a critical concept, the definition of social presence still lacks clarity, especially as it relates to distance education (Oztok & Brett, 2011). There are varying definitions for social presence across different fields of study. Lowenthal (2010) argues, "it is often hard to distinguish between whether someone is talking about social interaction, immediacy, intimacy, emotion, and/or connectedness when they talk about social presence" (p. 125). Along with the variety of definitions, the literature indicates that there are significant issues yet to be solved, including the methods of measuring social presence, the factors affecting social presence, and the relationship between social presence and learning (Biocca, Harms, & Burgoon, 2003; Russo & Benson, 2005). It is recommended that future research examine how the frequency of use and application of specific social media tools within a distance education are connected to social presence. For example, do students who use social media tools more frequently and more effectively have a stronger social presence?

Oztok and Brett (2011) identified several gaps in the literature including the lack of understanding of social presence from a qualitative standpoint. To date, social presence research on social presence has extensively been quantitative. While the present study did include qualitative components, more in-depth interviews would aid in better understanding the nature of social presence by exploring how social presence functions for individuals within a particular context. Therefore, more research within the domain of social presence is warranted.

CONCLUSION

Findings from this study confirm and reinforce the results of recent studies (Brady et al., 2010; DeSchryver et al., 2009; Holcomb et al., 2010; Schroeder & Greenbowe, 2009). Results indicate that the use of social media tools can have a positive impact on distance education courses. Data collected via a mixed-methods approach highlight statistically significant findings on pre-post measures in addition to providing data triangulation through interviews and qualitative measures. A majority of students in this study highlighted the educational advantages of various social media tools, from increased levels of collaboration to deeper levels of learning. Results from this study suggest that the use of social media tools, such as Twitter, Google+, and educational social networking sites, support and enhance social presence and communities of practices.

REFERENCES

Allen, I. E., & Seaman, J. (2007). *Online nation: Five years of growth in online learning.* Needhan, MA: Sloan Consortium. Retrieved on February 27, 2012, from sloanconsortium.org/publications/survey/pdf/online_nation.pdf

Anderson, T. (2004). Toward a theory of online learning. In Anderson, T., & Elloumi, F. (Eds.), *Theory and practice of online learning* (pp. 33–60). Canada: Athabasca University.

Anderson, T. (2005). Distance learning—Social software's killer app? *Proceedings from Conference of the Open and Distance Learning Association of Australia (ODLAA).* Adelaide, South Australia: University of South Australia.

Bai, H. (2003). Student motivation and social presence in online learning: Implications for future research. In C. Crawford, D. A. Willis, R. Carlsen, I. Gibson, K. McFerrin, J. Price, & R. I. Weber (Eds.), *Proceedings from The Society for Information Technology and Teacher Education International Conference* (2714-2720). Chesapeake, VA: AACE.

Barab, S. A., & Duffy, T. (2000). From practice fields to communities of practice. In Jonassen, D., & Land, S. M. (Eds.), *Theoretical foundations of learning environments* (pp. 25–56). Mahwah, NJ: Lawrence Erlbaum Associates.

Berners-Lee, T. (2006). *Developer works interviews: Tim Berners-Lee, Originator of the Web and director of the World Wide Web Consortium talks about where we've come, and about the challenges and opportunities ahead.* Interview transcription retrieved on February 1, 2012 from http://www.ibm.com/developerworks/podcast/dwi/cm-int082206txt.html.

Bielaczyc, K., & Collins, A. (1999). Learning communities in classrooms: a reconceptualization of educational practice. In Reigeluth, C. (Ed.), *Instructional-design theories and models: A new paradigm of instructional theory* (Vol. 2, pp. 269–292). Mahwah, NJ: Lawrence Erlbaum Associates.

Biocca, F., Harms, C., & Burgoon, J. K. (2003). Criteria for a theory and measure of social presence. *Presence (Cambridge, Mass.), 12*(5), 456–480. doi:10.1162/105474603322761270

boyd, d. m., & Ellison, N. B. (2007). Social network sites: Definition, history, and scholarship. *Journal of Computer-Mediated Communication, 13*(1), article 11. Retrieved from http://jcmc.indiana.edu/vol13/issue1/boyd.ellison.html

Brady, K. P., Holcomb, L. B., & Smith, B. V. (2010). The use of alternative social networking sites in higher educational settings: A case study of the e-learning benefits of Ning in education. *Journal of Interactive Online Learning, 9*(2), 152–171.

Brinkerhoff, J. (2006). Effects of a long-duration, professional development academy on technology skills, computer self-efficacy, and technology integration beliefs and practices. *Journal of Research on Technology in Education, 39*(1), 22–43.

Brook, C., & Oliver, R. (2003). Online learning communities: Investigating a design framework. *Australasian Journal of Educational Technology, 19*(2), 139–160.

Bruffee, K. A. (1993). *Collaborative Learning: Higher education, interdependence, and the authority of knowledge*. Baltimore, MD: John Hopkins University Press. doi:10.2307/358879

Cobb, S. C. (2009). Social presence and online learning: A current view from a research perspective. *Journal of Interactive Online Learning, 8*(3), 241–254.

Collis, B., & Moonen, J. (2008). Web 2.0 tools and processes in higher education: quality perspectives. *Educational Media International, 45*(2), 93–106. doi:10.1080/09523980802107179

Conrad, R.-M., & Donaldson, J. A. (2004). *Engaging the online learner*. San Francisco, CA: Jossey-Bass.

Correia, A., & Davis, N. (2008). Intersecting communities of practice in distance education: The program team and the online course community. *Distance Education, 29*(3), 289–306. doi:10.1080/01587910802395813

Cox, A. (2005). What are communities of practice? A comparative review of four seminal works. *Journal of Information Science, 31*(6), 527–540. doi:10.1177/0165551505057016

Dawson, S. (2006). A study of the relationship between student and communication interaction and sense of community. *The Internet and Higher Education, 9*, 153–162. doi:10.1016/j.iheduc.2006.06.007

Dede, C. (1996). The evolution of distance education: Emerging technologies and distributed learning. *American Journal of Distance Education, 10*(2), 4–36. doi:10.1080/08923649609526919

DeSchryver, M., Mishra, P., Koehler, M., & Francis, A. P. (2009). Moodle vs. Facebook: Does using Facebook for discussions in an online course enhance perceived social presence and student interaction? In C. Crawford, D. A. Willis, R. Carlsen, I. Gibson, K. McFerrin, J. Price, & R. I. Weber (Eds.), *Proceedings from The Society for Information Technology and Teacher Education International Conference* (329-336). Chesapeake, VA: AACE.

Dunlap, J. C., & Lowenthal, P. R. (2009). Tweeting the night away: Using Twitter to enhance social presence. *Journal of Information Systems Education, 20*(2), 129–136.

Fabro, K. R., & Garrison, D. R. (1998). Computer conferencing and higher-order learning. *Indian Journal of Open Learning, 7*(1), 41–54.

Farwell, T., & Krüger-Ross, M. (2012in press). Is there (still) a place for blogging in the classroom?: Using blogging to assess writing, facilitate engagement and evaluate student attitudes. In Seo, K. (Ed.), *Using social media effectively in the classroom: Blogs, wikis, twitter and more*.

Gable, R. K., & Wolf, M. B. (1993). *Instrument development in the affective domain: Measuring attitudes and values in corporate and school settings* (2nd ed.). Boston, MA: Kluwer Academic.

Garrison, D. R., Anderson, T., & Archer, W. (2000). Critical inquiry in text-based environments: Computer conferencing in higher education. *The Internet and Higher Education, 2*(2-3), 1–19.

Gunawardena, C. N., & Zittle, F. (1997). Social presence as a predictor of satisfaction within a computer mediated conferencing environment. *American Journal of Distance Education, 11*(3), 8–26. doi:10.1080/08923649709526970

Halic, O., Lee, D., Paulus, T., & Spence, M. (2010). To blog or not to blog: Student perceptions of blog effectiveness for learning in a college-level course. *The Internet and Higher Education, 13*(4), 206–213. doi:10.1016/j.iheduc.2010.04.001

Hew, K. F., & Brush, T. (2006). Integrating technology into K-12 teaching and learning: Current knowledge gaps and recommendations for future research. *Educational Technology Research and Development, 55*(3), 223–252. doi:10.1007/s11423-006-9022-5

Holcomb, L. B., Brady, K. P., & Smith, B. V. (2010). The emergence of "educational networking": Can non-commercial, education-based social networking sites really address the privacy and safety concerns of educators? *Journal of Online Learning and Teaching, 6*(2).

Hopkins, K. D., Stanley, J. C., & Hopkins, B. R. (1990). *Educational and psychological measurement and evaluation* (7th ed.). Englewood, NJ: Prentice-Hall.

Jenkins, H. (2006). *Confronting the challenges of participatory culture: Media education for the 21st century*. White paper for the MacArthur Foundation. Retrieved on July 1, 2008 from www.digitallearning.macfound.org

Jenkins, H., Clinton, K., Purushotma, R., Robinson, A. J., & Weigel, M. (2006). *Confronting the challenges of participatory culture: Media education for the 21st century*. MacArthur Foundation. Retrieved on February 27, 2012, from http://digitallearning.macfound.org/atf/cf/%7B7E45C7E0-A3E0-4B89-AC9C-E807E1B0AE4E%7D/JENKINS_WHITE_PAPER.PDF.

Kaplan, A. M., & Haenlein, M. (2010). Users of the world, unite! The challenges and opportunities of social media. *Business Horizons, 53*(1), 59–68. doi:10.1016/j.bushor.2009.09.003

Keengwe, J., & Kidd, T. T. (2010). Towards best practices in online learning and teaching in higher education. *Journal of Online Teaching and Learning, 6*(2), 533–541.

Kienle, A., & Ritterskamp, C. (2007). Facilitating asynchronous discussions in learning communities: The impact of moderation strategies. *Behaviour & Information Technology, 26*(1), 73–80. doi:10.1080/01449290600811594

Kirschner, P. A., & Lai, K.-W. (2007). Online communities of practice in education. *Technology, Pedagogy and Education, 16*(2), 127–131. doi:10.1080/14759390701406737

Krüger-Ross, M., Farwell, T., & Waters, R. D. (2012in press). (2012). Everyone's all a-Twitter about Twitter: Three operational perspectives on using Twitter in the classroom. In Seo, K. (Ed.), *Using social media effectively in the classroom: Blogs, wikis, twitter and more.*

Krüger-Ross, M., & Holcomb, L. (2011). Towards a theoretical best practices of Web 2.0 and web-based technologies. *Meridian, 13*(2). Retrieved on February 27, 2012, from http://www.ncsu.edu/meridian/winter2011/Krugerross/index.htm

Lave, J., & Wenger, E. (1991). *Situated learning: Legitimate peripheral participation*. Cambridge, UK: University of Cambridge Press. doi:10.1017/CBO9780511815355

Lawless, K. A., & Pellegrino, J. W. (2007). Professional development in integrating technology into teaching and learning: Knowns, unknowns, and ways to pursue better questions and answers. *Review of Educational Research, 77*(4), 575–614. doi:10.3102/0034654307309921

Lee, Y., & Choi, J. (2010). A review of online course dropout research: Implications for practice and future research. *Educational Technology Research and Development, 59*(5), 593–618. doi:10.1007/s11423-010-9177-y

Lenhart, A., & Fox, S. (2006). *Bloggers: A portrait of the Internet's new storytellers*. Pew Internet & American Life Project. Retrieved February 27, 2012, from http://www.pewinternet.org/Reports/2006/Bloggers.aspx

Lenhart, A., Purcell, K., Smith, A., & Zickuhr, K. (2010). *Social media and mobile Internet use among teens and young adults*. Retrieved on February 27, 2012 from http://pewinternet.org/Reports/2010/Social-Media and-Young-Adults.aspx

Li, C., & Bernoff, J. (2011). *Groundswell, expanded and revised edition: Winning in a world transformed by social technologies*. Cambridge, MA: Harvard Business Review Press.

Liedka, J. (1999). Linking competitive advantage with communities of practice. *Journal of Management Inquiry*, *8*(1), 5–16. doi:10.1177/105649269981002

Lilleker, D. G., & Jackson, N. (2008). *Politicians and Web 2.0: The current bandwagon or changing the mindset?* Paper presented at the Politics: Web 2.0 International Conference, April 17-18, 2008. London, UK: Royal Holloway, University of London.

Lowenthal, P. R. (2010). The evolution and influence of social presence theory on online learning. In Kidd, T. T. (Ed.), *Online education and adult learning: New frontiers for teaching practices* (pp. 124–139). Hershey, PA: IGI Global.

Maloney, E. J. (2007). What Web 2.0 can teach us about learning. *The Chronicle of Higher Education*, *53*(18), B26.

Nardi, B. A., Schiano, D. J., Gumbrecht, M., & Swartz, L. (2004). Why we blog. *Communications of the ACM*, *47*(12), 41–46. doi:10.1145/1035134.1035163

New Media Consortium & the EDUCAUSE Learning Initiative. (2007). *The horizon report*. Retrieved on February 27, 2012 from http://www.nmc.org/horizon/2007/report

Oztok, M., & Brett, C. (2011). Social presence and online learning: A review of research. *Journal of Distance Education*, *25*(3), 1–16.

Palloff, R. M., & Pratt, K. (2001). *Lessons from the cyberspace classroom*. San Francisco, CA: Jossey-Bass.

Pigliapoco, E., & Bogliolo, A. (2008). The effects of psychological sense of community in online and face-to-face academic courses. *International Journal of Emerging Technologies in Learning*, *3*(4), 60–69.

Richardson, J. C., & Swan, K. (2003). Examining social presences in online courses in relation to students' perceived learning and satisfaction. *Journal of Asynchronous Learning Networks*, *7*(1), 68–88.

Russo, T., & Benson, S. (2005). Learning with invisible others: Perceptions of online presence and their relationship to cognitive and affective learning. *Journal of Educational Technology & Society*, *8*(1), 54–62.

Salmon, G. (2005). *E-moderating: The key to teaching and learning online*. New York, NY: Routledge Falmer.

Searson, M., Dawley, L., Field, W., Owens, C., & Penny, C. (2011). *There's an app for that! The role of mobile learning in education*. Panel presentation at the Society for Information Technology & Teacher Education Annual Conference, Nashville, Tennessee.

Selwyn, N. (2000). Creating a "connected" community? Teachers' use of an electronic discussion group. *Teachers College Record*, *102*, 750–778. doi:10.1111/0161-4681.00076

Sloan Consortium. (2010). *Class differences: Online education in the United States*. Retrieved on February 27, 2012, from http://sloanconsortium.org/publications/survey/class_differences

Song, L., Singleton, E. S., Hill, J. R., & Koh, M. H. (2004). Improving online learning: Student perceptions of useful and challenging characteristics. *The Internet and Higher Education, 7*, 59–70. doi:10.1016/j.iheduc.2003.11.003

Squire, K., & Johnson, C. (2000). Supporting distributed communities of practice with interactive television. *Educational Technology Research and Development, 48*(1), 23–43. doi:10.1007/BF02313484

Swan, K. (2005). A constructivist model for thinking about learning online. In Bourne, J., & Moore, J. C. (Eds.), *Elements of quality online education: Engaging communities* (pp. 13–30). Needham, MA: Sloan-C.

Tello, S. F. (2007). An analysis of student persistence in online education. *International Journal of Information and Communication Technology Education, 3*(3), 47–62. doi:10.4018/jicte.2007070105

Thomas, D., & Brown, J. S. (2011). *A new culture of learning: Cultivating the imagination for a world of constant change*. Createspace.

University of Minnesota. (2008, June 21). Educational benefits of social networking sites. *ScienceDaily*. Retrieved January 20, 2009, from http://www.sciencedaily.com/releases/2008/06/080620133907.htm

U.S. Department of Education, National Center for Education Statistics. (1999). *Distance education at postsecondary education institutions: 1997-98*. NCES 2000-013, by Laurie Lewis, Kyle Snow, Elizabeth Farris, Douglas Levin. Bernie Greene, project officer.

U.S. Department of Education, National Center for Education Statistics. (2008). *Distance education at degree-granting postsecondary institutions: 2006–07* (NCES 2009-044).

Vonderwell, S. (2003). An examination of asynchronous communication experiences and perspectives of students in an online course: A case study. *The Internet and Higher Education, 6*, 77–90. doi:10.1016/S1096-7516(02)00164-1

Vrasidas, C., & Stock-McIssac, M. (1999). Factors influencing interaction in an online course. *American Journal of Distance Education, 13*(3), 22–35. doi:10.1080/08923649909527033

Walker, B. K. (2007). *Bridging the distance: How social interaction, presence, social presence, and sense of community influence student learning experiences in an online virtual learning environment*. Unpublished doctoral dissertation, The University of North Carolina at Greensboro, Greensboro, North Carolina.

Wellman, B. (1999). The network community: An introduction to networks in the global village. In *Networks in the global village* (pp. 1–48). Boulder, CO: Westview Press.

Wenger, E. (1998). *Communities of practice: Learning, meaning, and identity*. New York, NY: Cambridge University Press.

Woods, R. H. (2002). How much communication is enough in online courses? Exploring the relationship between frequency of instructor-initiated personal email and learners' perceptions of and participation in online learning. *International Journal of Instructional Media, 29*(4), 377–394.

Worthen, B. R., Borg, W. R., & White, K. R. (1993). *Measurement and evaluation in the schools*. White Plains, NY: Longman.

ADDITIONAL READING

Annand, D. (2011). Social presence within the community of inquiry framework. *International Review of Research in Open and Distance Learning, 12*(5), 40–56.

Aragon, S. R. (2003). Creating social presence in online environments. *New Directions for Adult and Continuing Education, 100,* 57–68. doi:10.1002/ace.119

Arbaugh, J. B., Cleveland-Innes, M., Diaz, S., Garrison, D. R., Ice, P., & Richardson, J. C. (2008). Developing a community of inquiry instrument: Testing a measure of the community of inquiry framework using a multi-institutional sample. *The Internet and Higher Education, 11*(3-4), 133–136. doi:10.1016/j.iheduc.2008.06.003

Boettcher, J. V., & Conrad, R.-M. (2010). *The online teaching surviving guide: Simple and practical pedagogical tips*. San Francisco, CA: Jossey-Bass.

Boubsil, O., Carabajal, K., & Vidal, M. (2011). Implications of globalization for distance education in the United States. *American Journal of Distance Education, 25*(1), 5–20. doi:10.1080/08923647.2011.544604

Byam, N. (1995). The emergence of community in computer-mediated communication. In Jones, S. G. (Ed.), *Cybersociety*. Newbury Park, CA: Sage.

Clark, R. C., & Mayer, R. E. (2008). *E-learning and the science of instruction*. San Francisco, CA: Pfeiffer.

Hara, N. (Ed.). (2009). *Communities of practice: Fostering peer-to-peer learning and informal knowledge sharing in the work place*. New York, NY: SpringerLink.

Hara, N., & Kling, R. (2000). Students' distress with a web-based distance education course. *Information Communication and Society, 3*(4), 557–579. doi:10.1080/13691180010002297

Haythornthwaite, C., & Kazmer, M. M. (Eds.). (2004). *Learning, culture, and community in online education: research and practice*. New York, NY: Peter Lang.

Hiltz, S. R., & Wellman, B. (1997). Asynchronous learning networks as a virtual classroom. *Communications of the ACM, 40*(9), 44–49. doi:10.1145/260750.260764

Lahaie, U. (2007). Strategies for creating social presence online. *Nurse Educator, 32*(3), 100–101. doi:10.1097/01.NNE.0000270226.84284.f8

Lakin, R. B. (2005). *Social presence: The secret behind online collaboration*. Retrieved April 20, 2008, from http://www.acenet.edu/AM/PrinterTemplate.cfm?Section=Home&CONTENTID=CM/ContentDisplay.dfm

Lehman, R. M., & Conceição, S. C. O. (2010). *Creating a sense of presence in online teaching: How to "be there" for distance learners*. San Francisco, CA: Jossey-Bass.

McInnerney, J. M., & Roberts, T. S. (2004). Online learning: Social interaction and the creation of a sense of community. *Journal of Educational Technology & Society, 7*(3), 73–81.

Moore, M. G., & Kearsley, G. (2005). *Distance education: A systems view* (2nd ed.). New York, NY: Wadsworth.

O'Sullivan, D. (2009). *Wikipedia: A new community of practice?* Burlington, VT: Ashgate.

Picciano, A. (2002). Beyond student perceptions: Issues of interaction, presence, and performance in an online course. *Journal of Asynchronous Learning Networks, 6*(1), 21–40.

Rovai, A. P., & Wighting, M. J. (2005). Feelings of alienation and community among higher education students in a virtual classroom. *The Internet and Higher Education, 8,* 97–110. doi:10.1016/j.iheduc.2005.03.001

Samaras, A. P., Freese, A. R., Kosnik, C., & Beck, C. (Eds.). (2009). *Learning communities in practice*. New York, NY: SpringerLink. doi:10.1007/978-1-4020-8788-2

Schwier, R. A. (2001). Catalysts, emphases, and elements of virtual Learning communities: Implications for research and practice. *Quarterly Review of Distance Education, 2*(1), 5–18.

Stuckey, B., & Smith, J. D. (2004). Building sustainable communities of practice. In Hildreth, P., & Kimble, C. (Eds.), *Knowledge networks: Innovation through communities of practice* (pp. 150–164). Hershey, PA: Idea Group.

Swan, K., & Shih, L. F. (2005). On the nature and development of social presence in online course discussion. *Journal of Asynchronous Learning Networks, 9*(3), 115–136.

Tu, C.-H., & McIsaac, M. (2002). The relationship of social presence and interaction in online classes. *American Journal of Distance Education, 16*(3), 131–150. doi:10.1207/S15389286AJDE1603_2

Wanstreet, C. E., & Stein, D. S. (2011). Presence over time in synchronous communities of inquiry. *American Journal of Distance Education, 25*(3), 162–177. doi:10.1080/08923647.2011.590062

Wei, C.-W., & Chen, N.-S. (2012). A model for social presence in online classrooms. *Educational Technology Research and Development, 60*(1), 1–17.

Wenger, E., McDermott, R., & Snyder, W. (2002). *Cultivating communities of practice: A guide to managing knowledge*. Boston, MA: Harvard Business School Press.

West, R. E. (2011). Insights from research on distance education learners, learning, and learner support. *American Journal of Distance Education, 25*(3), 135–151. doi:10.1080/08923647.2011.589775

Wubbels, T. (2007). Do we know a community of practice when we see one? *Technology, Pedagogy and Education, 16*(2), 225–233. doi:10.1080/14759390701406851

Zhao, X., & Bishop, M. J. (2011). Understanding and supporting online communities of practice: Lessons learned from Wikipedia. *Educational Technology Research and Development, 59*(5), 711–735. doi:10.1007/s11423-011-9204-7

KEY TERMS AND DEFINITIONS

Blog: A blog is an easy to edit and update website that orders a user's posts chronologically. Blogs are often cited as one of the first iterations of web-based, Web 2.0, and social media technologies because of the ease of access as well as other users' ability to leave "comments" – a function that has been integrated into many other social media technologies.

Communities of Practice: Groups of individuals who share a concern or a common goal for something they do and learn how to do it better as they interact regularly.

Distance Education: Field of education that covers all forms of teaching and learning where students and teachers interact via technologies at various geographical locations and at differing times. Within this definition includes all forms of e-learning, blended/hybrid learning, online learning, etc.

Google+: A social networking space sponsored by Google that allows for users to upload images and videos to share with various *Circles* or groups of people in their lives that they are connected to.

Social Media: Web-based technologies and applications that support the creation and exchange of user-generated content. Social media is considered a subset underneath Web 2.0 or web-based technologies.

Social Networking Sites: Online site that focuses on the building of social networks and connections. A social network consists of a personal profile, his/her social links, and a variety of additional services. An example of an educational social networking site is Ning in Education.

Social Presence: A construct used to describe the ability of learners to project their personal characteristics into the community of inquiry, thereby presenting themselves as 'real people.'

Twitter: Twitter is a microblogging service that provides users with 140 characters to share textual information. Videos and pictures may be shared via URLs as well. In addition to tweeting (the verb form for posting a message on Twitter), users can "retweet" another's tweet, mention another person and conduct a public dialogue, or privately message others. Twitter has become increasingly popular in mainstream media.

APPENDIX A

Table 3. Social Media in Distance Education Survey

	Strongly Disagree	Disagree	Neither Agree or Disagree	Agree	Strongly Agree
1. Social media enable me to communicate with peers and colleagues more frequently.	1	2	3	4	5
2. Social media enable me to communicate with peers and colleagues more effectively.	1	2	3	4	5
3. Social media tools enable me to discuss and share my views with peers.	1	2	3	4	5
4. Social media tools enable me to communicate with peers and colleagues who I would not otherwise be able to communicate with.	1	2	3	4	5
5. Social media enable more detailed, in-depth conversations with my peers.	1	2	3	4	5
6. I prefer using social media tools to communicate with my peers.	1	2	3	4	5
7. Social media tools enable me to express my thoughts more clearly and openly.	1	2	3	4	5
8. Social media tools enable me to collaborate with peers more frequently.	1	2	3	4	5
9. Social media tools enable me to collaborate with peers more effectively.	1	2	3	4	5
10. Social media tools enable me to collaborate with a wide audience.	1	2	3	4	5
11. Social media tools enable me to comment and discuss ideas with colleagues efficiently.	1	2	3	4	5
12. I prefer using social media tools to share and discuss ideas due to convenience.	1	2	3	4	5
13. I prefer to use social media tools for group work and collaborating with peers.	1	2	3	4	5
14. Social media tools enable me to reflect on my own learning.	1	2	3	4	5
15. Social media tools enable me to review and reflect on course material in a timelier manner.	1	2	3	4	5
16. Social media tools enable me more time to effectively reflect on others' comments.	1	2	3	4	5
17. Social media tools facilitate a more comprehensive understanding of topics.	1	2	3	4	5

continued on following page

Table 3. Continued

	Strongly Disagree	Disagree	Neither Agree or Disagree	Agree	Strongly Agree
18. Social media tools enable me to ask questions and obtain clarification more easily.	1	2	3	4	5
19. Social media tools enable me to review and reflect upon information & materials from varying viewpoints.	1	2	3	4	5
20. I prefer to seek help and clarification using social media tools.	1	2	3	4	5
21. Social media tools enable me to have a voice in an online class.	1	2	3	4	5
22. Social media tools enable me to have an identity in an online class.	1	2	3	4	5
23. Social media tools enable my peers to get to know me.	1	2	3	4	5
24. Social media tools enable me to get to know my peers.	1	2	3	4	5
25. Social media tools enable me to be an active member of an online course.	1	2	3	4	5
26. Social media tools enable me to be an effective member of an online class.	1	2	3	4	5

APPENDIX B

Student Interview Questions

1. What were the benefits of using social media tools in an online course?
2. What tools did you like best and why?
3. Did you prefer using a specific tool for a specific task? Please explain.
4. Do you feel that the use of social media tools allowed for you to have an identity and be a contributing member of the course?
5. How did the use of social media tools impact your learning in this course?
6. What were the drawbacks of using social media tools in an online course?
7. What were the biggest challenges to using social media tools in an online course?
8. Were there any tools that you did not like using? If yes, which tool(s) and why?
9. Would you like to continue using social media tools in future online courses? Why or why not?
10. What recommendations do you have for utilizing social media tools in an online class?

Chapter 6
Framing Non-Formal Education through CSR 2.0

Bogdan Pătruț
Vasile Alecsandri University of Bacău, Romania

Monica Pătruț
Vasile Alecsandri University of Bacău, Romania

Camelia Cmeciu
Danubius University of Galați, Romania

ABSTRACT

Schools and universities are not the only providers of knowledge any longer. Other types of organizations have become aware that a solid public-serving reason should lie beyond the firm-serving motive. "Doing well by doing good" has been the syntagm that prevails nowadays in the organizational discourse focused on corporate social responsibility (CSR) campaigns. This chapter has a twofold aim: to highlight two paradigmatic shifts (CSR 1.0 → CSR 2.0 & formal education → non-formal education), and to provide an analysis of the Web 2.0 practices and items and of the verbal and visual framing devices used in a CSR 2.0 campaign on non-formal financial education. Social media have provided the applications to put into practice the concept of edutainment specific to non-formal education since educators get a multifold identity, being, at the same time, generators and receivers of knowledge.

INTRODUCTION

Organizations exist only in so far as their members create them through discourse. This is not to claim that organizations are 'nothing but' discourse, but rather that discourse is the principle means by which organization members create a coherent social reality that frames their sense of who they are. (Mumby & Clair, 1997, p. 181)

The mutual interdependence between organizations and their stakeholders provides a feeling of belongingness and it is essential in the process of building a twofold identity (Cornelissen, 2005, p. 69): on the one hand, the organization identity through deep-structure elements (mission statements, vision, history) and on the other hand, the corporate identity through surface-structure elements (products, services, communication campaigns, employee behavior). This identity shaping of an organization and implicitly of its

DOI: 10.4018/978-1-4666-2851-9.ch006

stakeholders proves that organizations have turned into "mechanisms that enable a direct valorization (...) of people's ability to create trust, affect and shared meanings" (Arvidsson, 2005, p. 236). The process of sharing meanings lies on an invisible project, namely knowledge (Lester, 2005, p. 5). Nowadays knowledge and consequently education is not only associated with schools or/ and universities, it turns into "the invisible project" of organizations belonging to local communities. The permanent dialogue, achieved through educational campaigns, between organizations in a certain community proves that other types of organizations, such as banks, museums, theatres, "(…) have as much effectiveness in modernizing men as do schools" (Inkeles, 1983).

Since "learning would come about through the same processes of socialization", A. Inkeles (1983) highlights that educational organizations bear a twofold activity: on the one hand, the formal, explicit, self-conscious pedagogic activity which is inherent in schools and universities as organizations and on the other hand, the informal, implicit, and often unconscious activity which is performed in collaboration with other organizations or by other organizations. Thus organizations of any kind should be focused on what Adam Arvidsson (2005, p. 237) labels as "an ethical surplus", namely a social relationship, a shared meaning and an emotional involvement of the stakeholders. The performance of organizational actions connected to social, cultural, educational and environmental aspects bears an ethical and a responsible direction.

These implications of an ethical surplus have implied the (re)configuration of organization policies on openness, clarity and transparency (Garsten, de Montoya, 2008). These three attributes have two main outcomes:

- The existence of an endless negotiated flow between what should be made visible and what should be hidden in organizational texts, the multiple communication chan-

nels playing an important part in this process of (non)making visible. CSR 2.0 is the conceptual embodiment of the postmodern organization which has been integrating Web 2.0 instruments in its discursive visibility strategies.
- A social shift towards organizations' legitimacy, accountability, credibility (Golob & Bartlett, 2007; Huang & Su, 2009) and responsibility (Oprea, 2005; Capriotti & Moreno, 2007; An & Gower, 2009) by performing actions connected to social, cultural, educational and environmental aspects.

Within the context of new technologies which have shaped new ways of learning, sharing and collaborative knowledge construction, organizations seem to experience a shift from "collection to connection" (Luke, 2003, p. 400): the emphasis does not lie any longer on the abundant production of organizational texts which, most of the times, do not reach the stakeholders and are not provided with any feed-back, but it lies on a co-creating of meaning since organizations and stakeholders are both discursive producers having digital literacy. The importance of social media within the organizational communication was also highlighted in the 2011 European Communication Monitor (Zerfass et al., 2011), the five most important issues for communication management (p. 78) until 2014 being: coping with the digital evolution and the social web (54.9%), linking business strategy and communication (44%), dealing with sustainable development and social responsibility (37.2%), dealing with the demand for more transparency and active audiences (35.1%), and building and maintaining trust (30.1%).

BACKGROUND

According to Grunig and Repper (1992, p. 128), "organizations choose their markets, whereas publics arise on their own and choose organizations for attention". The question that prevails focuses on what organizations should do in order to catch the publics' attention. One syntagm which comes to one's mind belongs to Brad L. Rawlins (2005, p. 210), namely "doing well by doing good". It combines an organizational dichotomy based either on a financial profit through a production of goods and services, or a moral profit through a responsible attitude towards the society. According to the International Standards Organization[1], the corporate citizenship that postmodernity claims from organizations involves a transparent and ethical behavior that should (1) contribute to sustainable development, health and the welfare of society; (2) take into account the expectations of stakeholders; (3) be in compliance with applicable law and consistent with international norms of behavior; (4) be integrated throughout the organization and practiced in its relationships. Thus an organization turns from a represented participant through elements of corporate identity into an interactive participant (Cmeciu, Cmeciu, 2011, p. 166), having a corporate conscience (Bowen & Rawlings 2005, p. 205) and trying to educate its internal and external publics. Responsibility, the most salient word nowadays when it comes to defining organizations, has been assigned in two different syntagms (Visser, 2010, p. 14): CSR 1.0 (Corporate Social Responsibility) and CSR 2.0 (Corporate Sustainability and Responsibility). We will provide an insight into two paradigmatic shifts: on the one hand, from CSR 1.0 to CSR 2.0, and on the other hand, from traditional non-formal education to virtual non-formal education.

A Paradigmatic Shift from CSR 1.0 to CSR 2.0

Defined by the European Commission as "the integration by companies of social and environmental concerns in their business operations and in their interaction with their stakeholders on a voluntary basis"[2], CSR has been used within the organizational lexicon since the 1950s, developing in the 1990s when A.B. Carroll's (1991) four-layered pyramid (the economic, legal, ethical, and philanthropic dimensions) was widely used in the organizational management.

Despite the difficulty to find a unifying definition and means of measurement, A. Dahlsrud (2008) analysed 37 definitions of CSR and identified five main CSR components common to all definitions:1) the environmental, 2) social, 3) economic impacts businesses have in relation to CSR; 4) the voluntariness dimension that distinguishes CSR from legal compliance; and 5) the stakeholder dimension that introduces interaction and communication aspects.

Since "CSR communication has become an integral part of corporate reporting" and since "its impact on image building and stakeholder relationship management is widely accepted" (Bittner, Leimeister, 2011, p. 3), transparency has become the prevailing concept related to CSR. We will discuss the concept of transparency in CSR taking into account two aspects: a) CSR organizational texts, and b) the technological development.

a. **CSR Organizational Texts:** Considered "structured collections of texts embodied in the practices of talking and writing (as well as a wide variety of visual representations and cultural artefacts) that bring organizationally related objects into being as these texts are produced, disseminated and consumed" (Grant et al., 2004, p. 3), organizational discourses focus on the networks of social practices (Fairclough, 2005, p. 924). CSR campaigns based on different textual subsidies (advertisements, commercials, fliers, annual reports, web sites, social media) create a network of social practices mainly focused on a collaboration between: 1) one organization and other organizations, especially the non-profit organizations, 2) one organization and its internal public, 3) one organization and its (virtual) external public.

Within this framework based on networking, transparency is conceived (Garsten, Lindh de Montoya, 2008, p. 284) as a narrativizing tool which seems to be relational, situational, fluid, contested and negotiated. This constant interweaving of what should be made visible and what should be hidden especially in CSR reporting brings forth the problem of objectivity versus subjectivity. Following Rick Iedema and Ruth Wodak's framework for organizational discourse analysis (1999, pp. 12–13), the analysis of the CSR organizational discourse should be concerned with how objectivity is (1) constructed, achieved and contested, (2) how its transmission is ensured or prevented, and (3) what consequences of this are for interaction. The editors of the *Sage Handbook of Organizational Discourse* (2004) consider that the researchers studying (CSR) organizational discourses are mainly interested in the social constructionist effects of (non) verbal language in organizational settings. According to Michel Foucault (1984, p. 113–114), this "will to truth" that social constructionism relies on is but desire and power, which reminds us of Michel Foucault's metaphorical definition of visibility (1997, p. 200) as a trap. The power of organizational text producers lies in their ability of framing the social reality in such a way as to make stakeholders aware of some environmental and/ or social issues (see the framework of framing theories presented below).

b. **Technological Development:** We will tackle upon this issue of the evolution of technology (old media system → Web 1.0 → Web 2.0) taking into account the metaphorical definition provided to these concepts. George Lakoff's and Mark Johnson's *Metaphors We Live By* (1980) has already highlighted the fact that reality can be grasped in terms of conceptual metaphors (CM), assuming an interaction of at least two different domains

of knowledge: source-domain mapping some systematic set of correspondences upon the target-domain.

Throughout the years CSR discursive practices have been closely affected by the evolution of mass-media and McLuhan's famous syntagm ("The Medium is the Message") has turned into Baudrillard's syntagm ("Mass(age) is the message", 2007), focusing on a condemnation to "a «magical» practice and to a «spectacular» consumption" and to the fact that "image is as ideological and as power laden as word" (Jewitt, 2008, p. 252). This semantic change from medium to mass(age) can be explained in terms of the shift from traditional media system to new media. Starting from Dorothy's words ("Toto, I've got a feeling that we're not in Kansas anymore"), D. Wilcox (2009) offers a twofold metaphorical mapping (Pătruţ, Cmeciu, 2011, p. 24):

- On the one hand, the old media system as the Kansas territory, having the following features:
  ○ Centralization and top-down communication;
  ○ High price;
  ○ Gatekeeping focused on mediating the information;
  ○ One-way communication and limited feedback.
- On the other hand, the new media as the Oz territory, having the following features:
  ○ Widespread broadband;
  ○ Cheap/ free online publishing tools;
  ○ New distribution channels;
  ○ Mobile devices;
  ○ 24/7 news and information;
  ○ Democratized media.

One cannot forget the way in which Dorothy was brought to this new territory. The tornado was the vehicle which transported Dorothy and her dog into a totally new territory which despite its fascinating challenges, also hides some drawbacks (fragmentation, information overload, polarization, Dimitrova, 2007). Taking into account the last feature of new media mentioned by Wilcox, the democratized media triggers the metamorphosis of every human being into a possible online publisher.

The Web 1.0 stage or the beginning stage of the internet implies only communication via the email, the dial-up, high costs, websites which cannot be changed by other users. The Web 2.0 becomes a synonym of communication in real time, broadband internet (high speed, a better quality/price measure), blogs, podcasts, social networks, sites which create entire communities. While Web 1.0 is known as "The Read Only Web", Web 2.0 is known as "The Read Write Web" (O'Reilly, 2005). Defined as "a group of internet-based applications" (Kaplan, Haenlein, 2010, p. 61), social media "build on the ideological and technological foundations of Web 2.0" and "allow the creation and exchange of User Generated Content". The features of Web 2.0, that Wayne Visser (2010, p. 13) metaphorically considers to be "the seeds of a revolution" which is "as much a state of being as a technical advance", constitute the ingredients of the virtual public space (Goldberg, 2010) where online participation through user generated content seems to prevail.

This discrepancy between Web 1.0 and Web 2.0 is used as a source-concept by Wayne Visser (2010, pp. 14-15) in order to explain the differences between CSR 1.0 and CSR 2.0 (Table 1):

As the 2011 Global Social Media and CSR report[3] on the FTSE Global 500 shows, the advantages ('collective intelligence', 'collaborative networks', 'user participation', Visser, 2010, p. 15) that social media provide were exploited by 60% of the companies, the hierarchy of the forms of social activity being the following: RSS posts (107 companies), Embedded videos (102 companies), Twitter (56 companies), Facebook (44 companies), Youtube (40 companies), Blog (22 companies) and Podcasts (7 companies). On the

other hand, European Communication Monitor 2011 highlights that online communities are the most salient social media organizational channels, whereas podcasts, wikis and weblogs have lost relevance (Figure 1).

The salience of online communities highlights that the strategy of word-of-mouth has reached another level and that the bilateral symmetric model of communication (Grunig & Hunt, 1984) is still to be used since it is based on features (Grunig & White, 1992, pp. 43-44), such as: an interdependence between organizations and their environment, a moving equilibrium of the organization as an open system, equity, autonomy, decentralization, responsibility, and conflict resolution through negotiation.

Using the same principle of metaphorical mapping, Wayne Visser (2010, pp. 19-20) defines CSR 2.0 in terms of a journey and in terms of the DNA code:

- CSR 2.0 = SUSTAINABLITY (= DESTINATION) AND RESPONSIBILITY (= JOURNEY). Providing a diachronic perspective on the four CSR ages of greed,

Table 1. Discrepancies between CSR 1.0 and CSR 2.0 (Visser, 2010, pp. 14-15)

CSR 1.0	CSR 2.0
A vehicle for companies to establish relationships with communities, channel philanthropic contributions and manage their image.	Being defined by 'global commons', 'innovative partnerships' and 'stakeholder involvement'.
Included many start-up pioneers like Traidcraft, but has ultimately turned into a product for large multinationals like Wal-Mart.	Mechanisms include diverse stakeholder panels, real-time transparent reporting and new-wave social entrepreneurship.
Travelled down the road of "one size fits all" standardization, through codes, standards and guidelines to shape its offering.	Is recognizing a shift in power from centralized to decentralized, a change in scale from few and big to many and small; and a change in application from single and exclusive to multiple and shared.

Figure 1. European Communication Monitor 2011 (www.communicationmonitor.eu/ Zerfass et al. 2011, p. 103)

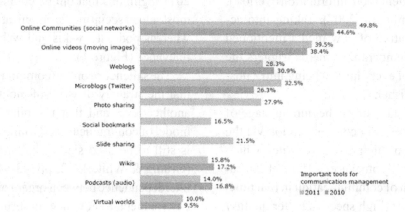

philanthropy, marketing, management, and responsibility, W. Visser (2010) considers that CSR 2.0 or systemic CSR implies a conjunction of *responsibility* which is "more about the journey – the solutions, responses, management and actions" (p.20) and of *sustainability* "conceived as the destination – the challenges, vision, strategy and goals" (p. 20).

- CSR 2.0 = DNA CODE. W. Visser (2010, p. 19) uses a mapping of the familiar source domain of a DNA code grounded in every human's experience onto the unfamiliar abstract target domain of CSR 2.0. Implicitly defining organizations as organisms, he identifies four responsibility bases that should prevail in every CSR 2.0-governed organization: value creation (capital investment, beneficial products, inclusive business), good governance (leadership, transparency, ethical practices), societal contribution (philanthropy, fair labour practices, supply chain integrity), environmental integrity (ecosystem protection, renewable resources, zero waste production). Creativity, scalability, responsiveness, glocality, and circularity are the five principles (Visser, 2010) upon which CSR 2.0 can be tested. Positioning themselves

as social businesses, organizations should respond to the community needs by thinking globally and acting locally. W. Visser (2010) considers that through education, training, and nourishing community and employee wellbeing, CSR 2.0 also lies an emphasis on the meaning of life and work alongside with ecological integrity and financial viability.

A Paradigmatic Shift from Traditional Non-Formal Education to Virtual Non-Formal Education

The literature on different types of education shows that formal education should be closely related to informal and non-formal education. In their study "Non-formal learning: mapping the conceptual terrain. A Consultation Report", Helen Colley, Phil Hodkinson & Janice Malcolm (2002) present several attempts to differentiate between formal, informal and non-formal learning: from pinpointing the term 'non-formal' as a substitute for the less precise 'informal' learning (Eraut, 2000), or from associating degrees of intentionality to the three types of education (the EC Communication on Lifelong Learning, 2001) to assuming that most learning takes place outside formal educational settings (Billett, 2001), or to perceiving learning as an organic or holistic process, engaging the whole person, thus blending the intellect, emotions, values and practical activities (Beckett, Hager, 2002).

Among all the distinguishing criteria mentioned in Colley and et al.'s study, we consider that intentionality plays an important part since it lies within learners' voluntary actions. The European Commission has used the following definitions[4] which focus on (the lack of) intentionality and (the lack of) being awarded a certification:

- **Formal Learning:** Is typically provided by education or training institutions, with structured learning objectives, learning time and learning support. It is intentional on the part of the learner and leads to certification.
- **Non-Formal Learning:** Is not provided by an education or training institution and typically does not lead to certification. However, it is intentional on the part of the learner and has structured objectives, times and support.
- **Informal Learning:** Results from daily activities related to work, family life or leisure. It is not structured and usually does not lead to certification. In most cases, it is unintentional on the part of the learner.

Another important criterion to distinguish between informal and non-formal learning is the setting where this process takes place. Haim Eshach (2007, p. 174) mentions that the syntagm "out-of-school" is too simplistic to highlight the difference between these two types of learning since both of them take place outside a formal setting. Hence the criterion of (visit) frequency should be taken into account: whereas informal learning is spontaneous and occurs in places within our day-to-day routine (street, home, playground, schools – free activities), non-formal learning has a structured form and occurs in places such as museums, zoos, botanical gardens, planetariums etc.

The cognitive aspects (gaining knowledge as a result of visits) and the affective aspects (enjoyable, long-lasting memories, positive attitude) of non-formal education (Eshach, 2007, pp. 178-179) show that this type of education which takes place out of schools but in an institutionalized environment lies on social constructivism which "(…) stretches us to think beyond narrow, curricular goals and to reach toward broad purposes of learning such as students' self-knowledge, development of identities, and belief that they can make a difference in the world" (Oldfather et al., 1999, p. 13).

Non-formal education as a form of social constructivism implies a twofold interaction:

- On the one hand, the dialogue between learners and non-formal educators. This dialogue should focus on two important concepts that have been linked to non-formal education: *empowerment* and *edutainment*. Non-formal education through its bilateral communication feature provides learners with "(…) an understanding of and control over social, economic, and/ or political forces in order to improve one's standing in society" (Kindervatter, 1979, in Moulton, 1997, p. 13). This non-formal means of acquiring new knowledge and skills has been perceived as a combination between the educational and the entertainment dimensions (Eshach, 2007, p. 172) thus providing a new term, namely *edutainment*.
- On the other hand, interaction with objects as semiotic resources. Even if researchers (Shortland, 1987, Wymer, 1991, in Eshach, 2007, p. 172) consider that bringing education and entertainment "under the same roof', the former will be "the loser", it is precisely this interaction with objects that turns learners from passive consumers of knowledge into active sign-makers and interpreters. The objects exhibited in the traditional non-formal settings (as museums,

zoos, botanical gardens, planetariums etc.) carry "a set of affordances" (Kress, van Leeuwen, 2006, p. 232) from which the non-formal educators select according to the learners' communicative needs and interests in a given context. The main advantage of learners' interaction with objects is "the hands-on" (Eshach, 2007) feature that exhibits carry. Interactivity with objects in non-formal educational settings lies on a multimedial experience (Kress, van Leeuwen, 2010, p. 67), a combination of senses in the process of interaction: sight, hear and touch.

The emergence of new media and social media has had an impact upon non-formal education as well. Gunther Kress (2003, p. 1) mentions two important factors which have influenced the new type of literacy: (1) the move from the long dominance of writing to the new dominance of the image, and (2) the move from the dominance of the medium of the book to the dominance of the medium of the screen. Whereas the medium of the book is specific to formal education, the medium of objects is specific to non-formal education. The (r)evolution in the uses and effects of this new type of literacy lies on the embedding of books and objects within the pervasive medium of the screen. Thus these new tools actually cause a shift from hands-on to eyes-on. New media and social media are characterized by multimodality and multimediality. Whereas multimediality focuses on synesthesia of two predominant senses (hear and sight) for social media which should compensate for taste, smell and touch, multimodality implies the affordances of each social media application which are provided in the context of two variables (Kaplan, Haenlein, 2010, p.62): social presence/ media richness and self-presentation/ self-disclosure (Table 2).

Blogs are multimodal mainly through two affordances, writing and images. Encompassing a variety of categories (from personal to organiza-

tional content), blogs constitute the perfect semiotic resource of transparency that is mainly used by company managers and employees.

Collaborative projects are the social media application where writing is the most pervasive monomodal element. Through wikis and social bookmarking applications, learners can participate in generating joint and objective contents about different objects promoted by organizations. Whereas writing is the modal element specific to collaborative projects, image and sound are the multimodal features of *content communities*.

Social networking sites have images, sound and writing as multimodal affordances. The profiles created through SNS constitute a resource of a twofold promotion: on the one hand, the promotion of the organization providing non-formal learning which can be quantified in the number of "likes" and "subscriptions", and on the other hand, the promotion of the participant-learners as being a member of the community which took part in the non-formal learning process. The non-formal learning that organizations provide through CSR 2.0 campaigns actually focuses on what boyd and Ellison (2008) define as social network sites, namely a place where users "articulate and make visible their social networks" (p. 211).

Table 2. Classification of Social Media by social presence/ media richness and self-presentation/ self-disclosure (Kaplan, Haenlein, 2010, p.62)

		Social presence/ Media richness		
		Low	Medium	High
Self-pre-sentation/ Self-dis-closure	High	Blogs	Social network-ing sites (e.g., Face-book)	Vir-tual social worlds (e.g., Second Life)
	Low	Collab-orative projects (e.g., Wikipe-dia)	Content communi-ties (e.g., YouTube)	Vir-tual game worlds (e.g., World of Warcraft)

Virtual social worlds use the greatest number of multimodal affordances since the residents of these worlds "show behavior that more and more closely mirrors the one observed in real life settings" (Kaplan, Haenlein, 2010, p. 64). The (re) production of a substitute of real life makes of virtual social worlds, alongside with *virtual game worlds*, the highest multimedial social media applications since participant-learners have the virtual possibility of tasting, smelling or touching objects which other applications slightly provide. Unlike virtual social worlds, *virtual game worlds* are the social media embodiments of traditional edutainment since organizations promote their objects (products/ services) by involving the learners into active participants in online role-playing game.

Despite "the out-of-school" feature, the traditional non-formal education remains an instance of "up-bottom" participation where the information is passed from the non-formal educators onto learners. As Nina Bonderup Dohn (2009, p. 345) highlights, Web 2.0 denotes activities, such as: collaboration and/or distributed authorship; active, open-access, "bottom-up" participation and interactive multi-way communication; continuous production, reproduction, and transformation of material in use and reuse across contexts; openness of content, renunciation of copyright, distributed ownership; lack of finality, "awareness-in-practice" of the "open-endedness" of the activity. The shift from "up-bottom" to "bottom-up" that characterizes Web 2.0 and that is embedded within the new context of education shows that (non-formal) educators get a multifold identity, learners becoming the new possible educators for other learners. This is actually why social media have been invented, namely "to meet new needs" (Kress, van Leeuwen, 2010, p.90). Within this context of the new type of non-formal education where learners turn into educators, the need that prevails is that of belongingness to a virtual community. It is "a cultural shift toward a more interpersonal function for search" (Zappavigna,

2011, p. 789), the search for content also implying a search of what "other people are saying online and forming communities of shared value". This collaborative process of generating knowledge is based on an interweaving between the goals of the Web 2.0 practices and those of education (Dohn, 2009, p. 349).

NON-FORMAL EDUCATION: CSR 2.0 CAMPAIGNS

The economic, legal, ethical, and philanthropic dimensions beyond every CSR activity, be it CSR 1.0 or CSR 2.0, should be integrated within the framework of campaigns which "are often driven by *reform* efforts, actions that seek to make life or society or both better, as defined by emerging social values" (Dozier et. al, 2001, p. 232). The KPMG International Survey of Corporate Responsibility Reporting 2011 shows that 95% of the 250 largest companies in the world (G 250 companies) now report on their corporate responsibility (CR) activities. It is clear that organizations have become aware of the impact that CSR has on their reputation and that "doing well by doing good", Brad L. Rawlins's syntagm (2005, p. 210) specific to CSR, should characterize their public communication campaigns. The final outcome of improving people's life and/ or society involves stirring one's awareness towards an issue. Considered "strategies of social control" (Paisley, 2001, pp. 5-6), public communication campaigns can be defined in terms of: (1) objectives, focusing on one group's intention to change another group's beliefs or behavior; (2) methods, focusing on a conventional and innovative mix of traditional, new and social media.

A campaign is based on a cognitive flow from a mere objective of informing towards a motivational objective which implies a change of attitude and behavior. This twofold change cannot be achieved unless the stakeholders are involved in a collaborative process of learning. The elements embedded within the meta-level ontological and the micro-level methodological shifts from CSR 1.0 to CSR 2.0 (Visser, 2010, pp. 18-19) highlight the salience that non-formal education plays in public communication campaigns.

On the one hand, the meta-level ontological shifts focus on a change from philanthropic to collaborative, from image-driven to performance-driven, from specialized to integrated, from standardized to diversified. On the other hand, the micro-level methodological shifts focus on a change from charity projects to social enterprise, from CSR departments to CSR incentives, from product liability to choice editing, from stakeholder groups to social networks. Thus the stakeholder gets a multifold identity: from a mere purchaser of a product/service (s)he turns, through the Web 2.0 practices present in campaigns, into a contributor to the process of networking with other stakeholders and a performer of some social, cultural, economic actions.

The major differences between CSR 2.0 campaigns lie on the field (social, cultural, education, health, environmental etc.) they are focused on and on the degree the Web 2.0 practices are used. Running a CSR 2.0 campaign implies that social media applications should be used as a bidirectional information delivery system where stakeholders play an active role in "the collaborative knowledge construction" (Dohn, 2009, p. 343) of an issue. Thus organizations which decide to use social media as methods in their CSR 2.0 campaigns should take into account the following ten pieces of advice (Kaplan, Haenlein, 2010, pp. 65-67): to choose carefully the proper social media application, to pick the application which allows participation, sharing, and collaboration rather than straightforward advertising and selling, to ensure activity alignment, to provide media plan integration, to provide access to all, to be active, interesting, humble, unprofessional, and honest.

Insights into CSR 1.0 & CSR 2.0 in Romania

Organizations have become more and more aware that any firm-serving motive should lie on a solid public-serving reason (Kim, Lee, 2012, p. 168). Alongside with tobacco, beer or fast food industries, banks can be labeled as socially stigmatized companies since they have been the target of public criticism for causing economic and financial issues. To generate stronger activism among consumers, to help people and young scholars in need, to get involved in environmental, cultural, education issues constitute a small sample of CSR activities through which firm-serving and public-serving motives are blending. Social media applications are the best means of making known these CSR initiatives. As the 2011 Global Social Media and CSR report on the FTSE Global 500 shows the 'banks' sector is the most productive (12%) in the use of social media in their CSR activities, followed by the 'oil and gas producers' (11%), the 'pharmaceutical and biotechnology' (6%) and the 'technology, hardware and equipment' (5%).

The use of social media in the banking services also prevails in Romania. According to a Zelist study (http://www.zelist.ro), in Romania, in the last six months of the year 2011 there have been more online comments and posts on the banking services (11 Romanian banks included in the study) than on the phone or car industries. The most frequently used social media applications were: Twitter (9674 twits), blogs (6279 posts), Facebook (5070 posts).

In the KPMG International Survey[5] of Corporate Responsibility Reporting 2011, Romania is placed in the "starting behind" quadrant because of the limited traction for communicating about their CR efforts and achievements. The concept of social responsibility in Romania should be closely linked to the abolishing of communism. The emergence of democracy after 1990 has constituted the perfect social, economic, and historical setting of establishing many NGOs associations and foundations which mainly had a humanitarian role (Udrea, Ionescu, 2007, p. 1), helping the disadvantaged categories (children, elder people, women). The investments of big transnational companies (Coca-Cola, Pepsi-Cola, Philp Morris etc.) in Romania had also brought the implementation of CSR aspects in Romanian companies' strategic management: community involvement, business behavior, relation with employees, workplace health, and relations with providers and clients. In the *CSR and Competitive ness European SMEs' Good Practice – National Report Romania* (2007), it is mentioned that after 2000, the involvement in actions of social responsibility mainly focused on restructuring the technologies for improving environment, adopting social measures for employees, developing good relations with local authorities, developing public-private partnership.

In the field of education, there are two online initiatives (*CSR Romania* - http://www.csr-romania.ro/, a common initiative of the foundation Forum for International Communications and of the Center for Sustainability and Excellence (CSE) and *Responsabilitate Socială/ Social Responsibility* - http://www.responsabilitatesociala.ro – an initiative of JTI Romania) which support organizations and governmental institutions to promote their CSR activities. Besides the monthly online newsletter provided, these two online CSR initiatives include case studies for different fields:

- http://www.csr-romania.ro/: education, entrepreneurship, disadvantaged social categories, environment, safety, health, community;
- http://www.responsabilitatesociala.ro: education, culture, environment, social and human rights.

In the field of education the responsabilitatesociala.ro site is the most active one. In Table 3 there

are included all the CSR campaigns on non-formal education promoted by banking organizations.

There are posted 31 case studies on education on www.responsabilitatesociala.ro, out of which the first two most salient organizations promoting education by means of CSR campaigns are: (1) banking services: 11 case studies are CSR campaigns (35%) and (2) telecommunications companies: 5 case studies (16%). The main issue that these CSR campaigns focused on has been nonformal financial education. A study of the World Bank in 2010[6] shows that the financial literacy in Romania is 30% and that 55% of Romanian citizens do not use financial products and services. Another conclusion of this study was that the

Table 3. CSR campaigns on education promoted by Romanian Banks (http://www.responsabilitatesociala.ro)

Year	Bank	CSR campaign
2010	OTP Bank Romania	Dreptul de a citi/ The right to read
2010	BRD Groupe Sociéte Generale	Săptămâna soldarității/ The week of soldarity
2010	RBS Romania	RBS Money Sense Romania
2009-2010	BCR	Start! Business 2009/ 2010
2009	BCR	BCR Speranțe/ BCR Hopes
2009	BCR	Şcoala de bani/ Money School
2008-2009	RBS Romania	Valori Europene / European Values
2008-2009	BCR	Finanțele mele/ My finances
2007-2008	RBS Romania	Educație pentru dezvoltare durabilă/ Education for Sustainable Development
2007	BRD Groupe Sociéte Generale	Youth Bank Cluj
2005-2006	RBS Romania	Valori Europene / European Values

Romanians aged between 16 and 24 years old are less capable of developing a long-term financial plan. Thus since 2009, Romanian banks have initiated CSR campaigns whose main aim was to provide non-formal financial education for different categories of stakeholders: highschool pupils, students, young adults and adults. These CSR campaigns on non-formal financial education involved a redesign of identities: bank employees turned into consultancy volunteers or teachers, the target public turned into real investors etc.

In Table 4, there are mentioned the Web 1.0 and Web 2.0 applications used by banks in promoting non-formal education. As it can be observed, CSR 1.0 applications through websites are the most salient ones, but since 2009 there have been used CSR 2.0 applications, such as blogs, Facebook, content community (YouTube).

Three of the CSR 2.0 campaigns on non-formal financial education used bloggers as "social media influencers" (Freberg et al., 2011, p. 90). Perceived as "a new type of independent third party endorser who shape audience attitudes through blogs, tweets, and the use of other social media" (Freberg et al., 2011, p. 90), bloggers have a twofold identity: either promoters of brands or organizations or hostile commentators.

MONEY SCHOOL: FRAMING OF NON-FORMAL FINANCIAL EDUCATION IN ROMANIA

This study will examine the way in which non-formal education was framed by BCR (Romanian Commercial Bank) and Rogalski&Grigoriu Agency in the CSR 2.0 campaign, *Money School*. Our choice has a threefold reason:

- Firstly, BCR is the most prominent user of social media applications in the banking services (Figure 2).
- Secondly, *Money School* is an integrated communication campaign where social media applications are salient;
- Thirdly, *Money School* won several awards: the SABRE Award (May 2010, the best program of financial education), the IPRA trophy for the best campaigns for social media (June 2010), and Golden Award for Excellence – Romanian PR Award (2010). This CSR 2.0 campaign was also present on the PR Cannes Lions 2010 shortlist.

Table 4. CSR campaigns on non-formal education using Web 1.0 and Web 2.0

Year	Bank	CSR campaign	CSR 1.0 & CSR 2.0
2010	OTP Bank Romania	Dreptul de a citi/ The right to read	*Online community* (www.estedreptulmeu.ro) blog posts, sharing (Youtube, Flickr), Facebook applications, the bloggers' involvement (debates on an issue "The book which marked your childhood")
2010	RBS Romania	RBS Money Sense Romania	The online guide of financial education (www.rbsmoneysense.ro)
2009-2010	BCR	Start! Business 2009/ 2010	The platform (http://www.start-business.ro/) of communication between the student teams and the BCR volunteers
2009	BCR	BCR Speranțe/ BCR Hopes	11 bloggers' involvement (posts on the stories of the disadvantaged children who are artistically gifted). Evaluation: 37 articles, 670 comments, over 10.000 views.
2009	BCR	Școala de bani/ Money School	Youtube (*How to get broke in 10 steps*), the platform (www.scoaladebani.ro), 11 bloggers' involvement (a competition between bloggers)
2008-2009	BCR	Finanțele mele/ My finances	The site (www.finantelemele.org) and the site for volunteers (www.voluntarcenter.ro)

Figure 2. 2011 – The social media analysis of the banking services (Source: http://www.zelist.ro)

2011: Analiza sectorului financiar bancar in social media  zelistmonitor

Instituti bancare	Presa	Bloguri	Twitter	Comentarii	Facebook	Forumuri	TOTAL*
BCR	10170 (477 surse)	1677 (602 surse)	2678 (719 surse)	260 (115 surse)	1192 (338 surse)	995 (19 surse)	16972 aparitii (2270 surse)
Unicredit	3226 (279 surse)	383 (180 surse)	438 (173 surse)	49 (29 surse)	168 (89 surse)	46 (7 surse)	4310 aparitii (757 surse)
Banca Transilvania	3927 (336 surse)	806 (375 surse)	1931 (490 surse)	174 (77 surse)	961 (247 surse)	708 (20 surse)	8507 aparitii (1545 surse)
CEC Bank	4859 (453 surse)	776 (476 surse)	534 (251 surse)	216 (82 surse)	808 (191 surse)	312 (17 surse)	7505 aparitii (1470 surse)
ING	4127 (315 surse)	678 (375 surse)	1454 (674 surse)	133 (80 surse)	549 (213 surse)	412 (52 surse)	7353 aparitii (1609 surse)
Raiffeisen	3883 (364 surse)	756 (349 surse)	508 (317 surse)	109 (34 surse)	549 (190 surse)	194 (31 surse)	6115 aparitii (1245 surse)
BRD	5542 (414 surse)	641 (363 surse)	1118 (184 surse)	122 (58 surse)	359 (16 surse)	194 (31 surse)	8264 aparitii (1413 surse)
Alpha Bank	2225 (224 surse)	147 (71 surse)	231 (92 surse)	11 (7 surse)	90 (46 surse)	41 (1 surse)	2745 aparitii (445 surse)
Bancpost	1577 (227 surse)	138 (88 surse)	246 (105 surse)	28 (21 surse)	182 (40 surse)	42 (7 surse)	2213 aparitii (488 surse)
Volksbank	1491 (196 surse)	139 (78 surse)	272 (101 surse)	15 (11 surse)	111 (54 surse)	29 (1 surse)	2057 aparitii (441 surse)
RBS Bank	1423 (197 surse)	138 (70 surse)	264 (115 surse)	16 (9 surse)	101 (43 surse)	57 (8 surse)	1999 aparitii (408 surse)

Theoretical and Methodological Framework

As we have mentioned in the beginning, "organizations exist only in so far as their members create them through discourse" (Mumb & Clair, 1997, p. 181). The ways in which members bring their insights onto organizational discourses constitute "socially constructed knowledges of (some aspect) of reality" (Kress & Van Leeuwen, 2006, p. 24). We will associate this social shaping of organizational reality to two theories: framing theories and the socio-cognitive approach to ideologies.

"Schemata of interpretation" (Goffman, 1974), frames are used by individuals to make sense of information or an occurrence (Goffman, 1974, p. 21), providing "principles for the organization of social reality" (Hertog & McLeod, 2001, p. 140). Considered "cultural structures with central ideas and more peripheral concepts and a set of relations that vary in strength and kind among them" (Hertog & McLeod, 2001, p.141), frames rely on the selection of "some aspects of a perceived reality" which are made "more salient in a communicating text, in such a way *as to promote a particular problem definition, causal interpretation, moral evaluation, and/or treatment recommendation* for the item described" (emphasis by R.M. Entman, 1993, p. 52). Unlike agenda-setting theories which focus on the impact of mass media content on the public agenda, framing theories also highlight the role that other social actors except mass media play in the selection and organization of the social reality according to their interests and/ or to others' benefits. In the promoting process that framing implies, the social actors use different verbal and non-verbal discursive devices which, in the end, will shape some meaningful clusters which impose strong relations among central concepts and some other peripheral concepts (Hertog & McLeod, 2001, p. 140).

Starting from the five framing devices (catchphrases, depictions, metaphors, exemplars, visual images) of Gamson and Lasch (1983) and developed by Zoch et al. (2008), we will develop a framework that implies a twofold analysis:

On the one hand, a content analysis of the non-formal CSR 2.0 school (*Money School*). It implies the identification of two topics (participants/ social actors and activities/ social practices) related to non-formal Web 2.0 education which are framed through:

1. **Verbal Framing Devices:**
   a. **Catchphrases:** A single theme statement, tag-line, title or slogan that is intended to suggest a general frame;
   b. **Depictions:** General description (any use of sensory language to create an impression about an idea), testimony (the claims or words of a third party in the description) and statistics (use of numbers that might describe or visualize an idea better).
2. **Visual Framing Devices:**
   a. **Iconic Images:** Images based on an analogy relation with referents from reality;
   b. **Indexical Images:** Images based on a correlation relation (an object serving as a pointer for another object);
   c. **Symbolic Images:** Images based on a conventional relation specific to a community.

On the other hand, a qualitative analysis of the two topics (participants and activities) related to non-formal CSR 2.0 school. We will use Teun A. van Dijk's integrated socio-cognitive analysis of ideologies (2000) based on a triangle (cognition, society and discourse). The novelty of this approach lies on the inclusion of the social practices of a particular group or community within the study of ideologies. This integrated socio-cognitive analysis will focus on four categories which supply the structure of ideologies (Van Dijk, 2000, p. 69): membership, activities, goals, position (group-relations). In our analysis we will adapt these categories to the CSR 2.0 school and we will use two types of groupings:

- **(1) Membership & (2) Position (Group-Relations):** School participants' identity defined through origin, appearance, belonging and their social position and networking;
- **(3) Activities & (4) Goals:** The virtual activities performed by the school participants, their final outcomes.

This framework will be used in order to answer the following research questions:

RQ1: To what extent did *Money School* inform, try to engage with, to mobilize and to provide an interactive experience for *Money School* participants?

RQ2: What types of virtual participants were involved in the non-formal education CSR 2.0 campaign (*Money School*)?

RQ3: What types of virtual activities were *Money School* participants involved into?

RQ4: Which are the most salient devices used for framing *Money School* participants and activities?

Money School: Web 2.0 Features

When presenting the CSR 2.0 campaign, *Money School*, for the Golden Award for Excellence at the Romanian PR Award, the representatives of the Romanian Commercial Bank and Rogalski&Grigoriu Agency said that *Money School* was created "as a peer competition and as an online community where people have the possibility of learning from the most trustworthy sources, namely people like them" (http://www.praward.ro/pr-award/editia-2010/rogalski-grigoriu-pr-bcr-scoala-de-bani.html). Releasing a new exchange currency ("Paraleu" – money saved to buy dreams) and celebrating the first "National Day without unnecessary expenses", BCR made people aware of their power to control their own financial wellness.

Since *Money School* won the IPRA trophy for the best campaign for social media (June 2010), the first research question (RQ1) focuses on the Web 2.0 items belonging to three practices: informing, involving & mobilizing, and interactivity.

Starting from Darren G. Lilleker et al.'s conceptual framework (2011) on Web 2.0 features and practices, we will provide a content analysis of *Money School* (Table 5). Each Web 2.0 item that is present for one of the four practices will be assigned the score "1" and each item that is absent will be assigned the score "0".

Even if *information* is specific to one-way content driven websites (Lilleker et al., 2001, p. 5), it can be embedded in social media practices through the Web 2.0 practice of weblogs which provide a high degree of self-presentation/ self-disclosure and a low degree of media richness/ social presence (see Table 2). Using weblogs as social media applications for CSR 2.0 campaigns, organizations have the possibility of integrating image-driven content with performance-driven content by creating what Wayne Visser (2010) labels as a social enterprise where web visitors can contribute through comments. This is actually the first step towards *interactivity*, the second Web 2.0 practice, which "encourages the visitor to interact both with the host, but also with other visitors" (Lilleker et al., 2001, p. 6). This flow of information in multiple directions is based on sharing experiences and it is embedded in Web 2.0 items, such as wiki, discussion forums, collaborative program, SNS, video/ photo comment facility etc. Taking into account Kaplan and Haenlein's classification of social media applications (see Table 2), we may say that interactivity lies on Web 2.0 items ranging from a high degree of self-presentation (comment facilities) to a low degree of self-presentation (collaborative projects).

Even if *interactivity* and *engagement* are intertwined (Lilleker et al., 2001, p. 6), engagement is linked to the notion of stickiness accomplished through Web 2.0 items, such as click-thrus,

sharing, audiovisuals and interactive games etc. *Mobilizing* focuses on generating resources (joining a competition, donating money for charity, registering as a supporter/ participant) from those already aware of the respective organization.

The content analysis of the *Money School* platform (Table 5) shows the following prominence of the Web 2.0 practices: *informing* (100%), *interactivity* (78.57%), *involving & mobilizing* (16.66%).

Since the message ("Înveți și câștigi!"/ "Learn and win!") of the *Money School* campaign was that each of us is responsible for the wellness of his/ her own family, saving money can be learned either from books, from those who are good at or from common people. *Money School* had the structure and content of a real school in the online environment (Figure 3): courses, exams, students, class mates, teachers and a class-master. Thus informing and interactivity are the most salient Web 2.0 practices.

The *Money School* platform had a twofold manner of providing information:

- On the one hand, through Web 1.0 non-interactive features of two course texts: "Guide of conversation between money and one's pocket" and "Guide of raising money".
- On the other hand, through Web 2.0 interactive features of 11 weblogs and one Youtube video.

One week (October, 8, 2009) before the beginning of the *Money School* campaign, the Youtube video ("How to get broke in ten steps") had a teasing effect by raising a real problem (getting broke) which each of us can get confronted with. Without providing the name of the bank which was behind this CSR 2.0 campaign, the Youtube video ended with the launching of a new currency (para-leu) considered to be the most valuable one since the money stays in the pocket. At the same time, those who registered for the courses were

Table 5. Money School: Web 2.0. items and practices

Practices	Web 2.0 items	Present (1) Absent (0)	Total
Informing	weblog	1	100%
	Youtube video	1	
Involving & Mobilizing	news rating facility	0	16.66%
	video TV Spots	0	
	videos of conferences	0	
	videos of appearances	0	
	videos of home/private	0	
	video rating facility	0	
	webcam feed	0	
	photo rating facility	0	
	games	1	
	competition	1	
	prioritise/rank function	0	
	personal events calendar	0	
Interactivity	blog comment facility	1	78.57%
	wiki	0	
	collaborative programme	1	
	collaborative organization history	0	
	collaborative features	1	
	links to SNS	1	
	promote via SNS	1	
	social bookmarking	0	
	chat facility with others	1	
	forum	1	
	video comment facility	1	
	video sharing channel	1	
	photo comment facility	1	
	product sharing market	1	

promised the first seats in the virtual classroom. The registering period coincided with a competition between bloggers, the *Money School* endorsers, who provided the most intelligent financial mechanism of solving a problem given by the class-master.

Besides the competition between bloggers, there were some other Web 2.0 items of mobiliz-ing the web visitors: a competition (the Pocket of Year 2010) and four lab applications (The Day with Unnecessary Expenses, Banking Scanner, Calculator Budget, Personal Inflation).

The comparison (Table 6) between the proposed objectives and the results of the campaign shows that the *Money School* Web 2.0 practices had the desired impact.

Figure 3. Money School platform (http://www.scoaladebani.ro/)

Money School: Virtual Participants and Activities

Unlike informal learning which occurs in places within our day-to-day routine, non-formal learning is intentional, has a structured form and occurs in institutional places. The *Money School* platform is such an organized environment, the Web 2.0 items providing a virtual setting where non-formal educators carry out financial activities with their learners.

The ideological domain of *Money School* is a site of generating knowledge which we will approach taking into account the categories of membership and group-relations (RQ2) and the categories of activities (RQ3).

Money School follows the prototypical structure of a real school where there is an apparent opposition between pupils (US) and teachers (THEM) due to one main "up-bottom" activity, namely teaching two main courses (How to spend money – "Guide of conversation between money and one's pocket" and How to invest money – "Guide of raising money"). Beyond this "up-bottom" participation, the *Money School* Web 2.0 items also provide a "bottom-up" participation

("The Open Lesson") where learners become the new possible educators for other learners.

The *Money School* participants are formed of two prototypical groups:

1. **Pupils:** Two-member teams;
2. **Teachers:** Class-master, bloggers, financial newspaper representatives (The Financial Newspaper, The Financial Week)

In order to show the participants' position within the *Money School* campaign, we will use Stephen Chen's social network analysis (2009, pp. 525-532). Starting from Fulk and Boyd's relational and structural properties of social networks, Stephen Chen provides a relationship between network properties and corporate responsibilities.

The *Money School* virtual participants can be grouped in a central small worlds network (Figure 4) where the central node is the class-master who together with The Financial Newspaper and the Financial Week forms the main small world of providing knowledge. The class-master's role is that of presiding the two courses and of coordinating the exams. Around this central small world there are 11 peripheral small worlds whose main node is a blogger.

Table 6. Money School: Objectives and results

		Money School proposed objectives	Money School evaluation results
Audience	unique *Money School* platform visitors during the six-week campaign	150,000	300,074
	Youtube views	-	9,696
	Facebook friends	-	1,453
	Twitter	-	50 twits 139 followers
Involving	Persons/ teams registering on the platform	10,000 persons / 5,000 teams	17, 422 persons / 8, 711 teams
	Participants claiming to have become more financially responsible due to *Money School*	30%	85%
	Participants considering *Money School* a useful platform	50%	84%

The 11 most known Romanian bloggers[7] had a double role which highlighted the interactivity practice. They were the heads of their classrooms and tuition providers. The future students had to vote the most intelligent solution provided by bloggers to the class-master's problem and the bloggers' debate on the issue of the social entrepreneur. For three weeks, the 11 bloggers created their own *Fan School* by providing tuition lessons on their blogs and explaining to his/ her mates the financial problems given by the *Money School* class-master. At the end of the *Money School* campaign, a top of the most influential *Money School* bloggers (Figure 5) was accomplished. As it can be observed, the most influential bloggers are not necessarily the most popular bloggers: Zozo has the greatest number of fans (504) but ranks on the 4th position of the most influential bloggers (final grade – 4.88), whereas Miruna has 76 fans but she is the first influential blogger (final grade – 9.82).

- **Blue Color:** The grade obtained by the bloggers' fans (according to their number, their presence during classes and their test results);
- **Red Color:** The grade obtained by the blogger to the financial and social problem;
- **Green Color:** The final grade.

Another important aspect of these peripheral small worlds should also be highlighted: each participant forming this cluster whose central node is a blogger has the structural property of a two-member subgroup, most of the time belonging to the same family. As it was shown in Table 6, 8, 711 subgroups registered as participants and 80% of them were between 20-40 years old. This transaction of information onto the subgroups/ teams emphasizes a direct responsibility of the Romanian Commercial Bank regarding the stirring of young families' and young persons' awareness in what their financial wellness is concerned.

The knowledge generated on the *Money School* platform focused on six main activities which highlight the concept of edutainment (empowerment + entertainment) specific to non-formal education. The six activities will be grouped as follows:

- **Macro-Activities:** Carried out by generic participants: teaching courses.
- **Micro-Activities:** Carried out by individual participants: taking part in lab applications, competing, writing for the school journal, taking part in the open lessons and placing products on the virtual market.

Figure 4. Money School: Central small worlds network

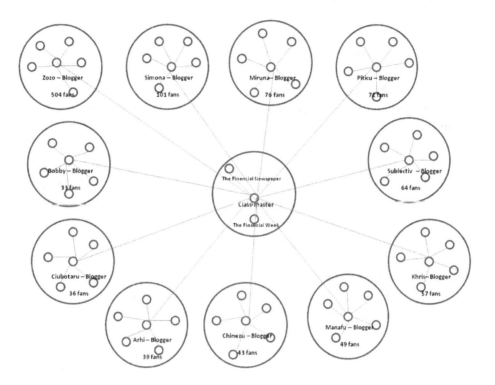

As it can be observed, micro-activities are more salient and this is obvious since the Web 2.0 items provide a "bottom-up" participation where the individual matters. When registering for the *Money School*, each team had to choose a name, as a means of visibility. For example, the first three winners of "The Pocket of the Year 2010" were Arc 178, Brokerii (Brokers) and Kubeti.

The macro-activity of teaching courses was performed by virtual teachers (The Financial Newspaper and The Financial Week) who provided a transaction content based on information regarding:

Figure 5. Money School – the most influential bloggers (http://www.scoaladebani.ro/)

- **Five Ways of Spending Money:** Monthly family budget, efficient means of using a bank, the costs of a credit, card administration, expenses administration using the current account;
- **Six Ways of Saving Money:** Wise saving, loaning through saving, life insurances, investment funds, personal investments).

The bloggers and the class-master as central nodes provided a transaction content based on information and influence which implies power (the class-master giving grades), advice (the bloggers as tuition providers) and prestige (bloggers as endorsers and opinion makers).

Writing for the school journal, taking part in the open lessons and placing products on the virtual market are three *Money School* micro-activities which focused on a "bottom-up" participation. Whereas the micro-activity of writing for the school journal generated 17 articles written by different endorsers from the field of communication, psychology, and sociology, the other two micro-activities had the team members as main content generators. *Money School* created 40 open lessons and classes on different topics (buying a house, investment rules, life insurances, etc.) and the participation focused on questions and answers.

The micro-activity of placing one's products on the virtual market focused on three main areas: demands, offers, and donations. The most salient activity was selling one's products. Out of the 24 products, the most advertised products on sale were jewelry and IT objects.

Money School: Verbal and Visual Framing Devices

The quantitative analysis of the *Money School* platform has a twofold aim: on the one hand, to highlight the way in which verbal and visual framing devices are used; on the other hand, to compare the way in which the *Money School* participants

and activities are represented through different verbal and visual framing devices.

In order to determine inter-coder reliability (Kappa), two coders coded the *Money School* platform and the coefficient of agreement was computed to 0.88, considered to be acceptable by researchers. The coding focused on two topics (Table 7):

- **Three Types of Participants:** Class-master, bloggers/ endorsers, students;
- **Six Types of Activities:** (a) teaching courses, (b) taking part in lab applications, (c) competing, (d) writing for the school journal, (f) taking part in the open lessons, (g) placing products on the virtual market.

We will discuss the findings in terms of the frequency of framing devices and in terms of the prominence in framing device use.

Frequency of Framing Devices

As it can be observed in Table 7, *visual framing devices* were more salient (96.67%) than *verbal framing devices* (3.33%). This salience of visual devices is due to the visual framing of *Money School* students (N=17,020).

Iconic images was the most commonly used framing device on the *Money School* platform, focusing on the analogical quality of the images. There were used two types of iconic images: (1) students' avatar images and (2) comic strips of all *Money School* participants. This overwhelming dominance of iconic images emphasizes two important aspects of Web 2.0 non-formal education:

- The intentionality feature of non-formal education is made visible through avatar images that each participant registering as a *Money School* student can create by himself/ herself;
- Involving and interactivity, two major Web 2.0 practices, are achieved due to the visual framing of each student.

Table 7. Verbal and visual framings of Money School participants and activities

		Money School **participants**			*Money School* **activities**						**Total**
		Class-master	**Bloggers**	**Students**	**(a)**	**(b)**	**(c)**	**(d)**	**(e)**	**(f)**	
Verbal framing devices	Catchphrases	2	0	0	14	4	0	0	0	0	20
	General descriptions	0	1	0	374	4	14	54	65	24	527
	Testimony	0	0	0	8	0	0	17	0	0	25
	Statistics	0	1	0	6	0	13	0	0	0	20
TOTAL1 **Verbal framing devices**		**2**	**2**	**0**	**402**	**8**	**27**	**71**	**65**	**24**	**592** **(3.33%)**
Visual framing devices	Iconic images	4	22	17,033	45	4	6	1	1	19	17,148
	Indexical images	0	0	0	3		4	0	0	0	4
	Symbolic images	0	0	0	7	3	0	0	0	0	10
TOTAL2 **Visual framing devices**		**4**	**22**	**17,033**	**55**	**7**	**10**	**1**	**1**	**19**	**17,165** **(96.67%)**
TOTAL 1 + TOTAL 2		**6**	**24**	**17,033**	**457**	**15**	**37**	**72**	**66**	**43**	**17,757**

General description was the second most frequently used device. If the students' iconic images were to be ignored, general descriptions (N=527 instances) were to be placed as the most commonly used device. This salience is closely linked to the non-formal learning that *Money School* focuses on. The two courses ("Guide of conversation between money and one's pocket" and "Guide of raising money") had 114 pages of information on financial responsibility.

Testimony is the third framing device (N=25 instances), focusing on (1) the experts on financial education (the Financial Newspaper, The Financial Week representatives as teachers) and on (2) the specialists in different fields (communication, psychology, sociology) writing articles for the *Money School* journal.

Catchphrases and *statistics* were the fourth most commonly used devices (N=20 instances). The framing device of statistics becomes a compulsory content item during *Money School* classes and exams since the students were taught how to make their own balance sheets of income and expenses. This device was used to stir the students' awareness on the important role that

family members can play in saving and investing money. The non-formal feature of the financial education provided by *Money School* has been verbally achieved through catchphrases (logo – "Înveţi şi câştigi!"/ "Learn and win!"; intertextual elements – reinterpretations of proverbs – "Bani albi pentru zile negre"/ "White money for a rainy day"/ "Save money for a rainy day"→ "Bani albi pentru zile albe"/ "White money for a sunny day").

Prominence in Framing Device Use

Iconic images were the most commonly devices used in framing the *Money School* participants, the students being the most visible virtual participants (N=17,033 instances). As we have mentioned above, comic strips were a visual characteristic of *Money School*. Comic strips function as iconic images with a twofold role:

- To stir the mental image of referents from reality;
- To provide a familiar and game-like setting which may stir some humorous memories from childhood.

The dressing code, the position and the gestures of the class-master and of the prototypical student (Figure 6) help the web visitor identify the setting of a real school. Facebook provides information about the *Money School* class-master: male, lives in Bucharest, Romania, born in 1976, and married. This Facebook profile information actually coincides with the profile of the target-public that this CSR 2.0 campaign addresses: young families (20-40 years old).

Considered "a form of play, comprising a social context, a cognitive process and an emotional response expressed through laughter" (Martin, 2007, p. 83), humor is verbally and visually framed on the *Money School* platform through catchphrases, iconic images and symbolic images. All these three framing devices are based on a self-enhancing humor that is considered a relatively healthy and adaptive type of humor (Martin, 2007, p. 211). This embodiment of humor mainly relies on intertextuality (reinterpretations of proverbs or well-known statements and pictorial metaphors).

Despite the fact that *general description* is the most commonly used device in framing teaching, this *Money School* activity is also framed through *catchphrases* (N=14) and *symbolic images* (N=7) which may function as triggers of students' attention. Most of the course texts embedded:

- **Verbal Intertextual Elements:** "Banii, oricât de puţini, aduc fericirea"/ "Little money brings happiness" (the reinterpretation of "Money doesn't bring happiness").
- **Visual Intertextual Elements:** Hyperboles and pictorial metaphors (Figure 7). Whereas hyperboles function as enhancing the qualities of a participant (the ant rolling a coin), pictorial metaphors (Forceville, 1996) provide a humorous visual composition of elements belonging to different conceptual fields (the human face being formed of eyes and cheeks and a mouth replaced by a wallet stacked with credit cards and bills).

The prominence in framing the activity of teaching (N=457 devices) is to be explained by the educational feature of this CSR 2.0 campaign. The second and the third most prominent *Money School* activities are also related to the learning process: writing for the school journal (N=72 devices) and taking part in the open lessons (N=66 devices). The game-like feature specific to the non-formal part of *Money School* is rendered through three activities (placing products on the virtual market – N=43 devices; competing – N=37 devices; taking part in lab applications – N=15 devices) mainly framed through *general descriptions* and *iconic images*.

Figure 6. The visual framing of the Money School student and class-master (http://www.scoaladebani.ro/)

Figure 7. Money School: Visual intertextual elements (http://www.scoaladebani.ro/)

CONCLUSION

CSR educational campaigns constitute means through which organizations can involve in the community by improving people's life and by stirring stakeholders' awareness towards an issue. Web 2.0 technologies have provided new ways of learning, sharing and collaborative knowledge construction where stakeholders turn from mere target-public into co-creators of meaning. Thus CSR 2.0 constitutes the perfect opportunity for organizations to create a virtual social reality where non-formal education through the empowerment and the entertainment of stakeholders seems to prevail. This involvement in the non-formal education of stakeholders through CSR 2.0 campaigns turns organizations into "social performers" (mckinney, 2005, p. 27).

The analysis of the non-formal financial education campaign, *Money School*, framed through CSR 2.0 practices showed that:

- Non-formal learning is based on multimodality, a blending between the medium of the book (the virtual activity of teaching) and the medium of the screen (the virtual activities of competing, of placing one's products on a virtual market);

- Non-formal learning implies cognitive aspects (gaining knowledge as a result of continuous virtual visits on the CSR 2.0 platform) and affective aspects (enjoyable virtual applications, competitions);

- Non-formal learning is verbally and visually framed through two main devices (general descriptions and iconic images) which highlight the cognitive aspect of CSR 2.0 campaigns and the analogy relation with participants from the real world;

- Non-formal education CSR 2.0 campaigns focus on a prominence of performance-driven intentions, of integrated Web 2.0 items and practices, and of social networks. The great number of participants in the virtual *Money School* classroom proves that this CSR 2.0 platform provided learners and educators a feeling of belongingness to an educational community.

REFERENCES

An, S.-K., & Gower, K. K. (2009). How do the news media frame crises? A content analysis of crisis news coverage. *Public Relations Review, 35*(2), 107–112. doi:10.1016/j.pubrev.2009.01.010

Arvidsson, A. (2005). Brands – A critical perspective. *Journal of Consumer Culture, 5*(2), 235–258. doi:10.1177/1469540505053093

Baudrillard, J. (2007). *In the shadow of the silent majority*. Cambridge, MA: MIT Press.

Bittner, E., & Leimeister, J. M. (2011). *Towards CSR 2.0 – Potentials and challenges of Web 2.0 for corporate social responsibility communication*. Paper presented at the annual meeting of the European Academy of Management (EURAM)

Bowen, S. A., & Rawlings, B. L. (2005). What is a conscience? In Heath, R. L. (Ed.), *Encyclopedia of public relations* (pp. 205–210). Thousand Oaks, CA: Sage Publications.

Capriotti, P., & Moreno, A. (2007). Corporate citizenship and public relations: The importance and interactivity of social responsibility issues on corporate websites. *Public Relations Review, 33*(1), 84–91. doi:10.1016/j.pubrev.2006.11.012

Chen, S. (2009). Corporate responsibilities in internet-enabled social networks. *Journal of Business Ethics, 90*(4), 523–536. doi:10.1007/s10551-010-0604-0

Cmeciu, C., & Cmeciu, D. (2011). New insights into corporate social responsibility: The semiotic act of experiencing a city through street naming. In Wasik, Z. (Ed.), *Unfolding the semiotic Web in urban discourse* (pp. 163–180). Frankfurt am Main, Germany: Peter Lang.

Colley, H., Hodkinson, P., & Malcom, J. (2002). *Non-formal learning: mapping the conceptual terrain*. A Consultation Report. Retrieved December 20, 2012, from http://www.infed.org/archives/e-texts/colley_informal_learning.htm

Cornellisen, J. (2005). *Corporate communications: Theory and practice* (2nd ed.). London, UK: Sage Publications.

Dahlsrud, A. (2008). How corporate social responsibility is defined: an analysis of 37 definitions. *Corporate Social Responsibility and Environmental Management, 15*(1), 1–13. doi:10.1002/csr.132

Dimitrova, D. (2007). New media technologies. In L. L. Kaid & C. Holtz-Bacha (Eds.), *Encyclopedia of political communication*. London, UK: Sage Publications. Retrieved March 16, 2009, from www.sage-ereference.com/politicalcommunication/Article_n434.html

Dohn, N. B. (2009). Web 2.0: Inherent tensions and evident challenges for education. *Computer-Supported Collaborative Learning, 4*(4), 343–363. doi:10.1007/s11412-009-9066-8

Dozier, D. M., Grunig, L. A., & Grunig, J. E. (2001). Public relations as communication campaign. In Rice, R. E., & Atkin, C. K. (Eds.), *Public communication campaigns* (3rd ed., pp. 231–248). Thousand Oaks, CA: Sage Publications.

Entman, R. M. (1993). Framing: Toward clarification of a fractured paradigm. *The Journal of Communication, 43*(4), 51–58. doi:10.1111/j.1460-2466.1993.tb01304.x

Eshach, H. (2007). Bridging in-school and out-of-school learning: formal, non-formal, and informal education. *Journal of Science Education and Technology, 16*(2), 171–190. doi:10.1007/s10956-006-9027-1

Fairclough, N. (2005). Peripheral vision: Discourse analysis in organization studies: The case for critical realism. *Organization Studies, 26*(6), 915–939. doi:10.1177/0170840605054610

Forceville, C. (1996). *Pictorial metaphor in advertising*. London, UK: Routledge. doi:10.4324/9780203272305

Foucault, M. (1977). *Discipline and punish: The birth of the prison*. New York, NY: Pantheon Books.

Foucault, M. (1984). The order of discourse. In Shapiro, M. J. (Ed.), *Language and politics* (pp. 108–138). Oxford, UK: Blackwell.

Freberg, K., Grahamb, K., McGaughey, K., & Frebergc, L. A. (2011). Who are the social media influencers? A study of public perceptions of personality. *Public Relations Review, 37*(1), 90–92. doi:10.1016/j.pubrev.2010.11.001

Gamson, W., & Lasch, K. E. (1983). The political culture of social welfare policy. In Spiro, S. E., & Yuchtman-Yaar, E. (Eds.), *Evaluating the welfare state: Social and political perspectives* (pp. 397–415). New York, NY: Academic.

Garrison, D. R., & Anderson, T. (2003). *E-Learning in the 21st century: A framework for research and practice*. London, UK: Routledge. doi:10.4324/9780203166093

Garsten, C., & Lindh de Montoya, M. (2008). In retrospect: the play of shadows. In Garsten, C., & Lindh de Montoya, M. (Eds.), *Transparency in a new global order: Unveiling organizational visions* (pp. 283–289). Cheltenham, UK: Edward Elgar.

Goffman, E. (1974). *Frame analysis: An essay on the organization of experience*. Cambridge, MA: Harvard University Press.

Goldberg, G. (2011). Rethinking the public/virtual sphere: The problem with participation. *New Media & Society, 13*(5), 739–754. doi:10.1177/1461444810379862

Golob, U., & Bartlett, J. L. (2007). Communicating about corporate social responsibility: A comparative study of CSR reporting in Australia and Slovenia. *Public Relations Review, 33*(1), 1–9. doi:10.1016/j.pubrev.2006.11.001

Grant, D., Hardy, C., Oswick, C., & Putman, L. (2004). Introduction: Organizational discourse: Exploring the field. In Grant, D., Hardy, C., Oswick, C., & Putman, L. (Eds.), *The Sage handbook of organizational discourse* (pp. 1–37). New York, NY: Sage. doi:10.4135/9781848608122.n1

Grunig, J. E., & Hunt, T. (1984). *Managing public relations*. New York, NY: Holt, Rinehart & Winston.

Grunig, J. E., & Repper, F. C. (1992). Strategic management, publics, and issues. In Grunig, J. E. (Eds.), *Excellence in public relations and communication management* (pp. 117–158). Hillsdale, NJ: Lawrence Erlbaum.

Grunig, J. E., & White, J. (1992). The effect of worldviews on public relations. Theory and practice. In Grunig, J. E. (Eds.), *Excellence in public relations and communication management* (pp. 31–64). Hillsdale, NJ: Lawrence Erlbaum.

Hertog, J. K., & McLeod, D. M. (2001). A multi-perspectival approach to framing analysis: A field guide. In Reese, S. D., Gandy, O. H., & Grant, A. E. (Eds.), *Framing public life: Perspective on media and our understanding of the social world* (pp. 139–162). Mahwah, NJ: Lawrence Erlbaum Associates.

Huang, Y.-H., & Su, S.-H. (2009). Determinants of consistent, timely, and active responses in corporate crises. *Public Relations Review, 35*(1), 7–17. doi:10.1016/j.pubrev.2008.09.020

Iedema, R., & Wodak, R. (1999). Introduction: Organizational discourses and practices. *Discourse & Society, 10*(1), 5–19. doi:10.1177/0957926599010001001

Inkeles, A. (1983). *Exploring individual modernity*. New York, NY: Columbia University Press.

Jewitt, C. (2008). Multimodality and literacy in school classrooms. *Review of Research in Education, 32*(1), 241–267. doi:10.3102/0091732X07310586

Kaplan, A. M., & Haenlein, M. (2010). Users of the world, unite! The challenge and opportunities of social media. *Business Horizons, 53*(1), 59–68. doi:10.1016/j.bushor.2009.09.003

Kim, S., & Lee, Y.-J. (2012). The complex attribution process of CSR motives. *Public Relations Review, 38*(1), 168–170. doi:10.1016/j.pubrev.2011.09.024

Kindervatter, S. (1979). *Nonformal education as an empowering process*. Amherst, MA: Center for International Education.

Kress, G. (2003). *Literacy in the new media age*. London, UK: Routledge. doi:10.4324/9780203164754

Kress, G., & van Leeuwen, Th. (2006). *Reading images. The grammar of visual design*. London, UK: Routledge. doi:10.1016/S8755-4615(01)00042-1

Kress, G., & Van Leeuwen, T. (2010). *Multimodal discourse. The modes and media of contemporary communication* (2nd ed.). London, UK: Bloomsbury Academic.

Lester, R. K. (2005). *Universities, innovation, and the competitiveness of local economies: Summary report from the local innovation project*. Retrieved March 20, 2010, from http://ekstranett.innovasjonnorge.no/Arena_fs/Local%20nnovation%20Project_MIT.pdf

Lilleker, D. G., Michalska, K. K., Schweitzer, E., Jacunski, M., Jackson, N., & Vedel, T. (2011). Informing, engaging, mobilising or interacting: Searching for a European model of web campaigning. *European Journal of Communication, 26*(3), 195–213. doi:10.1177/0267323111416182

Luke, C. (2003). Pedagogy, connectivity, multimodality, and interdisciplinarity. *Reading Research Quarterly, 38*(3), 397–403.

Martin, R. A. (2006). *The psychology of humor: An integrative approach*. Burlington, MA: Elsevier Academic Press.

McKinney, D. E. (2005). Annual community reports. In Heath, R. L. (Ed.), *Encyclopedia of public relations* (*Vol. 2*, pp. 27–28). Thousand Oaks, CA: Sage Publications.

McLuhan, M. (1964). *Understanding media: The extensions of man*. London, UK: Routledge & Kegan Paul.

Moulton, J. (2007). *Formal and nonformal education and empowered behavior: A review of the research literature. Prepared for the support and analysis in Africa (SARA) project, USAID*. Washington, DC: Academy for Educational Development, manuscript.

Mumby, D. K., & Clair, R. P. (1997). Organizational discourse. In van Dijk, T. A. (Ed.), *Discourse as social interaction (Discourse studies: A multidisciplinary introduction)* (*Vol. 2*, pp. 181–205). London, UK: Sage Publications.

O'Reilly, T. (2005). *What is Web 2.0? Design patterns and business models for the next generation of software*. Retrieved September 2, 2011, from http://www.oreillynet.com/ lpt/a/6228

Oldfather, P., West, J., White, J., & Wilmarth, J. (1999). *Learning through children's eyes: Social constructivism and the desire to learn*. Washington, DC: American Psychological Association. doi:10.1037/10328-000

Oprea, L. (2005). *Responsabilitate socială corporatistă*. Bucureşti, Romania: Tritonic.

Paisley, W. J. (2001). Public communication campaign: The American experience. In Rice, R. E., & Atkin, C. K. (Eds.), *Public communication campaigns* (3rd ed., pp. 3–21). Thousand Oaks, CA: Sage Publications.

Pătruț, M., & Cmeciu, C. (2011). Blogs–A means of consolidating the National Liberal Party identity. In G. Drulă, L. Roşca, & R. Boicu (Eds.), *The Role of New Media in Journalism: International Conference, NM-JUR-2011* (pp. 23-40). Bucureşti, Romania: Editura Universităţii din Bucureşti.

Rawlins, B. L. (2005). Corporate social responsibility. In Heath, R. L. (Ed.), *Encyclopedia of public relations* (pp. 210–214). Thousand Oaks, CA: Sage Publications.

Rennie, L. J., & McClafferty, T. P. (1996). Science centres and science learning. *Studies in Science Education, 27*(1), 53–98. doi:10.1080/03057269608560078

Tallinn, Estonia. boyd, d. m., & Ellison, N. B. (2007). Social network sites: Definitions, history, and scholarship. *Journal of Computer-Mediated Communication, 13*(1), 210–230.

Udrea, C., & Ionescu, A.-C. (2007). *CSR and competitiveness European SMEs' good practice – National report Romania.*

van Dijk, T. A. (2000). *Ideology – A multidisciplinary approach.* London, UK: Sage.

Visser, W. (2010). The age of responsibility. CSR 2.0 and the new DNA for business. *Journal of Business Systems. Governance and Ethics, 5*(3), 7–22.

Wilcox, D. L. (2009). Preserving reputation in the internet age. In A. Rogojinaru, & S. Wolstenholme (Eds.), *Current trends in international public relations* (pp. 13-27). Bucureşti, Romania: Tritonic.

Zappavigna, M. (2011). Ambient affiliation: A linguistic perspective on Twitter. *New Society and Media, 13*(5), 788–806. doi:10.1177/1461444810385097

Zerfass, A., Verhoeven, P., Tench, R., Moreno, A., & Verčič, D. (2011). *European Communication Monitor 2011: Empirical insights into strategic communication in Europe- Results of an empirical survey in 43 countries (Chart Version).* Brussels, Belgium: EACD, EUPRERA. Retrieved December 10, 2011 from www.communicationmonitor.eu

Zoch, L. M., Collins, E. L., Sisco, H. F., & Supa, D. H. (2008). Empowering the activist: Using framing devices on activist organizations' web sites. *Public Relations Review, 34*(4), 351–358. doi:10.1016/j.pubrev.2008.07.005

ADDITIONAL READING

Herring, S. (2004). Computer-mediated discourse analysis: An approach to researching online behaviour. In Barab, S. A., Kling, R., & Gray, J. H. (Eds.), *Designing for virtual communities in the service of learning* (pp. 338–376). New York, NY: Cambridge University Press. doi:10.1017/CBO9780511805080.016

Kent, M. L. (2008). Critical analysis of blogging in public relations. *Public Relations Review, 34*(1), 32–40. doi:10.1016/j.pubrev.2007.12.001

Thurlow, C., & Mroczek, K. (Eds.). (2011). *Digital discourse: Language in the new media (Oxford studies in sociolinguistics).* USA: Oxford University Press. doi:10.1093/acprof:oso/9780199795437.001.0001

van Dijk, J. (2006). *The network society.* London, UK: Sage.

Zappavigna, M. (2012). *Discourse of Twitter and social media: How we use language to create affiliation on the web.* London, UK: Continuum.

KEY TERMS AND DEFINITIONS

CSR 2.0: Corporate social responsibility (or corporate sustainability and responsibility) achieved through Web 2.0 items and practices which allow 'collective intelligence', 'collaborative networks', 'user participation'.

Edutainment: Education achieved through entertainment elements.

Framing Devices: Verbal and visual mechanisms used in order to represent certain social, cultural, economic, or political issues.

Ideology: The social practices of a particular group or community.

Intertextuality: The embedding of other verbal and visual texts within a new and coherent verbal and visual text.

Multimodality: The use of several affordances of social media applications in order to produce a coherent medium of communication.

Non-Formal Education: Intentional type of education which takes place in unconventional settings.

Organizational Identity: A blending of deep-structure elements (mission, vision) and of surface-structure elements (products, services, campaigns).

ENDNOTES

[1] The ISO guidance norms for CSR activities could be found in "Towards Greater Corporate Responsibility, the Conclusions of the EU-Funded Research", published by the European Commission in 2009. Retrieved December 16, 2009, from http://ec.europa.eu/research/research-eu.

[2] *Corporate Social Responsibility and Safety and Health at Work* (2004). Retrieved September 10, 2010, from http://bookshop.europa.eu/en/corporate-social-responsibility-and-safety-and-health-at-work-pbTE5904120/.

[3] *The Global Social Media and CSR* Report (2011). Retrieved January 5, 2012, from http://www.scribd.com/doc/56921419/The-Global-Social-Media-and-CSR-Report-2011

[4] Retrieved November 20, 2011, from http://ec.europa.eu/education/lifelong-learning-policy/informal_en.htm

[5] *The KPMG International Survey of Corporate Responsibility Reporting* 2011 takes into account two variables (quality of communication, level of process maturity) and divides global CSR activities according to four quadrants: (1) "leading the pack" (France, the Netherlands, UK, Spain etc.); (2) "scratching the surface" (USA, Japan, Brazil, Hungary etc.); (3) "getting it right" (China, South Korea); (4) "starting behind" (Finland, South Africa, Romania etc.). *The KPMG International Survey of Corporate Responsibility Reporting* (2011). Retrieved December 20, 2011, from http://www.kpmg.com/global/en/issuesandinsights/articlespublications/corporate-responsibility/pages/2011-survey.aspx,

[6] Retrieved November 20, 2011, from http://www.wall-street.ro/articol/Finante-Banci/88873/Avertisment-Avem-nevoie-urgenta-de-o-strategie-nationala-privind-educatia-financiara.html

[7] The 11 bloggers who were the *Money School* endorsers: Zoso - www.zoso.ro, Bobby Voicu - www.bobbyvoicu.ro, Simona Tache - www.simonatache.ro, Miruna - www.siblondelegandesc.ro, Chinezu – www.chinezu.eu, Khris - www.businessday.ro, Subiectiv - www.subiectiv.ro, Cristi Manafu - www.manafu.ro, Arhi - www.arhiblog.ro, Piticu - www.piticu.ro and Adrian Ciubotaru - www.adrianciubotaru.ro.

Chapter 7

Social Media Audit and Analytics:
Exercises for Marketing and Public Relations Courses

Ana Adi
Bournemouth University, UK

ABSTRACT

Beyond influencing the ways we communicate and we do business, social media is currently challenging traditional higher education in many respects: from the way in which courses are delivered and students interact with each other and with their lecturers to the content that the courses cover. In particular, the emergence of the social media specialist working in marketing-communications, creative industries or journalism, and their use of ever-changing content management and analytics tools require adaptation of courses to the constant changes in industry. Starting from two case studies of teaching social media auditing and analytics as part of courses taught in Belgium and Bahrain, this chapter aims to present a model exercise for marketing and public relations classrooms covering these topics. The discussion of the challenges of teaching social media audit and analytics emphasizes the need of more and constant collaboration between academia and industry as well as the need to ensure that students have a high level of media literacy before they embark on such a career route.

INTRODUCTION

It is an exciting time for communicators, academics and students. With social media uses going beyond the traditional business and educational fields and with its adoption rates increasing ex-

DOI: 10.4018/978-1-4666-2851-9.ch007

ponentially every year, educators have numerous opportunities to explore how social media change not only how practitioners, companies and publics communicate but also how they teach the discipline.

With calls for public relations professionals for instance to be social media ready (Falls, 2009) and indications that some might be still struggling with the impact of new media (Alfonso and de Valbuena Miguel, 2006; James, 2007), educators may need to review course curricula in light of new media developments and industry responses. After all, revisiting content would only be in line with academia's pledge to prepare students for their professional life and integrate practice in the classroom (Ehling, 1992).

While educators agree that active learning is the best method through which students can put theory into practice, Coombs and Rybacki (1999) suggest that public relations educators are rather slow to utilize new technology in the classroom. This lack of integration of new and social media in the teaching process – from the method of delivery to content – is also perceived by students (Hemmi, Bayne and Land, 2009) who include new technologies and electronic communication in their list with items which they associate with their weakest feeling of preparation. The same list includes, among others, understanding technology, setting performance criteria and design and layout.

Drawing on reflective practice and several case studies of implementing social media audit exercises as part of undergraduate courses, this chapter aims to fill the new media skills gap perceived by students as lacking in their preparation and deemed necessary by practitioners. In doing so, the chapter presents several models for social media audit exercises and how they have been used in different educational contexts. Although the primary focus of the exercise is on B2C the principles can easily apply to a B2B context. While the chapter examines the importance of evaluating current media activities from a strategic perspective, discusses the link between strategy, goals and objectives and how they reflect into a company's social media communication, its aim is to present a model exercise in its evolution and discuss its potential use in the classroom rather than evaluate its impact on teaching, learning and practice, the author considering it is to soon to see any effects on either areas.

DEFINING SOCIAL MEDIA, AUDITS, AND ANALYTICS

Social media is one of the newest concepts associated with new and emerging technologies and one of the fastest growing areas within the new media landscape. In her review of the impact of new media on public relations, Melanie James (2007) emphasizes that definitions related to new media remain fluid and continue to evolve, their key features including portability of data and mobility in communications. Like new media definitions, social media definitions are fluid as well. Heidi Cohen's (2011) collection of 30 definitions of social media offered by a group of social media, marketing and PR professionals and Econsultancy's (2009), a community for digital marketers, equally impressive list of 34 definitions are both good examples. While some definitions focus on platforms, formats, tools and specificities of the digital content production process, others provide reflections about social media as channels for communication and interaction between organizations and target audiences.

However different, most of the definitions recognize that communication through social media is in real-time and users generate the content that can be posted, transported, linked or aggregated from a platform to another. Among the platforms mentioned most often are Facebook, the social networking site with more than 640 million registered users, Twitter, the micro-blogging platform with more than 200 million registered users (Uehara Henrikson, 2011) and YouTube, the multi-media sharing site owned by Google where more than 48 hours of video are uploaded every minute (Bal, 2011).

Other characteristics of social media include a requirement for transparency, a potential for engagement and dialogue - either one-to-one, one-to-many or many-to-many -, a customer-centered approach and when used for marketing and communication purposes a need for strategy and coordination. The strategy however requires constant evaluation and analysis both of an organization's goals and objectives and but also of their implementation. Whether called a situational plan, research into past and current activities, background or audit, the evaluation and analysis of goals and objectives plays an important part within the communication/marketing plan as it helps map out the current strategy and compare it with what has been accomplished or how effectively it has been (WWF, n.d.). A social media audit therefore plays the same function. It assesses an organization's use of social media and compares it with an established set of goals and objectives.

As Gattiker (2011a) puts it a social media audit is "a formalized view of an organization's social media activities" that is undertaken in order to express an "opinion on the organization under annual assessment based on work done on a test basis". The audit should also be used to help benchmark a company's social media efforts and thus help them establish tactics to improve and metrics to assess future performance. Depending on the platform used and the goals and objectives to be evaluated, various tools can be used to measure, collect, analyze and report data. They are also referred to as analytics.

COMMUNICATION AND NEW MEDIA EDUCATION

There are currently many groups that explore how new technologies and social media are or can be integrated in the educational process. For instance, the Social Media Global Education Connection Project (SMGECP) provides "leadership, guidance, facilitation and resources to students, educators, and administrators in educational organizations who will promote and enable competent usage of social media by the world's citizens, workforces, educational institutions, and societies" (Eberhart, 2011). Edudemic, a group run by graduate students and teachers, seek to find "the best way to improve education using

social media" (Edudemic.com) while the digital media and learning initiative of the John D. and Catherine T. MacArthur Foundation explores how digital tools enable "new forms of knowledge production, social networking, communication, and play" (Digitallearning.macfound.org). The New Media Literacies Project of the Annenberg School of Communication and Journalism of the University of Southern California investigates the participatory practices in which youth engage while HASTAC (haystack)1 network brings together individuals and institutions "inspired by the possibilities that new technologies offer us for shaping how we learn, teach, communicate, create, and organize our local and global communities" (Hastac.org; Davidson, Goldberg and Jones, 2010).

These initiatives, it could be argued, are mostly concerned with new media literacies and collaborative learning rather than communication or public relations however their findings apply across disciplines. With their focus on authorship and content generation using a variety of digital media and tools for self-expression, advocacy, and research, and their questions about identity, ownership and legal and ethical concerns related to online activities, these initiatives help create new conceptual frameworks for studying "audiences and authors, messages and meanings, representations and realities that can deepen students' reflexivity, critical thinking and communication skills" (Hobbs & Jensen, 2009, p. 9). For communication and public relations courses these discussions are extremely important as an understanding of the boundaries and functions of social media can ensure effective and efficient communication.

Besides, there is little literature dedicated to teaching public relations and communication with new media and especially new media audits and analytics.

The Public Relations Review started a discussion about pedagogical experiments of those who "dare to keep up with the pace of change" in

Spring 2001. It was perhaps in reaction to writing like those of van Leuven (1999) or Coombs and Rybacki (1999). While van Leuven suggested that the core competencies that undergraduate students are required to master at the end of their degree course are changing, an increasing demand and emphasis being put on ethics, public relations management, public relations campaigns and visual and interactive communications, Coombs and Rybacki (1999) highlighted how slow PR education is in adopting technology. Although the Public Relations Review has since dedicated three special editions to PR pedagogy, in 2001, 2002 and more recently in 2011, only very few articles focus on technology in the classroom or innovative teaching that addresses new media challenges to the practice and profession of public relations.

Badaracco (2002), for instance, presents the case of teaching a Media, Religion and Cultural Identity course using technology to construct a learning community and to "turn the laboratory into a studio, where both teacher and student learned through performance" (p.149). The classroom was equipped with "two televisions with voice-activated cameras made possible team-teaching across three time zones" (p. 149). Video-teleconferencing systems, synchronous chat and threaded discourse using a common course site were other technologies used to enable students to talk both with each other and with US experts and faculty members about "all genres of media, including advertising, film, sitcoms, music, newscasts, newspapers" (p. 150). While innovative in delivery mode, Badaracco's article does not focus on integration of and impact of technology on public relations practice.

Boynton and Imfeld (2002 cited in Barry, 2005) explore how textbooks for undergraduate, introductory public relations courses address Internet technologies. Although the study looks at skills commonly used in textbooks and identify challenges facing the PR profession it does not however offer any innovative exercises for the classroom but only a warning that texts are outdated.

Barry (2005) investigates the new teaching methods that could be used in public relations education. His case study based on data gathered from the Ain Shams University School of Women in Egypt suggests that students look for more practical course work rather than theoretical knowledge, workshops and internships programs at media corporations being presented as more suitable methods for teaching public relations. Gaining computer skills and a good command of English language are competencies deemed necessary for a successful PR career.

Answering Barry's identified need, Swanson (2011) focuses on student-run public relations firms in USA undergraduate programs that are linked with capstone courses as a means to provide students with supervised work experience in public relations, "enhance student learning, maximize faculty support, build community relationships, and contribute to the overall health and vitality of the academic curriculum" (p.505). While student-run PR firms are certainly not the cure for every curricular problem, they require a different way of teaching and it can be assumed that through the work with real clients student inherently exposed to the challenges of technology. However, setting up student-run agencies can be a rather lengthy and complicated process and requires a general university courses set-up that allows for the professional practice to be evaluated in a manner that fits academic criteria and requirements.

Finally, Kent et al. (2011) present a case study of teaching web analytics as a tool for better strategic communication, examining the usefulness of analytical software for public relations and communication students and professionals. Their study uses analytic data from four organizations, "the websites include a professor's website, the Institute for Policy Studies (IPS) (an independent social cause organization), the city of Prague OK (a municipal, governmental website), and PR Romania (a professional information site)" (p. 538) and show how to it should be interpreted mentioning among others measurements like new vs.

returning visitors, bounce rates, adwords, landing pages, key words, or visitor loyalty. The authors suggest several activities that enable students to actively use and interpret data such as students interpreting the same set of organizational data while in class, or interpreting data on their own and writing up a strategic communication analysis for a fictive supervisor. "Such an assignment might involve explanations of what is happening and why, a short and long term organizational analysis, and tangible strategies and tactics that might be employed to improve the effectiveness of the website" (p. 541). While inspiring and up to date, Kent et al.'s suggestions remain generic leaving room for further exploration by those interested in integrating new and social media data in their classes.

SOCIAL MEDIA AUDITS: IN PRACTICE AND IN THE CLASSROOM

Although the academic literature might only marginally be focusing on social media audits and metrics, there are numerous resources and examples of practice on the web. Margaret Mc-Gann (2010), principal at 2M Communications Ink, dedicates a blog post to the communications audit, the reasons for completing one and offers twelve tips to conduct one. They include evaluation of recent communication and marketing materials, analysis and evaluation of media coverage and social media presence, one-on-one interviews with senior management, board members and key partners, focus groups with internal and external stakeholders and surveys for all stakeholders. She also recommends incorporating ongoing measurement tools into the communication plans.

Gattiker (2011b) from Commetrics.com emphasizes that social media audits need to be linked with the organization's strategy. In this respect, he recommends establishing an organization's level of maturity as reflected by their effective achievement of their strategic objectives. In his view, there are 5 phases that an organization using social media can find itself into:

- The novice or the discovery stage when only a few people participate with the purpose of "identifying consumer tech gadgets that could impact the business",
- The early adopter stage which is affiliated with the exploration and experimentation of tools, services and platforms undertaken by a small number of people with the aim of exploring ways to measure goal attainment,
- The evangelist stage associated with the practice, trial and connection phase when managers are open to change and new technologies and actionable metrics are developed in order to benchmark the organization,
- The adopter or the acceptance and focus on engagement stage when "successful pilot projects or evangelization leads to increasing use across the enterprise" and metrics are used and applied to assess key drivers and finally,
- The optimizer or cooperation and facilitation stage when "processes are improved and company seeks to expand adoption of its ecosystem in order to better serve stakeholders".

Like Gattiker, Kristi Bolsinger (2010) also suggests that social media audits have to reflect the needs of the organization undertaking them. Her example presents a list of elements included in the social media audits she performed. They include profile evaluation, branding, blog, content, tracking, promotions and tools as well as offline presence, conversation coverage and social touch-points.

Boame's (2010) model touches on similar elements like Bolsinger (2010) but makes the aim of the audit more obvious. Formulated as a series of questions, Boame looks at social media audits from a branding, integration, content, measurement, and overall campaign perspective. For instance, the branding social media audit focuses on the completeness of social media profiles, exclusive ownership, custom landing pages and overall consistency with the branding identity. The content audit explores the messages and feedback the company receives. The integration audit on the other hand analyzes how well connected and consistent are the organization's presences on various social media while the measurement audit concentrates on identifying platforms that provide the most leads or traffic.

Instead of a list of questions, Deidre Breakenridge (2011) proposes using a matrix to evaluate a company's social media based on the brand guidelines, engagement, strategy/purpose, frequency of posts, content shared and measurement where measurement indicates both what is being assesses as well as the tools, if any, used to collect and analyze the data.

Finally, the model proposed by Renegade (2010) starts from the organization's goals and then notes the presence of the organization on a variety of channels including the company website, microsites, blogs, social networks, microblogs, video, feedback, search or mobile in comparison with four major competitors. The model also includes a detailed evaluation list for Facebook, Twitter, search and blogs and comments preceded by a series of questions related to:

- **Planning and Competitive Issues:** The organization's social media goals, strengths and weaknesses of the current presence, the strategic role of each social media element in the context of the overall goals,
- **Infrastructure and Organizational Issues:** Impact measurements, tools, senior management engagement on social media, social media within the overall strategy,

- **Cultural Issues:** Social media policy, participation of staff and senior management in social media, access to social media.

Six Examples, Six Different Methods of Assessing Social Media

The variety of examples provided by professionals suggest that there is no agreed template for a social media audit and it emphasizes the fact that effective social media audits reflect the needs and goals of the organizations undertaking them. However, the lack of a single model also shows that social media audits still represent an exploratory practice for practitioners making them quite a challenging project if integrated as an exercise in communication classes.

Such approaches, although few, exist several educators and universities around the world including social media audits and analytics within their courses and as part of their assessment. The Social Media and Business Course offered by the Beedie School of Business of Simon Fraser University in Canada2 includes a social media audit exercise and so do Michigan State University3 and Southern University in the USA4 in the courses they offer. Other examples include Corrine Weisgerber's5 Social Media PR class whose social media audit represents 15% of the final grade, Barbara Nixon's social monitoring report6 developed for Southeastern University and Dr Regina K Water's Strategic Social Media for NonProfits and Business offered at Drury University which includes a social media campaign proposal. All these examples come mostly from the USA indicating that their practice is better documented but also that there is plenty of potential for adopting or developing similar exercises and tasks for other university courses in Europe and beyond.

Barbara Nixon and Corrine Weisegerber's exercises share commonalities in the sense that they propose a monitoring exercise which is aimed to observe an organization's communication as dynamic process as opposed to the social media audits proposed by practitioners that are more static due to their aim to capture the usage of social media by an organization at given time. However, both exercises go beyond the capturing of data requesting students to write a report in which they present the data obtained and explain what it means. They both concentrate on the main social media platforms: Facebook and Twitter but also include multimedia sharing platform Flickr, social networking site MySpace, message boards and analytic functions and alerts from Google.

Developed independent from the other social media audit exercises presented above, my exercises had the benefit of being offered not only to home students, but also to exchange students. Moreover, the exercise was presented in a variety of forms to students from the USA to Europe and the Middle East providing plenty of opportunities of reflection on the ubiquity of social media in the world as well as its different cultural and practical applications.

The sections to follow will present my experience with teaching social media audits and analytics, describe the exercises I developed to teach these concepts over the years and present the lessons learned from delivering them

SOCIAL MEDIA AUDITS AND ANALYTICS IN THE CLASSROOM

Belgium 2008: The Precursor

In summer 2008 I was invited to develop and teach a course about new media and using new media at Katholieke Hogeschool Zuid-West-Vlaanderen (KAHTO) in Kortrijk, Belgium. The course was to be offered to Erasmus exchange students from all over Europe studying in the Business and Languages School at KATHO. The group's academic background was heterogeneous ranging from communication to logistics and accounting. This influenced the decision to design learning outcomes focused on creating new media skills,

expanding the students' new media literacies and exposing to the newest developments in digital technologies and their impact on creative industries including journalism and public relations that enabled students to explore communication and new media related areas without having to have an in-depth knowledge of either subject.

Designed as an intensive course with only 15 hours of contact all covered throughout one week of teaching, the New Media course introduced students to concepts and definitions such as convergence and web 2.0 and provided them with examples and case studies. The course also required students to contribute to a blog, join Twitter and create a profile on LinkedIn, giving them an opportunity to explore through practice these three different new media environments. As part of the assessment students were asked to produce a team report assessing and reflecting on how international companies use new media, and websites and blogs in particular for their communication. Students were asked to find an international advertising company, public relations group, European institution or NGO and check their international and national sites looking for elements reflecting web 2.0 and convergence. They were also asked to compare and contrast the results while also looking at the company's mission, vision and objectives and discuss their findings. The focus of the students' reflections was thus on image consistency and cultural and technological differences between web presences of the same institution targeting two different audiences: an international one and a local one.

Lessons Learned

The exercise aimed to show students how complex online communications can be and how the target audience and their culture influence how a company presents itself through various websites. Considerations of whether links with cultural communication theories should be made were taken into account, however it was decided to keep the exercise at experimental and observation level as it reflected practice better. While theories provide a formula for real-life phenomena, it is challenging to include them in exercises that aim to replicate practice especially when presented in a condensed form such as the KATHO course was. This would require time for explanation and reflection so that an understanding of the theory is achieved before implementation in an exercise. With a class as diverse as the one at KATHO and a timeframe so short, when much of the attention was already dedicated to demystifying new media, integrating theory within the exercise could have confused the students. This does not mean that there is not any merit in integrating theory. On the contrary, for academic courses with an emphasis beyond applications of technology and potential uses for communication, theory can be the conceptual lens needed to analyse practice. This would ensure that the learning outcomes would expand from experience of tools and platforms to critical analysis and design of solutions that integrate theory in practice.

As the exercise aimed to reflect practice and integrate current online communication it was noted that future exercises should include social media analysis components as the number of websites showcasing social media connections was increasing.

Belgium 2009

A year later I rewrote the exercise to incorporate social media sites. Unlike the previous year when the students had to produce a report, the exercise was incorporated into a practice day when, during the 3 hours allocated to the classroom, the students had to gather their data and write up their report. Minimal instructions were given to the students combining a usability test with a social media audit image/presence audit making therefore possible the implementation of problem-based learning into the classroom and replicating the short deadlines and tight deliverables of marketing and communication agency pitches.

In this case students were randomly given the name of an organization. Their task was to:

- Find the organization's website using search engines,
- Check the organization's online presence,
- Identify what their mission and vision is and who their target audience might be,
- Identify whether they have any social media accounts and whether they visibly link to them from their website,
- Assess the audience and objectives of using social media as well as whether they are complimentary to or different from those of the website and
- Suggest improvements, if needed, both for the websites and the social media accounts.

In producing their arguments students had been introduced to and encouraged to use a series of analytics tools such as Google Insights for Search which enables comparison of search volume patterns across specific region, categories and timeframes, Twitgraph which provided a twitter network visualization for an account together with statistics reflecting the number of tweets, mentions, replies, links posted, twitter rank, conversation quotient and more or TweetStats that provided usage statistics for an account reflecting the timeframes and activity volume. At the end of the 3 hours students were asked to upload their report on one of the class blogs – Kathonewmedia. wordpress.com or Kathonewmedia.posterous.com where they can still be accessed today.

Lessons Learned

Introducing social media as well as free social media analytics tools provided students with a dynamic image of online communications. It challenged them to think both about the objectives of the companies they were auditing as well as about the relevance and reliability of the tools they were using. This enhanced their learning experience providing an opportunity for critical thinking, analysis as well as widening their understanding of how new media operates, expanding their new media literacies and improving their social media skills. It could be argued that the exercise wanted too much in too little time and this might be a very valid observation. The intention however was to create the situation of a company pitch with a tight deadline scenario when quickness of response, creativity and strength of argument can win the client. The ability to choose from a variety of data available as well as the ability to discern which tools serve the task at hand better, are essential when facing such scenarios. However, to increase the efficiency of the time used to produce the media audit, it was decided that future lectures will provide more detail and opportunities to discuss about and analyse the existing social media tools and how they can help measure how goals and objectives are reached.

Belgium 2010: The Improved Version

After 2 years of teaching and constantly improving the course and after having its contact hours double as a result of student demand and interest, the social media audit became part of a dedicated public relations practice day. In the first year of teaching the course, there were only three content-driven lectures – New media, definitions and landscape; New Media challenges for Journalism and New Media challenges for advertisers, marketers and public relations practitioners – the other two meetings being dedicated to guest lectures, class discussion and presentations. In the new format the number of lectures was maintained but each lecture day was followed by a full day of practice – journalist for a day; communicator for a day; job seeker for a day -. The lecture on new media and public relations was therefore adapted to include information about the strategic planning of communication using new and social media

emphasizing on a cyclic process that goes from listening or monitoring, to engagement, creation or content generation, buzz or dialogue and moves onto networking. The process also showcased a range of free tools that organizations could use to detect trends, monitor a brand, assess user sentiment, measure influence or evaluate volume of mentions. These include RSS, Google Insights for Search, Twitter Search, Trendistic – displays frequency of mentions on Twitter of searched keyword and enables its comparison with up to four other terms -, Backtype – blog and web search -, Twitscoop – Twitter trends and search - and social bookmarking sites. Emphasis was also put on explaining the complexity of the social media landscape and on identifying the functions and roles that different social media platforms – such as networking, professional networking, multimedia sharing and more – could play within an organizations' communication strategy.

Students were assigned a company. Their task this time combined search, usability, and message strategy. The aim of the audit was to assess the visibility of social media efforts and coherence and consistency with the company's brand and communication objectives. It required students to have an overall look at the assigned company's social media efforts but also evaluate each platform individually. While they were recommended to use a series of tools which were considered to provide the most in-depth data and whose algorithms of data retrieval could be identified, students were free to use any other tools as long as they justified their choice.

Search

The exercise asked students to google their company and note whether they find it straightaway and in which position within the Google results the link to the company is. Was the link to the website, a social media account? Who owned the website or the social media account?

Website

On the website, students were asked to identify the three main messages that the company aimed to transmit and assess their clarity. To identify the most frequently used words within the website, students were asked to create a word cloud using Wordle.net. This allowed them to compare whether the messages they identified found their keywords within the automated visualization. They were also asked to see if they could identify any links to social media accounts like Twitter, Facebook, Flickr, YouTube, MySpace.

Twitter

If students identified a Twitter account related with the company they were assessing, they were asked to check the number of followers for the account as well as the number of people the account followed. They were also asked to look at the company's bio and whether it was featured in any lists. Next, they were required to look at the messages, mentions and ReTweets (RTs) of the account as a way of identifying whether there is an algorithm, structure or strategy in the way the account was used. To verify their observations, students were encouraged to use Twitter Analyzer to verify the same information but also find out more about where the followers are located or how often they would engage with the account. Klout was used to assess the account's influence score and its location within the Klout matrix. To better see how users are connected to one another and perhaps uncover the source of some of the accounts' mentions students were directed to FlowingData7, a web application which upon input of a Twitter account automatically generated its network visualization. Finally, in a similar way to website and as a way to identify the words most frequently used and therefore identify the key messages transmitted through Twitter by the company, students were recommended to create another word cloud using wordle.net.

Facebook

If a Facebook group or Facebook page were found students were recommended to collect the following data: number of fans of the page or members in the group, number of likes, the description associated with the page which works as an equivalent of the Twitter bio and sometimes reflects the mission and vision of the company and the assumed objectives they aim to reach using the network, the frequency and type of links shared and the whether the page or group presented a conversational aspect or was a more like another channels through which the company would push information.

Blog

Since access to Google Analytics for a blog cannot be done without having access to the blog dashboard, students were asked to assess the structure, searchability, shareability and content of the blog as in easiness to use and browse, clarity of information, links with other social media presences and the official website, existence of a search option and the type and frequency with which information was shared on the blog.

Sentiment

Since students have looked at mentions and conversations and their nature, the sentiment analysis provided by SocialMention8 was recommended as an opportunity to verify, yet again, their findings. The website searches are reported both at web level as well as separately on blogs, microblogs, video and more. The results include mentions with links to the original posts, a percent calculation of strength meaning the likelihood that the brand/keyword is being a topic of discussion online, sentiment meaning the ratio of mentions that are positive compared to the negative, passion meaning the likelihood that people will write again about the brand/keyword and reach meaning the number of unique references to the brand/keyword compared to the total mentions. Other metrics provided by SocialMention include top keywords, top sources and top users writing about the keyword.

As an alternative for those whose audit focused mostly on Twitter, Twittratr9 provides a less in depth but equally helpful sentiment analysis bases on an input search.

The exercise thus organized provided students with several opportunities to verify their results and with an equal number of opportunities to question the accuracy, relevance and reliability of the tools they used in relation to the audit that they had to complete. Their recording and analysis of the website mission and vision, twitter bio, Facebook page/group description enabled them to identify the communication objectives associated with each presence as well as the target audience addressed. This also enabled them to verify the consistency of the messages. The use of Twitter analytics tools enables them to verify the data that they collected manually. Similarly, the use of SocialMention allowed them to cross check the statistics provided by the other tools.

Lessons Learned

With the information gathered, the students had to make recommendations. Their report, as in previous semesters, was to be uploaded on either one of the class blogs. The time students were allocated to conduct their research, gather the data and write up their report was three hours however they were given a chance to revisit it and amend it until the next day's class. While many of the students reported that they found the exercise interesting and useful they still indicated that the time awarded was too little for them to produce an in-depth report their lack of knowledge of the tools suggested or of the specificities of the social media landscape contributing to their delay. Providing them with a more prescriptive exercise helped direct and focus their work however their

feedback suggests that they were only marginally aware of the depth of the social media field and its influences on daily communications. This highlights once more the need for new and social media literacies to be incorporated into the classroom both within specialized subjects linked to the students' degree but also within interdisciplinary projects. This also suggests that practice and experimentation in the classroom provides students with a space for safe exploration where they receive guidance, support and explanations.

As with previous exercises, the aim was to introduce students to concepts and tools unique to online communication while providing them a controlled yet realistic environment to test them. Although focused mainly on how companies used the internet and social media to communicate about themselves and their services or with their clients, the exercises aimed to create awareness, increase digital media literacy and create digital media skills at the same time with presenting an experimental modal of analysis of online communication practices. The tools and platforms chosen reflected online trends and practices and therefore incorporated both popular platforms as well as emerging ones. Judging from the end of the course feedback received this mix of direct and indirect learning outcomes as well as the guided experimentation were among the points that the students appreciated most indicating that there is some merit in aiming for learning outcomes that go beyond the classroom and beyond assessment.

Bahrain 2011

The years I taught at KATHO in Belgium provided me with an invaluable testing ground for the social media audit exercise. One of the challenges I faced was due to the study background diversity of the class making it difficult at times to provide them with examples and exercises relevant to their degrees. One of the other challenges faced was that using free analytics tools meant that some were not available several months later. This was the case with many of the Twitter analytics tools after the change of the way Twitter makes data available to third party applications, were not operational anymore. Some of the functions of Flowing Data for instance could be performed by the 5K Twitter Browser by Neuro Productions10 and the sentiment analysis available via Twittratr's could be replaced with the one from Crowdeye11. Others like The Archivist by Mix Online12 that also enables Twitter data archival covers some of the functions that Twitter Analyzer offered.

The chance to revisit the social media audit exercise came when I joined the team developing the Applied Communication course at the Business School of Bahrain Polytechnic in Bahrain. Among the learning outcomes were the application of audience-focused strategies to written and oral communication and the analysis of the impact of information technology applications on communication. The social media audit exercise helped meet both learning outcomes by challenging students to identify the audiences targeted by local business via their new and social media presences as well as make them critically assess the impact of technology on communication. Despite the political unrest in Bahrain (Naughtie, 2011), the temporary closing of the university, the reopening only to teach a shortened semester and the management's decision to block access to social media sites on campus, it was decided to still give students the exercise. This required accessing the social media platforms from outside the campus and saving as screenshots the pages that the students were supposed to click through. This eliminated the interactivity of the exercise as well as any possibility of using any analytics tools. The exercise therefore was refocused on how local companies communicate with their target audience through social media sites.

The worksheet given to students is included below in its entirety in Box 1.

Lessons Learned

Although highly prescriptive, this exercise emphasized the need to define metrics and analytics to be used for social media. This can be done in an exploratory way allowing the students to identify them through their own searches and inquiries or pointing them out to them.

Bournemouth 2012: Preparing a Specialized Social Media Audit

The experience of the past years has been extremely valuable. Started as an exercise of assessing the impact of digital technologies on how companies communicate with their target audience, the social media audit has become over the years a specialized exercise that addresses several of the current pedagogy challenges all at once: it is problem-based, reflects practice, incorporates emerging technologies and tools and proposes an experimental approach to both new media and communication. In previous years, one of the suggested shortcomings of the exercise was the little time provided to complete it. Therefore, this year the social media audit was part of the final assessment of Digital Communication Strategies course offered to more than two hundred 2nd year marketing, advertising and public relations students at Bournemouth University. To make their task easier and their social media audit exercise more valuable the students benefitted from an entire semester of lectures and seminars discussing social media strategy, audits, return of investment, metrics and tools. Similarly, the students were required to find a client of their own either located in the Dorset area or located closer to their hometowns.

Unlike previous social media audit exercises the one implemented at Bournemouth University had for the first time a practice perspective – either marketing, public relations, advertising or branding. This was believed to support students to identify the business objectives of their client

Box 1. Social Media audit worksheet

OBSERVE:
Website:
   1. Find the Batelco[13] website
       a. Write down the procedure you used to find it (search engine, referral or URL)
   2. Analyze menu
       a. Based on what you see what are the audiences the website is targeting? Justify why.
       b. Based on what you see, what are the communication aims of the website?
       c. Based on what you see, what do you think Batelco would want its website visitors to do on the website and after visiting the website?
   3. Find the mission and/or vision of the company?
   a. What are the key messages (Who, says what, to whom?... what is the desired effect?)
   b. How do they compare with the general communication aims you have identified at point 2?
   4. Find links to social media sites.
   a. Note position within the homepage (consider visibility, clarity and ease to identify)
   b. Note how many links there are.
   c. Discuss – relevance and importance of links (how do they link with the website's communication aims?)

Social media
   1. Click on each of the social media links you see on Batelco's home page.
   a. Where do they take you? Are the links working?
   b. Categorize the social media platforms based on the type of content/information they share (e.g: networking, sharing...)
   2. Once you are on each social media page check:
   a. Information about the account/account holder (who owns/manages the account? Bio/about user section – e.g. check the info page on Facebook or the about me section on YouTube)

b. Facebook
       i. How many people like the page?
       ii. Can you identify any links to other websites/social media sites?
       iii. Identify the type of content and interactions that Batelco has through Facebook? (check the Facebook postings and the number of comments and/or likes they received; check the photos, videos and links shared and the reactions – comments/likes – they received)
       iv. What is the communication goal of Batelco's Facebook page?
       v. What are the key messages of Batelco's Facebook page?
       vi. Who is Batelco's Facebook target audience?

c. YouTube
       i. Check profile data: channel views, total upload views, subscribers, total videos uploaded, comments.
   1. Is this an old channel?

2. Is this a channel with a lot of views? (check ratio – channel views/subscribers)
   3. Evaluate the interaction between the channel's viewers and Batelco.
       ii. Can you identify any link to other websites/social media sites?
       iii. What is the communication goal of Batelco's YouTube channel?
       iv. What are the key messages of Batelco's YouTube channel?
       v. Who is Batelco's Facebook target audience?

d. Twitter
       i. Check profile data (tweets, followers, followed, lists)
   1. What is the ratio of followers/followed?
       ii. Who is Batelco following?
       iii. Who is following Batelco?
       iv. What is Batelco tweeting about? (check tweets, mentions and RTs)
   1. Evaluate the interaction between Batelco and its Twitter followers.
       v. Can you identify any link to other websites/social media sites?
       vi. What is the communication goal of Batelco's presence and activity on Twitter?
       vii. Who is Batelco's Twitter target audience?

SOME MORE QUESTIONS
   1. Is Batelco linking all its media (and social media) sites to one another?
   2. Are the social media presences consistently representing the Batelco brand image?
   3. How do the communication goals of Batelco's social media presences compare to one another and to Batelco's website?
   4. How to the key messages of Batelco's social media presences compare to one another?
   5. Are the social media presences covering at least one of Balteco's website key messages.

continued on following page

Box 1. Continued

Based on all the information you have gathered, you can now create your report presenting:
• Batelco's communication goals for their website and social media presences
• Batelco's key messages as presented through their official website and social media
• Your discussion about the impact of internet and social media on Batelco's communication strategy (compare audience targeted, communication goals and key messages)
• Your discussion about the impact of Internet and social media on Batelco's communication consistency (compare audience targeted, communication goals and key messages).

and link them or translate them more easily to social media related objectives. This decision was inspired by a variation of the exercise proposed to students at KATHO in May 2011 when students were provided with two exercise models for a social media audit: one from a public relations perspective and one from a branding and branding equity one (Adi, 2011). While the public relations exercise follows the same pattern as the one presented above with few changes when it comes to tools recommended, the branding exercise starts with a brand touchpoint (website, Facebook page or Twitter account) using it as a gateway for the brand's image assessment. The Twitter brand audit exercise is replicated below:

1. Check out Twitter account (observe account bio, the followers, follows, list ratio and the structure of the messages – tweets, RTs, mentions)
2. Go to Twitter Network by Neuro Productions and analyze the account's network (is it well connected with other accounts or not, is it's network interconnected…)
3. Go to TwitterGrader[14] to assess the account's influence score (alternative TwitAlyzer or Twinfluence)
4. Go to Twitter Sentiment[15] and Social Mention and compare the positive/negative mentions ratio of the brand/account. Analyze (qualitatively) the messages about the brand and identify associations with the brand. Are the tools correctly assessing positive/negative sentiment. Add depth to the analysis separating tweets based on their references

to price, performance or quality of brand/product.

Also, unlike in previous years when it was either the tools or the data available that shaped the way the way the exercise was formulated, the exercise at Bournemouth University focuses on strategic outputs and business communication. In this respect, the structure of the report and the process of the social media audit that is emphasized rather than the tools to be used and steps to be followed.

The following structure is therefore recommended:

• Introduction & Executive Summary
• Internal Review
   ◦ Business goals, objectives and target audience
   ◦ The company's goals, objectives and target audience for social media
   ◦ Tactic (e.g: platforms and tools used)
   ◦ Content (e.g.: messages, frequency, types; this could also include information about integration, sentiment, engagement)
   ◦ Metrics (e.g: mentions, followers, subcribers, likes…)
• *Optional: External Review/Competitor Analysis (helps benchmark your client)*
• *Optional: Perception map*
• Insights and recommendations including metrics and analytics that could be used to assess the client's progress should they wish to implement your recommendations

◦ E.g. objective increase engagement – tactics: launch a weekly questions – measure: increase in number of mentions, increase in number of RTs – tools: Crowdbooster or TwentyFeet.

In its current format, the exercise incorporates information from Bolsinger (2011), Beakenridge (2011), Shepherd (2010) and Renegade (2010) reflecting in part the structure and audit elements they propose to be incorporated in a social media audit. Compared to the version of the exercise developed for Bahrain, this exercise is more complex. Unlike the version for Bahrain where every step was explained, this exercise leaves room for a multi-faceted approach and invites more depth of the analysis. For instance, if public relations students were to take this exercise they would first have to explore and find out what social media presences the company they audit has as well as find out what the company's potential goals and objectives might be. When it comes to goals, they can be either: reputation management ones such as improve image of the company, relationship management such as improve communication with a specific group of the target audience or task management goals such as increase interaction or engagement on one of the platforms they are present on. Having identified the goals, the students should then try to assess what objectives are associated with them. This can be done through a combination of observation and interviews with the client. Once the objectives are identified and what outcomes - whether knowledge such as increase awareness, predisposition such as increase feedback or behavior such as increase number of fans that post content on the account Facebook page - are desired, the students not only will know what to concentrate on but also what metrics and analytics to choose.

For instance, should the goal be reputation management and the objective associated with an increase in the ratio of positive to negative references across social media, hence an opinion change outcome then the students would be looking at the number of mentions and RTs on Twitter, the number of likes and comments on Facebook, the number of comments on their blog or the number of shares of content they produce on social bookmarking sites that the company currently has. To assess whether the mentions are positive or negative, they could use tools like SocialMention, UberVu, TwitterSentiment or by collecting all the mentions and then assessing them for the tone and references they include. Complex algorithms for data collection and sentiment analysis are also provided by Prabowol and Thelwall (2009) and Godbole, Srinivasaiah, and Skiena (2007). Questions however about what content the company uploaded that led to the mentions collected should be raised, leading students into content audit which depending on how it is conducted could be linked with an integration audit checking consistency of messages, relevance to the target audience and the meeting of communication goals and objectives. To identify these goals, contact with the audited organization should be sought and interviews should be conducted with the people in charge of the organization's social media presence. If not, the alternative would be to work with perceived or assumed goals as they result from an analysis of the organization's communication patterns.

Alternatively, should the goal be reputation management and the objective associated with it is to foster dialogue the outcome envisaged would be an informational one. The measurements required for assessing such an objective should consider not only mentions, likes and shares but also engagement and reach. Lovett and Owyang (2011) suggest a formula for audience engagement that sums up the comments, shares and trackbacks and divides their sum to the total views. They also suggest a formula for conversation reach which consists in the division of the total number of people participating to the total audience exposure. However, while the formulas are simple and straightforward, deciding what one understands by total views or even by total audience exposure remains to be defined by each organization.

Taking another example, this time looking at a task management goal, with a raising awareness about a new range of services an organization provides associated goal, the audit should focus on the current awareness of the company's services. A series of metrics such as number of subscribers to the blog, number of followers, number of fans of the page could indicate awareness but the numbers would only capture the people who associate with the company and its services and not necessarily those who are aware of it. Awareness thus will be assessed also through the number of social bookmarks, number of shares of a link, number of RTs or even through the number of unique visitors to a blog.

The exercise requires students to do what all practitioners agree upon: that social media audits need to starts from the goals and business objectives of the company audited; the clearer the goals and objectives, the easier to identify the relevant and correct metrics and measurements as well as identify the potential tools and analytics platforms to use. Reputation goals can be assessed through engagement, reach and sharing metrics. Relationships goals can be evaluated by impact, active users, conversation reach metrics while task goals associated metrics depend on the task assigned but could include satisfaction scores, resolution time, number of queries and so on.

DISCUSSION AND CONCLUSION

Social media audits are "key for identifying priorities, benchmarking previous efforts, and planning for future efforts" (Owyang, 2009). Currently used to obtain insight or drive strategic decision, social media audits are being offered more often by communication agencies as part of their digital media services. This chapter provided a history of development of a social media audit exercise and presented it in its international context and

application. It is difficult to currently state what is the real impact of such exercises on teaching, learning, industry and practice as the exercises has not been implemented long enough in the same place as to enable data collection at student and client levels. However, the limited feedback received either in Belgium or in Bahrain indicate that the exercise is challenging and rewarding at the same time as it provides an opportunity to the students to engage with social media in a professional way, relevant to their field of study and future field of work. The paragraphs to follow will discuss the potential implications of implementing social media audit exercises into the classroom.

Introducing a social media audit exercise in communication related courses provides educators with an opportunity to reflect practice but gives students a change to be part of and experiment current trends within their own field of specialization.

Unlike cases when technology is introduced in the classroom to enhance interaction and collaboration, the social media audit exercise takes the student's and lecturer's work with technology at a different level. It enables them both to "geek out", to experiment with ideas, use platforms, test tools and observe and critically appraise their results. When used in relation to real clients and real problems, it makes the learning environment more fluid and by default more problem-based and hence more applied. This enabled technology to be relevant as it is integrated with other specialist knowledge related to the degrees the students pursue.

The social media exercise therefore, in either form, enables students to develop new media skills related to content generation and management while expanding their digital media literacies and inviting them to further consider ethics, management and integrated, interactive communication. By doing so, the exercises answer both Coombs and Rybacki's (1999) concern related to new media adoption by educators as well as Hemmi, Bayne and Land (2009) call to focus more on technology as a result of students' self-perception of weak preparation in this area. Moreover, it meets the promise of bringing practice into the classroom and preparing the students for their future employment.

While answering these challenges, the social media audit faces several challenges of its own. As the case studies presented here show, the adoption of and integration in the classroom of an experimental exercise requires a different mind-set of the educator, the students but also of the institution hosting the course. An experimental exercise like the social media audit cannot provide students with a set recipe or a step-by-step guide. As long as practitioners do not use a single template, it would be at the students' disadvantage to propose one. On the one hand, this brings a marking challenge as setting a standard could be difficult especially since metrics and analytic formulas change so quickly. On the other hand, this merges the educator's mission with the responsibility to present students with all the trends and alternatives and thus challenges them to constantly keep up to date with industry and consultancy practices. Only by doing that, the students preparation for the workforce will be enabled and the exercise will support them to be creative and flexible, able to find solutions both either by using the tools and data that is made available to them as well as by developing their own.

To prepare students for the dynamic and ever-changing world of digital and social media the exercises have to be experimental. They also have to be connected, realistic and up to date. The educators therefore need to become explorers and connectors with technology and with practitioners but also supporters of their colleagues' and their exploratory journeys. Teaching a social media audit like teaching new media and with new media is not about the tools or the process or the outcome: it is about all of them together, at once.

REFERENCES

Adi, A. (2011). *Social media: Exercises 4 PR & branding #HigherEd classes.* Retrieved January 11, 2012, from http://www.anaadi.net/2011/05/20/social-media-exercises-4-pr-branding-highered-classes/

Alfonso, G.-H., & de Valbuena Miguel, R. (2006). Trends in online media relations: Web-based corporate press rooms in leading international companies. *Public Relations Review, 32,* 267–275. doi:10.1016/j.pubrev.2006.05.003

Badarocco, C. H. (2002). The linked classroom as studio: Connectivity and the etymology of networks. *Public Relations Review, 28,* 149–156. doi:10.1016/S0363-8111(02)00121-2

Ball, M. (2011). *Social media man! (Infographic)* Retrieved August 3, 2011, from http://www.one-socialmedia.com/tag/youtube-statistics

Barry, W. I. A. (2005). Teaching public relations in the information age: A case study at an Egyptian University. *Public Relations Review, 31*(3), 355–361. doi:10.1016/j.pubrev.2005.05.020

Beakenridge, D. (2011). *The social media audit.* Retrieved January 9, 2012, from http://www.deirdrebreakenridge.com/2011/03/the-social-media-audit/#.TwsASUpWYXx

Bolsinger, K. (2010). *How to conduct a social media audit.* Retrieved January 9, 2012, from http://socialfresh.com/social-media-audit/

Boynton, L., & Imfeld, C. (2002). *Virtual issues in traditional texts: How introductory PR textbooks address Internet technology issues.* A paper presented in The AEJMC 2002 Convention in Miami Beach, USA.

Cahill, B. (2009, Spring). Your attention please: The right way to integrate social media into your marketing plans. *Public Relations Strategist*. Retrieved June 13, 2012, from http://www.prsa.org/intelligence/thestrategist/articles/view/6k-020925/102/your_attention_please_the_right_way_to_integrate_s

Cohen, H. (2011). *30 social media definitions*. Retrieved January 8, 2012, from http://heidicohen.com/social-media-definition/

Coombs, T. W., & Rybacki, K. (1999). Public relations education: Where is pedagogy? *Public Relations Review*, *25*(1), 55–63. doi:10.1016/S0363-8111(99)80127-1

Digitallearning.macfound.org. (n.d.). *About the initiative*. The John D. and Catherine T. MacArthur Foundation. Retrieved January 8, 2012, from http://digitallearning.macfound.org/site/c.enJLKQNlFiG/b.2029319/k.4E7B/About_the_Initiative.htm

Eberhart, T. (2011). *Level up! SMEDU chats start today. Topic: our Social Media Global Education Connection Project*. Retrieved January 8, 2012, from http://socialmediaclub.org/blogs/social-media-education/level-smedu-chats-start-today-topic-our-social-media-global-education-0

Edudemic.com. (n.d.). *About*. Retrieved January 8, 2012, from http://edudemic.com/about-2/

Falls, J. (August 10, 2009). Public relations pros must be social media ready. *Social Media Explorer*. Retrieved January 6, 2012, from http://www.socialmediaexplorer.com/online-public-relations/public-relations-pros-must-be-social-media-ready/

Gattiker, U. E. (2011). *Why do social media audits fail?* Retrieved January 9, 2012, from http://commetrics.com/?p=15222

Godbole, N., Srinivasaiah, M., & Skiena, S. (2007). *Large-scale sentiment analysis for news and blogs.* International Conference on Weblogs and Social Media, March 26-28, Boulder, Colorado, USA Retrieved from http://www.icwsm.org/papers/paper26.html on January 12, 2012.

Hemmi, A., Bayne, S., & Land, R. (2009). The appropriation and repurposing of social technologies in higher education. *Journal of Computer Assisted Learning*, *25*(1), 19–30. doi:10.1111/j.1365-2729.2008.00306.x

Hobbs, R., & Jensen, A. (2009). The past, present and future of media literacy education. *Journal of Media Literacy Education*, *1*, 1–11.

James, M. (2007). A review of the impact of new media on public relations: Challenges for terrain, practice and education. *Asia Pacific Public Relations Journal*, *8*, 137–148.

Kaplan, A. M., & Haenlein, M. (2010). Users of the world, unite! The challenges and opportunities of social media. *Business Horizons*, *53*(1), 59–68. doi:10.1016/j.bushor.2009.09.003

Kent, M. L., Carr, B. J., Husted, R. A., & Pop, R. A. (2011). Learning web analytics: A tool for strategic communication. *Public Relations Review*, *37*, 536–543. doi:10.1016/j.pubrev.2011.09.011

Lovett, J., & Owyang, J. (2011). *Social marketing analytics: A new framework for measuring results in social media*. Retrieved January 12, 2012, from http://www.slideshare.net/jlovett/social-marketing-analytics-7985404

McGann, M. (2010). *Communications audit: Why and how to do it*. Retrieved January 8, 2012, from http://2mcommunications.wordpress.com/2010/07/05/communications-audit-why-and-how-to-do-it/

Naughtie, J. (2011). *Will Bahrain's Arab Spring bear fruit?* Retrieved January 13, 2012, from http://news.bbc.co.uk/today/hi/today/newsid_9499000/9499462.stm

Owyang, J. (2009). The importance of social media audits. Retrieved January 13, 2012, from http://www.web-strategist.com/blog/2009/07/28/the-importance-of-a-social-media-audits/

Phillips, D., & Young, P. (2009). *Online public relations: A practical guide to developing an online strategy in the world of social media.* Kogan Page Publishers.

Phippen, A., Sheppard, L., & Furnell, S. (2004). A practical evaluation of Web analytics. *Internet Research*, *14*(4), 284–293. doi:10.1108/10662240410555306

Prabowol, R., & Thelwall, M. (2009) Sentiment analysis: A combined approach. *Journal of Infometrics, 3*(2), 143-157. Retrieved from www.cyberemotions.eu/rudy-sentiment-preprint.pdf on January 12, 2012.

Renegade. (2010). *Social media audit.* Retrieved January 9, 2012, from http://www.slideshare.net/RenegadeSMAudit/renegade-social-media-audit-4411127

Shepherd, A. (2010). *Social media audit: Understanding and implementation.* Retrieved January 11, 2012, from http://ashshepherd.com/blog/5-planning-and-process/24-social-media-audit-understanding-and-implementation

Swanson, D. J. (2011). The student-run public relations firm in an undergraduate program: Reaching learning and professional development goals through 'real world' experience. *Public Relations Review, 37*(5), 499–505. doi:10.1016/j.pubrev.2011.09.012

Uehara Henrikson, J. (2011). *The growth of social media: An infographic.* Retrieved September 1, 2011, from http://www.searchenginejournal.com/the-growth-of-social-media-an-infographic/32788/

Van Leuven, J. (1999). Four new course competencies for majors. *Public Relations Review*, *25*(1), 77–85. doi:10.1016/S0363-8111(99)80129-5

WWF. (n.d.). *WWF international communications department. Programme/project communications strategy template.* Retrieved January 9, 2012, from http://assets.panda.org/.../wwf_communications_strategy_template__t_.doc

KEY TERMS AND DEFINITIONS

Higher Education: Education that occurs at universities or colleges. It embraces specific studies to perform certain professions such as law, medicine, communications.

Micro Blogging: Is a broadcasting-blog like activity where the format in which the content is shared is typically smaller than a blog. The platform Twitter is an example of a micro-blog.

Social Media Analytics: The practice of gathering and analyzing data related to social media usage of a person or organization in order to identify usage patterns, customer opinion and insight to be used in determining business decisions including online communication strategy, customer service or marketing.

Social Media Audit: An evaluation of a person's or organization's current usage of social media platforms.

Social Media Metrics: Systems of measurement of social media activity; in social media some metrics are platform specific and are automatically generated.

Social Media: A group of Internet-based applications that build on the ideological and technological foundations of *Web 2.0*, and that allow the creation and exchange of *user-generated content* (Kaplan & Haenlein, 2010).

Social Networking: The activity undertaken through a website or platform where one connects with friends, family, peers or other people with whom they share personal or professional interests among others.

ENDNOTES

1 http://hastac.org/
2 http://beedie.sfu.ca/bbaportal/?cat=17
3 http://2011teachwithtech.blogspot.com/2011/07/social-media-syllabus.html
4 http://publicrelationsmatters.com/2011/01/21/social-media-monitoring-report/
5 http://socialmediaprclass.pbworks.com/w/page/34818752/SocialMediaAudit
6 http://www.scribd.com/doc/25388747/Social-Media-Monitoring-Report
7 FlowingData is no longer available however MentionMapp (http://mentionmapp.com) performs the same function
8 http://socialmention.com
9 http://twitrratr.com/
10 http://www.neuroproductions.be/twitter_friends_network_browser/
11 http://www.crowdeye.com/
12 http://archivist.visitmix.com/
13 Batelco is one of Bahrain's telecommunication companies.
14 http://tweet.grader.com/
15 http://twittersentiment.appspot.com/

Section 3
National Practices of Social Media in Higher Education

Chapter 8
Functions of Social Media in Higher Education:
A Case Study

Violeta Maria Şerbu
The Bucharest Academy of Economic Studies, Romania

ABSTRACT

This chapter aims to explore some critical functions that social media is playing for the internal processes included in an alternative higher education model – The Alternative University, developed in Romania, since 2007. This case study highlights the challenges and opportunities associated with using these new communication as well as information technologies in order to generate effective learning environments. The collaborative and student-centered traits of higher education models using social media for learning activities are mainly dealt with in this study. Functions such as connecting people, sharing knowledge, collaboratively generating knowledge, community building, management platform, accumulation and construction of knowledge, knowledge assessment, raising learning motivation, personal branding, and networking are identified as important assets of social media for their use in a higher education setting.

INTRODUCTION

The reality augmentation with the new information and communication technologies became more obvious with the birth of Web 2.0 and the Social Media phenomenon.

Web 2.0, defining the second wave of evolution of the Internet, which came after the dot-com bubble (O'Reilly, 2005) is perceived as the *social* web, or as Tim O'Reilly and John Battelle explained it in 2009, "is all about harnessing collective intelligence" because involves "building

DOI: 10.4018/978-1-4666-2851-9.ch008

applications that literally get better the more people use them" (O'Reilly & Battelle, 2009, p. 1).

The exponentially growth of technology also increased the social change rhythm: we are more mobile and the scale of participation has increased by orders of magnitude, thus the Web is becoming the world itself (O'Reilly & Battelle, 2009). In this perspective, Social Media is just the way people communicate in this wide connected world, this communication is now easier to carry, faster and more reachable than the traditional one (Asur & Huberman, 2010).

This communication-driven revolution, the so called *Social Media,* "touches nearly every facet of our personal and business lives" (Qualman, 2010, p. xiii). Higher education is no exception.

Higher education - perceived as a space for creating and sharing the most cutting-edge knowledge into society, is more and more influenced by this new media, either creating alternative models of higher education or transforming the old ones (Kamenetz, 2009). Social Media is blending students' learning environments and their knowledge "in one virtual world" (Robbins-Bell, 2008).

Initially regarded with skepticism, Social Media is now more and more integrated into the academic world, fulfilling a wide range of functions – from performing citations tools to academic community building instruments or learning platforms for students and also for the teaching staff (Junco & Cole-Avent, 2008; Hazari, North & Moreland, 2009; Li & Pitts, 2009; Violino, 2009).

Nevertheless, the traditional academic world is still reserved about using social media with profound educational purposes (Selwyn, 2009) and underestimates its potential in transforming the higher education landscape (Hazari, North & Moreland, 2009; Ras & Rech, 2009).

By choosing to research the uses of social media in the Alternative University case, we aim to explore its potential, analyzing the advantages that it brings - ease of use, availability, individual affordability and network effect, (Alexander &

Levine, 2008) but also its characteristics, such as "persistence, multiuser, avatars, and wide area network" (Robbins-Bell, 2008) and the bigger context of "new culture of learning" (Thomas & Brown, 2011).

Last but not least, we will present a case study of a non-traditional university that developed its own way of integrating social media in the educational model it had experimentally developed. The case study will focus on the main functions of social media (educational and non-educational), the principles that influenced the integration process, the limits of its use and also on the aspects relevant for future research.

ON SOCIAL MEDIA AND HIGHER EDUCATION

A New Way of Communicating and the Education Revolution

In a wider context, Social Media is regarded as *the latest trend in education,* (Violino, 2009) changing not only the way we consume information, but also the way we interact with each other and relate with information and knowledge (Kamenetz, 2009; Selwyn, 2011). New types of communication require new types of human behaviors and enact different kinds of needs.

The Internet has changed the way we think about technology and information, by "becoming a participatory medium, giving rise to an environment that is constantly being changed and reshaped by the participation itself" (Thomas & Brown, 2011, p. 42). Douglas Thomas and John Seely Brown (2011) speak about "a new culture of learning", facilitated by a "growing digital, networked infrastructure" that "is amplifying our ability to access and use nearly unlimited resources and incredible instruments while connecting with one another at the same time" (p. 18). This new type of learning is based on "potent tools" as Wikipedia, Facebook, YouTube, and online games that enable learning as a mix of "play, questioning and imagination" (p. 18). Therefore, Social Media leads to "making the general personal and then share our personal experience in a way that, in turn, adds to the general flow of knowledge" (p. 31). As the authors stated, "learning thus becomes a lifelong interest that is renewed and redefined on a continual basis" (p. 32).

An interesting fact is that some of the more significant trends in social-media supported learning are positioned outside the formal higher education system (p. 4). In this regard, "social media are socially disruptive technologies that prompt a range of deeply ideological (rather than purely technical) questions about the nature of institutionalized education" (Selwyn, 2011, p. 7).

Hence, new information and communication technologies are one of the main factors that put pressure on contemporary higher education. This enables higher education institutions to reform. More importantly, new types of higher education institutions arise, such as online programs or even more flexible forms of higher education, such as a *do-it-yourself university* (Kamenetz, 2009).

Do-It-Yourself University aims to develop a new kind of university, where students learn whatever they want, whenever and wherever they want to and with whoever they want and they will learn by doing (Kamenetz, 2009). This includes using the new information and communication technologies for learning purposes, but also requires independent study and self-directed learning.

Important social movements as those mentioned above are evolving worldwide. A relevant example is the *Edupunk* movement that fights against higher education institutions "lethargy and irresponsibility" and of financial means that are "cannibalizing their own mission" (Kamenetz, 2009, Kindle Location 1488). Kamenetz considers its origins in Ivan Illich ideology regarding the phenomenon of deschooling society. Edupunks argue that Internet-driven transformations will

change humankind history, liberating people from the bureaucratic world.

Higher education institutions, seen as the eternal "ivory tower", can be perceived as quite reluctant regarding this phenomenon. Though, we must note important initiatives such as the *OpenCourseWare* project of Massachusetts Institute of Technology (MIT). MIT has been a pioneer higher education institution, supporting the *open education movement* since 2001 when it decided to give free access to its courses and other knowledge created by the institution's community.

In the last decade, have developed many open education initiatives – free sharing video content, scientific articles, educational online games or augmented reality apps. These brought mobility, actionability, collaboration and real-time access of knowledge which allowed technology to become increasingly better at replicating the effects of physical proximity – by micro blogging services, immersive tridimensional environments or videoconferencing. Transforming education with this technologies is a cultural revolution but also a technical improvement in knowledge delivery. Kamenetz speaks about an Education Revolution that will strike traditional institutions to be more democratic and open and to better serve students and communities (Kamenetz, 2009, Kindle Location 1761).

Using Social Media in Higher Education

Furthermore, online education provisions are less expensive than brick-and-mortar ones. That transforms length and structure of university courses, offering new ways of customizing learning and universities administration (Kamenetz, 2009, Kindle Location 1146).

Nowadays, students are representatives of the Net Generation, being digital natives that come into the higher education with great experience in technology and Social Media – they are the first generation to grow up with technology integrated into their lives, from cell phones to instant messaging (Junco & Cole-Avent, 2008; Nikirk, 2009; Wankel, 2009). Thus, Net Generation *"reacts fast and multitasks, prefers an experimental working approach, is communicative, and needs personalized learning and working environments"* (Ras & Rech, 2009, p. 553). However, there is empirical research showing that social media and internet usage skills are not universal in students; therefore the digital divide is not only a matter of age but is also dependent of other contextual factors (Bennett, Maton & Kervin, 2008).

The students experience overcomes that of faculty or higher education administrators (Junco & Cole-Avent; 2008). That is why, it becomes more critical to harness technology in order to raise the students engagement and satisfaction and, at the same time, to improve the quality of their education (Junco & Cole-Avent, 2008; Li & Pitts, 2009; Violino, 2009). There are also financial reasons for successfully implementing these new technologies in higher education processes. The purpose thus becomes to consume less resource for more learning benefits.

The social environment that social media created is transforming education, which is becoming more interactive and flexible. As Ras & Rech (2009) were exemplifying, "reusing experiences from other students provides a first step towards building up practical knowledge and implementing experiential learning in higher education". (p. 553)

Social media are web 2.0 technologies that generate learning spaces (Hazari, North & Moreland, 2009; Ras & Rech, 2009). Those can be seen as tools for teaching and learning, "providing collaborative features and active learning opportunities in a web-based environment" (Hazari, North & Moreland, 2009, p. 187). In order to be truly effective, online learning must help facilitate the social process of learning, more specific, this involves providing "space and opportunities for students and faculty to engage in social activities" (Dunlap & Lowoenthal, 2009, p. 129).

Regarding the new social media integration in higher education, Robbins-Bell (2008) argues

that the barrier between the inside and the outside of the classroom is starting to break and this even enables the dialogue by raising the students' level of participation and contribution. In this regard, higher education institutions must follow "the <<rules of engagement>> in the online world in order to maximize their effectiveness" (Mattson & Barnes, 2009). But, due to the fact that students are multidimensional in talents, interests and abilities, communication tools must also be used differently in order to increase student involvement (Heiberger & Harper, 2009).

Social Media can be used for a multitude of purposes. For instance, higher education administrators could use it for staying connected to student networks, for promoting relevant events, and helping students feel safe and at home on campus (Heiberger & Harper, 2009).

Taking into account the above-mentioned reasons, we can observe that Facebook, created in 2004 is now one of the most frequently visited websites on college campuses and better at discussions functions than any web communication technology enabled by institutions (Schroeder & Greenbowe, 2009). In this respect, it is exploited for these kinds of purposes. For example, Facebook is supporting student integration, such as making friends inside the campus, "being the <<social glue>> that helped students settle into university life" (Madge & co., 2009, p. 141). Also, Facebook facilitates an "<<identity politics>> of being a student", providing the space where all the students' role conflicts with the formal prerequisites of higher education can be safely released and dissected with peers. (Selwyn, 2009) Another specific use of social media, with a more educational value is *"Web 2.0 storytelling"* that could be used both "as composition platform and as curricular object" (Alexander & Levine, 2008, p. 99).

The onlineuniversities.com 2011 info graphic regarding social media use in American higher education, called *Pros and Cons of Social Media in Education,* signals the fact that *"Social Media* is growing and not going anywhere. Many schools are now embracing the move. By understanding this movement, schools can make better choices on how to utilize Social Media in education" (mashable.com). Some interesting results showed the following: the number of college students using Facebook rose from 61% in 2008-2009 to 98% in 2010-2011; admission professionals are now using LinkedIn (from zero percent in 2008-2009 to 47% in 2010-2011); social media are used for sharing learning materials, making class announcements, consolidating institution's brand or professional development of teaching staff.

Among social media "successes" we are bound to mention: allowing teachers to control the online environment; making safer communities; encouraging collaboration through peer learning and working online opportunities; extending the invitation to produce content in a worldwide context "universities should have a focus and a clear idea on what they want students to see when they Google the school" (mashable.com).

Moreover, some "challenges" are reviewed – lack of knowledge of administrators institutional to make these accounts be more authentic; lack of features - "even a good webpage is useless if there aren't features that include on-to-one connection."; "it requires daily maintenance and interaction with students", taking in consideration that current and potential "students will judge the school based on their experience with the schools' Social Media accounts" (mashable.com).

According to the EDUCAUSE Center of Applied Research 2011 report, the main academic benefits of technology encompass four areas: "1. Technology gives students easy access to resources and helps them dispense with administrative tasks and keep track of academic progress; 2. Technology makes students more productive; 3. Technology helps students feel connected and 4. Technology can make learning a more immersive, engaging, and relevant experience", thus its major functions being that of *connecting, creating relationships,* and *online learning* (ECAR, 2011, p. 4).

CREATING COLLABORATIVE AND STUDENT-CENTERED LEARNING ENVIRONMENTS WITH SOCIAL MEDIA: THE ALTERNATIVE UNIVERSITY CASE STUDY

The Alternative University: Bringing the Education Revolution from the Grassroots

Worldwide, numerous discussions took place about a *"crisis" in the higher education system* and a series of transformations; one of the causes invoked was the lack of *an adequate educational model.* In Romania, higher education has expanded greatly over the last two decades, quantitatively, but also qualitatively, even if the results obtained are increasingly being challenged by stakeholders. One of the positive changes of the last two decades is *the development of professional student organizations,* noting an increased awareness among academic communities and other stakeholders regarding *their recognition as relevant educational partners.*

In this context, CROS (Resource Center for Student Organizations), was born as an initiative of former members of student organizations. Their main purpose was to *increase the impact of student organizations in society.* On a long term, CROS founders' mission is to *establish an alternative university, based on an innovative educational model.*

So far, their efforts of building this model consisted of establishing two communities of practices – one for students that are passionate about the human resources area and the other for communication enthusiasts, respectively *HRemotion* and *New Media School.* This involved building a philosophy on education as well as other particular learning programs to support this education.

The CROS educational model has *no fixed or predetermined curriculum,* being *student-centered* and *based on self-directed learning.* Instead, it includes three learning environments – an organization (for testing and practice), a specialized community of practice (for reflection and collaborative learning) and individualized counseling programs (for individual growing and support). Thus, the educational programs included in this model are of two types - *individual support* (which refers to self-directed learning, coaching, mentoring, workshops, networking or branding) and *social learning* (intergenerational summer school – *CROS Camp,* sharing meetings, training sessions, practical workshops, advanced practical courses, building community social events, online community platform, interactive library, access to external development opportunities such as internships) (Şerbu, 2011, pp. 338-347).

The mission of the Alternative University (AU) is *"to train people able to live a happy and fulfilled life, discovering and cultivating their talent and passion"* (CROS, 2011, p. 3). The vision behind is that a happy person is defined as one who *"has found his element"* - *"where his talents meet his passions",* and that person is able to learn and develop in an autonomous manner throughout life (CROS, 2011, p. 3). Among university's educational principles can be mentioned: *autonomy in learning, personalization of education, perceiving learning as an organic and nonlinear process, integrating learning with reality to acquire relevance and genuine motivation, defining learning as a social and collaborative process* (CROS, 2011, p. 3). One can notice a predominant orientation to social constructivism theories of learning, for example, the theory of communities of practice developed by Etienne Wenger and collaborators (Wenger, McDermott & Snyder, 2002), which were explicitly an inspiration in establishing the first community of the university.

The AU's educational model is only in its infancy, the majority of its educational programs have been in a pilot phase for the last four years, but there is considerable support and openness from the external environment - companies, students, and other stakeholders concerned with education that resonates with the principles and values transmitted by CROS members.

In the medium term, the University wants to be established as a small institution (with less than 1,000 students) focused mainly on learning; the education provided having "a strong component of personal development." The target audience is composed of "young people with a high degree of autonomy ", who do not want to choose a fixed specialization, preferring instead to seek their way of living in an autonomous, nonlinear and interdisciplinary manner. As stated by the founders of this model, AU importance will reside in the fact that it "will set the standard in: focusing on student autonomy, flexibility and customization, practical experience and connection with the socio-economic sector, integration of personal and professional development" (CROS, 2011, p. 12).

Social Media is perceived as an important component of the infrastructure of this educational model and also a lever for higher education innovation. Given the very limited resources of the organization that implements this model, it has developed a platform for information and personalized communication, using the freely available Internet information systems, facilitating a lean and efficient management and access to knowledge. Also, these tools have served to build a platform for communication, management and learning for students in the communities of practice.

Viewed in an integrated way – AU's educational principles and social media characteristics relation reflect in reality the features of the created educational model - open knowledge, richness of experience and learning resources, the dynamic of social interactions and knowledge generating conversations, facilitating the capitalization of human potential, attractive learning environments, education as an easy facilitating process supporting individual's autonomy, scaling learning at group or organization levels.

Research Methodology

Following qualitative research logic, we chose the study case as the most appropriate method to address the issue of describing the main features Social Media is playing in the implementation of the Alternative University educational model.

We selected this method as appropriate for this theme taking in consideration the view of Serge Moscovici and Fabrice Buschini, who considered that "a case study illustrates a special care to present the complexity of a phenomenon, focusing on natural, holistic, and phenomenological character of approach" (Moscovici & Buschini, [2003](2007), p. 196). At the same time, it is "an increasingly used method in educational research" (Antonesei, 2009, p. 52).

Thus, the research methodology is a descriptive one, respecting the specific requirements described by Yin [1984](2005), in order to answer the "how" and "why" questions, pointing out a contemporary phenomenon seen in a real life context. (p. 17) The study is also exploratory, widening the perspective on using social media in Higher Education.

The investigation was build around the following specific research objectives:

- Formulating a definition of Social Media in accordance with the educational philosophy of the studied educational model;
- Identifying the main functions, needs to address or determine the roles that social media play for specific processes of the investigated educational model;
- Revealing sets of examples of specific practices or subject related tools;
- Identifying and describing the limits of harnessing social media at the level of the researched educational model;
- Decrypting specific principles regarding the use of social media in the Alternative University educational model;

- Formulating dilemmas and conclusions on the studied subject.

Also, before collecting, analyzing and interpreting the data, two assumptions have been issued:

1. Social Media consist of a series of working and communication tools;
2. The learning function is not explicit, but implicit in the studied model.

Data collection sources were identified based on methodological suggestions offered by Yin ([1984](2005), p. 107), using three types of qualitative methods: observation (mainly participatory), interview (unstructured and semi structured) and document analysis. Also, there were accessed at least three similar data sources (interviews with minimum three people, observation of at least three relevant events or consultation of at least three relevant documents), thus ensuring research construct validity through triangulation (see Table 1).

During data collection some ethical measures have been taken, such as asking the consent of the participants for using data from the observed activities, the conducted interviews and also the performed content analysis and keeping the anonymity of all the individuals that participated in this research.

Regarding sampling procedures, the data sources were selected based on the waterfall approach, following a logical sequence of evidence (Yin, [1984](2005), p. 107). Firstly, the key stakeholders involved in implementing the educational model were interviewed and then accessed the other relevant sources they have recommended. Also, observations indicated the relevant documents to be analyzed. In general, we selected those documents which had a strategic component for the organization or its developed educational model or the ones with direct reference to online tools used by the students.

Table 1. Research methods and data collection

Method Category	Method Type	Data Sources
Interview	Unstructured interview - "Uses of Social Media in Implementing the Alternative University Model"	3 internal processes coordinators of the studied educational model
	Semi structured interview - "Knowledge Management Tools used by CROS organization"	4 of the studied educational model founding members
	Semi structured interview - "CROS as a learning organization"	5 of the studied educational model founding members
Observation	Semi structured participatory observation – "Using Social Media for the Alternative University Educational Model Processes"	3 relevant events (CROS's biannual strategic meeting, one working day at organization's building office, one educational program team meeting)
	Unstructured direct observation of social media uses by the organization in implementing the AU model	4 months (November 2011 - February 2012) of participating at organization's activities
Documents Analysis	Analyzing relevant content on the way of using social media by the implementing organization related	3 websites (one of the organization and each of its two communities); 11 wiki sites (collaborative) that serve to the organization's members and University' students; 17 collaborative documents (Google Docs) used by members and students; 3 Facebook pages (one of the organization and each of its two communities); 3 Twitter accounts (one of the organization and each of its two communities); 4 online discussion groups (one at organizational level, two at community level and one at an educational program team level).

The data collected from all sources and methods have been archived in a common online database, whose elements coincided with the specific research objectives. According to the instructions given by Robert K. Yin, we chose the described case development strategy for analyzing data collected and comparative synthesis and construction of explanations as specific techniques (Yin, [1984] (2005), p 135).

At first, data processing consisted of transcribing all the collected data (verbatim transcripts of interviews, observations notes taken during the observation and notes of the documents analysis). Subsequently, these texts were filtered by a code established under the seven elements extracted from specific research objectives:

1. Definition of Social Media,
2. Functions, roles and needs covered,
3. Examples of relevant practices or instruments,
4. Limits of using social media in the higher education model,
5. Specific principles of using social media in AU educational model,
6. The dilemmas of the explored phenomenon and
7. Some extracted conclusions.

The filtered content was inserted in a table, according to the seven variables defined, and then links were established between contents which conveyed the same idea, and generalizations to be made based on evidence testing, by triangulation.

These interpretations are the basis for developing a case description and corresponding explanations.

The final report was developed on the following structure: *CROS's way of defining Social Media, social media advantages, main functions of social media for CROS's educational model, CROS's specific approach of integrating Social Media in an educational setting, limits of this approach and concluding remarks.*

Defining Social Media

The research data revealed some specific ways of defining Social Media by the organization's members.

First of all, Social Media is perceived as *the virtual layer of the physical reality*, as one respondent said, "It is a natural way for replicating the existing conversation". Thus, it is a sort of mirror for the real world, reflecting its principles of action, values, relations or deficiencies. An evidence of this relation is that the online instruments that had the best results were generally the ones that resulted from a prior real event or action. Furthermore, when the "offline" situation goes wrong, it shows also in online (for the same environment or function). In the reverse situation, some online features can be replicated in a real setting, as the printed "like" button, posted on objects or even persons. As the Internet is becoming mobile, these ways of augmenting reality with a virtual layer will be more often. We can take the QR codes as examples.

This way of looking at Social Media widens the horizon of these environments impact, that of being more than "a set of social networking tools playing some small functions". Instead, these media are rather seen as "dynamics of people of a certain type, which is somewhat facilitated by this environment".

The relationship between these two perspectives - "amount of tools" versus "dynamic" or *phenomenon* was captured mainly in interviews

with members of the organization, so any online tool that has a social component is rather seen as an "instance" that "brings only one type of ingredient", and the environment, itself, consisting of all these networks and instruments to which individuals are connected, and forming a "potential" of "energy" that is manifested by these "instances". But this is a milieu in which most of us are living each day.

Additionally, Social Media reflects an "extensive conversation" *between* people, offering opportunities for reality augmentation, as it offers possibilities that have never been seen before in the physical environment - from connecting people very distant from each other physically or culturally, to unlimited possibilities of collaborative working compared to the physical work facilities, this being "a means by which people remain in contact even when they are not face to face".

These extended possibilities of human interaction, make the created environment a living and effervescent space, offering unlimited opportunities of expressing human creativity, all creations being in a continuous remix and easily transferred, retrieved and used by the people connected in the "network", serving both to social construction, and personal defining – "is not only a social space but conveys something about you as a person."

A sharing attitude (which is really the motto of the studied organization - CROS) reflects very well the way this set of social media is perceived - connecting people in order to share, to create something from scratch or by mixing different things. The spirit of initiative of young people, with the desire to build something together with similar people that is definitely relevant to the community that shares common value, resonates with the Social Media philosophy. The Internet is perceived as "the medium in which they unfold", responding to "the need to be connected, to build together."

Social media are also considered as a sense making instrument, because "with as many people sharing the same piece of information, it starts to get some kind of social importance." Thus, Social Media "is more than a new way to communicate, is a new way of thinking and interacting with the world."

Social Media Traits and Advantages

After analyzing the data, we could draw a number of features of Social Media. What is more, we can also find the advantages of these environments:

- Promotes open access knowledge;
- Provides multiple opportunities for collaboration;
- Knowledge is built flexibly and collaboratively, being remixed and gaining relevance by ratings, comments, or by the level of users access;
- Information is personalized - from the way of accessing it to the processing or presentation, responding to a variety of styles and informational creation and consumption needs;
- Has a high degree of flexibility in terms of functionality - from socially oriented functions (communication, connection, collaboration) to other more individually oriented (generally, the management of information relevant to individual, etc.);
- Also, is very adaptable, responding to a variety of specific needs (usually, translating specific functions from the real life in the virtual environment);
- Has easily modifiable content and features, allowing easy search and continuous redefining of knowledge and of the environment itself;
- Is more easy to correlate, as mash-ups of functions or tools - for example, the Google suite;
- Supports entrepreneurship and initiative (by group support, low cost information and work management);

- Provides powerful opportunities to disseminate information, due to high connectivity of these environments and automatically to their users;
- Replicates online what happens in the physical environment, especially the interaction between people, thus, being a mirror of the physical environment;
- It is a potential energy which may enormously potentiate initiatives and knowledge delivered in the physical environment.

Main Functions of Social Media in CROS's Educational Model

In the following, we draw a synthesis of the main functions that social media plays in the studied educational model. These functions are grouped by two separate criteria - one with reference to their immediate utility for stakeholders, and the second correlated with educational principles included in the studied model.

By Functionality

1. Connecting People

These environments connect individuals or groups of individuals dispersed in the physical environment ("from the other side of the world"), but who share common interests, needs, values, beliefs, etc. Thus, people can be aware of what others are doing and, at the same time, they can align their preferences or some similar or common initiatives. It is thus "a way to understand live what is happening in another context in which ... you are not part of."

There are many ways and tools corresponding to this function - in principle, all the social networks as Facebook and Twitter, where the user has an account which associates a profile and connects with other users' profiles. Thus, users connected to the network are closer to each other, having access to activities performed by others and can share activities, information and interests, either to act together, or simply to keep in touch. This function is responding, also, to the socialization needs of individuals. As interviewed subjects declared, this is "a means by which people remain in contact", accessing and building relevant connections together. This connects people and facilitates their communication.

Members, students and other stakeholders of the studied educational model are following each other constantly with the help of these online tools in order to keep connected - for example, by posting personal information on Facebook or Twitter, or sharing their location through tools such as Foursquare, Facebook Places or Google Lattitude.

2. Sharing Knowledge

Sharing news, things we like, our views, values, etc. is a reality of the recent years we are living in. Users of these environments are passing from the information consumer role to the one of knowledge distributor or producer.

Thus, by simply posting some information on your Facebook or Twitter profile, or writing an article on his or her personal blog, someone could generate complex and consistent interactions – such as a positive appreciation, the distribution of that piece of information on the network, formulating comments that can generate deep conversations, or just labeling the accessed content.

The shared content can be found in many shapes, and there are specialized tools for each, for instance, for text content as articles, presentations, magazines, actors included in the study access Slideshare, ISSU, Scribd; for the digital photography, they use Picasa or Flickr; for the video content, Qik, YouTube, Vimeo; for sharing geographical coordinates: Google Maps, Google Lattitude, Facebook Places, Foursquare etc.

Most times, the act of sharing some piece of information in the network generates an exchange - for example, a respondent recalls how the participants of a launching event transmitted

live *what they understood, what they felt and lived, (...) impressions, sensations, feelings*, based on positive appreciations or comments on each other's posts.

3. Collaborative Knowledge Generation

The possibilities for collaboration in these environments are perhaps the most attractive in terms of learning and knowledge development for any educational environment. From collaborative sites (wikis), as Google Sites, Ning or Wordpress blogging platform; collaborative working tools as the entire suite Google Docs - spreadsheets, docs, presentations, forms, drawings (for project management, designing events or documents, etc.); Prezi (for presentations or design events); MindMeister (for collaborative mind maps); Mendeley (for team research) or Picasa, Flickr, YouTube (for video or photo editing) – all of these media offers almost limitless creative opportunities (an interviewed member said about Yammer that "is brilliant for ideas"), experimentation, collaboration, editing or filtering information.

An illustrative example is the initiative to create an open handbook of the HRemotion community, which contains knowledge gained in this group, one that "any member of the community can edit, supplement, enhance, (...) to create an information resource for HR in student NGOs, putting together what we each have, in an organized form."

One advantage of this feature is that of *distance effectiveness* (for example, the using of chats or collaborative documents for a meeting of a project team, or the practice to open a collaborative scratchpad for any process, when working on drafts for new documents, articles, presentations or event design).

4. Collaborative Management Platform

One of the most valued features of Social Media in the studied educational model is the management facilities that it brings - at the organizational, project or process, and individual level. Thus, Google

Sites wikis are used by students as a control board of all the processes integrated in the model. Here we have the documented educational processes and the internal organizational management (e.g., planning and assessment weekly objectives), which are stored and archived as relevant data for these various actors (processes, events, decisions). These data are fingerprints of activities and knowledge produced in the interactions of the physical environment and remains archived, creating a kind of history of the knowledge evolution and progress at the community, organization or individual level.

Management platforms developed over time include a variety of services - from collaborative planning of events with a Google Calendar shared by individuals, teams or organization (also Doodle or Google Spreadsheet are used to set up meetings), to effectively and flexibly organize information as procedures, meetings minutes, partners database, useful contacts, budgets, etc. (with Google Sites, Google Docs, Dropbox - for accessing large data archived in personal computers, or even social bookmarking tools as Delicious or Stumble Upon, content syndication tools such as Google Reader), to a more managerial sense as project management with tool such as Manymoon, for all kinds of projects, or Mendeley, for research projects. They reflect the functions of the physical tools, trying to supplant these functions and even to augment it – "That stands for timetables, course material, and place to exchange information, personal learning environments or library". Also, this type of informational platform is "a support for reflection, analysis and synthesis, it helps you take decisions, think, put out some ideas, even if they remain in a document".

Some of the benefits of these platforms were mentioned - flexibility of information processing, real-time data operation possibilities (e.g., minutes taken during meetings), collaborative working possibilities, sharing options, integrating character (putting together different types of instruments and content), allowance of easy search

and customization of data processing, facilitating monitoring and evaluation, reality augmentation, extending learning processes – "We document some processes that happen offline and provide greater access to resources coming from offline."

5. Knowledge Assessment

As one respondent said, "With many people sharing the same piece of information, it starts to get some kind of social importance." This makes Social Media a tool of social validation and assessment and provides as well qualitative and quantitative feedback on knowledge conveyed by these media. This can be undertaken by using different forms of expression - *like*, *comment*, *reply* or *share* (through media such as Facebook, blogs, Twitter, YouTube, Foursquare, Delicious or Stumble Upon).

Another example of using social media in knowledge assessment are data metrics enabled by tools like Google Analytics or Facebook Insights, which provides evidence of data concerning the use of information, enabling and facilitating deep and complex analysis of their social relevance or their users. The fact that this knowledge is preserved as a trace, fingerprints or history of groups activity, allows an assessment of the activities progress, of processes and outcomes that were produce, even long after they have been completed.

6. Internal Communication Platform

The organization developed a communication platform connecting multiple social networks with restricted access to its members and students – such as Google discussion groups, Yammer, Facebook groups, Google Chat or Yahoo Messenger (rarely), Skype and other online communicating facilities such as the shared calendar that permit responding to an invitation.

Any newly formed team creates their own communication system, based on at least some of the above-mentioned tools, which allow, according to the statement of interviewees – "a very good and convenient combination between communication and information of the group." For example, Yammer, an internal communication channel used only by the organization's members, is regarded as a good channel for "information, quick decisions, resources, making fun of each other", facilitating an "easier internal communication."

7. External Communication and Branding

This is a widely mentioned function. For CROS, Social Media reflects the offline working principles of the organization or group of people, as a kind of "mirror of reality." According to respondents, they may reflect:

- "The criteria by which we do business, the spirit and vision we are building on the Alternative University;"
- "Communities, the idea of HR or the idea of communication and how to develop them and what's the level they have reached";
- The organization's message that "education may be some other way."

External communication channels - blogs, Facebook pages and profiles, Twitter profiles, all of which have a profile that conveys something about the identity of the organization and the educational model that is developed, represents, according to a respondent, "a way of promoting some things in a group of people with a common interest." One result of this function is that "somehow gathers around CROS people who have similar values." Thus, Social Media strives to enlarge the community and spread the vision, also, transmitting, communicating and promoting a lifestyle, enjoying the high spreading power of this message, facilitated by the phenomenon called "word of mouth."

In addition, content analysis revealed that the message is not the only one promoted, but it sup-

ports also a particular language (e.g., *community, sharing, learning, dream big, education, you, together, human resources, communication and management*) and reflects a new kind of society - "We speak a different language than our parents. We use pictures, sounds, movies and animations. And environments that we are sending it to are richer, open, bidirectional, social. It's more than a new way of communicating, is a new way of thinking and interacting with the world."

A member said that he gathers "people on Facebook as a kind of public", but communication is not just one-way - from the organization to the outside, but it also *generate* a quite consistent *conversation* with those external actors who resonate to the values found in CROS activities, Social Media being a stimulus for this conversation (with many features of expression).

This communication facilitates networking, developing and maintaining its existent and new network partners. It is also a means of building the identity of the university, growing credibility and recognition among stakeholders that form the public mentioned above. At the same time, social media are used as a channel for campaigning, such as raising donations or promoting events.

Social media enable brand building not only for the organization, but also for its members and students. In fact, this is mentioned as part of the educational model - through workshops, exchange of experience and by connecting to social networks, students build their own brand because this is "a space that is not only social but which conveys something about you as a person."

By the Educational Model Specific Necessities

1. Learning as Knowledge Construction and Accumulation

Social media facilitated learning is viewed from two perspectives - a *social* one, with reference to facilitated social interaction that produces learning and knowledge building and an *individual* one, in the sense that social media are knowledge vehicles that facilitate learning at the individual level, through accumulation of parts of that knowledge by individuals online.

Thus, these environments "can lead to valuable and intense conversations." The respondents gave us some examples that we find relevant, as Facebook, where "conversation happens a lot" or blogs that allow "deep conversations". Even Social Media use do not always has an explicit learning purpose, it still plays an important role to *continue the conversation* of students, conversation becoming unwittingly a support for the learning processes, designed "to support learning and social needs, and community expression." For example, inside the Facebook group of New Media School community a conversation was started about a commercial video competition that turned into a debate about the evaluation criteria of these types of ads and the elements that ensure their success.

One special characteristic of Social Media learning function is that information is built over time and with the contribution of all community members. A respondent said that Social Media helps to "collect and share resources", but "learning is the basic function." A dictum of students from both communities, engraved on an artifact from a previous summer school, says that "sharing is knowledge", correlating with a respondent's statement - "If you share what we find with others, learning experiences will be certainly more valuable."

Another learning feature of Social Media is that of providing support for building a personal learning environment, as well as an architecture allowing customized learning "but in a broader context." This personal architecture also leads to new ways of learning for individuals - a more self aware and autonomous learning, which requires, as a respondent stated, "learning to learn in a different manner." This supports entrepreneurship and initiative, making *students* the co-creators of their own *learning experience.*

Furthermore, CROS use social media for *knowledge augmentation*, enabling the completion or expansion of knowledge emerged from the physical environment – for instance, the completion of one sharing meeting outcomes with resources added by students that could not attend that meeting.

In addition, due to knowledge storage and processing functionality of Social Media, every learner has the chance to reflect on his own development, using these media as a *support for reflection, analysis and synthesis.*

2. Community Building and Socialization

Building communities as reliable learning environments, is one of the principles underlying the development of the studied educational model as mentioned above. Thus, Social Media is perceived as "a way to keep the conversation alive for people who are interested in the same subject", managing to "keep them in the dialogue from one event to another." This can be seen from several points of view:

- Ensuring the conversation "that links the group", which keeps community members "connected to each other", creating a kind of link members sometimes feel addicted to, as a member said - "When there is no activity on Yammer it feels as nothing happens in CROS."
- Facilitating interaction, creating a "shared learning space."
- Creating a *membership framework* (for example, in the design of these instruments are inserted identity elements such as photos of each member or valued symbols, a specific language, reflecting the spirit of each team or group in part, i.e. for HRemotion community, to *empower through knowledge sharing* and for New Media School *to be and do amazing things*);

- Being a personal space, enabling *a sense of intimacy and trust*;
- Responding to two important needs of people - that of "belonging to a group that shares common interests" and that of "building together."

Side of these advantages, Social Media *stimulates and facilitates the expression of each individual* - helps you manifest symbolically certain feelings, attitudes (e.g. the *like* button), but provides also the transmission of values, principles, beliefs, etc. among community members, based on socialization, thus creating a transfer from the individual to the community and also backwards from the community to the individual.

A specific feature of these communities of practice, unlike that of traditional communities, is that they are open and have different and more flexible memberships- so there is a core of members more involved and attached to the group activities, around which other members revolve at different distances. In this respect, "Social Media could link people around communities of practice", is expanding the wider circles of community on its outskirts, with potential members and partners. Worth mentioning is that this principle acts both at the community of students level but also at the level of members of the organization.

3. Strengthening Motivation for Learning

Motivation is the main support for learning, as expressed in the principles of the studied educational model (Şerbu, 2011).

Motivation function of Social Media is reflected, however, in several other complementary aspects:

On one hand, it is done by connecting to community social networking, but also by supporting the involvement and commitment from those connected to the network (students, members or other stakeholders). Thus, community extension and vision spreading is a way of supporting motivation and strengthening the "can do" or "can do better" attitudes, of becoming more ambitious. The challenge between members in order to overcome their performance is a common practice, Social Media being a support for it (e.g., *Blogging Challenge* competition held between two groups of members referring to the number of personal blogs unique visitors, or *The Game* competition, held between community members of New Media School, aiming to accumulate points for several tasks in order to strengthen the community with the help of the online environment).

The customizing options of these environments, the possibility of identity elements insertion in the design of these tools, gives a sense of ownership over accumulation and production of knowledge processes in these learning spaces, giving greater confidence and involvement. Also, these personalized environments heighten the sense of pride and belonging to the group. In this respect, each community discussions group has an automatic signature attached to each message released on the network, reflecting the view of that community, for instance, for the communication community it is "Together we learn to do every act of communication an Amazing one". Thus, the sending of motivational messages in the network aims "to transfer enthusiasm, values, and a vision."

Another important contribution of social media for students' motivation consists in providing recognition and appreciation by other members of the group. This creates a mechanism for positive reinforcement and rewarding of the efforts, a way of knowing "that what you do has some sort of value, that someone is appreciating that."

Also a motivating factor supported by social media is the *climate* facilitated by the social networks of communities, as a member interviewed said, it is "creating a family atmosphere." Thus, this virtual environment keeps "close together" the community members "because it allows posting all kinds of messages."

Specific Principles that Influence Social Media Integration in AU Model

Following these analyzes, we draw a set of specific principles of the Alternative University educational model that influence the integration of Social Media in the educational processes and its use.

The first principle relates to the integration of new instruments, namely *by continual experimentation*, at CROS each social medium being firstly tested and then shared within the organization or community, along with facilitating the awareness of its value. Organization's members can be integrated into the so-called group of *early-adopters* of new occurrences of Social Media, one of the motivations for this behavior being captured in one of the interviews - "more are more driven by needs, with limited resources, we always looked for innovative solutions to make things happen."

The same principle is found in the behavior of always updating, adding the newest hardware technologies which members have used since their appearance and are still using - iPhones, iPads, technologies based on Android, Kindles, etc. Also, they always test new experimental tools launched by Google, and seek to develop strategic partnerships with innovative companies in the industry (as Google, Adobe, or Sony).

Another CROS specific approach for using Social Media is *the customization and adaptation of the functionalities of these tools to specific needs* – from insertion of logos and custom designs, to searching ways of finding for new functionalities at the existing tools use. Also, everyone can build their own customized social networking platform - for example, it can used to build a personal learning environment.

Simple and flexible Social Media content and architecture development can also be revealed for this educational model. Everything is put online for easy accessing, editing, sharing and updating, the flexibility of these media fitting

with the organization's principles - "everyone in its natural rhythm."

As to the efficiency aspect, members have developed a number of features to streamline Social Media specific information flow, for example, by using labels, collaborative documents as scratchpads or defining principles and indicators of use of any online instrument or information - for instance, rethinking community platform after following principles - "useful - to meet the needs of its users, accessible - easy to use and access, desirable - to please." The results of these efforts are identified by a respondent: "we invested infinitely less than most - I mean money, time ... we invested less in building and promoting but our adoption rate is much higher."

The above-mentioned principles can be also separated from the data analyzed - from the way members use mobile technologies so that they can be always online or how they share relevant content (e.g., with a smart phone they can share on Facebook a photo taken with a phone connected to the Internet), to the attention on linking "offline" experiences (behaviors, workshops or social events) with the ones that are "online" (i.e., by posting photos of those events, the minutes to be completed and read by those who were not physically present, etc.). A member surprised this principle stating that the tendency is to see "what is the natural behavior that I tend to have and depending on that I choose if the instrument it's right for me or not." The aim is therefore that of linking experiences together in a way that makes sense and generates value.

An effect of the integration principle is the promotion of *Personal Learning Environments (PLE)* concept, which encourages students to take control of their own learning, and integrates all their sources and spaces with learning potential they have access to and feel that are relevant to their learning.

The collaborative spirit is reflected in many aspects of CROS activities - starting with organization's motto - "Sharing Attitude" or with the human resources community slogan - "Shared Knowledge is Power." This principle correlates very well with the operating principles of Social Media - open access to knowledge, knowledge sharing, collaborative working, knowledge assessment based on social relevance, communication with exponentially force of spreading. As for their effect on learning, in an article on the communication community's site was mentioned: "We realized that if we share with others what we have found, then our learning experiences will be more valuable."

Friendship, mentioned as a principle of using Social Media for CROS educational model, can be translated into "knowing each other on a personal level and learning well together." Two relevant examples are online social games (*The Game* and *53+*) initiated in each of the two communities of practice, with the aim "to know each other better, collaborate and become friends." Friendship spirit is found in a normal day, when people are physically together, but focused on their laptops to communicate to the outside, and yet intersecting in Social Media (e.g., someone puts a picture or announces an event on Facebook, and someone else, who is physically near him, working on something else, gives him a like, comment or shares his information).

Collaborative construction of knowledge and *ownership on knowledge* form a basic principle of the educational model, derived from social constructivist conception of learning. Thus, students are co-creators of the learning experiences, starting with choosing the working tools they will use. An example is the *Online Community Creation Kit* event, attended by all members of communities that came with suggestions and participated in building the online learning and working platform of the communities of practice. The importance of this event is argued by a member - "people, if not employed in the process and projects from the beginning, do not feel it as their own (...) let's think together what are our needs and what we want the platform represent for us (...) and to

build together, with all these instruments that are becoming increasingly user friendly, to be developers of our own online learning experiences."

CROS is a *values based organization* (Şerbu, 2011). The cultural layer of Social Media that interferes with educational processes is very important to ensure the desired learning outcomes. Respondents consider that this layer stands also as a basis of communicating efficiency in social networks, "without focusing on the fact that we clearly need to be in the minds of people around us, this is happening because we are somehow a network of people who believe and have some fundamental common values." Social Media became a vehicle of this culture, allowing both its propagation and its orientation.

CROS works primarily with the members of student organizations, these young people having a common value profile - voluntary, enthusiastic, creative, free spirit, sociable, self-consciously etc. Therefore, the values transmitted by using social media through the extended education community around CROS model resonates with this profile: innovation, collaboration, freedom, following your own passion, lifelong learning, dynamism, etc.

Limits of Using Social Media in the Alternative University Educational Model

After analyzing the collected data, we found a number of limitations of using Social Media for supporting AU educational model. It is worth mentioning that these limitations are not necessarily related to the functionality of these environments, but rather to their use within this educational model.

Examining the functioning of these tools in implementing AU educational model, we found the following limitations:

1.   They *require some development time and effort in order to be adopted*, a certain resilience

of the facilitators being necessary. CROS members analyze which is the optimal degree of push and pull in the growth of Social Media adoption levels among students. Most times, it is a matter of available time or energy of the facilitators, or of the natural growth rate of students or the community which cannot be forced to be adopted otherwise because it would become artificial or unsustainable - "You can do whatever you intend to do with this, if you grow up to that level (...) but it must be supported until it can grow up alone."

The best practices of adoption comes from two areas – it either covers a strong "offline" need (as Facebook covered the need to remain in contact with people with common hobbies and interests) or it benefits from a sustained effort of the facilitators of raising its adoption rate by the community (as the wikis collaboratively developed by the two communities of practice members). Unfortunately, according to the members interviewed, "at the moment, our communities are not really able to capitalize the online environment, they are still at half - we push more than they pull." A favorable indicator in this respect would be that of organizing a sharing meeting on Skype.

2. A problem that these environments can encounter on their way to support the educational model comes from the *existing differences between their users*, their different communication needs or different levels of knowledge. This reflects in the new members' integration process which can be biased by the large amount of data and the assaulting flow of information of this media. They need an induction period in order to discover their value and not perceiving it as something just to be taken for granted. The *Online Community Creation Kit* event, mentioned earlier, is a solution found by CROS members and one that could work in the long run.

Another shade of this problem lies in the different communication preferences of members - from simple and attractive tools (as Facebook) to a little more technical or complex (as Google Wave or, more recently, Google Plus) or between the highly interactive ones (Facebook) to the less interactive others (Twitter and blogs).

An aspect of this problem is that most users of the networks mentioned in the study are more consumers than producers of the disseminated information, a fact that can frustrate those making efforts in building knowledge (for example, those who write on blogs, put information on the discussion groups or constantly use the shared calendars).

3. In the spirit of innovation and experimentation that characterize CROS organization, the AU educational model Social Media platform development *requires numerous trial and error experiences* until the appropriate instruments are selected to be adopted by the community. For example, in order to choose a platform with good working and communication features for the communities, the Ning network was tested for several months, but has been adopted partially and only by some of the members. Subsequently, Google Sites proved to be more successful.

The solution built over time for this problem was to keep a limited number of instruments, generally one for a function, and to experiment until members realize which tool responds better to a specific need and then implement it till is stable and integrated. Usually, this strategy worked firstly within an experimenting group (few open-minded members or a team project tested it) and then it was transferred to the community and adopted by each new member.

4. *Information surplus and complexity* is another obstacle in integrating Social Media within the studied educational model. Many tools are appreciated by community mem-

bers, but are not used due to the complexity or negative reaction to informational surplus. Also, a disadvantage is the fact that organization abilities and discipline are necessary in order to use these tools properly. For instance, unlabeled or unfiltered collaborative files can be very disturbing for someone who has access to many of this kind, as well as using shared calendars that include too many events. Simplification and better organization, by setting rules of communication or data storage, are the key to successful management of this surplus information, the functionalities of these tools already allowing that or being in the process of amelioration, based on users' feedback.

One of the consequences related to information surplus is that they are quite time consuming. Furthermore, when these networks remain open while working, it can be highly distractive. CROS members are searching and disseminating solutions among communities concerning the elimination of these distractions, aiming to build a mental hygiene of work.

5. A number of *limitations pertaining virtual and physical environments relationships* could be drawn. Firstly, as data indicate, people's enthusiasm must be supported by "offline" events in order to lead to knowledge construction in the "online" environment. For example, in order to facilitate the exchange of practices between community members, first you need a physical meeting in which the individuals to talk face to face, and then analyze the data they produced and add new knowledge online.

This is because people still feel the need to socialize physically with their peers. When you meet someone on Facebook and you like what he or she does, you may feel the need to invite him or her to a discussion in the physical environment. Based on observations, we could identify that the basis for this behavior lies in the need for natural human gestures that cannot be entirely filled by the virtual environment, such as smiling, watching each other, touching, retrieval in a small space or playing purely physical habits such as eating or drinking a good tea, kinesthetic sensations that online cannot provide or replace.

Social Media often appears as a surrogate in relation to the physical environment that cannot always successfully compensate all "offline" functions. Some convincing arguments were extracted from collected data: it is *"a technique or resource that helps us to structure the learning, but not the process of learning itself"*; a deep conversation in the online environment cannot be generated as simple as in the physical one, ie. explaining the fundamentals of UA education; the content they carry cannot hold the same credibility that have, for example, scientific journals, so that information remains only *"a personal opinion, just one point of view, a perception"*; there are certain group work processes that can hardly be mediated, such as consultation on an event design; sending a message itself is distorted by the lack of emotional layers and of paraverbal and nonverbal elements as in the face to face communication; the need of connectivity through hardware infrastructure can be in itself a communication barrier for the physical interaction.

6. Proper functioning of social media *is dependent on a particular infrastructure,* that of being software or hardware. Firstly, you need an Internet connection - connection involving availability, costs, signal quality, etc. Then, it depends on the reliability of those online tools that are in most cases free or free versions of applications, which makes them prone to operational errors (bugs) or remain often without storage space for its free users.

Also, physical infrastructure is not neglected - to be connected even when you are mobile, you need smart phones, laptops or tablets, which require sufficient battery life to support networks access, but also to support the functionality of these mobile networks (e.g., Flash software to access mobile applications). Furthermore, that hardware can be sometimes exhausting for the human body (e.g., eye strain or tiring body positions, increasing temperature, a sedentary lifestyle etc.).

7.   Not least, one issue identified by respondents and also from the data collected through observations was the *weak integration of all accessed networks,* so it is somewhat hard to meet the diversity of individual or group of users needs. While social media are generally easily integrated and linked together, this requires some effort and a better understanding of each type of network functionality.

It may be noted, however, that integration of social tools exists between rather similar types (Google suite links together collaborative working tools, Facebook connects several communication needs - in dyads, group, mass, or a personal branding group or FriendConnect integrates multiple communication channels, etc.). But there is still the need of features integration, as a respondent was affirming "some tools are so well knitted that they are covering many needs at once." Though, he also argued that "there is no Facebook that can save your bookmarks or where you can access your video library... that are scattered and have to go separately for each function." In this perspective, the ideal would be "to have the Internet as a kind of tool (now it is a kit)."

FUTURE RESEARCH DIRECTIONS

This study only attempted to outline the boundaries of the problem of functions that Social Media can play throughout a higher education educational model, without pretending to achieved all essential aspects and taking in consideration the particular context in which it was analyzed. In this respect, *future studies* can be pursued and investigate other aspects such as:

- Elaborating methodologies for harnessing the relationships between physical and virtual environments (to adapt "working methods to the expected results", according to a respondent's statement);
- Identifying the border between social and personal for any of the used social media;
- Analyzing how that builds knowledge, skills and attitudes for those who use these media in an educational model;
- Documenting the relationship between social media features and AU educational model specific needs;
- Identifying ways in which can ensure students learning sustainability through Social Media;
- Measuring the return on investment for these media usage - what users receive in return for the time and energy invested daily on social networks).

CONCLUDING REMARKS

Following the results, we argue that Social Media can be viewed from at least three perspectives:

- *As a set of tools* that perform a variety of functions in people's lives. Some are more social (connection, communication, socialization, community building), others more operational (information, research, collaborative working, management, learning);
- *As a social phenomenon* that has an impact on contemporary human life. As a respondent said, "online (...) is very present in the lives of people we work with, and in our

lives or those who are CROS partners, participants and friends" and produce some positive effects, such as expanding conversation between individuals and groups, increasing efficiency and management of collaborative work processes, expanding the space of expression, etc., but also some negative ones, such as impaired concentration at work, increasing superficiality of sent messages or consumption information addiction;

- *As an environment or manifestation space*, reflecting both a mirror of reality (when the "offline" goes wrong, it shows also in "online", for the same environment or function) and a means to reality augmentation (extending communication, relationships, the way of working, knowledge itself or learning processes). It creates a mix of manifestation environments of individuals (eg, the relationship between virtual and real, "offline" and "online", between the personal and the social, etc.), managing more or less harmoniously to integrate into individuals' lives.

- In the end, looking at our *premises initially formulated*, we can conclude the following:

- The premise that *Social Media is composed of a series of working and communication tools* was confirmed, but much enlarged by the other two perspectives mentioned above (social phenomenon and manifestation environment) and also was nuanced with other functionality, such as contact, community building, management, motivation or learning.

- The second premise, that *the learning function is not explicit, but implicit in this model* is confirmed by the fact that these environments are viewed more as a support for the learning processes, but not with the same force to contribute to knowledge accumulation and construction as the "offline" events have now in the educational model studied.

REFERENCES

Alexander, B., & Levine, A. (2008). Storytelling emergence of a new genre. *EDUCAUSE Review, 43*(6), 40-56. Retrieved December 20, 2011 from http://net.educause.edu/ir/library/pdf/erm0865.pdf

Antonesei, L. (Ed.). (2009). *Ghid pentru cercetarea educației. Un "abecedar" pentru studenți, masteranzi, profesori*. Iași, Romania: Polirom.

Asur, S., & Huberman, B. A. (2010). Predicting the future with social media. In *International Conference on Web Intelligence and Intelligent Agent Technology*, Vol. 1 (pp. 492-499). Toronto, Canada: IEEE Press.

Bennett, S., Maton, K., & Kervin, L. (2008). The 'digital natives' debate: A critical review of the evidence. *British Journal of Educational Technology, 39*(5), 775–786. doi:10.1111/j.1467-8535.2007.00793.x

Centrul de Resurse pentru Organizații Studențești. (2011). *Universitatea Alternativă: Model educațional pilot*. Retrieved April 12, 2010, from https://sites.google.com/site/croshq/comunicare-si-parteneri/materiale-de-comunicare/PrezentareUAfinal.pdf?attredirects=0

Dahlstrom, E., de Boor, T., Grunwald, P., & Vockley, M. (2011). *The ECAR national study of undergraduate students and information technology*, (Research Report). Boulder, CO: EDUCAUSE Center for Applied Research. Retrieved December 20, 2011, from http://net.educause.edu/ir/library/pdf/ERS1103/ERS1103W.pdf

Dunlap, J. C., & Lowoenthal, P. R. (2009). Tweeting the night away: Using Twitter to enhance social presence. *Journal of Information Systems Education, 20*(2), 129–136.

Șerbu, V. M. (2011). *Paradigma învățământului centrat pe student. Abordarea etnografică a unei comunități profesionale*. Unpublished doctoral dissertation, University of Bucharest, Bucharest.

Hazari, S., North, A., & Moreland, D. (2009). Investigating pedagogical value of wiki technology. *Journal of Information Systems Education, 20*(2), 187–199.

Heiberger, G., & Harper, R. (2008). Have you Facebooked Astin lately? Using technology to increase student involvement. *New Directions for Student Services, 124*, 19–35. doi:10.1002/ss.293

Junco, R., & Cole-Avent, G. A. (2008). An introduction to technologies commonly used by college students. *New Directions for Student Services, 124*, 3–17. doi:10.1002/ss.292

Kamenetz, A. (2009). *DIY U: Edupunks, edupreneurs and the coming transformation of higher education*. Vermont: Chelsea Green Publishing.

Li, L., & Pitts, J. P. (2009). Does IT really matter? Using virtual office hours to enhance student-faculty interaction. *Journal of Information Systems Education, 20*(2), 175–185.

Madge, C., Meek, J., Wellens, J., & Hooley, T. (2009). "Facebook," social integration and informal learning at university: "It is more for socialising and talking to friends about work than for actually doing work. *Learning, Media and Technology, 34*(2), 141–155. doi:10.1080/17439880902923606

Mattson, E., & Barnes, N. G. (2009). *Social media and college admissions: The first longitudinal study*. Retrieved January 12, 2012, from http://www.umassd.edu/cmr/studiesresearch/mediaandadmissions.cfm

Moscovici, S., & Buschini, F. (Eds.). [2003]. (2007). *Metodologia științelor socioumane*. Iași, Romania: Polirom.

Nikirk, M. (2009). Today's millennial generation: A look ahead to the future they create. *Techniques: Connecting Education and Careers, 84*(5), 20–23.

O'Reilly, T. (2007). What is web 2.0: Design patterns and business models for the next generation of software. *Communications & Strategies, 65*(1), 17-37. Retrieved December 20, 2012, from http://ssrn.com/abstract=1008839

O'Reilly, T., & Battelle, J. (2009). *Web squared: Web 2.0 five years on*. Special report, Web 2.0 Summit. Retrieved December 20, 2012, from http://assets.en.oreilly.com/1/event/28/web2009_websquaredwhitepaper

Onlineuniversities.com. (in press). How higher education uses social media. *mashable.com*. Retrieved February 5, 2012, from http://mashable.com/2012/02/03/higher-education-social-media/

Qualman, E. [2009]. (2011). *Socialnomics: How social media transforms the way we live and do business*. Hoboken, NJ: John Wiley & Sons Inc.

Ras, E., & Rech, J. (2009). Using Wikis to support the Net Generation in improving knowledge acquisition in capstone projects. *Journal of Systems and Software, 82*(4), 553–562. doi:10.1016/j.jss.2008.12.039

Robbins-Bell, S. (2008). Higher education as virtual conversation. *EDUCAUSE Review, 43*(5), 24-34. Retrieved January 19, 2012, from http://net.educause.edu/ir/library/pdf/ERM0851.pdf

Schroeder, J., & Greenbowe, T. J. (2009). The chemistry of Facebook: Using social networking to create an online community for the organic chemistry. *Innovate: Journal of Online Education, 5*(4).

Selwyn, N. (2009). Faceworking: Exploring students' education-related use of "Facebook". *Learning, Media and Technology, 34*(2), 157–174. doi:10.1080/17439880902923622

Selwyn, N. (2011). Social media in higher education. *The Europa World of Learning 2012*, 62nd ed. Retrieved December 20, 2011, from http://www.educationarena.com/pdf/sample/sample-essay-selwyn.pdf

Thomas, D., & Brown, J. S. (2011). *A new culture of learning. Cultivating the imagination for a world of constant change*. Lexington, KY: CreateSpace.

Violino, B. (2009). The buzz on campus: Social networking takes hold. *Community College Journal*, *79*(6), 28–30.

Wankel, C. (2009). Management education using social media. *Organization Management Journal*, *6*(4), 251–262. doi:10.1057/omj.2009.34

Wenger, E., McDermott, R., & Snyder, W. (2002). *Cultivating communities of practice. A guide to managing knowledge*. Cambridge, MA: Harvard Business School Press.

Yin, R. K. [1984](2005). *Studiul de caz. Designul, colectarea și analiza datelor*. Iași: Polirom.

KEY TERMS AND DEFINITIONS

Alternative University: A higher education model established in Romania, based on training people able to live a happy and fulfilled life, discovering and cultivating their talent and passion.

Education Revolution: The social change of education enabled by the new information and communication technologies and humankind's knowledge evolution.

Functions of Social Media: Needs covered or roles they play for specific stakeholders.

Learning Environments: Real, virtual of mixed spaces of human manifestation where people share, process, build and gain new knowledge.

Social Media – as a Manifestation Environment: Perceiving Social Media as a mirror of reality and a means to reality augmentation.

Social Media – as a Set Of Tools: Perceiving Social Media as performing a variety of functions in people's lives.

Social Media – as a Social Phenomenon: Perceiving Social Media as having a significant impact on contemporary human life and producing positive or negative effects at this level.

Chapter 9

A Users' Perspective on Academic Blogging:
Case Study on a Romanian Group of Students

Mihai Deac
Babeş-Bolyai University of Cluj-Napoca, Romania

Ioan Hosu
Babeş-Bolyai University of Cluj-Napoca, Romania

ABSTRACT

There has been much research dedicated to the use of blogs in higher education, but a great deal of its enthusiasm is based on data that have the potential to be distorted by social desirability. The current chapter attempts a more balanced look at the use of educational blogs, taking into account the shortcomings, as well as the benefits of their proliferation amongst students. The authors write from the perspective of the blog users. Although their feedback is mostly positive, user behavior is also affected by fear of peer appraisal, lack of engagement, lack of trust, or unwillingness to share knowledge or to debate. In order to support our argumentation, the authors use traffic data from the educational blog "blogdeseminar," survey data from a convenience sample of Romanian students, and qualitative data from 11 interviews.

INTRODUCTION

As technology moves towards more and more integrated solutions for using the web, the telephone or the computer, there is a natural tendency to decrease the amount of time and attention people give to conventional ways of reading, studying and communicating. The development of Web 2.0, social media, e-books and phone applications for using the internet means that nowadays, the difference between an internet user and an administrator of content is virtually inexistent and also that online communication has become accessible

DOI: 10.4018/978-1-4666-2851-9.ch009

to everybody, from anywhere, at any time. Actual dialogue, rather than reading what others publish, is now, more than ever, possible. To add to this, the fact that the web and new media are more likely to be used by members of the younger generation is also difficult to debate against.

In this context, academic teaching is bound to be one of the areas where new media of all kinds would make an impact. Using it for learning and for directing student's preoccupation with the internet towards online platforms where they can actually find relevant information, where they can try collaborative studying and sharing their knowledge and resources, is vital for having an interested and informed group of students. Blogging can be one of the best tools to be used in such a direction.

While there has been some interest towards the use of social media and Web 2.0 within universities, the focus has been mainly on the way lecturers and students use social networks such as Facebook (Bosch, 2009, Akyıldız & Argan, 2011). Studies predictably show that students do not primarily use such tools for collaborative learning but rather for pleasure. Yet, they use the network in a variety of ways, some of them being more active than others. Some of Bosch's subjects even report that using the social network makes their lives easier, as checking academics on the same platform they use on a daily basis, for social reasons, turns out to be very practical. Also, using Facebook for academics enables students to help each other with learning resources, advice and administrative information, such as assignments, course venues, and time-table changes. There is also a discussion on benefits that teachers might draw from being able to contact students more efficiently, and in a more informal, comfortable environment.

New communication technologies greatly increase the possibilities for individuals to interact with others in the public sphere, but the question remains: how much does ITC contribute to the development of a culture of dialogue and debate within the educational environment? This question is legitimate since socio-psychological studies have underlined both positive and negative aspects regarding the use of academic blogs for learning purposes.

The educational blog, although under-exploited, occupies a strategic position within the current communicational landscape. The acknowledgment of this position is given by the combination of psycho-social, cultural and cognitive roles it fills and by the fact that it promotes both relational activism and reflexivity, stimulating consumption of the productions posted by others and inviting to ones' own content production. On that same note, the educational blog provides heightened interactivity by exploiting the connectivity existent between groups of individuals with common interests.

Finally, perhaps the most important aspect is that the educational blog could represent a model for continued social learning. The empirical studies that we quote further on, though not many, and sometimes not very detailed, underline the academic blogs' central attribute to be its' social value. They also point to aspects that should be improved, that should lead to better learning and various forms of collaboration.

Scholarly blogging has been the focus of some innovative research, as early as the first few years after blogs were developed. Even though the technology had been available since the late '90s, blogs had become large-scale online instruments only a few years after the turn of the millennium. Some of this research has been provided from the perspective of teachers and scholars (Flatley, 2005, Gregg, 2006). It is revealed that the teacher's job was, in some concerns, much more efficient. Professors were able to evaluate the level of involvement in group work and discussions in a much easier way. It is also argued that academic blogging can support the creation of a truly efficient system of scholarly debate between professors.

However, for this chapter, we engage on the endeavor to study academic blogging from a users' perspective, complete with benefits and shortcomings. The chapter aims to introduce a critical dimension to the study of academic blogging, different from the rather descriptive or over-enthusiastic literature that has been produced so far. The objectives for the current study are to determine patterns of use of the academic blog by the students and to discover whether it helps or hinders the development of dialogue and debate. More particularly, the chapter's objectives include:

- Determining schedules and periods of intense use
- Studying the type of content that is accessed - whether administrative information (assignments, time tables) or scholarly content is preferred
- Exploring the purpose of use, be it for mandatory assignments or for other academic discussions
- Describing the level of involvement by the users – passive readers or active contributors
- Assessing the level of cooperation between peers
- Gathering student perceptions on the efficiency of the blog as teaching instrument

BACKGROUND

Perceived Benefits

Most literature on the subject of academic blogging is very optimistic when evaluating the effects such web tools have on the learning process as a whole. Empirical studies almost invariably show positive reactions from students involved in classes where blogs had been introduced. Perhaps the most synthetic of approaches is the one proposed by Minocha (2009), who combines mostly qualitative data from 26 different case studies in the UK to draw conclusions about the

benefits and challenges that are connected to social software in higher education. The benefits largely outnumber the challenges, and they include: *Inspirational learning* (learning from others) *and reflective learning, Sense of achievement* (others can see and appreciate students' work), *Sense of control and ownership, Peer-to-peer support and feedback, Team working, Problem solving, Overcoming communication difficulties in face-to-face environments, Creating one's own e-portofolio, Collaborative learning etc.* (Minocha & Roberts, 2008, Minocha, 2009).

Further benefits of higher education blogging are acknowledged by Ducate & Lomicka (2008), who add to Minocha's list, the fact that there is no need for advanced HTML knowledge to be able to generate content, and the benefit of encouraging critical thinking. Supporting the same argument, one could say that blogs have the capacity to engage people in knowledge sharing and debate, leading to "collective knowledge generation" (Williams & Jacobs, 2004), which is more than just information. This is an advantage that seems to turn blogs into perfect learning tools for students. Williams & Jacobs (2004) are also responsible for reporting on one of the first initiatives in academic blogging, the BGSB MBA blog. Testimonials from this experience prove that it was a largely positive one. Students reported that although there was an initial fear of taking the risk to blog, they quickly came to realize that it was a good way to discuss concepts and it allowed the sharing of up-to-date information that would not have been possible in/during class. Also, the testimonials reveal that students had to spend more time reflecting on what they had to say (see also Martindale & Wiley, 2005, Brescia & Miller, 2006).

Some authors have found benefits of academic blogging using the Delphi method. Brescia & Miller (2006, p.48) determine which elements are considered to be the most important for students. First few elements are:

- The possibility to use it as a knowledge log and personal content management system
- The fact that what is learned in school can be expressed in the public eye, which is what happens in real life
- Overcoming fear of expressing yourself outside the safe environment of the classroom

It is worth noting that the possibility for interactivity is revealed to be only in seventh place within the rankings. In spite of this view, there are some examples of online platforms that have efficiently led students to share information and help each-other: the MIT Spartan Connect (De Andrea et al, 2012), the BGSB MBA blog and others.

Nevertheless, Brescia & Miller write from the perspective of scholars, while others have insisted that academic blogging is meant to shift responsibilities from teachers to students:

As indicated, we believe that the radical inversion of both the locus of responsibility, from teacher to student, and from institutionally owned technology to that which is publically available, has the potential to transform the quality of current networked learning. (Brett & Cousin, 2010, p.613)

The authors go on to praise the fact that Web 2.0 is open for all to contribute and participate. Yet, this view does not take into account the great amount of so-called "lurkers", passive users that do not contribute to the discussions and works of the blog (Williams & Jacobs, 2004). Foale & Carson (2006) are also inclined to put the emphasis on the fact that networked learning in general should be managed by students, rather than teachers. They paid a team of foreign language students to create and manage an educational blog. However, it would be interesting to see if such an educational resource could be developed without any extrinsic motivation. Martindale & Wiley (2005), who are some of the first authors to discover the uses of academic blogging, also militate for a student-led system, and they discover first hand that academic blogging should be developed outside the institution, completely free.

One of the few studies that did not offer a reward for student's participation is that of Blau et al (2009). Authors claim that tutors had a minimum involvement in the task that required students to post and comment on the posts published by their peers. The good news is that in this particular case, all posts in the academic blog received feedback. Also, the number of comments was higher than average. Yet, not any type of post received the same amount of feedback from peers. Comments varied depending on the type of information. Posts that were informative received far less comments. The results show that it is important to request opinions in your post and to have content that is perceived as personal. The posts estimated as near received significantly more comments compared to posts which were perceived as distant or strictly informative (Blau et al, 2009, p.240).

There are not many authors who describe the relationship between online and offline activity for a university course. Davi et al (2007) used the blog to discuss the in-class topics in advance, so when students came to class, they would be prepared and participation would grow. Data suggests that participation does indeed grow, although it is somewhat inappropriately measured, soliciting once again potentially socially desirable answers from the students.

Also on the part regarding benefits, Ducate & Lomicka (2008) explore the use of blogs for foreign language classes. It shows that at the time of the research, there was little to medium knowledge of the term "blog" among students. The research adopts a very particular angle on the topic, using blogs as a gateway towards other cultures. Contrary to some expectations, the authors discovered that some of the students who participated less in class, were willing to share many opinions and even personal details and issues online (Ducate & Lomicka, 2008, p.18). The blog has offered a relaxed setting where students could express their feelings. This rather surprising finding could be explained by the fact that in this case blogging was used solely to increase foreign language writing abilities, the topic/content being far less important. Therefore, one could talk about his/her feelings without fear of appraisal, and without underestimating his/her capacity to provide useful input. All things considered, feedback from the students involved was largely positive, pointing out one major advantage that refers to socialization, creating a community and learning about each-other. The same benefits are acknowledged by Yang (2009), on a very similar group: foreign language student teachers. Feedback from the research subjects pointed out the benefits of ease of access and engagement. Discussions were described as being more "inviting". Also, adding to Ducate & Lomicka's findings, student teachers stated that they were more comfortable in constructively criticizing their peers online, rather than discussing the issues face to face. (Yang, 2009, p.17).

Obviously, not all students use academic blogging in the same way. Derntl & Graf (2009) are the only authors who try to correlate posting behavior with preferred learning styles. We find their study to be one of the most relevant in the entire literature dedicated to the subject, as Derntl and Graf differ from most researchers in the fact that they did not establish blogging as a compulsory task for their students. However, they did provide a platform where students were encouraged to talk about one specific project, indicating the problems they encountered, solutions that could be useful to other colleagues etc. Their results in terms of student participation were, in these conditions, impressive: an average of 7.5 postings per student, during one semester, for one project. Learning style was not correlated with how often they used the blogging environment, which indicates that it is a tool with the potential to be used by all students. Posting is an entirely

different matter, as active learners proved to have higher posting rates than reflective learners. At the same time, the latter prefer to read the posts of other users over posting themselves, which is the exact opposite from active learners. Students also had the possibility to rate the posts of peers, and the aggregate scores were posted in a blog chart. Active learners used top rated blog charts more often, as they rely more on other student's opinions and assessments. There were also some differences between sequential and global learners, in terms of length of posts. However, since the study focused on a group of students with a technical background, a study on students from social sciences or humanities may have very different results. It is notable, that although 70% of the students hadn't used blogs before, they were open to this possibility after the course experience.

The way educational blogging is received and understood may well depend on the cultural setting involved in the study, too. In Romanian higher education, experience tells us that there is a subculture of doing the minimum that is required in class, in order to pass a course. Although other subcultures may be present among students, this particular current involves low participation if there is no extrinsic reward and little enthusiasm towards new, creative educational methods. To the best of our knowledge, there is only one Romanian author to have studied the use of various Web 2.0 instruments in higher education. Her conclusions partially differ from the above statement, claiming that most students *showed willingness and enthusiasm towards the large-scale introduction of Web 2.0 tools in the instructional process* (Popescu, 2010, p.96).

In summary, all of the above research talks about the upside of using academic blogs, which is largely supported by scholars. However, most of these case studies share a few points where their results are debatable. Although there have been many cases when blog benefits have been supported by data, we argue that most of them are not applicable in any scenario and that sometimes researchers tend to rely too much on data gathered from students through interrogative techniques. It is hard not to suspect that this data may be the result of socially desirable answers, at least in part. It is unlikely that one could play the roles of evaluator, mentor and objective researcher simultaneously, without that situation leading to errors. In some cases, the errors of judgment in the research design are obvious. Derntl (2008), for one, claims that there is a very strong correlation between the amount of blog postings that students made during a course, and their final evaluation, the conclusion being that academic blog postings by students are somehow responsible for higher academic performance. Yet, the obvious reason behind this result is the fact that the blogging activity had been an acknowledged evaluation factor. The students involved in Derntl's study did not post materials based on their own free will to evolve, but due to the fact that it was a compulsory activity within their class, and their marks depended on it. Therefore, stating that those who had a higher performance in blogging were also those who had higher marks is to state the obvious. The same problem is to be found in many other studies, where student's contribution is not entirely voluntary (Williams & Jacobs, 2004, Foale & Carson, 2006, Dippold, 2009). The conditions in which the studies take place may be the reason why Kim (2008, p.1345) felt compelled to notice that apparently very similar experiments lead to completely different results in terms of student contribution to the tasks involving academic blogging.

Another issue is the question why so few authors base their results concerning user's behavior on actual traffic data, rather than interrogative methods. In the world of research methodology, it is a well-known fact that what people say is different from what they do. Also, if interrogative methods such as surveys and interviews are to be applied, than those who operate with these instruments should be perceived as neutral observers. The blog creator and manager (the teacher) and the researcher should be different persons. Lastly, some of the studies (Derntl, 2008, Dron & Anderson, 2009) allowed posts to be private, therefore no actual dialogue was encouraged, and benefits regarding expressing one's self in public were not applicable.

Perceived Shortcomings

In order to have a balanced view on the topic, the shortcomings of academic blogging should also be pointed out. For a summary of these challenges, one could once more turn to Minocha (2009): *Negative comments or non-constructive feedback by fellow students* (arguments), *Selective commenting and being forced to comment, Lack of socialization* (not knowing each-other enough to comment), *Lack of trust of peer feedback, Lack of student engagement, Resistance to sharing artefacts in the public or collaborative space, Student over-enthusiasm or non-interest, Students' wish to remain anonymous in the public domain.* Adding to that, we find that an important factor behind these challenges may be student's under-estimation of one's own capacities (fear to contribute, preferring to be passive). This view seems to be shared by Williams & Jacobs (2004), who believe that this is one of the two possible motives explaining low participation, the other one being the fact that users do not perceive enough immediate benefits from blogging for school. The latter reason suggests a very pragmatic type of user, one that participates only as long as there is an extrinsic reward or an outside pressure on him. Derntl (2008) is one of the few to take into account the variance of user's participation to the blog. His results show that students tend to post just before a lab meeting or a deadline, in order to receive good evaluations, which supports the above hypothesis concerning the pragmatic type of student.

So, what sort of students are we actually dealing with? Do they understand the usefulness of academic blogs and act accordingly or do they act as if posting on the blog is just another "chore"? Based on the research brought forward so far, coupled with our own first-hand experience, we argue that there are four different types of student users of blogs:

- Those who use it because they understand its purpose of generating knowledge through debate
- Those who use it only to get higher marks and only if there is an outside pressure
- Those who don't use it because they fear peer evaluation and lack trust in their abilities to contribute
- Those who don't use it because they are not willing to make efforts for small or no rewards.

Fear of public evaluation is obvious in Dron & Anderson's results (2009), where it is shown that about 80% of students were passive users, making little to no contribution to the discussions. Moreover, given the choice on level of access on their published content, only one student made his post completely public. All others shied away from the public eye. One of the subjects that Davi et al (2007) dealt with puts it best: "Sometimes it was hard to write anything because you really had nothing to say or had a fear of saying something stupid". Popescu (2009) agrees that posting in public mode turns out to be frustrating for users, in some cases. Martindale & Wiley (2005) are less exact when evaluating participation, mentioning that only "one or two" of the students involved in class blogging, put up a blog of their own. Therefore, it would seem that for most students, blogging on academic topics is a closed chapter outside the context of an organized class. These findings are also supported by Davi et al (2007), who conclude that there is little evidence that blogs encouraged peer-to-peer interaction beyond discussion of the blog, either during class or outside of it.

On the matter of peer feedback, Dippold (2009) suggests viewing the matter from two different perspectives. In addition to studying fear of appraisals, one could also take into account that there might be reluctance to offering feedback. The main concern that Dippold's students had was the way to comment on other's work, without sounding "patronizing" or being perceived too negatively. Due to these problems, comments turned out to be generic, stating the obvious or "recounting their own experience related to the topic at hand" (Dippold, 2009, p.17). When asked which of the course tasks they enjoyed the least/most, students favored commenting on others work the least or almost the least, preferring to be on the receiving end of comments. Also, they relied only on feedback from the evaluator, considering peer feedback as unreliable.

Therefore, we can consider research on scholarly blogging to be quite ambivalent, many researchers admitting to advantages that this web tool brings with it, but not without taking into account negative reactions from users. This ambivalence is noticeable in Reviglio's work (2011), where roughly half of the students found the blog difficult to use (although they admitted to the benefit of archiving information from class), whereas the other half enjoyed learning something new and claimed to have adapted easily.

Overall, one cannot deny that the user's feedback on the topic is overwhelmingly favorable and also that the use of academic blogs by students may be intense (more so when a reward is involved). Yet there are question marks on the type of activity that students choose to have on the blog. Students may well be more interested in the posts, but they are far less willing to comment on them (Gregg, 2006). If users choose to remain passive, then many of the perceived benefits of academic blogging may be undermined.

ISSUES AND PROBLEMS APPLIED TO A ROMANIAN GROUP OF STUDENTS

Context and Objectives for the Current Research

As teachers at the department of Communication and Public Relations in Cluj-Napoca, we have had the chance to use various online instruments in order to reach students in the most efficient ways. There are three possibilities through which mediated teacher-student communication occurs in our case: (1) posting information and resources on the official website of the institution, which is not very time-effective since access to the server is restricted and a limited number of employees have access to it, (2) using yahoo groups, which have been the favored channels for communication by most teachers and students for the past 10 years, (3) using blogs, such as the one we have had running for the past year: blogdeseminar. wordpress.com. The blog is mostly used during the first semester of the academic year, and its users are almost entirely bachelor level students from Communication and Public Relations, on the one hand, and Advertising, on the other.

The blog specified earlier (3) is established as a high profile website, currently reaching a total of almost 40,000 page views, with daily averages that span between 150 and 350 views, and a record of 806 views in one day. During the past year, we have gathered traffic data that allow us to understand the way students use the blog for their courses. The increase in use of the blog is correlated with a decrease in the use of the yahoo groups, which were considered to be somewhat ineffective due to a series of reasons, such as (a) the huge amount of unstructured information that was preventing the system from working properly, (b) the lack of discipline and rules for using the group, (c) the difficulty to properly organize and archive messages. As such, much of the information and resources concerning part of the courses was moved onto the wordpress platform.

Data Collection

The data collection process was based on a methodological approach meant to intertwine qualitative and quantitative instruments. By using this approach, we tried to provide a detailed image regarding the educational blog in academic life. The data collection instruments were the questionnaire and the interview guide. The first was used to systematically collect information on the communicational patterns of behavior from those who access *blogdeseminar.wordpress.com*. The former was meant to reveal motivations and in-depth perspectives on user practices, also regarding *blogdeseminar*.

But a study such as this cannot rely solely on data gathered from students, since it can also use first-hand data regarding patterns of access from users by analyzing traffic data. Therefore, it was considered necessary to provide a third research method: content analysis of traffic data. This provides a methodological triangulation that leads to complementary images regarding the research subject.

The content analysis evaluates the frequency and type of interactions between users (posts, comments), frequency and duration of access and other timelines of use.

Quantitative Analysis of Traffic Data

Traffic data from blogdeseminar.wordpress. com shows us that users visit the blog especially when they are faced with a deadline. Right after the deadline has passed, there is a great drop in interest. The deadline for the turning in of the term paper for the first year was set to be the 8th of January. For the second year of studies, the deadline was the 13th of January. For both classes of students, the final written exam, for which they had to read materials that were available on the blog, was set on the 26th of January. Following the timeline in Figure 1, we notice how the use of the blog gradually grows, reaching its highest

Figure 1. The use of the blog timeline

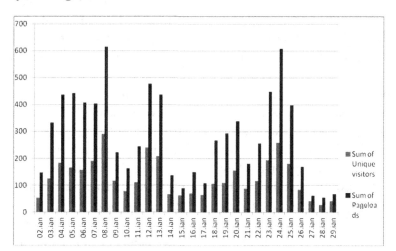

point on the day of the deadline, or the day before it, and then suddenly dropping.

This suggests that students have a tendency to postpone their compulsory activities until the last few days available, after which they lose all interest in reading or discussing academic topics. The patterns of use visible in Figure 2 show us that students do participate on the blog during the semester, but the level of interest shown towards it is about doubled during the period when they are nearing deadlines and evaluations.

Although the number of visitors is high, when it comes to analyzing the number of active users, the situation drastically changes. Comments are few and far between, even though students had been encouraged to share information and even had the possibility to substitute class activity points with online comments. During the whole semester that we had selected for the study, there were no more than 28 comments provided by students, by their own initiative. Taking into account that the target group is made up of about

Figure 2. The students do participate on the blog during the semester

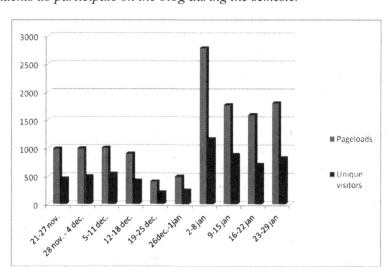

300 students (taking into account only those groups that received support for specific courses), that is an average of roughly 0.09 posts/student, which is much lower than what other researchers have achieved. Furthermore, none of these 28 comments led to any discussions between students, the only short dialogues remaining between the moderator-teacher and the respective students. Results are even more surprising if we look at the number of comments posted to receive activity points. Only 3 comments were posted in order to receive points, leading to the conclusion that the vast majority of students preferred to comment face to face, during seminars, or even not to comment at all. In some cases, the teachers were faced with situations when certain students could not attend class. Although we gave these students the possibility to recover the missed classes by posting on materials they had already read about, they invariably forfeited on that proposal. This goes to show that the students involved have a heightened fear of expressing themselves in the public sphere.

One of the groups of students involved was a class of 84, which had a very uncomfortable time-table, having to attend a seminar Friday, from 18:00 to 20:00. Taking that into account, they were the group that was most encouraged to post comments and links on the topic of the seminar, in order to provide an alternative for their physical presence in class (Table 1). 31 out of the 84 ended the class without scoring any activity points (online or offline), which were a compulsory part of their seminar. Therefore, even when faced with a situation when their grade depended on posting comments, they did not engage into any kind of dialogue. This is part of the reason why many of them ended up failing the entire course.

Looking further on the type of comments that users made, we notice that most of the comments take the form of questions addressed to the teacher-moderator, thus merely replacing e-mail communication. 12 of the 28 comments were utilitarian questions, regarding schedules and such. Very little of the comments provided raised

any scientific issues or started any debates. However, in 5 of the comments, links to useful scientific materials were provided.

The type of content that is accessed by users could also be separated in two distinct categories: administrative information (assignments, time tables) or scholarly content. Granted the fact that most of the content on the blog is utilitarian in content, there are however a number of posts that bring forward topics for debate. Two of these posts are good illustrations of what type of content attracts most users: (1) a post titled "False advertising – the case of Power Balance" and (2) "Herman and Chomsky – summaries from *Manufacturing Consent*". The first is focused around a topic for debate that has the potential to stray off from classic scholastic content, while the second is purely academic. Both are equally open to comments. Post (1) was published on the 7th of January, 2011. It led to some strong debates, manifested through 16 comments, some of which were written in a very aggressive, even insulting manner. One year after publishing, the post still gathers roughly 4.5 readers/day. However, it is safe to assume that these readers are not necessarily students included in our study, as a tracking analysis shows us that many of the readers are led to the post by targeted

Table 1. Type of comments provided by students

Type of comment	Number of comments
Utilitarian questions (about time-tables, changes of schedule, deadlines etc.)	12
Sharing links to articles/online books, sometimes providing comments on them	5
Thanking the teacher for providing information	2
Comments on peer posts	1
Questions regarding scientific content	3
Short summary of an article read by the student	1
Elaborate answer to teacher's comment on post	1
Spontaneous comments on various content	2
Questions about internship, on a related post	1

Google searches. The way in which the post is commented also leads us to believe that readers in this case were not always from the academic environment. However, it proves that the blog can become a platform for discussions outside the faculty. Posted one day earlier, post (2) only gathers about 0.4 readers/day over the same period as measured for post (1). It also spawned only 3 comments since its publishing, under the form of a short dialogue between the author and a person from outside of the academic environment. So, on a more scholarly topic, the attention received is much lower, suggesting that blog comments and activity depend a great deal on posting content that is not perceived as too formal or too academic.

Apart from this type of posting, the blog has the main goal of providing useful learning materials, mainly through the use of organized sets of topics and links to academic content. Students from the second year were evaluated based on what they read every week regarding the topics set on the blog page. Therefore, their mark depended somewhat on accessing the links section regularly. Once there is this pragmatic interest at stake, students access the blog, but they do so mostly based on immediate needs. The blog section where links to scientific materials were provided is accessed, during the normal part of the semester (leaving

aside the period right before the final evaluations and the period of the evaluations itself) receives on average 43.28 views/day, which is about 10 times more than the best school non-related post. Figure 3 shows that this use is dominated by a clear pattern.

Taking into account that students had seminar meetings on Monday afternoon, Thursday morning and Friday evening, when they were invited to discuss what they had read. In accordance with this schedule, the most page views of resource links are done Sunday and Monday, before the seminar when most groups were scheduled. Other high points are the days of Friday and Wednesday, right before the seminars. On the other hand, Tuesdays and Saturdays are the lowest points on the timeline, by far (Table 2). This pattern of use suggests once more that students tend to use the blog when there is an outside, immediate pressure to do so.

Quantitative Analysis Based on the Online Survey

To confirm some of the results from the traffic data analysis, an online survey was conducted through the month of February 2012. It is a time of evaluations for our students, an intense period

Figure 3. Unique blog visitors per day

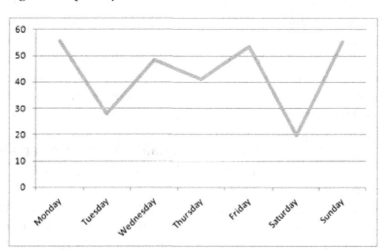

Table 2. Reasons for not posting

Reluctance towards communicating in the public space	15
Having nothing to say	22
Preferring face to face interaction	14
It is more efficient to just use the information provided than to contribute yourself	25
It is not worth making comments, because nobody will appreciate them	3
The blog does not offer sufficient possibilities for dialogue	1
Students just aren't interested in communicating this way	19
Other	4

of studying and taking exams. This is part of the reason that participation in our survey was low: 43 students answered the short questionnaire. The sample of students being unrepresentative and based on voluntary choice of participation, the answers may have been biased, in the sense that those who actually use the blog the most and have something to say about it may have been more inclined to answer. Thus, the results could show more favorable results than reality.

However, results give more insight into the patterns of use of the blog, and we come to realize that there is a positive attitude towards it, but the passive use is blamed on the its' structure. Students claim they would contribute more if the blog was built in a way that would encourage them more to do so, and if the blog was more active, not just supported by one teacher, with limited resources.

36 students mainly use the blog to fulfill their duties with respect to a certain course or seminar (Table 3). Some personal details show that they are experienced users of internet tools (of course there is a strong bias, as the survey was conducted using online forms): 40 use online social networks, 31 declare that they are members of virtual communities and 9 manage their own blog. So it is quite obvious that these students constitute a group that has the pre-requisites to learn using web tools. Interestingly enough, though, the answers show that our group is entirely made up of passive us-

ers, 28 having never posted anything, while 15 having done so rarely. Subjects were also asked to evaluate what may be the reasons why posting is on such a low level. Results in Table 2 prove that there is a general reluctance towards being active users, not predominantly because of fear of peer evaluation, but rather due to commodity and/or actually having nothing worth saying. This brings forward a very dark picture of student's interest in academic debate and sharing of knowledge.

Further into the survey results, students were shown once more to have a well developed utilitarian way of looking onto academic blogging. On a scale of 1 to 10, using the blog to get information on teachers' requests regarding deadlines and content of specific tasks received an average of 9.11, where 10 was used to denote the type of information that is accessed the most. Table 3 shows the detailed results of what students claim to use more often within the blog. The first three categories are by far the most accessed, as they refer to administrative or utilitarian content. In this case, answers were most definitely influenced also by the type of content that is actually available on the blog.

Overall, those who answered the questionnaire appreciated the blog as a useful tool: 24 stated it was very useful, 18 claimed it was rather useful and one person could not deliver an answer. If we were to base our conclusions solely on this type of feedback, the same way that many other researchers have done in the past, we would be presented with an overly optimistic view on academic blogging. Indeed, feedback from the students is positive, but the actual use of the blog proves that it is not a universal solution to solving issues of communication within an academic group.

Qualitative Data Analysis Based on Interviews

Evaluating the student-blog interaction from a qualitative stance was based on 11 single-respondent interviews, directed through a semi-structured

Table 3. Which type of information do you access? (scale from 1 to 10)

Information regarding deadlines and content of specific tasks received for certain courses	9.11
Information on seminar rules	7.11
Information on time-tables of teaching activities	6.76
Links to scientific materials	5.61
Information on internship possibilities	5.28
Information on various events	4.4
Information on employment possibilities	3.88
Articles and discussions on various topics	3.57
Links to extracurricular activities	3.45
Other	1.61

interview guide, which covered a few strategic dimensions for our research:

1. The first dimension regarded the role of the blog within learning activities; in this instance the themes brought forward for discussion with the blog users mainly concerned aspects regarding relationships with other students, with teachers, using the blog in addition to other social media;
2. The second level focused on perceptions of content and architecture of the blog; the accent was placed here on the way that posted information is used, appreciations regarding utility, accessibility and actuality of the information etc.;
3. One last dimension regarded the self-assessment of one's own behavior and level of activism in this type of e-learning, use of ITC for educational and non-educational purposes, online socialization.

Subjects were bachelor level students from the Communication and Public Relations, and Advertising specializations. Selection for the interviews was almost entirely random, yet keeping in mind that a heterogeneous group of individuals would be desirable. Heterogeneity was in fact obtained

in terms of degrees of experience with the blog, as well as in terms of general interest towards educational activities and attitudes towards using ITC in the educational area.

The statements affirmed within the interviews view the blog in an extremely positive manner, as an instrument or way of working with development potential and possibilities to be inserted in learning processes (Table 4). Yet, positive aspects are followed immediately by elements that show the blog to be under-exploited, its marginal position being connected to the logic by which the Romanian educational system is functioning for the time being (Table 5). The interviews clearly reveal that the practice of blog using is not institutionally encouraged; educational blogs are few and online debate is handled with restraint:

I use "blogdeseminar" to have access to relevant information on evaluation methods, but also for news on schedule modifications, exam dates etc.

(...) users also need to be educated. If you don't tell me to do it face to face, than I might not access the blog. In time, I need to get accustomed to see it, and for that I need face to face meetings.

Active use and interactions with *blogdeseminar* are correlated with high levels of activism and active presence in other social media, too. Passivity and restraint are traits of users who also have a hostile or neutral attitude towards blogs and social media in general:

I don't use social media of any kind. I don't have Facebook or Twitter accounts. It is my belief that social networks constrain you, you become too visible to strangers. I only make use of yahoo groups, where information regarding school is provided.

Other positions were identified, too. Some subjects go as far as to support the total substitu-

Table 4. Positive aspects drawn from interviews

Topic	Identified positive aspect
The role of the blog within the learning process	Information regarding evaluation processes Time-saving regarding bibliographic research Clear steps provided for the carrying out of individual projects Offering the possibility for fast and unmediated teacher-student interaction
Structure and content	Contents and information that help with day-by-day activities (deadlines, schedules, meetings etc.)
Attitudes and behaviors on using ITC	Providing content should be continuous, diverse and constant Contents produced by a large number of individuals, both students and professors

tion of face-to-face interactions with computer mediated communication:

If you're going to make me choose between reading something for a class or watching an online video, where the teacher explains a problem, I will always choose the second option. Instead of coming to school I would prefer to connect online and watch what I am interested in.

Fear of appraisal was revealed to be connected mostly to the fear of sounding patronizing or fear of rejection:

I have contributed less to some shared platforms (blogdeseminar, crpedia) because of the attitude that my colleagues have towards me. I no longer have the motivation to share ideas and information because I stop to think that they will say <there she goes again, commenting on whatever she can!>. I used to contribute, but those that appreciate it are very few.

The most pragmatic extract from the interview data reveals a student that is only led by reward systems. The honesty and simplicity in his argument are noteworthy:

As long as there is an interest, I will access the blog (if there are materials needed for school online, if I depend on it to get a grade). After the interest has gone, I don't access it anymore.

The positions expressed are dominated by the need of complementarity and balance between face-to-face relationships and mediated communication. Online platforms are meant to be used in balance with the classic learning methods, and they serve the purpose of rendering more flexible informational flows and stimulating cooperation for common cognitive accumulation.

SOLUTIONS AND RECOMMENDATIONS

The dynamic and interactive character, and the possibility of information exchange between participants are central elements that indicate attractiveness and utility for the blog. The marginal position that the blog holds stems also from the lack of positive experience in relation to the blogosphere. This is why the proliferation of test-blogs should be encouraged. These blogs would have

Table 5. Negative aspects and recommendations revealed from the interviews

Theme	Negative aspect/suggestion identified
The role of the blog within the learning process	It does not have to be a substitute for the face-to-face relationships between teacher and students. The blog contents are just a part of the elements use in the educational process The blog is rather informative and not enough oriented towards debate, exchange and dialogue
Structure and content	Should be completed with socialization and entertainment information An interface that would facilitate contacts between students should be made available Blog dynamics should be oriented towards a debates and discussions platform
Attitudes and behaviors on using ITC	Accessing those social media that regard entertainment and leisure For literature documentation – databases are preferred instead of debates and discussions Facebook and e-mail communication are preferred – acts of communication that are less visible in the public sphere A tendency to avoid public exposure (fear of appraisal, fear of labeling)

the role of providing experience, and promoting favorable attitudes towards the blog.

Furthermore, it becomes obvious that in order to be functional, the academic blog needs to completely distance itself from a formal registry of communication. If the blog publishes too much information perceived as formal, students will use it pragmatically and will remain passive. If we continue further on the path of formality, the blog becomes just another version of the institutional website, whereas its purpose should be to encourage freedom of expression without worrying about others evaluating ones' contribution.

LIMITATIONS AND FUTURE RESEARCH

The current study investigated the status and the role that the educational blog has within the landscape of learning and knowledge. The manner in which it was conducted has been exploratory and it certainly did not accomplish a comprehensive picture of implications and complexities of the blog's use in learning processes. Future research should explore and explain the deep connections that are established between the technology of communication and educational processes. Research interests should be directed towards the changes that take place on an organizational, cultural and inter-human relations level. Psychosociological perspectives regarding participation or involvement in information exchange and knowledge sharing are central elements to deciphering the less-known variables connected to new forms of cognition/learning/innovation. The role of the ITC is central in facilitating the production and dissemination of knowledge and innovation in educational processes, as well as in rethinking the type of interactions that develop between teacher and students, on the one hand, and between students, on the other.

REFERENCES

Akyıldız, M., & Argan, M. (2011). *Using online social networking: Students' purposes of Facebook usage at the University of Turkey*. Paper presented at the International Conference-Las Vegas.

Blau, I., Mor, N., & Neuthal, T. (2009). Open the windows of communication: Promoting interpersonal and group interactions using blogs in higher education. *Interdisciplinary Journal of E-Learning and Learning Objects*, *5*, 233–246.

Bosch, T. E. (2009). Using online social networking for teaching and learning: Facebook use at the University of Cape Town. *Communication*, *35*(2), 185–200.

Brescia, W. F., & Miller, M. T. (2006). What's it worth? The perceived benefits of instructional blogging. *Electronic Journal for the Integration of Technology in Education*, *5*, 44–52.

Brett, P., & Cousin, G. (2010). *Student led network learning design*. Paper presented at 7th International Conference on Networked Learning, 2010, Aalborg, Denmark.

Davi, A., Frydenberg, M., & Gulati, G. (2007). Blogging across the disciplines: Integrating technology to enhance liberal learning. *MERLOT Journal of Online Learning and Teaching*, *3*(3), 222233.

DeAndrea, D. C., Ellison, N. B., LaRose, R., Steinfield, C., & Fiore, A. (2012). Serious social media: On the use of social media for improving students' adjustment. *The Internet and Higher Education*, *15*(1), 15–23. doi:10.1016/j.iheduc.2011.05.009

Derntl, M. (2008). *Employing student blogs as reflective diaries in a lab course*. Paper presented at the proceedings of IADIS International Conference on Cognition and Exploratory Learning in Digital Age (CELDA 2008), Freiburg, Germany.

Derntl, M., & Graf, S. (2009). Impact of learning styles on student blogging behavior. *Advanced Learning Technologies* [IEEE CS Press.]. *ICALT*, *2009*, 369–373.

Dippold, D. (2009). Peer feedback through blogs: Student and teacher perceptions in an advanced German class. *ReCALL*, *21*(1), 18–36. doi:10.1017/S095834400900010X

Dron, J., & Anderson, T. (2009). Lost in social space: Information retrieval issues in Web 1.5. *Journal of Digital Information*, *10*(2).

Ducate, L. C., & Lomicka, L. L. (2008). Adventures in the blogosphere: From blog readers to blog writers. *Computer Assisted Language Learning*, *21*, 9–28. doi:10.1080/09588220701865474

Flatley, M. E. (2005). Blogging for enhanced teaching and learning. *Business Communication Quarterly*, *68*(1), 77–80. doi:10.1177/108056990506800111

Foale, C., & Carson, L. (2006). Creating a student driven self access language learning resource. *Joint BAAL/IRAAL Conference*, Cork, September 2006.

Gregg, M. (2006). Feeling ordinary: Blogging as conversational scholarship. *Continuum: Journal of Media & Cultural Studies*, *20*(2), 147–160. doi:10.1080/10304310600641604

Kim, H. N. (2008). The phenomenon of blogs and theoretical model of blog use in educational contexts. *Computers & Education*, *51*, 1342–1352. doi:10.1016/j.compedu.2007.12.005

Martindale, T., & Wiley, D. A. (2005). Using weblogs in scholarship and teaching. *TechTrends*, *49*(2), 55–61. doi:10.1007/BF02773972

Minocha, S. (2009). A case study-based investigation of students' experiences with social software tools. *New Review of Hypermedia and Multimedia*, *15*(3), 245–265. doi:10.1080/13614560903494320

Minocha, S., & Roberts, D. (2008). Social, usability, and pedagogical factors influencing students' learning experiences with wikis and blogs. *Pragmatics & Cognition*, *16*(2), 272–306.

Popescu, E. (2010). Students' acceptance of Web 2.0 technologies in higher education: Findings from a survey in a Romanian university. *Proceedings of DEXA 2010 Workshops*, (pp. 92–96). IEEE Computer Society Press.

Reviglio, M. C. (2010). La mediatizacion del discurso academico en los decires delos ingresantes a la Universidad. *Revista Latinoamericana de Comunicacion*, *11*, 33–37.

Williams, J. B., & Jacobs, J. (2004). Exploring the use of blogs as learning spaces in the higher education sector. *Australasian Journal of Educational Technology*, *20*(2), 232–247.

Yang, S.-H. (2009). Using blogs to enhance critical reflection and community of practice. *Journal of Educational Technology & Society*, *12*(2), 11–21.

KEY TERMS AND DEFINITIONS

Academic/Educational Blog: A blog that is built in order to guide a certain part of students activity within a course, the purpose being to encourage online debate, knowledge sharing and making information more available.

Blog: A pre-designed website that has the form of an online diary. The use of the blog does not require programming skills.

Collaborative Learning: A form of social knowledge that involves interactions between individuals and has information exchange at its core. The resources for this type of learning are determined by the availability and the capacity of those who take part in the exchange.

E-Learning: Acquiring knowledge and access to information by using informatics networks.

Fear of Peer Appraisal: Type of behavior that affects the sharing of opinions in the public space.

Mixed Mode Learning: Learning form that combines classic methods of teaching, learning in class, with forms of learning that include computer and web use.

Social Learning: Learning activities resulted from interactions developed in group situations or organizational environments. Social learning allows the transmission of rules and procedures through which individuals adapt and identify solutions for new contexts and situations.

Chapter 10
Uses and Implementation of Social Media at University:
The Case of Schools of Communication in Spain

María-Jesús Díaz-González
University of A-Coruña, Spain

Natalia Quintas Froufe
University of A-Coruña, Spain

Almudena González del Valle Brena
International University of Rioja (UNIR), Spain

Francesc Pumarola
Expert in Internet issues, Spain

ABSTRACT

There have been many contributions to scientific literature which have helped develop a theoretical framework in the field of education and Information Technologies. The contributions have come from the educational sciences and from the communication processes and collaboration perspectives. The purpose of this chapter is to make a contribution within the specific scope of university teaching and social media. In order to achieve this objective, a case study methodology was chosen to analyze the use and implementations of social media networks in Spanish Schools of Communication. The parameters used were chosen out of the same social media nature (potential use). The success of social media presence at Schools of Communications must follow an initial plan and a further control and supervision of the plan. The relationship of social media with the university community depends greatly upon the specific community manager's profile and commitment.

BACKGROUND

There is a vast body of scientific literature which contributes to developing a theoretical framework and conceptualization of Information and Communication Technologies (ICTs), originating both from the educational sciences and communication processes. Many contributions to social media are found with specific interests such as the business world, marketing, public relations and advertising. The recently published book by Bradley and McDonald (2011, 2012 for the Spanish transla-

DOI: 10.4018/978-1-4666-2851-9.ch010

tion) is an example of this. McAfee is another example of strong research in the field, however focused specifically on how IT changes the way companies perform, organize themselves, and compete (2009, Brynjolfsson & McAfee, 2011). Nevertheless, academic pieces specifically tacking the relationship between social media with university activities, as well as university teaching, are much more difficult to find. Therefore, the aimed in this chapter is to make a contribution in this field.

The chapter takes as a starting point the following social media concept: "an online environment created for the purpose of mass collaboration. It is where mass collaboration occurs, not the technology per se" (Bradley & McDonald, 2011, p. 10). That is to say, an online environment open to mass collaboration, one in which all participants that are invited may create, upload, classify, improve, discover, consume and share content without a direct intermediary partner. Lester offers an interesting literature review on the concepts of social media and digital generations, illustrated in an applied advertising project incorporating YouTube, Flickr, MySpace, Facebook, Twitter, Linkedin, Ning, Tagged, Google +, and other online social networking sites, as the foundation for an integrated marketing communication strategy (Lester, 2012). Following Orihuela's statement, communication technology changed along history. However, this change is now happening at an extraordinary speed rate. Changes used to happen over several generations and there was enough time to adapt cultures to each new technology; nowadays, we have a technological revolution every week. Social media are an integral part of today's youngsters' reality, they are part of their ecosystem, they are part of their closest culture. Social media entail connectivity, real time, multimedia, sharing, learning together and collaboration.

However, all these characteristics belong to the University, don't they? Exactly this is what social media are performing. Many of the values at the root of social media are university values: building up content, collaborating in order to generate content, efficiently distributing that content etc. And this content may very well be in the form of text, audio or video. These media allow to foster values that are very interesting to teachers such as collaboration, understood as being able to work in groups along with people who complement each other's talents, and not necessarily being friends among them. In real life, that is exactly what happens.

Social media are intuitive for youngsters; however, traditional university teaching methodologies are foreign to them. They have to make a strong effort in order to follow and these methodologies are far from their daily experiences. Furthermore, these media are free. Most of these applications are stored via cloud computing, and are available on a permanent basis. Everything has to be in the cloud: their contact list, their pictures, videos and above all, their favorite music (Orihuela, 2011). Along this line, the work by Gómez, Roses and Farias (2012) may be considered, about the academic use of social media by university students, taking University of Málaga, in Spain, as a case study. The abilities developed by university students in social media are coherent with those proposed by European Higher Education Area (EHEA): personal competences (self-learning and critical thought, diversity appreciation); instrumental (visual culture, information systems abilities); or systemic (research potential or case-based learning) (Alonso and López, 2008). How the same students perceive their own way of learning, points out that they feel comfortable in the Web. Michael Wesh experience developed in collaboration with 200 students at Kansas State University is very illustrative. Such experience was shared in YouTube and was titled *A Vision of Students Today* (Wesch, 2007). Another interesting experience is the one by Wodzick, Schwämmlein y Moskaliuk (2012) on StudiVZ, the German replica of Facebook, and recently published.

Let's state that university students are found in social media, and that these are appropriate and fit for higher education uses. A foreseen outcome is that no opposition should be encountered. However, the difficulty lies in how to contribute to that particular aim, on the University and academic side.

Regalado suggests (2011) that universities could show students how they are a good place to fulfill their dreams, and that social media must help universities display their value proposition so that dreams actually come true. Within the university realm, a vast quantity of interesting topics is prone to become social media content. Obviously, many employees at universities are highly educated labor, with a great potential for contribution. Regalado's recommendation is to look for a useful way of collaborative learning: social media followers and university employees: learning about business, technology, innovation, case studies, economy or any other subject; setting this dynamic is better than publishing content about undergraduate and graduate studies, as a main subject of social media. Furthermore, universities should be warm and approachable, and share interesting events happening on campus, such as concerts, sports, meetings, atmosphere, parties, how much fun students have etc. They may also publish job openings and opportunities for employment.

Remember, people buy dreams at your university, the dream to become a better person and transcend, is your institution ready to offer this? Tell the student how you will contribute to fulfill their dream (Regalado, 2011).

METHODOLOGY

The methodology chosen for this chapter has been that of the case study. This method best suits this research because it fits Yin's definition as "an empirical inquiry that investigates a contemporary phenomenon within its real life context; when the boundaries between phenomenon and context are not clearly evident; and in which multiple sources of evidence are used" (Yin, 1984, p. 23). The use of this methodological tool is determined by the proposed subject of study, because it meets the need to observe the phenomenon within its own context, Web 2.0. This method is thought to perform an intensive analysis of the institutional use of social media and their tools within the Spanish environment.

The sample is made up of all those Schools (publicly or privately owned) from the Spanish university system in which communication studies are provided (Journalism studies, Advertising Studies, Audiovisual Communication Studies). A total of 46 Schools have been selected. Our observation unit is the home web page of the selected School. From there the particular information about the present use of social media was extracted. In order to categorize social media, the following classification seemed the most suited:

1. Communications (blogs, micro blogs, chats, social networking, document sharing, forums, geolocation)
2. Collaboration (wikis, bookmarking and news)
3. Multimedia (snapshots, videos, music)

Following this categorization, the following table (Table 1) was drawn, as a working tool for subsequent analysis.

The research design started with the research questions to address, a key step in the case study method, such as in Yin (1994). When the research started out, the questions revolved around the following axes: which social networks are present at Communication Schools? What is the use of social media on the Schools part? How do users participate? Is conversation or dialogue actually achieved?

Table 1. Data as of 27th December, 2011; Prepared by the authors

SOCIAL MEDIA/TYPOLOGY	SERVICES	SCHOOL OF COMMUNICATION USING THEM
COMMUNICATION		
Blogs		Universidad Cardenal Herrera CEU Universitat Internacional de Catalunya (UIC) Universitat Ramon Llull Universidad de Sevilla
Micro blogs	Twitter	Universidad Autónoma de Barcelona Universidad de Navarra Universitat Ramón Llull Universitat Internacional de Catalunya (UIC) Universidad Pontificia de Salamanca Universidad de Girona Universidad de Alicante Universidade da Coruña Universidad Politécnica de Valencia Universidad Carlos III de Madrid
Social networks	Facebook	Universitat Internacional de Catalunya (UIC) Universitat Ramón Llull Universidad de Sevilla Universidad Católica San Antonio Murcia Universidad de Navarra Universidad País Vasco Universidad de Girona Universidade da Coruña Universidad Politécnica de Valencia Universidad Carlos III de Madrid
	Tuenti	Universidad Católica San Antonio Murcia Universidad Politécnica de Valencia Universidad Pontificia de Salamanca
Documents	Issuu	Universidad de Navarra
MULTIMEDIA		
Snapshots	Flickr	Universidad Pontificia de Salamanca Universidad de Girona Universidade da Coruña
Video	YouTube	Universidad de Navarra Universitat Internacional de Catalunya (UIC) Universitat Ramon Llull Universidad de Sevilla Universidad de Girona Universidade da Coruña
	Vimeo	Universidad Católica San Antonio Murcia Universidad de Girona

It was soon realized at an early research stage that the most recurrent social networks and tools were the following: Facebook (43%), Twitter (36%), YouTube (32%), RSS (21%) and Flickr (19%).To a lesser extent, one could find LinkedIn (10%), Blogs (13%) or Tuenti (13%). The pro-posed research entails parameters that are specific to social media nature. These are the following: to offer students the possibility of *expressing* themselves through text, video, audio, music etc.; the possibility of *communicating and of sharing*. And as a result of this, to offer students the possibility of *striking up a conversation* around their learning experiences, their academic interests and their creativity. "We are going from the Information Society towards the *Conversation Society*, and it is advisable to adapt to this new scenario" (Pumarola, 2011).

Two more analysis parameters were added because of their relevance to the present academic environment: generate positioning and image, and alumni relations (Regalado, 2011). With the results, quantitative and qualitative data are obtained that allow us to have a full vision of the topic studied. One month was the timeframe taken as a time reference, from 15th January 2012 to 15th February 2012, in order to analyze the Schools' activities in social media. It was not chosen by chance, but because that particular time period is best suited for this purpose. Academic activities have by then returned to normal, after the extended Christmas break (15th December to 7th January). A second reason for choosing this particular time period was the near deadline for submission of the research work. This meant having more actual data. Other key dates were discarded, such as course commencement, because a logical increase in social media activity might be present; not representative though of the day to day social media activity at Communication Schools. However, course commencement, as the starting point for the research, was taken indeed as a reference to track back previous records.

Having in mind the previous academic work observant participation technique,--from the users' point of view-- (Túñez & Sixto, 2011; Rúas & Dapena, 2011) a daily monitoring of records was undertaken. In order to do so, the authors' own personal profiles were used, except for Tuenti, a social network. In this case, a false profile, with false data was used. In the next section, the results of the analysis are shown. The results are descriptive and explanatory, coherent with the applied methodology.

CASE DESCRIPTION

Social Media: Blogs

Communication

Only five out of the 46 Schools in the simple use blogs as a social media tool to communicate on the Web (Table 2). Blogs are logs on the Web, created and maintained by people interested in the topic who feed it and share points of view.

The School of Liberal Arts and Communication (Facultad de Humanidades y Ciencias de la Comunicación) at Universidad Cardenal Herrera CEU in Valencia is the most active School in blogging. The University holds campuses in Valencia, Elche and Castellón, and offers undergraduate degrees in three areas: Advertising and Public Relations, Audio-visual Communication and Journalism Studies. The three areas offer their own blogs, accessed through the general univer-

Table 2. Data as 5th March 2012; Prepared by the authors

SCHOOL	BLOG	POSTS
Facultad de Humanidades y Comunicación Universidad Cardenal Herrera CEU	Advertising and Public Relations Audiovisual Communication Journalism	15
Facultad de Comunicación Blanquerna Universidad Ramón Llull	Communication blog	45
Facultad de Ciencias de la Comunicación Universidad Internacional de Cataluña	Milhistories; periodismesportiu.com; communication online	36
Facultad de Comunicación Universidad de Sevilla	Fcom blog-not available at the time of analysis	455

sity web site, Blogs at CEU, in combination with all other Schools' blogs.

The blog dedicated to Advertising and Public Relations registered ten entries. The content was diverse: prize awards announcements, pictures, contests, book launches, students training projects and practical assignments. The students entries had the greatest number of comments, for example one assignment about participating in a European contest to come up with creative ideas for promoting European food. Other entries that raised comments were teachers' conferences and talks. The blog is organized in three columns, on the right side there are Ad sites that take the user to promotional land pages about other courses within the School or in collaboration with other institutions. There are also spaces dedicated to organization of content by categories common to the field of advertising, contact e-mail address, calendar, and interesting links in the area.

The blog dedicated to Journalism did not have any entry during the studied period of time, and the last entry dated from 2010. On the other hand, the blog dedicated to Audiovisual Communication had 5 entries. The content focused on news about contests and prize awards, communicated by the School to the students. There are also two posts about film forum announcements. It also shows videos (mostly short film student projects).

Therefore, students do not take the advantage offered by their school to express themselves creatively through this social digital tool. They use it as a source of information about future events, contests and travel opportunities. The School seems to use the blogs for similar reasons, avoiding a possible conversation with their students. However, the space is at least open for them out there.

The School of Communication Blanquerna at Universitat Ramón Llull holds a blog for their communication students that may be accessed through the main university web page. It is a well-designed blog, linked to the School accounts in Twitter and Facebook and very actively fed

by the School. It had 41 entries in the main tab (agenda), covering topics as diverse as teachers' presentations, talks, conferences, announcements, interviews with important people in the field, data on communication sector, PhD Thesis *Vivas,* new undergraduate and graduate courses, registration periods etc. The main menu opens in six other sub menus or tabs, however, classifying the same content as in Agenda. There is one tab, Services, which opens up a different landing page, where audiovisual facilities may be reserved either by the faculty or by students or by the public. Such facilities include media lab, editing facilities, information technology facilities. An interesting characteristic is that this particular landing page has the option of changing languages (from Catalan to Castilian), whereas the main blog page does not (Catalan only).

The blog is managed by the School and it is used as an organizational communication tool, to promote its image and reputation. It does allow for participation through sharing (Twitter, Facebook, and other tools, such as e-Mail, Delicious, Reddit etc). On the right column there is a blog roll, with personal blogs by faculty and some students. Finally, it offers links to national and international mass media and other interesting links in the field of communication. Students do not often comment, and it seems much more like an official board for events and text.

The School of Communication at Universidad Internacional de Cataluña has a blog on Audiovisual Communication, which is called *milhistories.* It had only two posts at the time of analysis. The content is mostly about film reviews, openings, and TV series and gives the opportunity to share videos and interesting links, blog roll, and a dedicated space for comments. It is the only one in this category with this capability. However, there are no recent comments on the posts, the only one appearing were written back in 2011 by the same student. The blog is linked to the School Twitter account, and to RSS feeds.

The School also holds two other blogs, one about sports journalism and the other one dedicated solely to the students of a Digital Communications Degree. Both of them had no posts since the beginning of the academic year.

Social Media: Twitter

Micro-Blog

There are 10 Schools with some Twitter activity. They are registered with the following accounts:

- FCC UAB @FccUab (School of Communication Sciences, Facultad de Ciencias de la Comunicación, at Universidad Autónoma de Barcelona)
- Fac. de Comunicación @fcomnavarra (School of Communication, Facultad de Comunicación at Universidad de Navarra)
- FC Blanquerna @FCBlanquerna (School of Communication, Blanquerna- Facultad de Comunicación Blanquerna at Universidad Ramón Llull)
- milhistories @milhistories (School of Communication Sciences, Facultad de Ciencias de la Comunicación at Universidad Internacional de Cataluña)
- fcomsalamanca @fcomsalamanca (School of Communication, Facultad de Comunicación at Universidad Pontificia de Salamanca)
- EU ERAM @EUERAM (Audio-visual and Multimedia University School, Escuela Universitaria Audiovisual y Multimedia at Universidad de Gerona)
- Fac. Económicas UA @EconomicasUA (School of Economics, Facultad de Económicas at Universidad de Alicante)
- Campus Gandía UPV @campusgandiaupv (Polytechnic Upper School Gandía Campus, Escuela Politécnica Superior at Universidad Politécnica de Valencia)
- CienciasComunicación @C_Comunicacion (School of Communication Sciences, Facultad de Ciencias de la Comunicación at Universidad de La Coruña)
- Fac.HumComyDoc UC3M @FacHCD_uc3m (School of Liberal Arts, Communication and Documentation, Facultad de Humanidades, Comunicación y Documentación at Universidad Carlos III de Madrid)

The following table (Table 3) summarizes a sample of the schools' Twitter activity.

The analysis covers Twitter activity to see whether its use allows for communication, sharing and converse students' learning experiences, their academic interests or creativity. The School of Communication (Facultad de Comunicación at Universidad Pontificia de Salamanca), @fcomsalamanca, is an outstanding example in achieving communication, sharing and dialoguing with students. The analysis covered Twitter from 15th January to 15th February 2012. Its timeline published 310 messages, 137 tweets and 182 *retweets*. Of these, 148 (more than 46%) are conversations between the School and university members, questions and answers, or comments over several interest topics emerging from the social Web.

How does @fcomsalamanca achieve this much more activity over the rest of Spanish Schools of Communication? @fcomsalamanca frequently throws questions to followers, such as

- "We are already in the question time. Do you have any? #canalplusenfcomsalamanca 2:01 pm - 16 Jan 2012 via Twitter for iPad
- "Which is the best memory you keep about our teachers? We would like to know it today, St. Thomas Aquinas" (Patron Saint of Universities, well celebrated among Catholic universities)

Table 3. Data as of 20th February 2012; Prepared by the authors

SCHOOL	Twitter users	TWEETS	FOLLOWING	FOLLOWERS
Facultad de Ciencias de la Comunicación Universidad Autónoma de Barcelona	@FccUab	407	5	592
Facultad de Comunicación Universidad de Navarra	@fcomnavarra	2.458	56	4.733
Facultad de Comunicación. Blanquerna Universidad Ramón Llull	@FCBlanquerna	1.582	2.907	2.641
Facultad de Ciencias de la Comunicación Universidad Internacional de Cataluña	@milhistories *	36	20	24
Facultad de Comunicación. Universidad Pontificia de Salamanca	@fcomsalamanca	1.424	439	1.383
Escuela Universitaria Audiovisual y Multimedia Universidad de Gerona	@EUERAM	455	171	328
Facultad de Económicas Universidad de Alicante	@EconomicasUA	60	10	835
Escuela Politécnica Superior Universidad Politécnica de Valencia	@campusgandiaupv	732	143	643
Facultad de Ciencias de la Comunicación Universidad de La Coruña	@C_Comunicacion	43	61	88
Facultad de Humanidades, Comunicación y Documentación. Universidad Carlos III de Madrid	@FacHCD_uc3m	242	40	324

* @milhistories is inactive since 2011.

12:33 pm - 28 Jan 2012 via web
- "Would you like to spend a work day with four journalists from @el_pais?"
1:52 pm - 13 Feb 2012 via web
- "We join the celebration and we ask you: which are your best radio memories?"
7:08 pm - 13 Fe 2012 via web

Their followers answer directly or with a message on their own Twitter account, but they all mention @fcomsalamanca. The School is able then to find these messages and *retweet* them to its own timeline. Therefore, these tweets are shared and known by all @fcomsalamanca followers, and this becomes an opportunity for them to meet and to answer back each other's messages. During the analysis time period, 57% of published content were *retweets* of other pieces of conversation. Furthermore, the School answers every message

generating a proper written dialogue. Table 4 presents a summary of activity data on Twitter.

Connecting with alumni is another analysis parameter. The School of Communication (Facultad de Comunicación) at Universidad Pontificia de Salamanca keeps close contact with alumni and their activity. It is difficult to quantify the volume of that particular activity because users do not necessarily identify themselves as alumni. The School does not specify whether they talk to an alumni, should they refer to a particular person.

On 3rd February, 2012 the following conversation was happening on Twitter:

- My #FF to @fcomsalamanca for creating the list *lista@fcomsalamanca/antiguos-alumnos* (alumni), an excellent way to keep the relationship alive!
1:29 pm - 3 Feb 2012 via web

Table 4. Tweets and retweets may be classified under more than one category; Prepared by the authors

Retweets	182	Total messages: 319
Tweets	137	
		Percentage over total messages
Expressing themselves: video, picture, links, etc.	59	19%
Communicating	70	22%
Sharing	34	11%
Striking up a conversation	148	46%
Image and positioning of the School	46	14%
Contact with alumni	30	9%

- @rociosasca many thanks. We would like to increase this list. Any help is welcome.
  4:44 pm - 3 Feb 2012 via Twitter for iPad

The list *lista@fcomsalamanca/antiguos-alumnos* is a public list and it had a total of 300 members at the end of February 2012.

The School of Communication at Universidad de Navarra is the most followed one. Its Twitter account stands out to be a channel for studentship and faculty expression. Many of the text messages share pictures, videos, texts and links to the School web site. There are also many messages sharing positive and negative feelings, congratulations, opinions, etc. In these, people also state, though not necessarily share, certain content. In order to achieve the aim of becoming a channel for *expression and sharing*, @fcomnavarra retweets hundreds of messages coming from the faculty, alumni, about School events etc. and thus offers continuous feedback and portrays a dynamic image. Through Twitter @fcomnavarra spreads out information about activities, professional visits to the School, visiting lecturers, publications and other faculty credits, and their alumni achievements. All of this works out to enhance its marketing positioning and image.

When analyzing *expression and sharing content* functions, the Polytechnic Upper School at Universidad Politécnica de Valencia Twitter account, @campusgandiaupv, also stands out. Many are the messages to share students' academic projects, for example, a TV program for the local TV station:

- Tonight at 19.30! at Telesafor, @radiogandia: @Telegrafies, a TV program by our Campus' students.
  7:15 pm - 27 Jan 2012 via Hootsuite

Or short films by students:

- Look at these short films http://ow.ly/8uV5T by colleagues from Audiovisual Communication Studies
  4:08 pm - 16 Jan 2012 via HootSuite

On the other side of the spectrum, the School of Communication Blanquerna (Facultad de Comunicación Blanquerna) at Universidad Ramón Llull, @FCBlanquerna, uses its Twitter account to spread out very institutional, unidirectional messages. Their tweets announce events and other announcements to the academic community. This contributes to its *institutional image and communication*. The same objective is achieved by the School of Liberal Arts, Communication and Documentation (Facultad de Humanidades, Comunicación y Documentación) at Universidad Carlos III de Madrid, @FacHCD_uc3m. They use Twitter to communicate that one member of the faculty was awarded six Goya awards for one film (Goya are the most priced film awards in Spain). Other Schools use Twitter as a news board online, to communicate important information to students, such a as grades, schedules, grants, topics, or events. Twitter is one the social media considered to be most useful for universities because it allows for content disclosure, high interaction with people, sharing information and connecting with the target market (Regalado, 2011).

Social Media: Facebook

Social Networks

In order to analyze the social network Facebook, basic data appearing on the Schools' network profiles are shown. The activity generated on their walls is then analyzed along the established parameters. The research interest is focused on the profile walls, for they are the paradigmatic place with a real possibility for expressing one-self, for communicating, sharing and finally, generating dialogue with other users. Update status is observed, as well as shared links and interaction with the rest of users. Out of all Schools studied in this chapter, only nine of them are present on Facebook. This is really striking, since there are more than 15,000,000 Facebook users in Spain and the network has a penetration 33.6% within the Spanish population (Social Bakers, 2012). Three Schools embed a link to Facebook on their web site allowing sharing of content; however, the user does not land on a School specific Facebook profile or page. Therefore, it may lead the user to confusion, since they might expect to land on the School Facebook profile.

A special case is Universidad Politécnica de Valencia. Their Facebook page is not exclusive of Audiovisual Communication studies; it is the Gandía campus page. Therefore, its activity on the wall is intensive though sometimes hardly related to the School itself.

As shown on Table 5, the Spanish Schools are present on Facebook by using pages rather than profiles. The schools create a specific page in which they publish information interesting to them and to their followers. Whenever the schools

choose to be present by opening a user profile, this profile is usually a public one so that all web users may access it whether they are Facebook users or not. On the other hand, at the time of this research, only Universidad Internacional de Cataluña had adopted the new Facebook profile, called *biography*.

The number of friends or followers ranking is headed by the Facultat de Comunicació Blanquerna, with a total of 2,352 fans, followed by Facultad de Comunicación, Universidad de Navarra, with 2,232 followers. Therefore, more attention is paid to these particular schools in the analysis, since they have stronger user support (as for number of followers).

Facultat de Comunicació Blanquerna

This School updated the status fifteen times. Six updates were links shared by followers that would land on the School web site. The majority of these updates and links are shared by users through the share option. Nevertheless, the usual number of followers that shared a particular link was one, an insignificant figure against the 6,352 page fans. The content updated is used to communicate School activities to followers. The School shares links about students and teachers' initiatives, not necessarily related to academic content. It congratulates them by starting a conversation with them. For example, Professor Richard Wakefield's initiative "Advertising professionals involved" received several links and comments (see *Publicitarios implicados: 5 años comunicando valores*, 31st January, 2012, 10:41). However, page followers do not interact with the School, as one may think by the number of followers. Fan activity on the wall is limited to indicating whether they like whatever is published, an action that is performed by a small number of users. For example, out of all the links and updates published, the most liked one raises 25 likes only. This is a small number compared to the total number of page followers. Participation through comments is almost inex-

Table 5. Data as of 20th February 2012; Prepared by the authors

UNIVERSITY	SCHOOL	USER NAME	TYPE OF COMMENT	FRIENDS/ FOLLOWERS
Universidad Internacional de Cataluña	Facultad de Ciencias de la Comunicación	Facultat de Ciències de la Comunicació Uic	Biographic	594
Universidad Ramón Llull	Facultad de Comunicación. Blanquerna.	Facultat de Comunicació Blanquerna	Page	6,352
Universidad de Sevilla	Facultad de Comunicación	Facultad de Comunicación - fcom Sevilla	Page	891
Universidad Católica San Antonio Murcia	Facultad de Comunicación	Comunicación Audiov Ucam	Profile	561
Universidad de Navarra	Facultad de Comunicación	Facultad de Comunicación (UN)	Page	2,232
Universidad País Vasco	Facultad de Ciencias Sociales y de la Comunicación	Gkz Csc	Profile	415
Universidad de Gerona	Escuela Universitaria Audiovisual y Multimedia	Escola Universitària Eram	Page	146
Universidade da Coruña	Facultad de Ciencias de la Comunicación	Nécora Dixital	Page	183
Universidad Carlos III	Facultad de Humanidades, Comunicación y Documentación	Facultad de Humanidades, Comunicación y Documentación UC3M	Page	494
Universidad Politécnica de Valencia	Escuela Politécnica Superior	Campus de Gandia_Universidad Politécnica de Valencia	Page	1,590

istent. There are only three links/updates with comments (one or two comments). Blanquerna page menu is organized in eleven sub-menus (wall, information, friend activity, Blanquerna Communication, discovering the School, Site and Facilities, videos, Blanquerna through one click). Basic data and facts about the School are provided through these submenus.

Facultad de Comunicación (Universidad de Navarra)

The activity generated in the Facultad de Comunicación de Navarra is far more dynamic than in the rest of the researched schools (49 publications within the studied time period). The page also receives more feedback from followers than the rest of the schools. These publications may be classified according to post characteristics: update status, link sharing or add content. More than half

of the publications share links. Most links come from the same School web site, where one may read more about whatever content is shared. The topics of publications focus on teaching activities and academic events that happen within the School facilities, such as book launches, student initiatives, Patron Saint's day, prize awards, etc.

Users and followers participate by showing their interest for published links, especially through the like button. In any case, this is not a massive action: the update status / link that got more likes (54) was "Feliz día del Patrón de los periodistas: San Francisco de Sales" (Happy Journalists Patron Saint's Day: St. Francis of Sales). On the other hand, users do not often share links /update status published, and when they do, the number is not relevant (14 times). Users do not often comment on publications either. The most commented publication scored 10. The School page is organized in ten sub-menus: wall, information, your friends' activity, welcome, events, YouTube, Code of Conduct, Snapshots, Fcom active, Fcom professional. Through these menus the School expresses itself and communicates with followers.

There is less wall activity in the remaining Schools, a lot less than the previous two. However, there are similarities in the type of content published. Most of the wall publications focus on link sharing landing on different web pages, sometimes related to advertising and communication. This may be so to inform about new trends or topics, especially within the field of communication. For example, Nécora Dixital publishes interesting content for students in the field of audio-visuals, as does the School of Social Sciences and Communication of the Universidad del País Vasco. On the contrary, other Schools, such as the School of Communication of the Universidad de Sevilla, use their Facebook wall as news board, where facts and interesting data for students are published (activities, grants, registration periods, etc.)

Most commonly published content, appearing on almost every profile and pages, is related to the School activities; these activities are used to position the Schools within the Spanish university field. The student is the message recipient, more than prospects or alumni. Therefore, the School presence in Internet may be considered as a communication channel directed exclusively to the studentship and teachers. Some teachers do participate actively in the wall, sharing activities of interest, recommended or even their own academic publications. Profiles of friends or followers belong to teachers, students or alumni from the same School. Generally speaking, students do not often participate. Page followers participate with publication on the wall, but conversation is never achieved. They only express their likes or dislikes through the like or unlike buttons. Most of the Schools publish in Castilian, except for Facultat de Comunicació Blanquerna and Escola Universitària Eram (Catalan) and Facultad de

Ciencias Sociales y de la Comunicación del País Vasco (Basque).

As a conclusion, Facebook pages and profiles from the Schools in this research are used mostly to replicate links already present in the School blog or web site. There is no specific content generation for this particular social network. Therefore, the web site is the true source of content creation and expression. We can conclude that most of the capabilities for interconnectivity present in this network are not taken into consideration.

Social Media: Tuenti

Social Network

Tuenti is a Spanish social network which started up in 2006. It is said to be the Spanish Facebook. In January 2012, it reached 13 million registered users. It is highly popular among youngsters; minimum entry age is 16. However, Tuenti is a space to meet for adolescents in the range from 12 to 14 on a regular basis. Membership was on invitation only until November 2011. Access is now allowed when giving a mobile phone number. The organization has blogs in Spanish and in English, where more information about the network may be accessed (Tuenti, 2012)

Three Schools of Communication on our list have a Tuenti account.

- School of Communication (Facultad de Comunicación) at UPSA (Universidad Pontificia de Salamanca)
- Polytechnic Upper School Gandía Campus, (Campus de Gandía Escuela Politécnica Superior) at UPV (Universidad Politécnica de Valencia
- Audiovisual Communication Studies (Comunicación Audiovisual) at UCAM (Universidad Católica San Antonio de Murcia)

Universidad Politécnica de Valencia is the only institution using the page for converting prospects into students in a significant way. Its opening states "Official page, Gandía Campus (Universitat Politècnica de València). Here you will find information about our course offerings, facilities and events on campus". The page is used to develop a specific program called "University comes to your school". Members of the faculty give talks to secondary school students. The talk is recorded and uploaded in YouTube and Tuenti.

- Campus de Gandía UPV

University comes to your school: *Veles e Vents* Secondary School
Environmental Studies professor Jose Andrés Torrent gives the following talk about "Forest fires" at IES *Veles e Vents* de Grao de Gandía. Do you like it?
16 Feb, 15:49 Comment (UPV, 2012)

Social Media: Issuu

Documents

Facultad de Comunicación, at Universidad de Navarra is the only active School in this social space. They are registered as fcom-navarra.

Statistics

- **Profile Views:** 377
- **Documents:** 17
- **Document Views:** 129,191
- **Comments Made:** 0
- **Comments Received:** 2
- **Bookmarks Made:** 0
- **Bookmarks Received:** 48
- **Subscribers:** 20

Their membership dates from May 30, 2008, but it is seldom used. During the research period, no document was uploaded and the user had no "friends" yet.

Social Media: Flickr

Snapshots

The Schools of Communication with Flickr presence are the following three:

- School of Communication, (Facultad de Comunicación) at Universidad Pontificia de Salamanca (Salamanca, 2008).
- Audiovisual and Multimedia University School (Escuela Universitaria Audiovisual y Multimedia) at Universidad de Gerona (ERAM, 2008).
- School of Communication Sciences (Facultad de Ciencias de la Comunicación) at Universidad de La Coruña (Coruña, 2009).

None of the three schools seems to have the same focus when participating in this social medium. The School of Communication (U. P. Salamanca) Flickr is a picture gallery about themselves, their facilities, their faculty, invited faculty and other guests, students, alumni, and academic events. There are many pictures about events. As of February 2012, there were 11 albums with a total of 185 pictures. There is a high frequency of uploads, so that the pictures are recent. As a consequence, Flickr is a tool for marketing positioning and the School own image. The social tool also achieves the goal of sharing those *moments,* with the academic community and alumni connection. Nevertheless, it is always used as a unidirectional tool for communicating with followers and does not create conversation.

The Audiovisual and Multimedia University School (Escuela Universitaria Audiovisual y Multimedia at University of Gerona-ERAM) differs from the previous school in that Flickr is used as a channel for student expression: students show their photographic assignments. Thus, more intense sharing and communication is achieved. As of February 2012 this Flickr account had a total of 9 albums with 367 snapshots. Among those albums, there was one dedicated to students and another to pictures of the School facilities. Therefore, the School also uses Flickr as a positioning and image tool, to a lesser extent.

At the School Communication Sciences (Facultad de Ciencias de la Comunicación) at University of La Coruña, Flickr is considered as a space to share academic assignments or pieces of work. It is a *group board* and not a picture gallery managed under the School direction. Its opening text states: "The objective of this group is to become a space for all members of the School community interested in photography, info-graphics to *share their creative pieces of* work. Everybody is welcome, especially students and alumni, faculty and researchers, and administration personnel". Topics are open, though there are some specific contents that are especially welcomed:

- Pictures of events, or people, related to the School or the University
- Pictures about any topic related to the audio-visual communication field
- Computer generated images
- Pieces by students (assignments, final projects)

In spite of the clear and coherent social characteristics of the space, no significant results were found as of February 2012. The group amounts to a total of 25 members, and only five of them have shared their pieces of work. There are a total of 152 images and there is no conversation. This Flickr account has a special space dedicated to debate, though.

Social Media: YouTube

Video

Schools with dedicated channel in YouTube are summarized in Table 6.

Facultad de Comunicación at Universidad de Navarra has a dedicated channel with 6 reproduction lists and more than 200 subscriptions. The lists gather video content around course offerings (postgraduate degrees), events at the School, celebrations (50th anniversary), and prize awards, contests, and students testimonies. It is connected to their blog. It is the only School in the sample with activity in YouTube during the studied period. One of the most reproduced audio-visual piece is about the celebration of the Patron Saint's Day, with one comment as well. Other highly reproduced content are testimonies about student life at Fcom, course offerings and how good the degree is in future professional life.

Facultad de Ciencias de la Comunicación at Universidad de La Coruña holds a dedicated channel with several reproduction lists: Stopmotion, Animation 3D, Videoclips, Spots and Fiction. As with the previous one, content had not been updated in the last three months. Content was mainly creative work by students, but there are also interviews to key visitors and some School self-promotion. The number of subscriptions and the small number of videos uploaded lead us to think that the School makes little use of the social networking capabilities of the medium. The videos are produced both in Castilian and in Galician.

Facultat de Ciencias de la Comunicaciò at Universidad Internacional de Cataluña holds just a reproduction list under the main YouTube channel owned by the University. It is used to show creative works and assignments of communication students; however, there is another reproduction list, a general one within the main University channel that also gathers video works by students from all Schools. Therefore, students

Table 6. Data as of February 2012; Prepared by the authors

SCHOOL	USERNAME	SUBSCRIPTIONS	VIEWS	VIDEOS UPLOADED
Facultad de Comunicación Universidad de Navarra	fcomnavarra	276	412,630	113
Facultad de Comunicación. Blanquerna Universidad Ramón Llull	fcblanquerna	31	8,177	21
Facultad de Ciencias de la Comunicación Universidad Internacional de Cataluña	Uic	n.a0	426	33
Escuela Universitaria Audiovisual y Multimedia Universidad de Gerona	Univgirona/ escolaeram	40		
Facultad de Ciencias de la Comunicación Universidad de La Coruña	cienciascomunica- cion	45	37,932	94
Facultad de Comunicación Universidad de Sevilla	alumnosfcom	10	756	16

may also have their work uploaded in a different reproduction list. In any event, no video had been uploaded since October 2011. Although the list description clearly states that it is open to *show student work pieces* as well as descriptive films about the School facilities, the truth is that most of the content falls into the latter. Because of these two reasons, that it is only a reproduction list within the main university channel, and that most of the content depicts the School facilities, one may conclude that it main purpose is a reputational one. The language in this channel is Catalan.

Escuela Universitaria Audiovisual y Multimedia (ERAM) at Universidad de Gerona has its own channel. However, it was difficult to find since the School offers audio-visual and multimedia studies in collaboration with the University, but they are different organizations. ERAM had uploaded the latest video in January 2012, therefore a lot more recently than the rest of the Schools present in the sample. The content is mainly produced by the School production house, as TV content for the local TV channel in Girona, student work pieces, and promotional films on their own course offerings. Language wise, the channel is in Catalan.

Facultad de Comunicación Blanquerna at Universidad Ramón Llull has a smaller, less important presence: 5 reproduction lists, no uploaded videos

in the period of the analysis. The five reproduction lists correspond to five categories of videos: My top videos (miscellanea) Blanquerna (dedicated to corporate content about the School), Non-fiction (pieces of work).

Social Media: Vimeo

Video

There are only two Schools which hold their own channel in Vimeo: Escola Universitària ERAM and Facultad de Comunicación, Universidad Católica de San Antonio de Murcia. The first one, (escola. eram) has uploaded 63 videos where the students show their final audio-visual projects.

Facultad de Comunicación, Universidad Católica de San Antonio de Murcia holds one channel in Vimeo, with only five videos, related to the students' final audio-visual projects.

CONCLUSION

How do universities deal with social media obstacles and shortcomings? In order to contribute to the answer to this question, we have analyzed the use School of Communications in Spain make of social media. We believe that these institutions have the capacity to innovate, for they are in the right position to understand the social media phenomenon and to examine new trends.

First of all, how social media and social network are conceptualized is of great significance, as it is the precise understanding that this development is wider than just social networking in fashion, such as Facebook or Twitter. For the taking the correct starting point, a categorization and typology of social media are needed. Also, research parameters should be defined taking in extracted from the same social media nature and not from how they are used from the Schools practice.

Secondly, we consider that universities are organizations that must be present in social media, because they have content and vast knowledge to share, and gather a community made of student, alumni, faculty and researcher, that may meet and be enriched by these social media.

However, more research and case studies are necessary on how, why and with what purpose social media are used in universities. Although technology changes fast, higher education institutions such as universities are usually slow in their processing change, evaluating options and taking decisions. Consequently, universities and schools within them should not pursue social media presence per se, "because everybody else is". Their presence should account for a plan: what do we want from our presence, how are we going to communicate with and connect with my students and faculty, which tone of voice and language register we should use in the messages and which content will be shared and why. In order to do this, the person managing the social media at universities, responsible for its dynamism and responsiveness should of course be professionally educated (a community manager?) and know web analytics and KPIs; but most important of all, the person should be able to talk to students in their language and be identified with the organization.

Thirdly, what we have found does not correspond to these requirements, since what most of the Schools lack is conversation, studentship engagement, and use their social media mainly as a corporate communication tool. Their presence is concentrated within the most popular social media such as Facebook, Twitter and YouTube.

We believe that there is not enough presence for out of 46 institutions offering studies in Communication, only 10 are registered in Facebook and Twitter, and only 6 have a dedicated channel in YouTube. These Schools are at a first adoption stage of social media networks. According to the data, the Schools have not defined their usage yet. The Schools should consider using social media networks to interact and connect with students efficiently.

Fourthly, social media are mostly used as a channel to communicate and share the same content as it appears in their web sites. Lastly, having said that, some outstanding examples have been found, along the ability to get the academic community share their own created content. It is also prominent their ability to generate dialogue around learning abilities, personal and academic interests and experience, memories and dreams. We refer by this to the use of Twitter by School of Communication (Facultad de Comunicación) at Universidad Pontificia de Salamanca; and to the use of Facebook by School of Communication (Facultad de Comunicación) at Universidad de Navarra.

In order for these cases stop being exceptional, and that their example may be extended to the rest of the Schools of Communications, we recommend they devise a digital communications strategy in social media. It is also highly advisable to commit time and resources to the School profiling, or a professional community manager. This job position should be held by someone with the right educational background and social media background. The person must be able to speak to students in their own language and identify with the particular institution in which he or she works. Constant management of social media in which the School is present, quick answers, usual messages and one-to-one attention may be some of the key actions to achieve interactivity and connectivity with end users, students.

REFERENCES

Alonso, H., & Lopez, I. (2008). Adaptando asignaturas al EEES: El caso de Teoría y Técnica de la Publicidad. In I. Rodríguez (Ed.), *El nuevo perfil del profesor universitario en el EEES. Claves para la renovación metodológica*. Valladolid, España: Universidad Europea Miguel de Cervantes.

Bradley, J., & McDonald, M. (2011). *The social organization. How to use social media to tap the collective genius of your customers and employees*. United States: Gartner Inc. Harvard School Publishing Corporation.

Bradley, J., & McDonald, M. (2012). *La organización social. Convertir en resultados las oportunidades de las redes sociales*. Barcelona, España: Profit Editorial.

Brynjolfsson, E., & McAfee, A. (2011). *Race against the machine: How the digital revolution is accelerating innovation, driving productivity, and irreversibly transforming employment and the economy*. Lexington, MA: Digital Frontier Press.

Coruña, F. C. (2009). *Mural de grupo. Facultad CC Comunicación Coruña*. Retrieved February 24, 2012, from http://www.flickr.com/groups/cienciascomunicacion/

ERAM. E. (2008). *Galería de Escola ERAM*. Retrieved February 24, 2012, from http://www.flickr.com/photos/escolaeram/sets/

Gómez, M., Roses, S., & Farias, P. (2012). El uso académico de las redes sociales en universitarios. *Comunicar, 19*(38), 131–138.

Lester, D. (2012). Social media: Changing advertising education. *Online Journal of Communication and Media Technologies, 2*(1), 116–125.

McAfee, A. (2009). *Enterprise 2.0: New collaborative tools for your organization's toughest challenges*. Boston, MA: Harvard Business Press.

Orihuela, J. (9 June 2011). *Enseñar aprendiendo con medios sociales*. Retrieved October 24, 2011, from http://www.newmedia.ufm.edu/gsm/index.php/Orihuelaensenaraprendiendo

Pumarola, F. (15th November, 2011). *De la Sociedad de la información a la sociedad de la conversación*. Retrieved February 20, 2012, from http://gugleandoporlared.com/blog/2011/11/de-la-sociedad-de-la-informacion-a-la-sociedad-de-la-conversacion/

Regalado, O. (20th November 2011). *¿Cómo deberían usar las universidades las redes sociales?* Retrieved February 20, 2012, from http://www.dosensocial.com/2011/11/20/como-deberian-usar-las-universidades-las-redes-sociales/

Rúas, X., & Dapena, B. (2011). Los diputados del parlamento gallego en Facebook. *Revista Redmarka: Revista digital de marketing aplicado*. Retrieved February 23, 2012, from http://www.cienciared.com.ar/ra/usr/39/1254/redmarkan7v1pp77_106.pdf

Salamanca, F. D. (2008). *Galería de fcomsalamanca*. Retrieved February 24, 2012, from http://www.flickr.com/people/orionmedialab/

Social Bakers. (2012). *Spain Facebook statistics*. Retrieved February 24, 2012, from http://www.socialbakers.com/facebook-statistics/spain

Tuenti. (2012). *Blog English version*. Retrieved February 28, 2012, from http://blog.tuenti.com/en/

Túñez, M., & Sixto, J. (2011). Redes sociales, política y Compromiso 2.0: La comunicación de los diputados españoles en Facebook. *Revista Latina de Comunicación Social*, 210-246. Retrieved February 23, 2012, from http://www.revistalatinacs.org/11/art/930_Santiago/09_Tunez.html

UPV. C. G. (10th February 2012). *La Universitat al teu centre: IES Veles e Vents (Grao de Gandía)*. Retrieved February 25, 2012, from http://www.youtube.com/watch?v=csBUC19ZxeY

Wesch, M. (10th October 2007). *A vision of students today*. Retrieved February 27, 2012, from http://www.youtube.com/watch?v=dGCJ46vyR9o

Wodzick, K., Schwämmlein, E., & Moskaliuk, J. (2012). "Actually, I wanted to learn": Study-related knowledge exchange on social networking sites. *The Internet and Higher Education, 15*(1), 9–14. doi:10.1016/j.iheduc.2011.05.008

Yin, R. K. (1994). *Case study research: Design and methods*. Thousand Oaks, CA: Sage Publications.

ADDITIONAL READING

101Agencia. (11 January 2011). *Uso de las redes sociales en España y resto del mundo: Youtube*. Retrieved October 20, 2011, from http://www.youtube.com/watch?v=ikIwvc4tzoQ&feature=iv&src_vid=uitAUu7cVSw&annotation_id=annotation_914656

Area, M. (July 2008). *Las redes sociales en Internet como espacios para la formación del profesorado: Razón y palabra*. Retrieved October 24, 2011, from http://www.razonypalabra.org.mx/n63/marea.html

Castañeda, L. (2010). *Aprendizaje con redes sociales. Tejidos educativos para los nuevos entornos*. Sevilla, España: MAD.

De Haro, J. J. (2010). *Redes sociales para la educación*. Madrid, España: Anaya.

Espuny, C., & González, J. (2011). Actitudes y expectativas del uso educativo de las redes sociales en los alumnos universitarios. *Revista de Universidad y Sociedad del Conocimiento, 8*(1), 171–185.

Gutiérrez, A., Palacios, A., & Torrego, L. (2010). Tribus digitales en las aulas universitarias. *Comunicar, 34*, 173–181. doi:10.3916/C34-2010-03-17

Kalamas, M., Mitchell, T., & Lester, D. (2009). Modeling social media use: Bridging the communication gap in higher education. *Journal of Advertising Education, 13*(1), 44–57.

Noguera Vivo, J. M., Martínez Polo, J., & Grandío Pérez, M. M. (2011). *Redes sociales para estudiantes de comunicación*. Barcelona, España: UOC.

Richter, A., & Koch, M. (2008, May). *Functions of social networking services*. Paper presented at the COOP '08 Meeting: 8th International Conference on the Design of Cooperative Systems, Carry-le-Rouet, Provence, France.

Riemer, K., & Richter, A. (2010, June). *Tweet inside: Microblogging in a corporate context*. Paper presented at the meeting of the 23rd Bled eConference eTrust: Implications for the Individual, Enterprises and Society, Bled, Slovenia.

Schubert, P., & Koch, M. (2003). Collaboration platforms for virtual student communities. In *Proceedings of the 36th Hawaii International Conference on System Sciences*. Retrieved May 30, 2012, from http://ieeexplore.ieee.org/stamp/stamp.jsp?tp=&arnumber=1174571

Valenzuela, S., Park, N., & Kee, K. F. (2009). Is there social capital in a social network site? Facebook use and college students life satisfaction, trust and participation. *Journal of Computer-Mediated Communication, 14*, 875–901. doi:10.1111/j.1083-6101.2009.01474.x

Wankel, C. (Ed.). (2011). *Teaching arts and science with the new social media*. Bingley, UK: Emerald. doi:10.1108/S2044-9968(2011)0000003004

Wankel, L. A., & Wankel, C. (Eds.). (2011). *Higher education administration with social media: Including applications in student affairs, enrolment management, alumni affairs, and career centres.* Bingley, UK: Emerald.

Wankel, L. A., & Wankel, C. (Eds.). (2012). *Misbehaviour online in higher education.* Bingley, UK: Emerald.

KEY TERMS AND DEFINITIONS

Facebook: A social networking service and website launched by Mark Zuckerberg in February 2004 with the purpose of facilitating communication and content sharing among Harvard University students, where he was a student. As of May 2012, Facebook has over 900 million active users.

Higher Education: Education that occurs at universities or colleges. It embraces specific studies to perform certain professions such as law, medicine, communications.

Schools of Communication: Academic divisions within a university, aroung which studies of communication are grouped.

Social Media: An online environment open to mass collaboration, one in which all participants that are invited may create, upload, classify, improve, discover, consume and share content without a direct intermediary partner.

Twitter: Free microblogging tool with social networking

Universities: Higher education institution which comprises several Schools, research departments, colleges, institutes, vocational schools.

Chapter 11

Web Use in Public Relations Education:
A Portuguese Example

Sónia Pedro Sebastião
Technical University of Lisbon, Portugal & Center for Administration and Public Policies, Portugal

ABSTRACT

The chapter relates several of the difficulties associated with public relations as an academic subject. Bearing these obstacles in mind, a public relations academic program has been defined, along with, a teaching strategy using Web-based social media (blog and Facebook profile) to communicate with students. The main purposes of the research are: to understand how university students see public relations as a subject and to ascertain their attitude toward the importance of using web-based communication tools in the assessment of public relations disciplines. The results have shown that students understand that the use of Web-social media is important to their academic life and to their relationship with the teacher. Nevertheless, it is also admitted that the use of technological tools must be followed by motivation, interest in the subject of public relations, and in general, academic work.

INTRODUCTION

The use of technology in education has caught the attention of Media Literacy and Education researchers. In the last years, computers have been identified as an instrument that would change educators' goals and methods, although, practice has revealed the legal, financial and cultural difficulties of this promise. Besides computers have been seen as an add-on, and not as integral to the full educational process (Hargadon, 2009).

However, the advent of web 2.0 and the growing use of web-social media have changed

DOI: 10.4018/978-1-4666-2851-9.ch011

the relationship with information and personal learning. This set of software tools is profoundly altering both learning processes and outcomes (Hargadon, 2009) and a new approach is required.

The educational use of web-social media has rarely been studied or accepted, because of the remaining doubts about its "informality" and "publicness", privacy issues and diverting basis. Nevertheless, and as noted by Bosch (2009), some efforts have been made to understand how students feel about having teachers on *Facebook* and to perceive how this participation affects the student-teacher relationship, as well as how the use of web-social networks can be helpful to academic assignments.

This book chapter follows Bosch statement and will attempt to provide exploratory evidence about the usefulness of social media in educational field. Its main objective is to inform about the potential of web-social media in pedagogical approaches to subjects. We have used our teaching experience in public relations (but the same approach can be used for other subjects), and we present the results of our research based on a survey of three different classes, applied at three different time periods.

This chapter has been divided into four main parts: a critical appreciation of what has been said about social media and its use in education; a theoretical approach to public relations and to the difficulties in defining it as an academic subject; an explanation of public relations university program and its pedagogical approach; and empirical data collection and analysis about the use of the web for teaching public relations in a Portuguese public university.

1. SOCIAL MEDIA IN EDUCATION

Technology is ubiquitous in our everyday lives. Yet, and according to Abreu's K12 study, most schools lag far behind when it comes to integrating technology into classroom learning (Abreu, 2011). Many are just beginning to explore the true potential technology offers for teaching and learning. Since, and as recognized by Abreu (2011), it is an opportunity to use what students know, enjoy and are entertained by to create dynamic lessons, develop critical thinking, problem solving, collaboration and communication among students. Properly used, technology help students acquire the skills they need to survive in a complex, highly technological knowledge-based economy. Authors, such as: Griffith, & Liyanage (2008); DeSchryver, Mishra, Koehler, & Francis (2009) and Holcomb, Brady, & Smith (2010) have demonstrated that the benefits and drawbacks of using safe and secure social networking sites (SNS's) in an educational setting outweigh the costs.

Technology changes the way teachers teach, offering educators effective ways of reaching different types of learners and assessing student understanding through multiple means. It also enhances the student-teacher relationship. When technology is effectively integrated into subject areas, teachers grow into roles of adviser, content expert, and coach. Technology may help to make teaching and learning more meaningful and fun. While the creation and collaboration within social networks provide opportunities to bridge informal and formal education, stressing new uses for web social media (Abreu, 2011, p. 52).

As stated by Boss (2011), Seymour Papert was the first to recognize the potential of technology in the learning process. During the 1960s, after collaborating with Jean Piaget, Papert developed the Logo programming language and began introducing it to children, who were able to gain a deeper understanding of geometry concepts, gaining programming expertise, as well as showing an engagement in learning rare in more traditional classroom activities.

Since Papert's groundbreaking work, the tools available for learning have become increasingly powerful and widespread. At the same time, barriers to using technology have gradually diminished. Today's learning landscape includes a wide variety of tools, such as: personal computers, tablets, interactive whiteboards, digital video cameras, and a constantly expanding suite of web 2.0 tools. Disparities persist, however, between technology-rich schools and those that have limited access to outdated equipment (Boss, 2011).

How does technology enhance the learning process? According to Roschelle, Pea, Hoadley, Gordin, & Means (2001), it offers active engagement, the opportunity to participate in groups, frequent interaction and feedback, and connections to real-world contexts. Technology also expands what students can learn by providing them with access to an ever-expanding store of information. Yet the same researchers emphasized that merely making computers available does not automatically lead to learning gains. They describe technology integration as only one element in "what must be a coordinated approach to improving curriculum, pedagogy, assessment, teacher development, and other aspects of school structure." (Roschelle, Pea, Hoadley, Gordin, & Means, 2001)

Bransford, Brown, & Cocking (2000) add to these advantages the opportunity of building local and global communities that include teachers, administrators, students, parents, practicing scientists, and other interested people, and the expanding opportunities for teacher learning.

The pedagogical value of social media, as summarized by Hargadon (2009), is about the involvement of student, teachers, practitioners, and other interested parts, at the same level and in the same space, in the following goals and outcomes: participation; discussion; engagement; creativity; expression; authenticity; openness; collaboration; proactivity; critical thinking and personalized learning.

Nowadays, several organizations have been studying technology integration and its consequences in the learning process (including School Boards like the NSBA and Pew Internet & American Life Project). One of the most recent examples is the project Edutopia.org (The George Lucas Educational Foundation) that tries to learn how technology has changed education and how

educators can leverage new educational tools to personalize learning, encourage collaboration, and prepare students for the future.

According to Edutopia.org, effective technology integration is achieved when the use of technology becomes routine and transparent and when technology supports curricular goals. This integration must support four key components of learning: active engagement, participation in groups, frequent interaction and feedback, and connection to real-world experts.

Social media opens new possibilities for connecting learners and taking education in new directions. Although schools have been slow to bring social media into the classroom, many students are using digital tools on their own to create and publish content, connect with acquaintances, and pursue their own interests, in a more entertaining basis.

In sum, the integration of technology in the learning process and in classrooms seems to be gradual, in an attempt to minimize possible disadvantages related with the preconception of social media as entertaining, informal and insecure; and trying to benefit from the advantages of pervasiveness, familiarity and usefulness. If students have been greatly using social media in their everyday life, why not using it as part of the learning process?

In the following parts of this book chapter we will present the discipline of Public Relations and attempt to demonstrate how university students ascertain their attitude toward the importance of using web-based communication tools in its assessment.

2. PUBLIC RELATIONS THEORETICAL APPROACH

Public Relations are considered an academic subject since the beginning of the twentieth century thanks to the works of Ivy Lee, Newton Vail and Edward Bernays (apud Bernays, 1980). However, in the 1960s it started to be theorized and defined as a strategic management function rather than as a messaging, publicity, and media relations role (Grunig, 2006). This definition has revealed itself as a hard and long way because theories are ideas in the mind of researchers and, fortunately, the number of researchers in this field has been increasing.

Nevertheless, Public Relations is a social science discipline with some specificity (Bernays, 1980). Despite the use of social science research methods and having man as its main object, on the one hand, it is considered as an applied social science since part of its theory arises from its practice, and we may find several practitioners undertaking research and authoring books and papers clarifying about best practices and best ways to achieve comprehension and theoretical models. On the other hand, some marketeers (like Kotler), consider it as a technique of communication, used by organizations to promote themselves and their products. The different conceptions about Public Relations lead to a sort of panacea and harden the understanding of the discipline and of its teaching.

Updating a 1999's study, Pasadeos, Berger, & Renfro (2010) realize that public relations have matured in the last decade as a social science discipline. Their conclusion is deducted from: the increasing number of refereed journal articles; new research perspectives and topics; and theory development. Greenwood (2010) even states that public relations theory development is one of the fastest growing areas of public relations scholarship, motivated by three factors: the work of leading public relations scholars; the criticism of the existing theory; and the continuing research for a satisfying and unifying theoretical framework.

In a 2006 article, James Grunig mapped the evolution of the theoretical research on the strategic management role of public relations, identifying the contribution of the situational theory of publics in the late 1960s, followed by the application of organization theory to public relations (1976); the symmetrical model of public relations, and

evaluation of communication programs (late 1970s); concluding with the Excellence study (1992). Despite its US-centrism, this theoretical edifice is central to the acknowledgment of how the public relations function should be structured and managed to provide the greatest value to organizations, publics, and society.

Regardless of this existing body of theories, public relations discipline faces a problem of identity, i.e., of unified meaning. The difficulty in defining public relations can be related to the youth of the profession, if we consider its development tied to the generalization of democratic societies and with the society of information and communication (Castells, 1996; Van Djik, 1999; Fuchs, 2008); with the rapid change and complexity of societies (Giddens, 2002; Sriramesh, & Vercic, 2007); and with the complexification of organizations and of their demands on communication services. The social nature of public relations implies their adjustment to the context where they are implemented (Cancel, Cameron, Sallot, & Mitrook, 1997; Tench & Yeomans, 2009, p. 16), making difficult the definition of a paradigm.

In 1976, Harlow found 472 definitions of public relations presented between 1900 and 1976. If we updated his work today, maybe this number would triple. As a result of his research, Harlow devised a long and complex definition of public relations. According to it:

"Public relations is a distinctive management function, which helps establish and maintain lines of communication, understanding, acceptance and co-operation between an organization and its publics; involves the management of problems or issues; helps management to keep informed on, and responsive to, public opinion; defines and emphasizes the responsibility of management to serve the public interest; helps management keep abreast of, and effectively utilize, change; serving as an early warning system to help anticipate trends; and uses research and ethical communication techniques as its principal tool." (*apud* Tench, & Yeomans, 2009, p. 4)

In 1978, The World Assembly of Public Relations Associations agreed on this more succinct definition: "Public relations is the art and social science of analyzing trends, predicting their consequences, counseling organizational leaders and implementing planned programs of action, which will serve both the organization's and the public interest." And even more tidily, the UK's Institute of Public Relations framed this one-liner: "Public relations is the planned and sustained effort to establish and maintain good-will and understanding between an organization and its publics. "

The diversity of public relations definitions comes with the multiplicity of roles that the practitioner may have to take part in his professional life. (Tench, & Yeomans, 2009, pp. 28-29) Most public relations professionals perform a mixture of manager and technician work and we cannot predict which will be predominant in our students' future, so we have to prepare a general *curriculum* that they will have to deepen by themselves when integrated in the labor market.

We think that a young graduate can aspire to a technician role; and expertise plus years of practicing may lead them to the manager function. This path will depend on their communication skills, proactive nature, strategic-thinking capacities, performance and organizational perception of their value and role. (Berger, Reber, & Heyman, 2007; Shen & Toth, 2008)

In Portugal, we are also noticing an increasing number of adults (more than 35 years old) that have decided to go back to the university and graduate, to reinforce their theoretical background as basis to progress in their professional career or even change their professional area. In these cases, we have graduating students with business and market knowledge, strategic-thinking capacities and external contacts that only seek to develop their communication and technical skills, to gain leverage to ascend to managerial roles.

We understand the market requirements to educate students for public relations practice, nevertheless, our model must be multidisciplinary and general, because professions based in communication are changing. Besides, changes are also provoked by the global economy (Sriramesh, & Vercic, 2007) and the varying nature of organizational identities and responsibilities, as well as, by the new challenges presented by the growing constellation of new stakeholders. (Pasadeos, Berger, & Renfro, 2010)

The digital tools of communication have been gradually inserted in the establishment of "good-will" and understanding between the organization and its publics, following the digitalization of society and communicating environments. In the context of public relations, web media have been widely studied by Haig (2001), Phillips (2002); Phillips & Young (2009), Breakenrigde (2008) and Breakenrigde, & Solis (2009).

So the difficulty in teaching public relations is not only related to the difficulty in defining it, but mostly with the interpretation of values and changes in a complex set of individual and institutional interests. There are too many variables at stake: the theory and the practice; the teacher and the practitioner; academia universe and the market. In one word: the "stakeholders", that is, everyone that contacts with public relations and has some interest on it, either to benefit from its services, either to educate about it. Concerning this dilemma, Betteke van Ruler (2005) uses a metaphor synthesizing the constant divorce between the professionals and the scholars and emphasizes the importance of an agreement between the two sides of a common coin: recognition of public relations as a profession supported by a coherent teaching program. After all, public relations are not only a specialized management area, but a professional domain and a social phenomenon that need to be valued by society. (Grunig, 2000; Coombs, & Holladay, 2007) So the experts need to claim autonomy and ownership to define a professional identity and this requires a specific professional education *curriculum*. (Kruckeberg, 1998; L'Etang, 1999; Sriramesh, & Hornaman, 2006; Global Alliance, in progress)

Considering the need for an educational curriculum adapted to labor market requirements and scholar research we have prepared a university program and a pedagogical approach that we present in the next section.

3. PUBLIC RELATIONS UNIVERSITY PROGRAM AND PEDAGOGICAL APPROACH

Public relations are a social practice that considers and tries to explain transforming processes in society. (Coombs, & Holladay, 2007; Ihlen, van Ruler, & Fredriksson, 2009) The public relations management function is closely tied to ethics since it intends to create mutual understanding and promote dialogue and collaboration rather to manipulate and deceit. (Grunig, 2000; Bowen, 2005; Lieber, 2008)

Having those premises in mind, as a former communication technician and as a current public relations teacher, one started a plan to define the "best" program, the "best" teaching practices, the "best" connection to the practitioner's world and needs. Soon we realize that, the "best" is the enemy of action, and worse our best is never good enough in an interchangeable environment where organizations (Communication Consultancies and clients) act like individuals, adapting and reacting, other than, researching and planning.

Considering the global economy and the network configuration of markets, we decided to construct our program following the *European Communication Monitor: Trends in Communication Management and Public Relations* (2009) and the work of Holger Sievert (2009).

The demands made to a professional of public relations in terms of knowledge and skills are changing with the rhizomatic[1] configuration of the information society and with the digital para-

digm that characterizes it. In this context, we have realized that digital communication is growing in importance. Several practitioners have even asked us to deepen our attention in the teaching of digital competences in the use of digital tools, specially, social media. According to Portuguese and multinational public relations and communication practitioners[2], clients are requesting integrated communication campaign to promote their products and services. In consequence, skilled junior practitioners with no market experience, but with the understanding of the social media potential, are valuable assets for consultancies. We perceive that the best way to acquire these skills is using the mind set of "learning by doing", that is, using social media in our communication with students in a two way basis (working techniques, point 2 below).

In Holger Sievert's (2009) conception, shifts in the communicative environment, such as: new technologies and new forms of communication; the increasing importance of knowledge in the economy; the opaqueness of the commercial exchange; the globalization of the economy; the crescent complexity of decision taking; and the critical perception of communication consultants; demand qualifications to a professional of public relations, which can be grouped in four basic areas:

1. Knowledge of communication sciences (communication principles; theories and models of communication; ethics of communication, marketing, and public relations).
2. Working techniques (instruments; measurement and evaluation; specialisms).
3. Organization (research; planning; management).
4. Surrounding environment (SWOT; PEST; culture; financial; image and reputation).

However those are the contents that must frame a public relations university program. With the purpose of defining the teaching practice we have analyzed studies on public relations pedagogy, like: Kruckeberg (1998); L'Etang (1999); Coombs & Rybacki (1999); Badaracco (2002); Hardin, & Pompper (2004); Alexander (2004); Gower, & Reber (2006); Sriramesh, & Hornaman, 2006; DiStaso, Stacks, & Botanc (2009).

As a result, we come up with the need to contemplate the instructional delivery techniques of: dialogue/class discussion; exercises/application of ideas; lectures; small group discussion; group work; textbook; and powerpoint-type presentations; student assignments, such as: individual speeches/presentations; group presentations; elaboration of publicity materials; case studies analysis; written exercises; and analysis of scientific articles; textbook; and films; that were used as study guides to improve the students' learning methodology. (Lubbers, 2002)

The students' main difficulties were related to the inexistence of Portuguese-writing textbooks or scientific articles. Even if we are Portuguese researchers in the area we have to write our work in English, and students are not eager to study in English. The second difficulty was related to the students insecurity in organizing a Public Relations plan and adequate their purposes to their means. So when they were asked to organize a workshop inviting public relations' practitioners for a one hour and a half presentation they devised a plan for a one-day congress or with insufficient promotion resulting in a small audience in the event. Finally, students feel more insecure with production techniques: design and layout, new technologies use and understanding; observations that validate Gower, & Reber's (2006) results.

The strengths of the pedagogical approach was the group work, discussions and oral presentations, as well as, powerpoint-type presentations production. Our observation and discussion's analysis allow us to understand, on one hand, the students' passion with some technician roles, such as: production, work team and research development; and, on the other hand, the need to deepen their communication skills (oral, writing and multimedia).

These behavior observations have allowed us to adapt our program and assessment requests; however, we felt the need to improve our delivery methods and to use instruments for regular and equal delivery of pedagogical objects. So we have decided to use web social media and inquired our students about their information needs and attitudes about this new method. Our inquiry process and results are presented below.

4. THE USE OF WEB IN TEACHING PUBLIC RELATIONS

Our first approach was inspired in the gathered theory and in direct observation of student behavior, which allowed us to create a working basis on which the students could pronounce themselves in the second phase. Thus, for a better understanding of students' opinions, the second empirical approach includes the application of a self-completion questionnaire in the classroom, with anonymous responses. So in the second semester of the scholar year of 2009-2010, we have applied a direct survey to our students (class A and B) inquiring them about the utility and the content of those communication tools. The answers were used to improve our blog and adapt our program to the next scholar year (first semester, class C). Finally, by the end of the semester, we have applied the same survey to the class C to measure their opinion on the blog and *Facebook* profile, its utility and content.

Our target group is university students attending the bachelor degree of Communication Sciences in the Technical University of Lisbon. Normally, these students have between 18 and 22 years old, however we may have older students due to failed assessment and latter graduations (people in the labor market that decide to graduate). Student and young adults are one of the groups that uses internet the most in Portugal and especially web social media (Marktest, 2011).

4.1. First Approach

During the scholar year of 2008-2009, we have implemented a research process applied to university students, attending the third year of a bachelor degree in Communication Sciences. Our strategy was designed according to our perception of what matters for public relations teaching and for students to be successful in the subject. On one hand, the public relations' syllabus was divided in four basic areas: (1) communication sciences (communication principles; theories and models of communication; ethics of communication, marketing, and public relations); (2) working techniques (instruments; measurement and evaluation; specialisms); (3) organization (research; planning; management); and (4) surrounding environment (SWOT; PEST; culture; financial; image and reputation). On the other hand, the pedagogical approach considered the instructional delivery techniques of: dialogue/class discussion; exercises/application of ideas; lectures; small group discussion; group work; textbook; and powerpoint-type presentations; student assignments, such as: individual speeches/presentations; group presentations; elaboration of publicity materials; case studies analysis; written exercises; and analysis of scientific articles.

Considering the importance and the so-called simplicity of the use of technology and web-based social media, we tried to engage students in the discussion of matters associated with the computer mediated communication and reflections of it in public relations learning and practice. The emphasis was given to the shift in an engaging and relational perspective; and to the use of a weblog and *Facebook* profile for classes' support.

In the year 2009, the weblog was organized with the following data: program and rules of assessment; important dates for examinations, group presentations, case studies and scientific articles analysis; current issues on public relations; powerpoint-type presentations.

The *Facebook* profile was used to disclose some important information about assignments and evaluation; and a midlevel self-disclosure with some personal photographs at European cities (individual portraits); quotations; personal thoughts; film and music divulgation. The encounter of students on *Facebook* is an attempt to communicate and engage with them outside the controlled environment of classes (Mazer, Murphy, & Simonds, 2007). Nevertheless, we try not to be lame, personal or too intrusive. We avoid comments on personal subjects on students' murals or even in classes. Our aim was to increase proximity to students and promote a more positive classroom climate.

In sum, and trying to respond to Alexander's challenge (2004), we used weblog, a web-based social network profile (*Facebook*) and e-mail as web tools to engage and communicate with students. We have been using e-mail since the year 2004 noticing the increasing exchange of messages asking for face to face meeting or to clarify doubts about classes and group work. Though, in 2009 and 2010, e-mails have been preferably used to deliver individual and group assignments, powerpoint-type presentations and final reports for evaluation; appointments and doubts started to be arranged and clarified through *Facebook* private messages and chat.

4.2. Second Approach

In 2010 (second semester, March to June), we have survey the classes (first and third year of enrollment in bachelor degree in communication sciences) asking for students' opinion about the weblog and asking for suggestions to improve it. The survey was composed by closed and open questions. Open questions were about the weblog structure and suggestions of improvement and about students' opinion about the use of web social media in the relation teacher-student. After the collection, answers were coded by the researcher.

Considering our sample, we have collected 53 valid answers (about 50% of the students registered in the subjects). About 45,3% of the respondents have between 20 and 24 years (third year), and 47,2% have between 18 and 19 (first year). 67,9% are female and 32,1% are male. 92,5% have been using web for more than three years and consider themselves advanced (73,6%), average (15,1%) and expert (11,3%) web users. In average, they have 1 or 2 social network profiles (75,5%), mostly on *Facebook* (83%) and they access it at least once a day (84,9%). Finally, 92,5% have access to Internet at home and the remaining 7,5% have mobile broadband access.

All the inquired students declared that the weblog is important (55%) for the classes' organization. 45% even state that the weblog is very important.

Supporting their first answer, most students answer that they have been visiting the weblog at least once a week (58,5%); 24,5% declared to visit it occasionally; 15,1% stated to visit it at least three times a week and only 1,9% declared to visit the blog daily.

About 71,7% of the inquired students did not make any suggestions to improve the weblog. Yet, 17% of the inquired students asked for more educational objects, mostly, notes from lectures (see Figure 1).

Most inquired students (96,2%) declare to agree with web social media use in the relationship teacher-student. Students justified their opinion stating that it is more practical (26,4%), it increases the proximity to the teacher in less formal ways (24,5%), it is easier (17%) and quicker (17%). 7,5% of students do not justify their opinion and the ones that do not agree with web social media use, mostly, with *Facebook* use, in the relationship teacher-students, answered that it is not academic. They classify a *Facebook* profile as too informal and private.

When asked about how to learn web social media, 67,9% prefer to do it individually by exploration and 15,1% learn it with friends. 13,2% consider the importance of learning it with the teacher in classes. The remaining 3,8% stated that web social media can be learn anyway (by exploration individually, with friends and with teachers in class).

After collecting all students answers and discuss with them some remaining doubts, we have changed the weblog structure. The new weblog structure is as follow:

1. Author's textbook information;
2. Program and rules of assessment;
3. Important dates for examinations, group presentations, case studies and scientific articles analysis;

Figure 1. Suggestions of contents to add to the weblog (2010, in %)

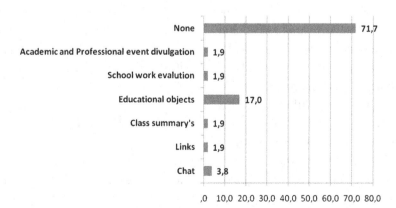

4. Important international and national events for researchers and students interested in Public Relations (BledCom, EUPRERA, ECREA, IAMCR, ICA, SOPCOM);
5. Papers for study support in Portuguese and English grouped in five categories: public relations definition, ethics, research and evaluation, specialisms, and trends;
6. Current issues of the public relations market;
7. Bibliographic and web references;
8. Previous writing examinations examples.

The weblog was also connected with the *Facebook* profile, providing a mural publication every time the weblog was updated with important information about classes; assignments; events and new publications; case studies and links.

4.3. Third Approach

In 2011 (first semester: September 2010 to January 2011), we have survey a new class (third year of enrollment in the bachelor degree in communication sciences) asking for students' opinion about the improved weblog and asking for new suggestions.

Considering our sample, we have collected 50 valid answers (about 80% of the students register in the subjects). Near 94% of respondents have between 20 and 24 years. 86% are female. All the inquired students have been using web for more than three years and consider themselves advanced (82%), expert (10%) and average (8%) web users. In average, they have 1 or 2 social network profiles (74%), mostly on *Facebook* (92%) and they access it at least once a day (92%). Finally, 78% have access to Internet at home, 20% have mobile broadband access and the remaining 2% accessed Internet using their mobile phone. This sample is slightly more aged, more used to access Internet and web social networks; besides they have a larger mobile access to Internet.

Similarly to the first sample, all the inquired students declared that the weblog is important

(46%) for classes' organization. The majority (54%) stated that the weblog is very important.

Despite the recognition that the weblog is very important for their success in public relations subject, this inquired sample visit the weblog with less frequency. Most students answer that they visit the weblog at least once a week (46%), but the percentage is substantialy inferior of the first sample (58,5%) and the percentage of students that declared to visit the weblog occasionaly increased from 24,5% to 28%. Considering other answers, 24% stated to visit the weblog at least tree times a week and 2% declared to visit the blog daily.

Like in the first sample, about 78% of the inquired students did not make any suggestions to improve the weblog. Yet, 16% asked for more educational objects, mostly, lecture notes; 2% asked for papers in Portuguese language and 4% for information about their grades (information provided by the university administrative services).

Like in the first application, a large majority of the inquired students (98%) declared to agree with web social media use in the relationship teacher-student. The students justified their opinion stating that it is more practical (34%), easier (20%), quicker (18%) and it increases the proximity to the teacher in less formal ways (16%). 10% of students do not justify their opinion and the 2% that do not agree with *Facebook* profile use in the relationship teacher-students answered that it is not academic.

Finally and when asked about how to learn web social media, 74% prefer to do it individually by exploration; 18% consider the importance of learning it with the teacher in classes; and the remaining 8% declared that they prefer to learn it with friends.

5. DISCUSSION

According to the answers of the two samples used in our exploratory study, we realize that thanks to time spent on *Facebook*, students are able to socialize and entertain themselves at the same time they discuss academic assignments. Besides, the use of web-social networks provides more immediate response and the pre-existing familiarity and user experience eases the information flow. Finally, the contact with the teacher in this environment provides the sense of participation in the same academic community, helping to break down barriers between student and teacher, because the web social network is a shared space, not controlled by traditional power hierarchies. But and as realized by Bosch (2009) inequalities remain in the access to this tools and in the use of it, not only provoked by economic and infrastructure access difficulties, but also because of the attitude through web-social networks: students may see it as entertainment and "private", they do not want educators controlling their "space" (boyd, 2007 and 2008); and teachers may find it equalizing and a peril to their authority in classrooms. (Bosch, 2009)

Yet, students' preferences confirm boyd's (2007) conception of mediated publics that engaged in conversations in digital environments rather than in assertions of power, or hierarchical recognitions of authority. Web social networks are supposed to be fun places and not "academic" ones. What has been confirmed by the declared students' occasional visits to the weblog. Those occasions are the beginning of the academic year and the evaluation moments, when students realize the need for bibliographic references or additional information to be successful in their assessment. According to weblog statistics collected with *wordpress*, the weblog was most visited in March (presentation, rules of assessment and project definitions) and May (writing examination and assignments delivery for evaluation) – see Appendix 2.

A large majority of the inquired students did not make any suggestions to improve the weblog. On the one hand, it may be a symptom of ignorance about the possible academic functionality of a weblog since usually the students use it as a digital diary for their jokes, ironies and prefer-

ences. When confronted with academic purposes, they lose the perspective of what is possible to ask for. But it can also be an indicator of indolence, lack of interest in the subject and short attention span, associated to information overload and to the multiplication of sites and spaces students are requested to be/visit. On the other hand, they have the notion that if they ask for more contents they will have to work on it and sometimes the subjects do not motivate them. So the weblog can be "too demanding" considering all the other "things" students have or want to do.

Despite the request of both samples for lecture notes, we still do not provide them in the weblog, because we have just published a textbook in Portuguese language that supports the classes. The problem is that the textbook has more than 200 pages and the notes from classes would have less than 100.

Regarding school work evaluation, it is a service provided by the university services in a private network platform. Students' request would imply the duplication of information in different web places.

The increasing number of students declaring that social media should be learned in classes with the teacher (second sample) may be due to sample composition. The first sample included students from the first year that did not attend the subject Communication and Digital Media (second year of enrollment) and are not aware of the full potential of learning web social media in classes. But it can also be due to students understanding of the "most right question" considering that they were questioned by a teacher.

Finally, with this research we have also learned that the use of technological tools must be followed by motivation, interest in the subject of public relation, and in the general academic work. In 2011, we had to teach an unenthusiastic and reckless class, and, despite our efforts, the results were not good.

So, while in 2009-2010 (first sample), almost 53% of the classes got good classifications (14 or

15)3 and almost 14% got very good marks (16-17) (see Figure 2); in 2010-2011 (second sample) 76% of the class had sufficient marks and 17% got good ones (see Figure 3).

The results of this study are exploratory, but they were very useful to define the weblog structure and the boundaries for using *Facebook* to communicate with students. The survey technique used has limitations, namely: the reliance on self-reports of phenomena, which may suffer from imprecision and deception; the mediation of language often insufficient to describe some realities; the open-ended limitations related with the impossibility of the researcher to predict all possible answers and the incapacity of students to present alternatives without time to reflect on the topic. Yet, and considering the sample size (a mean of 65% of the enrolled students), the clarity and consistency of the answers were very satisfying.

Future research in web use in the education of Public Relations will have to include an inquiry to our former students that have participated in this research so that we may understand if our teaching approach was fruitful for their professional life and collect additional suggestions to improve our academic strategy.

Final Remarks

DiStaso, Stacks, & Botanc (2009) declared that Public Relations is rapidly becoming a highly educated field in the United States and this encourages scholars to strengthen their programs everywhere. The new programs should reflect the practice of public relations as a globalized profession, including areas such as intercultural communication; strategic planning and internationalization; ethics; quantitative and qualitative research; media training and coaching; and skills in planning, writing, producing and delivering content to media and publics using multimedia techniques.

In the teaching ground that motivates this chapter, our purpose was to place more emphasis in a coherent and motivating pedagogy to help the understanding and strengthening of the public relations field. So we have cultivated the participation and active learning; integrated a practical project in traditional lecture formats; promoted dialogue between students and practitioners; used technology to improve on-site classrooms and communication with students.

Communication skills are vital to solve conflict (Plowman, 1998), but talking about them

Figure 2. Public Relations students' evaluation in regular assessment system (scholar year 2009-2010, 2nd semester)

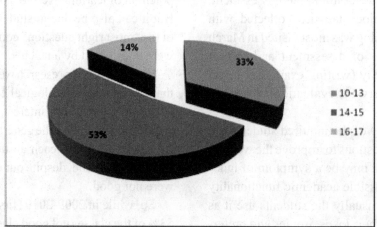

Figure 3. Public Relations students' evaluation in regular assessment system (scholar year 2010-2011, 1st semester)

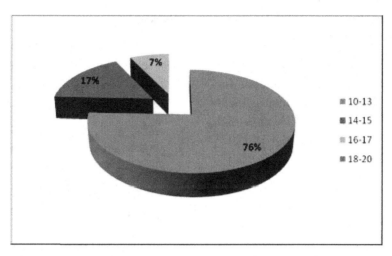

will not furnish the students those skills. The recognition of public relations as an important and strategic management function starts in the bench of university. As noted by Plowman (1998) and Grunig (2000) among others, for public relations practitioners to become members of the dominant coalition it is important to increase their education, their knowledge of communication theory and research methods, as well as, their knowledge about business practices and expertise. If we do not prepare our students they will not be able to do their work, scan the market or understand what they have to do to gain power in the organization.

We chose to start by giving them power in the classroom and by exemplifying how web-based technological tools can be "non-academic", "informal" and also useful and determinant to organize and keep them up to date on "serious" subjects.

REFERENCES

Abreu, B. S. (2011). *Media literacy, social networking, and the Web 2.0 environment for the K-12 educator*. New York, NY: Peter Lang Publishing.

Alexander, D. (2004). Changing the public relations curriculum: A new challenge for educators. *Prism*. Retrieved 13th July, 2010, from http://www.prismjournal.org/fileadmin/Praxis/Files/Journal_Files/Issue2/Alexander.pdf.

Badaracco, C. H. (Ed.). (2002). Special issue on innovative pedagogy. *Public Relations Review*, *28*(2), 135–208. doi:10.1016/S0363-8111(02)00119-4

Berger, B. K., Reber, B. H., & Heyman, W. C. (2007). You can't homogenize success in communication management: PR leaders take diverse paths to top. *International Journal of Strategic Communication*, *1*(1), 53–71. doi:10.1080/15531180701285301

Bernays, E. (1980). *Public relations*. Norman, OK: University of Oklahoma.

Bosch, T. E. (2009). Using online social networking for teaching and learning: Facebook use at the University of Cape Town. *Communication*, *35*(2), 185–200.

Boss, S. (2011). Technology integration: A short history. *Edutopia.org* (The George Lucas Educational Foundation). Retrieved 12th November, 2011, from http://www.edutopia.org/technology-integration-history.

Bowen, S. A. (2005). A practical model for ethical decision making in issues management and public relations. *Journal of Public Relations Research, 17*(3), 191–216. doi:10.1207/s1532754xjprr1703_1

boyd, d. (2007). Social network sites: Public, private, or what? *Knowledge Tree*. Retrieved from 1st February, 2011, http://www.danah.org/papers/KnowledgeTree.pdf

boyd, d. (2008). *Facebook*'s privacy trainwreck: Exposure, invasion, and social convergence. *Convergence: the International Journal of Research into New Media Technologies, 14*(1), 13-20.

boyd, d. m., & Ellison, N. B. (2007). Social network sites: Definition, history, and scholarship. *Journal of Computer-Mediated Communication, 13*(1). Retrieved 10th November, 2011, from http://jcmc.indiana.edu/vol13/issue1/boyd.ellison.html

Bransford, J. D., Brown, A. L., & Cocking, R. R. (Eds.). (2000). *How people learn: Brain, mind, experience, and school*. Washington, DC: National Academy Press.

Breakenridge, D. (2008). *PR 2.0: New media, new tools, new audiences*. New Jersey: FT Press.

Breakenridge, D., & Solis, B. (2009). *Putting the public back in public relations: How social media is reinventing the aging business of PR*. New Jersey: FT Press.

Cancel, A. E., Cameron, G. T., Sallot, L. M., & Mitrook, M. A. (1997). It depends: A contingency theory of accommodation in public relations. *Journal of Public Relations Research, 9*(1), 31–63. doi:10.1207/s1532754xjprr0901_02

Castells, M. (1996). *The information age: Economy, society and culture (Vol. I)*. New Jersey: Blackwell.

Coombs, T., & Rybacki, K. (1999). Public relations education: Where is pedagogy? *Public Relations Review, 25*(1), 55–63. doi:10.1016/S0363-8111(99)80127-1

Coombs, W. T., & Holladay, S. J. (2007). *It's not just PR*. Malden, UK: Blackwell Publishing.

Cutlip, S., Center, A., & Broom, G. (2000). *Effective public relations* (8th ed.). London, UK: Prentice-Hall.

Department of Trade & Industry and the Institute of Public Relations. (2003). *Unlocking the potential of public relations: developing good practice*. London, UK: European Centre for Business Excellence. Retrieved 24th June, 2010, from http://www.lombard-media.lu/pdf/0312_Potential-PR.pdf

DeSchryver, M. P., Mishra, M. K., & Francis, A. P. (2009). Moodle vs. Facebook: Does using Facebook for discussions in an online course enhance perceived social presence and student interaction? In C. Crawford, D. A. Willis, R. Carlsen, I. Gibson, K. McFerrin, J. Price, & R. I. Weber (Eds.), *Proceedings of Society for Information Technology and Teacher Education International Conference 2009*, (pp. 329-336). Chesapeake, VA: AACE.

DiStaso, M. W., Stacks, D. W., & Botanc, C. H. (2009). State of public relations education in the United States: 2006 report on a national survey of executives and academics. *Public Relations Review, 35*, 254–269. doi:10.1016/j.pubrev.2009.03.006

Fuchs, C. (2008). *Internet and society: Social theory in the information age*. New York, NY: Routledge.

Giddens, A. (2002). *Runaway world. How globalization is reshaping our lives*. London, UK: Profile Books.

Global Alliance. (in press). *Curriculum standards in public relations: Towards a global standard.* Retrieved 10th November, 2011, from http://www.globalalliancepr.org/project.php?id=3

Gower, K. K., & Reber, B. H. (2006). Prepared for practice? Student perceptions about requirements and preparation for public relations practice. *Public Relations Review, 32,* 188–190. doi:10.1016/j.pubrev.2006.02.017

Greenwood, C. A. (2010). Evolutionary theory: The missing link for conceptualizing public relations. *Journal of Public Relations Research, 22*(4), 456–476. doi:10.1080/10627261003801438

Griffith, S., & Liyanage, L. (2008). *An introduction to the potential of social networking sites in education.* In Emerging Technologies Conference 2008, Paper 9. Retrieved 12th November, 2011, from http://ro.uow.edu.au/etc08/9.

Grunig, J. E. (Ed.). (1992). *Excellence in public relations and communication management.* Hillsdale, NJ: Lawrence Erlbaum Associates, Inc.

Grunig, J. E. (2000). Collectivism, collaboration, and societal corporatism as core professional values in public relations. *Journal of Public Relations Research, 12*(1), 23–48. doi:10.1207/S1532754XJPRR1201_3

Grunig, J. E. (2006). Furnishing the edifice: Ongoing research on public relations as a strategic management function. *Journal of Public Relations Research, 18*(2), 151–176. doi:10.1207/s1532754xjprr1802_5

Haig, M. (2001). *E-PR: The essential guide to public relations on the Internet.* London, UK: Kogan Page.

Hardagon, S. (2009). *Educational networking: The important role Web 2.0 will play in education.* Retrieved 12th November, 2011, from http://www.stevehargadon.com/2009/12/social-networking-in-education.html

Hardin, M. C., & Pompper, D. (2004). Writing in the public relations curriculum: practitioner perceptions versus pedagogy. *Public Relations Review, 30,* 357–364. doi:10.1016/j.pubrev.2004.05.007

Holcomb, L. B., Brady, K. P., & Smith, B. V. (2010). The emergence of "educational networking": Can non-commercial, education-based social networking sites really address the privacy and safety concerns of educators? *MERLOT Journal of Online Learning and Teaching, 6*(2).

Ihlen, O., van Ruler, B., & Fredriksson, M. (2009). *Public relations and social theory: Key figures and ideas.* London, UK: Routledge.

Kruckeberg, D. (1998). The future of PR education: Some recommendations. *Public Relations Review, 24*(2), 235–248. doi:10.1016/S0363-8111(99)80053-8

L'Etang, J. (1999). Public relations education in Britain: An historical review in the context of professionalisation. *Public Relations Review, 25*(3), 261–289. doi:10.1016/S0363-8111(99)00019-3

Lieber, P. S. (2008). Moral development in public relations: Measuring duty to society in strategic communication. *Public Relations Review, 34*(3), 244–251. doi:10.1016/j.pubrev.2008.03.028

Lubbers, C. A. (2002). Using alternative teaching techniques to enhance student performance in the traditional introductory public relations course. *Public Relations Review, 28*(2), 157–166. doi:10.1016/S0363-8111(02)00122-4

Marktest. (2011). *Os Portugueses e as redes sociais.* Retrieved 25th November, 2011, from http://www.marktest.com/wap/a/n/id~1891.aspx\

Mazer, J. P., Murphy, R. E., & Simonds, C. J. (2007). I'll see you on Facebook: The effects of computer-mediated teacher self-disclosure on student motivation, affective learning, and classroom climate. *Communication Education, 56*(1), 1–17. doi:10.1080/03634520601009710

National Schools Board Association (NSBA). (2007). *Creating and connecting: Research and guidelines on online social and education-networking*. Retrieved 12th November, 2011, from http://www.nsba.org/site/docs/41400/41340.pdf.

New Media Consortium (NMC) & EDUCAUSE Learning Initiative. (ELI). (2002). *The horizon reports*. Retrieved 12th November, 2011, from http://www.nmc.org/horizon-project/horizon-reports

Pasadeos, Y., Berger, B., & Renfro, R. B. (2010). Public relations as a maturing discipline: An update on research networks. *Journal of Public Relations Research*, 22(2), 136–158. doi:10.1080/10627261003601390

Phillips, D. (2002). *On-line public relations*. London, UK: Kogan Page.

Phillips, D., & Young, P. (2009). *Online public relations: A practical guide to developing an online strategy in the world of social media*. London, UK: Kogan Page.

Plowman, K. D. (1998). Power in conflict for public relations. *Journal of Public Relations Research*, 10, 237–261. doi:10.1207/s1532754xjprr1004_02

Roschelle, J., Pea, R., Hoadley, C., Gordin, D., & Means, B. (2001). Changing how and what children learn in school with computer-based technologies. *The Future of Children*, 10(2), 76–101. doi:10.2307/1602690

Shen, H., & Toth, E. L. (2008). An ideal public relations master's curriculum: Expectations and status quo. *Public Relations Review*, 34, 309–311. doi:10.1016/j.pubrev.2008.03.030

Sievert, H. (2009, September). *Some ideas for new systematics*. Input to the Round Table "PR practices and qualifications. EUPRERA 2009, Bucharest.

Simon, M., Graziano, M., & Lenhart, A. (2001). *The internet and education*. Pew Internet & American Life Project Report. Retrieved 12th November, 2011, from http://www.pewinternet.org/Reports/2001/The-Internet-and-Education.aspx

Sriramesh, K., & Hornaman, L. B. (2006). Public relations as a profession: An analysis of curricular content in the United States. *Journal of Creative Communications*, 1(2), 155–172. doi:10.1177/097325860600100202

Sriramesh, K., & Vercic, D. (2007). The impact of globalization on public relations: A special section from the BledCom 2007 Conference. *Public Relations Review*, 33, 355–444. doi:10.1016/j.pubrev.2007.09.002

Tench, R., & Yoemans, L. (2009). *Exploring public relations*, 2nd ed. London, UK: Financial Times/ Prentice Hall.

Van Dijk, J. (2005). *The network society: Social aspects of new media* (2nd ed.). London, UK: Sage. (Original work published 1999)

Van Ruler, B. (2005). Commentary: Professionals are from Venus, scholars are from Mars. *Public Relations Review*, 31, 159–173. doi:10.1016/j.pubrev.2005.02.022

Zerfass, A., Tench, R., Verhoeven, P., Vercic, D., & Moreno, A. (2009). *European Communication Monitor 2008. Trends in communication management and public relations – Results and implications*. Brussels, Belgium: EUPRERA. Retrieved 12th October, 2009, from www.communicationmonitor.eu

ADDITIONAL READING

Buckingham, D. (2003). *Media education: Literacy, learning, and contemporary culture*. Cambridge, UK: Polity Press.

Davidson, C. N., & Goldberg, D. T. (2009). *The future of learning institutions in a digital age. (John D. and Catherine T. MacArthur Foundation Reports on Digital Media and Learning).* Massachusetts: MIT Press.

Davidson, C. N., & Goldberg, D. T. (2010). *The future of thinking: learning institutions in a digital age. (John D. and Catherine T. MacArthur Foundation Reports on Digital Media and Learning).* Massachusetts: MIT Press.

Davis, J. A., & Merchant, G. (2009). *Web 2.0 for schools: Learning and social participation.* New York, NY: Peter Lang.

Deal, T. E., Purinton, T., & Waetjen, D. C. (2008). *Making sense of social networks in schools.* Thousand Oaks, CA: Corwin Press.

Jenkins, H., Clinton, K., Purushotma, R., Robison, A. J., & Weigel, M. (2009). *Confronting the challenges of participatory culture: Media education for the 21st century.* Massachusetts: Massachusetts Institute of Technology.

Jensen, K. B. (2010). *Media convergence: The three degrees of network, mass and interpersonal communication.* New York, NY: Routledge.

Jonassen, D. H. (2004). *Handbook of research on educational communications and technology.* Hillsdale, NJ: Lawrence Erlbaum. doi:10.1111/j.1467-8535.2009.00969_7.x

Kiili, K. (2005). Participatory multimedia learning: Engaging learners. *Australasian Journal of Educational Technology*, *21*(3), 303–322.

Kress, G. R. (2003). *Literacy in the new media age*. London, UK: Routledge. doi:10.4324/9780203164754

Mayer, R. E. (2005). *The Cambridge handbook of multimedia learning.* New York, NY: Cambridge University Press. doi:10.1017/CBO9780511816819

Mayer, R. E., Fennell, S., Farmer, L., & Campbell, J. (2004). A personalization effect in multimedia learning: students learn better when words are in conversational style rather than formal style. *Journal of Educational Psychology*, *96*, 389–395. doi:10.1037/0022-0663.96.2.389

Mayer, R. E., & Massa, L. J. (2003). Three facets of visual and verbal learners: Cognitive ability, cognitive style, and learning preference. *Journal of Educational Psychology*, *95*, 833–846. doi:10.1037/0022-0663.95.4.833

Mayer, R. E., Moreno, R., Boire, M., & Vagge, S. (1999). Maximizing constructivist learning from multimedia communications by minimizing cognitive load. *Journal of Educational Psychology*, *91*, 638–643. doi:10.1037/0022-0663.91.4.638

Moreno, R., & Mayer, R. (1999). Cognitive principles of multimedia learning: The role of modality and contiguity. *Journal of Educational Psychology*, *91*, 358–368. doi:10.1037/0022-0663.91.2.358

Ponte, C., Azevedo, J., & Straubhaar, J. (Eds.). (in press). *Inclusão e participação digital (Portugal-Austin-EUA)*. Retrieved November 20, 2011, from http://digital_inclusion.up.pt/

Wellman, B., & Haythornthwaite, C. A. (2002). *The Internet in everyday life*. Oxford, UK: Wiley-Blackwell. doi:10.1002/9780470774298

Willett, R. (2006). *Digital generations: Children, young people, and new media.* New York, NY: Routledge.

KEY TERMS AND DEFINITIONS

Education: The process of teaching and learning, usually at school, college, or university, which includes the institutions and people involved with teaching.

Participation: The act of taking part in an activity; in its organization and/or opinion.

Pedagogy: The practice of teaching, using methods and techniques combined in a logic sense.

Public Relations: Social, organizational and communicative function which plan and sustain efforts to establish and maintain good-will and understanding between an organization and its publics.

Social Media: Web-based tools that allow users to develop a public or semi-public profile, electronically communicate with other users with whom they share a connection, and view and comment on their list of communications with other web users.

Survey: A set of questions that you ask a large number of people in order to find out about their declared opinions, beliefs or behavior.

Technology: Equipment, and ways of doing things that are based on modern knowledge about science and computers.

ENDNOTES

[1] The rhizomatic configuration allows for multiple, non-hierarchical entry and exit points in data representation and interpretation. Deleuze and Guatari (1987) oppose it to an arborescent conception of knowledge, which works with dualist categories and binary choices. A rhizome works with planar and trans-species connections, while an arborescent model works with vertical and linear connections. The rhizome can not be reduced to a structural model, defining itself as a map relatable in all its aspects, reversible and subject to constant change (1987, p. 13). In the authors words: "every rhizome contains lines of segmentarity according to which it is stratified, territorialized, organized, signified, attributed, etc., as well as lines of deterritorialization down which it constantly flees." (Deleuze & Guattari, 1987, p. 210)

[2] That we meet in EUPRERA's events and in Academic events in Portugal.

[3] In Portugal the numeric scale is from 1 to 20. The qualitative scale is: 1-9 (bad/excluded); 10 to 13 (sufficient); 14-15 (good); 16-17 (very good) and 18-20 (excellent).

APPENDIX 1

SURVEY (English Adaptation)

Q1: With which frequency did you visit the weblog http://smpsebastiao.wordpress.html to obtain information about PR subject?
1. Daily
2. A mean of 3 times a week
3. Once a week
4. Occasionally
5. Never

Q2: What is the importance of weblog for the organization of the subject?
1. Very important
2. Important
3. Indifferent
4. Little important
5. Not important

Q3: Which contents would you had to the weblog?

Q4: Do you know the teacher's profile on *Facebook*?
1. Yes
2. No (go to Q7)

Q5: Have you ever use FB to contact the teacher?
1. Yes
2. No (go to Q7)

Q6: How did you contact the teacher on FB?
1. Chat
2. Private message
3. Mural comment
4. Other. Which? _____

Q7: In your opinion, social web (blogs, social network) can be used in the relation teacher-student?
1. Yes
2. No

Q8: Why?

Q9: In your opinion, the use of social web should be learn preferably
1. Individually (by exploration)
2. In class (with the teacher)
3. With friends

Q10: For how low have you been using Internet?
1. Less than 1 year
2. 1 to 3 years
3. More than 3 years

Q11: How do you define your level of internet user?
1. Beginner

2. Average
3. Advanced
4. Expert

Q12: On a regular day, how many time do you spent online?
1. Less than 3 hours
2. Between 3 to 6 hours
3. More than 6 hours

Q13: How many profiles do you have on social networks?
1. 1
2. 2
3. 3 or more
4. None (go to Q16)

Q14: Which social network do you use the most (1 answer)?
1. *Facebook*
2. Hi5
3. LinkedIn
4. MySpace
5. Windows Live
6. Twitter
7. Other. Specify:

Q15: How often do you go the your most used profile?
1. Several times a day
2. Once a day
3. Once a week
4. Once a month
5. Rarely

Q16: Age
1. 15 – 19
2. 20 – 24
3. 25 – 29
4. 30 – 34
5. More than 35 years old

Q17: Genre
1. Male
2. Female

Q18: Main internet Access
1. Home
2. Mobile Phone
3. At school/work
4. Other place (street, coffee)
5. Anyplace (mobile broadband)
6. Other. Specify:

APPENDIX 2

Weblog Statistics (http://smpsebastiao.wordpress.com)

Table 1, Table 2, Table 3, Table 4.

- March / June – 1st semester, 1st survey administration
- September / December – 2nd semester, 2nd survey administration

Table 1. Months and Years

	Jan	Feb	Mar	Apr	May	Jun	Jul	Aug	Sep	Oct	Nov	Dec	Total
2008									152	2.079	1.466	962	4.659
2009	1.088	713	349	309	392	573	202	94	1.422	2.707	3.033	1.329	12.211
2010	1.596	292	2.485	1.700	3.640	1.428	530	199	1.478	2.817	3.116	2.585	**21.866**
2011	907												907

Table 2. Mean/day

	Jan	Feb	Mar	Apr	May	Jun	Jul	Aug	Sep	Oct	Nov	Dec	Total
2008									19	67	49	31	47
2009	35	25	11	10	13	19	7	3	47	87	101	43	33
2010	51	10	80	57	117	48	17	6	49	91	104	83	60
2011	52												52

Table 3.

Page Visits / 2010 (more than 10%)	Total Visits	% Total
Home Page	7269	33,24
Semiology (March/June)	3866	17,68
Culture (Sept / Dec.)	2851	13,04
Public Relations (all year)	2621	11,99
(…)		
TOTAL	21866	75,95

Table 4.

Post views / 2010 (better 7)	Total Views
Public Relations Portuguese textbook announcement	135
What's PR (by PR Conversations)	68
Image analysis introduction (book by M. Joly) - Semiology	58
Rules of Assessment	48
Ethics and Research on the Web (paper)	47
Facebook fashion (opinion & statistics)	41
PR ethics (paper by G. Gonçalves in Portuguese)	41
(…)	

Chapter 12
Social Media Usage among University Students in Malaysia

Norsiah Abdul Hamid
University Utara Malaysia, Malaysia

Syamsul Anuar Ismail
University Utara Malaysia, Malaysia

Mohd Sobhi Ishak
University Utara Malaysia, Malaysia

Siti Syamsul Nurin Mohmad Yazam
University Utara Malaysia, Malaysia

ABSTRACT

Social media are playing an increasing role in today's living. The social media platforms allow users to search, create, share, collaborate, and organise contents among them, and at the same time provide virtual self-presentation and self-disclosure of oneself. Social media were also claimed to give implications to human beings with regards to personality, yet these variables have not much been emphasised in previous studies. Thus, it is important to highlight the implications of social media on users' personality. Given the issues and challenges faced by the country in profiling the adoption of social media and its implications in view of the perspective of personality, it is timely and significantly important to undertake this research in Malaysia. The objective of this chapter is to discuss a research conducted recently to determine the relationships between social media and personality traits. The specific objectives of this study are to identify the profile of social media adoption among students in Malaysia, including duration, frequency of use, purpose, and person/s that introduced the social media, and to determine the relationships between social media and personality traits.

INTRODUCTION

The study in this chapter employed a cross-sectional survey using self-administered questionnaire which was distributed among university students who use social media via wired and mobile devices. The data was collected for the duration of one month with the total respondents of 405. Results show that the purposes of using social media can be associated with the students' learning needs such as for searching for information, communicating with friends/families, keeping in

DOI: 10.4018/978-1-4666-2851-9.ch012

touch with friends/families, entertainment, and completing the assignment task. The research also identified the relationships between frequency of use of various social media applications and the Big 5 personality traits. The findings of this research can be used by university lecturers to utilize the social media applications for teaching and learning purposes, as well as the social media providers to enhance the applications for the use by students.

What is Social Media (SM)? What is so interesting about it that makes people 'addicted' to it? How and why do people use it? Is there any implication of SM to the Malaysian society? These are among questions that arise with the emergence of new Internet applications called Social Media. Social media are playing an increasing role in today's living. It is such a common scenario today to see people browsing and surfing social networking sites, reading blogs or chatting by using laptops, mobile phones or other sophisticated devices anywhere and at anytime. Some people are even addicted to certain applications, such as online games. Undoubtedly, social media is one of the fastest growing segments on the web (Parra-López, Bulchand-Gidumal, Gutiérrez-Taño & Díaz-Armas, 2010). Among the most popular applications of social media are weblogs or blogs (i.e. Blogger and WordPress), social networking sites (i.e. Facebook, Twitter and MySpace), photos and videos (i.e. Flickr and YouTube), online encyclopaedia (i.e. Wikipedia), online bookmarking (i.e. Delicious), virtual social worlds (i.e. Second Life) and virtual game worlds (i.e. World of Craft). These social media platforms allow users to search, create, share, collaborate and organise contents among them while at the same time provide virtual self-presentation and self-disclosure of oneself.

A report by Gartner Inc. (21st October 2010) stated that the Asia Pacific social media market is highly diverse and in many places evolving rapidly. The growth of social networking in China, Japan and South Korea for instance, has been driven by strong consumer interest in online games, while India's social networking market has been spurred by demand for online dating and matchmaking sites. It is reported that more than 770 million people worldwide visited a social networking site in July 2009 (Nguyen, 2010). This figure increased 18 percent from the previous year. According to Gartner Inc. Report (13th January 2010), by the year 2012, Facebook will become the hub for social network integration and web socialisation. The report also predicted that Facebook will support and take a leading role in developing the distributed, interoperable social Web. Facebook claimed that its users are now reaching 500 million active users (Facebook, 2010). What is more interesting is that, if Facebook was a country, it could be the third largest in the world after China and India (Nguyen, 2010).

In Malaysia, the adoption of ICT and SM in particular has shown a significant growth in the last few years. Internet users in Malaysia alone comprised of 16 million in the first quarter of 2009, while the number of cellular subscriptions in the third quarter of the same year has reached 29.6 million (Malaysian Communications and Multimedia Commissions, 2010). 80% of affluent Malaysians (those with a household income above RM5,000 a month) use social networking sites; nine of the top 20 websites in Malaysia are social networking sites, and the top six sites are Yahoo!, Facebook, Google.com.my, YouTube, Google.com, and Blogger (Gibson, 2009). These show evidence that the demand for social media in Malaysia is growing. There are several social media established in Malaysia recently (i.e. youkawan.com, myfriends2u.com and ruumz.com) but the adoption is still low (record shows that the registered users for youkawan is only 801 members as at 23 November 2010) as compared to the use of Facebook, Friendster and Twitter which recorded 7.5 million users from Malaysia alone (Shawkath Azde, 12 November 2010).

STATEMENT OF PROBLEM

One important limitation in the existing literature on social media in Malaysia is a lack of understanding on its adoption and implications on end-user personality in Malaysia especially among the university students, most likely pertaining to the profile of the users of social media; what or how the social media are used for; and most importantly is which social media have significant relationships with personality. Yoo and Gretzel (2010) emphasised that it is necessary to examine the implications of personality in the context of social media since it has been found to be an important factor influencing a wide variety of human behaviours and choices. Furthermore, the majority of research on social media adoption and use solely focused on social networking sites (Correa, Hinsley & de Zuniga, 2010). Despite various applications of social media adopted by users, pattern shows that research on social media in Malaysia were only emphasised on blogs (e.g. Muhamad Nazri & Suhaimee, 2008; Zanariah, Siti Rohana & Norun Najjah, 2008) and social networking sites (e.g. Safurah, Khaizuran & Azmi, 2010). Other researches on media usage and impacts focused mainly on youths (Latiffah, Samsudin & Fauziah, 2009; Safurah et al., 2010) and this may not apply to the population at large and disregard other groups of potential users. Social media were also claimed to give implications to human beings with regards to personality, yet these variables have not much been emphasised in previous studies (Correa et al., 2010; Yoo & Gretzel, 2010). Thus, it is important to highlight the implications of social media on users' personality. Given the issues and challenges faced by the country in profiling the adoption of social media and its implications in view of the perspective of personality, it is timely and significantly important to undertake this research in Malaysia.

DEFINITIONS AND CHARACTERISTICS OF SOCIAL MEDIA

What is social media after all? Kaplan and Haenlein (2010) defined social media as "a group of Internet-based applications that build on the ideological and technological foundations of Web 2.0, and that allow the creation and exchange of User Generated Content" (p.61). Kaplan and Haenlein then categorised social media into six major types based on a set of theories, which are media research (media richness theory and social presence), and social processes (self-presentation and self-disclosure), namely collaborative projects, blogs, content communities, social networking sites, virtual game worlds and virtual social worlds. Kaplan and Haenlein even distinguished social media from Web 2.0 and user-generated content.

Eyrich, Padman and Sweetser (2008) view social media to consist of tools such as blogs, intranets, podcasts, video sharing, photo sharing, social networks, wikis, gaming, virtual worlds, micro-blogging/presence applications, text messaging, video conferencing, PDAs, instant message chat, social event/calendar systems, social bookmarking, news aggregation/RSS and e-mail. These applications were also supported by Taylor and Kent (2010) who opined that social media tools include interactive social networking sites, as well as blogs, podcasts, message boards, online videos and picture albums, and mobile telephone alerts. Moreover, social media are seen as user-friendly, inexpensive, scalable internet- and mobile-based technologies that allow for the sharing of user-generated materials (Fischer & Reuber, 2010). In particular, Kim, Jeong and Lee (2010) defined social web sites as "those web sites that make it possible for people to form online communities, and share user-created contents (UCC)" (p.216). Social media is always recognised as and used interchangeably with Web 2.0 and user-generated content (UGC) (Owyang & Toll, 2007); however Kaplan and Haenlein (2010) argued that it differs from those two concepts.

TRENDS IN SOCIAL MEDIA ADOPTION

In order to investigate the implications of social media on the personality, it is important to understand the trends in social media adoption. Among the major purposes of adoption of social media covers the socialisation needs, finding old friends, education, information seeking, promote products and services, job seeking, sharing information and spreading news on particular events, and playing games. There are quite a number of researches concentrated on the adoption of social media in areas such as *tourism* (Parra-López, Bulchand-Gidumal, Gutiérrez-Taño & Díaz-Armas, 2010; Xiang & Gretzel, 2009), *electronic government* (Bertot, Jaeger & Grimes, 2010), and *public relations* (Curtis, Edwards, Fraser, Gudelsky, Holmquist, Thornton, et al., 2010; Diga & Kelleher, 2009; Khaizuran, 2010; Taylor & Kent, 2010). Many prior researches focused on the usage and adoption of social media among targeted populations. College students for instance, reported using social networking websites to make new friends, locate old friends and to keep in touch with current friends (Raacke & Bonds-Raacke, 2008). A study on public relations (PR) practitioners (Diga & Kelleher, 2009) found that practitioners who frequently used social network sites were more likely to report feeling empowered to be promoted into their current positions. The information they gain from using social network sites may be used as a strategic tool, which can empower them to advance within organizations. The study also concluded that engaging in relationships through social network sites can build a practitioner's social capital, which may then boost status or prestige.

Similarly, Curtis et al. (2010) studied the adoption of social media by PR practitioners in the non-profit organisations by employing the *Unified Theory of Acceptance and Use of Technology* (UTAUT). Their survey measured social media adoption with relations to performance expectancy, effort expectancy, social influence, facilitating conditions, voluntariness of use, self-efficacy and anxiety. They found that social media tools are becoming beneficial methods of communication for PR practitioners and organisations with defined PR departments are more likely to adopt social media technologies and use them to achieve their organisational goals. However, PR practitioners are more likely to use social media tools if they find them credible. Another study on PR suggests that social media power far outweigh evidence of social media effectiveness as a communication tool (Taylor & Kent, 2010). They argued that very little evidence exists to date to support the claims about the power of social media made by the profession of PR.

Recent Pew Internet Project on teens and young adults usage of social media in the United States of America (Lenhart, Purcell, Smith & Zickuhr, 2010) found that since 2006 onwards, the popularity of blogs among teens and young adults has dropped, but the usage among older adults shows an increasing pattern. However, the use of social networking sites among teens and adults has increased, and Facebook was reported as the most commonly-used online social network as compared to MySpace and LinkedIn, while Twitter was the less used application. Similarly, the use of virtual worlds among teens is more common than young adults. Interestingly, among teens, the average person owned 3.5 gadgets out of five being queried, namely cellular phones, MP3 players, computers, game consoles and portable gaming devices. In contrast, the average gadgets ownership among adults is under 3. The report also revealed that teens are avid and clever creators of digital contents while adults have shown some increases in content creating activities. A study on adoption of social networking sites in Pakistan also shows an increasing dependency on the media among university students (Shaheen, 2008). Out of 295 respondents, 71% logged on to the sites daily and 85% trusted the information posted on their preferred web sites. In addition, 93% agree that during the state of emergency in Pakistan, these web sites created awareness among the Pakistani youth about their political rights. Shaheen also pointed out that the use of social networking sites may be an alternate medium to promote the freedom of speech in Pakistan and greater awareness about people's political rights among university students.

Although there has been a significant growth in the empirical studies related to social media, it is found that there is a lack of focus in the context of Malaysian population. Khaizuran (2010) for instance, reported an initial study on adoption of social media among PR practitioners in Malaysia. Only 33% of the respondents utilised blogs for PR activities while half of them used Facebook for the same purpose. A study on social media amongst youths in Malaysia (Safurah, Khaizuran & Azmi, 2010) revealed that more than half of the respondents used the World Wide Web everyday while 88% used Facebook daily. The reasons for using social networks varies, but the highest given reasons are to socialise with friends and seek information. The least used social media is microblogging. This finding was similar to that of Lenhart et al. (2010) which shown that blogging has not attracted much attention amongst youngsters. The study also revealed that social media have influenced the respondents in the areas of communication, entertainment, language and learning. The adoption of social media was also associated with human personality. Correa et al. (2010) found that people with greater levels of neuroticism and negative affectivity are more likely to engage in the social media activities. They also pointed out that anxious and nervous people use the social media services to seek support and company.

Social media has gained huge attention and trust by various parties, including the governments, businesses, civil societies and individuals. In ad-

dition, the benefits and threats of social media has also been emphasised by quite a number of publications (Bertot, Jaeger & Grimes, 2010; Kim, Jeong & Lee, 2010). Bertot, Jaeger and Grimes (2010) suggested four major potential strengths of social media towards anti-corruption in the government, namely collaboration, participation, empowerment and time. They argued that social media is beneficial since it provides collaboration and participation by the social interaction, whereas it can also be used to empower its users as it gives them a platform to speak and express their opinions. Social media also allow users to immediately publish information or news in almost real time manner. In contrast, social media also allow for infringement of copyrighted materials. Users can freely post copyrighted materials without authorization, or pornographic or other illegal contents (Kim, Jeong & Lee, 2010). This has forced site operators to hire staff to investigate and remove the material, or else being sued by copyright holders or even worse the site being banned by the government.

Recent case in Malaysia showed a university student, Wee Meng Chee (nickname 'Namewee') composed and sung a highly controversial song called 'Negarakuku' (adopted from Malaysia national anthem) and posted it on the YouTube. This song portrays his perspective of anti-government, disrespectful towards Islam and accused racism, which then forced him to remove the video amid pressure on July 2007. In 2010, again he made another music clip and uploaded on the YouTube criticising a school principal in Kulai Jaya. The clip contained obscene language condemning the school principal and the Education Ministry, and he was asked to give statement in Kuala Lumpur police station and also Cyberjaya Investigation Unit for two times later (Benjamin, Camoens & Kumar, 2010). This true case highlights the threats by social media which may give harm to the whole nation.

Undoubtedly social media exposed many risks and threats, hence give implications to the users. Children are the most highly risked group of users on the Net. Children tend to publish their personal information such as telephone number or home address on their profile, thus exposing themselves to strangers. Among the risks factors in social media include pornography, bullying, sending/receiving sexual messages, and going to meetings with contacts first met online (Livingstone, Haddon, Görzig, & Ólafsson, 2011). Kim, Jeong and Lee (2010) pointed out that social media sites have also led users to 'lose sense of what is appropriate and end up losing employment or college entrance opportunities'.

RELATIONSHIPS BETWEEN PERSONALITY TRAITS AND SOCIAL MEDIA

As the pool of research on ICT use grew, several scholars examined the influence of personality traits on Internet uses by utilizing the Five-Factor Model (or also known as the Big Five Model) (McCrae & Costa, 1997). The Big Five personality factors are generally acknowledged as relevant and valid dimensions of personality in various fields of research (Goldberg, 1992; Gelissen & de Graaf, 2006). The five personality factors are extraversion, agreeableness, conscientiousness, neuroticism and openness. Extraversion means that of a person who possesses characteristics as approachable, sociable, friendly, lively, optimistic and energetic, whereas agreeableness indicates a person with trustful, honest, tolerant, god-natured, forgiving and soft-hearted. High score on conscientiousness indicates a person as being responsible, efficient, organized, productive, thorough, achievement-oriented, self-disciplined and well-informed. Neuroticism relates to anxious and upset, unable to control anger and low self-esteem. Openness to experience indicates those who are explorative or imaginative, creative, appreciate artistic values, willing to try new things, can easily adapt to changes, and open to different ideas or opinions (Gelissen & de Graaf, 2006; Tengku Faekah, 2010; Yoo & Gretzel, 2010). In

Malaysia, belief in God is seen as significantly important in the life of human beings, thus the principle 'Belief in God' was made priority in the National Principles (Rukunegara). Furthermore, there is a long tradition of equating technology with spiritual qualities (Campbell & La Pastina, 2010). Hence, another important attribute which needs to be taken into consideration is spirituality and religiousness, and its implication on the SM users. In fact, different cultures may use unique employments of religion in relation to technology, suggesting that a culturally specific understanding should exist for such interactions (Campbell & La Pastina, 2010).

Early studies of individuals' online activities found those high in extraversion and low in neuroticism were not as heavy Internet users as their more introverted, more neurotic counterparts (Amichai-Hamburger, Wainapel & Fox, 2002). A study by Yoo and Gretzel (2010) suggest that personality is an important determinant of motivations and barriers to social media creation, as well as of specific creation behaviours. The study focused on the use and creation of travel consumer-generated media (CGM). The study also confirmed that the attitudes and behaviours of travel-related CGM creators are influenced by five big personality traits. Correa et al. (2010) studied the relationships between three dimensions of Big-Five personality traits namely extraversion, emotional stability and openness to experience and the social media use, particularly on social networking sites and instant messages. They found that extraversion and openness to experiences were positively related to social media use, while emotional stability was negatively related to social media use. What is more interesting is that the findings differed by gender and age. While extraverted men and women were both likely to be more frequent users of social media tools, only the men with greater degrees of emotional instability were more frequent users. Based on the previous studies done on personality and social media, it is timely that an in-depth investigation be undertaken to understand the implications of social media on end-user personality.

The main objective of this chapter is to discuss a research finding which aimed to determine the relationships between social media and personality traits. The specific objectives of the study are as follows:

1. To identify the profile of social media adoption among students in Malaysia, including duration, frequency of use, purpose, and person/s that introduced the social media.
2. To determine the relationships between social media and personality traits.

METHODOLOGY

The study employed a cross-sectional survey using self-administered questionnaire which was distributed among university students who use social media via wired and mobile devices. The data was collected in June 2011 for the duration of one month with the total respondents of 405. Questions are adapted from Pew Internet Report (Lenhart et al., 2010), Curtis et al. (2010), Yoo and Gretzel (2010) and some other related sources. In addition, to measure the 5-personality traits, items for each factor were adapted from the International Personality Item Pool (Goldberg, 1999; IPIP, 2008). The questionnaire consists of three parts. Part A pertains to the demographic profiles of the respondents while Part B on the profiles of social media adoption. Respondents were asked on ownership of ICT devices, types of social media being used, their experiences with social media, how frequent they usually used the media, their purpose of using social media, and other related questions. Part C will focus on the relationships of social media on personality of the respondents, particularly on the 5-personality traits, namely Extraversion, Openness, Agreeableness, Conscientiousness and Neuroticism. Descriptive and inferential analyses will be conducted to describe the participants' demographic profile, their profile of social media adoption, as well as to identify the relationships between social media and personality.

FINDINGS OF THE RESEARCH

The results of the study were analysed by using SPSS version 16 software. Among the key findings are as follows.

A. Demographic Profiles of the Respondents

Table 1 shows the demographic profile of the respondents. The total number of respondents involved is 405, in which 118 are male, while 287 are female students. The majority of the students are from the Malay ethnic (310), 51 are Chinese, 27 are Indians, 10 are from Sabah/Sarawak ethnics while the rest are others. Since they are undergraduate students, their age ranges from 19 to 26 years old.

Table 2 indicates the list of academic colleges of the students.

Table 1. Demographic profiles of the respondents (n=405)

Demographic	f (%)
Gender	
Male	118 (29.1%)
Female	287 (70.9%)
Race	
Malay	310 (76.5%)
Chinese	51 (12.6%)
Indian	27 (6.7%)
Sabah/Sarawak Ethnic	10 (2.5%)
Others	7 (1.7%)
Age	
19 – 22 years old	269 (66.4%)
23 - 26	136 (33.6%)

Table 2. Academic colleges and programs of the respondents (n=405)

Academic College	ƒ (%)
College of Arts & Sciences	160 (39.5%)
College of Business	170 (42.0%)
College of Law, Government & International Affairs	75 (18.5%)

B. Purpose of Using Social Media

There are various purposes of using social media among the students. Table 3 indicates that among the highest usage are for communicating with friends/families (95.6%), searching for information (87.9%), keeping in touch with friends/families (82.5%), entertainment (76.5%), and completing the assignment task (71.9%).

C. Who Introduced to Social Media?

With regards to the awareness and knowledge about social media, 93.3% stated that they have been introduced to social media by friends, while more than half (51.5%) been introduced by their families (Table 4). It is also important to highlight that 37% stated that their teachers or lecturers have introduced them to social media. This indicates that teachers and lecturers also play an important role in the social media adoption.

D. The Relationships between Frequency of Use of Social Media and Personality Traits

Table 5 shows the relationships between frequency of use of various social media applications and the Big 5 personality traits. The finding shows a significant relationship between students with Agreeableness trait and the use of photo sharing application. This means that students who are more compassionate and cooperative like to use photo sharing. Another interesting finding is the signifi-

cant negative relationship between Openness to experience and the use of social networking sites. It was found that the more openness the students in terms of emotion, adventure, art, unusual ideas, curiosity, and other related experience, the less likely they will use the social networking sites.

This is also the case for Conscientiousness and video conferencing relationship whereby a well-planned student with tendency to show self-discipline, act dutifully and aims for achievement will be less likely to use video conferencing. A Conscientiousness person is someone who is responsible, efficient, organized, productive, thorough, achievement-oriented, self-disciplined and well-informed. Therefore, in the case of video conferencing, the students who possessed this trait do not see this kind of application as their preferred medium. Social bookmarking has positive relationships with the Big-5 traits, in which significant values were found with Agreeableness (r (403) =.133), p < .01), Conscientiousness (r (403) =.159), p < .01), and Openness to

Table 3. Purpose of using social media

Purpose	Yes	No
Communicate with friends/families	387 (95.6%)	18 (4.4%)
Search for information	356 (87.9%)	49 (12.1%)
Keep in touch with friends/families	334 (82.5%)	71 (17.5%)
For entertainment	310 (76.5%)	95 (23.5%)
To complete the assignment task	291 (71.9%)	114 (28.1%)
To get new friends	275 (67.9%)	130 (32.1%)
To improve the communication skills	254 (62.7%)	151 (37.3%)
To improve the language skills	242 (59.8%)	163 (40.2%)
To improve the computer skills	211 (52.1%)	194 (47.9%)
To know what other people are doing	210 (51.9%)	195 (48.1%)

Table 4. Who introduced to social media?

	Yes	No
Friend	**378 (93.3%)**	27 (6.7%)
Family	**207 (51.1%)**	198 (48.9%)
Relatives	130 (32.1%)	**275 (67.9%)**
Teacher / Lecturer	150 (37%)	**255 (63%)**

experience (r (403) =.126), p < .05). Openness to experience indicates those who are explorative or imaginative, creative, appreciate artistic values, willing to try new things, can easily adapt to changes, open to different ideas or opinions (Gelissen & de Graaf, 2006; Tengku Faekah, 2010; Yoo & Gretzel, 2010).

There are also positive relationships between News aggregation/Really Simple Syndication (RSS) with Extraversion and Agreeableness, in which the significant values are (r (403) =.137), p < .01), and (r (403) =.107), p < .05). As discussed earlier, Extraversion means that of a person who possesses characteristics as approachable, so-

ciable, friendly, lively, optimistic and energetic, whereas agreeableness indicates a person with trustful, honest, tolerant, god-natured, forgiving and soft-hearted. The relationship between these two traits and the RSS means that students who possess these traits preferred to get the latest news since he/she is sociable, lively and energetic. This finding is consistent with Amichai-Hamburger and Ben-Artzi (2003) and Correa et al. (2010).

What is more interesting is that, this study found that there is no single relationship between Neuroticism and the use of social media among university students. Neuroticism relates to anxious and upset, unable to control anger and low self-esteem. This is in contrast with the previous studies by Correa et al. (2010) which found that people who are more emotionally stable will use social media less frequently, while anxious and worrisome individuals tend to use social media more frequently.

Table 5. The relationships between frequency of use of social media and personality traits

Social Media	EXT	AGR	CON	NEU	OPE
Blogs / Web blogs	.050	.013	-.088	.001	-.087
Podcast	.047	-.024	.006	.023	.049
Video sharing (i.e. YouTube)	-.002	-.026	-.013	.046	.012
Photo sharing (i.e. Flickr)	.013	.126*	.054	-.071	.015
Wikis	-.042	-.059	-.095	.093	-.016
Online Gaming	-.019	-.018	-.073	-.016	-.043
Email	.058	-.019	.024	-.016	.053
Social networking sites (i.e. Facebook, Twitter, Friendster)	-.050	-.037	-.052	.052	-.101*
Virtual worlds	-.006	-.053	-.069	.060	.007
Text messaging	.014	-.011	.058	-.058	.072
Video conferencing	-.076	-.045	-.100*	.071	-.053
Instant message chat	.035	-.032	.041	.007	-.057
Social event/calendar systems	.040	.012	.058	-.042	.090
Social bookmarking	.055	.133**	.159**	-.028	.126*
News aggregation/Really Simple Syndication (RSS)	.137**	.107*	.051	-.012	.096

EXT=Extraversion; AGR=Agreeableness; CON=Conscientiousness; NEU=Neuroticism; OPE=Openness.
** p <.01 (2-tailed); * p <.05 (2 tailed)

CONCLUSION

Overall, this chapter discussed a research conducted in a university setting which involved 405 undergraduate students. The aim of this research is to determine the relationships between social media and personality traits particularly in identifying the profile of social media adoption among students in Malaysia, including duration, frequency of use, purpose, and person/s that introduced the social media, and determining the relationships between social media and personality traits. The study employed a cross-sectional survey using self-administered questionnaire which was distributed among university students who used social media via wired and mobile devices. Results shows that the purposes of using social media can be associated with the students' learning needs such as for communicating with friends/families, searching for information, keeping in touch with friends/families, entertainment and completing the assignment task. The research also identified the relationships between frequency of use of various social media applications and the Big 5 personality traits. The finding shows a significant relationship between students with Agreeableness trait and the use of photo sharing application, and between Conscientiousness and video conferencing. There were also positive relationships between News aggregation/Really Simple Syndication (RSS) with Extraversion and Agreeableness while no single relationship between Neuroticism and the use of social media among university students. The findings of this research can be used by university lecturers to utilize the social media applications for teaching and learning purposes, as well as the social media providers to enhance the applications for the use by students.

REFERENCES

Amichai-Hamburger, Y., & Ben-Artzi, E. (2003). Loneliness and Internet use. *Computers in Human Behavior, 19*(1), 71–80. doi:10.1016/S0747-5632(02)00014-6

Amichai-Hamburger, Y., Wainapel, G., & Fox, S. (2002). On the Internet no one knows I'm an "introvert": Extraversion, neuroticism, and Internet interaction. *Cyberpsychology & Behavior, 5*(2), 125–128. doi:10.1089/109493102753770507

Benjamin, N., Camoens, A., & Kumar, M. (2010, Tuesday August 31). Namewee under probe over video. *The Star Online*.

Bertot, J. C., Jaeger, P. T., & Grimes, J. M. (2010). Using ICTs to create a culture of transparency: E-government and social media as openness and anti-corruption tools for societies. *Government Information Quarterly, 27*, 264–271. doi:10.1016/j.giq.2010.03.001

Campbell, H. A., & La Pastina, A. C. (2010). How the iPhone became divine: New media, religion and the intertextual circulation of meaning. *New Media & Society, 12*(7), 1191–1207. doi:10.1177/1461444810362204

Correa, T., Hinsley, A. W., & de Zuniga, H. G. (2010). Who interacts on the Web? The intersection of users' personality and social media use. *Computers in Human Behavior, 26*, 247–253. doi:10.1016/j.chb.2009.09.003

Curtis, L., Edwards, C., Fraser, K. L., Gudelsky, S., Holmquist, J., & Thornton, K. (2010). Adoption of social media for public relations by nonprofit organizations. *Public Relations Review, 36*(1), 90–92. doi:10.1016/j.pubrev.2009.10.003

Diga, M., & Kelleher, T. (2009). Social media use, perceptions of decision-making power, and public relations roles. *Public Relations Review, 35*(4), 440–442. doi:10.1016/j.pubrev.2009.07.003

Eyrich, N., Padman, M. L., & Sweetser, K. D. (2008). PR practitioners' use of social media tools and communication technology. *Public Relations Review*, *34*, 412–414. doi:10.1016/j.pubrev.2008.09.010

Facebook Statistics. (2010). *Statistics*. Retrieved from http://www.facebook.com/press/info.php?statistics

Fischer, E., & Reuber, A. R. (2010). Social interaction via new social media: (How) can interactions on Twitter affect effectual thinking and behavior? *Journal of Business Venturing*, *26*(1). doi:doi:10.1016/j.jbusvent.2010.1009.1002

Gartner Inc. (13 January 2010). *Gartner highlights key predictions for IT organizations and users in 2010 and beyond*. Stamford, CT: Author.

Gartner Inc. (21 October 2010). *Gartner says social media in Asia Pacific is developing in different directions to the U.S. and Europe*. Hong Kong, PRC: Author.

Gelissen, J., & de Graaf, P. M. (2006). Personality, social background, and occupational career success. *Social Science Research*, *35*, 702–726. doi:10.1016/j.ssresearch.2005.06.005

Gibson, D. (2009, 19 September 2009). Communication for the connected generation. *The Star Online*.

Goldberg, L. R. (1992). The development of markers for the big-five factor structure. *Journal of Personality and Social Psychology*, *59*(6), 1216–1229. doi:10.1037/0022-3514.59.6.1216

IPIP. (2008). *International personality item pool: A scientific collaborator for the development of advanced measures of personality traits and other individual differences*. Retrieved 12 May, 2011, from http://www.ipip.ori.org

Kaplan, A. M., & Haenlein, M. (2010). Users of the world, unite! The challenges and opportunities of social media. *Business Horizons*, *53*, 59–68. doi:10.1016/j.bushor.2009.09.003

Khaizuran, A. J. (2010). *Social media and the practice of public relations in Malaysia: Where do we stand?* Paper presented at the International Conference on Communication & Media 2010, Melaka.

Kim, W., Jeong, O.-R., & Lee, S.-W. (2010). On social websites. *Information Systems*, *35*, 215–236. doi:10.1016/j.is.2009.08.003

Latiffah, P., Samsudin, A. R., & Fauziah, A. (2009). Media consumption among young adults: A look at labels and norms in everyday life. [Malaysian Journal of Communication]. *Jurnal Komunikasi*, *25*, 21–31.

Lenhart, A., Purcell, K., Smith, A., & Zickuhr, K. (2010). *Social media and mobile Internet use among teens and young adults*. Washington, DC: Pew Research Centre.

Livingstone, S., Haddon, L., Görzig, A., & Ólafsson, K. (2011). *Risks and safety on the Internet*. Retrieved 25 June, 2012, from http://www2.lse.ac.uk/media@lse/research/eukidsonline/eukidsii%20(2009-11)/eukidsonlineiireports/d4fullfindings.pdf

Malaysian Communications and Multimedia Commissions. (2010). *National broadband initiatives*. Retrieved from http://www.skmm.gov.my/index.php?c=public&v=art_view&art_id=36

McCrae, R. R., & Costa, P. T. (1997). Personality trait structure as a human universal. *The American Psychologist*, *52*, 509–516. doi:10.1037/0003-066X.52.5.509

Nguyen, J. (2010). *The state of social networks* [Electronic Version]. Retrieved 1st November, 2010, from http://www.comscore.com/content/search?SearchText=social+media

Noor, M. N. M., & Saabar, S. (2008). *Blogsphere: Ruang kontra hegemoni? Analisis terhadap blog politik Malaysia terpilih dalam PRU 2008*. Paper presented at the Seminar Politik Malaysia.

Owyang, J., & Toll, M. (2007). *Tracking the influence of conversations: A roundtable discussion on social media metrics and measurement*. New York, NY: Dow Jones Inc.

Parra-López, E., Bulchand-Gidumal, J., Gutiérrez-Taño, D., & Díaz-Armas, R. (2011). Intentions to use social media in organizing and taking vacation trips. *Computers in Human Behavior*, *27*(2), 640–654. doi:10.1016/j.chb.2010.05.022

Raacke, J., & Bonds-Raacke, J. (2008). MySpace and Facebook: Applying the uses and gratifications theory to exploring friend-networking sites. *Cyberpsychology & Behavior*, *11*, 169–174. doi:10.1089/cpb.2007.0056

Safurah Abd, J., Khairuzan Abd, J., & Azmi Abdul, L. (2010). *Social media and our youths today: Exploring the impact of social media on Malaysian youths*. Paper presented at the International Conference on Communication and Media, Melaka.

Shaheen, M. A. (2008). Use of social networks and information seeking behavior of students during political crises in Pakistan: A case study. *The International Information & Library Review*, *40*, 142–147. doi:10.1016/j.iilr.2008.07.006

Shawkath, A. (2010, November 12). 7.5 juta pemilik akaun Facebook. *KOSMO*.

Taylor, M., & Kent, M. L. (2010). Anticipatory socialization in the use of social media in public relations: A content analysis of PRSA's Public relations tactics. *Public Relations Review*, *36*, 207–214. doi:10.1016/j.pubrev.2010.04.012

Tengku Faekah, T. A. (2010). *A structural model of the relationships between personality factors, perceptions of the school as a learning organization, workplace learning and job performance of teachers*. Unpublished doctoral thesis, College of Arts and Sciences, Universiti Utara Malaysia.

Xiang, Z., & Gretzel, U. (2010). Role of social media in online travel information search. *Tourism Management*, *31*, 179–188. doi:10.1016/j.tourman.2009.02.016

Yoo, K.-H., & Gretzel, U. (2010). Influence of personality on travel-related consumer-generated media creation. *Computers in Human Behavior*, *27*(2), 609–621. doi:10.1016/j.chb.2010.05.002

Zanariah, J., Siti Rohana, O., & Norun Najjah, A. (2008). *Political discourse in Malaysian blogs*. Paper presented at the Seminar Politik Malaysia.

KEY TERMS AND DEFINITIONS

Agreeableness: Often refers to courteous, flexible, good-natured, cooperative and tolerant individuals. Agreeable people are cooperative, cheerful and supportive of others.

Conscientiousness: Refers to the tendency to be organized, efficient, and systematic. Conscientious individuals are punctual, reliable, determined, and likely to have a strong need for achievement.

Extraversion: Extraversion encompasses sociability and talkativeness, and the ability to make friends with others. Extravert individuals show the tendency to be sociable, talkative and ambitious.

Neuroticism: Neuroticism often described using words such as fearful, anxious, pessimistic, worried and insecure. Neurotic individuals are depressed, anxious and unstable.

Openness to Experience: Refers to imaginative, curious, original, broad-minded, and intelligent. Individuals with high level of openness enjoy new things, knowledge and experience.

Personality Factors: Encompassing the broad five universal traits, namely Extraversion, Agreeableness, Conscientiousness, Neuroticism, and Openness to experience.

Social Media: A group of Internet-based applications that build on the ideological and technological foundations of Web 2.0 and that allow the creation and exchange of User-Generated Content.

Chapter 13
Social Media and Other Web 2.0 Technologies as Communication Channels in a Cross–Cultural, Web–Based Professional Communication Project

Pavel Zemliansky
University of Central Florida, USA

Olena Goroshko
The National Technical University: Kharkiv Polytechnic Institute, Ukraine

ABSTRACT

In recent years, cross-national web-based teaching projects have become very popular in many fields. During such projects, participants from different countries work together on collaborative tasks. Communications among project participants take place over the Internet, including via social media. In this chapter, the author reports the results of social media use in one such project, which brought together students from the United States and Ukraine. A pre and post project survey taken by the participants demonstrate the main opportunities and challenges afforded by social media to educators. The reporting and analysis of the survey results are preceded by a review of relevant literature, which contextualizes our findings.

DOI: 10.4018/978-1-4666-2851-9.ch013

INTRODUCTION

With the globalization of not only the world economies but also of world educational systems (Vaira 2004), cross-cultural and cross-national collaborative learning and teaching using online tools has become more possible. Projects, which bring together faculty and students from different countries, not only enrich the cultural experiences and awareness of participants, but also give learners valuable professional skills and competencies. (Herrington 2010). Among such skills are the abilities to work in virtual distributed teams, to understand and interact with representatives of other cultures professionally, and to manage complex communication projects, which span nations, continents, and time zones. (Maznevski and Chudoba 2000).

In the field of professional communication, one viable method of teaching students based in different countries is through web-based projects during which learners work in virtual teams on writing, design, and other professional communication tasks. The availability of a wide array of online communication and collaboration tools, from wikis and other collaborative writing spaces to free audio and video-conferencing solutions, has allowed many professional communication instructors and students to participate in such projects.

Students need to be exposed to other cultures and the ways in which professionals function in other cultures, because of the globalized nature of today's workplace. University graduates will be increasingly expected to function in environments which combine global and local traits. (Maznevski and Chudoba 2000). Therefore, experiencing teamwork with locally and remotely based colleagues, among other things, is important for the achievement of students' cross-cultural competencies.

Social media and Web 2.0 communication technologies have lowered the barrier to the development and implementation of such projects by reducing or completely eliminating the cost associated with this work. Because many of the technological tools needed for the success of such projects are either free or very cheap, the burden of developing and carrying out these projects has shifted from the financial sphere to the areas of participant training in the most effective pedagogical approaches to such projects as well as in the use of the wide range of available web technologies. Coupled with an already high rate of social media use by young people (Lenhart et al, 2010), the low cost of social media makes them a natural fit for international and intercultural educational projects conducted over the Internet.

The purpose of this chapter is to provide our audience with theory-grounded but practical and usable ways of developing and implementing their own web-based learning projects. To accomplish this goal, we describe and analyze a collaborative web-based professional communication project, which we taught to a group of American and Ukrainian students in 2009. Specifically, we conduct a critical analysis of the use of social media and other web communication technologies during the project. Sound practice should be grounded in theory. Therefore, our analysis is preceded by a review of literature on the subject of cross-national and cross-cultural virtual teaching and learning in professional communication and related disciplines. It is followed by a set of research and teaching recommendations for educators and practicing professionals. In the chapter, we explore the following questions:

- To what extent do social media and other web 2.0 tools not only serve as communication tools for virtual projects but shape the learning and teaching which happens during those projects?

- What best practices for the selection, configuration, and use of social media and web 2.0 tools for virtual projects exist?

This analysis and set of recommendations will be useful for scholars of professional communication, educators and education administrators, workplace trainers, and managers who wish to provide their employees with advanced communication and collaboration skills.

SOCIAL MEDIA AND CROSS-CULTURAL WEB-BASED LEARNING

In this section of the chapter, we review the literature relevant to the topic of social media in cross-cultural virtual learning. Our review consists of two sections: in the first section, we survey the fundamental theories and practices of social media and their role in the establishment and sustaining of communication channels over the web. We are particularly interested in the ability of social networks to influence and even regulate communication practices of users, including their ability to influence the "tie strength" between users (Haythornthwaite, 2005). In the second part of the literature review, we highlight the best practices in cross-national web-based projects in professional communication and investigate the main affordances and constraints of this mode of teaching and learning. Cross-national web-based projects are collaborations between learners located in different countries on various learning tasks. Participants of such projects work in virtual teams. Since this chapter focuses on the use of social media in such cross-national web-based learning projects, it is logical and necessary to include both topics in the review. It is also logical and necessary to include in the review a discussion of the application of social media to such cross-national web-based teaching and learning projects. The discussion of that topic concludes the review.

SOCIAL MEDIA AS ARTICULATORS OF ONLINE COMMUNICATION CHANNELS

In recent years, the role and functioning of social media in various academic and professional fields and as well as in the public sphere have been studied extensively. It has been shown that social media can help people stay in touch, mobilize them fight for social and political causes, and serve other important communicative and persuasive purposes. (Boyd and Ellison 2008).

However, one important aspect of social media, relevant to the project discussed in this chapter is social media's ability to not only serve as existing channels of communication, but also to play an active role in how those channels are created and used, including the opportunities and constraints they afford their users. At the center of this issue is the question of how exactly social media help users create and maintain relationships and communications, both socially and professionally. Latent tie theory developed by Haythornthwaite (2005) and other researchers of social media is a promising theoretical framework, which may allow us to better understand how the use of social media influences communication processes.

Two features of social media are relevant for this discussion: 1) the multi-directionality and simultaneity of communications that occur within social media; 2) their primary purpose of making existing connections and networks "visible" rather than of creating entirely new connections among users (Boyd and Ellison 2008).

1. Social Networks Allow for Multi-Directionality and Simultaneous Communication

Boyd and Ellison (2008) define social media sites as "web-based services that allow individuals to (1) construct a public or semi-public profile within a bounded system, (2) articulate a list of other users with whom they share a connection, and (3) view and traverse their list of connections and those made by others within the system." (no pag.) An important aspect of this definition for us is social media's ability to create multi-directional connections among users, thus enabling simultaneous communications between many people and often on unrelated topics. Such a way of communicating is not possible through such "web 1.0" tools as e-mail and others. This multi-directionality of communication on social media sites is important for the organization and management of web-based teaching projects because it creates multiple, simultaneous, and often hard-to-track communication channels and message exchanges. This multiplicity and multi-directionality of communication channels, in turn, potentially introduces a host of project management issues and questions into the set up and running of teaching projects that use social media.

The learning project discussed in this chapter required members, who were worked in virtual teams of four and five members, to communicate within those teams using social media and other means of electronic communication. A high level of multi-directionality and self-governance of communication within each virtual team was seen as necessary for the success of each team and was thus highly encouraged. This created both communication opportunities and challenges for the project participants, which are discussed in more detail later in the chapter.

2. Social Networks Make Existing Connections Visible

Haythornthwaite (2005) states that the primary purpose of most social networking sites is not to help people meet new people, but to add an online component to an already existing "offline" relationship. According to Haythornthwaite's "latent tie theory," the introduction of a new connection medium to an already existing group results in one or more of the following: 1) it creates latent ties among users; 2) it "recasts weak ties—both

fording new ones and disrupting existing associations" and 3) "has minimal impact on strong ties." (Haythornthwaite, 2005, 136). Boyd and Ellison (2005) agree with Haythornthwaite in that the primary purpose of social networking sites is to extend existing relationships, not to create new ones.

According to Haythornthwaite, stronger ties between users appear to result from the use of multiple means of communication, both face-to-face and over social networks. (136). Therefore, anyone who creates, administers, and assesses social-media based communication channels needs to keep this connection in mind. (142). Extending Haythornthwaite's argument, if the success of a web-based cross-national teaching project depends in part on the strength and quality of a communication "tie" between participants (and usually it does), then such projects would benefit from the creation and sustaining of such strong ties. Practical implications of this conclusion for our teaching project are discussed later in the chapter.

Ellison, Steinfeld and Lampe (2007) show that social networking sites are used mainly to maintain existing connections among users rather than to create new ones (n. pag.). This ability "can result in connections between individuals that would not otherwise be made…" (Boyd and Ellison 2007). Boyd and Ellison also show that establishing a long-distance connection is often not the primary goal of activity on social networking site, as most users communicate with the people to whom they have access in "real life." (Boyd and Ellison).

Preece and Schneiderman (2009) contradict Haythornthwaite, Boyd and Ellison, and others who claim that social networking online maintains existing relationships rather than creates new ones. Citing their own analysis of social networking sites as well as the research of others, Preece and Schneiderman (2009) develop the "Reader to Leader Framework" of social media use, in which they explain how a user of a social media site may evolve from passively consuming content posted by others to making occasional contributions in a variety of media (text, photos, videos), to then becoming a leader who "promote participation, mentor novices, and [set] and uphold policies." (Preece and Schneiderman 2009, 23).

Research by Preece and Schneinderman is important not only because it suggests that interactions among users of social networking sites are complex and can hardly be reduced to a single model, but also because it has significant implications for the work of distributed virtual teams. The mechanisms through which virtual teams develop and maintain leadership patterns is a crucial aspect of virtual team theory and practice (Sarker et al. 2009). Leaders of virtual teams can influence every aspect of the team's performance, including the effectiveness of communication among members, thus either ensuring the team's success or leading to its failure. Therefore, if there is indeed a mechanism, by which passive consumers of social media may become contributors and leaders, as Preece and Schneinderman suggest, perhaps specific techniques can be taught to students that would help them both develop as leaders in social networking learning and professional spaces and to become more effective members of virtual teams members through a better understanding of leadership dynamics of virtual teams.

This brief analysis of the nature and some of the properties of social networking sites has two important implications for the discussion of the teaching project later in the chapter. Firstly, as we state in our analysis of the cross-national web-based teaching project between US and Ukrainian students, social media became the main communication channel for the project participants, albeit somewhat unexpectedly for us, their instructors and perhaps for the students themselves as well. Because of that, all project participants, students and teachers alike, had to make adjustments to communications plans and strategies "on the fly." If the researchers of social media cited above are correct in their assessment of those media's ability to shape communication

practices of participants, then the communication practices and outcomes in our project were also impacted by the use of such media. Secondly, because of the impact that the use of social media can have on the teaching projects of the kind discussed in this chapter, teachers and trainers who are interested in the design and implementation of such project need to understand social media's effects on communication within such projects.

CROSS-NATIONAL WEB-BASED LEARNING

With the proliferation of low cost or free web communication and collaboration tools, cross-national web-based learning projects have become easier to organize and implement in recent years. During such projects, learners based in different countries collaborate on the creation of jointly written documents, multimedia artifacts such as websites or videos, and other kinds of deliverables. The majority of such projects described in literature appear to take place in professional communication and such related disciplines as business writing, translation studies, and others.

Most authors discussing cross-national web-based learning frame the need for such projects in terms of globalization and the importance of preparing students for functioning in a more globalized workplace as well as for being more "global" citizens (Herrington 2010). Many such projects emphasize the experiential nature of cross-national web-base learning and stress the importance of "real life" communication, collaboration, and problem solving skills that learners receive as they engage in cross-cultural web-based work (Mousten et al, 2010). Some scholars mention teaching learners hot to work in globally distributed teams as an explicit purpose of such projects. (Starke Meyerring and Andrews, 2006).

Herrington (2010) writes about "The Global Classroom Project" at the Georgia Institute of Technology. She notes that by engaging in cross-cultural internet-based projects, students achieve "experiential learning" which prepares them "for a future in which synthetic thinking that leads to innovative, imaginative problem solving and invention will be desirable and necessary" (516). In addition to giving students practical cross-cultural training, such projects teach them the "intangibles" of working in globalized environments.

Mousten et al. (2010) note the benefits of participating in such projects for students citing the ever-increasing importance of the ability to function in digital and web-based environments for professional purposes. Describing a ten year "Trans-Atlantic Project," which brought together teachers and students from the US, Denmark, Belgium, France, Italy, and other countries, they argue that participants of such projects learn not only how to communicate cross-culturally, but also increase their understanding of cross-disciplinarity, gain new and valuable professional experiences, and other benefits. (Mousten et al. 2010, 402).

Starke-Meyerring and Andrews (2006) describe an international teaching project involving a group of US and a group of Canadian students, which they taught. According to Starke-Meyerring and Andrews, "business professionals increasingly use digital tools to collaborate across multiple cultures, locations, and time zones. Success in this complex environment depends on a shared culture that facilitates the making of knowledge and the best contributions of all team members." (2006, 25). In order to ensure the success of the project, the two instructors implemented a variety of strategies, including "inclusive" communication techniques. (Starke-Meyering and Andrews 2008.) To facilitate communication among project participants, the authors designed a collaborative web space, which included blogs and other communication spaces, as well as allowed students to choose other means of getting and staying in touch, "notably e-mail and instant messaging." (Starke-Meyerring and Andrews, 2006, 32). Importantly, the students had a large degree of freedom in deciding which communication tools to use for their daily interactions with one another. (Starke-

Meyerring and Andrews, 2006, 32). To describe their approach to the design and implementation of the communication structures for the project, the authors use the phrase "structured independence". (Starke-Meyerring and Andrews, 2006, 36).

A vast majority of the authors who write about cross national web-based learning projects note the following factors which are crucial to the success of such projects:

- A focus on experiential learning. During experiential projects, students learn from the very act of participating in them and from being exposed to regular interactions with their counterparts in other countries.
- A carefully structured support system, which enables independent learning. In order for learning to occur, instructors need to create various support systems for the learners, including support systems for the use of various communication tools and strategies. Simultaneously, both instructors and students must patiently and deliberately develop the inter-personal and inter-team relationships needed for the success of such projects.
- A mixture of "core" and optional communication tools for all participants(Maznevski, 2000) (Lenhart, 2010). Research suggests that having a group of core communication instruments (blogs, wikis, e-mail, and so on) at the outset of the project may allow participants to transition into the project better (Starke-Meyering and Andrews 2006, 36).

SOCIAL MEDIA'S POTENTIAL TO INFLUENCE TEACHING AND LEARNING

So far, we have reviewed research on two topics: social media and cross-national web-based learning. In this section of the chapter, we bring these topics together by surveying the uses of social media in cross-national web-based learning projects.

Few authors of works dedicated to cross-national web-based learning explicitly discuss the use of social media in their projects. However, as we mentioned earlier, many authors do state the importance of giving learners flexibility in developing their own arsenal of communication tools and techniques. One direction in which this development can take place is towards social media. For example, many students who participated in our project gravitated towards social media services such as Facebook and others as their primary or secondary means of communication with their foreign counterparts.

The majority of cross-national web-based learning projects discussed in published literature includes a very significant writing component. Students who participate in those projects are either asked to create substantial written deliverables (reports, arguments, white paper, and so on), or engage into regular informal writing activities, such as blog posts, e-mails, and so on.

Kaufer et al. (2011) describe the web platform, which they created, called Classroom Salon. The platform's "Facebook-like features" allow students to collaborate on writing assignments. (Kaufer et al. 2011, 299). One important purpose of this platform is the building of communities around texts. Students are asked to upload drafts of their writing to the "Salon" web space," after which they are given time to read and comment on each other's work. (Kaufer et al. 2011, 299). The introduction of a "salon" into a writing classroom "changes the dynamic" of that classroom (Kaufer et al. 2011, 314) by allowing more time for peer-to-peer discussions of writing and by placing more responsibility for learning on the students. (Kaufer et al. 2011, 314-316). Moreover, students felt that the reading of drafts of papers had become a "more social activity," while teachers reported that using such a web platform made the reading of those drafts a "more accountable activity." (Kaufer et al. 2011, 316).

It follows from Kaufer et al.'s argument that a major purpose of a course or project centered around collaborative reading and commenting on texts is the building of a community of learners. The importance of building such communities has been noted by authors in writing studies professional communication, and distributed team theory. For example, see Bruffee (1984), Olaniran and Edgell (2008), Flammia (2011), and others. Such community building and the methods of achieving it may also be transposed, with modifications, to the arena of cross-national web-based learning.

To be sure, implementation of cross-national web-based projects presents educators with very specific challenges. Among such challengers is the need to accommodate cross-cultural differences between groups of participants, the requirement to accommodate possible variations in the participants' experiences with virtual team work, and their varying general comfort levels with collaborative work. However, the method of bringing features of social media into the writing classroom described by Kaufer et al. and the success with which their experiment went may present an opportunity to incorporate similar approaches to social media integration in cross-national web-based learning.

McLoughlin and Lee (2007) argue that the use of social media and other web 2.0 tools in learning can transform the whole learning experience. Like Kaufer et al., McLoughlin and Lee's work is not addressing the use of social media in cross-national web-based projects directly. Instead, they "investigate the affordances of Web 2.0 and social software and the choices and constraints they offer to…teachers and learners." (McLoughlin and Lee 2007, 664). After defining the term "social software" as "software that supports group interaction," McLoughlin and Lee enumerate the various educational affordances of such software. The main affordance, according to these authors, are the increased communication and interactivity among their users/learners (McLoughlin and

Lee 2007, 666). The ever-increasing popularity of social media make easier the gathering and sharing of information, the collaboration among learners, and content creation by users without significant technical expertise (McLoughlin and Lee 2007, 667). Also important is the ability of web 2.0 software to give learners more control over the choice of communication tools that they use. This new control, claim McLoughlin and Lee, may lead to an increased ability by educators to create more learner-centered pedagogies. (McLoughlin and Lee 2007, 668 669).

THE US-UKRAINE CROSS NATIONAL WEB-BASED TEACHING PROJECT

In this section, we describe and analyze a cross-national, web-based teaching project, which we taught in 2009. As a part of the analysis, we present the results of a pre and post-project survey, which were offered to the participants. While drawing large-scale conclusions and recommendations about the use of computer-mediated tools in general and social media in particular based on a limited study like this one, is not possible or necessary, we, nevertheless, believe that our small-scale research project offers useful results for those educators and trainers who are interested in carrying out similar efforts.

Research Questions

Our literature review demonstrates that while there exists a substantial body of research on the use of social media for communication and learning in general, little attention has been paid so far to the specific concerns related to social media in cross-national web-based projects. Our analysis attempts to begin filling that gap by exploring the following research questions:

- What are the best practices in the deployment and use of social web and other communication technologies in cross-cultural, web-based learning projects?
- What specific recommendations for the use of internet-based communication tools can we provide to other researchers and practitioners, both in education and in industry?
- Based on the answers to the first two questions, how can we move towards creating a theoretical and practical framework of web 2.0 and social media use in cross-national web-based learning project?

A Description of the Teaching Project

The project described here brought together ten students from the US and twelve students from Ukraine. The students worked in virtual teams of four or five members on the creation of joint written analyses of localized versions of websites of global companies. Each team comprised both Ukrainian and American participants. The US-based students were enrolled in an MS Program in Technical and Scientific Communication while the Ukraine-based students were members of a MA course in Marketing. The program, in which the Ukrainian students were enrolled, is taught in English, so their level of English-language proficiency was generally quite high.

While the "active" stage of the project, during which the students collaborated on the written analysis pieces lasted for five weeks, about one month before the start of this work, the students were given the list of required readings for the module. Several days before the start of the active stage of the project, students were introduced to the main theoretical framework, which they would follow during their analysis. This theoretical framework was the prototype theory of intercultural communication, covered by St. Amant in his article "A Prototype Theory Approach to International Web Site Analysis and Design" (2005). The article argues that "Cultural groups...can have different expectations of what constitutes acceptable website design" and that using prototype theory as a framework for analyzing and designing web sites for intercultural communication can improve those sites' effectiveness. (St. Amant, 2005, 176).

A variety of online communication tools were used during the project. Typically, initial contact between virtual teams was established by e-mail, after which the instructors encouraged students to select and use communication tools and channels that made the most sense to them as a group and that allowed them to fulfill their goals. During the course of the project, different teams used the following communication tools:

- E-mail
- Blogs
- Wikis
- Skype
- Facebook
- V Kontakte (a Russian social networking site similar to Facebook)

Project Schedule

Weeks 1-2

- A "large team" meeting via Skype was held. The purpose of this meeting was to get acquainted with the other team and to conduct a project overview as well as to introduce the participants to the project's communication protocols.
- Work on common readings for the project. All participants read a set of common texts on intercultural communication and website localization and conducted discussions of those articles within their groups. The two groups' respective instructors facilitated those discussions.

Weeks 3-4

- Virtual teams worked on reports analyzing localized version of the site of their choice. The writing and revision was done on wiki pages.
- During week 4 of the project, a Skype meeting was held to assesse the progress of the project and to trouble-shoot any problems.

Week 5

- The virtual teams produced final versions of their reports.
- At the end of week five, a group Skype meeting was held, during which each virtual team presented their work to the rest of the group.

As is evident from the project's structure, a variety of communication channels and strategies were planned for the project, ranging from large group Skype conferences to communications between virtual team members via social networks and e-mail, to collaborative writing on wikis and blogs.

Research Design

The 22 project participants were offered two online surveys. All of them responded, thus giving us 100% response rate. In our reporting of the results of the surveys in this chapter, we focus only on the data pertinent to the use of social media during the project. Other categories of data, obtained during the survey are outside of the scope of this chapter and are therefore not reported or analyzed here.

Pre-Project Survey

The purpose of the pre-project survey was to gauge the participants' expectations of the project. The questions in the survey were organized around the categories of a "SWOT" analysis, asking project participants to identify and discuss the main strengths, weaknesses, opportunities, and threats of the upcoming project, as their saw them. SWOT analysis is a popular assessment tool in business and management, so offering a survey based on SWOT categories was somewhat a natural choice for our project, given that one half of the project participants were business majors and that the other half had likely heard of SWOT Analysis before.

Obtaining these results allowed us to learn with what expectations the students entered and project. In addition, we believe that the survey was also useful for the students because it encouraged them to begin thinking critically about the work ahead.

The results of this pre-project survey, summarized in Table 1, show that US and Ukrainian students entered the project with slightly different expectations. While both groups were clearly interested in the opportunity to communicate and work with counterparts from another country, the Ukrainians understandably worried that their English may not be good enough. Also, interestingly, the Ukrainian participants anticipated a "digital divide" between the groups. While we saw no evidence of any digital divide between the two groups during the project, the fear that such a divide might happen, could have been important in the participants' choices of communication tools and of ways in which they used those tools.

Post-Project Survey

After the completion of the project, all participants were offered a second survey. The goal of this survey was to investigate the perceptions and impressions of the project by its participants. While the survey included such broad questions as "What did you like most/least about the project?" and "What did you think about the writing assignment which you were offered?", in our analysis here we choose to pay particular attention to those results of the survey which relate to communication among project participants, particularly to their use of communication channels and tools.

The three main areas around which the survey questions were grouped are as follows:

- General differences between online and face-to-face (f2f) communication, according to the students.
- The impact of online communications during the project on project and time management, according to the students.

Table 1. Results of the pre-project survey

	Strengths	Weaknesses	Opportunities	Threats
US-Based Students	Interest in intercultural communication and in web design	Lack of cross-cultural communication competencies. Differences in learning styles. Differences in time zones. General lack on experience in virtual collaboration.	Want to know more about Ukraine as a country and to work in virtual teams with Ukrainian students.	General lack of knowledge about Ukraine. Concern about their ability to finish the project on time.
Ukraine-Based Students	Mutual interest of the two groups in the topic of the project and in intercultural communication	Lack of cross-cultural communicative competencies. Differences in educational backgrounds. Differences in time zones.	Opportunity for additional English-language practice. Opportunity to learn about "other ways of learning." Opportunity to learn about "global business."	A perceived language barrier. Terminological discrepancies, given the different academic areas of the two groups. A perceived digital divide between two countries.

- Possible impact of the experience of communicating online during the project on the students' future professional and academic success.

A brief summary of the post-project survey results in presented in Table 2. As this summary shows, US and Ukrainian participants appeared to agree, among other things, that the lack of face-to-face contact tended to create communication difficulties. An important area of difference between the Ukrainians and the Americans are possible professional applications of their experience during the project. This difference could be explained by the fact that the two groups represented two different academic disciplines, marketing and international management on the Ukrainian side and professional communication on the US side, thus prompting each to look for future professional benefits of in their own field's set of values and practices.

DISCUSSION

The results of the surveys show that project participants both achieved a greater level of confidence in their ability to communicate and work online with others and were left somewhat frustrated by the process of establishing and maintaining professional relationships exclusively via social media and other online channels.

The first significant result from the study is the keen awareness, by members of both the US and Ukraine-based groups, of the differences between online and face-to-face communication. Such differences and their impact on the progress and results of the project were frequently mentioned in the post-project survey. However, they were not mentioned at all in the SWOT analysis, as an opportunity, difficulty, or threat to the project. The reasons for such prominence, in the respondents' minds, of the different nature of face-to-face and online communication in the post-project stage could be that, while all project participants had certainly used social media for social purposes, none of them had used it for academic or professional purposes prior to this project. Therefore,

Table 2. Results of the post-project survey

	General differences between online and f2f communication	The impact of online communications during the project on project and time management	Possible impact of the experience of communicating online during the project on the students' future professional and academic success
US-Based Students	The inability to communicate face-to-face. Occasional technical difficulties. The feedback on the writing is not "instant" due to the nature of online communications.	Trying to manage the project without interacting in person was difficult. Lack of frequent and regular interaction was a "challenge." Lack of confidence about the "correct" intercultural communication steps and protocols in online communication.	Learn to use and understand online documentation and instructions. Learn to give and receive feedback on writing "long-distance" and without the other person present "face-to-face."
Ukraine-Based Students	Time zone differences, a language barrier, and the need to constantly express oneself in writing presented some difficulties. Lack of face-to-face contact made the work more difficult.	Trouble initiating conversations with US students. Lack of time to develop trust and understanding about the project. Occasionally felt that communication difficulties "hindered" the overall progress of the project.	The development of project and time management skills and of creativity. Overcoming of fear of dialogue online in a foreign language.

it is possible that using social media to accomplish professional and academic tasks during this project compelled project participants to think more critically and articulate better the important distinctions between communicating face-to-face and online.

When compared, the results of the two surveys yield some rather predictable areas of correlation. For example, before the project, the Ukrainian students listed a possible "language barrier" as one of the threats to the overall success of the project. In the post-project survey, the Ukrainians also named language proficiency as one of the factors that could have hindered communication. The US students named the lack of the general knowledge about the most effective intercultural communication protocols and lack of experience in virtual collaboration as weaknesses in the first survey. In the second survey, the Americans named those same factors as possibly having a negative impact on the communication during the project.

One the other hand, what the participants called "terminological discrepancies" between countries and academic fields, in the SWOT analysis, predicting that those discrepancies could get in the way of effective communication, did not turn out to be a major negative factor. Instead, based on the results of the second survey, the participants appeared to be able to derive discipline-specific professional benefits for themselves out of the project. In other words, what had been perceived as a potential problem may have turned out to be a valuable learning experience.

Possibly the most significant outcome of the post-project survey is the participants' realization that it is very hard to build social and professional relationships "from scratch" using social media alone. As evident from Table 2, project participants named the inability to communicate face-to-face as one of the factors that hindered the progress of their work and made the achievement of satisfactory results slightly more difficult. Importantly, technical difficulties, although mentioned, were not considered to be a major negative factor that

hampered interactions. This leads us to believe that the factors of social media and other communication tool use that presented challenges to the students were the need to "connect" and collaborate with people whom they did not know personally, and the need to do it rather quickly. This finding correlates well with published research on social media. Preece and Schneiderman (2009), Haythornthwaite (2005), and Boyd and Ellison (2008), whose research we cited earlier in the chapter, all argue that social networks mainly maintain and sustain the relationships which are first built in real life via face-to-face communication.

If these researchers are correct and if the results of our survey are accurate, then educators and trainers wishing to create web-based projects similar to ours, would need to take this difficulty into account. According to Haythornthwaite, social networks "make existing connections visible." (2005, 130). However, the participants of our project had to rely on social media and other web-based communication channels to establish those very connections first.

In the pre-project survey, members of both US and Ukraine-based groups indicated that their perceived lack of general cultural knowledge about the other country could hinder the project. The responses in the pre-project survey demonstrate an interesting mixture of apprehension and anticipation of the project by the students, none of whom had ever participated in such endeavors before. However, in the post-project survey, the students did not mention a lack of such general cultural knowledge, preferring instead to focus on the challenges of online communication and other professional and linguistic issues. In other words, overall, the fact that the project participants came from two different countries and two distinct cultures alone did not seem to influence their perception of the success of the project. When respondents mentioned anxiety about not knowing the "correct" intercultural communication procedures and protocols, they typically spoke about those protocols and procedures specifically in relation to intercultural communication online rather than communication in general terms, as evident from Table 2.

Finally, it is also worth noting that the project was conducted entirely in English, a language, which was foreign to the 12 project participants based in Ukraine. While the general English language proficiency of the Ukrainian students was sufficient for the communication and collaboration tasks presented to them during this project, we can perhaps hypothesize that this fact may have complicated the use of social media and other web communication channels during the project further. For example, the "trouble initiating conversations with US students" reported by Ukrainian students in the post-project survey could have resulted from the lack of confidence in their English and not in the difficulty with using social media.

Overall, our surveys demonstrate that both participating in the project and using social media tools as primary ways of communicating during the project presented the students with both unique challenges and unique opportunities. Project participants achieved experiential learning by participating in a project, which allowed them a significant amount of freedom in selecting online communication tools and in shaping communication channels and protocols. As teachers of the project, we hope (and evidence from the survey results seems to support that hope) that the members of both US and Ukraine-based groups saw considerable value in the project, even despite the occasional frustrations and difficulties which they encountered.

FUTURE RESEARCH DIRECTIONS

The limitations of our research include a small size of the project and a small number of survey respondents, a short duration of the project, which limited the scope and amount of collected data, and the pilot nature of the project and of the surveys.

Due to these limitations, we see this project as a first step towards a fuller understanding of the mechanisms of online communication, including communication via social media, which are a part of such cross-national web-based teaching projects. We are interested in further research on this topic and invite fellow researchers and practitioners to consider the following questions for future research:

1. What specific strategies and approaches do by participants of cross-national web-based projects use to select social media and other online communication tools for use during the project?

Our surveys show that the communication tool sets available to our participants significantly influenced the flow and outcomes of the project. In designing the project, we tried to follow the published advice of identifying a few "core" communication channels for the participants while allowing them to identify any additional tools and channels that work best for them. The core communication tools offered to the participations were the wiki, in which the virtual teams created their texts, a class blog, Skype, and e-mail. In addition to those tools, different virtual teams chose to use Facebook and the Russian social networking site V Kontakte. Further research can help us identify the reasons and mechanisms through which different virtual teams choose different communication tools and combinations of tools for their work, and what factors influence those choices.

2. How do participants of such projects negotiate of social media-based communication and collaboration strategies and protocols? How do they then follow those protocols?

Another useful and fruitful direction for future research is an investigation of the steps and moves members of virtual teams make to establish and maintain communication channels. The following questions could be asked: a) who takes initiative in suggesting and establishing a new communication tool? b) what specific negotiations take place within a virtual team once a new tool has been suggested? c) how, if at all, do the protocols for using team-selected communication tools get formalized and enforced?

3.   What impact do cross-linguistic and cross-cultural factors, such as native/non-native speaker communications, have on overall nature and effectiveness of communication during such projects?

The research presented in his chapter does not directly address the factors and outcomes of cross-national web-based teaching projects that result in communication between individuals and virtual teams from different linguistic and cultural backgrounds. (Vaira, 2004) (Vaira, 2004) (Vaira, 2004)A useful way of investigating this area may be through a direct comparison between single and multiple-language virtual teams.

4.   What pedagogical and design options and approaches are available to educators and trainers in creating and implementing cross-national web-based projects, and how can the results of such research shape instructional design and teaching decisions?

In addition to providing valuable theoretical knowledge, the directions for research suggested above, would allow educators and workplace trainer to develop effective instructional designs and instructional methods for cross-national web-based teaching projects. The communication channels and tools which participants of such projects use to accomplish their goals shape the outcomes of such projects. Therefore, in order for these projects to lead to the outcomes desired by their designers and by their participants, instructional design must be based on a solid understanding of the properties, roles, and functions of communication tools, which are used during the project.

CONCLUSION

With an increasing globalization of professional activity and of education, it is likely that the popularity of cross-national web-based teaching projects will continue to grow. Simultaneously, with the continued popularity and possible expansion of the range of social media and other online communication tools which are available to the participants and teachers of such projects, anyone involved in this work will need an increasingly sophisticated understanding of the opportunities and challenges that these projects present. The research presented in this chapter builds on the existing knowledge about cross-national web-based learning and charts new directions for future investigations.

REFERENCES

Boyd, D. E. (2008). Social network sites: Definition, history, and scholarship. *Journal of Computer-Mediated Communication, 13*(1), 210–230. doi:10.1111/j.1083-6101.2007.00393.x

Bruffee, K. (1984). Collaborative learning and the conversation of mankind. *College English, 46*(7), 635–652. doi:10.2307/376924

Ellison, N. S. (2007). The benefits of Facebook friends: Exploring the relationship between college students' use of online social networks and social capital. *Journal of Computer-Mediated Communication, 12*(4). doi:10.1111/j.1083-6101.2007.00367.x

Flammia, M. (2011). *Using service-learning and global virtual team projects to integrate sustainability into the technical communication curriculum. Prodessional Communication Conference--IPCC* (pp. 1–9). IPCC.

Haythornthwaite, C. (2011). Social network and internet connectivity effects. *Information Communication and Society, 8*(2), 125–147. doi:10.1080/13691180500146185

Herrington, T. (2010). Crossing global boundaries: Beyond intercultural communication. *Journal of Business and Technical Communication, 24*(4), 516–539.

Kaufer, D. G. (2011). Bringing social media to the writing classroom: Classroom salon. *Journal of Business and Technical Communication, 25*(3), 299–321. doi:10.1177/1050651911400703

Lenhart, A. P. (2010). *Social media and mobile internet use among teens and young adults*. Washington, DC: Pew Research Center.

Maznevski, M. C. (2000). Bridging space over time: Global virtual team dynamics and effectiveness. *Organization Science, 11*(5), 473–492. doi:10.1287/orsc.11.5.473.15200

McLoughlin, C. L. (2007). Social software and participatory learning: Pedagogical choices with technology affordances in the web 2.0 era. *Proceedings ASCILITE* (pp. 664-675). Singapore: ASCILITE.

Mousten, B. M. (2010). Learning localization through trans-atlantic collaboration: Bridging the gap between professionsetween professions. *IEEE Transactions on Professional Communication, 53*(4), 401–411. doi:10.1109/TPC.2010.2077481

Olaniran, B. A. (2008). Cultural implications of collaborative information technologies (CITs) in international online collaborations and global virtual teams. In Zemliansky, P., & St.Amant, K. (Eds.), *The handbook of research on virtual workplaces and the new nature of business practices* (pp. 120–129). Hershey, PA: IGI Global. doi:10.4018/978-1-59904-893-2.ch010

Preece, J. S. (2009). The reader to leader framework: Motivating technology-mediated social participation. *Transactions on Human-Computer Interactions, 1*(1), 13–32.

St.Amant, K. (2005). A prototype theory approach to international website analysis and design. *Technical Communication Quarterly, 14*(1), 73–91. doi:10.1207/s15427625tcq1401_6

Starke-Meyerring, D. A. (2006). Building a shared virtual learning culture: An international classroom partnership. *Business Communication Quarterly, 69*(1), 25–49. doi:10.1177/1080569905285543

Vaira, M. (2004). Globalization and higher education organizational change: A framework for analysis. *Higher Education, 48*, 483–510. doi:10.1023/B:HIGH.0000046711.31908.e5

ADDITIONAL READING

Benkler, Y. (2006). *The wealth of networks*. New Haven, CT: Yale University Press.

Cohen, S. G., & Bailey, D. E. (1997). What makes teams work: Group effectiveness research from the shop floor to the executive suite. *Journal of Management, 23*, 239–290. doi:10.1177/014920639702300303

Ducate, L. C., & Lomicka, L. L. (2008). Exploring the blogosphere: Use of web logs in the foreign language classroom. *Computer Assisted Language Learning, 21*, 9–28. doi:10.1080/09588220701865474

Gurak, L. (1999). *Persuasion and privacy in cyberspace: The online protests over Lotus MarketPlace and the clipper*. New Haven, CT: Yale.

Haas, C., & Flower, L. (1988). Rhetorical reading strategies and the construction of meaning. *College Composition and Communication, 39*, 167–183. doi:10.2307/358026

Hamman, R. (2000). Computer networks linking network communities. In Werry, C., & Mowbray, M. (Eds.), *Online communities: Commerce, community action, and the virtual university* (pp. 71–95). Upper Saddle River, NJ: Prentice Hall.

Kaufer, D., & Carley, K. (1993). *Communication at a distance: The influence of print on socio-cultural organization and change*. Mahwah, NJ: Erlbaum.

Leonard, D. C. (1996). Using the web for graduate courses in technical communication with distant learners. *Technical Communication, 43*, 388–401.

Levy, M. (1998). Theory and design in a multimedia CALL project in cross-cultural pragmatics. *Computer Assisted Language Learning, 12*(1), 29–57. doi:10.1076/call.12.1.29.5716

Marginson, S. (2004). Don't leave me hanging on the Anglophone: The potential for online distance higher education in the Asia-Pacific region. *Higher Education Quarterly, 58*(2/3), 74–113. doi:10.1111/j.1468-2273.2004.00263.x

Myers, G. (2010). *Discourse of blogs and wikis.* London, UK: Continuum Press.

Nardi, B. A., Schiano, D. J., Gumbrecht, M., & Swartz, L. (2004). Why we blog? *Communications of the ACM, 47*, 41–46. doi:10.1145/1035134.1035163

Ougaard, M. (2004). *Political globalization: State, power and social forces.* Houndmills, UK: Palgrave Macmillan.

Qualman, E. (2009). *Socialnomics: How social media transforms the way we live and do business.* New York, NY: Wiley.

Richman, A., Noble, K., & Johnson, A. (2002). *When the workplace is many places: The extent and nature of off-site work today.* Watertown, MA: WFD Consulting. Executive Summary retrieved April 24, 2005, from http://www.abcdependentcare.com/docs/ABC_Executive_Summary_final.pdf

Rupert, M. (2000). *Ideologies of globalization: Contending visions of a new world order.* London, UK: Routledge.

Schneider, B., & Andre, J. (2005). University preparation of workplace writing: An exploratory study of the perceptions of students in three disciplines. *Journal of Business Communication, 42*, 195–218. doi:10.1177/0021943605274749

Shirky, C. (2008). *Here comes everybody: The power of organizing without organizations.* New York, NY: Penguin.

Starke-Meyerring, D. (2005). Meeting the challenges of globalization: A framework for global literacies in professional communication programs. *Journal of Business and Technical Communication, 19*, 468–499. doi:10.1177/1050651905278033

Suárez-Orozco, M. M., & Qin-Hilliard, D. B. (2004). Globalization: Culture and education in the new millennium. In Suárez-Orozco, M. M., & Qin-Hilliard, D. B. (Eds.), *Globalization: Culture and education in the new millennium* (pp. 1–37). Berkeley, CA: University of California Press.

Surowiecki, J. (2005). *The wisdom of crowds.* New York, NY: Anchor Books.

Wang, Y. (2004). Supporting synchronous distance language learning with desktop videoconferencing. *Language Learning & Technology, 8*, 90–121.

Wolfe, J. (2002). Marginal pedagogy: How annotated texts affect a writingfrom-sources task. *Written Communication, 19*, 297–333. doi:10.1177/074108830201900203

Zhang, P. (2008a). Toward a positive design theory: Principles for designing motivating information and communication technology. In Avital, M., Bolland, R., & Cooperrider, D. (Eds.), *Designing information and organizations with a positive lens* (pp. 45–73). Amsterdam, The Netherlands: Elsevier Advances in Appreciative Inquiry Series. doi:10.1016/S1475-9152(07)00204-9

Zhang, P. (2008b). Motivational affordances: Reasons for ICT design and use. *Communications of the ACM, 61*(11), 145–147. doi:10.1145/1400214.1400244

KEY TERMS AND DEFINITIONS

Social Media: Internet sites, platforms, and services, which allow users to communicate and share various kinds of content with each other. A key element of a social media site is the ability to create and maintain a user profile.

Cross-National, Web-Based Teaching Projects: Projects and similar activities, whose participants, located in different countries, work together, over the internet on learning tasks.

Experiential Learning: The process of learning and making meaning from direct experience. Many experiential learning projects privilege the direct experience of their participants over specific outcomes of learning projects, such as deliverables.

Virtual Distributed Teams: Groups of professionals or learners who are dispersed geographically and conduct their work over the Internet or through other long-distance means of communication.

Visible Connections in Social Media: The connections among users of social media, which are made visible and material through textual and other communications among users.

Core Communication Tools: The communication tools, which are given to the participants of a virtual learning project by instructors or other managers. These tools ate typically used during early stages of a project to establish initial connections among participants.

Optional Communication Tools: The communication tools, which participants of virtual learning projects find and learn to use during the project. Such tools supplement and, in some cases, replace the core tools.

Chapter 14
E–Learning Records:
Are There Any to Manage? If so, How?

Luciana Duranti
University of British Columbia, Canada

Elizabeth Shaffer
University of British Columbia, Canada

ABSTRACT

Through the lens of an archival theoretical framework, this chapter examines the digital outputs of the use of social media applications by students, faculty, and educational institutions, and discusses the need to control and manage their creation, use, maintenance, and preservation. The authors draw on a case study that explores the identification, arrangement, description, and preservation of students' records produced in an eLearning environment in Singapore and is used as a starting point to highlight and discuss the implications that the use of social media in education can have for the management and preservation of educational institutions' records as evidence of their activity and of students' learning, to fulfill legal and accountability requirements. The authors also discuss how the use of social media by educators in the classroom environment facilitates the creation of records that raise issues of intellectual property and copyright, ownership, and privacy: issues that can further impact their maintenance and preservation.

INTRODUCTION

The participatory nature of social media applications has challenged the way in which knowledge is traditionally imparted and learning developed, as educators can enlist any number of social media

tools to enhance "social learning" (Brown & Adler, 2008, p. 18) and engage students as participants in their education. As Armstrong and Franklin (2008) note, educational institutions report three key advantages to Web 2.0 use in higher education: 1. Affordances not present in other technologies such as co-creation and online collaboration; 2.

DOI: 10.4018/978-1-4666-2851-9.ch014

Students' engagement fostered by familiarity; and 3. No cost, as these technologies are often free and without the restrictions that accompany those offered by institutions (p. 3). Blogs, wikis, social networking sites (SNSs), discussion fora, virtual worlds, and other tools are utilized by faculty to deliver content in novel and engaging ways, and by students to meet course requirements and interact with one another and faculty in active learning environments. But, what do we know about the documentary products of these interactions and how to manage and keep them? The documentary by-products and outputs of these new and emerging pedagogical practices and engagements are replacing traditional academic records, such as exam papers, term essays, or multiple answers tests, and Paul Wu Horng-Jyh even believes that "the emerging pedagogical practices inevitably change the ways records are defined in a learning space" (2010, p. 68).

Through the lens of an archival theoretical framework, this chapter examines the digital by-products and outputs of the use of social media applications by students, faculty and educational institutions, and discusses the need to identify among them which constitute evidence of the learning process, and to control and manage their creation, use, maintenance and preservation. Further, it examines how issues of intellectual property and copyright, ownership and privacy can further impact their management through time. This discussion of the educational use of social media is situated in the learning, teaching and administrative activities of higher education (post-secondary) environments as the majority of current research on the educational use of Facebook and other social media tools primarily focuses on college and university student environments (Hew, 2011).

These authors primarily draw their observations from a case study conducted in the context of the third phase of the InterPARES (International Research on Permanent Authentic Records in Electronic Systems) Project, an international multidisciplinary research endeavour which aims at developing the theoretical and methodological knowledge essential to the long-term preservation of authentic records created and/or maintained in digital form (www.interpares.org). The case study explores the identification, arrangement, description and preservation of students' records produced in an e-learning environment in Singapore (Wu Horng-Jyh, 2010) and will be used as a starting point to highlight and discuss the implications that the use of social media in education can have for the management and preservation of the records of educational institutions which are to be kept as evidence of teaching and learning in order to fulfill legal obligations and accountability requirements.

Used to assess students' achievements and ability to meet course requirements, the by-products and outputs of the use of social media, although different from traditional record types, are still subject to the same retention and access rules, thus, this chapter will also propose ways of respecting such rules by implementing policies and procedures capable of ensuring that the digital records of e-learning can be treated and maintained as institutional records – clear from intellectual property challenges, and as evidence of teaching activity, learning progress, and institutional assessment of both teaching and learning, for the benefit and accountability of all parties involved and the memory of the future.

SOCIAL MEDIA AND EDUCATION

Web 2.0 and Social Media

Web 2.0 (often referred to as the read/write Web) is an evolution of the Web, a shift from an environment of passive consumers to one where individuals can readily create, contribute and collaborate with other users (O'Reilly, 2005). Used to refer to the participative Web, Web 2.0 is an umbrella term that encompasses the ideas underpinning social media applications and the technologies that have produced them (Anderson, 2007).

Social media, as defined by Kaplan and Haenlein (2010), are "a group of Internet-based applications [and services] that build on the ideological and technological foundations of Web 2.0, and that allow the creation and exchange of User Generated Content (UGC)" (p. 60). Social media are generally linked to ideas such as: individual production and user generated content; harnessing the power of the crowd; data on an epic scale; architecture of participation; network effects; and openness (Anderson, 2007). The expression "social media" encompasses a variety of applications and services such as blogs and microblogs, wikis, RSS feeds, podcasts, multimedia sharing, tagging and social bookmarking, and social networking services (Anderson, 2007). The key attribute of the majority of these social media applications is the ability to enable users to develop, contribute, collaborate and share user-generated content on the web and enterprise platforms. The democratic nature of social media technologies has afforded greater connection, collaboration and knowledge creation in interactions amongst citizens, organizations, and governments (Benkler, 2006).

Social media are consistently evolving with the ever-increasing ability to combine tools and information to create new forms of documents that are posing unprecedented challenges to traditional recordkeeping paradigms. (Dearstyne, 2007; Gerber, 2006).

Social Media in Higher Education

There is a paucity of research into the record creating/recordkeeping implications of social media use in education; however, several reports and journal articles were identified which investigate the potential and current use of social media in education, its goals and implications for use. Most research presented in this literature examines the use of social media for teaching and learning (Chapman & Russell; 2009, Armstrong & Frank-

lin, 2088; Becta, 2009; Hunter, 2009; Minocha, 2009). It seeks to understand how and if these technologies are currently being used and what is their potential to inform pedagogical practice of both instructors and learners. A large amount of the research/discourse into social media use in education focuses on Social Networking Services (SNS) and their potential use in this environment. SNS, as defined by boyd and Ellison (2007), are "web-based services that allow individuals to (1) construct a public or semi-public profile within a bounded system, (2) articulate a list of other users with whom they share connection, and (3) view and traverse their list of connections and those made by others within the system" (para. 4). For the purposes of this chapter we will expand our examination of educational use of social media beyond SNS to include a full range of social media tools and their potential for record creation. However, it is to be noted that many of the qualities that boyd and Ellison define as characteristics of SNS are also present in other social media tools and services such as blogs and microblogs, multimedia sharing sites, wikis, etc.

The growth of the personal Web, considered a trend in curriculum and pedagogy (Becta, 2009), and the consequent need of identifying and understanding the by-products and outcomes of its use, makes it necessary to understand the nature, characteristics and variants of such use. According to Haythornthwaite & Wellman (1998), academic communities support intricate hierarchies, rich organizational traditions and interpersonal ties utilizing many different channels of communication (as cited in Hewitt & Forte, 2008), but social media tools and services are often incorporated into higher education on an ad hoc basis (Chapman & Russell, 2009; Armstrong & Franklin, 2008; Hunter, 2008; Roblyer et al, 2010), complementing and potentially replacing traditional means of academic record creation and perhaps generating new and unique information artifacts. It is evident from the literature that these tools are adopted in educational environments that have moved, or are moving towards a constructivist pedagogy which shifts the role of the educator from a "deliverer" of education to students, to a "facilitator" of students' engagement with the material, away from a traditionally hierarchical environment. Huijser (2008) writes "Web 2.0 technologies both reflect and drive a blurring of the lines between students and university educators which has a potentially profound impact on learning and teaching in higher education" (p. 45). However, the very qualities that make social media attractive in an educational environment create serious challenges for the identification, management and preservation of the records of teaching and learning:

The recent, and undeniably massive, growth in adoption of various social software applications represents both an opportunity and a threat to institutions and educators: opportunity because the qualities which help these applications thrive, align well with social-constructivist and other contemporary theories of learning which have resonated strongly with online educators and learners and spared massive interest and growth in adoption; threat in part because they are often developed and adopted by learners outside the bounds of their formal relationships with institutions, and in part because they depend on network characteristics that can be in tension with the more 'closed' environments and online approaches found within most institutions (Huijser, 2008, p. 47-8).

Research indicates that SNS such as Facebook are being employed by educators to share information with students. Hew (2011) reports that "One lecturer used Facebook to communicate or pass important information to students because it was easier and quicker than to look for them in class. Another lecturer felt that Facebook helped students ask questions that they might not feel comfortable doing so in class" (p. 665). While the extent to which students in higher education are using SNS such as Facebook for educational purposes is not large at present (Hew, 2011; Kolek & Saunders, 2009; Madge et al., 2009; Mazer, Murphy & Simonds, 2009), there is an impetus

to increase formal incorporation of such tools into the higher education classroom (Munoz & Towner, 2011). Huijser (2008) argues that social media could potentially offer major opportunities for educational purposes, and that "educators could potentially seize on the ways in which these technologies are already being used by Generation Y, and appropriate and guide this usage into particular directions" (p. 46). Use of social media in higher education will continue to grow; however, there is no specific prediction as to the rate of growth (Chapman & Russell, 2009).

It is difficult to predict to what extent Web 2.0 will become integrated with the academic digital landscape and what impact it will have but respondents were generally positive that Web. 2.0 tools and services are here to stay and will increasingly be used. They thought that this would inevitably change the way students, staff and institutional services work, noting that using Web 2.0 poses its own challenges which need to be recognized, allowed for and addressed (Chapman & Russell, 2009, p. 25).

While students' preferences for using social media (particularly SNS) in higher education are mixed, it is evident that this trend will continue, making it necessary for educational institutions and faculty to negotiate this landscape in order to satisfy students differing expectations (Dahlstrom et al., 2011). "My generation is a social networking generation"—writes a student. "We devote most of our time to Tweeting and or reading tweets, it would help if we could communicate with our professors in this way because most of us aren't able to contact them during office hours" (Dahlstrom et al., 2011, p. 26). A landscape study examining the use of social media in higher education in Australia indicated that users prefer Web-based services that have already been adopted by their wider community and offer a greater ease of use and lower barriers to entry, including FaceBook, YouTube, Skype and Twitter (Hunter, 2009). As Chapman & Russell (2009) state: "if a large proportion of staff and/or students are using a service (e.g. Facebook) then IT services need to look at ways to support people who need to engage with that service" (p. 25). It is not just the responsibility of IT to react or, better, to be pro-active, but also of administrators, records managers and policy makers.

ARCHIVES, RECORDS, AND EVIDENCE

In archival theory, a record is "a document made or received in the course of a practical activity as its instrument or by-product, and set aside for action or reference" (Duranti, 2009, p.44). It has distinct attributes, which support the presumption of its authenticity and ensure its reliability and accuracy through creation, use, maintenance, and ultimately, preservation (www.interpares.org). The authenticity of digital records is dependent upon the protection through time of their identity and integrity. Persons and institutions keep the records they create in order to refer to them in subsequent action and to support accountability and compliance, that is, as evidence of their activities. In order for records to be used in their evidentiary capacity, they must be created, managed and preserved respecting applicable legislation, regulations, standards, codes of practice, procedures, and/or community expectations (Shepherd & Yeo, 2003). The evidentiary capacity of a record depends on its reliability and is assessed on the basis of its form, authorship, and procedure of creation. In a traditional educational environment producing traditional records all of these factors are easy to identify and assess; however, in a synchronous Web 2.0 environment, they become difficult to define and demonstrate and can pose challenges to effectively managing and preserving the records of eLearning over time.

Evidence is a relative term in legal terminology; it is the relation between two facts. The first fact is theoretical and necessitates proof (*factum probandum* or fact to be proven) and the second is

real, concrete, and serves to prove the theoretical fact (*factum probans* or proving fact). Evidence is the relation between the fact to be proven and the fact that proves it; as Meehan states, "evidence is not evidence simply because the rules say so" – "evidence is a word of relation and as such has no complete signification of itself" (Meehan, 2006, p. 136). In order to have evidentiary capacity, to be used as evidence that is, a record must be trustworthy, that is, able to stand for the facts it attests, make authentic claims, offer accurate content, have an identity that is certain and ascertainable, and have proven integrity. Only if all these qualities are present in a record, it can serve as the *factum probans* that supports the *factum probandum*.

There are questions regarding whether and when the by-products and outputs of social media use in e-learning processes are records, and how to ensure that, if and when they are records, they are trustworthy, that is reliable, accurate and authentic. Content created with external social media tools and services may be unable to act as a record of the learning process because it lacks one of more of the necessary characteristics of a record to start with. Digital information, to be regarded as having record nature, must 1) present fixed form and stable content, 2) be the indisputable by-product or outcome of a clearly defined act in the context of a process or procedure of any nature, 3) be clearly related to the other by-products or outputs of the same process or procedure in a cause-effect relationship (i.e. archival bond), 4) be indisputably linked to an originator,[1] an author,[2] a writer[3] and an addressee[4] (be they individual, multiple or collective), 5) to a creator[5] (e.g. the class, the course, the academic unit, the university), and 6) to a documentary, technological, procedural, provenancial, and juridical-administrative context (InterPARES 1 and 2).

In a social media environment each and every one of these necessary characteristics are hard to identify, demonstrate and, when present, maintain. Consider for example fixed form and stable content. A digital record has a fixed form if its binary content is stored so that the message it conveys can be rendered with the same documentary presentation it had on the screen when first saved, even if its digital presentation has been changed, for example, from Word to .pdf. A digital record has a fixed form as well if the same content can be presented on the screen in several different ways but in a limited series of pre-determined possibilities; in such a case we would have different documentary presentations of the same digital entity (e.g., statistical data viewed as a pie chart, a bar chart, or a table). This situation raises the issue of the difference between a stored record and a manifested record.

A "stored record" is constituted of the linked digital component(s)[6] that are used in re-producing the record, which comprise the data to be processed in order to manifest the record (i.e., content data and form data) and the rules for processing the data, including those enabling variations (i.e., composition data). A "manifested record" is the visualization of the record in a form suitable for presentation to a person or system. Sometimes, a manifested record does not have a corresponding stored record, but is re-created from fixed content data when a user's action associates these data with specific form and composition data (e.g., a record produced from a relational database). If the same user's action always results in the same documentary presentation with the same content, the manifested entity is considered to have fixed form and stable content, even when it does not have a corresponding stored record, and, if all other requirements for the existence of a record are present, it is a record. In contrast, when one stored record may be manifested in several documentary presentations, the creator has to determine whether the official record is the stored one or one or more of the manifested ones by assigning to the chosen entity a classification code and/or a retention period. There might be situations in which a stored record is never manifested, as is the case with interacting business applications, workflow generated and used to carry out experi-

ments, analyses of observational data carried out by interpreting software, etc. Also in this case, the creator determines which entities should be retained with other records of the same activity, manifested or not. Clearly, these decisions are based on the functions and activities in which the records participate, both as aggregates and as individual entities.

Stable content has a more intuitive explanation. A digital entity has stable content and can be considered a record, if all other conditions are satisfied, if the data and the message in it are unchanged and unchangeable, meaning that data cannot be overwritten, altered, deleted or added to. However, there are cases in which entities that demonstrate "bounded variability" can be said to have stable content. A digital entity has bounded variability when changes to its form are limited and controlled by fixed rules, so that the same query or interaction always generates the same result, and when the user can have different views of different subsets of content, due to the intention of the author or to the character of the operating systems or applications. While the first definition of stable content applies to static digital entities, the second is significant when the entities we are looking at are interactive.

A "static digital entity" is one that does not provide possibilities for changing its manifest content or form beyond opening, closing and navigating; for example, emails, reports, sound recordings, motion videos, and snapshots of web pages. These entities, if all other requirements are satisfied, are records, because they have fixed form and stable content. By contrast, an "interactive digital entity" presents variable content, form, or both, and the rules governing the content and form of presentation may be either fixed or variable. Interactive entities may or may not be records, depending on whether they are non-dynamic or dynamic. "Non-dynamic entities" are those for which the rules governing the presentation of content and form do not vary, and the content presented each time is selected from a fixed store of data. Examples are interactive web pages, online catalogs, and entities enabling performances: if the other conditions exist, they are records. "Dynamic entities" are those for which the rules governing the presentation of content and form may vary: these entities may be components of information systems or "potential records," in that they can become records if the digital system in which they exist, given the purpose that it fulfills, is supposed to contain records and is therefore redesigned in such a way that it will produce and manage records, or if the entities that should exist as records are moved to another system that only maintains digital records (i.e., static or non-dynamic entities). Examples of dynamic entities are: entities whose variation is due to data that change frequently (e.g., the design permits updating, replacement or alterations; it allows data collection from users or about user interactions or actions; or it uses these data to determine subsequent presentations); entities whose variation is due to data continually received from external sources and not stored within the system; entities produced in dynamic computing applications that select different sets of rules to produce documents, depending on user input, sources of content data, and characteristics of content (e.g., weather sites); entities produced by evolutionary computing where the software generating them can change autonomously (e.g., scheduling and modeling of financial markets; edutainment sites), etc. (Duranti & Thibodeau, 2006).

Thus, a digital entity that can be said to have fixed form and stable content according to the parameters outlined above is a document. While all records are documents, though, not all documents are records. Records must exhibit the other five characteristics mentioned earlier. The most important is the archival bond. The archival bond is a concept that is at the core of archival science. It is the network of relationships that each record has with the records belonging in the same aggregation.7 The archival bond is *originary*, because it comes into existence when a record is created (i.e., when, after being made or received, it is set

aside in the archives, or archival fonds[8] of the physical or juridical person who made or received it for action or reference), *necessary*, because it exists for every record (i.e., a document can be considered a record only if it acquires an archival bond), and *determined*, because it is qualified by the function of the record in the documentary aggregation in which it belongs. The archival bond first arises when a record is set aside and thereby connected to another in the course of action, but it is incremental, because, as the connective tissue that joins a record to those surrounding it, it is in continuing formation and growth until the aggregation in which the record belongs is no longer subject to expansion, that is, until the activity producing such aggregation is completed.

Besides determining the structure of the archival fonds, the archival bond is the primary identifying component of each record, as several identical documents become as many distinct records after they acquire the archival bond. The archival bond can be revealed by either the physical order of the records, their classification code or their registration number. The archival bond is also expression of the development of the activity in which the document participates, rather than of the act that the document embodies (e.g., appointment, grant, request), because it contains within itself the direction of the cause-effect relationship. Therefore, the archival bond determines the meaning of the record.

Finally, in order to establish whether the by-products and outcomes of the use of social media are records, it is also essential to establish in which way they participate in activities, if at all, in the context of the functions of their creator, and who are the persons linked to them as originators, authors, addressees, writers and creators (Duranti, 2009a).

Even if we are successful in ensuring that entities presenting the six characteristics of records are created during the e-learning process using social media, these records may still lack sufficient information to establish their integrity, authenticity, reliability and usability (NARA, 2010). Furthermore, if they do, protecting these qualities over time in social media environments may be difficult, as educational organizations may not have control over who has access to systems if information is hosted on third-party servers. The answers to these issues may only come from institutional policies prescribing what is to be considered a record in a social media environment, when such an entity is trustworthy, and how to keep it as such over time.

E-LEARNING, RECORD-MAKING, AND RECORDKEEPING

To resolve the record-related issues arising from social media use in higher education it is necessary to understand how social media are used pedagogically and to identify the by-products and outcomes of such use. How instructors and students, in the course of teaching and learning, use social media will determine what the by-products and outcomes of such use are. For example, assignments may be the outcomes of student work which are submitted to the teacher in a documentary form, whereas by-products may include correspondence, tweets, Facebook messages, etc., that is, any recorded output (whether intentional or not) of the interaction between students and teacher. Both outcomes and by-products should be capable of serving as evidence of course activity. The by-products would be evidence of the process of teaching and learning, while the products would be evidence of what has been learned (as manifested in assignments), with the latter being what is traditionally assessed.

In a traditional pedagogical environment, the outcomes that are evaluated are the students' products that demonstrate what the students in a particular context have learned: essentially, only those products are marked as assignments. In such a traditional juridical system, only similar outcomes would be considered the records of e-

learning, with the exclusion of the by-products. This is because the face-to-face learning paradigm is transferred to an e-learning environment without further translation. However, as social media are adopted into the e-learning environment, and pedagogical approaches become more constructivist, the potential for the by-products mentioned above to be assessable records of student learning is very real, with attention being paid to the quality of the interactions in the e-learning environment, the skill with which students navigate the environment or aid peers in doing so, and other similar measures of performance. Instructors who enlist Wikipedia as one learning environment, for example, may regard the acts of creating, editing and navigating on the Wikipedia platform as part of the basis of evaluation along with the actual article they produce (Kolowich, 2010; Jbmurray, 2009).

In the context of two examples, the authors are now going to examine the ways in which social media tools and services have begun to punctuate the landscape in higher education, to identify some of the ways in which this adoption and use pose challenges for records maintenance and preservation and test the educational institutions' ability to adhere to their ongoing administrative requirements and governing legislations and to interpret these through the lens of the archival concepts discussed above.

Professional Seminar, a Master's level course at the Nanyang Technological University in Singapore, is an example of a "Web 2.0 experimental learning environment" that incorporates both online and offline learning and utilizes social media (Wu Horng-Jyh, 2009). The course is modeled on constructivist pedagogy and incorporates social media tools, including blogs, fora and wikis, which the students are expected to use throughout the course for collaboration, communication and creation of content. The structure of the course has students first meeting in-person, after attending lectures by industry professionals, to discuss topics such as "leadership, communication, ethics and critical thinking," and then interact on the social media platform, which is expected to document "students' socializing, dialoging and sense-making efforts" (Wu Horng-Jyh, 2009). The digital objects that constitute the by-products of these interactions are required to be maintained, ensuring their reliability, authenticity, accessibility and usability over time, because they are considered evidence of student learning and are used by students in the construction of a final reflective report that aids in substantiating their learning outcomes (Wu Horng-Jyh, 2009). This course was one of the InterPARES 3 case studies. The case study included an examination of a system prototype that integrated web "archiving" and annotation functions, but this is beyond the scope of this chapter, which will primarily examine the "record-ness" of the student outcomes through the lens of the archival theory discussed above – examining the implications for e-learning records and their requirements.

The second example of social media use in higher education is provided by courses for the Master of Archives and Records Administration (MARA) programme at the School of Library and Information Science (SLIS) of San Josè State University. As well as teaching students about social media and its implications for archives, the SLIS programme incorporates social media into its Master's courses and provides opportunities for students to "apply social media skills and knowledge" (Franks, 2012). The programme requires students to complete a mandatory On-line Social Networking: Technology and Tools course at the beginning of their course of study. This course is designed to introduce students to a variety of "new and emerging technologies" used in contemporary online environments, including those they will be utilizing during the programme. The course includes several social networking platforms, content and learning management systems, web conferencing as well as immersive environments and trends in social computing (Franks, 2012). Because the courses at San Josè are solely online, it is necessary for

the success of faculty and students that both are well equipped to effectively use social media and other online teaching and learning technologies. "The student experience is enhanced and community is built through the use of social media and emerging technologies in and outside of the classroom" (Franks, 2012). The suite of social media tools and technologies used in the SLIS programme range from in-house technologies to external tools, such as Second Life, Google Docs and Facebook. Students primarily work within Desire2Learn (D2L), the University's learning management system where students upload their work to a personal ePortfolio. The D2L courses that contain content are stored as inactive records by the University for five years (although if the content contains links to readings and lectures, these are not captured). Work done outside of the D2L system is recorded in the system as either a grade or a graded rubric with grade (most often the latter) (Franks, 2012).

For each of the two examples we ask what are the digital entities regarded as the records of e-learning. The answer will depend on the juridical context of the course, its intended products, its pedagogical approach, and how it defines and evaluates student learning goals within the system in which it resides – either through outcomes (products), interactions (by-products), or a combination of the two. Wu Horng-Jyh (2010) believes that "The concept of record in the eLearning space is inevitably shaped by its underlying pedagogical theories, which confluence with the perspectives of the records authors, preservers, users, and creators in defining the records in such a space" (p. 67). As we move to examine each environment from a record creating perspective, it is important to remember that the example from the Nanyang Technological University is of a blended learning environment (both online and offline), whereas the San Josè State courses are 100% online.

As already stated, Nanyang Technological University's Professional Seminar course is modeled on the theory of Constructivist Pedagogy (Wu Horng-Jyh, 2010). According to Wu Horng-Jyh (2010), changes in pedagogical practice are brought about by the affordances of new technologies. The emergence of social media has facilitated a pedagogical paradigm of participation rather than instruction. This approach shifts the focus from the teacher as a "molder" to that of the teacher as a "facilitator," with students being moved from an environment that supports a deterministic instructional design approach to one where more responsibility is placed on the students to construct their own understandings through interactions with other students and instructors in the social media space. According to Wu Horng-Jyh (2010), the instructor's role is to provide the framework and guidelines where conversations, dialogue and consensus building can occur amongst students, only intervening when necessary to aid in navigating conflict through dynamic and in-situ interventions. In Wu Horng-Jyh's eyes, this shift inevitably redefines the concept of records in a learning space (2010). In such a learning environment, what is the evidence of e-learning? The amount and quality of interactions appear to carry greater weight than the products, and as the outcomes of e-learning are no longer the sole object of evaluation, which now includes the by-products of teaching, learning and interaction, it becomes necessary to maintain and preserve the latter as well as the former according to juridical norms. However, the broader juridical context of the educational institution may support a more traditional approach versus the value placed on by-products as evidence of learning. So, as Wu Horng-Jyh (2010) suggests, with these new pedagogical functions needing to be accounted for, the question to be posed to stakeholders (including instructors, learners, record-keepers and educational institutions) is: how is the learning process to be accounted for?

As the goal of the Professional Seminar course was to develop students' "soft skills", including leadership, communication and critical/creative

thinking, successful learning would be demonstrated by the engagement of students in a vibrant collaborative community where they involve each other in serious sense-making processes (Wu Horng-Jyh, 2010). Therefore, the teacher guided students in this engagement through participation in blogs, fora and wikis, all of which were hosted on the e-learning platform edveNTUre. While participation in these social media environments was encouraged, it was not mandatory. Only attendance in class and a short 500-word paper were mandatory, as the intended objective of the course was for students to focus on interacting through reflecting on the material and engaging with one another in the social media space. The intent was to have students assist one another in group forming and community building in the social media space, with those stronger in these "soft skills" aiding those who were not, providing an opportunity for teaching and learning amongst peers. Scaffolding work was also undertaken by the instructor when necessary to aid students in establishing a successful virtual learning community, by offering advice on organizing in the blog and/or discussing in the forum (Wu Horng-Jyh, 2010)..

The Professional Seminar utilized the SECI knowledge sharing functions (Nonaka, Toyama & Konno, 2000) – Socialization, Externalization, Combination and Internalization – to "guide students through a process of authenticating self-understanding, rationalizing and articulating thoughts, and norming and connecting on consensus, and then positioning and embodying their actionable knowledge through critical reflection, achieving a spiral of truly internalized knowledge" (Wu Horng-Jyh, 2010, p. 77). As such, the social media spaces of the course (blogs, wikis and fora) were populated by entries that could then be classified according to the SECI structure utilized by the Seminar (e.g. blog entries classified under Socialization as participants interact with one another and the speaker and share and exchange views). "By identifying these records, they form the basis of the formative assessment of the students' learning process, an emphasis over the conventional summative assessments" (Wu Horng-Jyh, 2010, p. 78). Additionally, these records, when aggregated, were utilized for evaluation of the success of the structure and format of the course and to inform curriculum development.

For the Professional Seminar course it was determined that the manifestations and interactions of the students on the blogs, fora and wikis were records of the course. "The inputs are actually recorded experiences or responses resulting from the users being triggered in the engagement with other users" (Wu Horng-Jyh, 2010, p. 84). They were considered records because:

1. They have fixed form and content;
2. They have explicit linkages to other records – for instance, comments are to a post in blogs and replies are to a thread in a forum discussion, within or outside of the digital system, through a classification code associates with SECI sense-making process;
3. The documents are kept in an eLearning platform with clear administrative context;
4. Each posting in blog, forum, wiki has an unambiguous writer and addressee, while the author is the instructor who prescribed the SECI learning spaces;
5. The action associated with these records are retrospective records of a collective "performance" that are designed according to a Constructivist Pedagogy and "conducted" by the instructor of the course (p. 85).

As mentioned earlier, linkages need to be maintained in order to ensure the archival bond is explicit and remains intact and that interactions and outcomes of e-learning activities are able to function as records when necessary. For the Professional Seminar course, the blog, forum and wiki postings were classified as Socialization,

Externalization, Combination and Internalization and arranged as "SECI spirals" with such aggregations viewed as "mini-series" of records representing the learning experience as expressed by students, as well as the students' performance. The metadata applied to such records must be sufficient to ensure their authenticity (i.e. identify and integrity) and reliability, and allowing for access to these records as they are preserved over time.[9]

Having examined in detail the hybrid course delivered in Singapore, it is much easier to identify the records produced in the delivery of the San José course. As noted, this course is entirely on line, thus all the records of teaching and learning are digital entities resulting either from the interaction student-teacher and student-student (by-products of the learning activity) or students' products/assignments (outcomes of learning activities). As the American juridical context considers all digital entities captured as records as having evidentiary capacity, the programme ensures such capture through the university central Information Technology storage system. However, although the intentional capture as records of both the by-products and outcomes of e-learning ensures that they can be used as evidence of e-learning, the fact that they are kept outside the original context fails to convey the characteristics of the process. Indeed, there is no easy answer to the question that Wu Horng-Jyh (2010) asked at the beginning of the InterPARES case study: how is the learning process to be accounted for? At this time, we are unable to account for it in any accurate way. If we download by-products and outcomes to a central system we lose context, and if we leave it in cyberspace we encounter the set of issues linked to any kind of cloud computing, including those related to preservation, security, privacy and confidentiality, intellectual property and copyright, and ownership. In both cases, we might have to destroy the records of e-learning right after having verified and assessed them to avoid incurring the series of problems outlined below.

BEYOND RECORDNESS

All records resulting from the teaching, learning, research and administrative activities of higher education institutions, after having been identified as such, must be maintained and preserved for their evidentiary capacity to serve a variety of purposes, including (but not limited to) evidence of student performance and assessment, of faculty teaching and research performance, and of the institutional activities and adherence to applicable laws, policies and standards. The role educational institutions play in the building of societal culture and social memory may also be gathered from their records. Maintaining and preserving them over time requires more than just the ability to back them up, as the continued authenticity and accessibility of digital records call for on-going actions of digital preservation.

Digital Preservation

Digital preservation comprises the strategies and frameworks, policies, principles, techniques, and tools that afford for the ongoing stewardship of digital materials.

Research into digital preservation has demonstrated that it is not possible to preserve digital materials, but only the ability to reproduce them. Reproduction involves taking a variety of actions on digital objects over time. These may range from simply generating a copy of an object to recreating it, in the case of complex entities. Over time, it is necessary to either migrate the digital object to new technological environments or emulate the original one. Such actions are to be carried out over the lifetime of the digital object to ensure continuing access and use. Research has developed models of digital preservation (e.g. Open Archival Information System OAIS & Chain of Preservation COP) that can operate across communities and domains.

However, digital preservation also encompasses social and cultural conventions, which

may be manifest through acts of selection and appraisal -- what is to be kept and how it should be kept; what gets included in or excluded from the recorded memory. Additionally, it requires an understanding of the rights and responsibilities involved in ongoing preservation and access to digital records, including those related to freedom of information and protection of privacy, as well as intellectual and economic rights and treaties. The effectiveness of digital preservation is predicated on the development of and adherence to agreed upon standards, benchmarks and practices and the creation of effective information policies, which by their nature can be value-laden.

Privacy and Confidentiality

Protecting the privacy and/or anonymity of users' activities is a serious issue in the context of social media use. Because social media operate via the web over the Internet, the information stored in social media applications resides in the cloud instead of the creator's computer hard drives. Information stored in the cloud may be located in countries and continents different from those in which it originates at any given time, and this may make it subject to the local laws and standards, raising questions for information security, access and privacy. Additionally, information residing in the cloud has to be protected not only in terms of ownership, but also for *what* it is. Information stored in the cloud – whether it is personal information, scientific data or other subject matter – has particular requirements attached to its management and is accompanied by a duty of care to safeguard its contents. Unauthorized access to digital information (be it data, documents or records) is a privacy concern for faculty and students interacting through social media applications and services, as is protecting any sort of information stored on the Internet. For example, the Freedom of Information and Protection of Privacy Act (FIPPA) applies to public institutions in British Columbia, Canada. It requires public bodies to protect personal information no matter where it resides, and with limited exceptions, ensure that personal information is only stored in and accessed from inside Canada (OIPCBC, 2012). "Under FIPPA, it is an offence to store or allow access to personal information outside of Canada unless it is authorized by the individual the information is about" (OIPCBC, 2012, p. 3). Other jurisdictions have similar legislation that applies to the collection, storage and use of personal information.

A study of 136 undergraduate students (79%/106 of which were on Facebook) asked students about their interactions with faculty on the SNS. Of the 102 students who responded to the question "Do you think faculty should be on Facebook?" 66% found it acceptable, while of the remaining 33% cited issues of privacy and identity management as concerns (Hewitt & Forte, 2006). While two thirds of the students reported that they were comfortable with faculty on the site, "several students noted that student profiles often contain information they do not want professors to see" (Hewitt & Forte, 2006). The use of social media applications must examine privacy on a variety of levels – protection of privacy amongst peers/instructors within the application; protection of data and personal information within the institutional system; and protection of data and personal information on the web at large. "The social network environment makes it easy to accidentally share information to an unintended audience" (Munoz & Towner, 2011).

Utilizing third party social media applications for educational purposes may have consequences for the protection of individual privacy, confidentiality and online identity. For example, Google's new privacy policy (effective 01 March 2012) will see the company apply one policy to user information across all of its applications. Instead of being "siloed" as in the past, information from one Google application can now be applied when users engage with another application. For example, Google suggesting whom to include

in the distribution of a Google Doc based on the users with whom one has shared information in the past or the syncing of location data to inform users that they may be late for a meeting based on their entries in Google Calendar.

Unlike a closed learning management system where students are safe to "experiment without consequences" (Downes, 2007), SNS are mediated public sites where the "'conversation' may be recorded indefinitely, can be searched, replicated, and altered and may be accessed by others without the knowledge of those in the conversation" (Cain, 2008). Many students already utilize a number of social media tools for their personal or social use – to communicate with friends and family, participate in communities of common interest, etc. The identity that students have constructed in these communities may be different from the one they would choose to show classmates, faculty or administrators (Armstrong & Franklin, 2008; Cain, 2008). This is often not an issue that higher education institutions have begun to seriously address. "Anecdotally, it appears that relatively few institutions have created formal policies on how to deal with Facebook and SNS in general, let alone for specific educational purposes" (Munoz & Towner, 2011). Enlisting third party applications for use in the classroom may have broader implications for student and faculty privacy that must be considered and mitigated against, and resources should be enlisted to ensure all parties are educated on the privacy and confidentiality concerns involved in utilizing these sites.

As Munoz and Towner (2011) report, "educational uses for SNSs have critics among faculty and students;" the primary reasons cited are privacy, safety and the erosion of professional boundaries (Munoz & Towner, 2011; Cain, 2007; Griffith & Liyanage, 2008). While social media offer the opportunity for networking to occur, as Downes (2007) points out, it "makes communication hypervisible, with potentially profound consequences" (para 7). Downes (2007) argues that "in this context, managing one's public profile becomes a vital skill and this is one area where education can play an important role" (para, 7). Making use of such sites optional is not enough. As social media makes its way into the classroom there is an opportunity to engage with students and ensure they are informed, savvy users of these tools. "Students should be able to recognize that there needs to be a division of one's personal and professional identity online and find ways to protect and manage their digital selves" (Munoz & Towner, 2011).

Intellectual Property, Copyright, and Ownership

Intellectual property and copyright laws and guidelines should be considered when social media is enlisted for use in higher education. Users of SNS such as Facebook are required to grant Facebook a license to use and display the user's content. Ownership of data stored in the cloud (where the majority of external social media sites are hosted) can fall prey to ambiguous service level agreements. Moreover, the ability to retain and/or destroy records can be a serious concern when institutional records are stored in the cloud.

Preservation activities can also pose complex challenges to the intellectual rights associated with those objects. The rights of the copyright owner are attached to the authentic digital object and, specifically, to its documentary form. Economic and moral rights are affected by the long-term digital preservation actions of repetitive transformative migration or emulation. It is still unclear what the full ramifications of digital preservations actions on records are.

Economic rights, according to Michael O'Hare (1982), are those that enable the copyright owner to gain commercially from the exploitation of that work. Moral rights, according to Mira Sundara Rajan (2004), are those that the author or creator retains over the integrity of a work that disallow distortion, mutilation or other modification of the work in a way that is prejudicial to the author's

reputation; they also include the right to be associated with the work as its author by name or under a pseudonym, the right to remain anonymous, and the right to refuse that the work to be used in association with a product, service or cause in a way that is prejudicial to the author's reputation. These moral rights are particularly at risk in a social media environment, especially those linked to the outcomes of the e-learning process.

SOLUTIONS AND RECOMMENDATIONS

As we are still at the early stages in the adoption of social media in higher education, we have the opportunity to ensure that effective and appropriate policies and procedures are put in place by higher education institutions to control the use of social media in the classroom and protect the records of e-learning. Such policies and procedures should aim to the proper identification, capture, retention and management of the by-products and outcomes of e-learning activities, in order to fulfill institutional obligations and preserve institutional social memory.

These policies and procedures should also address the issues earlier identified: reliability, security, privacy and confidentiality, as well as authenticity, accuracy, economic and moral rights, freedom of information and long-term preservation and access. Service agreements with external hosts of social media tools and applications need also to consider what happens to the records of e-learning if the hosting services cease to operate. Furthermore, guidelines for faculty, students and administrators on best practices for the use of social media tools in the classroom, in research teams and when engaging with peers need to be developed and implemented. Education around the implications of social media use, particularly with regard to issues of privacy, confidentiality, ownership of data, and intellectual property needs to occur at all levels to ensure social media are used safely and appropriately, and that the records resulting from their use can be captured and preserved as evidence of actions (Minocha 2009; Munoz & Towner, 2011; Chapman & Russell, 2009).

CONCLUSION

The ubiquitous use, the ease of access and the democratic nature of social media technologies have afforded greater connection, collaboration and knowledge creation through the interactions amongst students and educators. However, educational adoption of social media has proven to occur primarily on an ad hoc basis without the guidance of clearly established policies, procedures or best practices. Social media are continually evolving as technologies change and are utilized in new ways in higher education. The by-products and outcomes of the use of social media technologies are by their very nature ephemeral and collaborative, and much is unknown about them. Examining them from an archival point of view and understanding the record related issues linked to their creation and use will aid in identifying the risks in the use of social media in the classroom as well as the best ways for addressing them.

As stated in the introduction to this chapter, the ubiquitous use of social media in education is contributing to the production of students' academic records and altering their traditional makeup, but these technologies are still in the course of development. As the desire and drive to incorporate them into educational practices grows, it is necessary to study the products that are created as a result of this adoption. Limited empirical research exists that examines the impact of social media use on the records of teaching and learning, and because their nature encourages ad hoc adoption, it is necessary to gain an understanding of the attributes of the products social media generate if management and preservation of academic records are to be successfully undertaken.

REFERENCES

Anderson, P. (2007). What is Web 2.0? Ideas, technologies and implications for education. *JISC Technology and Standards Watch*. Retrieved from http://www.jisc.org.uk/media/documents/techwatch/tsw0701b.pdf

Armstrong, J., & Franklin, T. (2008). *A review of current and developing international practice in the use of social networking (Web 2.0) in higher education*. Franklin Consulting.

Becta. (2009). *Harnessing technology: Emerging technology trends*. University of Oxford (Department of Education).

Benkler, J. (2006). *The wealth of networks: How social production transforms markets and freedom*. New Haven, CT: Yale University Press.

Boyd, D. M., & Ellison, N. B. (2007). Social network sites: Definitions, history, and scholarship. *Journal of Computer-Mediated Communication*, *13*(1). Retrieved from http://jcmc.indiana.edu/vol13/issue1/boyd.ellison.html doi:10.1111/j.1083-6101.2007.00393.x

Brown, J. S., & Adler, R. P. (2008). Minds on fire: Open education, the long tail and learning 2.0. *EDUCAUSE Review*, (January/February): 17–32.

Cain, J. (2007). Online social networking issues within academia and pharmacy education. *American Journal of Pharmaceutical Education*, *72*(1).

Chapman, A., & Russell, R. (2009). Shared infrastructure services landscape study: A survey of the use of web 2.0 tools and services in the UK HE sector. *JISC Landscape Study*. Retrieved from http://blogs.ukoln.ac.uk/jusc-sis-landscape/

Dahlstrom, E., de Boor, T., Grunwald, P., & Vockley, M. (2011). *The ECAR national study of undergraduate students and information technology*. Boulder, CO: EDUCAUSE Center for Applied Research. Retrieved from http://www.educause.edu/ecar

Dearstyne, B. W. (2007). Blogs, mashups, and wikis oh my! *The Information Management Journal,* July/August, 24-33.

Downes, S. (2007). Places to go: Facebook. *Journal of Online Education, 4*(1). Retrieved from http://www.innovateonline.info/index.php?view=article%id=517

Duranti, L. (2009). From digital diplomatics to digital records forensics. *Archivaria, 68,* 39–66.

Duranti, L. (2009a). Diplomatics. In Bates, M., Maack, M. N., & Drake, M. (Eds.), *Encyclopedia of library and information science.* New York, NY: Marcel Dekker, Inc.

Duranti, L., & Thibodeau, K. (2006). The concept of record in interactive, experiential and dynamic environments: the view of InterPARES. *Archival Science, 6,* 13–68. doi:10.1007/s10502-006-9021-7

Franks, P. (2012). *Archives and archival studies in a social media world.* 4th Annual International Symposium Unpacking the Digital Shoebox: The Future of Personal Archives.

Gerber, R. S. (2006). Mixing it up on the web: Legal issues arising from internet 'mashups'. *Intellectual Property & Technology Law Journal, 18*(8), 11–14.

Griffith, S., & Liyanage, L. (2008). An introduction to the potential of social networking sites in education. In I. Olney, G. Lefoe, J. Mantei, & J. Herrington (Eds.), *Proceedings of the Second Emerging Technologies Conference 2008,* (pp. 76-81). Wollongong, Australia: University of Wollongong.

Haythornthwaite, C., & Andrews, R. (2011). *E-Learning: Theory and practice.* London, UK: Sage.

Haythornthwaite, C., & Wellman, B. (1998). Work, friendship and media use for information exchange in a networked organization. *Journal of the American Society for Information Science American Society for Information Science, 49*(12), 1101–1114. doi:10.1002/(SICI)1097-4571(1998)49:12<1101::AID-ASI6>3.0.CO;2-Z

Hew, K. F. (2011). Students' and teachers' use of Facebook. *Computers in Human Behavior, 27,* 662–676. doi:10.1016/j.chb.2010.11.020

Hewitt, A., & Forte, A. (2006). Crossing boundaries: Identity management and student/faculty relationships on Facebook. *Proceedings of the 2006 CSCW,* Banff, Alberta.

Huijser, H. (2008). Exploring the educational potential of social networking sites: The fine line between exploiting opportunities and unwelcome imposition. *Studies in Learning. Evaluation Innovation and Development, 5*(3), 45–54.

Hunter, J. (2009). A landscape study of shared infrastructure services in the Australian academic sector. *JISC Landscape Study.* Retrieved from http://ie-repository.jisc.ac.uk/439/1/Aust-SIS-Landscape-report-final.pdf

International Research on Permanent Authentic Records in Electronic Systems. (n.d.). Retrieved from www.interpares.org

Jbmurray. (2008). *Was introducing Wikipedia to the classroom an act of madness leading only to mayhem if not murder?* In Wikipedia. Retrieved February, 14, 2012 from http://en.wikipedia.org/wiki/User:Jbmurray/Madness

Kaplan, A., & Haenlein, M. (2010). Users of the world, unite! The challenges and opportunities of social media. *Business Horizons, 53*(1), 59–68. doi:10.1016/j.bushor.2009.09.003

Kolek, E. A., & Saunders, D. (2008). Online disclosure: An empirical examination of undergraduate Facebook profiles. *NASPA Journal, 45*(1), 1–25.

Kolowich, S. (2010, September 7). Wikipedia for credit. *Inside Higher Ed.* Retrieved from http://www.insidehighered.com/news/2010/09/07/wikipedia

Madge, C., Meek, J., Wellens, J., & Hooley, T. (2009). Facebook, social integration and informal learning at university: It is more for socializing and talking to friends about work than for actually doing work. *Learning, Media and Technology, 34*(2), 141–155. doi:10.1080/17439880902923606

Mazer, J. P., Murphy, R. E., & Simonds, C. J. (2009). The effects of teacher self-disclosure via Facebook on teacher credibility. *Learning, Media and Technology, 34*(2), 175–183. doi:10.1080/17439880902923655

Meehan, J. (2006). Toward an archival concept of evidence. *Archivaria, 61,* 127–146.

Melville, D., et al. (2009). Higher education in a web 2.0 world. *Committee of Inquiry into the Changing Learner Experience.* Retrieved from http://www.jisc.ac.uk/media/documents/publications/heweb20rptv1.pdf

Minocha, S. (2009). *A study on the effective use of social software by further and higher education in the UK to support student learning and engagement.* JISC. Retrieved from http://www.jisc.ac.uk/media/documents/projects/effective-use-of-social-software-in-education-finalreport.pdf

Munoz, C., & Towner, T. (2011). Back to the wall: Facebook in the college classroom. *First Monday, 16*(12).

National Archives and Records Administration (NARA). (2010). *Implications of recent web technologies for NARA web guidance.* Retrieved from http://www.archives.gov/recordsmgmt/initiatives/web-tech.html

O'Hare, M. (1982). Copyright and the protection of economic rights. *Journal of Cultural Economics, 6*(1), 33–48. doi:10.1007/BF00162292

O'Reilly, T. (2005). *What is Web 2.0? Design patterns and business models for the next generation of software.* O'Reilly website. Retrieved from http://oreilly.com/web2/archive/what-is-web-20.html

Office of the Information and Privacy Commissioner of British Columbia (OIPCBC). (2012). *Cloud computing guidelines for public bodies.* OIPBC.

Roblyer, M. D. (2010). Findings on Facebook in higher education: A comparison of college faculty and student uses and perceptions of social networking sites. *The Internet and Higher Education, 13,* 134–140. doi:10.1016/j.iheduc.2010.03.002

Shepherd, E., & Yeo, G. (2003). *Managing records: A handbook of principles and practice.* London, UK: Facet Publishing. doi:10.1108/00220410310506349

Sundara Rajan, M. (2004). Moral rights in information technology: A new kind of personal right? *International Journal of Law & Information Technology, 12*(1), 32–54. doi:10.1093/ijlit/12.1.32

Wu Horng-Jyh, P. (2010). Towards the preservation of web records: A case study of the capture, arrangement and description of a professional seminar eLearning space. *Archivi, 4*(1), 65–93.

Young, J. R. (2008). When professors create social network for classes, some students see creepy treehouse. *The Chronicle of Higher Education.*

ADDITIONAL READING

Brown, J. S., & Adler, R. P. (2008). Minds on fire: Open education, the long tail and learning 2.0. *EDUCAUSE Review,* (January/February): 17–32.

Duranti, L. (1997). The archival bond. *Archives and Museum Informatics, 11,* 213–218. doi:10.1023/A:1009025127463

Duranti, L. (1998). *Diplomatics: New uses for an old science*. Lanham, MD: Society of American Archivists, Association of Canadian Archivists, & Scarecrow Press.

Haythornthwaite, C., & Andrews, R. (2011). *E-learning theory and practice*. London, UK: Sage Publications.

Sundara Rajan, M. (2011). *Moral rights: Principles, practices and new technology*. New York, NY: Oxford University Press. doi:10.1087/20120212

KEY TERMS AND DEFINITIONS

Accessibility: The availability and usability of information.

Accuracy: The degree to which data, information, documents or records are precise, correct, truthful, free of error or distortion, or pertinent to the matter.

Archival Bond: The network of relationships that each record has with the records belonging in the same archival aggregation.

Authenticity: The trustworthiness of a record as a record; i.e., the quality of a record that is what it purports to be and that is free from tampering or corruption.

Chain of Preservation: A system of controls that extends over the entire lifecycle of records in order to ensure their identity and integrity over time.

Evidence: All the means by which any alleged matter of fact, the truth of which is submitted to investigation, is established or disproved.

Identity: The whole of the characteristics of a document or a record that uniquely identify it and distinguish it from any other document or record. With integrity, a component of authenticity.

Integrity: The ability of a record to convey the message it was intended to communicate when generated.

Reliability: The trustworthiness of a record as a statement of fact. It exists when a record can stand for the fact it is about, and is established by examining the completeness of the record's form and the amount of control exercised on the process of its creation.

Trustworthiness: The accuracy, reliability and authenticity of a record.

ENDNOTES

[1] The physical or juridical person assigned the electronic address in which the record has been generated and/or sent.

[2] The physical or juridical person(s) having the authority and capacity to issue the record or in whose name or by whose command the record has been issued.

[3] The physical or juridical person(s) having the authority and capacity to articulate the content of the record. It may be the same name as the author and/or originator of the record.

[4] The physical or juridical person(s) to whom the record is directed or for whom the record is intended.

[5] The physical or juridical person in whose *fonds* the record exists.

[6] "Digital components" are digital entities that either contain one or more records or are contained in the record and require a specific preservation measure.

[7] See for example Hilary Jenkinson, *A Manual of Archival Administration* (London: Percy, Lund, Humphries, and Co., 1937), p. 97 et seq.; Giorgio Cencetti, "Il fondamento teorico della dottrina archivistica," *Archivi* II, VI (1939): 40; and Elio Lodolini, *Archivistica. Principi e Problemi*, 6th edition (Milano: Franco Angeli, 1992), pp. 132 and 149. See also Elio Lodolini, "The War of Independence of Archivists," *Archivaria* 28 (Summer 1989): 38, 41.

8   An archival fonds is the whole of the records that a physical or juridical person accumulates by reason of its function or activity. (www.interpares.org)

9   Identity and integrity metadata according to InterPARES (www.interpares.org) include: Identity metadata: names of the persons concurring in its creation; date(s) and time(s) of issuing, creation and transmission; the matter or action in which it participates; the expression of its archival bond; documentary form; digital presentation; the indication of any attachment(s); digital signature; name of the person responsible for the business matter. Integrity metadata: name(s) of handling persons over time; name of person responsible for keeping the record; indication of annotations; indication of technical changes indication of presence or removal of digital signature; time of planned removal from the system; time of transfer to a custodian; time of planned deletion; existence and location of duplicates outside the system.

Section 4
The Impact of Social Media Technologies on the Academic Environment

Chapter 15
The Influence of Twitter on the Academic Environment

Martin Ebner
Graz University of Technology, Austria

ABSTRACT

In the last few years, microblogging has become a phenomenon of our daily lives. Communicating, sharing media files, as well as acting on digital social communities platforms using mobile devices assist our everyday activities in a complete new way. Therefore, it is very reasonable that academic environments are influenced arbitrarily too. In this publication, different settings for the use of microblogging are pointed out – for teaching and learning as well as for further scientific purposes such as professional conferences. It can be summarized that there are different possibilities to use microblogging in an academic context; each of them are new advantages for the academic life. The publication gives a short overview and a first insight into the various ways to use microblogging.

INTRODUCTION

Dominating platforms of the World Wide Web of the last years belong to the type called social networks. The most popular ones are Facebook, Twitter, and the newcomer Google+. First of all, a short look at the characteristics of a social network must be taken to understand the typical idea of such systems. According to Koch & Richter (Koch & Richter, 2008) social software is a web based information system of the Web 2.0 generation, which allows interaction within a community in various ways. In contrast to Web 1.0 technologies users are made possible to search, find, and connect to each other as well as exchange multimedia content in a very handsome and easy way. Schmid (Schmidt, 2006) stated that the software itself is not social per se; the people who are using it collaboratively are the moving power to make such

DOI: 10.4018/978-1-4666-2851-9.ch015

software become social. Koch & Richter (Koch & Richter, 2008) also defined the three crucial components of social software:

- **Identity and Network Management:** Allows user to create his/her own profile as well as the possibility to connect with each other.
- **Information Management:** Allows user to exchange, find, and rate their multimedia data.
- **Interaction and Communication:** Allows communication and interaction between users in various ways.

In the last years many different social networks were introduced to the World Wide Web community. Actually it has become hard to categorize them. Ebner & Lorenz (Ebner & Lorenz, 2012) carried out a model according to the described three crucial components. Each factor

displayed in the model represents one axis in a three-dimensional cube. Figure 1 shows different information systems like weblogs, wikis, or even microblogging systems with their representation and relation to social networks. For example, social bookmarking systems and wikis are excellent platforms for delivering information but of less interest for providing identity management or interaction amongst users. In opposite, instant messaging services (like MSN or Skype) allow excellent communication but are not appropriate for presentation of information.

Microblogs are very close to social networks according to the definition pointed out in Figure 1 due to their main components such as making friends, becoming ones followers, creating a user profile, and interacting with users via posts and direct messages. Furthermore various multimedia data can be uploaded in order to exchange it with other users (Haewoon et al., 2010). Templeton (Templeton, 2008) defines microblogging as a

Figure 1. Definition and overview of social software according to Ebner & Lorenz (2012)

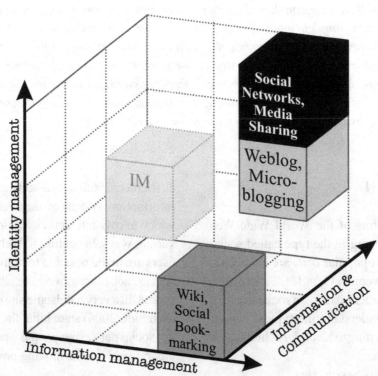

small-scale form of blogging made up from short, succinct messages, used by both consumers and businesses to share news, post status updates, and carry on conversations. Therefore a clear separation from weblogs (Rosenbloom, 2004) can be done, which are more used to write larger online essays with a personal touch to a specific topic.

Maybe the most well-known feature of microblogging systems is the restriction to 140 signs for each post remembering the short-message service of mobile phones. Nevertheless it must be asked, why this service gains such popularity and attracts so many active users. One of the success factors for sure is the simplicity to share ideas, daily situations, as well as multimedia files with anyone in the world. Assisted by mobile phones and the growing popularity of mobile Internet access the service becomes ubiquitous available. So, since 2007 a complete new way to interact and communicate with people independently of time and place has been established. The so called "living within a big personal information stream" becomes reality and is nowadays part of the information society. Dealing with information was never easier in the history of mankind in principle.

Of course, this progress influences also the work of researchers and teachers. Therefore this contribution provides an insight into related research studies into the microblogging platform Twitter in an academic environment. After a short introduction to Twitter explicit examples are given to demonstrate the possibilities for microblogging systems to be useful for teaching and learning as well as for daily research work. The results are discussed and summarized in the last chapters.

TWITTER

Twitter was not the first microblogging platform offered for free registration, but it is the most well-known and most used one so far. Twitter's weblog states the impressive numbers of 140 mil-

lion tweets sent per day in March 2011, or more than 460000 created accounts per day within the same time (Twitter, 2011). Finally the number of mobile users increased from 2010 – 2011 with 182%. A similar growth can only be noticed for the other two big social networks Facebook and Google+. But those both systems are not typical microblogging platforms at all.

Twitter and other microblogging platforms are characterized by:

- **A Concept of Shortness:** The number of signs for each post (in case of Twitter it is called "tweet") is usually limited to 140 signs.
- **A Concept of Friends and Followers:** Friends are accounts I am following and I am followed back by so called followers. There is no concept of a strong friendship; anyone can follow anyone in principle.
- **A Concept of Information Presentation:** Tweets of friends are presented just in an endless list with the newest post at the top. This kind of information stream can be split into different groups.
- **A Concept of Openness:** In general, all posts on Twitter are public. Users can hide their profiles, but it is more or less unusual.
- **A Concept of Web Services:** Already in a very early phase Twitter allowed third-party applications to connect with the service using a provided Application Interface (API). A high number of additional Twitter applications have been developed and made Twitter even much more powerful.

Overall it can be concluded that indeed a new service for a new kind of communication has been invented by microblogging. First scientific studies point out the communication aspect (Ebner & Schiefner, 2008) (McFedries, 2007). Beside the new communication culture other publications focus the reasons why people are using Twitter

(Java et al., 2007): for daily chats, for conversation, for sharing information, and for reporting news. Boyd (Boyd et al, 2010) mentioned the importance of so-called re-tweets for the social network. By repeating a message this message is offered to another network of followers and in that way distributed further. The power of re-tweeting could be massively monitored for example by the death of Michael Jackson (Kim & Gilbers, 2009), the election of Barack Obama, and further political events of great importance (e.g. revolutions such as the Arab Spring). Due to the fact that people are repeating messages or sending tweets using a special "hashtag" a massive information stream especially on the focused (hashtagged) item can be produced.

TWITTER IN ACADEMIC SETTINGS

Of course, this new communication possibility inspired the interest of researchers. A number of different studies appeared, asking, how Twitter can be used for learning (Grosseck & Holotescu, 2008) (Costa et al., 2008) or for further academic scopes (Reinhardt 2009). In the following, different academic scenarios are described, exemplifying the way Twitter has been used whether for teaching and learning purposes or for the researcher´s daily work.

Twitter as Tool for Mass Education

- **Didactical Approach:** Use of microblogging to allow instant feedback during face-to-face lecturing
- **Technical Issues:** Use of lecture hashtags to allow a collection of posts on a so called "Twitterwall" (http://twitterwall.tugraz.at)

Mass education is mainly a problem of Higher Education . Often one lecturer has to teach more than 100 students in big lecture hall. A well-known problem is that the interaction between teachers and students decreases therefore or even does not happen anymore. Anderson (Anderson et al, 2003) pointed out the three main reasons for that:

- **Feedback Lag:** With the number of attendees the feedback is dramatically increasing
- **Student Apprehension:** Students simply fear to get blamed by asking questions or doing some other interactions
- **Single Speaker Paradigm:** The only-one speaker syndrome leads to less active participation

There are different technological possibilities to overcome these problems, mainly through so-called Audience Response Systems (ARS). Such systems are a combination of hard- and software that allow giving the auditorium instant feedback by polling. The hardware mostly consists of a special developed "clicker" sending the signal to a server that is interpreting the answers and providing the result. With other words, installing such systems in huge lecture rooms is nearly impossible because of high hardware costs (every student would need a hardware clicker on his/her own) as well as high efforts for organization (the hardware must be given to learners each lecture and collected afterwards). Furthermore such systems can only be used for quizzes or polls, textual feedback is not possible.

At Graz University of Technology (TU Graz) a research work has been started to enhance the lecture room interactivity in a meaningful way. It was specified that learners must be able to use their own devices and the existing infrastructure environment of the lecture halls. Too, the application must be as simple to handle as possible. Due to the fact that Twitter is a daily used, primarily mobile application that is little limited by different devices a Twitterwall has been developed (Ebner, 2011).

By displaying the Twitterwall during the lecture students nowadays are able to ask questions, comment lecture content, or simply apply it for example by providing. On the left side of Figure 2 all tweets within a defined time frame are shown (e.g. the time the lecture takes place). On the right side all tweets that contain the lecture's hashtag (e.g. #gadi2011) and an additional hashtag (e.g. #question) are displayed. With this application it becomes easily possible to collect tweets and filter them according to different needs as well as to enhance the lecture interactivity. The first practical experiences showed that students use the Twitterwall especially to ask questions in a more or less anonymous way and to collect hyperlinks relevant to the lecture. The lecture's feedback was very positive due to the fact that the audience's response definitely increases compared to prior years. The next release of the Twitterwall will also allow to post without a Twitter account and also to rate tweets of other students to rank more important questions.

Twitter as Tool for Discussing beyond Face-to-Face Lectures

- **Didactical Approach:** Use of microblogging to post status updates of activities concerning the lecture outside classrooms
- **Technical Issues:** Use of an own microblogging platform (http://mblog.tugraz.at)

Another didactical approach is the use of microblogging to stay in contact with learners beyond the traditional face-to-face lectures. Especially Twitter with its communicational quality allows students to post status updates of their current activities concerning the lecture and report about what they are currently doing. In this case, lecturers can interact with students in real time, answer questions when they occur and discuss them.

Ebner (Ebner et al, 2010a) showed in a practical study that within a time period of 6 weeks students were using the microblogging platform very extensively. More than 11.000 recorded and analyzed posts (tweets) result in the fact that in

Figure 2. TU Graz Twitterwall (http://twitterwall.tugraz.at)

average each student wrote 7,5 tweets each day. Due to the fact that most of all updates were relevant to the lecture and served as assistance to students' communication, it was pointed out that microblogging assists the communication behavior in a very new way.

Figure 3 points out that "course-related work" posts are a minority – not more than 10-20% each day. Vice versa, updates belonging to the discussion subject, or just for small talk, or private content cover 60-70% of all updates per day. The lecturers as well as the authors of microblogging posts keep the dialogue beyond the classroom running which allows process-oriented learning and helps students to keep in touch with each other as well with the lecturers.

Furthermore, more than 60% of all posts contain the sign @, which means that the post is directly related to another person and more or less a personal message to him/her. This means that theses posts are from a directed communicative nature.

Finally, oral evaluations pointed out that many users unfamiliar with microblogging systems report an unwieldy information flow, known as information overload. So the need of different strategies for consuming massive information becomes an important task. Otherwise this kind

of information stream can also be described as constant murmuring in the background where the user takes an active part when he/she wants to do so.

The function of communication by this understanding is exclusively social – an exchange of trivial information. Malinowski (1922) referred to this as a "phatic function". It serves to keep in contact with others and as an assurance of group identity (Honeycutt, 2009).

Twitter as Tool for Exchange of Lecture Content (GADI)

- **Didactical Approach:** Use of microblogging to collect and exchange relevant lecture content in a fast and easy way
- **Technical Issues:** Use of a microblogging platform (e.g. http://mblog.tugraz.at) and a defined hashtag

According to that approach another practical example was carried out in the lecture called "Social Aspects of Information Technology". This course is an obligatory one for students of informatics during their bachelor program. It educates students to have a critical view on the ways informatics influence human society today. More than 200

Figure 3. Communication by subject (Ebner et al., 2010a)

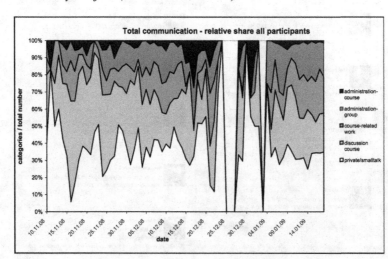

students attend this course every year to listen to about 17 presentations held by different experts in different fields: Topics are for example Human Computer Interaction, eHealth, Google, weblogs as well as virtual worlds or the use of informatics in civil engineering.

In recent years, students had to write two essays about topics of their own choice to pass the lecture. Based on the strict scientific rules a high amount of text documents had been composed. The big drawback of this method is that nobody is reading the text of the students but the teachers. From a very critical point of view it can be argued that the students´ work more or less equaled a concentrated version of the experts´ presentations. Therefore nearly no further discussion on the topics took place during the whole lecture. Hence a new didactical concept was needed to increase students' activity. Therefore four groups were introduced – Scientific Writer (still have to write a short essay), Scientific Reviewer (have to review the essays of the Scientific Writers), Blogger (have to write short blog posts about the topic of their choice) and Mircoblogger (have to write microblogs about the topic of their choice).

Figure 4 displays the relation between the four groups. With a special eye on the microblogging group it can be pointed out that these students have to search the Web for interesting and relevant content concerning the defined topics. Furthermore they have close contact to the blogger group for discussions and exchange of interesting information. Ebner and Maurer (Ebner & Maurer, 2008) stated that this didactical approach leads to a better performance of the course´s outcome. Furthermore students that are member of the microblogging group gave a very positive feedback; they reported that they felt constantly involved during the whole time period of the lecture. A pencil based evaluation carried out amongst the students resulted in the very interesting aspect that due to the fact that students read other contributions more often also informal learning effects occur as a result of blogging and microblogging activities.

Ebner and Maurer concluded in their final paper (Ebner & Maurer, 2008) that mainly three effects occurred:

- **Reflection:** Students attending the microblogging group wrote more reflective contributions in a personal and subjective style
- **Discussion:** Students of the blogging and microblogging groups commented more often than their colleagues of the other

Figure 4. Communication by category (Ebner & Maurer, 2008)

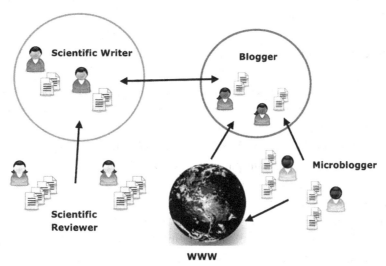

groups; their feedback and statements provided were more detailed.

- **Quality:** Teachers mentioned that the quality of the contributions increased arbitrarily to former years at all.

Twitter as Tool for Documentation and Retrieve of Information

- **Didactical Approach:** Use of microblogging for documentation of lecture issues or other relevant content
- **Technical Issues:** Use of a tool that allows collection of tweets, to store collected tweets offline and provide a search function (http://grabeeter.tugraz.at)

A very simple possibility to collect information is to use microblogging streams of different sources. In our contex different sources are meant to be events or lectures, a learning unit or simply a traditional face-to-face lecture with writing on blackboards, or showing something on the Internet, or using the projector for presenting learning content. In that way events are even documented on base of their microblogging activities. Due to the fact that students own smartphones or similar devices, it becomes quite easy to take pictures, browse hyperlinks, or simply take some notes during the lecture. For the later learning phase it would be advantageous to have just one application providing and organizing all notes taken in the course of an event. So the research idea was to develop a web-based application that can also be used offline for information retrieval and knowledge discovery based on a micro-content system like Twitter. In 2010 the application called "Grabeeter" (http://grabeeter.tugraz.at) has been launched. Grabeeter consists of two main parts (Mühlburger et al., 2010). The first part is a web application that retrieves tweets and user information from Twitter using the official Twitter API. The second part of Grabeeter consists of a client application developed in JavaFX technology for accessing the stored information on a client side.

Figure 5 shows a screenshot of the web application Grabeeter of a Twitter user. Once a user is registered within the application each single tweet of the user will be stored automatically in the Grabeeter database and can be accessed online via the web application as well as offline with the client application. On the right sidebar an export possibility of all tweets of the user is offered in the standard formats XML and JSON. An API allows third party applications to use the stored tweets for other purposes. Finally a short statistic shows how many posts of all tweets ever posted on Twitter are currently stored. With the help of Grabeeter the following approaches were made possible:

- Micro-content (e.g. a tweet) is achievable offline due to the fact that any tweet can be retrieved at anytime from a local hard-drive
- Micro-content is storable in a way that the user can distinguish between different events
- Micro-content is searchable along keywords, hashtags, time frames as well as different entities (URLs, @ ...)

Due to these facts Grabeeter become an application used by more than 1500 users very extensively to document their events especially in a learning or research context. Different research studies pointed out that also monitoring events became an interesting variant to use Grabeeter (Ebner et al., 2010b). Finally Twitter became also a useful tool to spread and store scientific messages (Letierce et al., 2010).

Twitter as Tool for Academic Conferences

A similar approach can be gained using the application called "Twitterwall". With Twitterwall the interaction in a huge lecture hall can be enhanced. But Twitterwall is for the usage during academic conferences too in order to collect and filter mi-

Figure 5. Grabeeter – Web application

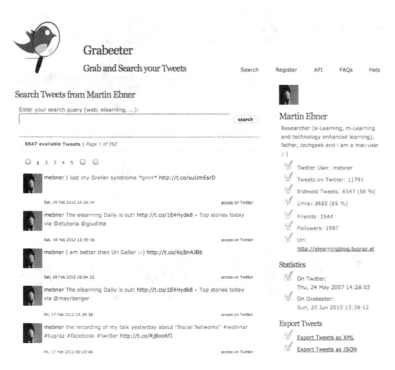

croblogging content. In 2008 (Ebner, 2009) for the first time, during the EdMedia conference tweets including the defined hashtag (#edmedia08) were collected to enhance the conference by virtual statements, opinions, pictures, hyperlinks, or just private discussion among conference participants. This special Twitter stream was displayed on several walls with simple projectors and screens. Besides those walls located at meeting points also a projection of the stream beside the keynote slides was provided. It could be shown that the "murmuring of the audience" during the talks made visible as well as additional information posted enhanced the live talk in a way never done before. A research study (Ebner, 2009) carried out that the audience use Twitter for comments to the presentation, for discussion, for collection of additional hyperlinks, and repeating statements.

Figure 6 gives an impression of the setting at EdMedia 2008. Since then the Twitterwall has become a standard surplus for every keynote speech at further EdMedia conferences and other conferences too. Furthermore the number of tweets regarding the conference did not only increase during the conference but also before and after the event (Ebner & Reinhardt, 2010). Hence it can be noticed that social networking turned out to be just more than a professional tool for communication during events. Figure 7 shows the result of a survey amongst participants of conferences (Reinhardt et al., 2009). Besides communicating with others, resources are shared through tweets, parallel discussions/events are followed, notes are jotted down, the online presence is established and enhanced, and organizational questions are raised. Figure 7 represents the main reasons why the surveyed conference delegates used Twitter while attending the learning event.

Microblogging at conferences is an additional way of discussing presented topics and exchanging additional information. It is not limited to the face-to-face audience or the location of the conference. Microblogging virtually allows anyone to actively participate in the thematic

Figure 6. Twitter stream beside keynote presentation at EdMedia 2008

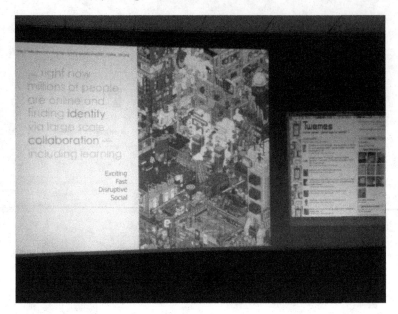

debates. Different research studies (Ebner, 2009) (Reinhardt et al., 2009) point out that several conference speakers and attendees are using Twitter for various purposes. Nowadays microblogging often is necessary to meet participants' needs for communication during academic events. Reinhardt (2009b) also pointed out the increasing dynamic of academic communities using social networks for their communication.

Twitter as Tool for Semantic Profiling and Visualization

A very new approach is to use posts for semantic profiling or keyword extraction to visualize crucial event topics.

As described before, conference participants tweet about what they have noticed, what they have remarked as interesting for their own needs.

Figure 7. Purposes of using Twitter by attendees (role) at conferences (Reinhardt et al., 2009)

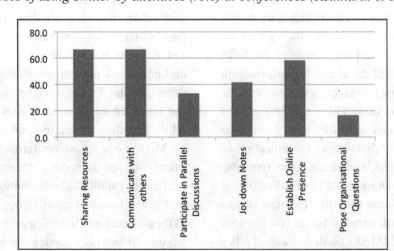

What if we could connect these users by using this information? An application is needed for a profiling of researchers. The fact that the data produced in social networks can have true value if properly annotated and interlinked between different services. It can be done by choosing community approved ontologies and linked open data resources. A second requirement is to create a suitable interface for further treatment of that information.

Using the described Grabeeter API an application to allow researchers on Twitter to connect with each other regarding to their profiles and interests has been developed, it is called "Researcher Affinity Browser" (De Vocht et al., 2011).

Figure 8 shows a screenshot of the Researcher Affinity Browser. The left column tells the different affinity facets that can be explored. The center view displays the results in a grid, an affinity plot, and a map. Details about a person and the person´s different affinities are to be seen in the bottom zone.

The Researcher Affinity Browser application retrieves a list of relevant users using the Researcher profiling API. The results are a current snapshot, not static data. Every time users produce new content on social networks, the analyzed data evolves with it. The relevance is measured according to the number of common entities (thus affinities) that are shared with the user. The different affinity facets are displayed on the left. Within the demo version users can explore three types of affinities: conferences, tags, and mentions. Activating a certain affinity narrows down and filters the list of matching persons.

Users can explore their matches in several ways. First there is the result table that displays detailed information about each person and how many affinities are shared. Second there is a map view and an affinity plot synchronized with the result table. The purpose of the map is to visualize the locations of the affiliations of the found persons. The affinity plot visualizes in a quick overview how "good" the affinity to the user is. One dimension shows the mentions, the other dimension shows the tags. The more to the top right corner a person's dot is plotted, the more affinity there is to the user.

Finally, users can double click on any person within the result list to get a tab that displays a profile with more information and allows them to get more insight into certain affinities of that person. They can also click on contact links to get in touch with that person. For example, if the profile of someone is extracted from Twitter, a link to the Twitter profile will be displayed.

Figure 8. Researcher Affinity Browser (http://affinitybrowser.semanticprofiling.net/)

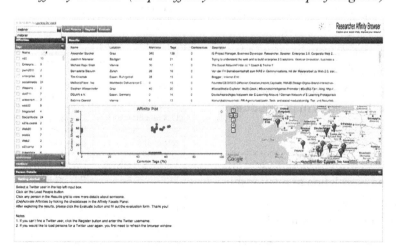

This application aims at gaining more knowledge and getting usable social data out of microblogs with a framework driven methodology based upon semantic web standards and tools. Some other efforts deal with the extraction of keywords of tweets and try to visualize them in a meaningful way to get a clue about what people are writing, who is writing, and which topics are focused (Ebner et al., 2011a). With the help of semantic web standards and linked data social networks like twitter will help to combine data in a complete new way as well as offering new insights and dependencies (Bojärs et al., 2008).

DISCUSSION

Twitter as well as microblogging in principle can be used in very different ways to enhance academic communication and cooperation. Table 1 gives a short overview about the described different research studies and points out the approaches used as well as its technical realization by TU Graz.

Table 1 points out that microblogging can be used for lecturing as well as for research purposes. All cases in common are that the possibility of updating a status online is not only a fast way but also a way to express feelings, statements or comments on other thoughts. So the nature of microblogging is primarily about communication between people of same interests (at academic conferences) or people with the same goal (lecture).

After thoroughly research studies over a long time period some crucial factors for using microblogging in academic environments can be carried out. It can be also seen as a kind of preconditions to get the community running:

1.   **Mobility:** Between microblogging and mobility is a strong correlation or relationship. Different research studies[1] pointed out that more than 50% of all users mostly access Twitter with a mobile device. Therefore microblogging is heavily used on the go or on the move as well as during waiting times. The foreground is more or less to get information from the stream or to post anything from a location. Smartphones with an on-board camera offer a very interesting option to share something with the community. Therefore especially for this purpose programmed apps are nowadays available (for example Instagram is a mobile photo community, which can only be used and shared with mobile phones) and allow us to deal with pictures in real time.

2.   **Communication:** Microblogging allows us to communicate in a short and efficient way as pointed out in different studies (Ebner et al., 2010). In the nature of a mobile society contact to each other is an important precondition. This allows to keep in touch with colleagues, teachers as well as students for exchanging thoughts, pictures, and statements or simply to ask questions.

Table 1. Overview about usage of microblogging in academic context

Academic environment	Approach	Technical implementation
Enhance interaction for mass education	Allow anonymous posts on a Twitterwall	http://twitterwall.tugraz.at
Discussion beyond face-to-face lecture	Provide a Twitter channel for communication	http://twitter.com + lecture hashtag
Exchange lecture content	Provide a Twitter channel or install an own platform	http://twitter.com + lecture hashtag
Documentation and information retrieval	Use an application that allows collection of posts	http://grabeeter.tugraz.at
Enhance academic conferences	Provide Twitter-walls at conferences for exchange	http://twitterwall.tugraz.at + conference hashtag
Become friend of researchers with similar interests	Semantic profiling	http://affinity-browser.semanticprofiling.net/

3. **Collection:** Finally a very interesting possibility is offered through microblogging, the use of hashtags, and the search possibility. A community (for example lecture participants) can save bookmarks, pictures or even videos by using an event hashtag. Because of the simple possibility to do such posts this is maybe one of the most effective ways to enhance lectures as well as conferences.

CONCLUSION

Mircoblogging became part of our daily life as well as other social network activities (Ebner et al., 2011b). Today it is quite normal do use a smartphone for writing posts, sharing photos or simply to communicate with a worldwide (academic) community. From this perspective the use of Twitter or similar software in higher education as well as academic context must be taken into account. As shown in this publication there are various possibilities to enhance lectures or scientific events (conferences) through sharing and collecting related content. Based on different research studies (Costa et al., 2008) (Grosseck & Holotescu, 2008) (Ebner et al., 2010a) this field of research seems well progressed – the next research step should point to semantic analyses of social networks, to address questions that can be answered in an implicit way. For example, what is the post of a specific person about, how can be a person assisted by linked data because of his/her posts. First research attempts were already done to combine people with same interest – researchers, teachers as well as learners (Thonhauser et al., 2012).

Microblogging is primarily about communication and we have to think how we can assist it in a meaningful way.

REFERENCES

Anderson, R. J., Anderson, R., Vandegrift, T., Wolfman, S., & Yasuhara, K. (2003). Promoting interaction in large classes with computer-mediated feedback. In *Designing for Change in Networked Learning Environments, Proceedings of CSCL 2003*, Bergen, (pp. 119-123).

Bojärs, U., Breslin, J., Finn, A., & Decker, S. (2008) Using the Semantic Web for linking and reusing data across Web 2.0 communities. *The Journal of Web Semantics, Special Issue on the Semantic Web and Web 2.0.*

boyd, d., Golder, S., & Lotan, G. (2010). Tweet, tweet, retweet: Conversational aspects of retweeting on twitter. In *Proceedings of the HICSS-43 Conference*, January 2010.

Costa, C., Beham, G., Reinhardt, W., & Sillaots, M. (2008). Microblogging in technology enhanced learning: A use-case inspection of PPE summer school 2008. In: *Proceedings of the 2nd SIRTEL Workshop on Social Information Retrieval for Technology Enhanced Learning.*

De Vocht, L., Selver, S., Ebner, M., & Mühlburger, H. (2011). Semantically driven social data aggregation interfaces for research 2.0. In *11th International Conference on Knowledge Management and Knowledge Technologies* (pp. 1-10).

Ebner, M. (2009). Introducing live microblogging: How single presentations can be enhanced by the mass. *Journal of Research in Innovative Teaching, 2*(1), 91–100.

Ebner, M. (2011). Is Twitter a tool for mass-education? *4th International Conference on Student Mobility and ICT*, Vienna, (pp. 1-6).

Ebner, M., Altmann, T., & Selver, S. (2011a). @ twitter analysis of #edmedia10– is the #informationstream usable for the #mass. *Form@re, 74*, 1–11.

Ebner, M., Lienhardt, C., Rohs, M., & Meyer, I. (2010a). Microblogs in higher education – A chance to facilitate informal and process oriented learning? *Computers & Education, 56*(1). ISSN 0360-1315

Ebner, M., & Lorenz, A. (2012). Web 2.0 als Basistechnologien für CSCL-Umgebungen. In Haake, J., Schwabe, G., & Wessner, M. (Eds.), *CSCL-Lernumgebungen. München, Germany.* Oldenburg.

Ebner, M., & Maurer, H. (2008). Can microblogs and weblogs change traditional scientific writing? *Proceedings of E-Learn 2008*, Las Vegas, (pp. 768-776).

Ebner, M., Mühlburger, H., Schaffert, S., Schiefner, M., Reinhardt, W., & Wheeler, S. (2010b). *Get Granular on Twitter - Tweets from a conference and their limited usefulness 1 for non-participants* (pp. 102–113). Key Competences in the Knowledge Society.

Ebner, M., Nagler, W., & Schön, M. (2011b). The Facebook generation boon or bane for e-learning at universities? In *World Conference on Educational Multimedia, Hypermedia and Telecommunications; 2011*, (pp. 3549–3557).

Ebner, M., & Reinhard, W. (2009). Social networking in scientific conferences – Twitter as tool for strengthen a scientific community. Workshop Science 2.0 for TEL, ECTEL, 2009.

Ebner, M., & Schiefner, M. (2008). Microblogging - More than fun? In I. A. Sánchez & P. Isaías (Eds.), *Proceedings of IADIS Mobile Learning Conference 2008*, Portugal, (pp. 155-159).

Grosseck, G., & Holotescu, C. (2008). Can we use Twitter for educational activities? In *Proceedings of the 4th International Scientific Conference eLSE eLearning and Software for Education*, April 2008

Haewoon, K., Changhyun, L., Hosung, P., & Moon, S. (2010). What is Twitter: A social network or a news media? *Proceedings of the 19th International World Wide Web (WWW) Conference*, April 26-30, 2010, Raleigh NC (USA), April 2010. Retrieved from http://an.kaist.ac.kr/traces/WWW2010.html

Honeycutt, C., & Herring, S. C. (2009). Beyond microblogging: Conversation and collaboration via Twitter. *Hawaii International Conference on System Sciences, 42nd Hawaii International Conference on System Sciences*, (pp. 1-10).

Java, A., Song, X., Finin, T., & Tseng, B. (2007). Why we Twitter: Understanding microblogging usage and communities. In *Proceedings of the 9th WebKDD and 1st SNA- KDD 2007 Workshop on Web Mining and Social Network Analysis*, (pp. 56–65). ACM

Kim, E., & Gilber, S. (2009). *Detecting sadness in 140 characters*. Web Ecology Project. Pub. 03. Retrieved from http://www.webecologyproject.org/2009/08/detecting-sadness-in-140-characters/

Koch, M., & Richter, A. (2008). *Enterprise 2.0: Planung, Einführung und erfolgreicher Einsatz von Social Software in Unternehmen. München.* Germany: Oldenbourg.

Letierce, J., Passant, A., Breslin, J., & Decker, S. (2010). Understanding how Twitter is used to spread scientific messages. In *Proceedings of the Web Science Conference*, Raleigh, NC, USA, (26-27 April 2010).

Malinowski, B. (1922). *Argonauts of the Western Pacific*. New York, NY: E.P. Dutton & Co. Inc.

McFedries, P. (2007). All a-Twitter. *IEEE Spectrum, 84*. doi:doi:10.1109/MSPEC.2007.4337670

Mühlburger, H., Ebner, M., & Taraghi, B. (2010). @twitter try out #Grabeeter to export, archive and search your tweets. *Research 2.0 Approaches to TEL* (2010), (pp. 76–85).

Reinhardt, W. (2009a) Visualizing the dynamics of communication of communities of practice on Twitter. In *Proceedings of the 3rd International Workshop on Building Technology Enhanced Learning solutions for Communities of Practice.*

Reinhardt, W. (2009b). *Tracking the dynamics of social communities - Visualising altering word clouds of twitter groups.* Special Track on Mash-Ups for Learning, ICL2009.

Reinhardt, W., Ebner, M., Beham, G., & Costa, C. (2009). How people are using Twitter during conferences. In V. Hornung-Prähauser & M. Luckmann (Eds.), *5th EduMedia Conference*, Salzburg, (pp. 145-156).

Rosenbloom, A. (2004). The blogosphere. *Communications of the ACM, 47*(12), 31–33.

Schmidt, J. (2006). Social software: Online-gestütztes Informations-, Identitäts- und Beziehungsmanagement. *Neue Soziale Bewegungen, 19*(2), 37–47.

strengthen a scientific. *Workshop Science 2.0 for TEL*, ECTEL 2009

Templeton, M. (2008). *Microblogging defined.* Retrieved from http://microblink.com/2008/11/11/microbloggingdefined/

Thonhauser, P., Selver, S., & Ebner, M. (2012). Thought bubbles - A conceptual prototype for a Twitter based recommender system for research 2.0. *iKnow 2012, Proceedings of the 12ᵗʰ International Confrerence on Knowledge Management and Knowledge Technologies.*

Twitter. (2011). *#numbers: Official Weblog of Twitter.* Retrieved from http://blog.twitter.com/2011/03/numbers.html

KEY TERMS AND DEFINITIONS

Mass Education: Lecture with more than 100 attendees.

Microblog: A new form of communication in the World Wide Web, similar to a Weblog, but restricted to 140 signs for each blog.

Microblogging: To post on a Microblogging plattform.

Twitter: The world best known microblogging platform.

ENDNOTES

[1] http://www.slideshare.net/mebner/social-networks-danger-big-business-or-simply-big-chance (last visited February 2012)

Chapter 16
Academic Perspectives on Microblogging

Gabriela Grosseck
West University of Timisoara, Romania

Carmen Holotescu
Politehnica University of Timisoara/Timsoft, Romania

Bogdan Pătruț
Vasile Alecsandri University of Bacău, Romania

ABSTRACT

This chapter introduces the phenomenon of microblogging and presents the most relevant options for educators, like: What is a microblog?; What is microblogging?; What can microblogging offer in terms of teaching/training? This chapter has a descriptive character, and it is structured into two large parts that provide a general-to-specific approach of both theoretical and practical aspects related to the microblogging phenomenon and the impact of microblogs in the educational space. Two case studies are also presented.

INTRODUCTION

The Web, as a socio-technical environment, comprises various means of interactions, as well as the social practices related to their use. In the online landscape structured on four axes of interactions: communication, collaboration, creation and curation, the microblogging is seen as a new social media revolution.

It is quite demanding to write about microblogging in general, and writing a comprehensive study on its dissemination and pedagogical potential can present even more problems. Even if this social media instrument has come into use only relatively recently (the first platforms appeared six years ago, in 2006), more and more educators, practitioners and researchers worldwide are actively involved in finding, testing and sharing educational uses for microblogging.

This chapter introduces the phenomenon of microblogging and presents the most relevant options for educators:

DOI: 10.4018/978-1-4666-2851-9.ch016

- What is a microblog/What is microblogging? What are the resources needed to create a microblog and to explore the microsphere?
- What can microblogging offer in terms of teaching/training, learning and researching?
- Are microblogs educational instruments? How can microblogging be integrated into pedagogical practices?
- What are the theoretical principles (essential for guiding the integration of microblogs into education) and what kind of best practice models are there?
- If there is a *blogology*, the study of the social aspects of blogs, why could we not have a *micrology*, as a pedagogy of microblogs, as well? Could this be the proper term for a discipline dealing with the educational potential of microblogs?

MICROBLOG, MICROBLOGGING: POSSIBLE DEFINITIONS

Microblogging is a term in common use since 2006, when Twitter and Jaiku were launched[1]. From an etymological perspective the word *'microblog'* (also, sometimes written with a hyphen: *micro-blog*) comes from the conjoining of the terms 'micro' and 'blog'. The first one is a common used prefix which means 'small' whereas the second term represents a webpage with a continuous, regular and chronological series of information (text and/or multimedia content) about one or more subjects.

In other words, by microblog we understand a blog of small sizes, 'a severe space' with size constraints, as specifies Merriam Webster[2] Dictionary, composed by posts of maximum of 140-200 characters, that may sometimes include links, images or video clips and are available to be read either by any internaut or just by a group of people, named followers.

The person who creates and maintains the entries is called 'microblogger', entries are called 'microposts' and the activity of writing is called 'microblogging'.

The 'lilliputian' character of the notes and the fact that they may be posted from wherever you are (online, by phone, ipads or tablets, sent as SMS, e-mail or instant messaging) has not only changed microblogging into a fast-food writing experience, circumventing the usual editorial rigor, but may be considered as a possible explanation for its popularity.

In a world of hundreds of microblogging platforms, the most popular applications include Twitter, Plurk, Edmodo, Tumblr, Identi.ca, Yammer, Shoutem, Weibo in China or Cirip.eu as the most notable Romanian platform.

Summing up, we can state that microblogging is another form of social media, recognized as *Real-Time Web Publishing* (Winer, 2009), which has won an impressive audience acceptance and surprisingly changed online expression and interaction for millions of users.

In this context, the idea that microblogging is a form/an extension of real-time blogging on a smaller scale, which creates an interaction between users *by means of various devices, technologies and applications*, makes the topic itself delicate when it comes to finding a comprehensive definition. We say this because microblogging, as a means to express any type of message quickly, was practiced in several ways before the emergence of the well-known microblogging platform Twitter. Such examples of miniature digital communications are:

- Saving an online resource using a service of social bookmarking like Delicious (or Diigo), accompanied by a short explanatory/descriptive text – within a certain limit of characters (it basically provides a 'diet' for increasing the size of messages),

- Taking notes on a web page with a notetaking software like Zotero, EverNote or other similar services[3],
- Describing an image with Flickr or a piece of news with Digg, can be considered interesting micro-posts, with unique content, even if some of them come from social sites with user-created content.

However, in education, the convergence of different types of social-presence technology (with microblogging in the top) became the link between teachers and students and also the direct contact with the world of educational actors or the needed experts. Thus, 'in academic life, microblogging is about the idea of continuous information on what you do, discover and experience', which in terms of devices and technology, and also in terms of learning mobility and participants in this process, define microblogging as a new form of mobile and social learning (Betta, 2007).

CLASSIFICATIONS

The format that is the closest to the microblog is the *tumblelog*, a less structured variant of a blog. Accent is placed on the flow of thoughts, as the author concentrates his/her ideas in short articles and adds colour to the content with pictures, music, videos, quotes and/or links. The main characteristic of a tumblelog is logical inconsistency, without categories, taxonomies, comments or even titles.

The first tumblelog ever created is considered to be Anarchaia.org, by Christian Neukirchen, a place where the author intended to post quickly, without spending too much of his time, about things that drew his attention. The most popular applications are Tumblr and Posterous (bought by Twitter in March, 2012).

Microblogging also provides the possibility to publish content in a multitude of formats, which thus gives the first criterion for microblogs typology:

- **Classic:** Only text-format content (in the beginning Twitter being the classic example), possibly including links;
- **Photo:** A content published in image formats (DailyBooth, Ifotoyou);
- **Video:** A microblog with content in video format (59sec-video);
- **Audio:** A microblog with content in audio format (audioboo.fm, blip.fm);
- **Linking/Sharing:** Short-URL services, for instance Delicious as a link compilation;
- **Multimedia:** A microblog with content in multimedia format (Cirip.eu).
- **Concept:** Posting topics and gather audience's opinions (Flipter); sharing emotions/feelings (feelblogr, IRateMyDay.com), location-based service (PingGadget – free conversation tool) etc.

There are also specific digital regimentations according to:

- **The Length of the Message:** There are variations when the message undergoes dramatic simplification. The well known is *nanoblogging*: the message consists of only one word. A concrete example of a micro concept taken to the extreme is adocu. Although we fail to see the interest presented by such an application, we nevertheless try to understand its usefulness: that of super-synthesis, an 'in extremis' concentration of ideas. Users can basically write as many characters as they wish, but they cannot use spaces.
- **The Device:** For instance mobile-only (qik).
- **The Social Presence Services:** Social networking sites such as Facebook, MySpace or LinkedIn include a microblogging feature as *status update*[4].
- **The Target Group:** Educational - scientifical community incuded (Edmodo, Cirip.eu, ScienceFeed), organisational (Yammer,

Swabr – an Enterprise Microblogging Company from Germany).

- **The Content:** Corporate, news (CNN), educational, broadcasting, brand (Pepsi), marketing, artistic, spammer, non-profit, etc.
- **The User:** Personal, multi-author, community – we can consider them niche microblogs (twingr).
- **The Language / Country:** Weibo in China.
- **The Openness of Platforms:** An open source microblogging platform is identi.ca.

Thus, premises for the appearance of new series of applications / current concepts were created, such as *micro-media* (for example blogs about the lifestyle in different countries), *micro-news* (opinions of the digital landsmen about subjects of interest or notes about ongoing world-events), *micro-health* (for example timeline of a person or population health in certain moments and/or places) or *micro-learning* (micro-perspectives in the context of education – learning, treaning and researching). Thus, an entire array of terms have been developed based on the *micro-* particle: micromessaging, microsharing, micromedia, microformats, microlinking, microcontent, etc. (therefore the issue became a subject to be studied from a linguistic point of view, too).

We will not insist upon one type of microblogging or another. Choosing a certain platform is ultimately a personal option that also depends on a series of factors (such as writing skills, technical skills, costs, etc.) that are equally important for the future microblog author.

Once they have been engaged in the microblogging phenomenon, many users decide to use *social aggregation* services such as FriendFeed or Profilactic, which actually focus on the 'quantitative side' of users' profiles (i.e. managing several accounts) as a premise for the qualitative analysis of their virtual identities. The virtual identity built

on various sites is collected via a pseudoblog containing the news related to a user from the social networks on which he/she owns accounts or from suggested URLs/RSS feeds. There is also a flipside: for instance there are applications that sends micro-posts to many social networks.

Before launching into microblogging, we advise educational actors to ask themselves whether this form of content publishing is appropriate/suitable to their identity / character / way of being and, subsequently, if they can / agree/ feel it is possible to include it in their (PLE/N or educational/didactical) activities. In many cases, microblogging can prove to be only a whim, a caprice, an useless investment, especially as it is an activity that requires a lot of time and information resources.

A BRIEF HISTORY OF THE MICROBLOGGING TERM

Online media contain instances of the word microblog/microblogging from as early as 2002[5]. Thus, Natalie Solent wrote the following on her blog, in a post dated 17 July 2002:

Only micro-blogging today. It's Sports Day. Oh, can I make a date with you all for about this time in the year 2012? By that time my offspring will be, I trust, all grown up, loaded with achievements and equipped with stratospheric levels of self-esteem. I will then feel free to tell some very funny stories about the egg and spoon race back in 2002.

Also in 2002, a few months before, Jeneane Sessum posted a note titled *Microblogging[6]*, in which she challenged Internet users to write about their personal experiences, thoughts, emotions, feelings, using only a few words and short sentences.

The term *microblogging*, however, only attracted general attention as a major communication channel in 2007, as a consequence of the fact that Twitter became the main star of the Southwest Conference in Austin, Texas. On huge screens, the creator of Twitter, Evan Williams, invited all conference participants to follow what was being presented and discussed. Williams did not invent a new means of text communication, but his campaign created the conditions needed for messages to become powerful[7]. As Passant et al. (2008) said, the 'recent social phenomena of Web 2.0, Twitter is the missing link between blogging and instant messaging'.

MICROBLOGGING PLATFORMS USED IN EDUCATION

Twitter

Twitter, the most popular microblogging system, was launched in July 2006 by Obvious Corp with the name Twttr, and was renamed in the fall of same year as Twitter. The initial idea dated back to 2000, when Jack Dorsey opened a LiveJournal account. In 2006, there were ten employees, coordinated by Evan Williams, the co-author of Blogger, Jack Dorsey, and Biz Stone.

This robust, elegant, and simple system has gained an important popularity, having 500 million users today, who send 200 million tweets per day. According to recent figures (Solis, 2012; Smith and Brenner, 2012), 46% of active users make mobile a regular part of their Twitter experience. More than 10 new accounts are created each second, and over a thousand tweets are consumed daily by an active user (Bernstein et al., 2010).

The users of Twitter, the *twitterers*, can tweet via the web, SMS/mobile, instant messaging clients, and by third party applications. The notifies can be received in real-time as SMS, IM or RSS.

In linguistics, sociolect refers to the language of a certain group which, using specific terms and interactions dynamics, is characterized by an intimate / personal / private culture. In a society where Web 2.0 has generated an unprecedented diversity in terms of online communication, by transferring this concept to the Social Web, we can start considering microblogging through Twitter as a specific social dialect, in which individual users are clearly singled out and engaged in conversations with others, creating a social network in only 140 characters. The posts can also embed images, video clips or presentations (created with SlideShare).

Twitter's co-founder Biz Stone argues that 'creativity comes from constraint' and also that 'you can change the world in 140 characters'[8].

The Twitter's original stated purpose was to answer the question "What are you doing?". Later, in 2010, reflecting the taxonomy of users as Java (2007) defined it (daily chatter, conversations, sharing information and reporting news), focused on the ongoings in the real world, the question became "What's happening?".

Each user is able to monitor the notes of other users, who will be listed in the profile, under *Following*, thus the user becomes *Follower* for them. Twitter suggests also to follow people with similar profile or you can browse users tweeting about different topics/categories (section @Connect of a user's profile).

The posts can be classified using hashtags, and you have the option to view either worldwide trends or local trends, based on your phone's location (section #Discover of a user's profile). Users can retweet or favorite tweets. Hashtags and retweets, now platform core features, originally were conventions adopted by twitterers, later being formally implemented by the Twitter staff.

Already a fabric of our digital culture. Twitter is now ingrained in our digital DNA and is reflected in our lifestyle and how we connect and communicate with one another. Twitter represents a promising intersection of new media, relationships, traditional media and information to form one highly connected human network. (Brian Solis, 2012)

The numerous mashups based on Twitter API have an important contributions for this platform popularity, together with the possibility to follow and interact with people worldwide and to be updated with what is happening around the globe, thus overcoming the geographical, economic or political barriers. For example tops may be made according to number of followers or retweeted posts, such mash-up applications being Tweepz, Twitaholic or WeFollow.

Among the minuses there are the impossibility to create groups (groups would preserve the whole history of interactions between members and private groups would assure the privacy) and also the limit of search history to four days, too short for some types of applications, such as following a topic or the reactions to an event. A partial solution for groups are the lists, which were implemented in 2009: a list aggregates together users, a complete tweet stream for everyone appearing on list's page. A user can create lists including users not followed and can follow lists built by other users.

On March 12, 2012 Twitter acquired the well known mobile blogging platform Posterous, so there are expected innovations in Twitter sharing and mobile features.

Concerning the educational area, a huge amount of academic papers related to integrating Twitter in teaching-learning have been written, starting with the pioneering period 2007-2008 (Java et al., 2007; Grosseck and Holotescu, 2008). Also there are organized conferences, courses and workshops on this topic. Today a growing number of teachers, students, universities, schools, other educational actors or scientific events have an identity on Twitter.

Twitter is a good tool for jumpstarting large-scale educational reform, it enables easy access to educational visionaries from all over the globe, and highlights where government policy is hopelessly inadequate across the world. (Justin Marquis, 2012)

The 2010 Faculty Focus survey of nearly 1,400 US higher education professionals found that more than a third (35.2%) use Twitter 'to share information with peers', 'as a real-time news source', 'to communicate with students' and 'as a learning tool in the classroom'. In a recent research, the authors revealed that almost a half (48%) of educational actors from Europe use a microblogging platform in the teaching-learning process or for personal development (Grosseck and Holotescu, 2010).

The study of Junco et al. (2011) demonstrated that to have impacts on real-world academic outcomes, namely student engagement and grades, the Twitter usage has to be designed and facilitated by faculty in order to support the principles for a good practice in (undergraduate) education (Chickering and Gamson, 1987):

1. **Student/Faculty Contact:** Contact congruent with students digital lifestyles to be provided;

2. **Cooperation Among Students:** Students ask each other questions, provide emotional support to each other, and create and schedule real-world study groups;

3. **Active Learning:** Assignments should help students relate the course material to their own experiences both inside and outside of the classroom;

4. **Prompt Feedback:** Not only for their assignments, but also for other questions and issues they could face;

5. **Emphasizing Time on Task:** Based on the Twitter stream, discussions and learning community building could continue outside the classroom and also after the course end date;

6. **Communicating High Expectations:** In student's academic work, learning projects, and out-of class activities;

7. **Respecting Diversity:** Different learning styles, also encourage students who otherwise may not be active participants in class to participate online.

Thus, based on their experience using Twitter with their online students, Dunlap and Lowenthal (2009) offer the following five guidelines:

1. Establish relevance for students
2. Define clear expectations for participation
3. Model effective Twitter use
4. Build Twitter-derived results into assessment
5. Continue to actively participate in Twitter.

Following these guidelines, the Twitter based learning community helped students attend cognitive presence ('interacting with teachers and other professional practitioners in Twitter, the students constructed meaning through sustained communication'), while faculties for teaching presence ('the teachers clearly engaged in interactions with students via Twitter attend to instructional management issues and students' knowledge building'. (Dunlap and Lowenthal, 2009).

In all verity, all these principles could be applied when other microblogging platforms are used.

Edmodo

Built on a microblogging model, Edmodo, launched in September 2008, is basically a private online social platform designed specifically for teachers and students to share ideas, files, events and assignments.

Teachers can publish assignments, receive and grade them when completed, maintain a class calendar, store and share files, conduct polls and quizzes, and send SMS alerts to students. Students can easily follow the class stream and see a summary (teacher' commentaries included) of their grades on all assignments (Nevas, 2010).

In March 2012 an API was published, already other applications being connected with Edmodo (Watters, 2012). The service is free (without ads) and gained an important popularity, having more than six million users, who integrate it in the teaching-learning process.

Case studies can be found in a special section of the site[9], or in many presentations on slideshare or academic papers (Giacomantonio, 2011), some of the most interesting being:

*   Conduct a live online Socratic seminar at an appointed date and time outside of school hour. Open the session to all keen to join and send invites, reading links and topic to colleagues and students in the school.
*   Groups can be formed for common study of material, pen pals, reading groups, current events.
*   Differentiation - use the small group feature to move students into and out of groups based on readiness and other factors and deliver appropriate questions to each small group. It's very easy to move students into and out of small groups so no one is 'stuck' in a group he/she doesn't belong.
*   Embedding presentation tools (glogster, Pixton Comics, voki, animoto, prezi, voicethread, word clouds).
*   Coaches and sponsors can use the calendar for important dates / matches / meets / games/practices. If a practice is cancelled or moved students can receive an immediate text message so they know.
*   Encourage students to read and help make their reading experience more engaging with an Edmodo book club.
*   Give your students an interactive educational experience through mobile devices.
*   Create a 'teacher lounge' where teachers within your school can discuss ideas and share content.
*   After the school year ends, keep in touch with students and help them stay connected with each other.

There were written also research papers having Edmodo as central topic: Nevas (2010) attempted to answer to the question 'How can the Edmodo microblog increase student engagement and performance through collaborative learning tasks? ', while Holland and Muilenburg (2011) described a study in which students participated in literature discussions on Edmodo, their initiative being encouraged and being supported by reciprocal teaching strategies.

Plurk

Launched in May 2008, by a company located in Canada, Plurk has a unique, relaxed and intuitive interface, showing updates, called *plurks*, in horizontal form through a scrollable timeline, which can be clicked and dragged left and right to reveal more dates.

Plurk is described by its implementation team as: 'a really snazzy site that allows you to showcase the events that make up your life in deliciously digestible chunks. Low in fat, 5 calories per serving, yet chock full of goodness'.

Sent online, or through instant and text messaging, *plurks* can contain media such as videos and images and also *qualifiers*, which are color coded verbs used to represent a though.

The Karma system, a metric for people's activity, encourages participation and continued conversation; more options and features are made available when Karma increases. 'Like' and 'Meh' buttons let users vote on statuses. According to Tu et al. (2011), there are four types of plurkers' behaviours: reality shows, mood bulletins, kiosks, and propaganda.

Plurk is most popular in Philippines and Taiwan (Narkhede et al., 2010). Although not so many educators are using Plurk in their activity, there are some active communities of edu-plurkers[10]. The features that are used more in educational setting are related to group friends in *cliques* with whom to share plurks and the threaded conversations.

One interesting succesful educational uses of Plurk is as an artificial intelligent software agent in an university course, so-called plurk robot. Others

activities carried out during the course included teaching, team-working, planning, designing (hardware and software), testing, debugging (or problem-solving), and applying (Shen, 2010).

Yammer

Yammer, asking 'What are you working on?', originally launched in September 2008 as an enterprise microblogging service, evolving to an enterprise social network, which has now more than three million users.

Its many educational uses are facilitated by characteristics such as: public and private groups, replies and threaded conversations, file and photo attachments, knowledge bases search, events, polls, and questions applications, Twitter and Microsoft SharePoint integration (Beliveau et al., 2011; Loh, 2011).

According to Yammer CEO David Sacks, 1,692 of the more than 100,000 organizations using Yammer are in the educational industry.

Yammer is unique because it allows schools to expand problem-based learning (PBL) opportunities, where students look up answers to questions and share information with the group, rather than memorizing lectures. It's what he calls the "brass ring" for teaching problem solving skills to health professionals. (Wecker, 2011)

One notorius use of Yammer in academic settings was proved by Australian Charles Sturt University as a flexible environment for a Community of Practice (CoP) about Information and Communication Technology, supporting blended learning in the light of social presence and organisational culture (Uys, 2010).

Identi.ca

Identi.ca is an open source microblogging service, opened in July 2008, which provides many features not currently implemented by Twitter, including

XMPP support, export and exchange of personal and friend data based on the FOAF standard, trackbacks, native video playback, OpenID, and groups, making the platform an interesting choice for collaboration.

Identica.ca is the first service to support OStatus (formerly OpenMicroBlogging) specification, an open protocol that allows different microblogging services to inter-operate and people on different social networks to follow each other (Van Buskirk, 2009). Status comes to support decentralized architectures, important fundamentals of the web, which were generally neglected by the microblogging applications.

Even there aren't so many references in the literature, identi.ca has gained success in higher education sector, see for example the group 'Women in Higher education'[11]. Likewise, a study conducted by Ebner et al. (2010) at University of Graz, Austria, aimed to investigate the use of microblogs, dissued the implementation of Identi.ca in Higher Education, by addressing the following research questions:

1. How are students using microblogging in the context of their course?
2. Can public and individual timelines using microblogging be used for documentation in the sense of 'process tracking by timeline' (process-oriented learning)?
3. Does microblogging foster informal learning?

The results of this study led to conclusions that microblogging is supporting process-oriented learning by a constant information flow between students and between students and teachers" (Ebner et al., 2010).

Cirip.eu

Cirip.eu is a microblogging platform designed for education and business, implemented by Timsoft, a Romanian company specialized in eLearning and mobile applications, under the coordination of the second author (Holotescu and Grosseck, 2011). Cirip.eu provides the following facilities:

•   Creating public or private user groups; collaboration groups can be established between the members of a class or a university year, for a course enhancement or to run an entire course, or for a conference, event, workshop, etc.; in a specific group section, the moderators can post announcements and materials, also can send alerts via SMS to members;

•   The possibility to embed multimedia objects in the notes: images, audio and (live) video files, presentations, files, livestreaming; thus the platform integrates a wide range of Web2.0 applications and social networks organized around educational resources; this integration is realized in order to encourage teachers and students to discover and integrate them in education;

•   Scenarios for learning and new pedagogical approaches in using social media in education can be captured and formally represented as learning design objects; the learning design objects can be shared, discussed, improved, and reused on the microblogging platform;

•   The possibility to monitor RSS feeds for sites, blogs, or activities on other social networks or search feeds;

•   Tags, statistics, personal and group tagclouds, representations of the users' interaction networks;

•   Polls and quizzes which can be answered online or by SMS;

•   Import and export notes from Twitter and other social media platforms.

The strong characteristic of Cirip is allowing the creation of a personal profile and/or a portfolio including ideas, projects, research, information resources, multimedia objects created individually or collaborativelys. Furthermore, all users' activities are developed in a dynamic manner and follow a continuous evaluation process by communicating with members of groups or of the platform. In this manner / way on Cirip each member can build not sonly a Personal Learning Environment but also a Personal Learning Network. From this perspective and according to classification of Stutzman (2009) and analysis of Cross and Conole (2009), Cirip is both a *profile-centric network,* and an *object-centric network* (a social network around multimedia objects). Thus, the objects of cirip:

- Are part of the communication-conversation flow of the platform;
- Are connecting Cirip with other social networking/Web2.0 applications organized around educational objects;
- Can be reused, validated, created or recreated individually or collaboratively - we can say Cirip offers an opening to Open Educational Resources – OERs;
- Are *meta-objects* meaning *objects of learning design (OLD).* The OLD specify learning scenarios, best practices for integrating new technologies (Cirip in particular) in education;
- And, by extension, public or private groups can be considered as *social objects.*

No matter the platform used[12] there are lots of educational uses of microblogging – limited only by the imagination and teachers' will to try this technology in didactical activities.

EDUCATIONAL USES OF MICROBLOGGING IN TERMS OF OPPORTUNITIES, CONTEXTS, CHALLENGES, ADVANTAGES, AND LIMITS / RISKS

Educational Opportunities

As the technology of microblogging is adopted in a variety of contexts, its usefulness becomes more and more compelling for educational actors, from schools and universities, from training and workplace learning. As a consequence, four microblogging platforms (Twitter, Edmodo, Yammer, and Cirip.eu) featured the last three tops 100 tools in education, compiled by the Centre for Learning & Performance Technologies UK from the proposals of hundreds learning professionals worldwide[13].

The aspects most emphasized in literature (Suster, 2010; Gavan, 2011) reveal that microblogging:

- Is a tool for sharing information and resources, bringing also comments and validation of them;
- Offers the opportunity to discuss / practice different types of online discourse, and to organize ideas and reflections;
- Creates instant and mindful communities in unexpected environments;
- Can be successfully used in the teaching-learning process;
- Promotes a collaborative virtual environment which fosters process-oriented learning;
- Facilitates the work of multidisciplinary groups;
- Is a useful tool for cooperation and collaboration in project management or for assessing peers and students opinions;
- Is a viable platform for meta-cognition;
- Is the preferred support for conferences or other events;

- Is used in the convergence of knowledge;
- Facilitates the creation of a personal learning network;
- Allows exploration of colloquial language (important in learning foreign languages);
- Can be a reference service in libraries;
- To get instant feedback from students;
- It's the ultimate 'wisdom of the crowds' curation application and also a curated RSS.

Didactical Contexts

Although most microblogging platforms are not perfect, different actors from the educational spectrum have found that microblogging can be successfully adopted and integrated in the teaching-learning process or in other didactical activities (Java et al., 2007; Parry, 2008; Reinhardt, Ebner, Beham and Costa, 2009; Grosseck and Holotescu, 2008; Dunlop and Lowhenthal, 2009; Borau et al., 2009; Ebner et al., 2010). As general uses / contexts of microblogging platforms in education can be underlined:

- **Learning Communities:** Communication on microblogs may enhance traditional courses, by exploring the potential of the microblog in a *formal and informal context*. It offers students the opportunity to discuss/exercise various types of online discourses (voice, aim, audience), to structure their ideas, reflections, it promotes discovery through serendipity. By incorporating in the instructional environment a social and a group component, we become more human, more polite, more available and visible for social activities.
- **Exploring Collaborative Writing:** Microblogging promotes writing as a pleasant activity, enhances the students' written expression skills, those for lecture, offers students the chance to pass from per-

sonal writing to public writing (evocation, realizing sense, reflection).
- **Collaboration between Schools, Universities, Countries:** Pupils, students, teachers share ideas, experiences, projects by social learning.
- **Instrument for Evaluating Opinions:** Used in the academic environment, microblogging applications develop, stimulate interactions on a certain topic, allowing the expression of ideas and feelings related to a situation or a life experience.
- **A Viable Meta-Cognition Platform:** A way of thinking about one's own way of thinking/learning/understanding.
- **Support for Conferences or Other Events (Learning Sessions, Workshops):** A very simple way for the participants in a scientific event to share thoughts about a certain session and the activities taking place during it, being thus useful for those who cannot participate, but also for future reflections.
- **Building a Personal Learning Environment (PLE)/Personal Learning Network (PLN) for Each Registered User or Accordingly to Howard Rheingold (2011):** It's not just about knowing how to find experts, co-learners, but about exploration as invitation to serendipitous encounter'[14].
- **Research and Dissemination Tool:** Microblogging proved to be one of the most popular tool used in a professional research context (see the next section). Twitter together with Skype, Google Docs, and YouTube (CIBER, 2010) are used intensively both 'to share information with peers' and 'as a real-time news source', being the most common activities of teachers (Faculty Focus, 2011).

Research Context

Perhaps one of the most debated use of microblogging in education is the research. Popular microblogging services used in research are: Twitter, Friendfeed, Cirip or ScienceFeed (http://www.sciencefeed.com). The last one is a microblogging platform dedicated to the online scientific community acting as a 'bridge between online scientific networking platforms, scientific databases' and scientists from all over the world.

At the question raised by researchers Mayernik and Pepe (2009) *'Can micro-blogging be used for field research?'* we noticed in the literature some answers of the most frequent uses for different research contexts such as the following (Ovadia, 2009; Costa, 2011; Gilpin, 2010; Grosseck and Holotescu, 2011):

- A new form of *scholarly communication*: 'answer other people's questions' or 'ask questions relevant to your practice', getting in touch with science journalists, science organizations or doctoral students, get advice on how to improve research;
- A new form of *authoring, publishing, researching*;
- A tool for *disseminating scientific information,* including the own results;
- A s*ocial collection* to manage:
  - *people* (e.g. to follow list of researchers on Twitter)
  - *messages* (favorite notes, to resend / to comment - @ / RT; D for scholarship authority or supporting critical discussions)
  - *hashtags* (social news, following scientific events) etc.;
- A *data repository* to collect:
  - *information* from science newsfeeds and from various individuals / institutions;
  - *links* to other valuable resources;

- A *search tool* 'more appropriate for capturing hyperrcurent information';
- An *outreach tool* aimed at promoting public awareness (and understanding) of science and making informal contributions to science education;
- A *platform for social micro-interactions* to connect people (building personal relationship with other researchers, co-colleagues) and also to engage in conversations with an active community of scientists;
- A *way to track trends-in-time* like natural disasters or political events, mentioned in messages;
- A *micro-peer method* for learning, reviews, feedback etc.

A recent study conducted last year by the first two authors indicates that academic uses of microblogging for research purposes range from searching for scholarly content to academic publishing (Grosseck and Holotescu, 2011):

- Search for scholarly content: academics are looking to discover new information, ideas or practices. By looking for specific ideas the researcher can scan easily the stream for news other than academic papers, science magazines, data bases, scientific discoveries etc.
- *Dissemination Channel* for promoting of own results / articles / projects or studies / formal products.
- Tool for *reviewing the literature, collecting and analyzing research data,* "for listening what other researchers are going to say" (Gilpin, 2010).
- Talking and *sharing experiences online,* communicating scholarly ideas, collaboration between colleagues, networks of stakeholders, and other contacts.
- Building a *network of contacts* for research opportunities, finding sponsors, reaching fellow specialists; thus the development of

319

a *Personal Research Network* (PRN) is appropriate not only for 'establishing professional expertise' but also for 'professional identity construction' (Gilpin, 2010).

- *Monitoring scientific events:* Nowadays following conferences and posting from scientific events (with a special hashtag) is a common practice; communication before, during and after the event, using microblogging as official, quasi-official or unofficial back-channel, for collaborative keynotes, and feedback.
- *Scholarly publishing and capturing contextual information.*

Other studies suggest that the researchers' behavior changed due to the *social participatory process* in micro-sphere stressing the need to create an online research profile on microblogging, what we called a *micro-scholarly identity 2.0.*

Potential Disadvantages

There are also some potential withdraws in using microblogging in educational settings, such as:

- Can be too distracting (or at least too distracting for some students, like someone with autism, attention deficit disorder, chronic fatigue syndrome etc.);
- Is a time-consuming task both for students and teachers who 'already have too many places to post messages or check for student questions/comments'[15];
- Can be addictive;
- (Sometimes) no social / educational value;
- Teachers are being 'on-call' virtually 24-7 and students can intrude into his/her private life;
- In classroom situations is better to have a private account (also students have to be warning and encouraging their anonymity and thoughtful postings otherwise);

- 'Creates poor writing skills and could be yet another classroom distraction's (Faculty Focus, 2011).

Regarding the research, the disadvantages, barriers or limits of integrated microblogging can be included into one of these categories:

- **Ethical Dilemmas:** Authority; coping with a large amount of information; the level of acceptability to collect, archive and analyze data from the stream; 'authenticity of crowd sourced information' (CIBER, 2010); intellectual property rights; new forms of peer review and approval, such as retweeting (for e.g. resending messages without giving credit); social citation sharing; trust etc.
- **Concerns about Quality:** Quality of ideas information/assurance (poor studies, no substantial academic/scientific values; banality); drain on resources; too time consuming; reliability and expertise of microbloggers; disorganized information (sometimes a chaotic stream); common language (the human chemistry is all adrift); poor linguistic conventions (for e.g. difficulty of writing a math formula); limited communication options (short messages - only the length of a SMS); week feedback etc.
- **Security and Privacy Concerns:** Information overload; noise; spam; juxtaposition with the personal life; confusing in following too many interactions; uncertainty of the identity of sender; plagiarism, lack of a code of microblogging ethics etc.

In order to actually reach the previously mentioned results and to limit the bad points, a well planned usage of microblogging in the teaching-learning process we suggest as necessary: the description of educational objectives, the orientation of education according to certain concrete landmarks, the construction of efficient learning situations, the planning of adequate evaluation tools.

Challenging Advantages

The authors' previous experience (Holotescu and Grosseck, 2010) in integrating microblogging in their academic courses enabled them to notice the following aspects related to students:

- Development of written communication skills and especially multimedia skills (in a variety of forms and contexts).
- Creativity and intellectual curiosity: Openness and receptivity to the new, communicating ideas, different perspectives on current technological reality (and not only).
- Information and media skills: Creating information in various forms and environments.
- Since students are offered managerial attributions in connection to their own learning, the degree of their personal and social responsibility is thus improved.
- Capacity to adapt.
- Development of critical and systemic thinking.
- Demonstration of interpersonal and collaboration skills: Through team-work, adapting to various roles and responsibilities.
- Identifying, creating and solving issues.
- Auto-formation: During courses we noticed the maintenance of a competitive spirit among participants.
- Entertainment (as a function of sensory stimulation): It is known that each online learning activity should include an entertaining component, which also facilitates learning in the real-world context.

On the other hand, the benefits of using microblogging for research purposes can be clustered in the following types:

- **Collective Intelligence:** Communication; collaboration with a wider audience of specialists, sharing ideas and perspective, interdisciplinary research; collecting / surveying / filtering data and resources.
- **Ambient Intelligence:** Visibility and validation of projects, results, professional portfolio, recognition.
- **Extension of the PRN – Personal Research Network:** Building and engaging (in) a relevant community of scholars/ of practice, beyond geographical, cultural and linguistic barriers; mentoring colleagues; transfer of knowledge between researchers; help in problem solving; build networks to support research (and researchers' career); access to OERs and collaborative applications.
- **Managing the Researchers' Projects:** Research publishing; tagging contents; getting notified using RSS feeds.
- **Developing as a Researcher:** Improving digital and professional skills and competencies help for academic career.

MICROBLOGGING AS A FORM OF MOBILE LEARNING

The wireless communications technology, considered the most popular, widespread and ubiquitous (personal) communications technology on the planet (Gagnon, 2010), includes a wide range of mobile devices/wireless terminals, starting from the already classic laptops, notebooks, PDAs, iPods, handheld, palmtops or tablet PCs to the various mobile phone models (with or without specifications such as: touchscreen, clamshell, sliding, possibility to capture images with an integrated camera, editing/sharing them, bluetooth, 3G, radio FM, music player/MP3, recording/rendering video content, Internet connexion, HTML browsers, email applications) and other intelligent devices such as the iPhone and iPad.

As mobile devices offer flexible access to the online resources and communication tools for learning, *mobile learning* (m-learning) open up access to flexible and collaborative learning modalities, anywhere and anytime, at the same time ensuring close relationships between learning in the workplace, at home, at school and/or in a community by anyone on any subject[16].

Even if m-learning is defined differently by different people, each definition focusing on features such as mobile technologies, mobility, individualism, ubiquitous, or e-learning (Keskin and Matcalf, 2011), in this context, the facilitation and the pedagogical design input of the teacher are critical (Laurillard and Pachler, 2007): ´m-learning, being the digital support of adaptive, investigative, communicative, collaborative, and productive learning activities in remote locations, proposes a wide variety of environments in which the teacher can operate´.

This type of learning can be used successfully by associating instant messaging with the SMS and the social networking communication, such characteristics having the microblogging applications. Whatever microblogging platform we use, we're witnessing a new paradigm blooming/expanding in the hands of our students (Feijóo, Pascu, Misuraca and Lusoli, 2009), ´the generation that has not known life without mobile phone´ (CDE, 2008).

The microblogging specific features for m-learning can be classified in the following categories: administration, reference, interaction, multimedia collaboration, meta-collaboration, localization, facilitation (Patten, Sanchez and Tangney, 2006; Holotescu and Gosseck, 2011).

Buchem and Camacho (2011) defined ten guidelines to designing a mobile learning course in higher education, which can be easily transfered to m-learning in microblogging context:

1. Engage students as co-designers of m-learning;
2. Involve other stakeholders to enable the uptake of m-learning;
3. Enable a socialising context for m-learning;
4. Facilitate communication and cooperation between and within teams;
5. Facilitate co-construction of m-learning content;
6. Find the optimal level of control by scaffolding;
7. Encourage the development of higher-order thinking skills;
8. Facilitate bridging different contexts;
9. Engage students in evaluation;
10. Find ways to increase sustainability.

MICROBLOGGING METRICS: ASSESSING STUDENTS' ACTIVITY

The activity, participation and interaction of students on different social media platforms (on microblogging too) during courses cannot be assessed or marked by using traditional assessment strategies and most university assessment procedures don't offer guidance related to identification, ownership, safety, privacy and recording-keeping of such Web 2.0 work produced for assessment (Gray et al., 2010a). After analysing 17 selected cases where academics have set assessable activities, establishing an inter-relation between learning objectives, assessment tasks and marking criteria, the authors of the study 'Students as Web 2.0 authors: Implications for assessment design and conduct' (Gray et al., 2010a) make the following recommendations for a quality assessment:

- Integration with other elements and forms of assessment should be clear;
- Is linked to specified learning objectives;
- Produces evidence of desired learning outcomes;
- Is supported by adequate instructions and marking rubrics;
- Encourages academic honesty;
- Provides explanatory and diagnostic feedback;
- Enables peer review and moderation of marking;
- Can be externally evaluated for curriculum accreditation and recognition of prior learning.

Teachers and educational actors interested in assessing students' activities on microblogging platforms could consult another work of Gray et al. (2010b), also part of the ´Assessment of student web 2.0 authoring' Edna Project[17], which contains good practice guidelines, in the form of three checklists:

- An affordances checklist, to support an appropriate fit between what web 2.0 activities entail and what assessment is trying to achieve;
- A processes checklist, to support individual and organisational learning throughout the cycle of assessment activities;
- A policies checklist, to support practices that make assessment safe and fair for students and staff.

Another notable research work on this topic is Assessment 2.0 (Tinoca, 2011), which defines e-assessment as ´all technology-enabled assessment activities where the design and student activities (complete, present, submit) must be mediated by technologies´. The conceptual framework for e-assessment adresses four dimensions: authenticity, consistency, transparency, and practicability.

A set of microblogging metrics ´Microsphere analysis indicators´, which can be used to assess students' activity and learning communities coagulation on microblogging platforms, are defined in Grosseck and Holotescu (2009):

1. **Popularity:** Relation between the number of followers of a user and the number of messages sent;
2. **Influence:** Based on number of followers and distribution of own messages (referenced or resent);
3. **Coagulation Index:** The covering / density of the network, the conversational coefficient, the reciprocity and the relevance;
4. **Exposure Index:** Set of the discussed elements, taking into consideration the topics approached by a person on her / his microblog;
5. **Geographical Distribution:** Analyses and exposes in a graphical form the signs of our online presence, thus practically drawing up a social map under continuous expansion, showing in detail the ways in which we interact and expose ourselves in a public space;
6. **Temporal Distribution:** Messages distribution on time;
7. **Online Social Presence:** Type and quality of messages.

The indicators were implemented on microblogging platform Cirip.eu, facilitating student assessment, and observations on the moderation and courses quality. Some interesting remarks can be noted on the interdependences between (Grosseck and Holotescu, 2010):

- The types/the complexity of objects integrated in messages;
- The types of communication – public / private group, learning/hobby/business/ socializing; as example, personal audio /

video interventions appear mostly in private groups;

- The coagulation degree of the community;
- The facilitation of the group moderator.

CASE STUDIES

Learning must not be limited to educational/school situations/contexts, but must reveal to students what it means to be successful in everyday life. This is why teachers must provide students with the most varied opportunities to practice their social skills, starting from a careful observation of these skills and choosing to practice certain situations in which students may be less competent or lacking in skills.

In the following there are presented two case studies that prove the theorectical background above mentioned.

Case Study 1: Developing Social Interactions through Microblogging

The binder of a social network is represented by *interrelations* (to be more precise, their *density*) and by their common aim, which result in *conversational* partnerships and *collective cohesion* (the degree of connectivity of each member to the others). Microblogs are, in fact, structures of relatively sustainable interactions between the actors that take part in exchange relationships. If many sociologists initially considered that the smallest element of a relational structure in the case of a social network are the *dyads* (in which the potential for communication is realised through the exchange of messages between two persons), the basic structural element was later established to be the triangular format of the *triads*, because social interactions are more sustainable than social contacts. The online environment brings along the new element of *user-generated content/user-shared content* in various forms/formats (texts, links, images, audio or video clips, etc.).

For students participating in courses held on the educational platforms Cirip.eu and Edmodo in the last three years by the authors microblogging proved to be a catalyst of social practices. Thus, these environments act like a new form of expression and social interactions, like minimalist tools capable of orchestrating complex social relationships that cannot be found in traditional social networks (compared to Facebook, for instance). However, microblogging is perceived by students with good digital skills as an almost virgin media territory, which they can freely explore. Consequently, we are talking about *collective consciousness* and *ambient intimacy*, about a space meant to host feelings that people cannot otherwise express publicly.

Thus, the user is seen as a ´psychological system´ defined by standard demographical characteristics (age, gender, education, residence, civil status etc.), who is integrated into a set of normalised, linguistic, socio-cultural and/or political and economic systems: behaviours, attitudes, motivations and practices of microblogging users, in terms of growth and change, social dynamics and group activities, handling aspects such as users' socio-cultural profiles, (online) identity, language, age, gender, etc.

Any of the following advantages can justify the importance of ensuring a digital social life on a microblogging platform from the perspective of a social network:

- *The capacity to create and develop a social network* until reaching a critical mass of the public interested in social interactions (colleagues, professionals, specialists, librarians, policy makers, social entrepreneurs and other educational actors).
- *The feeling of networking* seen from the perspective of one's adherence to the stream (one is part of the community and identifies oneself with it), influence (one has influence over the community and the other way around), integration and meet-

ing the necessities (one enjoys the others' support and one offers support in return) and sharing feelings (the connections between community members).

- *Redefining communication and social interactions.* The virtual space has promoted the transformation of traditional human relationships based on proximity and groups from the same communities to communities centred around virtual social networks that are scattered from a geographical point of view. Thus, it is not surprising that they mostly refer to the online migration of a consistent part of one's personal, social and professional life, in microblogging being more easy and fast.

- In a social network environment users *have control over their own identity,* an aspect which is entirely new and which is unimaginable in physical social relationships. For the first time, the social participants of interactions, who are engaged in the network, have unlimited access to sketching their identities, but they cannot control others, nor can others control them. Even if this phenomenon occurs in a virtual environment, it grows and manages to influence real, palpable aspects of day-to-day life.

- The individual's *freedom of movement.* Users are practically free to negotiate their presence within a certain group, which they can willingly follow or not. Even though this aspect may seem to be insignificant, it is not present when we refer to groups and communities in day-to-day life. Moreover, actual adherence to a microblogging platform has brought along two side effects: *differentiating one's own network* from others and the *positive credit* given to it.

- *Socialising naturally.* Virtual social networks offer one the possibility to have an online presence, to meet new people with the same interests and hobbies, to expand day-to-day online interests. In microblogging environment all is accomplished in a casual, natural, simple manner, devoid of artificial behavioural actions.

- *The network effect* is the phenomenon through which a service gains more value as more people use it. The members of your network (F/F circle) must work together to increase the 'network effect', i.e. to perform those activities that can create a synergy and help avoid the doubling of the effort within the network. Furthermore, the mutual trust and responsibility which every user contributes will encourage the information flow and synergy within the network, generating power and intelligence.

- *Creating a personal learning network.* Within a social network, learning can also occur by creating and forming connexions with other people and informational resources with the declared purpose of enriching the members' capacity to understand themselves, others, the effects of their behaviour on other people, group processes, etc.

Such a network is founded on interpersonal relationships characterised by a deep and highly expressive personal involvement. Thus the idea of *'shared knowledge'* is embraced, meaning that the things we know are incorporated in a personal network of connections that we form when we are in contact with others, with information resources and with the world. The possibilities supplied by new socially-oriented communication and collaboration tools are based on George Siemens' *theory of connectivism,* as an alternative approach to learning within a network.

- *Member filtering.* Once the profile has been created, users can communicate with any other person or with those members who accept communications from (un) known persons, according to the site operating rules.

- *Communication is interactive, varied and easy* due to a sum of new technologies meant to increase connectivity and diversity of the applications within social networks. As a matter of fact, communication relationships on a microblogging platform have a degree of laterality that is quite high.
- Microblogging is in a state of *permanent change*, both in terms of technology or software used, as well as in terms of direct manifestations (an aspect that confers them new features periodically, from the interface to applications, which are either kept or not, depending on users' reaction).
- *Connecting to the community's requests.* There are social groups that provide opportunities for increasing adult participation in social campaigns, by means of user-generated content and the specific niche of comments and the online exchange of views regarding various issues.
- Using *collective intelligence* (in ´nodes´). In several cases, the distinct number of users is the number that makes them interesting, that increases the content available or ensures their quality.
- *Ease of access to certain user information.* Certain online social networks represent enormous databases that provide a great amount of information on a great number of users. For microblogging this is a strong feature. For instance, companies looking to employ personnel by looking / scanning to Twitter profile can select candidates from a much wider area than by organising an interview to which only some of the people participate.
- *Participation* (investment of time, actions and effort in network activities*).* Twitter for e.g. is known for the fact that it serves millions of enthusiasts and people who want to make new acquaintances. Although the

key element is *trust*, which derives from the respect invested in the chosen community, in the microblogging space, the same importance must be given to the following:

- ◦ *Permeability* (The extent to which it allows or not for new members to be added – F/F ratio)
- ◦ *Flexibility* (the degree of informality and freedom), as well as
- ◦ *Intimacy* (the degree of the members' mutual closeness).
- *The temporal dimension,* as a key value of the 21st century, is an omnipresent notion in our digital numerical lives. Time offers a competitive advantage in comparison to other services and thus becomes a very important aspect, especially in the case of social presence services such as Twitter. The temporal dimension that is, to a certain extent, also applicable to services used to keep records of daily activities - *lifelog* (like Life2Front) or to create *collaborative chronologies* (such as xTimeLine), is estimated to become a powerful differentiating criterion for online content editors, which will play a central role in social applications.
- Microblogs can provide a powerful environment in order to improve *the way in which certain cultural and social aspects are perceived.* For instance, a critical culture and social relationships in the network make cultural acts be much more transparent and malleable.

Taking into account our own observations/ experiences (as members of several microblogging platforms, both educational and professional) and compiling information from specialty literature, the authors have identified several (potential) issues/limits faced by microblogs as social networks, summed up by means of the following disadvantages:

- Currently, social networks *do not grant people enough freedom to build and create their own worlds*, which is exactly what users want to do.
- Microblogging entails the acceptance of a *sociological fragmentation* of their members in order to classify and coordinate them within certain types of activities that require a common interest, within certain areas of mutual correspondence and sometimes even according to age or gender categories.
- *Permanent expansion* may lead to the loss of a main topic, which might subsequently cause a loss in the number of users.
- *Exclusivity*. Microblogging services are not exactly permissive (the case of academic/scientific/research platforms).
- *Inequality of participation*. At the basis of this phenomenon lies the reality of the passive participation of the greatest part of microbloggers. Thus, although the basic ingredient of a social network is interaction, a significant number of users prefer to explore and experiment with the network individually instead of becoming directly involved in one community or another. According to the principle of Vilfred Pareto, 20% of Internet users account for 80% of the content. They act according to what has become known as the *90:9:1 rule*:
- 90% of users will remain passive (i.e. they will read, observe, but not contribute – they are *lurkers*);
- 9% will occasionally participate in the content created, as they dedicate most of their time to other priorities;
- 1% will be active, participate frequently and be responsible for most of the contributions.
- A direct consequence is *micro-networkitis*, the fatigue caused by being present and follow too many users on a microblogging platform.

- *Anonimity*. Through the millions of users that they have worldwide, microblogginng platforms can potentially connect a vast, almost limitless world of people and resources. Generally, a user's *profile* comprises a series of information published by the person, in addition to feedback received from other users, which can be quantified in various ways according to the specific features of the network. What matters is the qualitative approach of these identities.
- On the other hand, when the microblogging is used excessively, there is a tendency that can be defined as a certain feeling of irritation and/or aggression exhibited by some users.
- *Disclosing personal information* such as one's short bio (name, qualifications, interests, hobbies, possibly photographs or the refusal to disclose such data) may deny one access to communication/collaboration.
- *Identity theft*. Due to the popularity of such services, cyber-criminals might take advantage of this information in order to obtain other material benefits.
- *Manipulation, extortion*. Within micrologging, certain people will always stand out from the great mass of users: public personas, celebrities, leaders of political parties, etc. They can direct users towards certain goals. When improperly used, microblogs become powerful instruments for generating social changes (see the recent political movements from Moldova, Iran, Egypt or London riots).
- *Pretexts for personal exposure. As useful instruments for testing human shallowness*, microblogs help feed dreams and give the impression that the big world is actually much smaller. Moreover, because microblogging focus on creating social interactions with other people, social inclusion (membership to a group/community), on the need to pay and receive attention,

negative feedback may cause people to become uninhibited or become engaged in lewd or inadequate behaviour.

- *Access with harmful intentions.* Microblogging policies on comments are generally quite open and permissive. More often than not, divergent opinions, even if critical, lead to constructive discussions.
- *Viral contamination:* Members of networking sites often receive invitations to follow accounts with which they have nothing in common.
- *Wasted time:* For instance workplace productivity may be affected by this tempting and time-consuming environment.
- *Social spam:* Unsolicited messages from members of the network.
- And, last but not least, a certain *hostility* when it comes to introducing social networks into various organisations, manifested especially among educational institutions. The consequences of such a refusal become irrelevant, however, given that 1 out of 3 students is using this type of socialisation in order to communicate and share knowledge.

Other unforeseeable negative human consequences that may occur are:

- Social corrosion: due to the ´invasion´ of social interaction sites in digital life, the ´weakening´ of connections might determine their vulnerability;
- Social isolation or absenteeism and social autism (It is easy to ignore anyone);
- Certain social allergies as reactions to rude or reckless behaviour of ´friends´ (which may become more severe through repeated exposure).

The activities presented next serve the very purpose of developing social skills using a microb-

logging platform as a social network environment, by preparing students for a better interaction with their peers and the world, especially in order to provide easy access on the future labour market (students are also encouraged to propose their own topic, using web 2.0 tools/social media):

- Week-end thoughts: Write a statement/ message (with a specific hashtag on a specific topic).
- Who am I? (´Explain yourself´ in 140 characters or through a CC image, audio/video clip etc.)
- Who are you? What makes you special? (create a self story with a digital tool like photopeach, prezi, capzles, glogster, animoto etc.)
- *What book I read/*Book on the nightstand/ Book of your Childhood (see the note on Edmodo, http://www.edmodo.com/ post/43491940).
- Me_in_Music/What am I listen to (use blip. fm to post your favorite songs or artists).
- The Fair of (famous) quotes/Sayings/ reflections.
- *Celebrating together* Spring, Autumn, Christmas, Eastern, The End of Year etc. (for e.g. My Christmas tree – include in the message pictures, video clips, presentations with our own/our towns' Christmas trees).
- *A haiku a day* (Keeps low grades away ☺).
- *Travelling through time:* imagine (your) life on a particular period of time (using an animation web 2.0 software/one can develop further using a mobile phone and augmented reality).
- *Text me* (using mobile phone to post on microblog answers to polls, photos or mini-videos capturing students everyday life-facts – lifestreaming with qik, poll with polleverywhere or wiffiti, fun with qr codes apps etc).

- *Motivational poster.* We proposed a combination word - picture (Creative Commons) to be associated with microblogs and/or microblogging and posted on the flow (see 'Metaphors for microblogging on PhotoPeach'http://photopeach.com/album/montoq?ref=est).

- *Curate the web:* a collaborative collection of resources using particular hashtags, enlarged and used after the courses end.

- *Translation of videos* (posted for e.g. on dotsub.com, where the transcript can be translated collecting the translated phrases tweeted by students). See 'Twitter in Plain English, translation collaborative exercise by students' at http://dotsub.com/view/665bd0d5-a9f4-4a07-9d9e-b31ba-926ca78.

- *Visual Statements/Internet Meme* using notes on a Flickr image. Starting from a tag cloud application like wordle.net, a tag-cloud with the words that appeared most frequently in tweets during the course.

- *Participate with students at local event* (tweetmeme) or scientific events (see the next study case about microreading the stream).

A particular attention has to be paid to stories in 140 characters. Digital storytelling is defined as telling stories and sharing information with multimedia tools and resources (Yuksel et al., 2011) (Figure 1 and Figure 2). It means recounting (using more or less details) their own actions or their colleagues', teacher' actions and/or educational activities, interactions developed within the group or other events that students take part

Figure 1. Digital storytelling exercises on cirip.eu platform (sources: http://www.cirip.ro/status/2876246, http://www.cirip.ro/status/2877810)

Figure 2. Digital storytelling exercise on Edmodo; (public link) http://www.edmodo.com/post/24761405

in (such as conferences or other scientific events) and conveying the information in a casual manner during the class.

Conveying information through stories is a very good method, because information is stored in the students' memory for a longer period of time this way, as compared to information occurring in another context (moreover, it becomes possible for them to learn by following an event). Stories improve organisational learning (the university as an organisation), highlight common values and sets of rules; they represent an excellent means of capturing, encrypting and transmitting tacit, high-value knowledge, while also playing an excellent role in knowledge sharing and organisational change.

The aim of each activity is to develop creative thinking, team work, social skills, communication skills and to promote interaction, etc.

Examples:

- **Personal Discovery Stories:** Tell how you discovered a lesson.
- **Success or Failure Stories:** Tell how you achieved (or not) something.

- **Biographies or Autobiographies:** Tell a story about yourself or another person from start to finish.
- **Picture Stories:** Tell a story in 5 images.
- **Collective stories, Imagine If … stories, Fiction (Time travellers), etc**

All exercises allocate sections for evaluation, for talks with students:

- What techniques/technologies did you use? Why?
- What skills did you use? Active listening, watching passively, etc.
- How important was it for you to participate in this game?

Case Study 2: Micro-Learning from the Stream

Even at a first glance there seems to be only a linguistic connection between microblogging and conferences/events, the recent literature registered an increased number of papers that analyse the *usage of microblogging as a community event*

Figure 3. An interactive mindmap of events types used suitable for microblogging technology, embedded in a note on the microblogging platform cirip (source http://www.cirip.ro/status/3484961?lg=en)

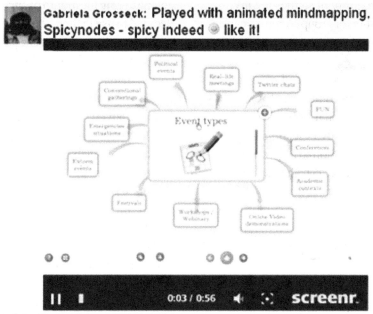

too (Figure 3). The usage may fall in one of the following categories:

- *Information interfaces* (Sutton, 2010; Kwak, Lee, Park and Moon, 2010; Mendoza, Pobleteand Castillo, 2010);
- *Communication* before, during and after the event (Balcom, 2007; Reinhardt, Ebner, Beham and Costa, 2009; Ebner and Reinhardt, 2009; Ebner et al, 2010) between participants, organizers, presenters and audience;
- *Monitoring the event* for non-participants (reporting/online coverage the event) (Ebner et al, 2010; Saunders et al, 2009);
- *Presentation* (Mitchell, 2009);
- *Collaborative keynotes* (Hart, 2010);
- *Participation/engaging audience* (Atkinson, 2009; Harry, Green and Donath, 2009);
- *Live-blogging session / instant discussions* (Ebner and Reinhardt, 2009);

- *Live annotations of a broadcast media event* (Shamma, Kennedy, Churchill, 2009);
- *Official/quasi-official/unofficial backchannel* (Ebner and Reinhardt, 2009);
- *Persistent / mobile / mobilizing backchannel* (McNely, 2009);
- *Messages transcription / twitter subtitling* (Du, Rosson, Carroll and Ganoe, 2010);
- *Back-chatting* (Yardi, 2006/2008; Osmond, 2009);
- *For evaluation* (Ebner et al., 2010; Shamma, Kennedy, Churchill, 2010),

and may also belong to a variety of settings: professional, academic / educational, scientifical, or for specific organisational purposes (McNely, 2009; Letierce et al, 2010).

These events use different digital / social media technologies / applications / platforms and several formats (e.g., (un) keynotes, multi / poster sessions, workshops, roundtable discussions, social events, etc.). Usually the participants use *hashtags* for the events / topics findability across different social platforms.

While the vast majority of studies are investigating the use of Twitter for group communication, the impact on group participants, quantitative analysis of message types, and motivational aspects, there are few research and case studies that address the use of microblogging for learning from informal conversational flow.

In this context, this study case aims to examine how the micro-connection to a specific event can enhance the learning experience of students enrolled in formal university courses. We tried to answer at this research question by exploring the integration of the *PLE Conference 2010* information flow into the microblogging platform cirip.eu.

Framework

In the 2nd semester of the academic year 2009-2010, the first two authors have run the following courses in private groups: ´Computer Assisted Instruction´ with freshmen of the Pedagogy Department of West University of Timisoara, respectively ´Multimedia´ with college juniors of University Ion Slavici and ´New Educational Technologies´, a continuous training course for teachers at University Politehnica of Timisoara.

Social Learning and Personal Learning Environments (PLE) were common topics of the three courses curriculum, and related materials were presented in the courses groups. Also, six students, divided in two working teams, taking part in the ´Multimedia´ course, had to develop collaborative projects related to PLE.

During the semester the first PLE Conference was planned out, and eventually took place in Barcelona during the month of July 2010. The teachers decided to use in their courses, for documentation and research the conference-related content and informal interactions on different social networks.

On January 8th, 2010, when the first call of papers for the PLE Conference (http://pleconference.citilab.eu) was launched, the *PLE / PLE Conference in Barcelona* group was open on cirip.eu, at http://cirip.ro/grup/plebcn and remained active until the last echo of this event faded away (Figure 4).

The members of this group were students, and also teachers, practitioners in education, trainers, and other persons interested in the PLE domain. The aims of the group were:

- To be a source of *real-time information, connections* with practitioners worldwide;
- To constitute *a framework for learning / communication / sharing in the PLE domain* for the students enrolled in these courses, but also for other members interested in this domain;
- To offer an environment for *strengthening knowledge in this domain* and *new PLE related experiments* for the authors;
- To offer access to all the group content, visualizations and statistics for *future reflections and studies.*

The group messages consist of:

- *tweets* referring to the PLE Conference, imported using the Twitter search API (the

Figure 4. The first message in the PLE group, source: http://cirip.ro/status/2180463

PLE / PLE Conference in Barcelona : cristinacost @timbuckteeth
@josiefraser @mariaperif: Oh Yeah! Time 4 a get together! ;-)
PLE conference 8-9 July! http://twurl.nl/705z5k #ple_bcn
posted on Friday 08 January 2010 22:40:14 from twitterAPI

searched terms are PLE_BCN or 'PLE Barcelona' or 'PLE Conference' or 'ple-conference.citilab.eu');

- *Blogs posts* which mention the conference, found using the Twingly search engine API, by searching 'PLE Conference Barcelona';
- *Multimedia notes* sent by the cirip members who joined this group.

This way the group was a *backchannel* of the PLE Conference and its messages reflected the interaction/debate on cirip.eu and in a worldwide community concerning PLE and conference. The actual number of messages on twitter and blogs could have been higher than the ones imported, the difference could be explained by Twitter and Twingly APIs limitations, but also by the specificated search terms. The content of the group and its information flow on PLE were enlarged with:

- *Specific requirements* for students' activities and *materials* related to PLE posted by

the facilitators in the group *Announcements* section;
- *Feeds/search feeds* on PLE topic monitored by the group members using the platform corresponding facility; they are delicious.com feeds with ple, pln, ple_bcn tags, also the feed corresponding to the collection built by the group members, using the ple_Cirip tag.

Students' Activities

Students' activities related to documentation and collaborative projects were organized in five stages and were hosted online by the PLE group, and by the private spaces of the two working teams; a few activities were also discussed face-to-face (f2f) in the laboratories. In completing their tasks, the students used the advanced facilities of the microblogging platform cirip.eu (Figure 5).

Because the semester ended prior to when the conference was held, participation in the PLE group during and after the conference was an

Figure 5. Message sent by a student, embedding a slideshare presentation (source: http://www.cirip.ro/status/2206463)

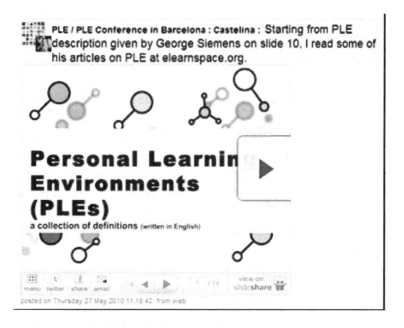

optional activity, performed especially by students interested in the fields of PLE and social learning for diploma thesis.

Students' activities were grouped in five stages ((M) are specific activities for Multimedia course):

1. *Preliminary documentation – online and f2f*
   a. Preliminary documentation related to PLE and task understanding
   b. Familiarisation with the PLE group, understanding the stream integration
   c. Open private groups for the two working teams (M);
2. *Documentation and interactions in the PLE group - online*
   a. Follow group messages (online or by SMS), identify key experts, main discussion topics, types of messages and resources;
   b. Commenting interesting posts and resources;
   c. Send (multimedia) messaging containing new resources;
   d. Interact with colleagues, facilitators, other group members;
   e. Track specific feeds - online or by SMS
   f. Participate in a survey related to possible definitions of PLE (M) - online or SMS reply;
   g. Each team has closely followed two key actors, identifying their work, entering virtually in their 'research laboratories' (M);
3. *Collaborative work – online and f2f* (M)
   a. Comment a video related to PLE by sending messages in the two teams' groups; the messages were exported as a .srt file by the specific facility of the platform, and used to subtitle the video published on dotsub.com
   b. Final projects published as collaborative Google docs, embedded in messages; the projects evaluated a few

multimedia resources, and the work of the followed experts;
4. *Activities evaluation – online and f2f*
   a. Conclusions related to the value of the PLE resources discovered
   b. Discussions on how students' own PLEs were developed and enlarged during the interaction with the stream;
5. *Optional activities - online*
   a. interactions and documentation during and after the conference.

By using the cirip.eu platform, we explored a new and challenging form of social learning, a new dimension of openness: *learning from the stream*, integrating a conference stream in higher education courses. The aim of our study was to make a preliminary evaluation, our findings can only lay the foundation for the elaboration of further and more thorough research. However, our explorative study leaded to several positive results.

Students taking part in different courses from three different universities have interacted with the stream, having common activities; thus this experiment is an affirmative answer to the question 'their tweets can reach other communities, in addition to their own?' (Letierce et al, 2009).

Stream integration in the PLE group allowed an uniform interaction, with the same communication mechanisms used by the students in the course group. Continuous facilitation and communication with students were needed because we could not estimate a priori the development of the ongoing stream volume, dynamics, and content.

Students appreciated that learning from the stream proved to be a novel and efficient method for documentation and research on PLE, meaning openness to real-time and valuable content, resources, and also an opportunity to follow experts and practitioners, being an illustration of open and social learning.

The *scenario* of learning from the stream was presented as a *mindmap* in the learning design group (Holotescu and Grosseck, 2010); the discussions with teachers, students, practitioners revealed other educational contexts in which such stream integration can be achieved, but also alternative and additional applications that can be used for integration.

The archived content and interactions, statistical data, and visualisations, can be accessed at http://cirip.ro/grup/plebcn, and used in future courses, documentation, and studies. Therefore, the group can be considered not only a *time capsule* for the worldwide practitioners' interaction concerning PLE and the PLE Conference, but also a *learning experience*, important in PLE documentation. Moreover, we can speak about a *learning serendipity*, which may provide substance for further research projects.

FINAL THOUGHTS

Microblogging is here to stay: as an effective tool for professional development and for collaboration with students and peers, that can change the rules of the teaching-learning process and models good pedagogy responsive to student's learning needs and challenging teachers to revisit their roles as educators. It also incorporates innovative characteristics or allows for mash-ups identified by the Horizon Report 2012 as emerging technologies likely to have a large impact over the coming three years in education around the globe: cloud computing, mobile and tablet computing, social reading, adaptive learning environments or augmented reality (NMC Horizon Report, 2012).

For the time being, microblogging is a source of intellectual optimism, a fact of life, which will increasingly become a fact of learning at all ages and levels of education. Thus, the current debates on whether or not to introduce microblogging into (higher) education are useful but ultimately worthless without experience, creativity and innovation – the desire to think of the educational process in completely new terms. We also hope that the present chapter represents an invitation to future reflections and studies for reviewing, expanding and validating the theoretical basis of using microblogging by all educational actors.

REFERENCES

Atkinson, C. (2009). *The backchannel: How audiences are using Twitter and social media and changing presentations forever.* New Riders Press.

Balcom Group. (2007). Retrieved from http://www.thebalcomgroup.com/node/124

Beliveau, L., et al. (2011). *New possibilities for teaching and learning: Yammer.* Retrieved March 1, 2012, from https://wiki.itap.purdue.edu/display/INSITE/Yammer#Yammer-YammerinEducationalSettings

Bernstein, M., Kairam, S., Suh, B., Hong, L., & Chi, E. H. (2010). A torrent of tweets: Managing information overload in online social streams. In *Proceedings CHI 2010 Workshop on Microblogging.* Retrieved from http://www.parc.com/content/attachments/torrent-of-tweets.pdf

Betta, C. (2007). *Social networking and academic life. Research Assignment, Literature Report.* Delft University of Technology.

Borau, K., Ullrich, C., Feng, J., & Shen, R. (2009). Microblogging for language learning: Using Twitter to train communicative and cultural competence. In Spaniol, M. (Eds.), *ICWL 2009, LNCS 5686* (pp. 78–87). Berlin, Germany: Springer-Verlag. doi:10.1007/978-3-642-03426-8_10

Buchem, I., & Camacho, M. (2011). *M-project: First steps to applying action research in designing a mobile learning course in higher education* (pp. 123–135). London Mobile Learning Group.

CDE, Center for Digital Education. (2008). *A connected life: A look at mobile strategies for schools, colleges and universities*. E-Republic.

Chickering, A. W., & Gamson, Z. F. (1987). Seven principles for good practice in undergraduate education. In *AAHE Bulletin*, (pp. 3–7).

CIBER, University College London and Emerald Group Publishing Ltd. (2010). *Social media and research workflow*. Retrieved from http://www.ucl.ac.uk/infostudies/research/ciber/social-media-report.pdf

Costa, C. (2011). *The Twitterati ... Workshop on Twitter for researchers*. Retrieved from http://virtual-doc.salford.ac.uk/pgrs/2011/02/25/the-twitterati/.

Cross, S., & Conole, G. (January 2009). *Learn about learning design*. Institute of Educational Technology, The Open University (UK). Retrieved from http://ouldi.open.ac.uk/Learn%20about%20learning%20design.pdf

Du, H., Rosson, M., Carroll, J. M., & Ganoe, C. (2009). I felt like a contributing member of the class: Increasing class participation with classcommons. In *Proceedings of the ACM 2009 International Conference on Supporting Group Work* (Sanibel Island, Florida, USA, May 10 - 13, 2009). GROUP '09. ACM, New York, NY, (pp. 233-242).

Dunlap, J. C., & Lowhenthal, P. R. (2009). Instructional uses of Twitter. In Lowenthal, P. R., Thomas, D., Thai, A., & Yuhnke, B. (Eds.), *CU online handbook: Teach differently. Create and collaborate*. University of Colorado Denver.

Ebner, M., Lienhardt, C., Rohs, M., & Meyer, I. (2010). Microblogs in higher education—A chance to facilitate informal and process oriented learning? *Computers & Education, 55*, 92–100. doi:10.1016/j.compedu.2009.12.006

Ebner, M., Mühlburger, H., Schaffert, S., Schiefner, M., Reinhardt, W., & Wheeler, S. (2010a). Getting granular on Twitter tweets from a conference and their limited usefulness for non-participants. *Proceedings of the WCC 2010 Conference* (track "Key Competencies in the Knowledge Society"). Retrieved from http://www.wcc2010.org

Ebner, M., & Reinhardt, W. (2009). Social networking in scientific conferences – Twitter as tool for strengthen a scientific community. In *Proceedings of the 1st International Workshop on Science 2.0 for TEL* (2009).

Feijóo, C., Pascu, C., Misuraca, G., & Lusoli, W. (2009). The next paradigm shift in the mobile ecosystem: Mobile social computing and the increasing relevance of users. *Communications & Strategies, 75*, 57–77.

Focus, F. (2011). *Social media usage trends among higher education faculty*. Special Report: A Magna Publication. Retrieved from http://www.facultyfocus.com/wp-content/uploads/images/2011-social-media-report.pdf

Focus, F., & Report, S. (2010). *Twitter in higher education 2010: Usage habits and trends of today's college faculty*. Magna Publication.

Gagnon, D. J. (2010). Mobile learning environments. *EDUCAUSE Quarterly, 33*.

Gavan, P. L. W. (2011). Micro-blogging and the higher education classroom: Approaches and considerations. In Wankel, C. (Ed.), *Teaching arts and science with the new social media: Cutting-edge technologies in higher education* (*Vol. 3*, pp. 365–383). Emerald Group Publishing Limited.

Giacomantonio, L. (2011). *20 ways to use Edmodo*. Retrieved from http://www.slideshare.net/seyfert6/20-ways-to-use-edmodo

Gilpin, D. (2010). Working the Twittersphere: Microblogging as professional identity construction. In Z. Papacharissi (Ed.), *The networked self: Identity, community and culture on social network sites*. New York, NY: Routledge. Retrieved from http://asu.academia.edu/DawnGilpin/Papers/120301/Working_the_Twittersphere_Microblogging_as_professional_identity_construction

Gray, K., Thompson, C., Sheard, J., Clerehan, R., & Hamilton, M. (2010a). Students as Web 2.0 authors: Implications for assessment design and conduct. *Australasian Journal of Educational Technology, 26*(1), 105–122.

Gray, K., Waycott, J., Clerehan, R., Hamilton, M., Richardson, M., Sheard, J., & Thompson, C. (2010b). *Web 2.0 authoring tools in higher education learning and teaching: New directions for assessment and academic integrity: A framework for field-testing and refining good practice guidelines in Pilot projects at Australian universities during Semester One 2010.*

Grosseck, G., & Holotescu, C. (2008). *Can we use Twitter for educational activities?* Paper presented at the 4th International Scientific Conference eLearning and Software for *Education*, April 17-18, 2008.Bucharest, Romania.

Grosseck, G., & Holotescu, C. (2009), *Indicators for the analysis of learning and practice communities from the perspective of microblogging as a provocative sociolect in virtual space*. In 5th International Scientific Conference eLSE – eLearning and Software for Education, Bucharest, 9-10 April 2009.

Grosseck, G., & Holotescu, C. (2010). Microblogging multimedia-based teaching methods best practices with Cirip.eu. In *Procedia - Social and Behavioral Sciences, 2*(2), 2151-2155. WCES 2010 Conference: Innovation and Creativity in Education. Istanbul, 4-8 February 2010.

Grosseck, G., & Holotescu, C. (2011). *Academic research in 140 characters or less*. Paper presented at 7th International Scientifiv Conference eLearning and Software for Education, Bucharest, April 28-29 2011. Retrieved from http://adlunap.ro/eLSE_publications/papers/2011/1590_1.pdf

Harry, D., Green, J., & Donath, J. (2009). *Backchan.nl: Integrating backchannels in physical space*. In CHI 2009, April 4–9, 2009, Boston, MA, USA.

Hart, J. (2010). *Using Twitter in a face-to face workshop*. Retrieved from http://janeknight.typepad.com/socialmedia/2010/05/using-twitter-in-a-facetoface-workshop.html

Hart, J. 2011). *Social learning handbook*. Retrieved March 12, 2012, from http://sociallearningcentre.co.uk/activities/how-to-use-twitter-for-social-learning/

Holland, C., & Muilenburg, L. (2011). Supporting student collaboration: Edmodo in the classroom. In M. Koehler & P. Mishra (Eds.), *Proceedings of Society for Information Technology & Teacher Education International Conference* 2011 (pp. 3232-3236). Chesapeake, VA: AACE. Retrieved from http://www.editlib.org/p/36816

Holotescu, C., & Grosseck, G. (2010). Microblogging-based teaching methods. Examples of good practices with Cirip.Eu. *Procedia Social Sciences, 2*(2), 2151-2155. Retrieved from http://www.sciencedirect.com/science/article/pii/S187704281000337X

Holotescu, C., & Grosseck, G. (2010a). *Learning to microblog and microblogging to learn: A case study on learning scenarios in a microblogging context*. In The 6th International Scientific Conference eLearning and Software for Education Bucharest, April 15-16. 2010.

Holotescu, C., & Grosseck, G. (2011a). M3-learning - Exploring mobile multimedia microblogging learning. *World Journal on Educational Technology, 3*(3), 168–176.

Holotescu, C., & Grosseck, G. (2011b). Cirip.Eu – An educational microblogging platform around objects2.0. *Form@re Open Journal, 74.*

Internet Reports, I. T. U. (2005). *The internet of things.* Retrieved from http://www.cahk.hk/Event/30/30.asp

Java, A., Song, X., Finin, T., & Tseng, B. (2007). Why we Twitter: Understanding usage and communities. In *WebKDD/SNA-KDD '07: Proceedings of the 9th WebKDD and 1st SNA-KDD 2007 Workshop on Web Mining and Social Network Analysis,* (pp. 56-65).

Junco, R., Heiberger, G., & Loken, E. (2011). The effect of Twitter on college student engagement and grades. *Journal of Computer Assisted Learning, 27*(2), 119–132. doi:10.1111/j.1365-2729.2010.00387.x

Keskin, N., & Matcalf, D. (2011). The current perspectives, theories and practices of mobile learning. *Turkish Online Journal of Educational Technology, 10*(2).

Kwak, H., Lee, C., Park, H., & Moon, S. (2010). *What is Twitter, a social network or a news media?* In WWW 2010, April 26–30, 2010, Raleigh, North Carolina, USA.

Laurillard, D., & Pachler, N. (Eds.). (2007). *Pedagogical forms of mobile learning: Framing research questions. Mobile learning: Towards a research agenda* (pp. 33–54). London, UK: WLE Centre, Institute of Education.

Letierce, J., Passant, A., Decker, S., & Breslin, J. G. (2010). *Understanding how Twitter is used to spread scientific messages.* In Web Science Conf. 2010, April 26-27, 2010, Raleigh, NC, USA.

Loh, T. (April 12, 2011). *Stop, drop and roll out Yammer.* Blog post. Retrieved March 2, 2012, from http://blog.yammer.com/blog/2011/04/emergency-preparedness-with-yammer.html

Marquis, J. (March 12, 2012). *Is Twitter the driving force behind upcoming educational challenge?* Blog post. Retrieved March 12, 2012, from http://www.onlineuniversities.com/blog/2012/03/is-twitter-the-driving-force-behind-upcoming-educational-change/

Mayernik, M., & Pepe, A. (2009). *Microblogging from the field: Capturing contextual information in highly mobile research.* Retrieved from http://research.cens.ucla.edu/events/?event_id=231

McNely, B. (2009). *Backchannel persistence and collaborative meaning-making.* In SIGDOC'09, October 5-7 2009. Bloomington, IN: ACM.

Mendoza, M., Poblete, B., & Castillo, C. (2010). *Twitter under crisis: Can we trust what we RT?* In 1st Workshop on Social Media Analytics (SOMA 10), KDD '10 Workshops, ACM, Washington, USA (July 25, 2010).

Mitchell, O. (2009). *How to present with Twitter (and other backchannels).* Retrieved from http://www.speakingaboutpresenting.com/wp-content/uploads/Twitter.pdf

Moran, M., Seaman, J., & Tinti-Kane, H. (2011). *Teaching, learning and sharing: How today's higher education faculty use social media.* Pearson Learning Solution and Babson Survey Research Group. Retrieved from http://www.pearsonlearningsolutions.com/educators/pearson-social-media-survey-2011-bw.pdf

Narkhede, P., Rajesh, P., & Kumar, S. (2010). Analysis on general profile of Plurk users. In *Rev Systems,* Bangalore. Retrieved from http://www.slideshare.net/bexdeep/plurk-analysis-4136802

Nevas, B. (2010). *Inquiry through action research: Effects of the Edmodo microblog on student engagement and performance*. Retrieved from http://www.scribd.com/doc/27372047/Edmodo-Research

NMC Horizon Report Project. (2012). *Short list, higher education edition*. Retrieved from http://horizon.wiki.nmc.org/file/view/2012-Horizon.HE-Shortlist.pdf

Ovadia, S. (2009). Exploring the potential of Twitter as a research tool. *Behavioral & Social Sciences Librarian*, *28*(4), 202–205. doi:10.1080/01639260903280888

Parry, D. (2008). *Twitter for academia*. Blog post. Retrieved from http://academhack.outsidethetext.com/home/2008/twitter-for-academia

Passant, A., Hastrup, T., Bojars, U., & Breslin, J. (2008). Microblogging: A semantic and distributed approach. In *Proceedings of the 4th Workshop on Scripting for the Semantic Web*, Tenerife, Spain, June 02, 2008.

Patten, B., Sanchez, A., & Tangney, B. (2006). Designing collaborative, constructionist and contextual applications for handheld devices. *Computers & Education*, *46*, 294–308. doi:10.1016/j.compedu.2005.11.011

Reinhardt, W., Ebner, M., Beham, G., & Costa, C. (2009). How people are using Twitter during conferences. In V. Hornung-Prahauser & M. Luckmann (Eds.), *Creativity and Innovation Competencies on the Web, Proceeding of 5 EduMedia Conference* (pp. 145-146). Salzburg.

Saunders, N., Beltrão, P., Jensen, L., Jurczak, D., Krause, R., Kuhn, M., & Wu, S. (2009). Microblogging the ISMB: A new approach to conference reporting. *PLoS Computational Biology*, *5*(1), e1000263. doi:10.1371/journal.pcbi.1000263

Shamma, D., Kennedy, L., & Churchill, E. (2009). *Tweet the debates*. Paper presented at WSM'09 October 23, 2009, Beijing, China.

Shamma, D., Kennedy, L., & Churchill, E. (2010). *Twetgeist: Can the Twitter timeline reveal the structure of broadcast events?* Paper presented at CSCW 2010, February 610, 2010, Savannah, Georgia, USA.

Shen, T. W. (2010). *Plurk intervention on artificial intelligent learning for higher education*. Paper presented at 2010 Conference on Teaching Excellence, 29-30 Nov. 2010. Retrieved from http://tec.tcu.edu.tw/et2010/paper/27.pdf

Smith, A., & Brenner, J. (2012). *Twitter use 2012*. A report by Pew Research Center. Retrieved from http://pewinternet.org/~/media//Files/Reports/2012/PIP_Twitter_Use_2012.pdf

Solis, B. (2012, 27 February). *The state of Twitterverse 2012*. Blog post. Retrieved March 1, 2012, from http://socialmediatoday.com/node/457621

Stutzman, F. (2009). *Information seeking during a life transition*. AOIR 2009 Doctoral Colloquium, Milwaukee. Retrieved from http://fredstutzman.com/papers/AOIRDC2009_Stutzman.pdf

Suster, M. (29 December 2010). *The power of Twitter in information discovery*. Retrieved March 1, 2012, from http://www.aonetwork.com/AOStory/Power-Twitter-Information-Discovery-0

Sutton, J. (2010). Twittering Tennessee: Distributed networks and collaboration following a technological disaster. In *Proceedings of the 7th International ISCRAM Conference* – Seattle, USA, May 2010.

Tinoca, L. (2011). *Assessment 2.0*. Retrieved from http://www.slideshare.net/luistinoca/assessment-20-10291238

Tu, B.-M., et al. (2011). Applying the perspective of technology sensemaking to Plurk user behaviors: An exploratory study. In *HICSS '11 Proceedings of the 2011 44th Hawaii International Conference on System Sciences.*

Uys, D. P. (2010). Blended learning in the ICT-enabled learning and teaching community of practice at Charles Sturt University. In *Proceedings of World Conference on Educational Multimedia, Hypermedia and Telecommunications 2010* (pp. 258-267). Chesapeake, VA: AACE. Retrieved from http://www.editlib.org/p/34647

Van Buskirk, E. (2009, August 10). Open source 'Twitter' could fend off the next twitpocalypse. *Wired.* Retrieved from http://www.wired.com/epicenter/2009/08/twitpocalypse

Watters, A. (6 March 2012). *Edmodo makes the move from Social network to Educational platform.* Blog post. Retrieved March 12, 2012, from http://hackeducation.com/2012/03/06/edmodo-makes-the-move-from-social-network-to-education-platform/

Wecker, M. (2011, October 24). Yammer trumps Facebook for some graduate students. *US News Education.* Retrieved from http://www.usnews.com/education/best-graduate-schools/articles/2011/10/24/yammer-trumps-facebook-for-some-graduate-students

William, R. (2011). *Edmodo.* Blog note. Retrieved from http://richardeducate.blogspot.com/2011/07/2nd-project-edmodo.html

Winer, D. (September 22, 2009). *What is the real time web?* Retrieved from on March 14, 2012, from http://scripting.com/stories/2009/09/22/whatIsTheRealtimeWeb.html

Yuksel, P., Robin, B. R., & McNeil, S. (2011). *Educational uses of digital storytelling around the world.* Retrieved from http://digitalstorytelling.coe.uh.edu/survey/SITE_DigitalStorytelling.pdf

ENDNOTES

1 Jaiku, purchased by Google in 2007, was shut down in January 2012.

2 Microblogging definition at Merriam Webster: http://www.merriam-webster.com/dictionary/microblogging.

3 A comparison of notetaking software can be found at http://en.wikipedia.org/wiki/Comparison_of_notetaking_software.

4 There are also location-based services (that identify and publish a person's location), such applications being Plazes, Foursquare, or Hotlist (the location has a status component too, for sharing information about user's current activities).

5 See for details http://www.wordspy.com/words/microblogging.asp

6 See for details http://allied.blogspot.com/2002/04/microblogging.html

7 See for details: http://www.blogschmog.net/2007/11/17/a-brief-history-of-microblogging/

8 See for details: http://c2mtl.com/biz-stone-talks-in-montreal-%E2%80%93-c2-mtl-loves-the-sound-bytes/

9 See for details http://blog.edmodo.com/2011/07/06/ideas-for-using-edmodo-add-yours/

10 Edu-plurkers communities can be found at http://plurk4educators.com and http://groups.diigo.com/group/plurking-educators.

11 See for details http://identi.ca/womeninhighered

12 We did not refer to Twiducate, a private social network like a microblogging platform, because it is used more for elementary and secondary students, http://www.twiducate.com/.

13 C4LPT (2012). *Top 100 Tools 2007-2011,* http://c4lpt.co.uk/top-tools/top-100-tools.

14 Rheingold, Howard (hrheingold), "Explore – it's not just about knowing how

to fiind experts, co-learners, but about exploration as invitation to serendipitous encounter", 2 January 2011, 4:38 AM Tweet. https://twitter.com/#!/hrheingold/status/21394804449480704.

[15] As one professor put it, 'I have no interest in adding yet another communication tool to my overloaded life.' (Faculty Focus, 2011)

[16] The Tim Kelly's 4A vision: ´anywhere, anytime, by anyone and anything´ (ITU, 2005)

[17] See Edna Project: http://www.groups.esa.edu.au/course/view.php?id−2146

Chapter 17

The Impact of Social Media on Scholarly Practices in Higher Education:
Online Engagement and ICTs Appropriation in Senior, Young, and Doctoral Researchers

Antonella Esposito
University of Milan, Italy

ABSTRACT

This chapter reports selected findings from a small-scale, exploratory study aiming to provide a snapshot of actual modes of uptaking new digital tools for research purposes. The study consists in an interview project, carried out in a large Italian university and constituted by semi-structured interviews to 14 senior, young, and doctoral researchers, working in humanities, social sciences, medicine, and physics subject areas. Whereas the most popular attitude is a pragmatic and efficiency-driven approach in selecting and using old and new tools, a few isolated profiles of digital scholars emerge, championing the construction of their digital identity along with networked modes of knowledge production and distribution, despite the lack of legitimation of their own research context.

INTRODUCTION

New technologies are challenging "cultures in higher education" (Elhers & Schnekenberg 2010), that is the way academics and students research, learn and teach at the university. The growing complexity of the current digital landscape is producing an increasing overlap of modes of working and learning in university (Weller, 2011) and is affecting academic 'scholarship', that is faculty's expertise and practice of discovery, engagement and teaching. Indeed in the last two

DOI: 10.4018/978-1-4666-2851-9.ch017

decades researchers have increasingly build their expertise and conducted their inquiries in digital environments, enabling an increasing convergence between scientific and humanistic research work, based on data- and information-intensive, distributed scholarship, as well as on a more collaborative, interdisciplinary approach (Borgman, 2007). However, in recent times, discussions about forms and legitimation of digital scholarship's practices (e.g. Pearce, Weller, Scanlon et al., 2010) – have been informed by reflections on the disruptive action of Web 2.0 approach (Anderson, 2007) or social Web (Boulos & Wheleer, 2007) and related tools - and its impact on the traditional assets of academic scholarship and scholarly communication practices. The new relationship between participatory media and scholarly practices is developing a form of digital scholarship that some define as 'networked participatory scholarship', referring to "scholars' participation in online social networks to share, reflect upon, critique, improve, validate, and otherwise develop their scholarship". (Veletsianos & Kimmons, 2012)

Indeed, in the literature focusing on changing scholarly practices, opinions seem to be polarised on the one side on an ideological take on innovative potentialities of digital tools towards a more extended culture of sharing (Weller, 2011) and a participatory approach in teaching and learning (Veletsianos, 2010); on the other side on a range of empirical findings (e.g. Schonfeld & Housewright, 2010; Harley, Acord, Earl-Novell et al., 2010; Procter, Williams & Stewart, 2010) that show how cautious and minority is the approach to new technologies among researchers and how resilient is their attitude to change the current scholarly communication asset. On the one hand emergent profiles of "digital, networked, open" (Weller, 2011) researchers are drawn from a range of individual pioneering cases scattered in the academic world; on the other hand, capacity and opportunity for 'digital' doctoral and young researchers to revolutionize current research practices are proven to be highly controversial

(James, Norman, De Baets et al., 2009; Harley et al., 2010; British Library/JISC, 2011). Here it seems to occur the same discrepancy between the discourse on the "state-of-the art" and that on the "state-of-the-actual", recently argued by Neil Selwyn (2011), referring to educational technologists' accounts of revolutionary use of digital tools and actual evidence on technology adoption from educational settings. In fact it is worth recalling that also issues of Web 2.0 impact on teaching and learning are largely treated with an "essentialist view" (Brown, 2012), that is focusing on general potentialities of new technologies, without considering how academics perceive social media in their own contexts and with respect to their beliefs about teaching.

The proposed chapter is located within this gap and intends to add to empirical knowledge in the field of current and emerging digital scholarship's practices, by illustrating first hand accounts from a non probabilistic sample of individual university scholars, working in specific disciplinary fields and communities and coping with an increasingly complex digital landscape.

Drawn from an unpublished MRes dissertation study[1], the chapter aims to report selected findings from semi-structured interviews to 14 senior, young and doctoral researchers, working in Humanities, Social Sciences, Medicine and Physics areas, in a large Italian university. This small-scale, exploratory study considers the viewpoint of digital scholarship's practices, that is research practices - such as information access, authoring, sharing, networking, publishing - mediated by 'old' and 'new' technologies. The goal is to draw a 'snapshot' of actual modes of uptake of new digital tools for research purposes, highlighting emergent profiles of 'digital scholars' and new demands from faculty for institutional support and training. In particular, the chapter intends to shed light on changing research practices in higher education, probing comparable behaviours of technology use in different subject areas and highlighting relations with teaching and learning approach. Interviews' accounts aim to reveal reasons why faculty are adopting tools and behaviours they state to adopt, more than merely inquiry what they are doing with technology. Results are discussed in relation with large scale empirical studies and referring to: the framework of ICTs appropriation in diverse disciplinary areas by Fry (2006); the typologies of online engagement – the continuum Visitor/Resident - devised by White & Le Cornue (2011).

The chapter concludes hoping for further research on the theme and in particular focuses on rethinking of doctoral students' training in digital environments as a priority from an institutional perspective.

BACKGROUND

The following sections provide an overview of theoretical and empirical studies among which the reported study is located: discourses on the celebrated potentialities of social media and models of evolving profiles of scholars and forms of scholarship are supplemented with theoretical frames to gain insights on subject-bounded ICTs appropriation and individual propensity towards a certain type of online engagement. Finally, findings from a range of large scale international inquiries of ICTs adoption for research purposes are discussed, in order to provide readers with enough elements to interpret the instance being researched.

Social Media: Identity and Typologies

'Social media' is a buzz word that has recently outclassed in popularity the expression 'Web 2.0 tools' and that generically refers to a varied and ever evolving cluster of cloud-computing software tools and environments being developed in the last decade: in other words, it deals with technologies and services distributed by interconnected virtual servers across the web. They provide basic free access and use to end users, have simplified and consistent navigational features, are cross-platform and everywhere accessibile through smart phones and any mobile computing device. However, this broad term encompasses remarkably different tools, that indeed often scholars have attempted to frame, aiming to reduce confusion in educators.

Suter, Alexander & Kaplan (2005) conducted a review of the attributed meanings to social media and identifies three diverse perspectives to intend this term:

Social software as a tool (for augmenting human social and collaborative abilities), as a medium (for facilitating social connection and information interchange), and as an ecology (for enabling a 'system of people, practices, values, and technologies in a particular local environment'). (Suter et al., 2005, p. 48)

Crook, Cummings, Fisher et al. (2008) focus on tools' characteristics to distinguish functions such as media sharing sites, in which users can create and sharing multimedia content; blogging, in which single/multiple users can write a web-based journal and receive comments; wiki spaces, in which users can have different levels of access to read, share and edit pages; social networking sites, that provide ways for structuring social relations among members, allowing the set up of 'subgroups'. Elsewhere, Siemens & Tittenberg (2009) propose to group social media according to six different typologies of actions being enabled by such tools:

1. Access to resources (e.g. through a wiki space or Google Reader).
2. Online presence (e.g. running a blog or using a geolocator in a smartphone).
3. Digital identity (e.g. curating own personal/professional profile in a social networking site).

4. Aggregating resources (e.g. through devoted services such as Netvibes or Scoop.it, or personalizing a blog or a general-purpose social networking site as Facebook).

5. Content creation (e.g. through a blog or a wiki, but also through a media production service).

6. Interacting in synchronous or asynchronous mode (e.g. using microblogging services such as Twitter or audio/video conferencing tools such as Skype).

On the other hand, Dabbagh & Reo (2010) draw attention to the charachteristics of multifunctionality belonging to social media, that in their view should be thought as a continuum, being inflected according three main levels of utilization: management of personal information; configuration of sharing of resources, social networking activity.

In fact, Conole & Alevizou (2010, p. 11) notice how social media have been evolving, becoming always more integrated each others, through common functions such as "tagging, commenting, rating, syndication and the development of relationships ('friendship')". So, the ensemble of social media can be intended as a "platform for dialogue and collaboration and user-generated content as a mutually added value component for community building" (ib.). This suggests that social media have been enabling a "social revolution" rather than a technological one (Downes, 2005) and leads to consider as more approaprate for these emergent technologies the interpretative perspective of an 'ecology' of tools and practices.

Social Media as Change Agents in Education

In the last decade the rapid spread of 'social media' has in fact changed the idea of the Web from that of a product provided by software developers to users/consumers to a concept of web as "an artifact evolving according to shifting user engagement" (Brown, 2012, p. 50). This new generation of software tools – as a whole reported as 'Web 2.0' or 'social web' - are seen as embedding the "powerful ideas" (Anderson, 2007, p. 2) of a new approach to knowledge production and distribution: architecture of participation, collaboration, user-generated content, openness as 'philosophy' and work practices drawn from the open source movement. These value-laden digitally-mediated practices – that are at the same time drivers and result of the social web approach – are considered as many change agents, in an ecological perspective of co-evolution of societal changes, arising from a digital generation and pedagogical innovations (Brown & Adler, 2008; Dabbagh & Reo, 2010). Social media would constitute for instance an enabling context for 'open scholarship' (Anderson, 2009), that is for a participatory approach in teaching and learning, whose tenets refer to a "pedagogy of abundance" (Weller, 2011) of free resources, means and data to be investigated, to an increasing complexity of problems to be faced collaboratively and a need to contrast a trend towards the 'commodification' of knowledge. Moreover, the social Web "begins to resemble to an academic world" (Haythonthwaite, 2009) since it embeds similar learning practices. So, a move to the participatory culture featuring Web 2.0 approach "may, in learning, be a transformation to an inquiry culture taught, practiced and used at all levels of education" (ib.). The envisioned close relation between networked-based modes of knowledge production and distribution and academic cultures of teaching, learning and research makes social media as the enabling locus in which the formation of both digital learner and future academic is at work. This leads for instance to apply the learner-centric pedagogical perspective of 'heutagogy' – generally speaking "the ability to play with form and question existing structures" (Garnett, 2010) – to the "process concerned with thinking about new knowledge", in order to enhance quality of 'epistemic cognition' in doctoral students working in the social web era.

However, these progressive views, including a series of popular metaphors (e.g. 'digital natives' by Prensky, 2001; 2009) related to the coming-to-age digital generation, have to come to terms with a body of empirically-based inquiry, that show a diverse and nuanced landscape of university students (e.g. Jones & Cross, 2009; Bullen & Morgan, 2011). Long-term research – such as the LLIDA Project (2009) across UK universities - probed that students in higher education are actually changing their digital behaviours, but show a variety of communication, collaboration, experiential learning and problem-solving approaches that can not be merely reduced to one model of 'digital learner'. On the contrary, higher education students can be critically seen as learners being situated in discipline-grounded knowledge building approaches as well as in combinations of tools and tecniques that fit academic practice and professional development (Sharpe, Beetham & de Freitas, 2010): at the same time they need to become well acquainted with this complex digital landscape and to develop critical thinking about that.

On the other hand, there is a lack of field research focusing on academics' perception of social media for teaching and learning (Brown, 2012), and also regards to changing research practices it is claimed that "the field is in dire need of empirical data" (Veletsianos, 2011), hoping for research agendas to be informed with the investigation of actual digital research practices across higher education settings.

In fact, without empirical investigations as informed basis, both fields of inquiry are at risk to be affected by the same argument of 'potentialities of social media': an analysis of digital scholarly practices may be in danger of becoming another "edtech bubble" (Selwyn, 2010, p. 11), that is a "self-contained, self-referenting, and self-defining" (ib., p. 11) debate which tends to attribute value-driven 'digital' behaviours belonging to a group of early adopters in specific disciplines (e.g. educational technology), to all subject areas, every

national and local university contexts and irrespective of any individual researchers' attitude towards technology use. As a further example of that, in the next section two diverse but complementary conceptualizations of 'scholar' and 'scholarship' are reported, as interesting frames that are likely to shed light on emerging phenomena of digitally-mediated scholarly practices, but that need to be empirically verified and theoretically integrated with issues such as discipline-bounded relation and personal propensity to ICTs adoption.

The Evolving Notions of Scholar and Scholarship

Among the number of threads on debate on the evolution of scholarship in the digital age, for the purpose of this chapter the author particularly considers the notion of 'digital scholar' (Weller, 2011) and the dimension of 'co-creating learning' (Garnett & Ecclesfield, 2011) as characterizing emerging forms of 'being academic' in the social media era. Whereas Borgman (2007) - in her seminal work on the evolution of scholarship in the digital age - focuses on digital infrastructures as enabling new data-driven research practices and as a consequence scholarly community's adaptive behaviours, on the other hand contributions to the notion of 'digital scholarship' by authors such as Pearce, Weller et al.'s (2010), Weller (2011) and Veletsianos & Kimmons (2012) strongly rely on the use of Web 2.0 tools by individual researchers, who increasingly act as networked researchers, beyond the discipline- and institution-bounded conventions and constraints.

In particular, Martin Weller (2011) conducts an accurate review of emerging scholarly practices that make use of the social Web and tentatively defines an emergent profile of "digital scholar" as "someone who employs digital, networked and open approaches to demonstrate specialism in a field" (2011, chapter 'Digital, networked and open'). He chronicles the appearence of each of these attributes across researchers' practices since early 90's. However, more radically, he draws on the democratisation of the social web to envision that a "well-respected digital scholar may well be someone who has no institutional affiliation" (ib.), because the networks and the online identity researchers are able to establish are becoming more and more important for one's scholarly reputation. Moreover, he explicitly holds a close relation between digital scholarship and 'openness', that is a more extended culture of sharing in academia:

Digital scholarship is more than just using information and communication technologies to research, teach and collaborate; it also includes embracing the open values, ideology and potential of technologies born of peer-to-peer networking and wiki ways of working in order to benefit both the academy and society. (Weller, 2011, chapter 'The nature of scholarship')

On the other hand, Garnett & Ecclesfield (2011) focus on the epistemological transition being enabled by the current networked environments, that foster a blurring distinction between knowledge production and knowledge transmission in higher education. They work on a significant conceptual re-thinking of the popular Boyer's (1990) model of scholarship, articulated in the dimensions of 'discovery', 'integration', 'application' and 'teaching'. Garnett & Ecclesfield add the dimension of 'co-creating', that refers to the participation process of both teachers and students (and practitioners) to the "permanent Beta" (2011, p. 13) of knowledge, through a collaborative creation of learning. Indeed, such a new dimension becomes constitutive and informs all the four dimensions in Boyer's model of scholarship, including that of 'discovery', reformulated in a "co-creation of research agendas" (2011, p. 14) that originally updates the traditional role of researcher and goes beyond Boyer's institution-centric approach. This position is explicitly inspired by the Open Scholarship movement (Anderson, 2009) and is linked to arguments endorsing a close relationship between 'e-research' (here being used as an alternative

term with respect to 'digital scholarship') and 'e-learning' (Borgman, 2006; Haythornwaythe, 2009).

However, it is acknowledged by these authors that such an evolution in scholarship is still 'emergent' and can be better understood within an ecological framework of "digital scholarship resilience matrix" (Weller, 2011), in which both conservative motifs and drivers of innovation should be identified at governmental, institutional, disciplinary and individual level.

ICTs Appropriation and Subject Areas

This ecological perspective permits to introduce the discourse of how the different disciplinary cultures relate to technology use for research, and then to gain understanding on a likely adoption of new tools and environments by individual scholars.

To this end, a study of Fry's (2006) is considered, since it focuses on how "the local work organization and communication practices of scholars within specialist fields influences the use of networked digital resources" (2006, p. 302) both in formal and informal communication. He applies the use of digital networks to a framework in which disciplinary cultures are characterized by different degrees and interplay of 'mutual dependence' and 'task uncertainty', as many analytical elements to consider social and epistemic aspects in scholarly practices.

For instance, whereas there is high level of 'task uncertainty' (scarce agreement of research priorities) and low level of 'mutual dependence' (researchers hardly made use of colleagues' outputs), an individualistic culture is more likely to be developed. Fry links such variations in cultural attitudes in different subject areas to diverse modes of appropriation of ICTs by researchers:

(Academic) fields that have a highly politicized and tightly controlled research culture will develop a coherent field-based strategy for the uptake and use of ICTs, whereas domains that are pluralistic and have a loosely organized research culture will appropriate ICTs in an ad-hoc localized manner. (Fry, 2006, p. 303)

It would seem fairly easy to assign the former type of behaviour to scientific areas such as Physics, in which there is strong agreement about research priorities and sharing and re-use of colleagues outputs, whilst the latter one is more likely to occur in Humanities area. However, to identify bounded academic fields with specific cultural features is at danger of oversimplification, due to the increasing high specialization and interdisciplinarity of research areas (Becher & Trowler, 2001; Trowler, Saunders & Bamber, 2012). On the other hand, Fry's framework leads attention to the opportunity to empirically probe whether a different propensity towards innovative ICT-mediated research approaches may be implied for researchers working in domains either embedding a "coherent field-based strategy for the uptake and use of ICTs" or an appropriation of ICTs "in ad-hoc localized manner".

Prevailing Academic Activities and Online Engagement

Issues of ICTs uptake in different disciplinary fields should also consider motivations of individual researchers with respect to prevailing activities in their career (LSE Public Policy Group, 2011, pp. 38-58) and to their own attitude towards online engagement with emerging tools (White & Le Cornu, 2011).

In the conceptual schema of a 'balanced scorecard' (LSE Public Policy Group, 2011, pp. 38-58), six evolving fields of activities of scholars' career are identified: research (building of inquiry skills through training opportunities and theoretical and empirical studies); authoring (publication of research outputs); teaching; administration (engagement in bureaucratic and coordination activities); networking, celebrity (management

of one's 'personal branding'). Engagement on a particular subset of such dimensions depends on one's career development's phase, as well as the diverse professional orientation and choices by individual researchers. A doctoral student is likely to mainly curate dimensions of 'research', 'authoring' and to a degree ''networking', whilst a senior researcher is likely to be progressively engaged in all the six dimensions. However, there could be a particular stress on networking and celebrity or on administration or authoring according to the diverse professional orientation by some individual researchers.

I argue that there might be a close relation between the engagement in a particular subset of such fields of activities and the selection and the patterns of adoption of technologies by the individual researcher. In particular, the increasing convergence between the dimensions of 'networking' and 'celebrity' (LSE Policy Group, 2011, p. 45), as enabled by networked environments, sheds light on new forms of research impacts that might be undertaken by the individual researcher and thus on related motivations in ICTs uptake:

Celebrity has hugely increased in importance relative to networking interactions. Whereas once academics relied on people knowing them and their work personally in order to gain citations from other academics, now what matters is how easy it is to find someone's work – and how many versions of it there are out there in different channels to be picked up and noticed by other academics and researchers. (LSE Policy Group, 2011, p. 45)

In this sense, social and participatory media – that opens up new spaces of personal intervention (vs institutional ones) - would seem to better fit researchers working within disciplines in which an individualistic attitude towards technology is more common and the appropriation of ICTs is more likely to occur in "ad hoc localized manner".

However, it is worth considering the motivating role of different online engagement undertaken by individual researchers with respect to 'old' and 'new web-based technologies, and being inflected according to personal and institutional level. In fact, some recent reflections (White & Le Cornu, 2011; White, 2012) whilst help to overcome the discourse of the generation factor in the adoption of new web-based tools, focusing instead on the diverse type of online engagement being enabled by the emergent environment of the social Web. This is thought as constituted by new kinds of computing applications that are better explained with the metaphor of 'place', that is of "a sense of being present with others" (White & Le Cornu, 2011) rather than that of 'tool', that is "a means to an end". This implies for the authors a shift paradigm from a type of online engagement by individuals as 'Visitors', who use the Web as a shed from which selecting the appropriate tool if needed for a specific purpose, to an attitude as 'Residents', who intend the Web as "a place to express opinions, a place in which relationships can be formed and extended" (ib.), and where content and persona (or digital identity) overlap. The Visitors / Residents typology is considered by White & Le Cornu as a continuum in which individual's digital behaviour can be located: the propensity towards the former or the latter can be valued within a frame of digital literacies, that is referring to the whole skills set required by the context and subject area in which the individuals usually carry out their activities. Given that, it can be argued that a researcher aiming to get more research impact by intersecting 'networking' and 'celebrity' dimensions is likely to be more successful by adopting a Resident approach rather than a Visitor one. This provides a perspective on researchers' motivation in using digital tools that may to a degree prescind from disciplinary conventions for ICTs appropriation. For instance, it might happen that a young researcher with a prevailing Resident approach in online engagement gives more value to 'networking' field of activities against their peers, by relating her own behaviour to advantages for 'research' and 'authoring' dimensions.

Empirical Studies on Scholarly Adoption of Digital Tools

Recent large-scale studies – carried out across UK and US - particularly focus on social media in research activities and agree that there is very limited evidence of the spread among faculty of the celebrated new channels of communication (Harley et al., 2010; Procter et al., 2010; Schonfeld & Housewright, 2010). On the contrary, traditional channels, such as conferences, seminars, often made more efficient by the transition to digital but otherwise largely unchanged – remain the most important ways in which faculty communicate both formally and informally. (Schonfeld & Housewright, 2010, p. 25)

Web 2.0 tools (e.g. blogs, RSS feeds, wikis, twitter) are not cited as popular mechanisms and are even seen as a "waste of time because they are not peer reviewed" (Harley et al., 2010, p. 25). This is also confirmed by small-scale inquiries, such as Kraker & Lindstaedt's (2011) carried out in the e-learning research field and Pearce's audit (2010) within the Open University, in UK.

On the one hand Procter et al.'s study reveals that "The process of experimentation and innovation is currently highly localised and dispersed, and likely to be protracted" (2010, p. 8). On the other hand, CIBER's one – explicitly surveying social media adopters – states that "Social media have found a place in the research workflow for many academics and are proving their worth" (2010, p. 16).

More interestingly, Procter et al. (2010) and CIBER (2010) investigate reasons why researchers are likely to adopt any of social media tools:

The services most likely to succeed are those where researchers are actively involved in uncovering, exploring and exploiting new capabilities, and adapting them to their own purposes, in accordance with the broader cultures and contexts and contexts in which they undertake their work. (Procter et al., 2010, p. 8)

Moreover, whereas working with peers based in other institutions may be a driver in the adoption of new technologies (CIBER, 2010, p. 21), the most important barriers to uptake of digital tools are reported to be the "lack of clarity over the precise benefits that might accrue to the researcher" (CIBER, 2010, p. 25) and the fact that "few services have achieved yet the critical mass needed to achieve the positive network effect that stimulate pervasive use by particular communities". (Procter et al., 2010, p. 7)

Whereas Harley et al. (2010) consider mid-career scholars as profiles more likely to pilot and adopt social media for research purposes, on the other hand they generally conclude that: "It is premature to assume that Web 2.0 platforms geared toward early public exposure of ideas or data, or open peer review, are going to spread among scholars at the most competitive institutions". (Ib., p. 15)

Focusing on demographic factors, in UK universities the adoption of Web 2.0 technologies is proven to be increasingly spread across PhD students (JISC/British Library, 2011). In general, early career researchers (James et al., 2009) are probed to use a number of 'old' (including 'email' as the key tool) and 'new' tecnologies: in particular, they show great flexibility in adapting their digital behaviours to supervisors' and peers' technological preferences. However, findings related to the frequency of usage of new tools reserve some surprises in favour of older generations of researchers (Procter et al., 2010), whilst elsewhere (JISC/British Library, 2011) also a scarce creativity in ICT use is attributed PhD students. Moreover, a survey addressing scholars in a range of international academic contexts (CIBER, 2010) prefers to apply the innovation types' model by Rogers (1995) to identify 'early adopters' of social Web tools across generations of academics, rather than featuring any younger generations' innovative approach. On the other hand it is increasingly acknowledged that social media embed a variety of potentialities for doctoral education (Millan & Bromage, 2011), that these tools are already affecting doctoral research process towards a more collaborative approach (Zaman, 2010) and play a key role in the identity building endeavour by prospective researchers (Coverdale, 2011). However, for doctoral candidates (James et al. 2009, p. 36) a local research environment being hostile towards tech innovations (e.g. innovations being perceived by senior scholars as frivolous or time-wasting) and the lack of institutional support (e.g. the blocking of social media web sites) are as many factors that can hold new researchers back from the adoption of new tools. Likewise, considering research universities in US context, Harley et al. (2010) hold that is unlikely that young scholars can actually innovate research practices, because these apprentice researchers usually rely on behaviours and discipline-bounded conventions followed by senior scholars, in order to advance in their career. On the other hand, there is some evidence (Ferguson, Clough & Hosein, 2010) that also PhD students that adopt innovative practices in their doctoral journey (such as regularly running a blog as a research journal), when they start their academic career and are involved in funded projects, may have to change their approach to social media, due to external constraints that impose limitations to sharing practices whilst a study is underway.

To conclude this brief review, it is worth noting that most studies focusing on emergent media fail to get the whole picture of technology adoption in research practices, because they often do not appropriately link 'old' with 'new' tools and patterns of adoption, overlook studies on ICTs in research before the social web (see Fry, 2006), and omit to consider the role being played by well-established institutional digital environments and tools such as personal webpages, digital libraries, email accounts, research information systems (Bitter & Muller, 2011).

THE INTERVIEW PROJECT

Methodology and Sampling Strategy

The reported research embeds an exploratory and qualitative approach, aiming to gain a snapshot of faculty's views in different subject areas and to draw prevalent behaviours and trends. To this purpose, an interview project was undertaken by using semi-structured face-to-face individual interviews as data gathering method and reporting technique. The participants in this investigation were individual researchers working in specific disciplinary fields and communities, in a single university. The interview approach relates to the notion of 'active inteview' by Holstein and Gubrium (1995, p. 141), who consider meanings as being produced through "collaborative accomplishments" between interviewer and interviewee. Interviews data were analyzed through comparison with previous empirical studies and by examining any implications for emerging modes of knowledge production and distribution, differences in ICTs appropriation in diverse subject areas and related problems of legitimation and motivation in part of individual researchers.

The study was carried out across the University of Milan, that is one of the largest public and multidisciplinary universities in Italy and entails a range of research areas. The author's condition as an "insider" at the University of Milan allowed her for an effective use of convenience and snowball sampling strategies to recruit research participants. So, firstly she contacted one researcher for each subject area, selecting among people she knew as examples of scholarly behaviour in digital environment and/or she was told to be interested in discussing the topic being researched. These early interviewees acted as many gatekeepers in their subject area and led her to identify other colleagues it would be worth interviewing. The initial aim was to select a group of 12 informants, and to interview at least three academics for each area,

preferably belonging to different generations (e.g. a senior researcher, a young researcher, a doctoral student). Cases and interviewees were selected on the basis of the expectations of information content they were likely to provide (Flyvbjerg, 2004, p. 426). The construction of the sample was progressively guided by the goal of "maximizing variation" (Larsson, 2009, p. 31) of opinions, searching for examples of specific research practices as undertaken in digital environments within different work contexts and traditions of disciplinary conventions. This approach is apparent in the choice of the four broad subject areas: Humanities, Social Sciences for soft sciences, Physics and Medicine for hard sciences. Each subject area in turn represents distinctive research needs and practices, but a particular attention was applied in order to not select interviewees working in the same discipline, department or project. Moreover, whereas it was possibile, one researcher was selected from an interdisciplinary context (e.g. Informatics for Humanities) and/or from a research setting located at the boundary between the university and external research institutes. Furthemore, in order to pursue the goal of maximizing variation, the number of interviewees raised to 14, increasing from 3 to 4 informants for Humanities and Medicine. Below a list of the interviewee' profiles is reported (Table 1).

Interviews to Senior, Young, and Doctoral Researchers

This section provides an account of selected findings drawn from the dissertation study undertaken from January to October 2011. The part of the interview schedule considered for the present chapter was planned to answer the following research question: What are current uses of digital tools and environments for research purposes in a higher education context?

Specifically, participants were asked to provide information about what tools they currently use

Table 1.

Subject	Discipline	Typology
Humanities	Medieval Philosophy	Senior Researcher
Humanities	Informatics for Humanities	Young researcher
Humanities	Language and Culture of the Ancient Greece	Young researcher
Humanities	(Digital) Archeology	Doctoral researcher
Social Sciences	Sociology of cultural processes	Doctoral researcher
Social Sciences	Social Research Methods	Senior Researcher
Social Sciences	Human Resources Management	Senior Researcher
Physics	Theoretical Physics	Senior Researcher
Physics	High Energies	Doctoral researcher
Physics	Optics	Young researcher
Medicine	Dentistry	Senior Researcher
Medicine	Anatomy	Young researcher
Medicine	Psychology	Young researcher
Medicine	Translational Medicine	Young researcher

and for which scholarly or non scholarly practices; how they perceive such tools; whether and to what extent new digital tools affect boundaries of their research communities and contribute to shape an idea of 'digital researcher'.

Common and Emergent Tools for Research Work

Email service and digital library result to be the most utilized tools (beyond basic desktop software) across the totality of interviewees, irrespective of subject areas, age groups, personal attitudes and specific work context. In addition, a variety of technological devices and software applications are named, as emergent tools in everyday life and for specific research activities.

Skype is being used by 12 out of 14 interviewees, whilst 5 researchers have a profile in Facebook (but 1 only for private purposes), 3 in Twitter and/or Linkedin, and 2 in Academia.Edu. Social citation tools such as Zotero and CiteULike are respectively mentioned 3 and 2 times, as well as Dropbox among document sharing tools and Google Docs as a co-writing instrument. Two interviewees state to run a blog for research purposes (one is a contributor in a multi-authored blog). Applications such as Basecamp, Quora, Endnote and Doodle were named only once and by the same researcher. Devices such as smart phones are named 3 times, tablet/e-readers (IPad) in 2 cases and e-readers-only (Kindle) only in one case.

In fact, email has become over time a manifold instrument that goes far beyond the original function of one-to-one communication tool (Physics, #1): most researchers explicitly still prefer to rely on this 'old' technology to networking and to co-edit a multi-authored paper. Moreover digital library, enabling an immediate access to a plenty of published research, actually makes researchers more aware of "how much we have not read yet on a defined topics" (Humanities, #1) and "boost interdisciplinary argumentation, just through the cross-reading of papers". (Physics, #1)

However, the landscape becomes more nuanced when choices of further devices occur and any relationship between everyday life and technological needs at work is considered. So, certain types of common instruments, such as an audio/video recorder, may be an integral part of everyday life of a Social Science researcher (#2), whilst a number of 'general purpose' devices may serve a range of specialized functions for another investigator:

Currently I use a Kindle to read e-books; an IPad, that supports Unicode, to read classic texts in Greek language; a smartphone to syncronize home and work activities, including time spent in digital library and to keep in contact with students, if needed. (Humanities, #3)

In three cases researchers explain that they are non-users of social networking sites because they do not feel any need to manage their private contacts through digital networks (e.g. Facebook): likewise, in three cases interviewees maintain that there is no necessity in their professional life to use the latest mobile phones, and that there is too much commercial pressure on this.

Among new generation tools, undoubtedly Skype results to be as the most favorite one, since it is commonly used to multiply opportunities to meet distant peers and/or faculty/doctoral students (Social Sciences, #1, #2; Medicine #4), whilst others (Humanities #2; Medicine #3; Physics, #2, #3) especially find it very useful to quickly solve problems whereas collaborative projects are at stuck or to re-negotiate collective decisions at the beginning of a new task in the work plan.

Blogging activity is scarcely spread and is not acknowledged at all as a rewarding and/or recommended activity, sometimes even as a means for postgraduate students to practice their scholarly writing:

I would be cautious about blogging for post-graduate students, especially in scientific areas: they first need to listen to experts, for a long time, then they will be able to express their opinions. The scientific method embeds specific constraints and instruments that you must acquire, before being able to build on. You cannot overlook such prerequisites. It might be a danger for students to expose themselves too early. The danger is just to make it public a loosely-scaffolded approach, a little scientific one. (Medicine, #3)

Another faculty, within the same area (Medicine, #1), runs a blog on health care as an extra work, because he was asked by the scientific society which he belongs to.

However, in a Social Sciences context one researcher runs a blog for musing in informal way on his own research agenda (#3), whilst another one is used to contribute to a multi-authored blog:

This collective blog can be considered as the 'showcase' of some research threads being undertaken within my department. It hosts posts that are indeed structured as many papers, and includes comments on these works and sometimes guest posts. Therefore to a degree it is also a means for networking, to extend the boundaries of our research community (Social Sciences, #1).

How Digital Tools and Networks Are Perceived

Among the interviewed researchers the most common approach in the adoption of technologies to support inquiry work generally appears to be quite pragmatic and efficiency-driven:

The use and choice of a digital tool is definitely functional to my research needs, questions and to the specific sample being researched: it doesn't matter how difficult a new tool is, if it can help and suits the research situation, I am willing to spend the needed time… this is the key (Medicine, #3).

Attributes such as "speed", "completeness of information" (Humanities, #3), "facilitation of existing practices" (Social Sciences, #2; Medicine, #4) characterize the way of intending technologies as means to solve practical issues. This attitude easily becomes adaptability to a new tool (e.g. DropBox for Medicine #2, #4, Humanities #2 for a transdisciplinary project) when this provides the appropriate facility at no cost in terms of time demand.

However, a subgroup of researchers (Social Sciences, #3; Humanities, #3; Humanities, #4) seems to be more inclined to experiment new tools as well as is interested in building an academic digital identity:

I use a range of tools and environments, that I am used to classify as frequent, academic, personal tools, often being used in mobile mode (IPad, BlackBerry) and for a variety of objectives, such as to manage projects, online surveys, blogging, microblogging, bookmarking, scheduling of meetings, etc. Above all I use Twitter as a 'knowledge feeder' drawing from an international network: it works better for me in this function than other social networking tools. Instead, in Facebook I usually discuss research topics, studies, personal opinions, 'views of the world', with people I am familiar with, including my students. On these themes my blog hosts more personal reflections: a 'readership' is being created by linking posts to Twitter. Finally I use Linkedin to attract new contacts around my professional extra-academia commitments (Social Sciences, #3).

In other cases, interviewees generally prefer to keep their private networks separated from the research ones:

It happens that someone asks me to join my network in Facebook: however, whereas an informal information exchange is likely to become a research collaboration I prefer to move to other means, such as email or Skype, to go in depth with discussion in a more private setting. (Humanities, #2)

However, the exploratory attitude undertaken by the individual researcher does not seem to be so rewarding in certain disciplinary fields:

I have a profile on a number of popular technologies, such as sites for social networking, social bookmarking, social citation... but so far I have not be able to identify any real benefits for my research work...for instance, I used CiteULike for a while, to exchange references. But I realized that a few Classicists are used to feed references, so my permanence there was worthless and I was not able to draw anything significant for my research. (Humanities, #3)

It is worth noting that such contextual hindrances do not prevent this researcher from originally curating a digital identity in literature-focused networks "in which I can play a different role that does not affect my responsibility as a university researcher". (Humanities, #3)

Otherwise, the emergent state-of-the-art of her own disciplinary context fosters collaboration via digital networks for a (doctoral) researcher in 'digital archeology':

First of all at the National Research Council - where I am based - there is an intense team working activity, that is for instance highlighted in the use of Google Docs for co-writing any documents. But, more importantly, in our field it is vital to search for new contacts and closely collaborate at a distance with the international community of open source software developers, for co-programming graphics and modeling tools that enable us to build virtual museums of archeological sites. As 'digital archeologists' we are still a relatively small number of researchers and so we are open to look for other experiences, solutions, outputs, browsing any kind of sites, mailing lists and communities on the Web. (Humanities, #4)

For two doctoral researchers social networking environments represent the informal bridge between professional and academic experiences (Social Sciences, #1; Humanities, #4) and to share their engagement between different research institutions they are dealing with. More interestingly, these doctoral researchers state to find in the online networking activity even a way to somewhat compensate for the methodological training that the university seems not to properly provide (Social Sciences, #1; Humanities, #4). Otherwise, online activities undertaken by a doctoral student in Physics (#2), being involved in a prestigious international project, are totally absorbed and structured by formal and informal interactions within a large but project-bounded community of about 500 researchers scattered all over the world.

On the other hand, among older researchers it is possible to identify a more disenchanted attitude towards emergent social technologies, that are seen to a degree as redundant with respect to means being developed in the previous decades.

In hard sciences we researchers faced the emotional impact of ICTs many years ago, in early 90s. Now many practical, technical and communication needs are mostly fulfilled. So, we are not particularly impressed by these emergent tools, or even, feel somewhat indifferent to social media. (Physics, #1)

Likewise, the celebrated affordances for networking and collaborative working of new social tools are seen as already experienced and fulfilled by using email and Web 1.0 facilities:

No doubt that without Internet at least two important initiatives in my early academic career would have not occurred: a collective book on qualitative social research, in which most contributors I firstly contacted by email, after sifting names from a publisher's catalogue. I did not meet them in person while structuring and writing chapters. Likewise, a small network of research in qualitative methods was set up fifteen years ago and is still currently and effectively managed only via email, including the organization of one yearly conference and the editing process of our journal's issues. (Social Sciences, #2)

In places, the emerging social spaces are considered as "quite distracting, definitely a waste of time" (Social Sciences, #2) and "playful...there are more efficient means to communicate and have impact" (Medicine, #4). More importantly, one senior researcher highlights how the level of awareness of the underlying logic of tools is in danger of being overlooked by students adopting ultimate 'plug and play' technologies:

I have been working with a classification system that I have been built over time, along with my own method to analyze texts. It is a tool that perfectly

suits my kind of research, but I don't believe it could be useful to share it with my students. I mean, such instruments are useful if you build them on your own specific needs. They work well only if you design them. I realize I belong to a privileged generation of researchers, firstly because we have the critical awareness of how much ideology is embedded in the mainstream tools; secondly, since we have our hands made dirty by building those tools really necessary for the specific research activity to be undertaken. Personally it takes more time to learn the logic underpinning a commercial software. (Humanities, #1)

Boundaries of Own Research Community

The question whether the boundaries of one's own research community is being challenged by networked environments was the most difficult one to reflect on for interviewees. Traditional channels appear to be paramount across all disciplines:

The most important communication channels to create new contacts are still definitely seminars and conferences: in such contexts you are likely to start professional relationships that you might want to furtherly cultivate via Skype or email. Anyway, at the very beginning you need to encounter in person researchers whose work you know 'via papers'...you need to exchange information about their research methods, work approach... in other words, you need to get acquainted with people before collaborating with them in a project. (Medicine, #3)

This view is particularly shared among interviewees in soft sciences (Humanities, #1, #3; Social Sciences, #2), in which the model of the "isolated scholar" is said to be prevailing. The occasional use of subject-focused mailing lists in Humanities (#3) merely addresses a scope to exchange information. It is also true that for some in these areas (Humanities, #2; Social Sciences

#1; #3), participation in social media is thought as enabling researchers to get in contact with new audiences, and even to discover new kinds of expertise among non-academic thinkers.

Anyway, means and modes to create and expand one's own research community appears as substantially unchanged also in researchers who make an intensive use of communication technologies:

I don't believe that digital environments really challenge the boundaries of my research community, that it is mainly based on a direct acquaintance of peers. My research community consists in an international network of colleagues and collaborators that I have being get to know over years. Indeed my daily use of social media aims to gain insights on a number of perspectives on reality, to receive hints and suggestions to further reflect on reality. (Social Sciences, #3)

For doctoral students the notion of 'community of research' assumes a sense of 'community of practice' (Wenger, 1998), in which building their own 'being scholar', by interacting with senior researchers. The continuing face-to-face relation apprentice/mentor is perceived as paramount in areas such as Medicine (#3) and Physics (#2). However, the doctoral researcher in Physics (#2) reports to additionally experience a significant permanence in a project-based online network that in fact represents an extension of the traditional instance of a community of practice. Otherwise, above it was reported that to a degree doctoral students interviewed in Humanities (#4) and Social Sciences (#1) autonomously rely on digital networks to significantly integrate their *in situ* research training.

The Digital Researcher

When asked about their own idea of 'digital researcher' the interviewees neatly split up between

who, especially in Humanities area, does not attribute a key role to technologies in their scholarly practices and on the contrary who, in hard sciences, think that the label 'digital' is pleonastic, due to decades of computational technologies' use.

However, some different attitudes stand out in soft sciences:

I am not be able to see among my colleagues, also in international contexts, a predisposition, an interest in making use of any tech applications, even if the use of these ones can apparently facilitate a certain phase of the research process. However, personally I feel a 'digital researcher', because I actually make an intensive use of digital services to conduct my research, from the access to databases of classic texts to thesaurus to bibliography search engines. Moreover, I have been undertaking a constant relation with computer science colleagues or software developers, discussing technical solutions and future projects. (Humanities, #3)

There is a way of thinking of a 'digital researcher' dealing with our views of the world. Indeed the world of my research ideas is strongly affected and is continuously fed with all that is being shared on the Web, through digital mechanisms. (Social Sciences, #3)

Indeed in my field the idea of a 'digital archeologist' could make sense, because there are still a few investigators attempting to 'renew' archeology's study. On the one hand a digital researcher utilizes new tools to collaboratively model new methods that broaden the knowledge of archeological sites and finds. On the other hand, this approach also enables researcher to think of very new and effective ways to make a large lay audience aware of an extraordinary cultural heritage. So, I think that the commitment of a digital researcher should encompass a focus on popularizing archeology and dealing with a wider community. (Humanities, #4)

The young researcher in Humanities (#3) comes to terms with the 'digital researcher' label relating it to the availability of a great deal of digital resources that constitute her ordinary work environment. However, her own attitude towards technology issues contrasts her own disciplinary context, that is still scarcely inclined to utilize technologies to support research.

The senior researcher (Social Sciences, #3) shows a full awareness that the networked environment is becoming a condition that significantly informs one's own approach to social inquiry. Indeed he also claims that his own interest and presence in social media are perceived as an "odd thing" by his colleagues and that such a behaviour is 'tolerated' only because he has already gained a solid reputation in his field and is well acquainted with the internal dynamics of the university.

Finally, the research student in Archeology (Humanities, #4) advances an idea of 'digital researcher' as a bearer of innovation, under different aspects, suggesting a style of learning to be a researcher that much relies on collectives and networks.

DISCUSSION

The presented study has some apparent limitations, since it has a focus on a small group of disciplines, that cannot account for the related broad subject area; utilizes a single inquiry method, by exclusively relying on individual researchers' views; and it does not investigate contextual factors and specific disciplinary conventions. However, the detailed report of findings provide an informed basis that allows to highlight patterns and exceptions in digital behaviours in part of academics, in order to provide that 'snapshot' that was the initial aim of the study. In fact, interviews data show a general picture of research practices in which the uptake of technologies by researchers mostly underlies a functional and efficiency-driven approach to digital tools and environments and

gives some evidence of a poor diffusion of and a cautious interest in Web 2.0 tools to support inquiry activities, in line with findings from large-scale empirical studies. Focusing on individual appropriation of ICTs, selection and patterns of use of technologies among informants reveal an approach that mostly matches the Visitor's attitude rather then the Resident's one (White & Le Cornu, 2011): the majority of researchers across the disciplines consider fit the 'Visitors' approach, because they seem to mainly conceive technologies as tools to be used, if needed, in specific situations and for defined purposes. Their conception of the Web refers to the metaphor of a 'shed' rather than to that of a social space. Introduction of new digital tools and environments mainly occurs whereas these are able to improve efficiency in existing practices and have a clear utilization: this general approach is exemplified by the popular uptake of Skype as a means to make meetings at a distance more cost-effective. However, collected data also highlight differences in disciplinary cultures' interpretation of digital research practices: for instance, social scientists see blogging as a means to disseminate own research papers or even as an instrument to produce new knowledge; otherwise, in scientific disciplines blogging is even perceived as a risky practice for doctoral students, engaged to a step-by-step and hierarchical acquisition of a robust scientific methodology.

On the other hand, among Humanities and Social Sciences' researchers in the sample there are a few champions of an eclectic and self-legitimating approach to new technologies of communication, despite the respective disciplinary contexts are fairly indifferent to the potential of new digital tools/environments. Only these champions hold an idea of a 'digital researcher' that resemble the definition of 'digital, networked and open' scholar by Weller (2011), since they also endorse the moral responsibility of a more extended culture of sharing in academia and engaged in undertaking tentative open practices such as blogging, social networking and a participatory attitude in teaching. In fact, these few researchers show a more exploratory approach towards emergent tools and in fact attempt to combine both Visitor and Resident type of online engagement, by building their own digital identity in various social media. Furthemore, these researchers particularly seem to find in the teaching dimension – supported by technology-mediated environments - an opportunity to exploit a participatory attitude towards students that approaches a sense of 'open scholarship' as 'co-creating' mode of knowledge production and distribution (Garnett & Ecclesfield, 2011).

Otherwise, the doctoral researcher (in Archeology) embodies a more integrated mode to be "digital, networked and open", in her commitment as an apprentice scholar focusing on 'research' (learn and scaffold research methods), 'networking' and to a degree 'authoring' activities, whereas 'authoring' means both writing reports and co-modeling inquiry work instruments within the community of software developers. In fact her online engagement as 'Resident' is enabled by an emergent disciplinary field in which there is alignment among the personal uptake of old and new technologies, the methodological challenges to be faced, the work condition across two different institutions, the inherent transdisciplinarity of the original field and even the production of the final research output (a virtual museum).

This latter example - supported by the use of digital networks by other PhD students to integrate their current training – suggests that among future researchers there are niches of "silent experts in how, where and by whom want to be educated" (Williams, Karousou & Mackness, 2011), whose technology-mediated learning practices constitute a sort of "learning black market" (White, 2012) that would be worth furtherly exploring.

Moreover, findings reveal that there are differences in the uptake of digital scholarship's practices according to modalities of ICTs appropriation inherent to diverse disciplinary areas, as interpreted by Fry's (2006) framework. So, on the one hand, researchers working in subject areas in which a systematic approach to ICTs use (e.g. Physics, Medicine) is prevalent, are more likely to assume stable, structured and shared digital behaviors, within a collaborative work asset. Under such a condition of ICTs appropriation, community and scholarly rules are stronger factors than individual subjects' attitudes to determine adoption of new tools and new practices. Although this behaviour is shared among interviewees in hard sciences, the current experience of a doctoral student in Physics is the clearest instantiation of such systematic approach to ICTs use: he mostly relies on means and practices shared in a large online community to learn and practice research methods and to actively contribute to a collective project. However, it is argued that whereas this kind of digital frame easily supports new and well-established researchers and make them 'digital scholars' as default, at the same time it is less enabling in the case of exploiting individual researchers' technological attitudes and initiatives addressing communication and informal publishing activities. This is likely to weaken any influence by individual 'early adopters' of new technologies on a thorough scholarly system that effectively works.

On the other hand, interviewees in subject areas in which work practices tend to be more individualistic and approach to ICTs is generally molded in an "ad-hoc localized manner" (e.g. Humanities, Social Sciences), are more likely to occasionally assume highly autonomous digital behaviors and to pilot new tools and networking practices, at an individual level. However, such new practices have more difficulty to become mainstream, because they are not grounded in a collaborative division of labour (Borgman, 2007).

FUTURE RESEARCH

Further research is needed in order to sample and investigate champions of digital and open practices in a range of disciplines, to gain in-depth understanding on motivations and patterns of practices and probe any link or gap between ICTs adoption for core disciplinary work and for teaching purposes. Furthemore, whether and to what extent digital tools and networks are affecting the transition 'from student to researcher' is an issue that deserves a particular attention, since doctoral education is of paramount interest from an institutional perspective, due to the range of pressures on universities for educating more creative and performing researchers. In this line, academic literacies need to be reconsidered, in function of the emergent digital scholarship, in order to provide guidelines to well-established researchers and students that tentatively adopt digital tools and social media for activities such as testing new ideas, practicing peer review and scholarly writing, collaborating in e-research projects, building networks, searching and sharing resources.

Moreover, another possible inquiry-based development can be referred to the design of innovative online communities of practices, as already the doctoral researchers' accounts in this exploratory study seem to suggest. In addition, taking cue by some PhD champions of digital scholarship in the reported interviews, a further research direction could focus on doctoral e-researchers intended as digital learners playing a role as many "silent experts" (Williams et al., 2011) experiencing a transition process towards their 'being a researcher', with or without support from a more or less digitally resilient university context, peers and disciplinary culture. Studying their networked learning practices as many "niche of co-evolution" (Nardi & O'Day, 1999) could lead

to make explicit their innovative contribution to the doctoral community as a whole.

CONCLUSION

The presented findings apparently show that most intervieewed researchers across all age levels and subject areas are used to select and adopt old and new tools to solve "busy-ness" (Katz, 2010) of scholarship, relying on existing practices. However, a few isolated profiles of new 'digital scholars' emerge, championing the building of their own digital identity together with new modes of knowledge production and distribution, despite the lack of legitimation of their own research context. In fact, such emergent profiles match well-established researchers in soft sciences, whose intensive use of social media for research purposes is aligned with a participatory approach in teaching. Moreover if, also in this case, the generational factor seems not to be useful to explain different attitudes towards new technologies, it can be said that some doctoral researchers – under specific disciplinary and environmental conditions – autonomously adopt social neworking sites to supplement and broaden their research training, since currently their university context does not seem to properly provide it. Furthermore, the permanence of these doctoral researchers in the social Web allows to envision change occurring in their mode of knowledge production and distribution in line with Garnett & Ecclesfield's (2011) dimension of "co-creating learning" that would inform scholarship's activities in the age of social media. However, what it is also highlighted from these findings is the apparent broad gap between a 'late majority' (Rogers, 1995) of researchers that do not use or are practically indifferent to the opportunities to adopt new tools and a small minority of 'early adopters' (ib.) that have a varied and to a degree sophisticated approach to social web, separating and/or blending personal, academic and professional level of use. On the other hand, it is argued that the added value – in terms of impact - that the new communication channels can provide to quickly disseminate and make own research products and activities more visibile (LSE Policy Group, 2011), can constitute a transversal motivation to different inquiry fields' conventions and individual propensity to a certain kind of online 'engagement'. In this perspective, an institutional commitment to provide considered information, training, support and regulations would be a necessary conditions so far these tools can effectively co-evolve along with researchers' needs and expectations.

REFERENCES

Anderson, P. (2007). *What is Web 2.0? Ideas, technologies and Implications for Edcation*. JISC Report. Retrieved October 10, 2010, from http://www.jisc.ac.uk/whatwedo/services/techwatch/reports/horizonscanning/hs0701.aspx

Anderson, T. (2009). *The open access scholar*. Presented at the Open Access Week 2009, Athabasca University. Pdf and audio recording. Retrieved June 8, 2011, from http://hdl.handle.net/2149/2320

Bitter, S., & Muller, A. (2011). Social networking tools and research information systems: Do they compete? *Proceedings of the ACM WebSci'11* [online], June 14-17 2011, Koblenz, Germany, (pp. 1-4). Retrieved June 20, 2011, from http://journal.webscience.org/533/

Borgman, C. (2006). What can studies of e-learning teach us about collaboration in e-research? Some findings from digital library studies. *Computer Supported Cooperative Work*, *15*(4), 359–383. doi:10.1007/s10606-006-9024-1

Borgman, C. (2007). *Scholarship in the digital age: Information, infrastructure, and the Internet*. MIT Press.

Boulos, M., & Wheleer, S. (2007). The emerging Web 2.0 social software: An enabling suite of sociable technologies in health and health care education. *Health Information and Libraries Journal*, *24*(1), 2–23. doi:10.1111/j.1471-1842.2007.00701.x

Boyer, E. (1990). *Scholarship reconsidered: Priorities of the professoriate*. Retrieved October, 23, 2010, from https://depts.washington.edu/gs630/Spring/Boyer.pdf

British Library/JISC. (2011). *Researchers of tomorrow: A three years (BL/JISC) study tracking the research behavior of 'Generation Y' doctoral students. Second annual report 2010-2011*. Retrieved June 30, 2011, from http://www.jisc.ac.uk/news/stories/2011/06/researchersoftomorrow.aspx

Brown, J. S., & Adler, R. P. (2008). Minds on fire: Open education, the long tail, and learning 2.0. *EDUCAUSE Review*, *43*(1), 16–32.

Brown, S. A. (2012). Seeing Web 2.0 in context: A study of academic perceptions. *The Internet and Higher Education*, *15*, 50–57. doi:10.1016/j.iheduc.2011.04.003

Bullen, M., & Morgan, T. (2011). Digital learners not digital natives. *La Cuestion Universitaria, 7*, 60-68. Retrieved January 25, 2012, from http://www.lacuestionuniversitaria.upm.es/web/articulo.php?id_articulo=84

Collis, B. (2012). *Digital learners: Will they surprise us?* Key note talk given at the TIES 2012 conference, Barcelona, 1-3 February. Retrieved February 15, 2012, from http://ties2012.eu/en/pg-videos.html

Coverdale, A. (2011). *Negotiating doctoral practices and academic identities through the adoption and use of social and participative media*. Paper presented at ECEL 2011, Brighton, 10-11 November 2011.

Crook, C., Cummings, J., Fisher, T., Graber, R., Harrison, C., Lewin, C., et al. (2008). Web 2.0 *technologies for learning: the current landscape – Opportunities, challenges and tensions*. Report Becta. Retrieved May 25, 2012, from http://partners. becta.org.uk/uploaddir/downloads/page_documents/research/web2_tech nologies_learning.pdf

Dabbagh, N., & Reo, R. (2010). Back to the future. Tracing the roots and learning affordances of social software. In Lee, M., & McLoughlin, C. (Eds.), *Web 2.0-based e-learning: Applying social informatics for tertiary teaching* (pp. 1–20). Hershey, PA: Idea Group Inc. doi:10.4018/978-1-60566-294-7.ch001

Downes, S. (2005, October 16). E-learning 2.0. *eLearn Magazine*. Retrieved August 21, 2011, from http://www.downes.ca/post/31741

Ferguson, R., Clough, G., & Hosein, A. (2010). *Shifting themes, shifting roles: The development of research blogs*. Paper presented at the conference: 'Into Something Rich and Strange' - Making Sense of the Sea-Change. The 17th Association for Learning Technology Conference (ALT-C 2010), 7-9 September 2010, Nottingham, UK. Retrieved June 25, 2011 from http://oro.open.ac.uk/22962/

Fry, J. (2006). Scholarly research and information practices: A domain analytic approach. *Information Processing & Management, 42*, 299–316. doi:10.1016/j.ipm.2004.09.004

Garnett, F. (2010, 18 October). Heutagogy & the craft of teaching. *The Heutagogic Archives*. Retrieved 20 December, 2011, from http://heutagogicarchive.wordpress.com/2010/11/18/heutagogy-the-craft-of-teaching/

Garnett, F., & Ecclesfield, N. (2011). A framework for co-creating open scholarship. *ALT-C 2011 Proceedings Papers: Thriving in a Colder and More Challenging Climate* [open access version], (pp. 5-17). Retrieved September, 5, 2011 from http://repository.alt.ac.uk/2177/

Harley, D., Acord, S. K., Earl-Novell, S., Lawrence, S., & King, C. J. (2010). *Assessing the future landscape of scholarly communication: An exploration of faculty values and needs in seven disciplines*. UC Berkeley: Center for Studies in Higher Education. Retrieved July 15, 2010, from http://escholarship.org/uc/item/15x7385g

James, L., Norman, J., De Baets, A.-S., Burchell-Hughes, I., Burchmore, H., Philips, A., et al. (2009). *The lives and technologies of early career researchers*. JISC report. Retrieved July 5, 2011, from http://www.jisc.ac.uk/publications/reports/2009/earlycareerresearchersstudy.aspx#downloads

Jones, C., & Cross, S. (2009). *Is there a Net generation coming to university?* Paper presented at the conference ALT-C 2009 "In dreams begins responsibility" - Choice, Evidence and Change, 8 - 10 September 2009, Manchester. Retrieved August 20, 2011, from http://repository.alt.ac.uk/645/

Katz, R. N. (2010). Scholars, scholarship, and the scholarly enterprise in the digital age. *EDUCAUSE Review, 45*(2), 44-56. Retrieved July 20, 2011, from http://www.educause.edu/EDUCAUSE+Review/EDUCAUSEReviewMagazineVolume45/ScholarsScholarshipandtheSchol/202341

LLIDA. (Learning Literacies for the Digital Age) framework wiki. (2009). *JISC Project*. Retrieved April 15, 2011, from http://caledonianacademy.net/spaces/LLiDA/index.php?n=Main.FrameworkOfFrameworks

LSE Public Policy Group. (2011). *Maximising the impacts of your research: A handbook for social scientists,* [Consultation draft 3 online]. Retrieved July 7, 2011, from http://blogs.lse.ac.uk/impactofsocialsciences/2011/04/14/maximizing-the-impacts-of-your-research-a-handbook-for-social-scientists-now-available-to-download-as-a-pdf/

Millan, N., & Bromage, A. (2011). An initial approach to the integration of Web 2.0 technologies in the research environment. *Interactive Technology and Smart Education*, *8*(3), 148–160. doi:10.1108/17415651111165384

Nardi, B., & O'Day, V. (1999). *Information ecologies: Using technology with heart*. Cambridge, MA: MIT Press.

Pearce, N., Weller, M., Scanlon, E., & Kinsley, S. (2010). Digital scholarship considered: How new technologies could transform academic work. *Education, 16*(1). University of Regina. Retrieved May 15, 2011, from http://www.ineducation.ca/article/digital-scholarship-considered-how-new-technologies-could-transform-academic-work

Procter, R., Williams, R., & Stewart, J. (2010). *If you build it, will they come? How researchers perceive and use Web 2.0*. Research Information Network. Retrieved February 20, 2011, from http://www.rin.ac.uk/system/files/attachments/web_2.0_screen.pdf

Rogers, E. M. (1995). *Diffusion of innovations* (4th ed.). New York, NY: Free Press.

Schonfeld, R. C., & Housewright, R. (2010). *Faculty survey 2009: Key strategic insights for libraries, publishers, and societies*. Ithaka Report. Retrieved July 25, 2010, from http://www.ithaka.org/ithaka-s-r/research/faculty-surveys-2000-2009/faculty-survey-2009

Selwyn, N. (2010). *The educational significance of social media: A critical perspective*. Key note talk at the ED-MEDIA 2010 Conference, Toronto. Retrieved August 20, 2010, from http://www.scribd.com/doc/33693537/The-educational-significance-of-social-media-a-critical-perspective

Selwyn, N. (2011). Finding an appropriate fit for me: Examining the (in)flexibilities of international distance learning. *International Journal of Lifelong Education*, *30*(3), 367–383. doi:10.1080/02601370.2011.570873

Sharpe, R., Beetham, H., & de Freitas, M. (2010). *Rethinking learning for a digital age: How learners are shaping their own experiences*. London, UK: Routledge.

Siemens, G., & Tittenberg, P. (2009). *Handbook of emerging technologies for learning*. University of Manitoba.

Suter, V., Alexander, B., & Kaplan, P. (2005). Social software and the future of conferences—Right now. *EDUCAUSE Review*, *40*(1), 46–59.

Veletsianos, G. (2010). Participatory scholars and 21st century scholarship. *George Veletsianos's blog*. Retrieved July 18, 2010, from http://www.veletsianos.com/2010/04/06/participatory-scholars-scholarshi/

Veletsianos, G., & Kimmons, R. (2012). Networked participatory scholarship: Emergent techno-cultural pressures towards open and digital scholarship in online networks. *Computers & Education*, *58*(2), 766-774. Retrieved November 6, 2011, from http://www.veletsianos.com/2011/11/06/networked-participatory-scholarship/

Weller, M. (2011). The digital scholar: How technology is transforming scholarly practice. London, UK: Bloomsbury Academic. Retrieved September 16, 2011, from http://www.bloomsburyacademic.com/view/DigitalScholar_9781849666275/book-ba-9781849666275.xml

Weller, M. (2011). Digital, networked and open. In *The digital scholar*. Bloomsbury Academic. Retrieved September 16, 2011, from http://www.bloomsburyacademic.com/view/DigitalScholar_9781849666275/chapter-ba-9781849666275-chapter-001.xml;jsessionid=466C69AA7FAE21941D713D8324F68744

Weller, M. (2011). The nature of scholarship. *The digital scholar*. Bloomsbury. Retrieved September 16, 2011, from http://www.bloomsburyacademic. com/view/DigitalScholar_9781849666275/chapter-ba-9781849666275-chapter-004.xml;jsession id=13C1CCC4B35C0F37EDE362F5B7718D5D

Weller, M. (2011). Digital resilience. In *The digital scholar*. Bloomsbury Academic. Retrieved September 16, 2011, from http://www. bloomsburyacademic.com/view/DigitalSchol-ar_9781849666275/chapter-ha-9781849666275-chapter-014.xml;jsessionid=466C69AA7FAE21 941D713D8324F68744

White, D. (2011, 30th September). The learning black market. *TALL Blog: Online education with the University of Oxford*. Retrieved February 10, 2012, from http://tallblog.conted.ox.ac.uk/index. php/2011/09/30/the-learning-black-market/

White, D., & Le Cornu, A. (2011). Visitors and residents: A new typology for online engagement. *First Monday, 16*(9). Retrieved September 15, 2011, from http://firstmonday.org/htbin/cgiwrap/ bin/ojs/index.php/fm/article/view/3171/3049

Williams, R., Karousou, R., & Mackness, J. (2011). Emergent learning and learning ecologies in Web 2.0. *The International Review of Resaerch in Open and Distance Learning, 12*(3). Retrieved January 20, 2012, from http://www.irrodl.org/index.php/ irrodl/article/view/883

Zaman, M. (2010). Doctoral programs in the age of research 2.0. In Anandarajan, M. (Ed.), *E-research collaboration: Theory, techniques and challenges* (pp. 233–245). Springer. doi:10.1007/978-3-642-12257-6_14

ADDITIONAL READING

Ajjan, H., & Hartshorne, R. (2008). Investigating faculty decisions to adopt Web 2.0 technologies: Theory and empirical tests. *The Internet and Higher Education, 11*, 71–80. doi:10.1016/j. iheduc.2008.05.002

Bukvova, H. (2011a). Scientists online: A framework for the analysis. *First Monday, 16*(10). Retrieved September 12, 2011, from http://firstmonday.org/htbin/cgiwrap/bin/ojs/index.php/fm/ article/view/3584

Bukvova, H. (2011b). Taking new routes: Blogs, web sites and scientific publishing. *ScieComInfo, 7*(2). Retrieved September 12, 2011, from http:// www.sciecom.org/ojs/index.php/sciecominfo/ article/view/5148

Carmichael, P. (2011). Networking research: New directions in educational inquiry. *Continuum*.

Clancy, K. (2011, 14 December). Networking, scholarship and service: The place of science blogging in academia. *Scientific American*. Retrieved December 20, 2011, from http://blogs.scientifi-camerican.com/context-andvariation/2011/12/14/ science-blogging-in-academia/

Collis, E., & Hide, B. (2010). *Use and relevance of Web 2.0 resources for researchers*. Paper presented at ELPUB2010. Publishing in the networked world: Transforming the Nature of Communication, 14th International Conference on Electronic Publishing 16-18 June 2010, Helsinki, Finland. Retrieved October 20, 2010 from http://elpub.scix. net/cgi-bin/works/Show?_id=119_elpub2010

Duval, E., Ullmann, T. D., Wild, F., Lindstaedt, S., & Scott, P. (Eds.). (2010). *Proceedings of the 2nd International Workshop on Research 2.0*. At the 5th European Conference on Technology Enhanced Learning: Sustaining TEL. Barcelona, Spain, September 28, 2010, CEUR-WS.org/Vol-675. Retrieved December 30, 2011, from http:// ceur-ws.org/Vol-675/

Ebner, M., & Reinhardt, W. (2009). *Social networking in scientific conferences. Twitter as a tool to strengthen a scientific community.* Paper presented at the Workshop Science 2.0 for TEL, ECTEL 2009. Retrieved August 20, 2010, from http://oa.stellarnet.eu/open-archive/browse?resource=2197_v1

Faculty Focus. (2009). *Twitter in higher education: Usage habits and trends of today's college faculty.* Retrieved January 15, 2010, from http://www.facultyfocus.com/free-report/twitter-in-higher-education-usage-habits-and-trends-of-todays-college-faculty/

Faculty Focus. (2010). *Twitter in higher education 2010: Usage habits and trends of today's college faculty.* Special Report. Retrieved October 12, 2011, from http://www.facultyfocus.com/free-reports/twitter-in-higher-education-2010-usage-habits-and-trends-of-todays-college-faculty/

Fitzpatrick, K. (2011). *Planned obsolescence: Publishing, technology, and the future of the academy.* New York, NY: New York University Press.

Genoni, P. (2010). An investigation of digital scholarship and disciplinary culture in Oman. *Library Hi Tech, 38*(3), 414–432.

Genoni, P., Merrick, H., & Willson, M. (2005). The use of the Internet to activate latent ties in scholarly communities. *First Monday, 10*(12). Retrieved December 15, 2011, from http://firstmonday.org/issues/issue10_12/genoni/index.html

Grosseck, G., & Holotescu, C. (2011). *Academic research in 140 characters.* Paper presented at the 7th International Scientific Conference eLSE "eLearning and Software for Education, Bucharest, April 28-29 April 2011. Retrieved December 12, 2011, from http://www.scribd.com/doc/54084667/Academic-research-in-140-characters-or-less

Halavais, H. (2006). Scholarly blogging: Moving toward the visible college. In Bruns, A., & Jacobs, J. (Eds.), *Uses of blogs* (pp. 117–126). New York, NY: Peter Lang.

Harvey, J. (2011, 1 December). Scholarly networking and open access – Are we asking the right questions? *Research to Action.* Retrieved December 10, 2011, from http://www.researchtoaction.org/%E2%80%98scholarly-networking%E2%80%99-and-open-access-are-we-asking-the-right-questions/

Heap, T., & Minocha, S. (2011). *The experiences of academic and research bloggers: A phenomenological enquiry.* Paper presented at the 30th International Human Science Research Conference: Intertwining Body-Self-World, 27-30 July 2011, St. Catherine's College, Oxford University, UK. Retrieved January 4, 2012, from http://oro.open.ac.uk/28484/

Heinze, N., Joubert, M., & Gilet, D. (2010). Connecting early career researchers: Investigating the needs of Ph.D. candidates in TEL working with Web 2.0. In *Proceedings of the 2nd International Workshop on Research 2.0 at the 5th European Conference on Technology Enhanced Learning: Sustaining TEL*, Barcelona, Spain, September 28, 2010, CEUR-WS.org/ 675, (pp. 86-92). Retrieved December 30, 2011, from http://ceur-ws.org/Vol-675/

Holliman, R. (2010). From analogue to digital scholarship: implications for science communication researchers. *Journal of Science Communication, 9*(3). Retrieved February 5, 2012, from http://oro.open.ac.uk/23218/

Holliman, R. (2011). Telling science stories in an evolving digital media ecosystem: From communication to conversation and confrontation. *Journal of Science Communication, 10*(4). Retrieved December 30, 2011, from http://jcom.sissa.it/archive/10/04/Jcom1004%282011%29C01/Jcom1004%282011%29C04

Kalb, H., Bukvova, H., & Schoop, E. (2009). The digital researcher: Exploring the use of social software in the research process. *Sprouts: Working Papers on Information Systems, 9*(34). Retrieved December 20, 2011, from http://sprouts. aisnet.org/9-34/

Kjellberg, S. (2010). I am a blogging resarcher: Motivations for blogging in a scholarly context. *First Monday, 15*(8). Retrieved August 28, 2010, from http://www.uic.edu/htbin/cgiwrap/bin/ojs/index.php/fm/article/view/2962/2580

Letierce, J., Passant, A., Breslin, J., & Decker, S. (2010). Understanding how Twitter is used to spread scientific messages. *Proceedings of the WebSci10: Extending the Frontiers of Society On-Line*, April 26-27th, 2010, Raleigh, NC. Retrieved July 10, 2010, from http://journal.webscience. org/314/

Luzon, M. J. (2009). Academic weblogs as tools for e-collaboration among researchers. In Kock, N. (Ed.), *E-collaboration: Concepts, methodologies, tools and applications*. Hershey, PA: IGI Global. doi:10.4018/978-1-60566-652-5.ch037

Masover, J. (2008). What do scholars mean by scholarly networking? *Project Bamboo Wiki*. Retrieved December 12, 2011, from https://wiki.projectbamboo.org/pages/viewpage.action?pageId=3113159

Meyer, K. A. (2010). A comparison of Web 2.0 tools in a doctoral course. *The Internet and Higher Education, 13*(4), 226–232. doi:10.1016/j.iheduc.2010.02.002

Mollett, A., Moran, D., & Dunleavy, P. (2011). *Using Twitter in university research, teaching, and impact activities*. LSE Public Policy Group. Retrieved October 10, 2011, from http://blogs. lse.ac.uk/impactofsocialsciences/2011/09/29/twitter-guide/

Nicholas, D., Clark, D. I., Rowlands, I., & Jamali, H. R. (2009). Online use and information seeking behaviour: Institutional and subject comparisons of UK researchers. *Journal of Information Science, 35*(6), 660–676. doi:10.1177/0165551509338341

Nielsen, M. (2011). *Reinventing discovery. The new era of networked science*. Princeton University Press.

Oliver, M. (2012). Technology and change in academic practice. In Trowler, P., Saunders, M., & Bamber, V. (Eds.), *Tribes and territories in the 21st century. Rethinking the significance of disciplines in higher education*. London, UK: Routledge.

Pearce, N. (2007). *Technology use across a campus: An analysis of the uptake of ICT across faculties within a single university*. Unpublished report, Center for e-science, Lancaster University, United Kingdom. Retrieved February 17, 2012, from http://www.ncess.ac.uk/events/conference/programme/workshop1/?ref=/programme/thurs/1bPearce.htm

Powell, D. A., Jacob, C. J., & Chapman, B. J. (2011). Using blogs and new media in academic practice: Potential roles in research, teaching, learning, and extension. *Innovative Higher Education* [online first]. Retrieved January 15, 2012, from http://dx.doi.org/10.1007/s10755-011-9207-7

RIN. (2009). *Patterns of information use and exchange: Case studies of researchers in life sciences*. Retrieved October 20, 2010, from http://www.rin.ac.uk/our-work/using-and-accessing-information-resources/patterns-information-use-and-exchange-case-studie

RIN. (2011). *Reinventing research? Information practices in the humanities*. Retrieved October 20, 2010, from http://www.rin.ac.uk/our-work/using-and-accessing-information-resources/information-use-case-studies-humanities

Santiago Campión, R., Navaridas Nalda, F., & González Menorca, L. (2012). *Web 2.0 y educación superior: Su utilización por parte de docentes universitarios*. Paper presented at the conference TIES 2012, Barcelona, 1-3 February 2012.

Schmiede, R. (2009). Upgrading academic scholarship: Challenges and chances of the digital age. *Library Hi Tech*, *27*(4), 624–633. doi:10.1108/07378830911007727

Snee, H. (2008). *Web 2.0 as a social science research tool*. British Library/ESCR. Retrieved September 20, 2010, from http://www.bl.uk/reshelp/bldept/socsci/socint/web2/report.html

Taraborelli, D. (2008). Soft peer review: Social software and distributed scientific evaluation. In P. Hassanaly, A, Ramrajsingh, D. Randall, P. Salembier, & M. Tixier (Eds.), *Proceedings of the 8th International Conference on the Design of Cooperative Systems*, Carry-le-Rouet, 20-23 May 2008 (pp. 99-110). Retrieved October 30, 2011, from http://eprints.ucl.ac.uk/8279/

Timmis, S., Joubert, M., Manuel, A., & Barnes, S. (2010). Transmission, transformation and ritual: An investigation of students' and researchers' digitally mediated communications and collaborative work. *Learning, Media and Technology*, *35*(3), 307-322. Retrieved February 7, 2012, from http://bristol.academia.edu/SueTimmis/Papers/1283112/Transmission_transformation_and_ritual_an_investigation_of_students_and_researchers_digitally_mediated_communications_and_collaborative_work

Veletsianos, G. (in press). Higher education scholars' participation and practices on Twitter. *Journal of Computer Assisted Learning, in press*. Retrieved October 24, 2011, from http://www.veletsianos.com/2011/10/24/what-do-scholars-do-on-twitter/

Wellmann, B., Koku, E., & Hunsinger, J. (2006). Networked scholarship. In J. Weiss, J. Nolan, J. Hunsinger, & P. Trifonas (Eds.), *International handbook of virtual learning environments*, (pp. 1429-1447). Springer. Retrieved January 17, 2012 from http://www.scribd.com/doc/34595375/Networked-Scholarship

Wilks, L. (2009). *It's like a permanent corridor conversation: An exploration of technology-enabled scholarly networking at The Open University*. Project Bamboo Report. Retrieved December 20, 2010, from https://wiki.projectbamboo.org/display/BPUB/Open+University+Scholarly+Networking+Report

KEY TERMS AND DEFINITIONS

Digital Scholar: The term indicates emergent profiles of researchers adopting social media to conduct, peer critique, write up and disseminate own research and contribute to others' inquiry.

Digital Scholarship: Range of uses of the social Web for knowledge production and distribution activity of researchers across disciplines. The term is otfen utilized to indicate activities and experimentations related to 'digital humanities'.

ICTs Appropriation: The term refers to patterns of adoption and sense making of technology characterizing users belonging to different traditions and cultures of research disciplines.

Open Scholarship: It is a value-laden approach that promotes and extended culture of sharing (content, methods, data, research and teaching practices) that has always characterized higher education, although differently inflected according to the variety of disciplines.

Scholarly Practices: Spectrum of activities usually undertaken by academics and independent researchers, such as acquiring and experimenting inquiry methods, managing research projects, teaching, publishing and networking.

Scholarship: Broad term encompassing methods, discipline and attainment of scholars, including reference to teaching and learning competences and approaches.

Social Media: New generation of software tools – also named as Web 2.0 or social Web tools – that are accessible from any web-based or mobile platforms/devices and enables users to become active participants in content production and sharing across digital networks.

ENDNOTES

[1]   The dissertation"*Research practices in transition: investigating the relationship between digital scholarship and open scholarship in higher education settings"* was submitted in October 2011 for the requirements of the Master of Research in Educational and Social Research, Institute of Education, University of London.

Chapter 18
Digital Literacy for Effective Communication in the New Academic Environment:
The Educational Blogs

Ruxandra Vasilescu
Spiru Haret University, Romania

Manuela Epure
Spiru Haret University, Romania

Nadia Florea
Spiru Haret University, Romania

ABSTRACT

"The fixity" of knowledge - the accumulation of fixed elements of knowledge - no longer meets the requirements of nowadays society. The capacity of change, adaptation, and constant updating of these elements according to individual needs, but also to the needs of the various contexts the knowledge, must be used as a prerequisite of social integration for the graduate. Education stepped into the era of deep reforms based on new concepts: student-centered learning, informal education, and personal learning environment. Thus, to teach means to model and to demonstrate; to learn means to practice and to consider. The information technology provides the new student with the learning environment he/ she needs in the new context, and it connects him/her rapidly to the up-to-date information and to the rest of the world. Finding new ways of recreating student community on the background of the change of the student structure, the profile of the new student, his/ her interests and individual learning habits, on the one hand, and the main challenges of the workforce training/retraining for the current and future information society, on the other hand are the main concerns of this chapter. Due to the spectacular extension of the Internet use, the blog is a solution for the development of the student community, for social interaction and serves as an alternative or extension of classroom discourse.

DOI: 10.4018/978-1-4666-2851-9.ch018

INTRODUCTION

No doubt we are experiencing today a rapid transformation of the learning process and the stakeholders involved in it need to clearly define their role. Teachers, students, parents, future employers are facing the knowledge "wave" coming through the Internet, and they are starting to realize that the traditional learning methods are not enough or appropriate in the new "digital world".

Traditional learning, consolidated over the years, has outstanding results in enriching the world knowledge heritage, but today it seems to become less effective (for teachers) and not at all attractive (for students).

The Lisbon Strategy and the Bologna Process in the European Union set forth the main objectives such as reforming and even transforming the higher education systems, so as they should be more flexible, more coherent, more transparent and more open to the society needs. In this context, the National Qualifications Framework in Higher Education was established in Romania (CNCIS)1 as a unique instrument setting the structure of qualifications and assuring national recognition and the international compatibility/comparability of the qualifications acquired in the higher education system. Due to this framework, all the learning results acquired in the higher education system may be recognized, measured and related (bachelor studies, master and doctoral studies) and the coherence of the qualifications and certified titles is assured.

Within this framework, the professional and transversal competence acquired after the completion of the level 6 studies (bachelor) also subordinates the *social interaction competences* training.

In the first part of the chapter we will show how from the didactic point of view for certain content areas all the disciplines, irrespective of the specialization, support the development of the transversal competence of social interaction. Thus, we will elaborate on the C7 descriptor derivation – 'Getting acquainted with the roles and specific

activities of the team work and task distribution for the subordinate levels' in the specific descriptors that may be adapted to the scientific content of any discipline for the bachelor level. Here is the exemplification of the phrasing of the following structures, to materialize this working principle: *competence, contents, minimum performance standards, information and methodological resources, examples of learning activities and assessment items.*

The second part deals with digital literacy, as an imperative of our society. Facing digital society means in fact to accept the need of a digital literacy, for young and old people, teacher or student, the learning process never ends life-long learning in the digital society is a must. The means of presentation and debate in the student virtual environment are particularized by the web transmission path: faculty site, Blackboard e-learning platform, teachers' blogs, yahoo groups, facebook, twitter etc. is approached in the third and fourth parts, with particular focus on educational blogs.

1. DEVELOPING AND ASSESSING TRANSVERSAL COMPETENCE OF SOCIAL INTERACTION

1.1. National and International Legislative Framework of Higher Education Qualifications

The main challenges of the European workforce training/retraining for the current and future information society reshape the complex university teaching process.

The Lisbon Strategy and the Bologna Process in the European Union set forth the main objectives such as reforming and even transforming the higher education systems, so as they should be more flexible, more coherent, more transparent and more open to the society needs. In this context, the *National Qualifications Framework in Higher Education* was established in Romania (CNCS) as a unique instrument setting the structure of qualifications and assuring national recognition and the international compatibility/comparability of the qualifications acquired in the higher education system. Due to this framework, all the learning results acquired in the higher education system may be recognized, measured and inter-related (bachelor studies, master and doctoral studies) and the coherence of the qualifications and certified titles is assured.

Based on Order No. 4.430 of 29 June 2009 on the use of the National Qualifications Framework in Higher Education (NQFHE), the NQFHE conceptual-methodological model is compatible with the European Qualifications Framework (EQF), mainly with the learning outcomes specified by this framework for skills levels 6(bachelor), 7 (master), 8 (doctorate). Within this framework, the professional and transversal competence acquired after the completion of the level 6 studies (bachelor) also subordinates the *social interaction competences* training.

The recommendation of the European Parliament and of the European Council of 23 April 2008 on the establishment of the European Qualifications Framework for life-long learning, in the Official Journal of the European Union C 111 of 6 May 2008 (2008/C 111/01, annex 1), key concepts operating within EU are clarified by concise definitions. These key concepts are taken over also by the *Methodology for the implementation and use of the National Qualifications Framework in Higher Education* (NQFHE), i.e.: qualification, learning outcomes, knowledge, skills and competence.

In the first part of the chapter we will show how from the didactic point of view for certain content areas all the disciplines, irrespective of the specialization, support the development of the transversal competence of social interaction. Thus, we will elaborate on the C7 descriptor derivation – '*Getting acquainted with the roles and specific activities of the team work and task distribution for the subordinate levels*' in the specific

descriptors that may be adapted to the scientific content of any discipline for the bachelor level. Here is the exemplification of the phrasing of the following structures, to materialize this working principle: *competence, contents, information and methodological resources, examples of learning activities and minimum performance standards for evaluating TC 7 via social media tools.*

1. *Qualification* is a formal outcome of an assessment and validation process, which is obtained when a competent body determines that an individual has achieved specific learning standards. Therefore, qualification is official recognition of the value of individual learning outcomes for employment and continuing education and training, by an act of education (diploma, certificate) that gives the legal right to practice a profession/trade.

2. *Learning outcomes* means that recognizes, understands and is able to do on completion of the learning process. These are defined in terms of knowledge, skills and competences. Therefore, learning outcomes are the set of knowledge, skills and competences that a person has acquired and is able to demonstrate after completion of learning on a school cycle.

3. *Knowledge* is the result of assimilation, by learning the information. Knowledge is the body of facts, principles, theories and practices in a particular field of work or study. As EQF, knowledge is described as theoretical and/or factual.

4. *Ability* means the ability to apply and use knowledge to carry out tasks and solve problems. Similarly EQF, skills are described as cognitive (involving the use of logical, intuitive and creative thinking) or practical (involving manual dexterity and the use of methods, materials, tools and instruments). Ability operators include certain types of

structures, from skills to the skills of interpretation and problem solving.

5. *Competence* is the demonstrated ability to select, combine and use the appropriate knowledge, skills and other acquisitions (values and attitudes) in order to successfully solve a particular category of work or learning and professional development or personal conditions of effectiveness and efficiency. Similarly EQF, competence is described in terms of responsibility and autonomy.

Skills are classified into two categories: professional skills and transversal competences.

The *professional competence* means the proven ability to select, combine and use the appropriate knowledge, skills and other acquisitions (values and attitudes) in order to successfully solve a particular category of work or learning, circumscribed profession, in terms of effectiveness and efficiency. Thus, skills are all unified and dynamic knowledge and skills. Knowledge is expressed by the following descriptors: knowledge, understanding and use of specific language (1), explanation and interpretation (2). In their turn, skills express themselves by the following descriptors: application, transfer and problem solving (3), critical and constructive reflection (4), creativity and innovation (5).

Each qualification related to a specific cycle (bachelor, master, doctorate) is defined in the general description of learning outcomes and is expressed by:

- General skills that are developed in the broader field of study;
- Specific skills that are developing within a narrow course.

Transversal competences are those capabilities that transcend a particular field, the study program, with a transdisciplinary nature. They consist of teamwork skills, communication skills, oral and written language / foreign information and communication technology-ICT, problem solving and decision making, recognition and respect for diversity and multiculturalism, learning autonomy, initiative and entrepreneurship, openness to lifelong learning, and development of values and ethics, etc. As purchases are values and attitudes that transcend a particular area / study program, is expressed by the following transversal skills descriptors: autonomy and responsibility (6) social interaction (7), personal and professional development (8). Our analysis will illustrate the generic descriptor no.7 - *social interaction*, providing the main milestones for the description and evaluation of transversal competences.

1.2 The Conceptual and Methodological Description of Qualifications in Higher Education

Learning outcomes and their descriptors are essential for analysis, description and interpretation of higher education qualifications in a frame of reference called *conceptual and methodological model*. This model NQFHE is compatible with the view of the European framework EQF 7, mainly by the learning outcomes specified for qualification levels 6, 7 and 8. Structure and content descriptors model capitalize the framework of qualifications for the European higher education, but also some elements of the most popular European models (models France, Ireland, the UK etc.). Meanwhile, the Romanian model NQFHE has its own identity, it integrates categories and types of skills, skill levels and specific descriptors. The essential elements of the model are reflected in the matrix NQFHE license (annex. 1).

NQFHE matrix includes: skill levels, learning outcomes expressed through knowledge, skills and competence level descriptors for higher education qualifications. Level descriptors for each learning outcome details the generic descriptors for each type of competence for each level of qualification: bachelor, masters and doctorate. From a structural matrix integrated skills and competences NQFHE cross each of the two categories of skills having the legitimacy and importance of performing. They are a couple jointly expressing professional effectiveness and efficiency of the graduate studies program. Professional skills are expressed through comprehensive knowledge and skills covering dimension for any qualified professional. The matrix is structured transversal competences: the role and skills of personal and professional skills. They consider the social context and group of professions and awareness of the need for professional development. Level descriptors introduced in the matrix indicate activities, expected results and performance for each skill level. They allow describing qualifications and also set landmarks needed to assess the level of achieving or obtaining learning outcomes.

The matrix is an integrative approach to higher education qualifications and offers two perspectives of analysis: vertical and horizontal. *The vertical analysis* indicates progress from stage professional skills knowledge and understanding (generic descriptor 1), the core of a result of learning, creativity and innovation to the point (generic descriptor 5), and transversal skills (generic descriptors 6, 7 and 8). In this way, skills are examined and described in terms of generic descriptors from 1-5 and transversal competences are examined and described in terms of generic descriptors 6, 7 and 8. Thus, the vertical perspective emphasizes that a learning outcome can be achieved if the landings were made subordinate and consolidated. *Horizontal analysis* reflected a generic descriptor relative to the three university courses: Bachelor, Master and PhD. In this case, descriptors highlight skills and increase professional qualification. Note that the model deals with a different kind of progress, suggesting adding value to each type of learning outcome, with the transition from one level to another university qualification. The horizontal perspective shows that each type of learning outcome, for the three cycles, necessarily integrate previous levels.

From those two analytical perspectives, one can say that each result of learning has a relative autonomy, being subject to previous acquisitions, both horizontally and vertically.

1.3. Social Interaction - Generic Descriptor no. 7 - Cross-Reference for the Assessment Skills of Social Media Tools

It is widely recognized that the introduction of modern communication technologies in teaching, learning and assessment has a major impact in redefining the competences. In this context, we will show below how, in terms of teaching, in some content areas, subjects, regardless of specialization, support the development of transversal competences of social interaction. In this respect, we present the derivation of the level descriptor Transversal competence 7 (TC 7) - "Getting acquainted with roles and specific activities of teamwork and assignment of tasks to subordinate levels" in specific descriptors that can be adapted to the scientific content in a discipline in the 3rd year of studies for the bachelor's degree (Table 1). Working to realize this principle, the formulations of the following structures illustrate: *competence, information and methodological resources, minimum performance standards* for evaluating TC 7 - *Social interaction through social media tools.*

The methods of presentation and discussion in the students' virtual environment are customized by the web path of transmission: the faculty website, Blackboard, teachers' blogs, yahoo groups, facebook, twitter, etc.

TC 7: *Familiarity with the roles and specific activities of teamwork and assignment of tasks to subordinate levels*

TC 7.1: Knowledge and setting / taking roles in a team, depending on specific activities and content depending on the psycho-individual particular features (skills of planning, organizing, coordinating, etc.)

Table 1. Transversal competences

Transversal competence	Minimum performance standards for evaluating transversal competence 7 - Social interaction through social media tools (Blackboard, blog, yahoo groups)
TC 7.1.	By the end of the course, all students will be able: - To assume at least one role in the team depending on the specific content (organizer, resources scout, evaluator, monitor, final analyst);
TC 7.2.	- To observe labour discipline and the effort of the other members of the team (relevant information accuracy, punctuality, work deadlines, etc.)
TC 7.3.	- To explain correctly and completely at least one training activity, at least one learning task for subordinate levels;
TC 7.4.	- To follow the working directions and methodology, so that each unit of learning objectives be achieved within planned term;
TC 7.5.	- To receive feedback from at least three team mates (e.g. trusted colleague, eager to learn, contributed to the success of the workload, etc.);
TC 7.6.	- To work with at least two other students from other universities / other specialties at home or abroad to perform their learning activities, self-instruction or personal development, applying effective techniques in a multidisciplinary working team;
TC 7.7.	- To draw up a (self) evaluation of own work based on a SWOT analysis highlighting the achievement of feedback activities and the identification of difficulties and introducing the immediate improvement measures.

TC 7.2: Clarification of behaviour rules specific for a system of moral, cultural and civic values, applying the ethical standards and best practices rules in order that the work discipline and the effort of the other team members should be respected (relevant information accuracy, punctuality, respect for deadlines, etc..);

TC 7.3: Correct and complete explanation of the training, learning tasks for the subordinate levels;

TC 7.4: Compliance with the methodologies and guidelines, so that the objectives be achieved within the planned term;

TC 7.5: Creates with the working team with colleagues, a positive emotional climate characterized by trust, acceptance, tolerance, willingness to learn, regardless of the role within the team (coordinator or performer);

CT 7.6: Collaborate with other students from other universities / other specialties at home and abroad to perform their learning activities, of self-instruction or personal development, applying effective techniques in a multidisciplinary working team on different hierarchical levels;

CT 7.7: Carrying out feedback activities, highlighting the identification of difficulties and the introduction of improvement measures proposed in designing future activities.

Below there is a variant form of minimum performance standards for assessing transversal competences by social media tools, the discipline of Business Correspondence – 3rd academic year, advanced level.

Contents:

Unit 1: Communication Ability

Unit 2: Business communication and business discourse

Unit 3: Varieties of English; preliminary Correspondence: Letter of inquiry

Unit 4: Contracts, Oral communication: Negotiations

Unit 5: Post-contract Correspondence: Letter of Complaint, Adjustment, Reminder

Minimum performance standards for assessing TC skills derived from TC 7 (7.1 TC... TC 7.7.):

Making a work of synthesis and integrated review

Possible titles:

- Key concepts in business works: Pre-contract, Contract, Post-contract;
- Business discourse;
- Another topic of synthesis, on the course syllabus.

Suggested learning activities:

- Making working groups based on the email address with username and password: Blackboard e-learning platform, Teachers' blogs, yahoo groups, facebook, twitter etc.
- Assigning tasks on workstations and coordination teams;
- Organizing the work in the group, setting appropriate tasks to cover topical content;
- Making lecture notes, maps, conceptual, intuitive schemata;
- Communication by e-mail with other students from other universities in the country and all over the world;
- Documentation and appropriate associations between images and text;
- Writing free or structured essays (fictional / imagined or real / experienced);
- Research on establishing a historical or current review on the selected theme;
- Identifying authentic texts (diaries, narratives, stories), commenting and integrating them into topics studied;
- Proposal of questionnaires for research issues identified for the study of the theme;
- Phrasing questions for more difficult content;
- Selected information to be presented in a poster or wall suggestive headlines;
- The final presentation of works per group in an exhibition, a brochure, a symposium, a book, a website, etc.
- Methodological Resources (Traditional and Digital): Lessons based on structured multimedia content (open source or licensed), demonstration, individual study, exercises, case studies, simulations, dramatized/decision-making games applica-

tions (online), research/assisted discovery, browsing, cooperative learning, team activities (online) teaching assistance activities (synchronous and/or asynchronous), problem solving, learning individual e-learning, assisted e-learning, c-learning (cooperative e-learning), info-learning (information e-learning), m-learning (mobile phone e-learning), extended by downloading online content, tests (evaluation or self-evaluation, online or offline), "free" e-learning platform, platform for assisted e-learning; team activities platform; platform for simulation or role playing games, virtual lab, learning by reading, learning by doing, learning through research, learning in informal context, etc.

Socializing competences may develop in language learning through simulation activities, dramatized/decision-making games applications (online) which by the requirements of a *digital game project* - a computer game (like "EthnoQuest"), simulating the roles and appropriate response, is both used to develop language competences per level groups and for carrying out specific intercultural education: cultural bilingualism, religious beliefs, habits, etc. (de Haan, J.2011, creators, Fiona, 2011, 35-46). We find that all these ways of carrying through socializing activities based on social media resources are able to develop and provide a genuine learning autonomy. But this level is reached only by those who have benefited in the early stages of training and education of a direct and individualized learning guidance by the teacher.

New information technologies can perform functions in terms of *competence training*. This is possible only by performing the following steps: users' acknowledgement of the structuring of the competences aimed at by a certain skills training / certification level; teacher mediation by formulating attractive, consistent learning tasks, dosed in time and degree of difficulty and be centered on achieving competences specified in the target training profile; gaining awareness of their degree by reference to minimum standards of competence achievement (minimum accepted performance evaluation).

The educational system has passed beyond its "re-industrialization time" in the late 90s. In this context, Pierre Moeglin (1998, 104) points out that training always involves more than simply acquiring skills; it is a very complex process that the *functionalism of an instrumentalized society may not fully realize*. However, in view of the development based on profitability and modernization criteria, all educational systems have purchased more and more modern resources in the neo-industrial beginning of the century, marked by the collocation "knowledge-based society". The modernization and relaunching provided by the new equipment, without adequate adaptation to specific structures of the teaching process involves the risk of distortion and even cancellation of the conscious, systematic, organized learning processes. Using varied synchronous and asynchronous communication ways, these technologies continue to grow and become increasingly more interactive. However, we support the development of the combined approaches of learning, so that they can more elderly persons, who are technophobes or have limited access to social media tools:

Whilst these technologies continue to improve and become more interactive, there is nothing which beats a blended approach to learning. So don't get too carried away yet, there is still considerable value in communicating face to face and of course, we should not disadvantage those learners who are technophobes or simply do not have access to such resources. (Linda Wilson, 2009, 211).

The way we rank the learning outcomes at the end of a training program is closely related to the coordination arrangements to acquire a set of competences, methods developed by teachers - people specifically prepared for this purpose.

Therefore, societies an in particular education systems, through successful schools (e.g. English, Australian, Danish) are constantly developing best management practices of the teaching process by specific techniques for the best exploitation of social media resources. Teacher mediation guarantees the acquisition of continuing education bases, namely those formative structures of a certain level of training competences that enable successful adaptation to dynamic changes in society. Activated later on the labour market, these competences prove their long term, increased economic efficiency.

2. PARADIGM SHIFT FROM TRADITIONAL KNOWLEDGE TO DIGITAL LITERACY

Education plays a vital role both in an economic and social context. EU offers a wide range of opportunities to its citizens for living, studying and working in other countries bringing a major contribution to cross-cultural understanding, personal development and the realization of the EU's full economic potential. Every year, well over a million EU citizens of all ages benefit from EU-funded educational, vocational and citizenship-building programs. Looking on EU Education figures, the major gaps can be easily seen, such as: less than 1/3 of the Europeans aged 25-34 have a university degree (comparing with 40% in USA and over 50% in Japan). The fact is Europe has around 4,000 higher education institutions, with over 17 million students and 1.5 million staff of whom 435,000 are researchers - and still the European universities rank poorly in global terms – only 2 are in the world top 20, which is quite unsatisfactory[2].

The EU Commission recommends stronger action at the European level to implement the necessary reforms to modernize European universities. As *key actors* in a knowledge economy and knowledge society, universities face many challenges and have to make the necessary reforms to fully participate in the global market place in the fields of teaching, research and innovation. The challenges facing higher education are similar across the EU and there are clear advantages in working together.

In a digital society, universities should play an important role: to *promote knowledge* by achieving greater involvement of all parts of society. In a knowledge-based society, it is vital for universities to step up communication and dialogue with those affected by their activities and with the whole of society.

It is quite relevant: the future starts today and we need to be part of it. That means to understand the challenges, to assume an active role in designing the teaching & learning process in order to enable the young generation with new skills and competencies to help them better integrate in the knowledge society. In fact the key question is: *what do our students need to learn today to be prepared for tomorrow?*

Many scholars have written and policy-makers have debated in the recent past years about knowledge society challenges and the teachers' role in the new context of rapid development of the information technologies. In order to better understand this paper's aim, it could be useful to explore the literature and to emphasize the more suitable concepts' definitions and underpinning approaches of the paper's subject.

The concept of "information society" was used for the first time in Japan (Kohyama, 1968) and in the 1970's the authors of the computer-related texts referred to an "information society" and they use word like " computerized society" (Martin, Norman, 1970, Rothman, Masmann, 1972). In the late 1980's the metaphor "information society" had become a concept that included the essence of a culture dominated by information and by the information technology (IT).

The "information society" concept was replaced in 1990's by the "knowledge society" which referred to the economic system where ideas or knowledge functioned as commodities.[3] At EU level, the concept was promoted along with the Lisbon Declaration, 2000 when looking through the eyes of political institutions, the year 2010 becomes the focal point for achieving the "most competitive and dynamic knowledge-based economy in the world capable of sustainable economic growth with more and better jobs and greater social cohesion"[4].

Digital society can be defined as a society or community that is well advanced in the adoption and integration of digital technology into daily life at home, work and play, and has advanced in the adoption of the connected or new economy. Many governments around the world see the development of a digital society as an essential aspect of continuing economic development.

Digital citizenship is the ability to participate in the society online. The British sociologist T.H. Marshall defines citizenship as endowing all members of a political community with certain civil, political and social rights of membership, including " the right to share to the full in the social heritage and to live the life of a civilized being according to the standards prevailing in the society" (Marshall, 1992). Digital citizens are those who use the Internet regularly and effectively on a daily basis.

The current spread of new technologies and the emergence of the internet as a public network seem to be carving out fresh opportunities to widen this public knowledge forum. Might we now have the means to achieve equal and universal access to knowledge, and genuine sharing?[5]

The idea of the information society is based on technological breakthroughs. The concept of knowledge societies encompasses much broader social, ethical and political dimensions. While information consists of intentionally structured and formatted data, knowledge consists of cognitive states needed to interpret and otherwise process information (David & Foray, 2003). In this sense it can be considered that any educational system is a knowledge society. When an educational group invests effort toward sharing and producing new knowledge, such as a group of teachers that work with each other to improve their teaching, we can refer to them as a knowledge society, especially those that use all the tools (ICT) to facilitate their goals (Hargraves, 2003).

A knowledge economy depends upon information as well as the intellectual capital of economic communities, the role of the education institutions in this context is obvious: to produce a high quality intellectual capital. Producing a high quality intellectual means, in general, to achieve a certain level of competence in the most relevant areas of today's society, in particular, in the ICT, so one can speak about ICT literacy and more recently, digital literacy, which enable individuals to engage in computer supported cooperative work with growing importance in the knowledge society.

Learning in the knowledge society was defined in Europe by the Bologna Process which propagates 10 action lines to lead us to a European standardization of study programs. At the same time with the Bologna Process a European Information Society is to be created by implementing modern electronic infrastructure and high-quality services accessible for all EU citizens. One of the important directions to build a true European Information society is the "use of new multimedia technologies and the Internet to improve the quality of learning by facilitating access to resources as well as remote exchanges and collaboration " [6]

No doubt we are experiencing today a rapid transformation of the learning process and the stakeholders involved in it need to define exactly their role. Teachers, students, parents, future employers are facing the knowledge "wave" coming through the Internet, and they are starting to realize that the traditional learning methods are not enough or appropriate in the new "digital world".

Traditional learning, consolidated over the years, has outstanding results in enriching the world knowledge heritage, but today it seems to become less effective (for teachers) and not at all attractive (for students).

Europe and the whole world is living in a society where our actions (including learning) are frequently mediated by digital tools and objects that interfere with us are more and more shaped by digital interventions (books = e-books, board = interactive board, teacher = virtual teacher, classroom=virtual classroom etc). Learning in the knowledge society should be seen quite differently and the traditional approach of this process must be left behind, the today's reality forces us to rethink our roles as teachers, students and parents.

Learning is the key to success—some would even say survival—in today's society. The rapid evolution of the knowledge society poses a difficult challenge to educators and policy makers. Many publications about the education in the twenty first century emphasize that students must acquire knowledge-based skills, and the most suitable is a "student-centered" didactical or pedagogical approach (Jonassen, 1999).

To support economic development, the education system shall encourage the personal growth of the European citizens in the following areas (Schoop, Bukvova & Lieske, 2006):

1. **Skills:** Technical, social and personal competences giving a secure foundation for life enable individuals to work in groups and to use existing Information and Communication Technologies (ICT). The explosion of information implies using systems that require new skills for accessing, organizing and retrieving information (Spitzer et al.1998)
2. **Adaptability:** The ability to learn about and adjust to new situations
3. **Mobility:** The skills required in today's multicultural society - the ability to work and communicate with others across national boundaries.

The higher education institutions should adapt their educational programs in order to enable their graduates to acquire the above-mentioned skills categories. *What changes to traditional teach-*

ing and learning processes are demanded by the knowledge society challenges?

Education and critical thinking are crucial in building real knowledge societies. Education has numerous functions in modern societies: intellectual and democratic training, acquisition of professional skills, knowledge production, etc (Cohen, 2005). On the other hand, young people are bound to play a major role because they are often among the first to use new technologies and to help establish them as familiar features of everyday life.

In order to answer to the previous question, we need to understand the meaning of the concept "well educated". Michael Barber offered a model to explain this concept:

Well educated= E(T+K+L),

where K is from knowledge, T from thinking, L for leadership (leading both yourself and others) and E for ethical underpinning. The Barber's model is going beyond knowledge and critical thinking and integrates the leadership skills and ethical aspects of the learning process, in the knowledge society.

To achieve the goal of producing "well educated" graduates a major contribution will have the ICT tools in supporting the teaching/learning process:

- Transforming the classroom practice: The teaching process is possible to be customized according to the needs and aspirations of the individual learners;
- expanding access to quality learning
- increasing collaboration amongst teachers, students, parents and communities.

Individuals are encouraged to explore the new possibilities to learn, not only during the school years, but also along their entire life. The society dynamics shows that today more and more individuals are willing to develop skills that enable them to benefit from most of the digital society opportunities.

While the education ICT investment is growing, its potential to transform teaching and learning has yet to be fully unleashed.

Education institutions are just beginning to feel the impact of a powerful new force: digital technology. The impact that technology is beginning to have on *pedagogy*, particularly in the traditional classroom has, in the long run, far greater significance.

Virtual education has been growing rapidly, and yet the change in the traditional classroom is, by comparison, moving slowly, dependant as it is on acceptance by individual teachers.

Using the computer in the traditional classroom was quite easily accepted, just because it was demonstrated that ordinary tasks were more efficiently solved. Providing the syllabus, course content, communication with students are some of these accepted tasks. Still, many teachers are concerned as to whether technology is simple and reliable enough to use more sophisticated learning tasks.

The new multimedia technologies and the Internet are supposed to improve the quality of learning, by facilitating access to resources as well as remote exchanges and collaboration, the ICT technologies can contribute to the quality of education and training and the Europe's move to a knowledge-based society.

Increasingly, better and better software is emerging which allows students to take part in more engaging and effective learning - computer mediated and allows teachers to have a better learning content management. Digital content and networked applications offer direct opportunities to enhance learning, to stimulate collaboration between teachers and to make the learning content more attractive to students.

Thoughtful scholars have estimated that in a few years the use of such software will become commonplace, truly transforming the way of learning takes place in most settings in traditional classrooms on campus and online.

Insofar, the implementation of ICT tools in the teaching/learning process seems to have a "white" face that includes great benefice to all parties involved and at the same time a "dark" face related to increasing evidence of misuse and abuse of these technologies in schools. Look around yourselves, and you will see students using cell phone during class time, plagiarizing information while preparing their home work, playing games on the computer instead of participating in class discussions and the list is far from being complete.

However, the today's usage of the new ICT technologies in education raises some *ethical issues* and there are claims that the learning performance is not directly dependent of the amount of ICT investment in educational institutions.

Creating the Digital Society is not a utopia, actually it is a quite real fact and it needs to be defined in terms of concepts and rules. Facing digital society means in fact to accept the need of a digital literacy, for young and old people, teacher or student, the learning process never ends life-long learning in the digital society is a must.

ICT literacy has traditionally been defined in terms of the technical skills related to IT, whereas information literacy is usually defined in terms of information functions. If we view the intersection of these two domains with a third, a particular subject or knowledge domain, then we can define the intersection as ICT literacy. (Anderson, 2008- Venn diagram Figure 1).

We live today in a society invaded by the digital; the objects we encounter are entirely shaped by the digital intervention (e.g. From mobile phones to smart phones, from walkman to MP3 player, from PC to iPads) that means it is compulsory to be digital literate.

Starting from the "computer age" (Dertouzos & Moses, 1979), passing through the "information society" (1990) to achieve the "knowledge/ information revolution"(Gates, 1995) can suggest that social change is determined by technology, in fact technology is the product of human action and interaction, and the result of a " learning to do" process. But having access to technology in

Figure 1. Venn diagram of applied ICT literacy (Source:De Joke Voogt, Gerarld A. Knezek- International Handbook of Information technology in primary and secondary education, Springer Science+ Business Media, 2008, p.18)

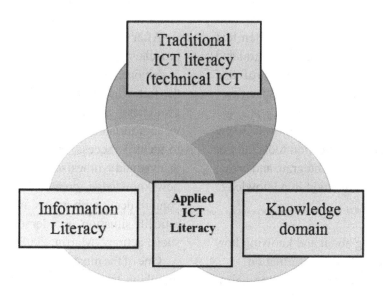

nowadays' global society is not for everyone; in this hierarchical and unequal society, the "digital divide" appears which adds another dimension to inequalities which have already long existed. In the age of globalization, digital technology has become essential to accomplish the official, commercial and personal activities and individuals must be aware of the need to stay active, to learn and to re-create themselves constantly.

The idea of literacy expresses one of the fundamental characteristics of participation in society, and the widening application of the word has seen it used to characterize all of the necessary attributes of social being. (Martin, 2008)

The literacy concept can be defined as an evolving one, Claire Belisle (2006) characterized this evolution using *three models*:

1. **The Functional Model:** Presents literacy from simple cognitive and practical skills such as reading and writing to a more developed ones such as skills required for functioning effectively within the community
2. **The Socio-Cultural Practice Model:** According to this model, to be literate is to have access to cultural, economic and political structures of society
3. **The Intellectual Empowerment Model:** Argues that literacy not only provides means and skills to deal with written text and numbers within a specific cultural and ideological contexts, but it brings profound enrichment of human thinking capacities.

ICT literacy can be defined as follows: "using digital technology, communication tools, and/or networks to access, manage, integrate and create information in order to function in a knowledge society"

- **Access:** Knowing about and knowing how to collect and/or retrieve information
- **Manage:** Applying an existing organizational or classification scheme

- **Integrate:** Interpreting and representing information: summarizing, comparing, contrasting
- **Evaluate**: Making judgment about the quality, relevance, usefulness or efficiency of information
- **Create:** Generating information (US National Research Council Report- NRC, 1999)

Focusing on work in schools, Hobbs (1998) defines literacy as "the ability to access, analyze, evaluate and communicate messages in a variety of forms". In the view of this definition, the student is being actively engaged in the process of analyzing and creating messages.

In this context is it possible to talk about *digital literacy*? The concept was introduced by Paul Gilster, who defined it as: "the ability to understand and use information in multiple formats from wide range of sources when it is presented via computers". As fundamental act of cognition, literacy becomes digital literacy when the computer screen is interfering between individuals and networked medium. Moreover, Glister identifies critical thinking as the core skill of digital literacy and emphasizes the need of a critical evaluation of what we found on the Web, rather the technical skills required to access it.

After a deep analysis of various of the approaches proposed by scholars, policy-makers, practitioners and educators, Allan Martin proposed the following definition: "*Digital literacy* is the awareness, attitude and ability of individuals to appropriately use digital tools and facilities to identify, access, manage, integrate, evaluate, analyze and synthesize digital resources, construct new knowledge, create media expressions and communicate with others, in the context of specific life situation, in order to enable constructive social action."(Martin, 2008)

One of the most influential examples of thinking about the new digital literacy comes in the form of the *Shift Happens* video, created originally by Karl Flisch in 2006. This is possibly the most widely viewed and circulated statement of the requirements of the techno-zealot agenda. It has been translated into many different languages, redesigned by commercial companies and shown all over the world at educational events with any kind of technology focus and often without. The version available on YouTube lists over 5 million views at the time of writing. In his own words, Flisch's original aim was to create something which would provoke discussion amongst teachers who were not technologists. 'I was hoping by telling some of these 'stories' to our faculty, I could get them thinking about – and discussing with each other – the world our students are entering. To get them to really think about what our students are going to need to be successful in the 21st century, and then how that might impact what they do in their classrooms. '

More and more our life goes digital, let's become digital literate! Were educators can interfere and support this process? How the future may look like?

Neil Postman predicted so accurately in his book *Amusing Ourselves to Death*, where he noted the impact that telegraphy had on American culture through the rapid dissemination of news. "The abundant flow of information had very little or nothing to do with those to whom it was addressed; that is with any social or intellectual context in which their lives were embedded. Coleridge's famous line about water everywhere without a drop to drink may serve as a metaphor of a decontextualised information environment: In a sea of information, there was very little of it to use."

Many new technologies are so powerful and work so quickly, that they have disrupted the accepted practice of academics and scholars in peer reviewing and evaluating colleagues' work, replacing scholarship with marketing practice and tools. One of the myths propagated by enthusiasts for technology is that the nature of learning has fundamentally changed as a result of wider technological change. They call for a new range of skills, sometimes referred to as 'digital literacy'.

The effective use and dissemination of knowledge through technology in all kinds of professions and vocations, has become vital for anyone seeking professional recognition or success. The competencies and skills that an educated person will need in 20 years will be markedly different from what school systems currently provide. What shall we do? The *multiliteracy* could be the answer.

Studies that evolved from the New London Group (1996) explored the nature of literacy in the 21st Century. The New London Group coined the concept of 'multiliteracies'. Multiliteracies help us determine what it means to be a literate person in contemporary society, a much broader view of literacy than portrayed by traditional language-based approaches. This view takes into account the "multiple modes of communication to which each of our senses is attuned and multiple ways in which knowledge and skills can be passed" (Williamson, 2005).

What kind of competence will be needed in the future? Kay et al. is proposing a Next Generation Users Competence (NGUS) Figure 2 Model which is explaining the link between digital literacy and digital independence. In the near future, any individual should be able to build himself a personal e-confidence through participation, enquiry and to produce (create) valuable assets for him and for the society.

The above model is comparable to the EQS model, as defined above.

The reality of innovation in schools is that energetic and enthusiastic teachers will always seek out new ideas and tools to improve their performance in order to be able to assist young people to gain their personal e-confidence.

There is also recognition that web world is transforming the way we go about many activities. The model, Figure 3, originated by Genny Dixon of e-Skills, illustrates the interplay between the online / offline and the collaborative dimensions. For example, what was once much more private (such as buying books or insurance) has been enhanced by the involvement of strangers in the form of ratings and reviews. This significantly

Figure 2. Next Generation Competency Model (Source: David Kay, Bob McGonigle, Barbara Tabbiner, Walter Patterson- Next generation users skills, 2008, www.digital2010.org)

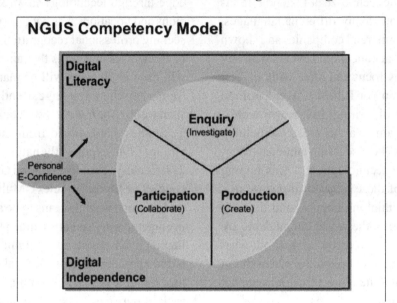

changes the everyday requirements for 'digital literacy.'

Studies are showing that the traditional way of learning has "dramatically' changed, the role of the teachers has changed too, and the today's challenge is the increasing of the learning effectiveness in the context of the new digital interference in the learning process. International Society for Technology in Education, USA has established clear standards about what students should do in order to be more effective in learning and more productive in the digital world (Figure 4 - USA technological standards.).

3. PROFILE OF THE NEW STUDENT

The boom of the *information technology* and the *change of the student population structure*, of 'marketization' of higher education – the so-called 'academic capitalism' age (Slaughter and Leslie, 1997) – and of flexibility, 'the fixity' of knowledge, the accumulation of fix elements of knowledge no longer meet the requirements of the society. The capacity of change, adaptation

and constant updating of these elements according to individual needs, but also to the needs of the various contexts where the knowledge must be used is a prerequisite of social integration for the graduate. In 1990, Barr brilliantly forecast the future of education, as: independent, individualized, interactive, interdisciplinary and intuitive. Education is supposed to change according to the structure of the new generations. Generation Y, the generation born with the computer, has specific features which claim specific changes in education to fit their expectations. This generation, as compared to the previous Generation X, is:

- **Familiar with and Reliant on Communication Technologies (Technosavvy):** Use and integrate technology in all forms into their lives
- **Short Attention Spans:** The instant click of a mouse is the info rate they are ready to accept, every topic should be short and to the point
- **Multitaskers:** While listening to a topic, they may send an e-mail or an SMS or look up something on the mobile net at the same

Figure 3. Dixon e-skills model (Source: www.learningtechnologies.ac.uk.org and www.e-skills.com)

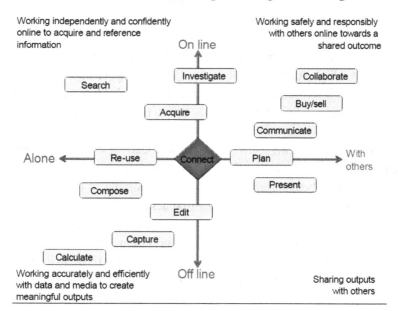

time, which does not mean they are not interested in the topic under discussion; but time is too precious not to make the best of it

- **Filter and Consume Info Quickly:** Easily select information and are able to process it immediately and apparently, effortless.

Figure 4. USA technological standards - Increasing learning effectiveness (Source: NTSE - National Educational Technology Standards Copyright © 2007 International Society for Technology in Education –USA)

NETS[3] - "What students should know and be able to do to learn effectively and live productively in an increasingly digital world"

1. Creativity and Innovation - Students demonstrate creative thinking, construct knowledge, and develop innovative products and processes using technology.

2. Communication and Collaboration - Students use digital media and environments to communicate and work collaboratively, including at a distance, to support individual learning and contribute to the learning of others

3. Research and Information Fluency - Students apply digital tools to gather, evaluate, and use information.

4. Critical Thinking, Problem-Solving & Decision-Making - Students use critical thinking skills to plan and conduct research, manage projects, solve problems and make informed decisions using appropriate digital tools and resources

5. Digital Citizenship - Students understand human, cultural, and societal issues related to technology and practice legal and ethical behaviour.

6. Technology Operations and Concepts - Students demonstrate a sound understanding of technology concepts, systems and operations.

- **Information Must Apply Directly and be Relevant for them:** Skype, ICQ, MySpace, Facebook are *the* channel of communication for them, where they select the information they need at a high-speed rate, any background or general information is irrelevant, therefore, useless and left aside.

Every generation has specific thinking patterns, different from the previous generations, but this generation processes and thinks about the information at hand subject to the technological supply. Their learning preferences, their motivation and expectations from education are different and while they are seen as 'growing without values', they have something new to offer: directness, pragmatic goals, high expectations, fast achievements. The new generation's features show its readiness to match the new competency model described above. Moreover, they are not only ready but also eager to investigate by themselves, to collaborate, to create, to share knowledge, using any way of communication they are used to. It is the education system which needed to adapt to the new models, both of competency and of student and provide the students the conditions to develop into attaining *professional competence*.

It was imperative for education to step into the era of deep reforms based on the new concepts: student-centered learning, informal education, digital literacy, personal learning environment, stating that "to teach means to model and to demonstrate; to learn means to practice and to consider". Sometimes, the early involvement of the student, immediately after high school graduation, in social life requires major alterations in the teaching/learning and assessment methods. The information technology provides to the new type of student with the learning environemnt he/she needs in the new context, connects him/her rapidly to the up-to-date information and to the rest of the world.

Recent studies show that there are over 7 million Internet users in Romania and that the Romanians are area leaders of online chat. As for blogs, in Romania there are over 10,000 active blogs and over 3 million blog readers (source: SATI - Internet Study of Rating and Traffic).

For the generations that have grown with the computer, the Internet and the communication space provided by the Internet is no mistery, on the contrary it is a close friend. Alienating and anti-social for some, the Internet is deemed by the young generation as an open gate to the world, a compression of time and space, impossible to be achieved by any other ways and means. The immediate community is no longer sufficient, the information got by the traditional ways (parents, school, reading) is limited and time-consuming. As the world of the future is a world of performance, where the value added by every individual matters, as education becomes more and more available and expands, competitiveness is increasing, the requirements of the society are higher. This social pressure has caused considerable changes in the profile of the new student: *Homo Sapiens* has turned early 2nd millennium in *Homo Zappiens* (a concept introduced by the University of Manitoba in the paper presented on 7 June 2007). The students of the 21st century are:

- Active information processors;
- Solve problems very quickly;
- Network with friends;
- Communicate informally;
- See school as irrelevant;
- Want control on what they are doing;
- Hyperactive, have a short period of concentration;
- Learn from the human and technical networks.

These are the features of a whole generation, irrespective of culture and traditions; and information technology has forged common traits and expectations in the young people worldwide.

The radical changes caused by the information technology which enables access to complex knowledge and concentrated information and by the requirements of the knowledge-based society resulted in the 'dissolution' of the university community and empty classrooms. While being an effect independent from the will of the stakeholders in the educational process, the disappearing university community may be recovered by creating the web community; and the blog may be a viable solution for it on the one hand, and for the extension of the classroom discourse on the other hand.

4. EDUCATIONAL BLOG: AN EFFICIENT WAY OF SOCIAL INTERACTION

Though some say that the first blog (an abbreviation of 'weblog') was the first website developed by Tim Berners-Lee in 1991, yet the first blog in its current format appeared in 1996, developped by Dave Winer. In the educational area, where the blog is seen as a means of conveying knowledge, the blogs are called *k*(nowledge)-*logs*. The blog is a *new space of communication*, a place of conversation, with a functional and rapid format and a *multimedia contents*: audio, video, animation (EDUBLOG). The contents and purposes of the blogs differ considerably. In 2002, Blood defined 3 basic types of blogs:

1. **Filters:** Blogs which include national and international events
2. **Personal Journals:** Blogs that contain the blogger's activities and feelings
3. **Notebooks:** Blogs with personal or external contents, characterized by longer essays.

The blogs are socially interactive and 'community'-type. Krishnamurty (2002) provided us with a more comprehensive classification of the blogs, and distinguished four categories (quadrants):

1. Online personal journals

2. Support groups (friends)
3. Filters
4. Metafilters, collaborative contents (educational blog)

The metafilter or the 'community blogs' are the blogs where anybody can post commentaries, that have characteristics similar to the asynchronous discussion forums, a text-based form of computer-mediated interactive communication, but it is not limited to that.

The commentaries, the entries are chronologically arranged. The page of the group/year is turned from a simple instrument into the group's/year's image as a discourse community. The first mention of a Romanian blog in a Romanian newspaper occurred 5 and a half years ago. Since then the number of loyal blog consumers has constantly grown and is still growing, due to its specific advantages as an extension of one's personal brand or, more recently, a profitable job.

As a *genre*, the blog enables the computer-mediated interactive and text-based communication, seen as a fundamentally different type of communication on the Internet as compared to the HTML documents, quite static, having an unique author, which are the standard web communication means.

Yates and Orlikowski (1992) analysed the electronic communication under the form of the e-mail, as a continuation of the 'memo' genre, highlighting the fact that the e-mail has reshaped the genre by its technical format and the usage rules. They elicited the traditional models of the genre and started from Miller's definition (1984) of the genre: 'as a rhetoric action based on recurrent situations'. On the one hand, Swales (1990) characterized the genre as "'a category of communicative events having in common a set of communicative purposes', and similar structures, stylistic fractures, contents and target-audience." From this point of view, the blog is hosting neutral language register conversation, with few abbreviations. The blog is acknowledged by the Internet users. Adopting this point of view and comparing the blog with other genres – electronic and traditional – the blog is part of a wider communicative domaine, with specific usage rules and its own development. We cannot say that the blog derives from only one source, such as the e-mail, but it is rather a hybrid of existing genres, unique by its combination of features of the source genres it adapts.

The edublog has considerable *advantages*: keeping up with the students, learning new technologies to maintain the student's interest, observing the individual results/progress, developing adequate forms of assessment for the technology-assisted learning, maintaining the relationship school/home, involves the student into conversation and makes them learn, develops a learning community, encourages the expression of one's own opinions, knowing the student's personality outside the classroom, knowing the student's personality outside the classroom, collective projects (in writing), the students may participate actively in the knowledge building process, increased interactivity. The edublog enhances interaction, widens the social group, enables *collaboration* and *creation* within the virtual team. Due to such advantages, it matches the C7. descriptor of the transversal competences in the *National Qualifications Framework Matrix of Higher Education: Familiarity with the roles and specific activities of teamwork and sharing of tasks to subordinate levels.*

There are *disadvantages* also, such as: scepticism on the benefits of technology for the educational process: alienating (desocializing) factor, time-consumer, encouraging plagiarism, aspects related to information security, the teachers must make an additional effort to get acquainted with and integrate technology into the teaching process, Internet addiction,. it is difficult to find the relevant info when one needs it, it is a remote means of communication, prior instruction of the users is required, but the advantages outnumber and are more important than the disadvantages.

The use of the new technologies has shifted the interest from the acquissition of knowledge to the acquisition of skills, competences required to attain the purpose of learning.

In Romania, the edublogs are quite popular, mostly due to centralized university projects, and to individual initiatives of the teachers or of the students. The easy way of opening, using and maintaining a blog and the fact that a blog requires from the users minimum of digital literacy has made it a common tool in education, both in higher education and in high schools. Most of the Romanian edublogs have been opened first by the faculties of informatics and they are very active, but they are now common with the other faculties too. Most of the blogs in Romanian universities are a public space for comment and notifications, less about study guides or online teaching and learning; these are services yet to be experimented.

We at Spiru Haret University, a private university, have also adapted to the new profile of the student and to the requirements of the employers in point of graduates' professional competences, therefore the blogs are nothing but unusual; there are student blogs (e.g. http://spiruharet-ro. blogspot.com/2008/04/universitatea-spiru-haret. html) or official blogs (e.g. http://focus.hotnews. ro/universitatea-spiru-haret, http://www.radioo-mega.ro/8371-universitatea-spiru-haret-targu-jiu-este-acreditata.html) of the filter type, or metafilters like www.ruxandravasilescu.blogspot.com,. The latter is an educational blog for the Business English class made by the students to diversify the learning methods, to get to each other better and exchange points of view freely, without the restrictions self-imposed in the classroom. Some of the students went beyond simply sharing opinions and information on homework and class activity and felt free to share with the virtual team their hobbies and interests, revealing their complex personality and skills in their attempt to connect and due to the sense of belonging to a team.

Students are active on all these blogs because they feel encouraged to express the points of view they cannot express in the classroom for various reasons. On the other hand, they feel that their voice is better heard, therefore the rhetoric of blogs is self-censored, responsible and common sense. Moreover, their voice is heard within a community they want to share and to belong to. The blogosphere continues to expand in higher education, as an effective aditional tool in instruction and teacher-student relationship, considering also the fact that most students get a job while studying and face-to-face learning is no longer a daily option for them.

CONCLUSION

This paper highlights the idea of the possibility to adapt the social interaction competences listed in the European legislative documents, through generic and specific level descriptors, but also through good practice nationally and locally valued. Therefore, the study provides a benchmark for developing the Subject Description to identify the competences subordinate to transversal competence of social interaction (TC 7), by encouraging the teaching, learning, research and development opportunities, training and evaluating them, both for the bachelor degree, as well as for the master's degree and doctoral studies. It can also be a source of expertise and information for decision makers to recognize the social interaction competences acquired in informal context, through social media (re)sources.

The blog, as a modern tool to support teaching and learning, enables a view upon the world from a personalized, creative, uncensored perspective. Therefore it has been embraced willingly both by the teachers, aware of the importance of adapting to the changes required by the technology boom and to the specific features of the new generation, and by the students. The edublog enhances interac-

tion, widens the social group, enables *collaboration* and *creation* within the virtual team. Due to such advantages, it matches the C7. descriptor of the *National Qualifications Framework Matrix of Higher Education: Familiarity with the roles and specific activities of teamwork and sharing of tasks to subordinate levels.*

The use of the new technologies in education shifted the focus from knowledge acquisition to skills and competences acquisition required for attaining the purpose of learning. Nowadays the blog is getting more and more fans and due to its generous multimedia contents it is able to successfully support the educational process.

REFERENCES

Academic Ranking of World Universities. (n.d.). *Shanghai index*. Retrieved from http://www.arwu.org/aboutARWU.jsp

Anderson, R. E. (2008). Implications of the information and knowledge society for education. In Voogt, J., & Knezek, G. (Eds.), *International handbook of information technology in primary and secondary education* (pp. 5–22). Springer. doi:10.1007/978-0-387-73315-9_1

Belisle, C. (2006). Literacy and the digital knowledge revolution. In Martin, A., & Madigan, D. (Eds.), *Digital literacies for learning* (pp. 51–67). London, UK: Facet.

Blood, R. (2002). *The weblog handbook: Practical advice on creating and maintaining your blog.* Cambridge.

Cohen, M., Adelman, L., Bresnick, T., Freeman, M., Salas, E., & Riedel, S. (2007). Dialogue as medium(and message) for training critical thinking. In R. Hoffman (Ed.), *Expertise out of the context-Proceedings of the Sixth International Conference on Naturalistic Decision Making*, (pp. 219-229). Lawrence Erlbaum Associates.

Creaser, F. (2011). The merits of using "Ethno-Quest" as an English language learning tool and a medium of cultural transmission. European Association for Computer Assisted Language Learning (EUROCALL). *The EUROCALL Review, 19*. Retrieved from http://www.eurocall-languages.org/review/19/No19.pdf

David, P. A., & Foray, D. (2003). Economic fundamentals of the knowledge society. *Policy Futures in Education- An e-Journal, 1*(1),

de Haan, J. (2011). Teaching and learning English through digital game projects. *Digital Culture and Education, 3*(1), 46–5.

Dertouzos, M. L., & Moses, J. (1979). *The computer age: A twenty year view*. Cambridge, MA: MIT Press. doi:10.1080/07377366.1982.10401297

Dixon e-skills Model. (n.d.). Retrieved from www.learningtechnologies.ac.uk.org and www.e-skills.com

Eur-Lex. (2005). *Mobilising the brainpower of Europe: enabling universities to make their full contribution to the Lisbon Strategy. Opinion of the committee of the Regions on the communication from the commission.*

European Counci. (2000). *Presidency conclusions of the Lisabona European Council, 2000.* Retrieved from http://www.consilium.europa.eu/uedocs/cms_data/docs/pressdata/en/ec/00100-r1.en0.htm

Hargraves, A. (2003)- *Teaching in the knowledge society*. New York, NY: Teachers College.

Herring, S. C., Scheidt, L. A., Bonus, S., & Wright, E. (2005). Weblogs as a bridging genre. *Information Technology & People, 18*(2), 142–171. doi:10.1108/09593840510601513

Jakobi, A. P. (2007). The knowledge society and the global dynamics in education politics. *European Educational Research Journal, 6*(1). doi:10.2304/eerj.2007.6.1.39

Jonassen, D. H. (1999). *Computers as mind tools for schools: Engaging critical thinking* (2nd ed.). Upper Saddle River, NJ: Merrill.

Kay, D., McGonigle, B., Tabbiner, B., & Patterson, W. (2008). *Next generation users skills*. Retrieved from www.digital2010.org

Kohyama, K. (1968). *Introduction to information society theory*. Tokyo, Japan: Chuo Koron.

Lankshear, C., & Knobel, M. (2008). Digital literacies: Concepts, policies and practices. In Allan, M. (Ed.), *Digital literacy and the "digital society"*. New York, NY: Peter Lang Publishing.

Martin A. (2005). DigEuLit- A European framework for digital literacy: A progress report. *Journal of eLiteracy, 2.*

Martin, J., & Normann, A. R. D. (1970). *The computerized society*. Bethesda, MD: World Future Society.

Moeglin, P. (Ed.). (2003). *Industriile educaţiei şi noile media*. Iaşi, Romania: Polirom.

Nelson, T., & Fernheimer, J. (n.d.). *Welcome to the blogosphere: Using weblogs to create classroom community*. Retrieved from http://www.cwrl.utexas.edu/whitepapers/030822-1

NTSE. (2007). *National educational technology standards*. USA: International Society for Technology in Education.

Ribble, M. S., Bailey, G. D., & Ross, T. W. (2004, September). *Digital citizenship – Addressing appropriate technology behaviour, learning & leading with technology*. ISTE-International Society for Technology in Education, USA.

Rothman, S., & Mosmann, C. (1972). *Computers and society*. Chicago, IL: Science Research Associates, Inc.

Schoop, E., Bukvova, H., & Lieske, C. (2006). *Blended learning arrangements for higher education in the changing knowledge society*. Retrieved from www.qucosa.de/.../2009_Riga_Schoop.pdf

Spitzer, K. L., Eisenberg, M. B., & Lowe, C. A. (1998). *Information literacy- Essential skills for the information age*. Syracuse, NY: ERIC Clearinghouse on Information and Technology.

Starr, R. H., & Murray, T. (2005, October). Education goes digital- The evolution of online learning and the revolution in higher education. *Communications of the ACM, 48*(10), 59–64.

Tyner, K. R. (1998). *Literacy in a digital world- Teaching and learning in the age of information* (pp. 18–20). Lawrence Erlbaum Associates, Inc.

Uso-Juan, E. (2006). The compensatory nature of discipline-related knowledge and English-language proficiency in reading for academic purposes. *Modern Language Journal, 90*(2), 210–227. doi:10.1111/j.1540-4781.2006.00393.x

Voogt De, J., & Knezek, G. A. (2008). *International handbook of information technology in primary and secondary education*, (p. 18). Springer Science+ Business Media.

Williams, B. J., & Jacobs, J. (2004). Exploring the use of blogs as learning spaces in the higher education sector. *Australasian Journal of Educational technology, 20*(2), 232-247.

Wilson, L. (2009). *Practical teaching: A guide to PTLLS & DTLLS*. Andover, MD: Cengage Learning EMEA.

KEY TERMS AND DEFINITIONS

Conceptual Model and Methodological NQFHE: The National Qualifications Framework in Higher Education (NQFHE), the NQFHE conceptual-methodological model is compatible with the European Qualifications Framework (EQF).

Digital Literacy: The awareness, attitude and ability of individuals to appropriately use digital tools.

Educational Blogs: Blogs maintained for the purpose of classroom instruction.

Life-Long Learning: The continuous building of skills throughout one's life.

Personal Learning Environment: Systems that help learners to take control of and manage their own learning.

Student-Centered Learning: Education focusing on the needs of students.

Transversal Competence: Those capabilities that transcend a particular field, the study program, with a transdisciplinary nature.

ENDNOTES

[1] ORDER no. 4.430 of 29 June 2009 on the use of the National Qualifications Framework in higher education, published in the Official Journal of Romania no. 545 of 5.08.2009, pp. 23-42.

[2] Academic Ranking of World Universities - Shanghai index -http://www.arwu.org/aboutARWU.jsp

[3] R.E. Anderson- "*Implications of the information and knowledge society for education*"- International Handbook of Information Technology in Primary and Secondary Education, Springer, 2008

[4] European Council- *Presidency Conclusions of the Lisbon European Council, 2000* http://www.consilium.europa.eu/uedocs/cms_data/docs/pressdata/en/ec/00100-r1.en0.htm_

[5] *Towards knowledge societies*- UNESCO Publishing, Paris, 2005

[6] European Commission *e-learning Glossary Term* http://elearningeuropa.info

APPENDIX

Extract from the National Qualifications Framework Matrix of Higher Education

Table 2.

Table 2. Types of learning outcomes and qualification descriptors for the "bachelor degree"

Learning outcomes		Generic descriptors	Level Descriptors - bachelor degree -
Trans-versal compe-tences (descrip-tors 6-8)	Personal and professional competences development	8. Personal and pro-fessional development	C8. Awareness of the need for training, effective use of resource and learning techniques for personal and professional development
	Role compe-tences	7. Social Networking	C7. Familiarity with the roles and specific activities of teamwork and sharing of tasks to subordinate levels
		6. Autonomy and responsibility	C6. Responsible performance of professional duties, under conditions of limited autonomy and qualified assistance
PRO-FES-SIONAL COM-PE-TENCE (descrip-tors 1-5)	Skills (functional –action dimen-sion):	5. Creativity and in-novation	C5. Professional project development using established principles and methods in the field
		4. Critical and con-structive reflection	C4. Appropriate use of standard evaluation criteria and methods to assess the quality, merits and limitations of processes, programs, projects, concepts, methods and theories
		3. Application, transfer and problem solving	C3. Application of basic principles and methods to solve problems / situa-tions defined, typical field conditions qualified support
	Knowledge (cog-nitive dimension):	2. Explanation and interpretation	C2. Use basic knowledge for explanation and interpretation of various types of concepts, situations, processes, projects, etc. associated domain
		1. Knowledge, under-standing and use of specific language	C1. Knowledge, understanding concepts, theories and basic methods of the field and area of specialization, their appropriate professional use

Chapter 19
Implementation of Augmented Reality in "3.0 Learning" Methodology:
Case Studies with Students of Architecture Degree

Ernest Redondo
Polytechnic University of Catalonia, Spain

Albert Sánchez
Polytechnic University of Catalonia, Spain

Isidro Navarro
Polytechnic University of Catalonia, Spain

David Fonseca
Ramón Llull University, Spain

ABSTRACT

This chapter discusses the impact of using social media resources and new emerging technologies in teaching and learning processes. The authors of this chapter focus on Spanish architecture-education framework by analyzing three case studies carried out by students finishing architecture and building degrees. Students' interaction with this resources is assessed, as well as their derived academic results, and the degree of satisfaction from students and teachers using these resources and technologies. To conduct the study, the authors worked with Web based freeware applications, such as Dropbox, blogging systems, Moodle, YouTube, Wikipedia, and Google Maps. Mobile devices, such as smartphones and tablets PCs, were used to test QR-Codes (Quick Response Codes) and Augmented Reality technology based applications as Junaio and Ar-Media Plugin.

INTRODUCTION

The emergence of new communications technologies in all areas of society has created a new situation in the classroom: we can integrate these technologies into the dynamic role of education, or we can avoid them. But its implementation becomes increasingly common. Particularly representative is the use of Smartphones in the classroom as a new system of communication and interaction among students, as we can see in the next sections.

DOI: 10.4018/978-1-4666-2851-9.ch019

Websites and social media applications such as Twitter, WhatsApp, and so on, are used to create and exchange user-generated content. Social media is ubiquitously accessible and enables, by scalable communication techniques, to establish and build new social relationships. This fact continues in computer class, where students are easily disconnected from the teaching through distractions such as blogs, emails, and multimedia content sharing, a situation that we often see in our classrooms.

This situation is a reality. In today's mediated society (where the use of mobile and social services is extended to all diary situations), it is necessary to reformulate the teaching and learning methodologies, and to implement changes allowing the student to follow their studies using friendly technologies. As we can see in this chapter, several studies have shown that the integration of "social media", as an element in the teaching process, allows greater integration into student's learning pace and leads a better comprehension of all explained concepts related to the course and teaching material. Howard Rheingold (Rheingold, 2011), in his -opening keynote of the ACM-CHI 2011 in Vancouver, Canada, affirmed that these technologies and their application allow and include mindful participation, collaboration, critical consumption, and all basic skills in the new digital teaching systems. This new situation allows improvement of the school experience and satisfaction in the learning process (Richardson and Swan, 2003; So and Brush, 2008; Wise, Chang, Duffy and Del Valle, 2004; Dziuban, Moskal, Brophy and Shea, 2007). There are several studies and implementations in the use of social media systems and visual interaction in the pre-university education and higher education, especially in areas where the use of visual information is very important such as in the frameworks of multimedia, design, communication, or architecture. We can find examples in sports education (Wagner, 2011), medicine (Billings, Halstead, 2008), and even to the legal education (Russo, Squelch and Varnham, 2010).

The introduction of "Learning 3.0 methods," was a widely discussed concept in the past conference Learning 3.0, 2011. Over the last few years, these new cooperative technologies have been incorporated into all academic frameworks, offering new educational opportunities. But it seems to be a novelty in architecture studies. These methods allow the use of newest multimedia content, such as three-dimensional (3D) visualization models, immersive environments, new publication and presentation systems using social media, document-managing and editing tools, and other applications linked to the capacity of the technologies used.

In the specific framework of the architecture degree, these new technologies provide new tools for the representation of architectural forms and their content. These new tools such as, mobile devices, 2D codes or markers, and mobile-learning or augmented reality systems (AR), facilitate new ways to access information and provide us opportunities for teaching under the concept of 3.0. In our case, by the use of mobile technology, students have generated exhibitions and presentations that combine physical and virtual content linked with QR codes, a real 2D object to interact with virtual objects in the scene.

In this chapter, we will present three case studies carried out in the Architecture and Building Engineering faculties of both the BarcelonaTech University of Catalonia and the Ramon Llull University, in the Campus of Architecture in Barcelona and Tarragona. The main objective of this work in progress, as summarized in this chapter, is to improve the academic performance of students by introducing technologies they already use in their daily lives, even for leisure outside of university.

BACKGROUND

New Learning Strategies: Toward the Concept of "Learning 3.0"

The main features of Learning 3.0 are the interactions of the user with the content, communication technologies incorporation, the use of new contexts for education, immersive environments contribution, and the awareness of sharing and recording student's own generated contents with their colleagues. The definition of Learning 3.0 includes technology because it involves the provision of collaborative tools such as blogs and Wikis, etc., (Moran, Seaman, Tinti-Kane, 2011); mobile-device interaction (using all type of devices such as iPhones, Android mobiles, Wiis, iPods, etc.); new environments for training as virtual simulation environments (Second Life, AR, etc.); and connectivity tools for location searching (e.g. 2D codes, Google Maps, etc.). The integration of mobile devices combined with multimedia applications provides students immediate access to information, unlike traditional methods, and expands their experience beyond the academic environment (Redondo et al. 2012).

We cannot forget that we are in a society of "native digitals", suppose kind of users with skills in handling certain devices, applications and services. It is the responsibility of teachers to train students, who are basically immature, in acquiring the skills necessary to use these technologies ethically and making "good practices of use", situations that students are not used on. Some data confirm the need for teachers to implement new systems related to technology and social media. This data can be found in several recent studies from the Spanish primary and secondary school level (Pedró, 2011), to general European level (Konrad and Ally, 2009; Kaufmann and Meyer, 2008). In similar studies, we can see that over 92% of pre-university students attend schools with computer and Internet access. About 50% use the computer to perform routine tasks. More than 75% of teachers use a computer every day for class preparation as well as for administrative and private uses. In Spain, 46.3% of mobile users use a Smartphone, which makes Spain the second country, only behind the United Kingdom, in number of customers using such devices in Europe. The predominant uses are listening to music (32.6% of all mobile users), using applications (35.4%) and accessing the Internet (34.7%). Men dominate with 58.8% in the use of such terminals, a slightly lower percentage than in the dominant use of the iPad tablet which is located in a 62.4% in the case of men (OTR Press, 2011).

The combination of computer and mobile devices with an Internet connection (Smartphones and tablets) generates staggering results: Approximately 80% of social network users are between 12 and 35, approximately 50% work and study, and 32% of these users are university students, 32% in secondary and 9% have finished university studies (actually in masters, PhD programs, etc.). The age group between 18 to 35 years is dominant in the use of mobile devices (OTR Press, 2011).

Focusing on the university framework and the use of social networks in Spain, 97.7% of young people who start any college degree are part of a social network, being the most popular: Tuenti with 90% of students and Facebook with over 75% of new college students. Most of them are connected daily and the students think that is pleased that the companies have presence in social networks (Top Position, 2011). Over two thirds (68.7%) consider social networks important or very important in their lives.

The presented data are limited to the Spanish academic framework, and it can be a future study evaluate if it can be extrapolated to any other industrialized country. It is inconceivable that academic training at this level may not be able to create an empathy with the student. For that, we must start – if we have not already done so – to migrate from the traditional "lecture" to the type of training that encourages students to collaborate using familiar technologies and that advances development through the specific content of each subject. Only in this direction will we be able to create a new wave of sympathy and gain more attention from the students, thus resulting in better educational achievement, as discussed in the results of the case studies proposed.

From E-Learning to Mobile Learning: "Mlearning"

We can explain "M-Learning" as a subfield of e-distance education learning, which includes the e-learning strategies based on the use of computers and network. M-Learning can go a step further by enabling teaching via wireless networks and mobile devices, allowing learning to take place anywhere and ensuring teacher-student interaction always exists (Tsvetozar, 2004). This is what is known as situational teaching, where the device detects the context and provides the relevant information. In combination with a collaborative model, participation and sharing within the network can generate new knowledge (Naismith, 2004). Initially, (this involved the use of certain devices such as notebooks, tablet-PCs, PDAs or mobile phones with Wi-Fi in outdoor environments (for example, in college campuses) over distances below 100 meters and with few advantages (Sharples, 2000; Motiwlla, 2005).

The use of touch-screens Smartphones and medium-sized tablets or iPads equipped with 3G, GPS and long-life batteries allowed this concept of progress towards new acquisitions of technological and pedagogical skills, in spite of the visibility limitations of screen. From a positive point of view, one might note that the constant demand for these devices for commercial and recreational uses, as well as advances in the technology, has allowed the cost of these gadgets to drop, allowing greater access to them by the final users.

Under this assumption, there are few documented teaching experiences. Within the framework of medical education, the availability of get-

ting medical information anywhere interactively through mobile interactive learning objects has been studied -MILOs- (Holzinger, 2005). Also some applications have been reported for language learning (Chinnery, 2006) and for university organization management through PDAs (Corlett and Sharples, 2005), equivalent to Athena Mobile, UPC, allowing schedules consultation, calendars, messaging and teaching materials. There are also some teaching strategies outdoors, such as in archaeological or historical environments (Ibañez and Asensi, 2006; Ardito and Lanzilotti, 2008; Giroux and Moulin, 2002) or even in the of geology and natural sciences (Safran, 2010; Yuh-Shyan Chen, 2004). However, a qualitative assessment of the results and teacher recommendations is still pending, it is necessary to highlight the case of education in architecture and urban planning, where the location of a building or city and its context are essential for understanding and design all type of geographical information (Norberg-Schulz, 1971; Lynch, 1966). This is where M-Learning becomes a fundamental tool and not merely a documented experience.

QR and BIDI Codes

The basis of the technology underlying the bi-dimensional code system defined by ISO/IEC in the 18004:2000 standard, and the first studies of its application on mobile phones are in the works of Kurosawa (2003), Ohbuchi, Hanaizumi and Hock (2004), Kato and Tan (2005), and Falas and Kashani (2007). The Quick Response Code (QR Code) is a two-dimensional code developed by Denso Wave in 1994 with the primary aim of being a symbol that is easily interpreted by scanner equipment. The main mission of this code is store information (numeric, alphanumeric or Kanji symbols). The main advantage of this code in front of other types is that carry meaningful information in the vertical direction as well as the horizontal, for this reason, QR code can carry up to several hundred times the amount of data carried by ordinary bar codes.

The most common data linked to a QR Code are: URL information (Website, Google maps location, iTunes link, YouTube video, Social Media data, etc.), text (basic text, SMS, email address or message, vCard, etc.), or numeric data (Phone Number, coordinates, etc.). In our experiments the students can link information related to the project, the architect, their WebPages or blogs, and technical information using this free technology and allowing ubiquitous connections and interactions.

The application of QR codes to the field of education has been documented in Korea's education system and e-learning environment. We find in Japan and Taiwan some experiences in teaching languages using this type of codes as examples of integration in the educational framework (Susono and Shimomura, 2006). Recently, some authors (Saravani and Clayton, 2009; Ramsden, 2009) have discussed its implementation and potential in the field of M-learning. Other authors (Walsh, 2010) have reviewed its application in bibliographic environments and libraries. In the field of architecture, Liu and Lee (2009) have used it for interaction and location inside buildings, and other studies (Tavares and Marambio, 2010) have proposed its use in museums by defining a specific profile for each visitor and designing a system that responds to that person's specific location information.

There is also documented work of equal value in the field of visual communication and architectural education (Redondo, 2010), except in academic environments where ICT (Information and Communication Technologies) have had great impact, for example in systems of representation and drawing architectural. This meeting point between ubiquitous computing, M-learning, e-learning, and visual communication in the architecture-education environment is the initial point of this teaching experiment.

Augmented Reality Technology (AR)

The technology we are going to evaluate and incorporate into the teaching processes, is AR. Its creators (Milgram, J, 1994) define AR as a virtual reality variation in which the user can see the real world with virtual objects mixed or superimposed. In contrast to virtual reality, AR does not replace the real environment but rather uses it as a background. The final result is a dynamic image of a 3D virtual model superimposed onto a real-time video of the environment. This scene is shown to the user via a computer screen or other devices such as projectors, a digital board, special glasses, or a 3G cell phone. This sensitive experience is essential for the rising of this technology. The main problem in architecture and building construction is to solve the problem of how to integrate virtual objects with real images. The overlap must be accurate and at the right scale in order to achieve its hypothetical situation and size matching in a real scene.

Beyond the superimposition of a virtual model onto a real environment, AR technologies are usable in a wide range of applications such as in engineering and construction. The technology offers potential advantages in all stages of the construction processes, from the initial planning and conceptual design to the management and maintenance of building systems throughout their lifetimes. We believe AR could be useful in staking tasks or facilities control too, as far as, this technology could facilitate the interpretation of drawings, technical documentation and other specifications. These systems can also generate a real image superimposed onto a specific stage of the construction process and, by connecting to a database, could show different levels of information based on each user's queries.

This technology, recently commercialized, covers different areas. If we focus on our specific fields of study, we would emphasize the book-edition applications, where trackers are added to show additional information. One of the first examples is the Magicbook (Billinghurts, Kato and Poupyrev, 2001). In the educational framework we can find specific applications for math and geometry (Kaufmann, 2002). But, in the field of architecture, the use of AR is anecdotic; the precedents in this field are the indoor studies (Malawi and Srinivasan, 2004). At the Tinmith project, outdoors architectural projects have been designed using AR (Piekarski, 2001). Other semi-immersive proposals that incorporate AR over screens in the study of urban projects include Arthur (Broll, 2004), the Luminous Table (Ben, 2001) or the Sketchand+Benchworks (Seichter, 2005), where different data-entry devices were combined in a virtual theatre. More recently, different tests on building renovations have been realized (Tonn, 2008). In urban planning, we would mention Kato and Tachibana (2003), with different implementations in the infrastructure of the construction engineering. In our opinion, the quantum leap and dissemination of this technology is due to its accessibility via mobile phones, thanks to the libraries ARToolkitPlus (Wagner, 2007). Mobile AR software applications have been appearing continuously; for example, MARA from Nokia or Layar, the first AR application of generalist use that is available for both iPhones and Android OS-based phones. In 2010, Junaio, the first markerless open-use application, appeared. It works with multimedia content (videos, renders, and 3D models) with a registration process based on real-environment image recognition instead of preset patterns.

DESCRIPTION OF THE CASE STUDIES AND METHODOLOGY

The project was developed in the context of the Architecture degree (UPC-Barcelona Tech), and aims to become a leading teaching experience in Training 3.0 in the field of architecture. Learning 3.0 was developed and implemented over time, and the contents of this chapter are the result of specific case studies. The students involved are in their third year of architecture degrees and are developing practices for representing modern architecture icons. The studies have been approached from a qualitative point of view, and from different proposals related to specific subjects, including the study of specific cases and projects per year. In 2011 the proposal cases were:

The first teaching project aims to create an exhibition to represent work undertaken by teams of students on a three-year degree of architecture at the University of La Salle. The project's theme is examples from the Case Study Houses located in California. The exhibition consists of a set of panels that show the graphics and documents related to each project. The visitor can find the exhibition in the exhibition space of the university or virtually through mobile devices.

The second case, a synergy between traditional technologies and AR was proposed in order to visually build up hybrid (virtual and real) scenes for architectural proposals. Two teaching workshops were held at the School of Building Engineering of Barcelona and at the BarcelonaTech University during 2011. Working in pairs, students were required to create collaborative scenes using marker-based tracking-free software. They blended the physical and virtual worlds so that real objects (markers) interacted with three-dimensional digital content and increased shared understanding. The first teaching experience was a feasibility study carried out in the framework of the platform BEST BCN (Board of European Students of Technology at Barcelona). We evaluated the possibility of using this technology in learning processes. The second activity focused on implementing new digital technologies into the building construction and maintenance processes of the Graphic Expression III course. Third-year students used virtual models of the existing technical infrastructure of their building to integrate them into a building information-management system.

Finally, the third project is related to the virtual reconstruction of the architecture of several

Venezuelan colonial buildings using 3D low-cost modeling systems, development of the process of disclosure, multimedia publishing in social networks, displaying the results in situ by 2D codes, and the visualization using mobile phones. This is part of a strategy to attract students to publicly recognize and appreciate their architectural heritage while being instructed in the techniques of restoration through the virtual reconstruction. The experiment is being conducted with architecture degree students from the Central University of Caracas, Venezuela.

Case 1: AR Implementation in Architecture Learning: Towards "3.0 Learning"

As we have remarked previously, the new technologies allow more knowledge and better approach to understanding the spatial models linked to general architectural projects. The barriers imposed by Computer Assisted Design programs (also known as CAD software, for example AutoCAD, MicroStation, AllPlan, etc.), such as the need for installation, complex commands, and large formats, and the high technical requirements, can be gradually replaced by user-friendly interfaces that enable intuitive and fast navigation and interaction with 2D and 3D models. This functions in all kinds of mobile technologies, allowing a better understanding of space by both the professional and student, and enabling them to integrate all the concepts "in situ." In addition, the opportunities for training can be diverse. The training process can be online thanks to school intranet.

Learning 3.0 concepts are designed to enable users to meet their project objectives Learning 3.0. Its implementation is designed to get project's objectives (Figure 1). By using popular devices, access to the process is easy. Finally, it is necessary to offer different ways to access to information to achieve greater success and spread.

Main Objectives and Working Methodology (Case 1)

The main objective of this case study is the definition of the methodological steps required in the implementation of AR visualization of the basic features of the architectural project. The project has been developed in the course of representation systems, a third-degree course in architecture at the Faculty of Architecture La Salle, on the campus of Tarragona. Both teachers and students have worked on the project proposed to assess the main advantages and disadvantages in the adoption of this technology for the visual and performing training of this particular type of contents.

The proposals for such implementation phases over a semester (duration of the course) are as follows:

Phase 1: Collection of graphic and document files from selected project. In this phase, the students have to generate 2D and 3D models using a CAD format and collect all types of information using the Internet.

The analysis of the projects was developed in the early months of the course, and the different types of documents were developed for each type of content by using different software and supports. The students must locate the Internet links that will be used to create QR codes, and all information must be organized on an Internet site for public access (Figure 2). We have used Dropbox as the application for students to manage all the documentation that will be provided to visitors in different public formats. Finally, for AR applications, the documents will be placed according to teacher's instructions (size, color, name, etc.) and all components will be created in the user channel using Junaio software. The main types of content the students must generate are a text and image recompilation about the project and the architect, other projects of the architect (photos, explanations, etc.), 2D and 3D models

Figure 1. Design of "learning 3.0 project"

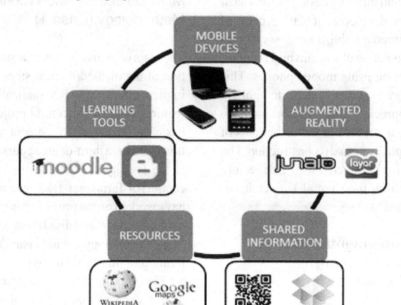

of the project design with CAD-BIM formats, a 3D stereoscopic image of the project, and a 3D model prepared for viewing in AR.

Phase 2: Creating QR codes. In this phase, the teacher explains basic concepts about the different types of 2D codes, the evaluation of different generator and readers' software, and finally the generation of a QR Codes linking to the information generated by the students. In this phase, the students must search for the appropriate link and add it to the QR code generator. The code will be saved as a digital-format image for later inclusion in the panels. These codes are related directly to the Internet and project documentation.

Phase 3: Designing the panels with the above information and QR codes. In this phase, the instructor provides a format and the order of the panels, including text, images, graphics, videos, blogs, and all useful information. The

presentation should be the composition of the following panels (Figure 3):

1. Main panel with the project name, architect, and basic information of the students linked with QR code of the course inside a personal blog;
2. QR code to show the situation and location with Google Maps;
3. Presentation of the Architect with a short text and an image of significant projects and a QR code that includes a link to a website with information about the architect;
4. Presentation of the project with a picture, a QR code that includes a link to a website with information from the project, and a link shows related videos of YouTube;
5. Graphic documentation in CAD-BIM format of the project and a QR code that includes a link to the original format documentation on the Internet, stored in a public folder of Dropbox;

Figure 2. Example of QR code generation

6. Presentation with 3D images of the project and a QR code that includes a link to the original image in JPG format stored in the previous folder;

7. Generation of basic volumes to view with AR, a QR code that contains a direct link to the application of AR (Junaio), and an image-viewing application to recognize the object in the mobile device.

Phase 4: Public presentation with an exhibition and an updated corporative blog. In the last phase of the project, all students will present their work in two models: as an exhibition at the school using photographic paper on a rigid support (size 20 x 20 cm) with each sheet mounted as cubes in a 3D experience (Figure 4), and as an exhibition on the Internet, where each group will show their work on their blogs with interactive links (Navarro, 2011).

Figure 3. Panels with the information and the QR-code links

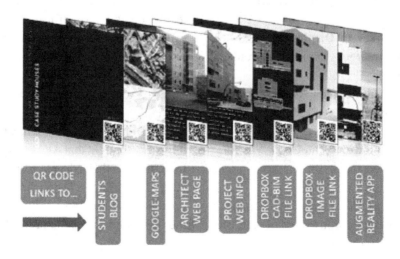

Figure 4. Physical cube panels with the contents and QR-code links

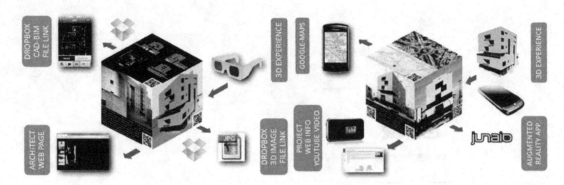

If we resume the applications needed to generate and read 2D codes and AR used in this project, we need:

- **QR Code Generator:** BeeTagg Multicode System;
- **QR Code Reader:** Kaywa Reader; Zxing QR.

Other applications that will manage the transfer of information are:

- **Dropbox File Manager**

To view all type of documentation generated, we need:

- **Viewer of Geographic References:** Google Maps;
- **Internet Browser to Display Web Page References:** Internet Explorer, Firefox, Google Chrome;
- **Viewer of Augmented Reality Files:** Junaio Augmented Reality, Layar Developer Section, AndAR;
- **DWG Files Viewer:** AutoCAD WS or AutoCAD (at least v.2010).

In Figure 5, we can see an example of a panel with a QR Code combined with a point of view of the architecture project that represents a BIDI code linked with an AR model using the configuration of the front view of the project.

Solutions and Recommendations (Case 1)

In this project, we were able to evaluate the various skills related to student self-learning and the use of advanced display technologies. Focusing on the architectural framework, we emphasized interaction skills with software tools, the ability to abstraction of the volume in AR, three-dimensional accuracy of the result and the footprint in the process of project definition.

In fact, the use of new technologies encourages students' attention in the learning process in a very practical and intuitive way, because these technologies are often used daily. We must put special attention in the ability of abstraction in 3D, because it is a skill that is being formed, and these tools help expedite that process.

Over 80% of the students tested affirmed that AR is a very good technology for viewing and understanding models of architectural projects, but only 45% thought that AR was a good technology for improving their education on architecture. Only 22% of the students tested thought that AR could improve their academic skills. We can affirm that the non-uniform results are possibly due to the

Figure 5. Example of panel with AR contents

lack of practice with this technology. However, the easy and quick mode to obtain final results increases their interest on improving the possible errors. These results are possibly related to the habit of using multimedia and gaming systems in which the outcome of each action has an immediate effect (a future lines to which the user must respond.

The project definition process is the ultimate goal, which is why it is interesting methodologies such as that applied in this case to find new systems of representation in architecture. This may prevent the project-result analysis from having the visual impact initially expected.

Case 2: Augmented Reality Technology for Visual Analysis, and its Application on Building Construction

In the present case, the interior spaces of existing buildings could be considered; for example, there may be a need to know about the building loads of an area, its thermal behavior, or the location of certain facilities. These aspects of the building could all be rendered as virtual models, once overlaid to real space, should contribute to a better understanding of the building, as well as to a greater efficiency in the construction processes, rehabilitation or building maintenance tasks. Two teaching experiences were had at the School of Building Construction of Barcelona and at the BarcelonaTech University of Catalonia. The strengths and weaknesses of the first experience were incorporated into the next activity. We aimed to assess the use of AR technology in the learning processes of the future building-construction engineers by applying a set of tools related to this technology.

The first teaching experience was a feasibility study carried out in the framework of the platform BEST Barcelona (Board of European Students of Technology - BCN), which brings together students from over 80 countries. It was held at the School of Building Construction of Barcelona (EPSEB) with international students of various

European nationalities who were studying architecture and related studies in building construction. We proposed a synergy between the traditional technologies used to show virtual models and AR. This would be accomplished by using several low-cost AR applications to visually build up hybrid (virtual and real) urban spaces and architecture proposals. We evaluated the possibility of using this technology indoors on learning processes. We worked indoors and outdoors where the students modified an existing architecture proposal, and we introduced occluders for a better integration of the scene in its actual location.

After receiving highly positive feedback, we tried to extend it to construction and building maintenance processes; thus, the second case is the result of some of the previous experiments. It was a supervised activity aimed to implement new digital technologies into the learning processes of the Graphic Expression III course at the same school in Barcelona. The goal was the implementation of AR technology in the teaching of engineering and building courses, particularly in regard to adding technical information. Third-year students implemented virtual models from the existing infrastructure of their building and integrated this into an information-management building system. They should have been able to communicate to other participants a greater knowledge and technical information of the building where they were working. They should somehow "complete" their real space with some constructive and technical information in order to contribute to a better understanding of the building and to increase the efficiency of the construction processes, rehabilitation or building maintenance.

Main Objectives and Working Methodology (Case 2)

The goal, therefore, was twofold: first, to evaluate the possibility of using this technology in indoor environments linked to construction and maintenance processes, so that the user could acquire more technical knowledge of their environment,

and second, to apply these emerging techniques to develop new and alternative teaching methods that result in greater efficiency and better academic performance than do the traditional methods. Every experience was divided into two parts: in the first one, students attended some lectures about the fundamentals of the technology, such as recording systems, rendering, occlusion, tracking systems. In addition, they were shown some examples of common applications implemented in different areas to ensure they were aware of the possibilities offered by the use of this technology. In a second stage, we developed practical exercises. All of them were carried out using free software and educational licensed or low-cost applications as Armedia, buildAR, Sketchup, and Junaio. Students created virtual models to be represented on mobile devices such as laptops, netbooks, and, if possible, UMPC and last-generation phones. These devices have all become useful tools for the use of AR. They are now equipped with more sensitive cameras and faster processors that can handle complex 3D image-processing routines, and they incorporate accelerometers, compasses, gyroscopes, and positioning and locating systems. All these features, often present in modern Smartphones, have made them prospective non-immersive AR platforms.

To carry out the exercises, some common steps were followed. After introducing the activity to be performed, each participant selected a site or an interior area, recreated a virtual architectural proposal, and chose different levels of information layers to display. It was assumed that the knowledge of the virtual object modeling had already been acquired during their training as engineers or architects. Once resolved and discussed in each specific case, the registration, texturing, lighting and occlusion problems, all of them typical and inherent in this kind of technology, we proceeded to register the model in its actual location using optical marker-based recognition systems. We avoided the use of optical marker-less recognition systems because they are more sensitive to changes in environmental light conditions; in previous experiments, natural features were unrecognizable and the scene was unstable and useless.

Finally, students were asked to make a presentation that included a description of the different "augmented" spaces. This served as a mechanism for checking the effectiveness of this technology in the learning process. Papers submitted were graded, and specific questionnaires were conducted, in parallel. These were aimed at evaluating the degree of satisfaction with the activity and course content. The total time taken changed in every experience, from one week (Case 1) to two days (Case 2).

Experience 1: Feasibility Study: This study required students to create a "collaborative" scene in which they were able to develop a virtual proposal for the expansion of the engineering school. They were asked to work in pairs to view and explain it by using AR technology. The scene was generated within the working class, and was intended to replace the classic systems currently in use for similar proposals. This first exercise was intended to familiarize students with the use of flat markers and software. Each marker was associated with one student proposal, a virtual architectural model in three dimensions, to be displayed within a virtual base model. We used SketchUp 8, in its free version. This program allows the user to import

nearby geo-referenced buildings models, which students used as base models. As an AR application, we used a SketchUp plug-in from AR-Media, also in its free version. The plug-in allowed the simultaneous use of several markers associated with each of the students proposals. This feature was critical to making the collaborative scene possible. The free version of the plug-in contained all the possibilities of the paid version but is restricted to 30 seconds for viewing the scene (Figure 6).

After that, students were asked to "augment" the real space where they were and design virtual proposals to evaluate some changes in that area. The scene was generated in an interior space, but outside the classroom, so the display devices were restricted to mobile devices (in this case, to laptops equipped with additional webcams). We used Sketchup 8 in its free version, and the plug-in from AR-Media, which was helpful in allowing the work with the "occluders," environmental elements not visible in the scene but allowed to hide parts of the virtual model. This feature helped to make the scene more believable. Each student chose a random indoor space in the school and chose different levels or layers of information to display. They modeled their proposals, previously tested in the classroom, to perform a scene that was the result of merging the real environ-

Figure 6. Examples of a collaborative scene creation from Exercise 1 using different models

Figure 7. Examples of an augmented scene created from Exercise 2 using different models and indoors spaces

mental information with their virtual superimposed models (Figure 7).

Until then, we had relied on the most widely used configuration for the performance of AR applications: a pattern-based recognition system that uses the ARToolKit libraries or MXRToolKit. In the last activity, however, we worked with the idea of superimposing virtual information on outdoor spaces, using buildings facades as markers to superimpose information (Figure 8). The use of flat patterns was not possible because of the workplace scale (distance camera-marker) and because the physical environment was altered by the marks (which require a considerable size in order to be recognized at a distance). The scene was generated, as we said, in outdoor spaces, and students were required to display their proposals onto an existing facade. This exercise was intended to familiarize students with using real images as markers. We used the BuildAR program, which is based on optical recognition of real images. Its free version is fully functional but does not allow the scene to be recorded or shared once generated. Each student had a laptop and an external webcam.

In this exercise, the pictures were rarely unrecognizable due to the less favorable light conditions or light conditions that had changed since the photo was taken. This suggests that these systems are more sensitive to light conditions changes and may be useless. The complexity of the tracking algorithm calls for more powerful computer software. This is why, in the second experience, we worked with flat pattern-based tracking systems.

In short, in this practice we evaluated the suitability of the use of flat markers as elements to interact with three-dimensional digital content and its ability to increase understanding of the proposals. The results extracted from the questionnaire responses were very positive. And we were encouraged to continue with the idea of applying the technology in a more concrete field. The average global opinion of students was 8.34 out of 10. We can find a video of the student's activity in http://www.youtube.com/watch?v=o696Jp58bUk

Experience 2: Adding Technical Information:
In this second experience, students had to "augment" the space where they were with virtual information, modeling proposals for

Figure 8. Examples of an augmented scene on outdoor spaces

intervention in that area, providing it with additional technical information (facilities, structures, etc.) that could be useful for future actions. The scene was generated in an interior space, but outside the classroom, so that the display devices should be mobile. As mentioned in the first experience, AR-Media free version plug-in, was used. It allowed to work with "occluders" environmental elements that were not visible in the scene but allowed to hide parts of the virtual model, and helped to make the scene more believable. Each student selected a school space, and modeled their proposals. 90% of students were able to follow the exercise. Designed their proposal, modeled on the environment from nearby models, and view their results on the desktop using flat patterns. They were able to explain a space with additional information to the actual site where they were (Figure 9).

Exercise was useful to verify the feasibility of the use AR technology, indoor, linking it to processes of construction and building maintenance tasks, completing somehow, real space information.

As we see in the example above, iron reinforcement of the beams and pillars, and different facilities were modeled, scaled, and positioned. Those virtual models, once overlapped to real space, contributed to a better understanding of the building, and could help to a greater efficiency in construction processes, rehabilitation or building maintenance tasks.

In short, in this practice we evaluated the suitability of the use of flat markers as elements to interact with three-dimensional digital building content and its ability to increase understanding of student's proposals. Results extracted from the questionnaire responses were very positive. Over 75% of students agreed or strongly agreed with AR could be useful on building and architectural areas, and they considered that AR Technology will be useful in their immediate future as an engineer. Only 6% of students were totally disagreeing with AR technology usefulness. The final global assessment in this case was 7.70 out of 10.

Solutions and Recommendations (Case 2)

Students were required to work in a final presentation that should include a description of the

Figure 9. Indoor spaces Augmented with technical information

different "augmented" spaces they had work in. It was useful for checking the effectiveness of this technology in the learning process. In parallel a questionnaire was conducted specifically oriented to assess the degree of satisfaction of the activity and to get a global opinion of the technology applied. So, questionnaire was divided into three sections. First, we asked about personal issues, age, gender, level and type of training, the prior knowledge about various programs, etc., in the second section we asked about the content and course material that students worked with, and finally, we surveyed on the usability and usefulness of the technology learned. The implementation of the use of AR technology in different environments, as explained above, gave very different results, because of students' creative freedom, and their different backgrounds (similar than Case 1).

According to their responses, it was demonstrated that the AR Technology implementation on learning processes improved their spatial skills and encouraged their creativity. But regardless of the evaluation of their response, it would be advisable to evaluate quantitatively the improvement of student's academic performance. There would be necessary to conduct an exercise with traditional methods, and a second one using tools similar to those used AR in this case.

All activities helped the students to improve their competitions and skills on graphical computer science, beyond current knowledge of traditional technologies. AR technology allows them to view their proposals inside a virtual model, which would not otherwise have been possible. They get familiarized with the use of markers as elements to interact with three-dimensional digital content and the technology helped them to increase understanding of their proposals.

Finally, due to the importance that students have given to the software used, we should take into account that there is no specific application in the field of maintenance and building construction. So, in future work we are developing a customized

application to be used on mobile devices. It will be specially designed for use indoors and will be real images optical recognition based. With it, students will be able to create and manage models and channels of information. This application will allow choosing their own bookmarks, based on real images of the environment, and each image will act as a marker to see layer of information (structure, facilities, materials...). Various models will be linked to the same image, so that with one marker it will be possible to visualize different stages of the construction processes.

Case 3: 3D Virtual Reconstruction and Visualization of Venezuelan Colonial Architectural Using QR-Codes: Work in Progress

The Venezuelan religious architectural heritage has survived in part of the economic speculation, but the situation is very serious because of missing the resources. The country is still standing a few colonial churches, some of which have been preserved with restoration sponsored by government agencies, but they are the exception. Only in Caracas they have documented six churches of the seventeenth century, which left standing only the Cathedral and the Church of San Francisco and the rest of the country more than 200, of which only 50 have been restored. The preservation of this heritage is a necessity that presents new perspectives based on multimedia technologies that make it accessible to students of Architecture. These are the main reasons driving this study, following which generates the need to train new architects who can carry out this work and do it that would attract them. The use of scarce resources at the institutional level can be compensated by the use of the most common technology as most of the students, about 85%, have the means provided for carrying out this experiment, cell phones 3G, laptops with high graphics capabilities and knowledge in the use of virtual modeling applications and rendering acquired a self-taught, with separate regular users of social networks as a way of relating with others and for training professional.

Main Objectives and Working Methodology (Case 3)

The main objective of this project is to verify the reality of teachers education in a methodological approach to knowledge and virtual recovery of the architectural heritage in Venezuela disappeared after conducting a feasibility study which was first digitally reconstruction of temple disappeared from San Jacinto in Caracas (1595-1821). The selection of the specific project is a basic example of religious and architectural summit in Venezuela and the relationship between the Canary Islands and Venezuela, highlighting in its "Mudéjar" wooden deck, a technology that lasted until the nineteenth century as opposed to the rest of Latin America.

Based on the traditional methods of historical research and architectural review of the literature sources, archaeological excavations, mapping urban, paintings, photographs of the temples and altars contemporaries, we defined a typological model and generated a low cost methodology, applicable to teaching for data acquisition, visual simulation and dissemination by computer using QR codes and Youtube. These strategies specific to ICT, which are considered attractive for our students, will be applied by them to other temples disappeared, like St. Paul, also in Caracas. The second objective is to test whether the use of these strategies in a whole new to them, enable them to learn to understand, analyze, build, document and evaluate this architecture.

We will develop two case studies, the first for the grade level in Architecture from the School of Architecture and Urbanism at the Central University of Venezuela, in the subject: Design, Expression Workshop, History of Architecture, Computing, and second to the grade level of the

Master in Conservation and Restoration of Monuments, in the subject: Restoration and Conservation Workshop. The first aimed at students with little base and the second one focused on training specialists in the field. In the first group of students, given their basic training, we will proceed to work on the first temple of San Jacinto, using part of the feasibility study materials. In the second work we will use the second temple.

From our previous experiences in similar projects, the pilot test was tested at the University of Guadalajara, Mexico in 2010 (Redondo, Navarro, Sanchez and Fonseca, 2001), we are talking about teaching of 15 active days at most, equivalent to 11 classroom sessions of 5 hours each, during the first process we will present the building under study and documentation available, in the second class we will visit the actual location of each building disappeared and students will take photographs and notes in response to the explanations teachers in various subjects. The third day, the methodologies and criteria for virtual modeling and start the construction process are describing. The fourth and fifth days were devoted to supplement students' education in CAD, virtual modeling and rendering, the sixth day students are expected to visit the archives and university libraries in the city to get some documentation. Final days the students will must generate the models, QR Codes and all digital documentation to upload in Youtube with the help of assistant professor of History, Construction and Representation (Figure 10). Last day the group we will go to the place where we can find the information to validate all information and to answer a final test to evaluate the experience by the students.

Well, the same is proceed to answer a series of surveys, both at the beginning, middle and end of activity where at first, each student is asked to describe their priority knowledge of mobile devices to be used, on applications of modeling and on the issue, assessing the usability of the devices, speed, comfort when watching the videos, to build virtual models of the questionnaire,

Figure 10. 3D models and example of navigation with QR codes related to the reconstruction of Saint Jacinto Church in Caracas, Venezuela

share experiences, knowledge about the issue of recovery of the architectural heritage disappeared and if it helps the experience Instead of viewing it on putting it in context.

Are proposed to select a group of students of Architecture degree and a Master that will make up the experimental course where ICT technologies applied within the program of the academic course material to be defined by the Faculty of Architecture and Urbanism, Central University of Venezuela and a second control group in each grade that will follow a normal course. It is recommended that each of the groups exceeds the minimum of 15 students to make significant population sample and to extract reliable statistics.

Solutions and Recommendations (Case 3)

Actually, we can affirm that this project is in designing phase. From the responses to usability questionnaires we expect to obtain a high value in the simple use of QR code technology and mobile devices, and in usefulness of this kind of applications for education. High values are also expected in information sharing and on architectural projects evaluation. This hypothesis is based on previous experiences that have taken high usability rates on this kind of systems performance. For this particular experiment, the assessments will be made by five degrees, from 1 to 5, where 1 is

the worst rating valuation system and 5 maximal satisfactions. Value 3 defines the value "does not know/no answer", and we will use the analysis by t-Student variable given the small sample.

We should monitor especially the possible problems that arise in conducting this experiment: control of population with access to device able to manage and display information, battery life and its relation to the size of the screens and the ability to display selected models, the added difficulty in outdoor viewing screens, and no doubt the difficulty of maintaining the codes on both places and their coexistence with meteorological factors such as vandalism.

To assess the suitability of this project, we are raising to leave the plates with QR codes "in situ" and evaluate, if curiosity and knowledge of the rest of the population mean that the information is accessed, for which regular monitoring the number of times that has been watched on Youtube.

FUTURE RESEARCH DIRECTIONS

Handheld displays employ a small display that fits in a user's hand. All handheld AR solutions to date opt for video see-through. Initially handheld AR employed fiduciary markers, and later GPS units and MEMS (Micro-Electro-Mechanical Systems) sensors such as digital compasses and six degrees of freedom accelerometer–gyroscope.

Today SLAM (Simultaneous Localization and Mapping) systems are starting to come into use. This technology makes possible to build and track a simple 3D model of the world around you in real time, using only the device's built-in camera working out a map of the environment in real time. Besides that, this new tracking technology allows for a much more stable, robust and versatile user experience than existing techniques for calculating a mobile device's position in the real world, which usually use compass, GPS and accelerometer, or pre-defined visual markers. And will be tested on future works.

Related to indoor scenes, in futures works, we should paid attention to one of the weaknesses in AR scenes, that is, lighting immersion. Because most of the times overlaid models lacks realism and does not integrate into the scene enough to be credible.

The problem lies in the different conditions of light between the real environment and the virtual model. And it is especially important indoors and interior design proposals, where an object which is not integrated in its environment may be unlikely and unattractive. Current tools do not allow Augmented Reality to simulate the ambient light conditions and export the model.

One solution to this problem could be the use of rendered textures incorporating light conditions from surrounding. To project the shadow of the virtual object in the real environment, there should be created a virtual object identical to the environment. This object had the object's shadow as texture simulating light conditions, and should be transparent where it is not projected. The use of "occluders" must be considered and developed in future works, for a better integration of the scene.

In the latter case study, we have chosen the Bidi Code technology on wireless Internet connection because of its accessible level. In this sense if it is not possible to consider a job with a large sample of student population because of the cost of the devices, but at finally has been shown that there is a population with experience in such

technology, such information based on the data that during the two days that the label was showed in its place, more than 70 people downloaded the information from YouTube, which reveals another unintended reality is the interest and real access that users have the technology.

CONCLUSION

We can affirm that the combination of practical "on site" testing, using current technologies of AR, combined with the study and classification of information, and how it is generated and displayed, as well as the establishment of the theoretical basis of this technology to use with mobile devices in the field of architecture and building construction, allowed spatial skills improvement for analysis and description of existing buildings, encouraging creativity and helping to recreate and modify more consistent proposals in real time and in their real environment.

In relation to the use of devices based on optical recognition systems for registering virtual models in indoor spaces versus outdoor models, and based on the results of our experiments, we highlight some of indoor advantages: High accuracy achieved with the 3D registration (near to 1cm), objects generated by computer can easily be linked with markers; the possibility of implementing elements of interaction (based on distances and rotations between marks); and the economy of the systems (as they often are GPL licensed and registration only requires a webcam). However, we must also take into account its limitations, for example, the strong dependence of the light conditions, the working local scale (distance camera-pattern) and the fact that the physical environment is altered by the marks, especially critical in the case of existing buildings. So, marker-less based optical tracking system might be more appropriate. Another option could be GPS tracking based systems, but llimited accuracy of these systems won't allow you to place labels and billboards as precisely as you'd like. AR calculated measurements are only approximations, and may frustrate end users experience because they expect a high degree of accuracy and precision.

REFERENCES

ACM. (2011). *CHI-Conference on Human Factors in Computing Systems*, January 10, 2012. Retrieved from http://chi2011.org/index.html

Ardito, C., Lanzilotti, R., Pederson, T., & Piccinno, A. (2008). Experiencing the past through the senses: An m-learning game at archaeological parks. *IEEE MultiMedia*, *15*(4), 76–81. doi:10.1109/MMUL.2008.87

Ben-Joseph, E., Ishii, H., Underkoffler, J., Piper, B., & Yeung, L. (2011). Urban simulation and the luminous planning table: Bridging the gap between the digital and the tangible. *Journal of Planning Education and Research*, *21*, 196–203.

Billinghurst, M., Kato, H., & Poupyrev, I. (2011). The MagicBook - Moving seamlessly between reality and virtuality. *IEEE Computer Graphics and Applications*, *21*(3), 6–8.

Billings, D. M., & Halstead, J. A. (2008). *Teaching in nursing: A guide for faculty*. Lavoisier SAS.

Broll, W., Lindt, I., Ohlenburg, J., Wittkämper, M., Yuan, C., & Novotny, T. … Strothmann, A. (2004). *ARTHUR: A collaborative augmented environment for architectural design and urban planning. Proceedings of Seventh International Conference on Humans and Computers* (HC 2004), (pp. 102-109).

Chinnery, A. (2006). Cold case: Reopening the file on tolerance in teaching and learning across difference. In Howe, K. (Ed.), *Philosophy of Education 2005* (pp. 200–208).

Chun-Hung, L., & Lee, C.-F. (2009). The design of a mobile navigation system based on QR codes for historic buildings. *Proceedings of the 14th International Conference on Computer Aided Architectural Design Research in Asia*, Yunlin, Taiwan, (pp. 103-112).

Corlett, D., Sharples, M., Chan, T., & Bull, S. (2005). A mobile learning organiser for university students. *Journal of Computer Assisted Learning*, *21*, 162–170. doi:10.1111/j.1365-2729.2005.00124.x

Dziuban, C., Moskal, P., & Brophy, J. (2007). Student Satisfaction with asynchronous learning. *Journal of Asynchronous Learning Networks*, *11*(1), 87–95.

Falas, T., & Kasanami, H. (2007). Two-dimensional bar-code decoding with camera-equipped mobile phones. *Proceedings of the Fifth IEEE International Conference on Pervasive Computing and Communications Workshops*, PERCOMW, (pp. 597-600). Washington, DC: IEEE Computer Society.

Holzinger, A., & Maurer, H. (2005). E-learning-Modelle für die Hochschule: Ein best practice-Beispiel aus der Bauingenieurwissenschaft. *OCG Journal*, *30*(4), 22–23.

ISO/IEC 18004. (2000). *Information technology – Automatic identification and data capture techniques—Bar code symbology—QR code*. (ISO/IEC JTC1/SC31, 2000).

Kato, H., Tachibana, K., Tanabe, M., Nakajima, T., & Fukuda, Y. (2003). A city-planning system based on augmented reality with a tangible interface. *Proceedings of the Second IEEE and ACM International Symposium on Mixed and Augmented Reality* (ISMAR´03), (pp. 340-341).

Kato, H., & Tan, K. T. (2005). 2D barcodes for mobile phones. *Proceedings of 2nd International Conference on Mobile Technology, Applications and Systems*, (p. 8).

Kaufmann, H., & Meyer, B. (2008). Simulating educational physical experiments in augmented reality. In *ACM SIGGRAPH ASIA 2008 Educators Programme on - SIGGRAPH Asia '08*. New York, NY: ACM Press. doi:10.1145/1507713.1507717

Konrad, M.-H., & Ally, M. (2009). Mobile learning. Transforming the delivery of education and training. In Ally, M. (Ed.), *Der anaesthesist* (*Vol. 58*). AU Press.

Kurosawa, K., Miyamoto, K., Nagase, Y., Ikegami, H., Sato, K., & Otsubo, M. (2003). *Mobile phones application LSI design using c based design methodology.* Tech. Report 4, NEC Corporation.

Liu, T.-Y., Tan, Y.-H., & Chu, Y.-L. (2007). 2D barcode and augmented reality supported English learning system. *Proceedings 6th IEEE/ACIS International Conference on Computer and Information Science* (ICIS 2007), Melburne, Australia, (pp. 5-10).

Lynch, K. (1966). *La imagen de la ciudad.* Buenos Aires, Argentina: Infinito.

Malkawi, A., & Srinivasan, R. (2004). Building performance visualization using augmented reality. *Proceedings of the Fourteenth International Conference on Computer Graphics and Vision*, (pp. 122-127).

Marambio, A., Corso, J., Lucena, J., & Roca, J. (2010). Nuevas formas de accesibilidad a través de aplicaciones con realidad virtual y aumentada en el museo marítimo de Barcelona: Proyecto PATRAC. *Architecture. City and Environment*, *13*, 145–160.

Milgram, P., & Takemura, H. (1994). *Augmented reality: A class of displays on the reality-virtuality continuum.* Presented at Telemanipulator and Telepresence Technologies. doi:10.1117/12.197321

Moran, M., Seaman, J., & Tinti-Kane, H. (2011). *Teaching, learning, and sharing: How today's higher education faculty use social media.* Boston, MA: Pearson Learning Solutions.

Motschnig-Pitrik, R., & Holzinger, A. (2002). Student-centered teaching meets new media: Concept and case study. *Journal of Educational Technology & Society*, *5*(4), 160–172.

Naismith, L. (2004). *Literature review in mobile technologies and learning. NESTA Futurelab series, report 11.* Bristol, UK: NESTA Futurelab.

Navarro, I. (2011). *Learning 3.0: Mobile-learning, augmented reality...in architecture.* Tech Architecture La Salle Blogging. Retrieved October 15, from http://blogs.salleurl.edu/tech-architecture/2011/05/19/hola-mundo/

Norberg-Schulz, C. (1971). *Existence, space and architecture.* London, UK: Praeger Publishers.

Ohbuchi, E., Hanaizumi, H., & Hock, L. A. (2004). Barcode readers using the camera device in mobile phones. *Proceedings of the 2004 International Conference on Cyberworlds* (CW'04), (pp. 260-265).

Pedró, F. (2011). La tecnología y la educación: Una dosis de realismo. *El País.* Retrieved December 20, 2011, from ww.elpais.com/articulo/educacion/tecnologia/educacion/dosis/realismo/elpepusocedu/20111121elpepiedu_1/Tes

Piekarski, W., & Thomas, B. (2001). Tinmith-Metro: New outdoor techniques for creating city models with an augmented reality wearable computer. *First International Symposium on Wearable Computers* (ISWC '01), (pp. 31-38).

Press, O. T. R. (2011). Los hombres son los principales usuarios de iPad. *Diario de Sevilla.* Retrieved December 16, 2011, from http://www.diariodesevilla.es/article/tecnologia/964075/los/hombres/principales/usuarios/ipad.html

Ramsden, A. (2011). *The potential of QR codes in education.* JISC Emerge User & Innovation Programme Meeting. Retrieved August 15, 2011, from http:77www.slideshare.net/andyramsden/potential-qr-codes-education-emerge-20098-presentation

Redondo, E., Fonseca, D., Sánchez, A., & Navarro, I. (2012). Augmented reality in architecture degree new approaches in scene illumination and user evaluation. *Journal of Information Technology and Application in Education, 1*(1), 19–27.

Redondo, E., Navarro, I., Sánchez, A., & Fonseca, D. (2011). Visual interfaces and user experience: augmented reality for architectural education: One study case and work in progress. *Communications in Computer and Informatic Science, 166*(3), 355–367. doi:10.1007/978-3-642-21984-9_31

Rheingold, H. (2011). *Exploring social media literacies in teaching and learning: Howard Rheingold's keynote at CHI 2011.* Interactive Multimedia Technology Blog. Retrieved January 10, 2012, from http://interactivemultimediatechnology.blogspot.com/2011/05/exploring-social-media-literacies-in.html

Richardson, J. C., & Swan, K. (2003). Examining social presence in online courses in relation to students' perceived learning and satisfaction. *Journal of Asynchronous Learning Networks, 7*(1).

Russo, C. J., Squelch, J., & Varnham, S. (2010). Teachers and social networking sites: Think before you post. *Journal of Law and Social Justice, 5*(5), 1–15.

Sanna, R., Pintus, A., Giroux, S., & Moulin, C. (2002). Mobile lessons: Lessons based on georeferenced information. In M. Driscoll & T. Reeves (Eds.), *Proceedings of World Conference on E-Learning in Corporate, Government, Healthcare, and Higher Education,* (pp. 331-338).

Saravani, S. J., & Cayton, J. (2009). A conceptual model for the education deployement of QR codes. *Proceedings ASCILITE,* Auckland, (pp. 919-922).

Seichter, H., & Schnabel, M. A. (2005). Digital and tangible sensation: An augmented reality urban design studio. *Proceedings of the 10th International Conference on Computer Aided Architectural Design Research in Asia* (CAADRIA 2005), Vol. 2, (pp. 193-202).

Sharples, M. (2000). The design of personal mobile technologies for lifelong learning. *Computers & Education, 34,* 177–193. doi:10.1016/S0360-1315(99)00044-5

So, H. J., & Brush, T. A. (2008). Student perceptions of collaborative learning, social presence and satisfaction in a blended learning environment: Relationships and critical factors. *Computers & Education, 51*(1), 318–336. doi:10.1016/j.compedu.2007.05.009

Susono, H., & Shimomura, S. (2006). Using mobile phones and QR codes for formative class assessment. In Mendez-Vilas, A., Solano, A., & Mesa, J. A. (Eds.), *Current developments in technology-assisted education.* Badajoz, Spain.

Tavares, D. M., & De Paula-Caurin, G. A. (2010). *Proposal for the use of QR code in supply chain management.* Production Online Magazine.

Tonn, C., Petzold, F., & Bimber, O., Grundhö, Fer, A., & Donath, D. (2008). Spatial augmented reality for architecture designing and planning with and within existing buildings. *International Journal of Architectural Computing, 6*(1), 41–58. doi:10.1260/147807708784640126

Tsvetozar, G., Evgenia, G., & Smrikarov, A. (2004). *M-learning - A new stage of e-learning.* International Conference on Computer Systems and Technologies, CompSysTech.

Wagner, D., & Schmalstieg, D. (2007). ARToolKitPlus for pose tracking on mobile devices. *Proceedings of the 12th Computer Vision Winter Workshop* (CVWW'07), (pp. 6-8).

Wagner, R. (2011). Educational technology: Social media tools for teaching and learning. *Athletic Train Education Journal, 6*(1), 51–52.

Walsh, A. (2010). QR codes-using mobile phones to deliver library instruction and help at the point of need. *Journal of Information Literacy, 4*(1), 55–64.

Wise, A., Chang, J., Duffy, T., & Del Valle, R. (2004). The effects of teacher social presence on student satisfaction engagement, and learning. *Journal of Educational Computing Research, 31*(3), 247–271. doi:10.2190/V0LB-1M37-RNR8-Y2U1

Yuh-Shyan, C., Tai-Chien, K., & Jang-Ping, S. (2005). Realizing outdoor independent learning with a butterfly-watching mobile learning system. *Journal of Internet Technology, 6*(1), 77–87.

KEY TERMS AND DEFINITIONS

Augmented Reality: Visual technology that allows merge virtual information (2D or 3D) with real scene.

Best BCN: Is a local BEST (Board of European Students for Technology) group, that tries to organize complementary formation courses through BEST network of 78 local groups implemented in more than 25 European countries.

BIM: Building Information Modeling, a new system of development architectural projects with informatics tools.

CAD: Computer Aided Design, traditional methodology of using computer systems to assist in the creation of 2D and 3D models.

Learning 3.0: New collaborative system where all the education community (teachers and students) are recipients of the information and also generators of it.

M-Learning: Subfield of e-distance education learning, which includes the e-learning strategies based on the use of computers and network.

Mobile Devices: Portable devices with advanced futures and Internet connection such as Smartphones and Tablets.

Native Digitals: New type of users living with technologies from birth.

Occluders: Virtual objects, identical to real objects, which are not shown in a scene. They have de ability of hiding all other visible virtual objects behind, as if they were hidden by the real ones, causing the occlusion effect.

Chapter 20
Digital Social Media Detox (DSMD):
Responding to a Culture of Interconnectivity

Theresa Renee White
California State University, Northridge, USA

ABSTRACT

This chapter presents the findings of an empirical, qualitative, one-day intervention, in which 25 college students were invited to leave all digital technology at home and participate in ten hours of face-to-face communication. The project involved alternative activities providing an opportunity for students to socialize and interact without the distraction of digital technology, while affording the investigators an opportunity to observe patterns of social behavior and communication. Those findings are offered to illuminate the potential effects of overuse of digital social media, the pedagogical challenges in a contemporary educational environment, and the social problems we face as a result.

INTRODUCTION

College students in the United States are now more technologically sophisticated than ever (Jones & Shao, 2011). As our technological landscape continues to change and grow, students are faced with an endless stream of opportunities to interact online, both scholastically and socially. The effects of digital social media on young people have been the subject of much scholarly discussion in recent years (Jones & Shao, 2011; Carr, 2010; Junco, 2010). Researchers such as Mayfield (2008) have studied the ways in which social media technologies (texting, email, Facebook and Twitter, and on-line video games) might interfere with the development of communication and

DOI: 10.4018/978-1-4666-2851-9.ch020

social skills; and how those skills, in turn, affect academic performance and the ability to engage in an increasingly digitized world. This empirical study aims to explore how technologically mediated social relations change individuals and their society, and how educators can enhance pedagogical strategies to address these changes. I attempt to answer the question at the individual level, where choices about using technology are made and consequences experienced, while simultaneously focusing on the role of higher education in mitigating the potentially addictive and unfavorable outcomes of social media dependency.

New research suggests that the problem of social media overuse and the lack of ability to speak in public forums might be graver than previously thought. Three recent studies, one conducted by the University of Maryland (2010), another representing a follow-up by twelve universities led by the International Center for Media & the Public Agenda (ICMPA) (Deluca, 2011), and yet another by the private research firm InterSperience, suggest that actual addiction to the internet is a growing risk (Murphy, 2011). All three studies found that students experience withdrawal symptoms when asked to stay offline for up to 24 hours. Participants in the studies reported "shaking, tremors, and headaches," as well as feeling "upset and lonely"—classic physical and emotional symptoms of addiction, similar to those reported by smokers and coffee drinkers trying to quit their habits.

Socialization is one of the main appeals of the Internet (Douglas et al., 2008; Preece, 2000; Wellman & Giulia, 1999), but as social media grows, dependency on it often develops pathologically. The connection between social and public skills, and potentially addictive behavior, warrants examination.

This chapter presents the findings of a Digital Social Media Detox – an empirical, qualitative, one-day intervention, in which 25 college students were invited to leave all digital technology at home and participate in ten hours of face-to-face communication. The project involved alternative activities that ranged from traditional spelling bees to nature walks, providing an opportunity for students to socialize and interact without the distraction of digital technology, while affording the principal investigator and a team of trained assistants an opportunity to observe patterns of social behavior and communication. Those findings are offered to illuminate the potential effects of overuse of digital social media, the pedagogical challenges in a contemporary educational environment, and the social problems we face as a result. While there have been several studies that have documented the excessive use of social media tools and the ways in which educators are utilizing those tools in an academic environment, this project is unique and adds to a growing body of literature that documents face to face interaction between college students *without* the distraction of interconnectivity. Moreover the study highlights the potential for internet addiction, and the consequences of distracted thinking and superficial learning, which can turn into pathological compulsion to only pay attention via social media tools. Most importantly, this study highlights how, despite the distracting "anxiety of disconnection," students can rediscover the pleasure of face-to-face connection.

LITERATURE REVIEW

The frequent use of digital and social media in higher education has received mixed reviews, and offer many paradoxes, with respect to its usefulness in enhancing students' learning experiences in and out of the classroom, its ability to provide a forum that bolsters creativity amongst college students, as well as its distractibility in and out of the classroom (Blankenship, 2011; Watkins, 2009). Some college professors claim noticeable increases in students' contributions to discussions and the creative ways they respond to homework assignments using social media (e.g., posting on blogs, online video, podcasts, and wiki) to communicate back to professors. For example, Jeremy Feibig, assistant professor of theater at Fayetteville State University in North Carolina, found an interactive online video game useful in teaching theatre to students. In his class, students are able to enter a virtual replication of Shakespeare's Global Theater and use characters they create to get a more realistic sense of what it would be like to view a play in that arena, and perform plays by using the chat function to input their lines (Blankenship, 2011).

Another study (Junco, 2011) indicated that when a group of college students were required to use the on-line social network, Twitter, for class, results showed that Twitter granted students a more rich class discussion and allowed students to extend conversations that would not have been practical in the hour-long class sessions. Twitter also created a means for students to ask questions and receive quick answers. And, most importantly, the results showed that through Twitter, students did not have traditional classroom boundaries and felt more comfortable engaging in discussion with one another.

Other arguments in favor of social media in academia include that social media allow students who do not participate verbally in class, due to feeling shy or uncomfortable, to feel less anxious to participate by typing or writing responses. In one study, researchers surveyed over 1,000 college and university faculty in the United States and found that over fifty percent use social media in their teaching, and thirty percent use it as a means of communicating with students (Blankenship, 2011). The real benefits, says Howard Rheingold, a professor who teaches a course on virtual communications and social media at UC Berkeley and Stanford University, are "…greater student engagement, greater student interest, students taking more control of their education, and more responsibility for their education" (Blankenship, 2011).

Many remain skeptical that the use of social media adds to students' learning, claiming it has the opposite effect --it distracts and leads to poorer performance in school (Blankenship, 2011; Watkins, 2009; Keim & Clark, 2009).

Digital connectivity gives us powerful new tools for finding information, expressing ourselves and conversing with others, however, Carr (2010) argues that, "It also turns us into lab rats constantly pressing levers to get tiny pellets of social or intellectual nourishment" (p. 117). Moreover, Carr (2010), borrowing from Elliot's *Four Quartets*, contends that, "the state of being 'distracted from distraction by distraction'---is very different from the kind of temporary, purposeful diversion of our mind that refreshes our thinking when we're weighing a decision" (p. 119). Increased use of technology leads to a certain degree of multitasking, which may be detrimental to the learning process, particularly when students simultaneously type notes, read emails, surf the web, and talk on the phone (Watkins, 2009). Studies have shown that in general, students who are Facebook users tend to have lower grade point averages (GPA's), a method of computing a numerical value for letter grades (e.g., 4=A, 3=B, 2=C, 1=D) in school by assigning each a numeric value and averaging the number, than those who do not use Facebook. A study conducted by Kirschner and Karpinski (2010) found that college students who were on Facebook had GPAs ranging from 3.0 to 3.5 on a 4.0 scale, compared to those of nonusers ranging from 3.5 to 4.0 on a 4.0 scale. Although strictly correlational, the implications of these findings might indicate that multitasking between homework and social networking sites affects performance in school.

Merzenich (2008) argues that the heavy use of the internet and online tools has neurological consequences. Carr (2010) notes that, "Dozens of studies by psychologists neurobiologists, educators, and Web designers point to the same conclusion: when we go online, we enter an environment that promotes cursory reading, hurried and distracted thinking, and superficial learning" (p. 116). Carr (2010) sums it up best:

What we're not doing when we're online also has neurological consequences. As the time we spend scanning Web pages crowds out the time we spend reading books, as the time we spend exchanging bit-sized text messages crowds out the time we spend composing sentences and paragraphs, as the time we spend hopping across links crowds out time we devote to quiet reflection and contemplation, the circuits that support those old intellectual functions and pursuits weaken and begin to break apart (p. 120).

Social networking also affects performance outside of school in social settings. Networking sites have been seen both as a benefit and a detriment to the perception of social capital, a term broadly referring to the resources accrued through social relationships. Ellison, Steinfield, and Lampe (2007) found a positive correlation between Facebook usage and the accumulation of social capital – in contrast to earlier studies, which found that networking sites establish and reinforce "weak ties" in bridging social capital among individuals and members of a group. And yet, the perception remains that the Internet deemphasizes personal development and expression, sublimating individual expressions of identity into group expressions. Author Mark Bauerlein (2008) suggests that the constant feeling of connectedness the Internet provides has eroded the individual's ability to be alone, while preventing the development of real-life social skills. This sentiment is echoed in Turkle (2011) when she states, "We build a following on Facebook or MySpace and wonder to what degree our followers are friends. We recreate ourselves as online personae and give ourselves new bodies, homes, jobs, and romances. Yet, suddenly, in the half-light of virtual communities, we may feel utterly alone. As we distribute ourselves, we may abandon ourselves" (p. 12).

Thus, for a generation growing up on the Internet, the experience of socializing online impacts the development of social skills at a crucial developmental stage. Huang (2011), a clinical psychologist based in Los Angeles, explains, "We're developing a whole generation of kids that have no interpersonal skills. They're having relationships, they're breaking up over the Internet, and they're not interacting with one another" (p. 28). She contends that a researcher at the University of Maryland believes we are creating a "generation of narcissists," as young people grow up online, without developing the social skills and general sense of empathy that results from face-to-face communication. Similarly, author Jonathan Franzen has suggested that the Internet provides a narcissistic paradigm for users. In his 2011 commencement address given at Kenyon College, Franzen noted: "The ultimate goal of technology is to replace the natural world that's indifferent to our wishes – a world of hurricanes and hardships and breakable hearts, a world of resistance – with a world so responsive to our wishes as to be, effectively, a mere extension of the self" (Franzen, 2011).

According to the Pew Internet & American Life Project (Lenhart, et al., 2010), fully 72% of online 18-29 year olds use social networking websites---nearly identical to the rate among teens, and significantly higher than the 39% of internet users ages 30 and up, who use these sites. Given that the predominant users of social media are college age, institutions and educators have increasingly incorporated a variety of technological tools into higher education in a bid to keep up with students' norms and expectations (Jones, 2011). Yet as institutions and educators equip themselves with the latest technology in efforts to improve pedagogical capabilities, students' opportunities to engage with others face-to-face diminish, both inside and outside of the classroom context. The appeal of constantly available, useful and/or fun interactive tools turns into potentially pathological compulsions to only pay attention via those tools. In fact, Internet Addiction Disorder (IAD) has been identified and classified as such in some countries.

Block (2008) writes that some of the most interesting research on Internet addiction has been done in South Korea:

After a series of 10 cardiopulmonary-related deaths in Internet cafés and a game-related murder, South Korea considers Internet addiction one of its most serious public health issues. Using data from 2006, the South Korean government estimates that approximately 210,000 South Korean children (2.1%; ages 6-19) are afflicted and require treatment. About 80% of those needing treatment may need psychotropic medications, and perhaps 20% to 24% require hospitalization. Unfortunately, Internet addiction is resistant to treatment, entails significant risks, and has high relapse rates (p. 32).

In the United States, Internet Addiction Disorder (IAD) has been considered for inclusion in the *Diagnostic and Statistical Manual of Mental Disorders* (DSM-5), though the studies diagnosing behavioral addictions are not yet satisfactory. According to psychologist Elizabeth Hartney (2011), researchers have scrambled to formulate diagnostic criteria for Internet addiction for the upcoming fifth edition of the DSM-5, but do not yet have adequate knowledge for its inclusion. There are, however, four discernible components to possible Internet addiction: "excessive" use of the Internet; withdrawal; high tolerance; and negative repercussions.

A study conducted by the Pew Research Center's Internet & American Life Project (Smith, 2011) reports that exceptionally widespread cell-phone texting is endemic among college age students. 83% of American adults own cell phones and three-quarters of them text with those phones. Only 31% said they preferred texts to talking on the phone. However, young people skew the averages. The nationally representative phone survey of adults ages 18 and older showed young adults are avid texters. "Cell owners between the

ages of 18 and 24 exchange an average of 109.5 messages on a normal day—that works out to more than 3,200 texts per month—and the typical or median cell owner in this age group sends or receives 50 messages per day, or 1500 messages per month" (p. 2).

Recent studies (Poldrack, 2011) have also argued that continual use of technology tools actually changes our brains: "The brain systems that drive us to habitually check our devices and crave new messages are exactly the same ones that drive drug abusers to wreck their lives in search of the next hit. In the case of both drugs and digital devices, our brains are faced with a degree of stimulation (chemical or informational, respectively) that is unprecedented throughout evolution, and our powers of self-control are simply too weak to overcome the urges that are created by these innovations. Turkle (2009) refers to this as "an anxiety of disconnection" – a kind of panic because the technology is part of their identity, their selves.

The public implications of these trends are disquieting. In her early work on the subject, Turkle (1995) acknowledged some therapeutic benefits to video gaming, as well as a connection between the non-linear aspect of online media and the ways that women tend to think. Nonetheless, in the intervening years, Turkle has come to find the effects of young people's preference for social media interaction as troubling for society:

What I'm seeing is a generation that says consistently, 'I would rather text than make a phone call.' Why? It's less risky. 'I can just get the information out there. I don't have to get all involved; it's more efficient. I would rather text than see somebody face-to-face'. There's this sense that you can have the illusion of companionship without the demands of friendship. The real demands of friendship, of intimacy, are complicated. They're hard. They involve a lot of negotiation (p. 12).

Her point is that those who have grown up with these toys and conveniences, have had the option not to engage in some of the more difficult challenges in adolescence, have not had to learn some basic skills, and that is a concern.

PRESENT STUDY: DIGITAL SOCIAL MEDIA DETOX

Traditional verbal communication is a crucial factor for success in college, as well as in interpersonal relationships, and in the workplace (Lucas, 2007; Stevens, 2005; Hawkins, Duran and Kelly, 1991). Social media can be very useful to a college student, however, when abused beyond leisure and networking, it can act as a hindrance to communication skills, success in college, and beyond. As Turkle (2009) put it succinctly, "how are we going to convince our children that we are giving them a world where the problems are more complex than ever – education, the environment, politics…and also tell them that actually you can get it in mind-size bites, little haiku bits of information directly off the Web?" (p. 2).

As a professor of Public Speaking and Communication at a large university in Southern California, I first became interested in the effects of the virtual environment after noticing increased verbal communication difficulties for many of the students in my undergraduate classes. The course attracts students from varied academic majors, as well as cultural and socioeconomic backgrounds, because it fulfills a general education requirement and is mandatory for matriculation. At the beginning of each semester there are clear expectations that I share with students regarding the multiple speaking assignments required in the course. Though there has always been a propensity for even the most gregarious, out-going students to shy away from the scrutiny inherent in this form of interaction, their reactions to public exposure in their presentation assignments (in a safe classroom environment) were profound. It was a common occurrence to see students experiencing labored

breathing, profuse sweating, and blanking out in the middle of sentences, unable to recover. One student had to run out of the room and vomit; another got dizzy and crumpled to the floor. One actually fainted, requiring a paramedic team to be called to the classroom. Why, I wondered, in a world where communication is more constant than ever before, are students exhibiting such panic when called upon to give a classroom presentation?

It was my hypothesis that the multifaceted forms of online communication and social networking familiar to students had preempted most face-to-face interaction; thereby, interfering with their ability to speak in public, and to communicate in general. Such interference could potentially negatively affect not only student performance in my class, but also affect their success beyond the classroom as they navigate the job market, personal and professional relationships, and adult social and civic lives.

Methods

The Digital Social Media Detox (DSMD) workshop was a ten-hour intervention requiring participants to forego any technological devices. The day was organized into separate workshop activities, which were designed to address and evaluate students in terms of face-to-face communication; verbal and written communication skills; multi-tasking; ability to recall information; and the ability to identify context-specific appropriate behavior for the educational environment, in the job market and in interpersonal relationships. The intervention was designed not only to see how students fared when separated from social media, but also to assess how their relationship to social media has affected their ability to socialize and communicate in authentic, real-life situations.

This is an empirical study utilizing qualitative triangulation research methods, including pre and post surveys, journal writings, and videotaped interviews and focus groups. Data were collected from a convenience sample of undergraduate students enrolled in a Fundamentals of Public

Speaking course at a mid-size university in Southern California. The students were primarily freshman, with approximately 10% identifying as sophomores or juniors. Of the 25 participants, 40% (N=10) were male and 60% (N=15) were female, with a mean age of 20. Thirty-two percent (N=8) of the students described themselves as Latino/Hispanic; 20% (N=5) African American; 16% (N=4) Asian American and 12% (N=3) Caucasian. The majority of the participants were from Southern California, and all were students enrolled in the freshman level course during the spring 2011 semester. Prior to the intervention, students had no knowledge of the impending activities that were scheduled during the program. The day began with students completing a pre-survey, engaging in journal writing, and participating in a video-taped focus group moderated by the principal investigator. Participants were then divided into groups and rotated through the workshop activities, comprising nature walks, word-play games, spelling bees and interactive exercises. There was a second journal writing session at midday, after which participants resumed workshop activities. The day ended with a post-program survey, journal writing session and another videotaped focus group. The entire intervention was videotaped, with students periodically stepping away from the workshop activities to give on-camera interviews to share their insights, what they noticed about their behavior in the absence of technology, as well as their responses to the day's events.

In sum, two surveys were given – one pre-program at the start of the day and one post-program at the end of the day. Three journal-writing sessions were administered – one pre-program session, one midday session, and one post-program session. Two videotaped focus groups also bookended the intervention, and students were required to write a two-page essay highlighting their experience participating in the Digital Social Media Detox program, which was due two weeks later.

Results

Pre-Program Survey

The pre-program survey was a two-page questionnaire that asked students to calculate how much time they spend using various digital and social media, (i.e., how often they text, check their phones, log on to Facebook and Twitter), their primary motivation for going online, and which websites and other forms of media they use most frequently. The majority of the respondents said they watched television infrequently; it seems the small screen has been passed over for an even smaller one, as most students said they spent most of their time online. One student wrote that she was on the internet "the majority of time I'm awake," while others reported going online "very often", "about 30 times a day," and "7-8 hours a day." It appears that students use Facebook more than any other form of media, though texting was frequently cited. Twelve students admitted to texting more than 80 times a day, with only two reporting texting less than twice a day.

When asked what they are doing while online, students gave answers ranging from homework to leisure activities. About half the participants said they use the Internet for research and other school-related needs, in addition to using the Internet for entertainment and socializing. Only one student said she uses the Internet exclusively for homework purposes. Other students said they check email, go on Facebook, chat with friends, and watch YouTube frequently throughout the day. One student wrote that he goes online "to keep up with what everyone else is doing...."

It has been noted that socialization is one of the primary appeals of the Internet (Thorne, Black and Sykes, 2009; Singh, Kwon and Pereira, 2003), and this sample group corroborates that idea. Given the amount of time spent both online and texting, we can deduce that students are using multiple technologies simultaneously. The effects of such multitasking upon attention span, and the increased

Digital Social Media Detox (DSMD)

inability to concentrate have been prevalent in previous studies (Mokhtari et al., 2011; Wallis, 2010), but very few qualitative, empirical studies that encourages face-to-face interaction, explores inhibited communication skills and internet addition, have been documented, and thus deserve further exploration.

Post-Program Survey

The post-program survey prompted students to take stock of the day's experience, including what they learned about their relationship with technology, and if they anticipated any changes in their behavior moving forward. The majority of the students said they felt more comfortable speaking to someone face-to-face than they had at the beginning of the day. Students stated: "talking to people is not all that bad," "social media isn't as important as I've made it," and "it's okay to communicate verbally." Participants said the experience of spending 10 hours without their phones was "liberating," "nice without the leash," as well as "bittersweet" and "actually fun." One student said, "I was panicking in the beginning, but I learned to control it," while another wrote, "It like opened my eyes to a whole new world." Many of the students said they would try to use less social media in the future. They wrote that social media can be detrimental to "verbal communication, spelling, even confidence," that it can "make people lazy, less social," and that they worry about its effects on future generations.

Focus Groups

During the pre and post focus groups, the moderators identified students reaching for their phone and exhibiting obvious anxiety due to the disconnectivity. One student stated, "I keep reaching for my phone just to see what time it is, because I, and most students, use it as a clock. Now I have no idea of the time." Another indicated that he was only able to tell time by looking at the direction of

the sun, and as a result he felt as though, "I'm in rehab and about to go into relapse." One student indicated that if she forgot her phone, no matter how far away from home she was, she would immediately go back to retrieve it, as she had to have it by her side.

On the contrary, however, the moderators noticed an ease in terms of communication and friendly banter between the students as the day progressed. Quiet contemplation was omnipresent as students took time out just to be "silent." Based on the participant's responses from the pre and post focus group, it was evident that the students had developed a new level of camaraderie and collaborative engagement. One student noted that she could determine, "all of us have come together and are closer as a result of this program." Another student stated: "We talked more and got to know one another. Who would have known we have so many eccentric and interesting people in our class." The program also seemed to stimulate creativity as the students were observed spontaneously playing a guitar that one student brought, singing and telling jokes and generally enjoying one another's company. The students also exhibited comfort in disclosing personal information and appeared to reconnect with their ability to problem solve and to think of innovative strategies to enhance socialization. In essence, the moderators noticed that the program reinforced peer communication and contributed to a more relaxed level of engagement and interaction.

Essays

Essays were to be turned in to the professor by the students two weeks after the Digital Social Media Detox intervention was completed. This extended period of time afforded the students an opportunity to reflect on the event and the changes, if any, that they incorporated into their lives as a result of having participated in the research project. Most of the students chose to write about the experience of not having access to technology during the event and what that experience taught them. Students considered the initial shock of not having their phones---"It was like I was missing a third arm. My phone, that extension of myself, was gone"– a shock that dissipated for most as the day wore on. But, for some, the anxiety was only mitigated when they were reunited with their phone at the end of the day: "I checked my pockets, and felt what I imagine a heart attack would feel like. I didn't feel that familiar bulge. My phone was not there, and for a split second I felt completely naked. That is how I felt every thirty to forty minutes throughout my detoxification experience."

A few students wrote of their surprise upon realizing how deficient their spelling skills were during the word games played that day. One student said, "One of the most shocking things I learned about myself during the digital social media detox day, was how horrible of a speller I am. I didn't realize how bad my spelling was until that moment. I misspelled embarrassing, how ironic." Students related their poor spelling to computer auto-correct functions. One student wrote: "As for college students in the future and even some in the present, I believe that social media will lead to a decline in grammatical skills due to the fact that most devices correct your incorrectly spelled words." Other student responses included: "The spelling bee was probably the worst experience from the whole program because I found out I did not know how to spell certain words by memory, probably due to the fact that the internet has given us a lot of tools to spell-check words and grammar," and "When it was time for activities during the event I really noticed that digital social media does have a big influence. I felt it has a big influence because when it came to the spelling game I could not spell any words. I really got sad because here I am in a university and I could not even spell words. I think that sub-standard vocabulary has a lot to do with computers and cell phones."

The majority of the participants wrote about how the detox made them aware of their own social skills and social behaviors, with respect to social media. One student said the seminar "opened my eyes to how much I have let social media and technology take over my life," while many others wrote about how they realized they could have fun without social media: "This experience has taught me how much fun we can have interacting with others by not just using our fingers to type and communicate"; "I realized how much I missed playing like a kid. When we played red light/green light and duck duck goose, honestly I had a blast"; "the games and the nature walk we participated in showed me how plain, simple, activities that do not involve an iPhone were quite fun."

Most importantly, many students felt that the experience enabled them to connect with others in a meaningful way that social media does not allow. One student wrote, "I just seemed to get more and more comfortable with everyone around me because I was learning things I didn't know about them," while another said, "I was having fun with my classmates whom I had never really spent time with before." The experience made one student wonder, "How many more people am I missing out on due to being consumed with social media?" Others commented on the nature of the social interactions they experienced that day: "It seemed like I connected with the majority of the people in that room on a different level. If it were not for this project I probably would not have engaged in half the conversations that I did. I made a genuine connection with some of my classmates that I truly cherish. Normally before class starts all of the students are engaged with their phones and we have simple, polite conversations, but nothing like the conversations we shared last weekend." Students attributed the connections they made to the absence of technology, without realizing the irony inherent in the idea that social media detracts from the social experience. One wrote,

"I found it very interesting that by not having access to technology and social media at this time, forced us to interact with one another more than we would normally, and we managed to learn a thing or two about one another," while another said, "As people get caught in the whirlwind of social media, they lose sight of one of the most important aspects in a person's life: personal interactions and relationships." One student concluded that, "It is apparent that social media is the brick wall that we have built between ourselves and others. College-age users of social media 'socialize' by narrowing themselves to shallow or one-way communication."

Students exhibited great concern about the extent to which digital social media will affect future generations; the "digital natives" who will have never known life without the Internet. One student indicated that, "I won't be surprised if people---the future generations---aren't able to keep face-to-face conversations with others." Other students stated: "if we don't actually communicate with other people, our ability to speak in public is going to decline, and I think the younger generation will be deprived from making these kinds of connections with their peers as they mature. They will be consumed by technology and some factors needed to build a relationship will not be instilled in them." Still another student wrote: "Meeting face to face seems almost extinct."

Many students said they had tried to limit the time they spent online since attending the detox program, because they had become aware, as one student said, of "how much time I spend doing nothing and staring at my screen." But not all of the participants felt that the detox was beneficial, or even necessary. One student wrote:

I need Facebook. Not like a crack head. But without it, I would lose contact with a lot of people I truly care about. . . I think Facebook is a tool. And a great one. I think it can be abused, but I really don't have sympathy for those who do. . . I have real goals to accomplish. And I'll do that with, or without, Facebook.

Another gave this more even-handed statement:

In retrospect, as someone who is a computer science major and a person who wants to participate in the technological revolution that is taking place in our society, I say this: I love technology and social media. They have made our lives easier, but the Digital Social Media Detox Program showed me one very important thing that I will carry with me now and into the future---that it's okay to let go of technology and digital social media. I can't let it dominate my life and that I should make more time to enjoy the physical world around me more than cyberspace, and I should stop looking at the iPhone and get to know the people around me. I think that is very important because in the end it will lead to a happy and healthy future.

Face-to-Face Communication

Many of the students found they were surprised at the ease and efficiency of face-to-face communication, after having disconnected from their technological devices. In one of the afternoon focus groups, one student said he "actually got to know people". Another, who described himself as shy, commented that he laughed more than he had in a long time: "I've laughed a lot today. I haven't laughed in awhile. . . I'm socially awkward in a huge gathering or crowd, as I usually go to my phone out of nervousness, but today it was different. I felt I was able to come out of my shell." It seems that not having the phone as a crutch to rely upon helped this young person connect with the world.

Potential for Addiction

Some of the students reported feeling edgy or shaky the longer they went without contact with the outside world. A member of the film crew noticed the students eyeing a cell phone belonging to a member of the production team, "like crack heads in a rehab house." Some participants shared past experiences of addiction. One woman described how she had "lost" three months of her life playing the video game, "Black Ops: Call of Duty". She stopped eating (she is now a nutrition major) and sleeping. She went to the bathroom during "Intermission," a forced break in the game, and took longer breaks only to nap. She said, "For three months I lost myself because of the video game." When asked how she stopped, she replied, "I beat the game." Another student said he sometimes texted 1,000 times a day, and has received cell phone bills for 8000 texts a month, noting that, "I feel lost, lonely and deprived when I don't connect via my devices."

Dating

Students apparently feel more comfortable with the faceless properties of digital communication in the early stages of dating. In the videotaped focus group, two students readily admitted to initiating contact with a member of the opposite sex via text message before making a phone call. It seems that texting is used in such situations to verify that further contact would be welcomed or not rebuffed. One student wrote in his essay that "when I ask for a girl's number [in order to call her], I feel I have to justify that approach by saying it's because I don't have Facebook". To the extent that social media allows young people to avoid awkward or difficult moments, social media inhibits the learning of skills that could allow them to negotiate their public lives with more grace and less pain.

FUTURE RESEARCH

Educators can take from this study a sense that, as much as college students like, use, and depend on social media, they can like, use, and depend on face-to-face interaction, if they are convinced of its value and its at-risk status. Participants in this study did not realize what they were losing

when devoting so much time to social media, and so much less time to face-to-face interactions. As Turkle notes (2009), social media dependency is not a substance addiction, the kind that closes down our ability to function until we stop using it. This dependency is more about how young people choose to spend the 24 hours they have in every day. Her concern is that college students are not doing certain things that are developmentally necessary because they cannot put down their technology. An analogy might be cigarette smokers in the mid-20th century who only saw the increased, glamorous use of cigarettes in popular culture, learning too late of the diseases that came from smoking (Cigarettes, 2011). To respond, educators can incorporate the *use* of digital social media (e.g., twitter, tumbler, Facebook) for classroom interaction, as well as provide opportunities to *replace* digital social media with *required* face-to-face interaction, as exemplified by the detoxification event. This can provide college students with multiple opportunities to engage in both communicative approaches, and can thus choose which format is most appropriate for different circumstances. Turkle (2009) emphasizes the public good to be gained:

By putting the premium on what's fast, [social media] takes away from education the ability to reason with your students about complicated things. That's why they shouldn't be doing everything virtually. That's why they should come to universities and be in a community. And most important, it takes away from the future our best way of thinking about complexity, which really is to study very long stories and try to put them together. The great paradox of the Internet is that it promises a greater potential for sociability, while apparently compromising our basic social skills the more we use it (p. 3).

The students exhibited an awareness at the day's end that social media was negatively affecting their ability to communicate, both orally and in writing. Though they placed blame on the media, and not on themselves, they all still seemed to feel that one of the benefits of social media was the ability to keep in touch and network with others. Compromise between "too much" and "not enough" media use seemed possible. As Jones and Shao (2011) note in their large-scale study of college students, "The gap between students and their teachers is not fixed, nor is the gulf so large that it cannot be bridged. In many ways the relationship is determined by the requirements teachers place upon their students to make use of new technologies and the way teachers integrate new technologies in their courses" (p. 20).

We cannot know how social media will continue to shape the millennial generation as its members grow into their 20s, 30s, and beyond. But for now, the negative effects of the Internet on young people's public interaction do not appear to be irrevocable. The participants in the Digital Social Media Detox program were eager to get back to their phones at the day's end, but they all managed to live without Internet access for a day. One student wryly remarked, "I'm not going to die" as a result of being technologically disconnected for a day. To the contrary, most students expressed joy and gratitude about connecting with each other in this "new" and personal way. Friendships were made on that day within a group that had been taking class together for nearly the whole semester by that point. Many of them said they wished the program had been held earlier in the semester so they could have gotten to know each other sooner. It was instructive to watch and hear how connections were being made the old-fashioned way. Jones, et al., (2009), concluded that college students continue to be early adopters of new internet tools and applications relative to general U.S. internet–users. The strong argument can be made, based on this study, that the two forms of interaction can balance each other. Participants made it clear that they have relationships that require social media (Facebook, smart phones, texts) with people who are not local; if there is great distance between communicators, social media actually strengthens these social worlds. Participants also made it clear that they want and need face-to-face interaction. If feeling safer at the start of a dating process makes someone more likely to date, how is that bad? Maybe the point is that everyone should "detox" now and then, to ensure that they can, because pathological dependency is real. Many college students find out the hard way what the boundaries are between appropriate and inappropriate use of the Internet and various digital social media. Individuals must learn to choose when and how to use it. They must be aware of the tendency towards personal pre-occupation and public isolation. Educators are in a position to help college students develop patterns of behavior that include both kinds of human interaction. The New Media Consortium (NMC) Horizon Report: 2012 Higher Education Edition, contends that educational institutions are embracing face-to-face/online hybrid learning models as a way to leverage the online skills learners have already developed, independent of academia. The report also indicates that there is new emphasis in the classroom on more challenge-based and active learning methods. Educators are leveraging technologies such as tablets and smartphones to connect curriculum with real life issues.

Technology challenges our human values by distancing us from each other, even if it connects us electronically. A civic life - a life connected to the public realm to which we belong -- requires that we are aware of ourselves in that context. We each have to figure out what our human values are -- whether on our own at 3 a.m., or in moments of difficulty, or during quiet contemplation of films, literature, poetry, and our lives. Many pleasures become pleasures through acquired skills. We know this. We must, as educators, ensure that our students know this as well.

REFERENCES

Baron, N. (2008). *Always on: Language in an online and mobile world.* New York, NY: Oxford University Press.

Bauerlein, M. (2008). *The dumbest generation: How the digital age stupefies young Americans and jeopardizes our future (or, don't trust anyone under 30).* New York, NY: The Penguin Group.

Blankenship, M. (2011). How social media can and should impact higher education. *Education Digest: Essential Readings Condensed for Quick Review, 76*(7), 39–42.

Block, J. (2008). Issues for DSM-V: Internet addiction. *The American Journal of Psychiatry, 165,* 306–307. doi:10.1176/appi.ajp.2007.07101556

Carr, N. (2010). *The shallows: What the internet is doing to our brain.* New York, NY: W. W. Norton & Company.

Carr, N. (2011, April 4). Interview by project information literacy. The age of perpetual distraction. *Project Information Literacy "Smart Talks," 6.* Retrieved March 30, 2012, from http://projectinfolit.org/st/carr.asp

Chan, A. (2011, July 26). The web: Just as addictive as cigarettes and booze. *Huffington Post.* Retrieved from http://www.huffingtonpost.com/2011/07/26/internet-addictivealcohol-smoking-addiction_n_910214.html

Cigarettes – Glamour of Smoke. (2009, September 23). Retrieved December 5, 2011 from http://cigarettes-.wikispaces.com/Glamour+of+Smoke

Deluca, J. (2010). *24 hour unplugged.* College Park, MD: University of Maryland. International Center for Media & the Public Agenda. Retrieved on December 30, 2011, from the http://withoutmedia.wordpress.com.

Denzin, N. K., & Lincoln, Y. S. (1994). *Handbook of qualitative research.* Thousand Oaks, CA: Sage Publications.

Douglas, A. C., Mills, J. E., Niang, M., Stepchenkova, S., Byun, S., Ruffini, C., & Blanton, M. (2008). Internet addition: Meta-synthesis of qualitative research. *Computers in Human Behavior, 24*(6), 3027–3044. doi:10.1016/j.chb.2008.05.009

Elliot, T. S. (1943). *Four quartets.* New York, NY.

Ellison, N., Steinfield, C., & Lampe, C. (2007). The benefits of Facebook 'friends': Social capital and college students' use of online social network sites. *Journal of Computer-Mediated Communication, 12,* 1143–1168. doi:10.1111/j.1083-6101.2007.00367.x

Fackler, M. (2007, November 18). In Korea, a boot camp for web obsession. *New York Times.* Retrieved from http://www.nytimes.com/2007/11/18/technology/18rehab.html?pagewanted=all

Franzen, J. (2011, May 28). Liking is for cowards: Go for what hurts. *New York Times.* Retrieved on December 30, 2012, from http://www.nytimes.com/2011/05/29/opinion/29franzen.html?pagewanted=all

Future of media education. (2010). *Program theme presented at University film & video association conference 2011.* Retrieved from http://www.ufva.org/conference/2011/theme

Hagedorn, W. B., & Young, T. (2011). Identifying and intervening with students exhibiting signs of gaming addiction and other addictive behaviors: Implications for professional school counselors. *Professional School Counseling, 14*(4), 250–260. doi:10.5330/PSC.n.2011-14.250

Hartney, E. (2011, September 15). What is internet addiction? Symptoms of internet addiction. *About.com Guide.* Retrieved from http://addictions.about.com/od/internetaddiction/a/What-Is-Internet-Addiction.htm

Hawkins, L., Duran, R. L., & Kelly, L. (1991). The relationship of interpersonal communication variables to academic success and persistence in college. *Communication Quarterly, 39*(4), 297–308. doi:10.1080/01463379109369807

Huang, T. (2011, July 26). *Interview by C. Williams* [Video recording]. Internet Deprivation Can Lead to Real Withdrawal Symptoms, NBC. Los Angeles, CA. Retrieved on January 7, 2012, from http://drtaji.blogspot.com/2011/07/internet-deprivation-can-lead-to-real.html

Jones, C. (2011). Students, the net generation and digital natives: accounting for educational change. In Thomas, M. (Ed.), *Deconstructing digital natives*. New York, NY: Routledge.

Jones, C., & Shao, B. (2011). *The Net generation and digital natives: Implications for higher education*. New York, NY: Higher Education Academy.

Jones, S., Johnson-Yale, C., Millermaier, S., & Seoane-Perez, F. (2009, October 5). Everyday life, online: U.S. college students' use of the internet. *First Monday, 14*(10).

Junco, R. (2010). The effect of twitter on college student engagement and grades. *Journal of Computer Assisted Learning, 27*(2), 1-14. doi:10.1111/j.1365- 2729.2010.00387.x

Junco, R. (2011). The relationship between frequency of Facebook use, participation in Facebook activities, and student engagement. *Computers & Education, 58*(1). doi:doi:10.1016/j.compedu.2011.08.004

Keim, N., & Clark, J. (2009 October). *Public media 2.0 field report: building social media infrastructure to engage publics: Twitter vote report and inauguration report '09*. Retrieved on December 18, 2011, from http://www.centerforsocialmedia.org/sites/default/files/documents/pages/TVR_Inaug09_Oct.pdf

Kirschner, P., & Karpinski, A. (2010, November). Facebook and academic performance. *Computers in Human Behavior, 26*(6), 1237–1245. doi:10.1016/j.chb.2010.03.024

Lebel, J. (2010, March 5). *5 examples of how schools are using social media to enhance learning* [Web log post]. Retrieved on April 18, 2010, from http://blog.thekbuzz.com/2010/03/5-examples-of-using-social-media-to-enhance-learning.html

Lenhart, A., Purcell, K., Smith, A., & Zickhur, K. (2010, February 3). *Social media and mobile internet use among teens and young adults*. Pew Internet & American Life Project website. Retrieved December 5, 2011, from http://www.pewinternet.org/Reports/2010/Social-Media-and-Young-Adults.aspx

Mayfield, A. (2008). *What is social media?* Retrieved December 18, 2011, from http://www.iCrossing.com/ebooks

McGonigal, J. (2011). *Reality is broken: Why games make us better and how they can change the world*. New York, NY: The Penguin Press.

Merzenich, M. (2008, August 11). Going Googly. *On the Brain with Dr. Mike Merzenich*. [Web log post]. Retrieved December 30, 2011, from http://merzenich.positscience.com/?p=177

Mokhtari, K., Reichard, C., & Gardner, A. (2011). The impact of Internet and television use on the reading habits and practices of college students. *Journal of Adolescent & Adult Literacy, 52*(7), 609–619. doi:10.1598/JAAL.52.7.6

Murphy, S. (2011, July 6). Tech withdrawal similar to giving up drinking, smoking. *Tech News Daily*. Retrieved December 30, 2011, from http://www.technewsdaily.com/2937-internet-addictions-similar-to-tobacco-addictions.html

Murray, J. (2011, November 21). Do students know more about technology than their teachers? We ask education experts for their verdicts. *The Guardian*. Retrieved from http://www.guardian.co.uk/education/2011/nov/21/multiple-choice-students-teachers-technology?newsfeed=true

Poldrack, R. (2011, October 12). May I have your attention: The brain, multitasking, and information overload. *Project Information Literacy Smart Talk, 9*. Retrieved from http://projectinfolit.org/st/poldrack.asp

Preece, J. (2000). *Online communities: Designing usability, supporting sociability*. Chichester, UK: John Wiley & Sons. Retrieved from www.ifsm.umbc.edu/onlinecommunities

Qualman, E. (2010). *Socialnomics: How social media transforms the way we live and do business*. Hoboken, NJ: John Wiley & Sons.

Rushton, K. (2011, February 28) Texting too distracting? Using cell phones creates problems for students. *The Oracle: West Springfield High School Newspaper*. Retrieved from http://www.theoracleonline.org/news/2011/02/28/texting-too-distractingusing-cell-phones-creates-problems-for-students/

Singh, N., Kwon, I., & Pereira, A. (2003). Cross-cultural consumer socialization: An exploratory study of socialization influences across three ethnic groups. *Psychology and Marketing, 20*(10), 867–881. doi:10.1002/mar.10100

Smith, A. (2011, September 9). *Americans and text messaging*. Pew Internet & American Life Project website. Retrieved November 18, 2011, from http://www.pewinternet.org/Reports/2011/Cell-Phone-Texting-2011.aspx

Stevens, B. (2005). What communication skills do employers want? Silicon Valley recruiters respond. *Journal of Employment Counseling, 42*(1), 2–10. doi:10.1002/j.2161-1920.2005.tb00893.x

Thorne, S., Black, R., & Sykes, J. (2009). Second language use, socialization, and learning in internet interest communities and online gaming. *Modern Language Journal, 93*(S1), 802–821. doi:10.1111/j.1540-4781.2009.00974.x

Turkle, S. (1995). *Life on the screen: Identity in the age of the internet*. New York, NY: Simon & Schuster Paperbacks.

Turkle, S. (2009). Interview Sherry Turkle [Television series episode]. *Frontline*. Los Angeles, CA: PBS. Retrieved from http://www.pbs.org/wgbh/pages/frontline/digitalnation/interview/turkle.html

Turkle, S. (2011). *Alone together: Why we expect more from technology and less from each other*. New York, NY: Basic Books.

Wallis, C. (2010). *The impacts of media multitasking on children's learning and development: Report from a research seminar*. New York, NY: The Joan Ganz Cooney Center as Sesame Workshop.

Watkins, S. C. (2009, August 24). Interview by M. Beja: How students, professors, and colleges are, and should be, using social media. *Wired Campus*. Retrieved on December 30, 2011 from http://chronicle.com/blogs/wiredcampus/how-students-professorscolleges-areshould-be-using-social-media/7787

Wellman, B., & Gulia, M. (1999). Net surfers don't ride alone. In Wellman, B. (Ed.), *Networks in the global village* (pp. 331–366). Boulder, CO: Westview Press.

ADDITIONAL READING

Bull, G., Thompson, A., Searson, M., Garofalo, J., Park, J., Young, C., & Lee, J. (2008). Connecting informal and formal learning: experiences in the age of participatory media. *Contemporary Issues in Technology & Teacher Education*, *8*(2). Retrieved from http://www.citejournal.org/vol8/iss2/editorial/article1.cfm

Campbell, R., Martin, C. R., & Fabos, B. (2011). *Media essentials: A brief introduction*. Boston, MA: Bedford.

Correa, T. (2009). *Who interacts on the web? The intersection of users' personality and social media use,* (pp. 248-253). Elsevier. Retrieved from http://www.elsevier.com/locate.comphumbeh

Crystal, D. (2008). *Texting: The gr8 db8*. New York, NY: Oxford University Press.

De Zengotita, T. (2005). *Mediated: How the media shapes your world and the way you live in it*. New York, NY: Bloomsberry Publishing.

Espejo, R. (2008). *Should social networking site be banned?* Detroit, MI: Greenhaven Press.

Fogg, B. J. (2007). Persuasive technology: Using computers to change what we think and do. doi:10.1145/763955.763957

Fogg, B. J., & Nass, C. I. (1997). Silicon sycophants: The effects of computers that flatter. *International Journal of Human-Computer Studies*, *46*, 551–561. doi:10.1006/ijhc.1996.0104

Fogg, B. J., & Nass, C. I. (1997). *How users reciprocate to computers: an experiment that demonstrates behavior change* [Extended Abstracts]. CHI97 Conference of the ACM/SIGCHI. New York, NY: ACM Press.

Hanson, T. (2010). Cell phones, text messaging, and Facebook: Competing time demands of today's college students. *College Teaching*, *59*(1), 23–30. doi:10.1080/87567555.2010.489078

Jones, S. (2002, September 15). *The internet goes to college: How students are living in the future with today's technology*. Pew Internet & American Life Project. Retrieved February 17, 2012 from http://www.pewinternet.org/reports/toc.asp?Report=71

Jones, S. (2003). *Let the games begin,* (pp. 2-14). Pew Internet & American Life Project. Retrieved from http://www.pewinternet.org

Junco, R. (2010). The effect of Twitter on college student engagement and grades. *Journal of Computer Assisted Learning*, *27*(2), 1–14. doi:doi:10.1111/j.1365-2729.2010.00387.x

Klein, J. D. (1993, July 1). Adolescents' risky behavior and mass media use. *Pediatrics*, *92*(1), 24–31. Retrieved from http://pediatrics.aappublications.org/content/92/1/24.short

Lenhart, A. (2009, April 10). *Teens and social media: An overview*. Pew Internet & American Life Project. Retrieved February 17, 2012, from http://isites.harvard.edu/fs/docs/icb.topic786630.files/Teens%20Social%20Media%20and%20Health%20-%20NYPH%20Dept%20Pew%20Internet.pdf

Levinson, P. (2009). *New new media*. Boston, MA: Allyn & Bacon.

Li, C., & Bernoff, J. (2008). *Groundswell: Winning in a world transformed by social technologies*. Boston, MA: Harvard Business Press.

Lucas, S. (2007). *The art of public speaking* (10th ed.). New York, NY: McGraw-Hill.

Madden, M. (2011). *Women maintain their foothold on SNS use and older Americans are still coming abroad*, (pp. 2-14). Pew Internet & American Life Project. Retrieved from http://www.pewinternet. org/reports/2011/social-networking-sites.aspx

Mastronardi, M. (2003). Adolescence and media. *Journal of Language and Social Psychology*, *22*(2), 83–93. doi:10.1177/0261927X02250059

McLaren, P. (1988). Schooling the postmodern body: Critical pedagogy and the politics of enfleshment. *Journal of Education*, *170*(3), 53–83.

Nakamura, L. (2008). *Digitizing race: Visual culture of the internet*. Minneapolis, MN: University of Minnesota Press.

Osuagwu, N. G. (2009). *Facebook addiction: The life and times of social networking addicts*. New York, NY: Ice Cream Melts Publishing.

Partridge, K. (2011). *Social networking*. New York, NY: H.W. Wilson.

Poe, M. (2011). *A history of communications: Media and society from the evolution of speech to the internet*. Cambridge, UK: Cambridge University Press.

Qualman, E. (2009). *Socialnomics: How social media transforms the way we live and do business*. Hoboken, NJ: Wiley.

Steyer, J., & Clinton, C. (2012). *Talking back to Facebook: A common sense guide to raising kids in the digital age*. New York, NY: Scribner.

Tuten, T. L. (2008). *Advertising 2.0: social media marketing in a Web 2.0 world*. Westport, CT: Praeger.

Vandewater, E. A., Rideout, V. J., Wartella, E. A., Huang, X., Lee, J. H., & Shim, M. (2007, May 1). Digital childhood: Electronic media and technology use among infants, toddlers, and preschoolers. *Pediatrics, 119*(5), e1006-e1015. doi: 0.1542/peds.2006-1804.

KEY TERMS AND DEFINITIONS

Addiction: Physical and psychological dependence on something.

Dependency: Relying and being controlled by someone or something, in this case social technology.

Interpersonal Communication: Interactive contact and exchange of information between two or more people.

Multitasking: The simultaneous execution of multiple duties or activities.

New Media: Refers to digital technologies.

Public Life: The complex or aggregate of relationships of people in society, especially those relationships involving authority or power.

Social Media: Includes the various online technology tools that enable people to communicate easily via the internet to share information and resources. Social media can include text, audio, video, images, podcasts, and other multimedia communications.

Social Networking: The use of dedicated websites and applications to communicate informally with other users, or to find people with similar interests to oneself.

Compilation of References

Abreu, B. S. (2011). *Media literacy, social networking, and the Web 2.0 environment for the K-12 educator*. New York, NY: Peter Lang Publishing.

Academic Ranking of World Universities. (n.d.). *Shanghai index*. Retrieved from http://www.arwu.org/aboutARWU.jsp

ACM. (2011). *CHI-Conference on Human Factors in Computing Systems*, January 10, 2012. Retrieved from http://chi2011.org/index.html

Adi, A. (2011). *Social media: Exercises 4 PR & branding #HigherEd classes*. Retrieved January 11, 2012, from http://www.anaadi.net/2011/05/20/social-media-exercises-4-pr-branding-highered-classes/

Ahlqvist, T., Bäck, A., Heinonen, S., & Halonen, M. (2010). Road-mapping the societal transformation potential of social media. *Foresight, 12*(5), 3–26. doi:10.1108/14636681011075687

Akyıldız, M., & Argan, M. (2011). *Using online social networking: Students' purposes of Facebook usage at the University of Turkey*. Paper presented at the International Conference-Las Vegas.

Alexander, B., & Levine, A. (2008). Storytelling emergence of a new genre. *EDUCAUSE Review, 43*(6), 40-56. Retrieved December 20, 2011 from http://net.educause.edu/ir/library/pdf/erm0865.pdf

Alexander, D. (2004). Changing the public relations curriculum: A new challenge for educators. *Prism*. Retrieved 13th July, 2010, from http://www.prismjournal.org/fileadmin/Praxis/Files/Journal_Files/Issue2/Alexander.pdf.

Alfonso, G.-H., & de Valbuena Miguel, R. (2006). Trends in online media relations: Web-based corporate press rooms in leading international companies. *Public Relations Review, 32*, 267–275. doi:10.1016/j.pubrev.2006.05.003

Allan, B. (2007). Time to learn? E-learners' experience of time in virtual communities. *Journal of Management Learning, 38*(5), 557–572. doi:10.1177/1350507607083207

Allen, I. E., & Seaman, J. (2007). *Online nation: Five years of growth in online learning*. Needhan, MA: Sloan Consortium. Retrieved on February 27, 2012, from sloanconsortium.org/publications/survey/pdf/online_nation.pdf

Allen, I. E., & Seaman, J. (2011). *Going the distance: Online education in the United States, 2011. Sloan Online Survey Series*. United States: Babson Survey Research Group.

Allwardt, D. E. (2011). Teaching note. Writing with wikis: A cautionary tale of technology in the classroom. *Journal of Social Work Education, 47*(3), 597–605. doi:10.5175/JSWE.2011.200900126

Alonso, H., & Lopez, I. (2008). Adaptando asignaturas al EEES: El caso de Teoría y Técnica de la Publicidad. In I. Rodríguez (Ed.), *El nuevo perfil del profesor universitario en el EEES. Claves para la renovación metodológica*. Valladolid, España: Universidad Europea Miguel de Cervantes.

Amichai-Hamburger, Y., & Ben-Artzi, E. (2003). Loneliness and Internet use. *Computers in Human Behavior, 19*(1), 71–80. doi:10.1016/S0747-5632(02)00014-6

Amichai-Hamburger, Y., Wainapel, G., & Fox, S. (2002). On the Internet no one knows I'm an "introvert": Extraversion, neuroticism, and Internet interaction. *Cyberpsychology & Behavior*, *5*(2), 125–128. doi:10.1089/109493102753770507

Anderson, P. (2007). What is Web 2.0? Ideas, technologies and implications for education. *JISC Technology and Standards Watch*. Retrieved from http://www.jisc.org.uk/media/documents/techwatch/tsw0701b.pdf

Anderson, R. J., Anderson, R., Vandegrift, T., Wolfman, S., & Yasuhara, K. (2003). Promoting interaction in large classes with computer-mediated feedback. In *Designing for Change in Networked Learning Environments, Proceedings of CSCL 2003*, Bergen, (pp. 119-123).

Anderson, T. (2005). Distance learning—Social software's killer app? *Proceedings from Conference of the Open and Distance Learning Association of Australia (ODLAA)*. Adelaide, South Australia: University of South Australia.

Anderson, T. (2009). *The open access scholar*. Presented at the Open Access Week 2009, Athabasca University. Pdf and audio recording. Retrieved June 8, 2011, from http://hdl.handle.net/2149/2320

Anderson, R. E. (2008). Implications of the information and knowledge society for education. In Voogt, J., & Knezek, G. (Eds.), *International handbook of information technology in primary and secondary education* (pp. 5–22). Springer. doi:10.1007/978-0-387-73315-9_1

Anderson, T. (2004). Toward a theory of online learning. In Anderson, T., & Elloumi, F. (Eds.), *Theory and practice of online learning* (pp. 33–60). Canada: Athabasca University.

An, S.-K., & Gower, K. K. (2009). How do the news media frame crises? A content analysis of crisis news coverage. *Public Relations Review*, *35*(2), 107–112. doi:10.1016/j.pubrev.2009.01.010

Antonesei, L. (Ed.). (2009). *Ghid pentru cercetarea educației. Un "abecedar" pentru studenți, masteranzi, profesori*. Iași, Romania: Polirom.

Ardito, C., Lanzilotti, R., Pederson, T., & Piccinno, A. (2008). Experiencing the past through the senses: An m-learning game at archaeological parks. *IEEE MultiMedia*, *15*(4), 76–81. doi:10.1109/MMUL.2008.87

Armstrong, J., & Franklin, T. (2008). *A review of current and developing international practice in the use of social networking (Web 2.0) in higher education*. Franklin Consulting.

Arnaud, M. (2000). *How to improve group interactions in open and distance learning configurations*. [Electronic Version]. International Federation of Information Processing Conference. Retrieved October 3, 2003, from http://www.ifip.or.at/con2000/iceut2000/iceut02-01.pdf

Arrington, M. (2005, September 7). 85% of college students use Facebook. *TechCrunch*. Retrieved January 22, 2012, from http://www.techcrunch.com/2005/09/07/85-of-college-students-use-facebook/

Arvidsson, A. (2005). Brands – A critical perspective. *Journal of Consumer Culture*, *5*(2), 235–258. doi:10.1177/1469540505053093

Asur, S., & Huberman, B. A. (2010). Predicting the future with social media. In *International Conference on Web Intelligence and Intelligent Agent Technology*, Vol. 1 (pp. 492-499). Toronto, Canada: IEEE Press.

Atkinson, C. (2009). *The backchannel: How audiences are using Twitter and social media and changing presentations forever*. New Riders Press.

Ausubel, D. (1963). *The psychology of meaningful verbal learning*. New York, NY: Grune and Stratton.

Ausubel, D. P. (1978). In defense of advance organizers: A reply to the critics. *Review of Educational Research*, *48*, 251–257.

Badaracco, C. H. (Ed.). (2002). Special issue on innovative pedagogy. *Public Relations Review*, *28*(2), 135–208. doi:10.1016/S0363-8111(02)00119-4

Badarocco, C. H. (2002). The linked classroom as studio: Connectivity and the etymology of networks. *Public Relations Review*, *28*, 149–156. doi:10.1016/S0363-8111(02)00121-2

Bai, H. (2003). Student motivation and social presence in online learning: Implications for future research. In C. Crawford, D. A. Willis, R. Carlsen, I. Gibson, K. McFerrin, J. Price, & R. I. Weber (Eds.), *Proceedings from The Society for Information Technology and Teacher Education International Conference* (2714-2720). Chesapeake, VA: AACE.

Baird, D. (2006). Learning 2.0: Digital, social and always-on. *Barking Robot*. Retrieved June 3, 2010 from http://www.debaird.net/blendededunet/2006/04/learning_styles.html

Baird, D., & Fisher, M. (2010). Social media, Gen Y and digital learning styles. In Dasgupta, S. (Ed.), *Social computing: Concepts, methodologies, tools and applications*. Hershey, PA: IGI Global Publishing.

Bakshy, E., Marlow, C., Rosenn, I., & Adamic, L. (2012). The role of social networks in information diffusion. *Facebook, Inc*. Retrieved January 15, 2012 from http://www.scribd.com/facebook/d/78445521-Role-of-Social-Networks-in-Information-Diffusion

Balasubramanian, K., Clarke-Okah, W., Daniel, J., Ferreira, F., Kanwar, A., & Kwan, A. ... West, P. (2009). *ICT's for higher education: Background paper from the Commonwealth of Learning*. Paris, France: UNESCO Retrieved June 5, 2012, from http://unesdoc.unesco.org/images/0018/001832/183207e.pdf

Balcom Group. (2007). Retrieved from http://www.thebalcomgroup.com/node/124

Ball, M. (2011). *Social media man! (Infographic)* Retrieved August 3, 2011, from http://www.onesocialmedia.com/tag/youtube-statistics

Barab, S. A., & Duffy, T. (2000). From practice fields to communities of practice. In Jonassen, D., & Land, S. M. (Eds.), *Theoretical foundations of learning environments* (pp. 25–56). Mahwah, NJ: Lawrence Erlbaum Associates.

Baron, N. (2008). *Always on: Language in an online and mobile world*. New York, NY: Oxford University Press.

Barrett, H. (2005). *Digital storytelling research design*. Retrieved March 14, 2012, from http://electronicportfolios.com/digistory/ResearchDesign.pdf

Barrett, H. (2006). Researching and evaluating digital storytelling as a deep learning tool. In C. Crawford, et al. (Eds.), *Proceedings of Society for Information Technology and Teacher Education International Conference 2006* (pp. 647–654). Chesapeake, VA: AACE.

Barry, W. I. A. (2005). Teaching public relations in the information age: A case study at an Egyptian University. *Public Relations Review, 31*(3), 355–361. doi:10.1016/j.pubrev.2005.05.020

Baudrillard, J. (2007). *In the shadow of the silent majority*. Cambridge, MA: MIT Press.

Bauerlein, M. (2008). *The dumbest generation: How the digital age stupefies young Americans and jeopardizes our future (or, don't trust anyone under 30)*. New York, NY: The Penguin Group.

Beakenridge, D. (2011). *The social media audit*. Retrieved January 9, 2012, from http://www.deirdrebreakenridge.com/2011/03/the-social-media-audit/#.TwsASUpWYXx

BECTA. (2006). *Safeguarding children in a digital world. Developing a strategic approach to e-safety*. BECTA Publication. Retrieved February 13, 2008, from http://publications.becta.org.uk/download.cfm?resID=25933

Becta. (2009). *Harnessing technology: Emerging technology trends*. University of Oxford (Department of Education).

Belisle, C. (2006). Literacy and the digital knowledge revolution. In Martin, A., & Madigan, D. (Eds.), *Digital literacies for learning* (pp. 51–67). London, UK: Facet.

Beliveau, L., et al. (2011). *New possibilities for teaching and learning: Yammer*. Retrieved March 1, 2012, from https://wiki.itap.purdue.edu/display/INSITE/Yammer#Yammer-YammerinEducationalSettings

Benjamin, N., Camoens, A., & Kumar, M. (2010, Tuesday August 31). Namewee under probe over video. *The Star Online*.

Ben-Joseph, E., Ishii, H., Underkoffler, J., Piper, B., & Yeung, L. (2011). Urban simulation and the luminous planning table: Bridging the gap between the digital and the tangible. *Journal of Planning Education and Research, 21*, 196–203.

Benkler, J. (2006). *The wealth of networks: How social production transforms markets and freedom*. New Haven, CT: Yale University Press.

Bennett, S., Maton, K., & Kervin, L. (2008). The 'digital natives' debate: A critical review of the evidence. *British Journal of Educational Technology*, *39*(5), 775–786. doi:10.1111/j.1467-8535.2007.00793.x

Berger, B. K., Reber, B. H., & Heyman, W. C. (2007). You can't homogenize success in communication management: PR leaders take diverse paths to top. *International Journal of Strategic Communication*, *1*(1), 53–71. doi:10.1080/15531180701285301

Bernays, E. (1980). *Public relations*. Norman, OK: University of Oklahoma.

Berners-Lee, T. (2006). *Developer works interviews: Tim Berners-Lee, Originator of the Web and director of the World Wide Web Consortium talks about where we've come, and about the challenges and opportunities ahead.* Interview transcription retrieved on February 1, 2012 from http://www.ibm.com/developerworks/podcast/dwi/cm-int082206txt.html.

Bernstein, M., Kairam, S., Suh, B., Hong, L., & Chi, E. H. (2010). A torrent of tweets: Managing information overload in online social streams. In *Proceedings CHI 2010 Workshop on Microblogging*. Retrieved from http://www.parc.com/content/attachments/torrent-of-tweets.pdf

Bertot, J. C., Jaeger, P. T., & Grimes, J. M. (2010). Using ICTs to create a culture of transparency: E-government and social media as openness and anti-corruption tools for societies. *Government Information Quarterly*, *27*, 264–271. doi:10.1016/j.giq.2010.03.001

Betta, C. (2007). *Social networking and academic life. Research Assignment, Literature Report*. Delft University of Technology.

Bielaczyc, K., & Collins, A. (1999). Learning communities in classrooms: a reconceptualization of educational practice. In Reigeluth, C. (Ed.), *Instructional-design theories and models: A new paradigm of instructional theory* (Vol. 2, pp. 269–292). Mahwah, NJ: Lawrence Erlbaum Associates.

Billinghurst, M., Kato, H., & Poupyrev, I. (2011). The MagicBook - Moving seamlessly between reality and virtuality. *IEEE Computer Graphics and Applications*, *21*(3), 6–8.

Billings, D. M., & Halstead, J. A. (2008). *Teaching in nursing: A guide for faculty*. Lavoisier SAS.

Biocca, F., Harms, C., & Burgoon, J. K. (2003). Criteria for a theory and measure of social presence. *Presence (Cambridge, Mass.)*, *12*(5), 456–480. doi:10.1162/105474603322761270

Bitter, S., & Muller, A. (2011). Social networking tools and research information systems: Do they compete? *Proceedings of the ACM WebSci'11* [online], June 14-17 2011, Koblenz, Germany, (pp. 1-4). Retrieved June 20, 2011, from http://journal.webscience.org/533/

Bittner, E., & Leimeister, J. M. (2011). *Towards CSR 2.0 – Potentials and challenges of Web 2.0 for corporate social responsibility communication*. Paper presented at the annual meeting of the European Academy of Management (EURAM)

Blankenship, M. (2011). How social media can and should impact higher education. *Education Digest: Essential Readings Condensed for Quick Review*, *76*(7), 39–42.

Blau, I., Mor, N., & Neuthal, T. (2009). Open the windows of communication: Promoting interpersonal and group interactions using blogs in higher education. *Interdisciplinary Journal of E-Learning and Learning Objects*, *5*, 233–246.

Block, J. (2008). Issues for DSM-V: Internet addiction. *The American Journal of Psychiatry*, *165*, 306–307. doi:10.1176/appi.ajp.2007.07101556

Blood, R. (2002). *The weblog handbook: Practical advice on creating and maintaining your blog.* Cambridge.

Bojärs, U., Breslin, J., Finn, A., & Decker, S. (2008) Using the Semantic Web for linking and reusing data across Web 2.0 communities. *The Journal of Web Semantics, Special Issue on the Semantic Web and Web 2.0.*

Bollman, M., & Wright, J. (2008). Professors and students come Facebook to Facebook. *Lee Clarion*. Retrieved February 3, 2012, from http://www.leeclarion.com/life/2008/09/17/professors-and-students-come-facebook-to-facebook/

Bolsinger, K. (2010). *How to conduct a social media audit*. Retrieved January 9, 2012, from http://socialfresh.com/social-media-audit/

Borau, K., Ullrich, C., Feng, J., & Shen, R. (2009). Microblogging for language learning: Using Twitter to train communicative and cultural competence. In Spaniol, M. (Eds.), *ICWL 2009, LNCS 5686* (pp. 78–87). Berlin, Germany: Springer-Verlag. doi:10.1007/978-3-642-03426-8_10

Borgman, C. (2006). What can studies of e-learning teach us about collaboration in e-research? Some findings from digital library studies. *Computer Supported Cooperative Work, 15*(4), 359–383. doi:10.1007/s10606-006-9024-1

Borgman, C. (2007). *Scholarship in the digital age: Information, infrastructure, and the Internet*. MIT Press.

Bosch, T. E. (2009). Using online social networking for teaching and learning: Facebook use at the University of Cape Town. *Communication, 35*(2), 185–200.

Bosco, J. (2010). *Participatory learning in schools: Square peg, round hole*. 2010 Digital Media Learning Conference. Retrieved March 5, 2010, from http://www.scribd.com/doc/33297174/Participatory-Learning-in-Schools-Square-Peg-Round-Hole

Boss, S. (2011). Technology integration: A short history. *Edutopia.org* (The George Lucas Educational Foundation). Retrieved 12th November, 2011, from http://www.edutopia.org/technology-integration-history.

Boulos, M., & Wheeler, S. (2007). The emerging Web 2.0 social software: An enabling suite of sociable technologies in health and health care education. *Health Information and Libraries Journal, 24*(1), 2–23. doi:10.1111/j.1471-1842.2007.00701.x

Bowen, S. A. (2005). A practical model for ethical decision making in issues management and public relations. *Journal of Public Relations Research, 17*(3), 191–216. doi:10.1207/s1532754xjprr1703_1

Bowen, S. A., & Rawlings, B. L. (2005). What is a conscience? In Heath, R. L. (Ed.), *Encyclopedia of public relations* (pp. 205–210). Thousand Oaks, CA: Sage Publications.

boyd, d. (2007). Social network sites: Public, private, or what? *Knowledge Tree*. Retrieved from 1st February, 2011, http://www.danah.org/papers/KnowledgeTree.pdf

boyd, d. (2008). *Facebook*'s privacy trainwreck: Exposure, invasion, and social convergence. *Convergence: the International Journal of Research into New Media Technologies, 14*(1), 13-20.

boyd, d. m., & Ellison, N. B. (2007). Social network sites: Definition, history, and scholarship. *Journal of Computer-Mediated Communication, 13*(1). Retrieved 10th November, 2011, from http://jcmc.indiana.edu/vol13/issue1/boyd.ellison.html

boyd, d., Golder, S., & Lotan, G. (2010). Tweet, tweet, retweet: Conversational aspects of retweeting on twitter. In *Proceedings of the HICSS-43 Conference*, January 2010.

Boyd, D. M., & Ellison, N. B. (2008). Social network sites: Definition, history, and scholarship. *Journal of Computer-Mediated Communication, 13*(1), 11.

Boyer, E. (1990). *Scholarship reconsidered: Priorities of the professoriate*. Retrieved October, 23, 2010, from https://depts.washington.edu/gs630/Spring/Boyer.pdf

Boynton, L., & Imfeld, C. (2002). *Virtual issues in traditional texts: How introductory PR textbooks address Internet technology issues*. A paper presented in The AEJMC 2002 Convention in Miami Beach, USA.

Brabazon, T. (2007). *The university of Google*. Aldershot, UK: Ashgate.

Bradley, J., & McDonald, M. (2012). *La organización social. Convertir en resultados las oportunidades de las redes sociales*. Barcelona, España: Profit Editorial.

Bradley, J., & McDonald, M. (2011). *The social organization. How to use social media to tap the collective genius of your customers and employees*. United States: Gartner Inc. Harvard School Publishing Corporation.

Brady, K. P., Holcomb, L. B., & Smith, B. V. (2010). The use of alternative social networking sites in higher educational settings: A case study of the e-learning benefits of Ning in education. *Journal of Interactive Online Learning, 9*(2), 152–171.

Bransford, J. D., Brown, A. L., & Cocking, R. R. (Eds.). (2000). *How people learn: Brain, mind, experience, and school*. Washington, DC: National Academy Press.

Breakenridge, D. (2008). *PR 2.0: New media, new tools, new audiences*. New Jersey: FT Press.

Breakenridge, D., & Solis, B. (2009). *Putting the public back in public relations: How social media is reinventing the aging business of PR*. New Jersey: FT Press.

Brescia, W. F., & Miller, M. T. (2006). What's it worth? The perceived benefits of instructional blogging. *Electronic Journal for the Integration of Technology in Education, 5*, 44–52.

Brett, P., & Cousin, G. (2010). *Student led network learning design*. Paper presented at 7th International Conference on Networked Learning, 2010, Aalborg, Denmark.

Brinkerhoff, J. (2006). Effects of a long-duration, professional development academy on technology skills, computer self-efficacy, and technology integration beliefs and practices. *Journal of Research on Technology in Education, 39*(1), 22–43.

British Library/JISC. (2011). *Researchers of tomorrow: A three years (BL/JISC) study tracking the research behavior of 'Generation Y' doctoral students. Second annual report 2010-2011*. Retrieved June 30, 2011, from http://www.jisc.ac.uk/news/stories/2011/06/researchersoftomorrow.aspx

Broll, W., Lindt, I., Ohlenburg, J., Wittkämper, M., Yuan, C., & Novotny, T. … Strothmann, A. (2004). *ARTHUR: A collaborative augmented environment for architectural design and urban planning. Proceedings of Seventh International Conference on Humans and Computers* (HC 2004), (pp. 102-109).

Brook, C., & Oliver, R. (2003). Online learning communities: Investigating a design framework. *Australasian Journal of Educational Technology, 19*(2), 139–160.

Brown, J. S., & Adler, R. P. (2008). Minds on fire: Open education, the long tail, and learning 2.0. *EDUCAUSE Review, 43*(1), 16–32.

Brown, S. A. (2012). Seeing Web 2.0 in context: A study of academic perceptions. *The Internet and Higher Education, 15*, 50–57. doi:10.1016/j.iheduc.2011.04.003

Bruffee, K. (1984). Collaborative learning and the conversation of mankind. *College English, 46*(7), 635–652. doi:10.2307/376924

Bruffee, K. A. (1993). *Collaborative Learning: Higher education, interdependence, and the authority of knowledge*. Baltimore, MD: John Hopkins University Press. doi:10.2307/358879

Bruner, J. (1990). *Acts of meaning*. Cambridge, MA: Harvard University Press.

Brynjolfsson, E., & McAfee, A. (2011). *Race against the machine: How the digital revolution is accelerating innovation, driving productivity, and irreversibly transforming employment and the economy*. Lexington, MA: Digital Frontier Press.

Buchem, I., & Camacho, M. (2011). *M-project: First steps to applying action research in designing a mobile learning course in higher education* (pp. 123–135). London Mobile Learning Group.

Bugeja, M. (2006). Facing the Facebook. *The Chronicle of Higher Education, 52*(21), C1–C4.

Bullen, M., & Morgan, T. (2011). Digital learners not digital natives. *La Cuestion Universitaria, 7*, 60-68. Retrieved January 25, 2012, from http://www.lacuestionuniversitaria.upm.es/web/articulo.php?id_articulo=84

Burmark, L. (2004, May/June). Visual presentations that prompt, flash & transform. *Media and Methods, 40*(6), 4–5.

Caballe, S., Xhafa, F., & Barolli, L. (2010). Using mobile devices to support online collaborative learning. *Mobile Information Systems - Mobile and Wireless Networks, 6*(1), 27–47.

Cahill, B. (2009, Spring). Your attention please: The right way to integrate social media into your marketing plans. *Public Relations Strategist*. Retrieved June 13, 2012, from http://www.prsa.org/intelligence/thestrategist/articles/view/6k-020925/102/your_attention_please_the_right_way_to_integrate_s

Cain, J. (2007). Online social networking issues within academia and pharmacy education. *American Journal of Pharmaceutical Education, 72*(1).

Cain, J., Scott, D. R., & Akers, P. (2009). Pharmacy students' Facebook activity and opinions regarding accountability and e-professionalism. *American Journal of Pharmaceutical Education, 73*(6), 1–6. doi:10.5688/aj7306104

Campbell, H. A., & La Pastina, A. C. (2010). How the iPhone became divine: New media, religion and the intertextual circulation of meaning. *New Media & Society, 12*(7), 1191–1207. doi:10.1177/1461444810362204

Cancel, A. E., Cameron, G. T., Sallot, L. M., & Mitrook, M. A. (1997). It depends: A contingency theory of accommodation in public relations. *Journal of Public Relations Research*, *9*(1), 31–63. doi:10.1207/s1532754xjprr0901_02

Capriotti, P., & Moreno, A. (2007). Corporate citizenship and public relations: The importance and interactivity of social responsibility issues on corporate websites. *Public Relations Review*, *33*(1), 84–91. doi:10.1016/j.pubrev.2006.11.012

Carr, N. (2011, April 4). Interview by project information literacy. The age of perpetual distraction. *Project Information Literacy "Smart Talks,"* 6. Retrieved March 30, 2012, from http://projectinfolit.org/st/carr.asp

Carr, N. (2010). *The shallows: What the internet is doing to our brain*. New York, NY: W. W. Norton & Company.

Cassidy, E. D., Britsch, J., Griffin, G., Manolovitz, T., Shen, L., & Turney, L. (2011). Higher education and emerging technologies: student usage, preferences and lessons for library services. *Higher Education and Emerging Technologies*, *50*(4), 380–391.

Cassidy, J. (2006). Me media. *New Yorker (New York, N.Y.)*, *82*(13), 50–59.

Castells, M. (1996). *The information age: Economy, society and culture (Vol. I)*. New Jersey: Blackwell.

CDE, Center for Digital Education. (2008). *A connected life: A look at mobile strategies for schools, colleges and universities*. E-Republic.

Centrul de Resurse pentru Organizaţii Studenţeşti. (2011). *Universitatea Alternativă: Model educaţional pilot*. Retrieved April 12, 2010, from https://sites.google.com/site/croshq/comunicare-si-parteneri/materiale-de-comunicare/PrezentareUAfinal.pdf?attredirects=0

Chan, A. (2011, July 26). The web: Just as addictive as cigarettes and booze. *Huffington Post*. Retrieved from http://www.huffingtonpost.com/2011/07/26/internet-addictivealcohol-smoking-addiction_n_910214.html

Chapman, A., & Russell, R. (2009). Shared infrastructure services landscape study: A survey of the use of web 2.0 tools and services in the UK HE sector. *JISC Landscape Study*. Retrieved from http://blogs.ukoln.ac.uk/jusc-sis-landscape/

Charnigo, L., & Barnett-Ellis, P. (2007). Checking out Facebook.com: The impact of a digital trend on academic libraries. *Information Technology and Libraries*, *26*(1), 23–34.

Chen, S. (2009). Corporate responsibilities in internet-enabled social networks. *Journal of Business Ethics*, *90*(4), 523–536. doi:10.1007/s10551-010-0604-0

Chen, Y.-S., Kao, T.-C., & Sheu, J.-P. (2005). Realizing outdoor independent learning with a butterfly-watching mobile learning system. *Journal of Educational Computing Research*, *33*(4), 395–417. doi:10.2190/0PAB-HRN9-PJ9K-DY0C

Chickering, A. W., & Gamson, Z. F. (1987). Seven principles for good practice in undergraduate education. In *AAHE Bulletin*, (pp. 3–7).

Chinnery, A. (2006). Cold case: Reopening the file on tolerance in teaching and learning across difference. In Howe, K. (Ed.), *Philosophy of Education 2005* (pp. 200–208).

Chun-Hung, L., & Lee, C.-F. (2009). The design of a mobile navigation system based on QR codes for historic buildings. *Proceedings of the 14th International Conference on Computer Aided Architectural Design Research in Asia*, Yunlin, Taiwan, (pp. 103-112).

CIBER, University College London and Emerald Group Publishing Ltd. (2010). *Social media and research workflow*. Retrieved from http://www.ucl.ac.uk/infostudies/research/ciber/social-media-report.pdf

Cigarettes – Glamour of Smoke. (2009, September 23). Retrieved December 5, 2011 from http://cigarettes-.wikispaces.com/Glamour+of+Smoke

Clough, G. (2010). Informal learning with mobile and social technologies: Framework for analysis. In E. Brown (Ed.), *Education in the wild: Contextual and location-based mobile learning in action* (pp. 4–6). A report from the STELLAR Alpine Rendez-Vous workshop series. Retrieved March 7, 2012, from http://www.lsri.nottingham.ac.uk/ejb/preprints/ARV_Education_in_the_wild.pdf

Cmeciu, C., & Cmeciu, D. (2011). New insights into corporate social responsibility: The semiotic act of experiencing a city through street naming. In Wasik, Z. (Ed.), *Unfolding the semiotic Web in urban discourse* (pp. 163–180). Frankfurt am Main, Germany: Peter Lang.

Cobb, S. C. (2009). Social presence and online learning: A current view from a research perspective. *Journal of Interactive Online Learning, 8*(3), 241–254.

Cohen, H. (2011). *30 social media definitions*. Retrieved January 8, 2012, from http://heidicohen.com/social-media-definition/

Cohen, M., Adelman, L., Bresnick, T., Freeman, M., Salas, E., & Riedel, S. (2007). Dialogue as medium(and message) for training critical thinking. In R. Hoffman (Ed.), *Expertise out of the context-Proceedings of the Sixth International Conference on Naturalistic Decision Making*, (pp. 219-229). Lawrence Erlbaum Associates.

Colley, H., Hodkinson, P., & Malcom, J. (2002). *Non-formal learning: mapping the conceptual terrain*. A Consultation Report. Retrieved December 20, 2012, from http://www.infed.org/archives/e-texts/colley_informal_learning.htm

Collis, B. (2012). *Digital learners: Will they surprise us?* Key note talk given at the TIES 2012 conference, Barcelona, 1-3 February. Retrieved February 15, 2012, from http://ties2012.eu/en/pg-videos.html

Collis, B., & Moonen, J. (2008). Web 2.0 tools and processes in higher education: quality perspectives. *Educational Media International, 45*(2), 93–106. doi:10.1080/09523980802107179

Conrad, R.-M., & Donaldson, J. A. (2004). *Engaging the online learner*. San Francisco, CA: Jossey-Bass.

Coombs, T., & Rybacki, K. (1999). Public relations education: Where is pedagogy? *Public Relations Review, 25*(1), 55–63. doi:10.1016/S0363-8111(99)80127-1

Coombs, W. T., & Holladay, S. J. (2007). *It's not just PR*. Malden, UK: Blackwell Publishing.

Copley, J. (2007). Audio and video podcasts of lecture for campus-based students: Production and evaluation of student use. *Innovations in Education and Teaching International, 44*(4), 387. doi:10.1080/14703290701602805

Corlett, D., Sharples, M., Chan, T., & Bull, S. (2005). A mobile learning organiser for university students. *Journal of Computer Assisted Learning, 21*, 162–170. doi:10.1111/j.1365-2729.2005.00124.x

Cornellisen, J. (2005). *Corporate communications: Theory and practice* (2nd ed.). London, UK: Sage Publications.

Cornu, B. (2007). *Being a teacher in the knowledge society.* Presentation. European, Distance and E-Learning Network (EDEN). Conference, Stockholm 2007. Retrieved February 10, 2011, from http://www.eden-online.org/contents/conferences/OCRCs/Poitiers/Keynotes/Cornu.ppt

Correa, T., Hinsley, A. W., & de Zuniga, H. G. (2010). Who interacts on the Web? The intersection of users' personality and social media use. *Computers in Human Behavior, 26*, 247–253. doi:10.1016/j.chb.2009.09.003

Correia, A., & Davis, N. (2008). Intersecting communities of practice in distance education: The program team and the online course community. *Distance Education, 29*(3), 289–306. doi:10.1080/01587910802395813

Coruña, F. C. (2009). *Mural de grupo. Facultad CC Comunicación Coruña*. Retrieved February 24, 2012, from http://www.flickr.com/groups/cienciascomunicacion/

Costa, C. (2011). *The Twitterati ... Workshop on Twitter for researchers.* Retrieved from http://virtual-doc.salford.ac.uk/pgrs/2011/02/25/the-twitterati/.

Costa, C., Beham, G., Reinhardt, W., & Sillaots, M. (2008). Microblogging in technology enhanced learning: A use-case inspection of PPE summer school 2008. In: *Proceedings of the 2nd SIRTEL Workshop on Social Information Retrieval for Technology Enhanced Learning.*

Couillard, C. (2009). *Facebook: The pros and cons of use in education*. Unpublished doctoral dissertation, University of Wisconsin-Stout, US.

Coverdale, A. (2011). *Negotiating doctoral practices and academic identities through the adoption and use of social and participative media*. Paper presented at ECEL 2011, Brighton, 10-11 November 2011.

Cox, A. (2005). What are communities of practice? A comparative review of four seminal works. *Journal of Information Science, 31*(6), 527–540. doi:10.1177/0165551505057016

Creaser, F. (2011). The merits of using "EthnoQuest" as an English language learning tool and a medium of cultural transmission. European Association for Computer Assisted Language Learning (EUROCALL). *The EUROCALL Review, 19.* Retrieved from http://www.eurocall-languages.org/review/19/No19.pdf

Crook, C., Cummings, J., Fisher, T., Graber, R., Harrison, C., & Lewin, C. ... Sharples, M. (2008). *Web 2.0 technologies for learning: The current landscape – Opportunities, challenges and tensions.* BECTA Publication. Retrieved January 15, 2011, from http://dera.ioe.ac.uk/1474/1/becta_2008_web2_currentlandscape_litrev.pdf

Cross, S., & Conole, G. (January 2009). *Learn about learning design.* Institute of Educational Technology, The Open University (UK). Retrieved from http://ouldi.open.ac.uk/Learn%20about%20learning%20design.pdf

Curtis, L., Edwards, C., Fraser, K. L., Gudelsky, S., Holmquist, J., & Thornton, K. (2010). Adoption of social media for public relations by nonprofit organizations. *Public Relations Review, 36*(1), 90–92. doi:10.1016/j.pubrev.2009.10.003

Cutlip, S., Center, A., & Broom, G. (2000). *Effective public relations* (8th ed.). London, UK: Prentice-Hall.

Dabbagh, N., & Reo, R. (2010). Back to the future. Tracing the roots and learning affordances of social software. In Lee, M., & McLoughlin, C. (Eds.), *Web 2.0-based e-learning: Applying social informatics for tertiary teaching* (pp. 1–20). Hershey, PA: Idea Group Inc.doi:10.4018/978-1-60566-294-7.ch001

Dahlsrud, A. (2008). How corporate social responsibility is defined: an analysis of 37 definitions. *Corporate Social Responsibility and Environmental Management, 15*(1), 1–13. doi:10.1002/csr.132

Dahlstrom, E., de Boor, T., Grunwald, P., & Vockley, M. (2011). *The ECAR national study of undergraduate students and information technology.* Boulder, CO: EDUCAUSE Center for Applied Research. Retrieved from http://www.educause.edu/ecar

Davi, A., Frydenberg, M., & Gulati, G. (2007). Blogging across the disciplines: Integrating technology to enhance liberal learning. *MERLOT Journal of Online Learning and Teaching, 3*(3), 222233.

David, P. A., & Foray, D. (2003). Economic fundamentals of the knowledge society. *Policy Futures in Education-An e-Journal, 1*(1).

Davis, C. H. F., III, Deil-Amen, R., Rios-Aguilar, C., & Gonzalez Canche, M. S. (2012). *Social media in higher education: A literature review and research directions.* The Center for the Study of Higher Education. Printed by University of Arizona and Claremont Graduate University. Retrieved June 5, 2012, from http://works.bepress.com/cgi/viewcontent.cgi?article=1003&context=hfdavis

Dawson, S. (2006). A study of the relationship between student and communication interaction and sense of community. *The Internet and Higher Education, 9,* 153–162. doi:10.1016/j.iheduc.2006.06.007

de Haan, J. (2011). Teaching and learning English through digital game projects. *Digital Culture and Education, 3*(1), 46–5

De Vocht, L., Selver, S., Ebner, M., & Mühlburger, H. (2011). Semantically driven social data aggregation interfaces for research 2.0. In *11th International Conference on Knowledge Management and Knowledge Technologies* (pp. 1-10).

De Wever, B., Van Keer, H., Schellens, T., & Valcke, M. (2011). Assessing collaboration in a wiki: The reliability of university students' peer assessment. *Journal of Internet and Higher Education, 14,* 201–206. doi:10.1016/j.iheduc.2011.07.003

DeAndrea, D. C., Ellison, N. B., LaRose, R., Steinfield, C., & Fiore, A. (2012). Serious social media: On the use of social media for improving students' adjustment. *The Internet and Higher Education, 15*(1), 15–23. doi:10.1016/j.iheduc.2011.05.009

Dearstyne, B. W. (2007). Blogs, mashups, and wikis oh my! *The Information Management Journal,* July/August, 24-33.

Dede, C. (1996). The evolution of distance education: Emerging technologies and distributed learning. *American Journal of Distance Education, 10*(2), 4–36. doi:10.1080/08923649609526919

Deluca, J. (2010). *24 hour unplugged*. College Park, MD: University of Maryland. International Center for Media & the Public Agenda. Retrieved on December 30, 2011, from the http://withoutmedia.wordpress.com.

Demski, J. (2009). Facebook training wheels. *The Journal, 36*(4), 24–28.

Denzin, N. K., & Lincoln, Y. S. (1994). *Handbook of qualitative research*. Thousand Oaks, CA: Sage Publications.

Department of Trade & Industry and the Institute of Public Relations. (2003). *Unlocking the potential of public relations: developing good practice*. London, UK: European Centre for Business Excellence. Retrieved 24th June, 2010, from http://www.lombard-media.lu/pdf/0312_Potential-PR.pdf

Derntl, M. (2008). *Employing student blogs as reflective diaries in a lab course*. Paper presented at the proceedings of IADIS International Conference on Cognition and Exploratory Learning in Digital Age (CELDA 2008), Freiburg, Germany.

Derntl, M., & Graf, S. (2009). Impact of learning styles on student blogging behavior. *Advanced Learning Technologies* [IEEE CS Press.]. *ICALT, 2009*, 369–373.

Dertouzos, M. L., & Moses, J. (1979). *The computer age: A twenty year view*. Cambridge, MA: MIT Press. doi:10.1080/07377366.1982.10401297

DeSchryver, M., Mishra, P., Koehler, M., & Francis, A. P. (2009). Moodle vs. Facebook: Does using Facebook for discussions in an online course enhance perceived social presence and student interaction? In C. Crawford, D. A. Willis, R. Carlsen, I. Gibson, K. McFerrin, J. Price, & R. I. Weber (Eds.), *Proceedings from The Society for Information Technology and Teacher Education International Conference* (329-336). Chesapeake, VA: AACE.

Dexter, S., Anderson, R., & Becker, H. (1999). Teachers' views of computers as catalysts for changes in their teaching practice. *Journal of Research on Computing in Education, 31*(3), 221–239.

Diga, M., & Kelleher, T. (2009). Social media use, perceptions of decision-making power, and public relations roles. *Public Relations Review, 35*(4), 440–442. doi:10.1016/j.pubrev.2009.07.003

Digitallearning.macfound.org. (n.d.). *About the initiative*. The John D. and Catherine T. MacArthur Foundation. Retrieved January 8, 2012, from http://digitallearning.macfound.org/site/c.enJLKQNlFiG/b.2029319/k.4E7B/About_the_Initiative.htm

Dimitrova, D. (2007). New media technologies. In L. L. Kaid & C. Holtz-Bacha (Eds.), *Encyclopedia of political communication*. London, UK: Sage Publications. Retrieved March 16, 2009, from www.sage-ereference.com/politicalcommunication/Article_n434.html

Dippold, D. (2009). Peer feedback through blogs: Student and teacher perceptions in an advanced German class. *ReCALL, 21*(1), 18–36. doi:10.1017/S095834400900010X

DiStaso, M. W., Stacks, D. W., & Botanc, C. H. (2009). State of public relations education in the United States: 2006 report on a national survey of executives and academics. *Public Relations Review, 35*, 254–269. doi:10.1016/j.pubrev.2009.03.006

Dixon e-skills Model. (n.d.). Retrieved from www.learningtechnologies.ac.uk.org and www.e-skills.com

Dohn, N. B. (2009). Web 2.0: Inherent tensions and evident challenges for education. *Computer-Supported Collaborative Learning, 4*(4), 343–363. doi:10.1007/s11412-009-9066-8

Dorner, R., Grimm, P., & Abawi, D. (2002). Synergies between interactive training simulations and digital storytelling: A component-based framework. *Computers & Graphics, 26*, 45–55. doi:10.1016/S0097-8493(01)00177-7

Douglas, A. C., Mills, J. E., Niang, M., Stepchenkova, S., Byun, S., Ruffini, C., & Blanton, M. (2008). Internet addition: Meta-synthesis of qualitative research. *Computers in Human Behavior, 24*(6), 3027–3044. doi:10.1016/j.chb.2008.05.009

Downes, S. (2005, October 16). E-learning 2.0. *eLearn Magazine*. Retrieved August 21, 2011, from http://www.downes.ca/post/31741

Downes, S. (2007). Places to go: Facebook. *Journal of Online Education, 4*(1). Retrieved from http://www.innovateonline.info/index.php?view=article%id=517

Dozier, D. M., Grunig, L. A., & Grunig, J. E. (2001). Public relations as communication campaign. In Rice, R. E., & Atkin, C. K. (Eds.), *Public communication campaigns* (3rd ed., pp. 231–248). Thousand Oaks, CA: Sage Publications.

Dron, J., & Anderson, T. (2009). Lost in social space: Information retrieval issues in Web 1.5. *Journal of Digital Information, 10*(2).

Du, H., Rosson, M., Carroll, J. M., & Ganoe, C. (2009). I felt like a contributing member of the class: Increasing class participation with classcommons. In *Proceedings of the ACM 2009 International Conference on Supporting Group Work* (Sanibel Island, Florida, USA, May 10 - 13, 2009). GROUP '09. ACM, New York, NY, (pp. 233-242).

Ducate, L. C., & Lomicka, L. L. (2008). Adventures in the blogosphere: From blog readers to blog writers. *Computer Assisted Language Learning, 21*, 9–28. doi:10.1080/09588220701865474

Dunlap, J. C., & Lowental, P. (2009). Horton hears a Tweet. *EDUCAUSE Quarterly Magazine, 32*(4). Retrieved June 5, 2012, from http://www.educause.edu/EDUCAUSE+Quarterly/EDUCAUSEQuarterlyMagazineVolum/HortonHearsaTweet/192955

Dunlap, J. C., & Lowenthal, P. R. (2009). Tweeting the night away: Using Twitter to enhance social presence. *Journal of Information Systems Education, 20*(2), 129–136.

Dunlap, J. C., & Lowhenthal, P. R. (2009). Instructional uses of Twitter. In Lowenthal, P. R., Thomas, D., Thai, A., & Yuhnke, B. (Eds.), *CU online handbook: Teach differently. Create and collaborate.* University of Colorado Denver.

Duranti, L. (2009). From digital diplomatics to digital records forensics. *Archivaria, 68*, 39–66.

Duranti, L. (2009). Diplomatics. In Bates, M., Maack, M. N., & Drake, M. (Eds.), *Encyclopedia of library and information science.* New York, NY: Marcel Dekker, Inc.

Duranti, L., & Thibodeau, K. (2006). The concept of record in interactive, experiential and dynamic environments: the view of InterPARES. *Archival Science, 6*, 13–68. doi:10.1007/s10502-006-9021-7

Dziuban, C., Moskal, P., & Brophy, J. (2007). Student Satisfaction with asynchronous learning. *Journal of Asynchronous Learning Networks, 11*(1), 87–95.

Eberhart, T. (2011). *Level up! SMEDU chats start today. Topic: our Social Media Global Education Connection Project.* Retrieved January 8, 2012, from http://socialmediaclub.org/blogs/social-media-education/level-smedu-chats-start-today-topic-our-social-media-global-education-0

Ebner, M. (2011). Is Twitter a tool for mass-education? *4th International Conference on Student Mobility and ICT,* Vienna, (pp. 1-6).

Ebner, M., & Maurer, H. (2008). Can microblogs and weblogs change traditional scientific writing? *Proceedings of E-Learn 2008,* Las Vegas, (pp. 768-776).

Ebner, M., & Reinhardt, W. (2009). Social networking in scientific conferences – Twitter as tool for strengthen a scientific community. In *Proceedings of the 1st International Workshop on Science 2.0 for TEL* (2009).

Ebner, M., Altmann, T., & Selver, S. (2011). @twitter analysis of #edmedia10 – is the #informationstream usable for the #mass. *Form@re, 74*, 1–11.

Ebner, M., Lienhardt, C., Rohs, M., & Meyer, I. (2010). Microblogs in higher education – A chance to facilitate informal and process oriented learning? *Computers & Education, 56*(1). ISSN 0360-1315

Ebner, M., Mühlburger, H., Schaffert, S., Schiefner, M., Reinhardt, W., & Wheeler, S. (2010). Getting granular on Twitter tweets from a conference and their limited usefulness for non-participants. *Proceedings of the WCC 2010 Conference* (track "Key Competencies in the Knowledge Society"). Retrieved from http://www.wcc2010.org

Ebner, M., Nagler, W., & Schön, M. (2011). The Facebook generation boon or bane for e-learning at universities? In *World Conference on Educational Multimedia, Hypermedia and Telecommunications; 2011,* (pp. 3549–3557).

Ebner, M. (2009). Introducing live microblogging: How single presentations can be enhanced by the mass. *Journal of Research in Innovative Teaching, 2*(1), 91–100.

Ebner, M., Lienhardt, C., Rohs, M., & Meyer, I. (2010). Microblogs in higher education—A chance to facilitate informal and process oriented learning? *Computers & Education, 55*, 92–100. doi:10.1016/j.compedu.2009.12.006

Ebner, M., & Lorenz, A. (2012). Web 2.0 als Basistechnologien für CSCL-Umgebungen. In Haake, J., Schwabe, G., & Wessner, M. (Eds.), *CSCL-Lernumgebungen. München, Germany*. Oldenburg.

Ebner, M., Mühlburger, H., Schaffert, S., Schiefner, M., Reinhardt, W., & Wheeler, S. (2010). *Get Granular on Twitter - Tweets from a conference and their limited usefulness 1 for non-participants* (pp. 102–113). Key Competences in the Knowledge Society.

Economist Intelligence Unit (ECI). (2008). *The future of higher education: How technology will shape learning*. A Report from the Economist Intelligence Unit, London.

Edudemic.com. (n.d.). *About*. Retrieved January 8, 2012, from http://edudemic.com/about-2/

Elliot, T. S. (1943). *Four quartets*. New York, NY.

Ellison, N. B., Steinfield, C., & Lampe, C. (2007). The benefits of Facebook "friends:" Social capital and college students' use of online social network sites. *Journal of Computer-Mediated Communication, 12*(3), 1. Retrieved January 30, 2012, from http://jcmc.indiana.edu/ vol12/issue4/ellison.html

Ellison, N. S. (2007). The benefits of Facebook friends: Exploring the relationship between college students' use of online social networks and social capital. *Journal of Computer-Mediated Communication, 12*(4). doi:10.1111/j.1083-6101.2007.00367.x

Entman, R. M. (1993). Framing: Toward clarification of a fractured paradigm. *The Journal of Communication, 43*(4), 51–58. doi:10.1111/j.1460-2466.1993.tb01304.x

ERAM. E. (2008). *Galería de Escola ERAM*. Retrieved February 24, 2012, from http://www.flickr.com/photos/escolaeram/sets/

Eriksen, T. H. (2001). *Tyranny of the moment: Fast and slow time in the information age*. London, UK: Pluto.

Eshach, H. (2007). Bridging in-school and out-of-school learning: formal, non-formal, and informal education. *Journal of Science Education and Technology, 16*(2), 171–190. doi:10.1007/s10956-006-9027-1

Eur-Lex. (2005). *Mobilising the brainpower of Europe: enabling universities to make their full contribution to the Lisbon Strategy. Opinion of the committee of the Regions on the communication from the commission*.

European Counci. (2000). *Presidency conclusions of the Lisabona European Council, 2000*. Retrieved from http://www.consilium.europa.eu/uedocs/cms_data/docs/pressdata/en/ec/00100-r1.en0.htm

Evans, C. (2008). The effectiveness of m-learning in the form of podcast revision lectures in higher education. *Computers & Education, 50*, 491–498. doi:10.1016/j.compedu.2007.09.016

Eyrich, N., Padman, M. L., & Sweetser, K. D. (2008). PR practitioners' use of social media tools and communication technology. *Public Relations Review, 34*, 412–414. doi:10.1016/j.pubrev.2008.09.010

Fabro, K. R., & Garrison, D. R. (1998). Computer conferencing and higher-order learning. *Indian Journal of Open Learning, 7*(1), 41–54.

Facebook Statistics. (2010). *Statistics*. Retrieved from http://www.facebook.com/press/info.php?statistics

Fackler, M. (2007, November 18). In Korea, a boot camp for web obsession. *New York Times*. Retrieved from http://www.nytimes.com/2007/11/18/technology/18rehab.html?pagewanted=all

Fagerberg, T., & Rekkedal, T. (2004). Enhancing the flexibility of distance education – Designing and trying out a learning environment for mobile distance learners. In T. Rekkedal, A. Dye, T. Fagerberg, S. Bredal, B. Midtsveen, & J. Russel (Eds.), *Design, Development and Evaluation of Mobile Learning at NKI Distance Education 2000-2005* (pp. 173–183). Bekkestua, Norway: NKI Forlaget. Retrieved March 6, 2012, from http://www.dye.no/articles/mlearning/m_Learning_2000_2005.pdf#page=173

Fahey, T. (1995). Privacy and the family. *Sociology, 29*, 687–703. doi:10.1177/0038038595029004008

Fairclough, N. (2005). Peripheral vision: Discourse analysis in organization studies: The case for critical realism. *Organization Studies*, *26*(6), 915–939. doi:10.1177/0170840605054610

Falas, T., & Kasanami, H. (2007). Two-dimensional barcode decoding with camera-equipped mobile phones. *Proceedings of the Fifth IEEE International Conference on Pervasive Computing and Communications Workshops*, PERCOMW, (pp. 597-600). Washington, DC: IEEE Computer Society.

Falls, J. (August 10, 2009). Public relations pros must be social media ready. *Social Media Explorer.* Retrieved January 6, 2012, from http://www.socialmediaexplorer. com/online-public-relations/public-relations-pros-must-be-social-media-ready/

Farwell, T. M., & Waters, R. D. (2010). Exploring the use of social bookmarking technology in education: An analysis of students' experiences using course-specific Delicious.com account. *Journal of Online Learning and Teaching*, *6*(2), 398–408.

Farwell, T., & Krüger-Ross, M. (2012in press). Is there (still) a place for blogging in the classroom?: Using blogging to assess writing, facilitate engagement and evaluate student attitudes. In Seo, K. (Ed.), *Using social media effectively in the classroom: Blogs, wikis, twitter and more*.

Feijóo, C., Pascu, C., Misuraca, G., & Lusoli, W. (2009). The next paradigm shift in the mobile ecosystem: Mobile social computing and the increasing relevance of users. *Communications & Strategies*, *75*, 57–77.

Ferguson, R., Clough, G., & Hosein, A. (2010). *Shifting themes, shifting roles: The development of research blogs*. Paper presented at the conference: 'Into Something Rich and Strange' - Making Sense of the Sea-Change. The 17th Association for Learning Technology Conference (ALT-C 2010), 7-9 September 2010, Nottingham, UK. Retrieved June 25, 2011 from http://oro.open.ac.uk/22962/

Fischer, E., & Reuber, A. R. (2010). Social interaction via new social media: (How) can interactions on Twitter affect effectual thinking and behavior? *Journal of Business Venturing*, *26*(1). doi:doi:10.1016/j.jbusvent.2010.1009.1002

Fischman, J. (2008, October 13). Dear Professor, students want to chat with you. *The Chronicle of Higher Education*. Retrieved January 24, 2012, from http://chronicle. com/wiredcampus/article/3384/dear-professor-students-want-to-chat-with-you

Fisher, M. (2004). *Designing courses and teaching on the Web: A "how to" guide to proven, innovative strategies*. Lanham, MD: Rowman & Littlefield Publishing Group.

Fisher, M., & Baird, D. (2006). Making mobile learning work: Utilizing mobile technology for collaboration, assessment and reflection in higher education. *Journal of Educational Technology Systems*, *35*(1), 3–30. doi:10.2190/4T10-RX04-113N-8858

Fisher, M., Coleman, P., Sparks, P., & Plett, C. (2006). Designing community learning in web-based environments. In Khan, B. H. (Ed.), *Flexible learning in an information society*. Hershey, PA: Information Science Publishing. doi:10.4018/978-1-59904-325-8.ch004

Flammia, M. (2011). *Using service-learning and global virtual team projects to integrate sustainability into the technical communication curriculum. Prodessional Communication Conference--IPCC* (pp. 1–9). IPCC.

Flatley, M. E. (2005). Blogging for enhanced teaching and learning. *Business Communication Quarterly*, *68*(1), 77–80. doi:10.1177/108056990506800111

Fletcher, J. K., & Ragins, B. R. (in press). Stone center relational theory: A window on relational mentoring. In Ragins, B. R., & Kram, K. E. (Eds.), *The handbook of mentoring: Theory, research, and practice*. Thousand Oaks, CA: Sage. doi:10.4135/9781412976619.n15

Foale, C., & Carson, L. (2006). Creating a student driven self access language learning resource. *Joint BAAL/IRAAL Conference,* Cork, September 2006.

Focus, F. (2011). *Social media usage trends among higher education faculty*. Special Report: A Magna Publication. Retrieved from http://www.facultyfocus.com/wp-content/ uploads/images/2011-social-media-report.pdf

Focus, F., & Report, S. (2010). *Twitter in higher education 2010: Usage habits and trends of today's college faculty*. Magna Publication.

Forbes, D. (2011). Beyond lecture capture: Student-generated podcasts in teacher education. *Waikato Journal of Education, 16*(1), 51–63.

Forceville, C. (1996). *Pictorial metaphor in advertising*. London, UK: Routledge. doi:10.4324/9780203272305

Foucault, M. (1977). *Discipline and punish: The birth of the prison*. New York, NY: Pantheon Books.

Foucault, M. (1984). The order of discourse. In Shapiro, M. J. (Ed.), *Language and politics* (pp. 108–138). Oxford, UK: Blackwell.

Franks, P. (2012). *Archives and archival studies in a social media world*. 4th Annual International Symposium Unpacking the Digital Shoebox: The Future of Personal Archives.

Franzen, J. (2011, May 28). Liking is for cowards: Go for what hurts. *New York Times*. Retrieved on December 30, 2012, from http://www.nytimes.com/2011/05/29/opinion/29franzen.html?pagewanted=all

Freberg, K., Grahamb, K., McGaughey, K., & Frebergc, L. A. (2011). Who are the social media influencers? A study of public perceptions of personality. *Public Relations Review, 37*(1), 90–92. doi:10.1016/j.pubrev.2010.11.001

Frydenberg, M. (2006). Principles and pedagogy: The two P's of podcasting in the information technology classroom. In *Proceedings of the Information Systems Education Conference 2006*, Vol. 23 (Dallas).

Fry, J. (2006). Scholarly research and information practices: A domain analytic approach. *Information Processing & Management, 42*, 299–316. doi:10.1016/j.ipm.2004.09.004

Frymier, A., & Thompson, C. (1992). Perceived teacher affinity- seeking in relation to perceived credibility. *Communication Education, 41*(4), 388–399. doi:10.1080/03634529209378900

Fuchs, C. (2008). *Internet and society: Social theory in the information age*. New York, NY: Routledge.

Future of media education. (2010). *Program theme presented at University film & video association conference 2011*. Retrieved from http://www.ufva.org/conference/2011/theme

Gable, R. K., & Wolf, M. B. (1993). *Instrument development in the affective domain: Measuring attitudes and values in corporate and school settings* (2nd ed.). Boston, MA: Kluwer Academic.

Gagnon, D. J. (2010). Mobile learning environments. *EDUCAUSE Quarterly, 33*.

Gamson, W., & Lasch, K. E. (1983). The political culture of social welfare policy. In Spiro, S. E., & Yuchtman-Yaar, E. (Eds.), *Evaluating the welfare state: Social and political perspectives* (pp. 397–415). New York, NY: Academic.

Garnett, F. (2010, 18 October). Heutagogy & the craft of teaching. *The Heutagogic Archives*. Retrieved 20 December, 2011, from http://heutagogicarchive.wordpress.com/2010/11/18/heutagogy-the-craft-of-teaching/

Garnett, F., & Ecclesfield, N. (2011). A framework for co-creating open scholarship. *ALT-C 2011 Proceedings Papers: Thriving in a Colder and More Challenging Climate* [open access version], (pp. 5-17). Retrieved September, 5, 2011 from http://repository.alt.ac.uk/2177/

Garrison, D. R., & Anderson, T. (2003). *E-Learning in the 21st century: A framework for research and practice*. London, UK: Routledge. doi:10.4324/9780203166093

Garrison, D. R., Anderson, T., & Archer, W. (2000). Critical inquiry in a text-based environment: Computer conferencing in higher education. *The Internet and Higher Education, 2*(2-3), 87–105. doi:10.1016/S1096-7516(00)00016-6

Garsten, C., & Lindh de Montoya, M. (2008). In retrospect: the play of shadows. In Garsten, C., & Lindh de Montoya, M. (Eds.), *Transparency in a new global order: Unveiling organizational visions* (pp. 283–289). Cheltenham, UK: Edward Elgar.

Gartner Inc. (13 January 2010). *Gartner highlights key predictions for IT organizations and users in 2010 and beyond*. Stamford, CT: Author.

Gartner Inc. (21 October 2010). *Gartner says social media in Asia Pacific is developing in different directions to the U.S. and Europe*. Hong Kong, PRC: Author.

Gattiker, U. E. (2011). *Why do social media audits fail?* Retrieved January 9, 2012, from http://commetrics.com/?p=15222

Gavan, P. L. W. (2011). Micro-blogging and the higher education classroom: Approaches and considerations. In Wankel, C. (Ed.), *Teaching arts and science with the new social media: Cutting-edge technologies in higher education* (*Vol. 3*, pp. 365–383). Emerald Group Publishing Limited.

Gelissen, J., & de Graaf, P. M. (2006). Personality, social background, and occupational career success. *Social Science Research*, *35*, 702–726. doi:10.1016/j.ssresearch.2005.06.005

Gerber, R. S. (2006). Mixing it up on the web: Legal issues arising from internet 'mashups'. *Intellectual Property & Technology Law Journal*, *18*(8), 11–14.

Giacomantonio, L. (2011). *20 ways to use Edmodo*. Retrieved from http://www.slideshare.net/seyfert6/20-ways-to-use-edmodo

Gibson, D. (2009, 19 September 2009). Communication for the connected generation. *The Star Online*.

Giddens, A. (2002). *Runaway world. How globalization is reshaping our lives*. London, UK: Profile Books.

Gilpin, D. (2010). Working the Twittersphere: Microblogging as professional identity construction. In Z. Papacharissi (Ed.), *The networked self: Identity, community and culture on social network sites*. New York, NY: Routledge. Retrieved from http://asu.academia.edu/DawnGilpin/Papers/120301/Working_the_Twittersphere_Microblogging_as_professional_identity_construction

Gils, F. (2005). *Potential applications of digital storytelling in education*. 3rd Twente Student Conference on IT, University of Twente, Faculty of Electrical Engineering, Mathematics and Computer Science, Enschede.

Global Alliance. (in press). *Curriculum standards in public relations: Towards a global standard*. Retrieved 10th November, 2011, from http://www.globalalliancepr.org/project.php?id=3

Godbole, N., Srinivasaiah, M., & Skiena, S. (2007). *Large-scale sentiment analysis for news and blogs*. International Conference on Weblogs and Social Media, March 26-28, Boulder, Colorado, USA Retrieved from http://www.icwsm.org/papers/paper26.html on January 12, 2012.

Goffman, E. (1974). *Frame analysis: An essay on the organization of experience*. Cambridge, MA: Harvard University Press.

Goldberg, G. (2011). Rethinking the public/virtual sphere: The problem with participation. *New Media & Society*, *13*(5), 739–754. doi:10.1177/1461444810379862

Goldberg, L. R. (1992). The development of markers for the big-five factor structure. *Journal of Personality and Social Psychology*, *59*(6), 1216–1229. doi:10.1037/0022-3514.59.6.1216

Golob, U., & Bartlett, J. L. (2007). Communicating about corporate social responsibility: A comparative study of CSR reporting in Australia and Slovenia. *Public Relations Review*, *33*(1), 1–9. doi:10.1016/j.pubrev.2006.11.001

Gómez, M., Roses, S., & Farias, P. (2012). El uso académico de las redes sociales en universitarios. *Comunicar*, *19*(38), 131–138.

Gower, K. K., & Reber, B. H. (2006). Prepared for practice? Student perceptions about requirements and preparation for public relations practice. *Public Relations Review*, *32*, 188–190. doi:10.1016/j.pubrev.2006.02.017

Graetz, K. A. (2006). The psychology of learning environments. In Oblinger, D. G. (Ed.), *Learning spaces* (pp. 6.1–6.14). Educause.

Grant, D., Hardy, C., Oswick, C., & Putman, L. (2004). Introduction: Organizational discourse: Exploring the field. In Grant, D., Hardy, C., Oswick, C., & Putman, L. (Eds.), *The Sage handbook of organizational discourse* (pp. 1–37). New York, NY: Sage. doi:10.4135/9781848608122.n1

Gray, K., Waycott, J., Clerehan, R., Hamilton, M., Richardson, M., Sheard, J., & Thompson, C. (2010). *Web 2.0 authoring tools in higher education learning and teaching: New directions for assessment and academic integrity: A framework for field-testing and refining good practice guidelines in Pilot projects at Australian universities during Semester One 2010*.

Gray, D. E. (2004). *Doing research in the real world*. Los Angeles, CA: Sage.

Gray, K., Thompson, C., Sheard, J., Clerehan, R., & Hamilton, M. (2010). Students as Web 2.0 authors: Implications for assessment design and conduct. *Australasian Journal of Educational Technology*, *26*(1), 105–122.

Greenwood, C. A. (2010). Evolutionary theory: The missing link for conceptualizing public relations. *Journal of Public Relations Research*, *22*(4), 456–476. doi:10.1080/10627261003801438

Gregg, M. (2006). Feeling ordinary: Blogging as conversational scholarship. *Continuum: Journal of Media & Cultural Studies, 20*(2), 147–160. doi:10.1080/10304310600641604

Griffith, S., & Liyanage, L. (2008). An introduction to the potential of social networking sites in education. In I. Olney, G. Lefoe, J. Mantei, & J. Herrington (Eds.), *Proceedings of the Second Emerging Technologies Conference 2008*, (pp. 76-81). Wollongong, Australia: University of Wollongong.

Grosseck, G., & Holotescu, C. (2008). *Can we use Twitter for educational activities?* Paper presented at the 4th International Scientific Conference eLearning and Software for *Education*, April 17-18, 2008.Bucharest, Romania.

Grosseck, G., & Holotescu, C. (2009), *Indicators for the analysis of learning and practice communities from the perspective of microblogging as a provocative sociolect in virtual space*. In 5th International Scientific Conference eLSE – eLearning and Software for Education, Bucharest, 9-10 April 2009.

Grosseck, G., & Holotescu, C. (2010). Microblogging multimedia-based teaching methods best practices with Cirip.eu. In *Procedia - Social and Behavioral Sciences, 2*(2), 2151-2155. WCES 2010 Conference: Innovation and Creativity in Education. Istanbul, 4-8 February 2010.

Grosseck, G., & Holotescu, C. (2011). *Academic research in 140 characters or less.* Paper presented at 7th International Scientifiv Conference eLearning and Software for Education, Bucharest, April 28-29 2011. Retrieved from http://adlunap.ro/eLSE_publications/papers/2011/1590_1.pdf

Grosseck, G., Bran, R., & Tiru, L. (2011). Dear teacher, what should I write on my wall? A case study on academic uses of Facebook. *The 3rd World Conference on Educational Sciences*, 2011, February 03-07, Vol. 15, (pp. 1425-1430). Istanbul, Turkey: Bahcesehir University.

Grunig, J. E. (2000). Collectivism, collaboration, and societal corporatism as core professional values in public relations. *Journal of Public Relations Research, 12*(1), 23–48. doi:10.1207/S1532754XJPRR1201_3

Grunig, J. E. (2006). Furnishing the edifice: Ongoing research on public relations as a strategic management function. *Journal of Public Relations Research, 18*(2), 151–176. doi:10.1207/s1532754xjprr1802_5

Grunig, J. E. (Ed.). (1992). *Excellence in public relations and communication management*. Hillsdale, NJ: Lawrence Erlbaum Associates, Inc.

Grunig, J. E., & Hunt, T. (1984). *Managing public relations*. New York, NY: Holt, Rinehart & Winston.

Grunig, J. E., & Repper, F. C. (1992). Strategic management, publics, and issues. In Grunig, J. E. (Eds.), *Excellence in public relations and communication management* (pp. 117–158). Hillsdale, NJ: Lawrence Erlbaum.

Grunig, J. E., & White, J. (1992). The effect of worldviews on public relations. Theory and practice. In Grunig, J. E. (Eds.), *Excellence in public relations and communication management* (pp. 31–64). Hillsdale, NJ: Lawrence Erlbaum.

Gunawardena, C. N., & Zittle, F. (1997). Social presence as a predictor of satisfaction within a computer mediated conferencing environment. *American Journal of Distance Education, 11*(3), 8–26. doi:10.1080/08923649709526970

Hadwin, A. F., & Philip, H. (2001). CoNoteS2: A software tool for promoting self-regulation. *Educational Research and Evaluation, 7*(2-3), 313–334. doi:10.1076/edre.7.2.313.3868

Haewoon, K., Changhyun, L., Hosung, P., & Moon, S. (2010). What is Twitter: A social network or a news media? *Proceedings of the 19th International World Wide Web (WWW) Conference*, April 26-30, 2010, Raleigh NC (USA), April 2010. Retrieved from http://an.kaist.ac.kr/traces/WWW2010.html

Hagedorn, W. B., & Young, T. (2011). Identifying and intervening with students exhibiting signs of gaming addiction and other addictive behaviors: Implications for professional school counselors. *Professional School Counseling, 14*(4), 250–260. doi:10.5330/PSC.n.2011-14.250

Haig, M. (2001). *E-PR: The essential guide to public relations on the Internet*. London, UK: Kogan Page.

Hakkarainen, P. (2007). *Promoting meaningful learning through the integrated use of digital videos.* Doctoral dissertation, University of Lapland. Acta Universitatis Lapponiensis 121. Rovaniemi, Finland: University of Lapland, Faculty of Education.

Hakkarainen, P., Saarelainen, T., & Ruokamo, H. (2007). Towards meaningful learning through digital video supported, case based teaching. *Australasian Journal of Educational Technology, 23*(1), 87–109.

Halic, O., Lee, D., Paulus, T., & Spence, M. (2010). To blog or not to blog: Student perceptions of blog effectiveness for learning in a college-level course. *The Internet and Higher Education, 13*(4), 206–213. doi:10.1016/j.iheduc.2010.04.001

Hamilton, E., & Freenberg, A. (2005). The technical codes of online education. *E-Learning and Digital Media, 2*(2), 104-121. Retrieved June 5, 2012, from http://dx.doi.org/10.2304/elea.2005.2.2.1

Hardagon, S. (2009). *Educational networking: The important role Web 2.0 will play in education.* Retrieved 12th November, 2011, from http://www.stevehargadon.com/2009/12/social-networking-in-education.html

Hardin, M. C., & Pompper, D. (2004). Writing in the public relations curriculum: practitioner perceptions versus pedagogy. *Public Relations Review, 30,* 357–364. doi:10.1016/j.pubrev.2004.05.007

Hargraves, A. (2003). *Teaching in the knowledge society.* New York, NY: Teachers College.

Harley, D., Acord, S. K., Earl-Novell, S., Lawrence, S., & King, C. J. (2010). *Assessing the future landscape of scholarly communication: An exploration of faculty values and needs in seven disciplines.* UC Berkeley: Center for Studies in Higher Education. Retrieved July 15, 2010, from http://escholarship.org/uc/item/15x7385g

Harris, P., Connolly, J. F., & Feeney, L. (2009). Blended learning: Overview and recommendation for successful implementation. *Industrial and Commercial Training, 4*(3), 155–163. doi:10.1108/00197850910950961

Harry, D., Green, J., & Donath, J. (2009). *Backchan.nl: Integrating backchannels in physical space.* In CHI 2009, April 4–9, 2009, Boston, MA, USA.

Hart, J. (2010). *Using Twitter in a face-to face workshop.* Retrieved from http://janeknight.typepad.com/socialmedia/2010/05/using-twitter-in-a-facetoface-workshop.html

Hart, J. 2011). *Social learning handbook.* Retrieved March 12, 2012, from http://sociallearningcentre.co.uk/activities/how-to-use-twitter-for-social-learning/

Hartney, E. (2011, September 15). What is internet addiction? Symptoms of internet addiction. *About.com Guide.* Retrieved from http://addictions.about.com/od/internetaddiction/a/What-Is-Internet-Addiction.htm

Hawkins, L., Duran, R. L., & Kelly, L. (1991). The relationship of interpersonal communication variables to academic success and persistence in college. *Communication Quarterly, 39*(4), 297–308. doi:10.1080/01463379109369807

Hayes, T., Ruschman, D., & Walker, M. (2009). Social networking as an admission tool: A case study in success. *Journal of Marketing for Higher Education, 19*(2), 109–124. doi:10.1080/08841240903423042

Haynesworth, L. (2009). Faculty with Facebook wary of friending students. *The Daily Princetonian.* Retrieved January 23, 2012, from http://www.dailyprincetonian.com/2009/02/18/22793/

Haythornthwaite, C. (2011). Social network and internet connectivity effects. *Information Communication and Society, 8*(2), 125–147. doi:10.1080/13691180500146185

Haythornthwaite, C., & Andrews, R. (2011). *E-Learning: Theory and practice.* London, UK: Sage.

Haythornthwaite, C., & Wellman, B. (1998). Work, friendship and media use for information exchange in a networked organization. *Journal of the American Society for Information Science American Society for Information Science, 49*(12), 1101–1114. doi:10.1002/(SICI)1097-4571(1998)49:12<1101::AID-ASI6>3.0.CO;2-Z

Hazari, S., North, A., & Moreland, D. (2009). Investigating pedagogical value of wiki technology. *Journal of Information Systems Education, 20*(2), 187–199.

Heiberger, G., & Harper, R. (2008). Have you Facebooked Astin lately? Using technology to increase student involvement. *New Directions for Student Services, 124,* 19–35. doi:10.1002/ss.293

Hemmi, A., Bayne, S., & Land, R. (2009). The appropriation and repurposing of social technologies in higher education. *Journal of Computer Assisted Learning, 25*(1), 19–30. doi:10.1111/j.1365-2729.2008.00306.x

Herring, S. C., Scheidt, L. A., Bonus, S., & Wright, E. (2005). Weblogs as a bridging genre. *Information Technology & People, 18*(2), 142–171. doi:10.1108/09593840510601513

Herrington, T. (2010). Crossing global boundaries: Beyond intercultural communication. *Journal of Business and Technical Communication, 24*(4), 516–539.

Hertog, J. K., & McLeod, D. M. (2001). A multiperspectival approach to framing analysis: A field guide. In Reese, S. D., Gandy, O. H., & Grant, A. E. (Eds.), *Framing public life: Perspective on media and our understanding of the social world* (pp. 139–162). Mahwah, NJ: Lawrence Erlbaum Associates.

Hewitt, A., & Forte, A. (2006). Crossing boundaries: Identity management and student/faculty relationships on Facebook. *Proceedings of the 2006 CSCW*, Banff, Alberta.

Hew, K. F. (2011). Students' and teachers' use of Facebook. *Computers in Human Behavior, 27*, 662–676. doi:10.1016/j.chb.2010.11.020

Hew, K. F., & Brush, T. (2006). Integrating technology into K-12 teaching and learning: Current knowledge gaps and recommendations for future research. *Educational Technology Research and Development, 55*(3), 223–252. doi:10.1007/s11423-006-9022-5

Hirschorn, M. (2007). About Facebook. *Byliner: The Atlantic.* Retrieved February 9, 2012, from http://byliner.com/michael-hirschorn/stories/about-facebook

Hobbs, R., & Jensen, A. (2009). The past, present and future of media literacy education. *Journal of Media Literacy Education, 1*, 1–11.

Hodas, S. (1993). *Implementation of the K-12NREN: Equity, access, and a Trojan horse.* ERIC Document ED, 358829.

Hodas, S. (1996). Technology refusal and the organisational culture of schools. In King, R. (Ed.), *Computerization and controversy* (2nd ed., pp. 197–217). doi:10.1016/B978-0-12-415040-9.50106-8

Holbrook, J. (2011). Making the decision to provide enhanced podcasts to post-secondary science students. *Journal of Science Education and Technology, 20*, 233–345. doi:10.1007/s10956-010-9248-1

Holcomb, L. B., Brady, K. P., & Smith, B. V. (2010). The emergence of "educational networking": Can non-commercial, education-based social networking sites really address the privacy and safety concerns of educators? *MERLOT Journal of Online Learning and Teaching, 6*(2).

Holcomb, L. B., Brady, K. P., & Smith, B. V. (2010). The emergence of "educational networking": Can non-commercial, education-based social networking sites really address the privacy and safety concerns of educators? *Journal of Online Learning and Teaching, 6*(2).

Holland, C., & Muilenburg, L. (2011). Supporting student collaboration: Edmodo in the classroom. In M. Koehler & P. Mishra (Eds.), *Proceedings of Society for Information Technology & Teacher Education International Conference* 2011 (pp. 3232-3236). Chesapeake, VA: AACE. Retrieved from http://www.editlib.org/p/36816

Holotescu, C., & Grosseck, G. (2010). Microblogging-based teaching methods. Examples of good practices with Cirip.Eu. *Procedia Social Sciences, 2*(2), 2151-2155. Retrieved from http://www.sciencedirect.com/science/article/pii/S187704281000337X

Holotescu, C., & Grosseck, G. (2010). *Learning to microblog and microblogging to learn: A case study on learning scenarios in a microblogging context.* In The 6th International Scientific Conference eLearning and Software for Education Bucharest, April 15-16. 2010.

Holotescu, C., & Grosseck, G. (2011). Cirip.Eu – An educational microblogging platform around objects2.0. *Form@re Open Journal, 74.*

Holotescu, C., & Grosseck, G. (2011). M3-learning - Exploring mobile multimedia microblogging learning. *World Journal on Educational Technology, 3*(3), 168–176.

Holzinger, A., & Maurer, H. (2005). E-learning-Modelle für die Hochschule: Ein best practice-Beispiel aus der Bauingenieurwissenschaft. *OCG Journal, 30*(4), 22–23.

Honeycutt, C., & Herring, S. C. (2009). Beyond micro-blogging: Conversation and collaboration via Twitter. *Hawaii International Conference on System Sciences, 42nd Hawaii International Conference on System Sciences*, (pp. 1-10).

Hopkins, K. D., Stanley, J. C., & Hopkins, B. R. (1990). *Educational and psychological measurement and evaluation* (7th ed.). Englewood, NJ: Prentice-Hall.

Hosein, A., Ramanau, R., & Jones, C. (2010). Learning and living technologies. *Learning, Media and Technology*, *35*(4), 403–418. doi:10.1080/17439884.2010.529913

Huang, T. (2011, July 26). *Interview by C. Williams* [Video recording]. Internet Deprivation Can Lead to Real Withdrawal Symptoms, NBC. Los Angeles, CA. Retrieved on January 7, 2012, from http://drtaji.blogspot.com/2011/07/internet-deprivation-can-lead-to-real.html

Huang, Y.-H., & Su, S.-H. (2009). Determinants of consistent, timely, and active responses in corporate crises. *Public Relations Review*, *35*(1), 7–17. doi:10.1016/j.pubrev.2008.09.020

Huijser, H. (2008). Exploring the educational potential of social networking sites: The fine line between exploiting opportunities and unwelcome imposition. *Studies in Learning. Evaluation Innovation and Development*, *5*(3), 45–54.

Hung, D. (2002). Forging links between communities of practice and schools through online learning communities: Implications for appropriating and negotiating knowledge. *International Journal on E-Learning*, (April-June): 2002.

Hunter, J. (2009). A landscape study of shared infrastructure services in the Australian academic sector. *JISC Landscape Study*. Retrieved from http://ie-repository.jisc.ac.uk/439/1/Aust-SIS-Landscape-report-final.pdf

Huntsberger, M., & Stavitsky, A. (2006). The new "podagogy": Incorporating podcasting into journalism education. *Journalism and Mass Communication Educator*, *61*(4), 397–410. doi:10.1177/107769580606100405

Iedema, R., & Wodak, R. (1999). Introduction: Organizational discourses and practices. *Discourse & Society*, *10*(1), 5–19. doi:10.1177/0957926599010001001

Ihlen, O., van Ruler, B., & Fredriksson, M. (2009). *Public relations and social theory: Key figures and ideas*. London, UK: Routledge.

Inkeles, A. (1983). *Exploring individual modernity*. New York, NY: Columbia University Press.

Instructional Technology Council. (2010). *Distance education survey results: Tracking the impact of elearning at community colleges*. Instructional Technology Council. Retrieved May 1, 2010 from http://www.scribd.com/doc/31893631/Trends-in-eLearning-Tracking-the-Impact-of-eLearning-at-Community-Colleges

International Research on Permanent Authentic Records in Electronic Systems. (n.d.). Retrieved from www.interpares.org

Internet Reports, I. T. U. (2005). *The internet of things*. Retrieved from http://www.cahk.hk/Event/30/30.asp

IPIP. (2008). *International personality item pool: A scientific collaborator for the development of advanced measures of personality traits and other individual differences*. Retrieved 12 May, 2011, from http://www.ipip.ori.org

ISO/IEC 18004. (2000). *Information technology – Automatic identification and data capture techniques—Bar code symbology—QR code*. (ISO/IEC JTC1/SC31, 2000).

Ito, M., Horst, H., Bittanti, M., Boyd, D., Herr-Stephenson, R., Lange, P., & Robinson, L. (2008). *Living and learning with new media*. Chicago, IL: MacArthur Foundation.

Ituma, A. (2011). An evaluation of students' perception and engagement with e-learning components in a campus-based university. *Active Learning in Higher Education*, *12*(1), 57–68. doi:10.1177/1469787410387722

Jakobi, A. P. (2007). The knowledge society and the global dynamics in education politics. *European Educational Research Journal*, *6*(1). doi:10.2304/eerj.2007.6.1.39

James, L., Norman, J., De Baets, A.-S., Burchell-Hughes, I., Burchmore, H., Philips, A., et al. (2009). *The lives and technologies of early career researchers*. JISC report. Retrieved July 5, 2011, from http://www.jisc.ac.uk/publications/reports/2009/earlycareerresearchersstudy.aspx#downloads

James, M. (2007). A review of the impact of new media on public relations: Challenges for terrain, practice and education. *Asia Pacific Public Relations Journal, 8*, 137–148.

Java, A., Song, X., Finin, T., & Tseng, B. (2007). Why we Twitter: Understanding microblogging usage and communities. In *Proceedings of the 9th WebKDD and 1st SNA- KDD 2007 Workshop on Web Mining and Social Network Analysis*, (pp. 56–65). ACM

Jbmurray. (2008). *Was introducing Wikipedia to the classroom an act of madness leading only to mayhem if not murder?* In Wikipedia. Retrieved February, 14, 2012 from http://en.wikipedia.org/wiki/User:Jbmurray/Madness

Jenkins, H. (2006). *Confronting the challenges of participatory culture: Media education for the 21st century*. White paper for the MacArthur Foundation. Retrieved on July 1, 2008 from www.digitallearning.macfound.org

Jenkins, H., Clinton, K., Purushotma, R., Robinson, A. J., & Weigel, M. (2006). *Confronting the challenges of participatory culture: Media education for the 21st century*. MacArthur Foundation. Retrieved on February 27, 2012, from http://digitallearning.macfound.org/atf/cf/%7B7E45C7E0-A3E0-4B89-AC9C-E807E1B0AE4E%7D/JENKINS_WHITE_PAPER.PDF.

Jewitt, C. (2008). Multimodality and literacy in school classrooms. *Review of Research in Education, 32*(1), 241–267. doi:10.3102/0091732X07310586

Johnson, L., Smith, R., Levine, A., & Haywood, K. (2011). *The 2011 horizon report*. Austin, TX: The New Media Consortium. Retrieved February 16, 2012, from http://net.educause.edu/ir/library/pdf/HR2011.pdf

Johnson, K. A. (2011). The effect of Twitter posts on students' perceptions of instructor credibility. *Learning, Media and Technology, 36*(1), 21–38. doi:10.1080/17439884.2010.534798

Jonassen, D. H. (1995). Supporting communities of learners with technology: A vision for integrating technology with learning in schools. *Educational Technology, 35*(4), 60–63.

Jonassen, D. H. (1999). *Computers as mind tools for schools: Engaging critical thinking* (2nd ed.). Upper Saddle River, NJ: Merrill.

Jonassen, D. H., & Hernandez-Serrano, J. (2002). Case-based reasoning and instructional design: Using stories to support problem solving. *Educational Technology Research and Development, 50*(2), 65–77. doi:10.1007/BF02504994

Jonassen, D. H., Howland, J. L., Moore, J. L., & Marra, R. M. (2003). *Learning to solve problems with technology: A constructivist perspective*. Upper Saddle River, NJ: Merrill Prentice Hall.

Jones, C., & Cross, S. (2009). *Is there a Net generation coming to university?* Paper presented at the conference ALT-C 2009 "In dreams begins responsibility" - Choice, Evidence and Change, 8 - 10 September 2009, Manchester. Retrieved August 20, 2011, from http://repository.alt.ac.uk/645/

Jones, C. (2011). Students, the net generation and digital natives: accounting for educational change. In Thomas, M. (Ed.), *Deconstructing digital natives*. New York, NY: Routledge.

Jones, C., & Shao, B. (2011). *The Net generation and digital natives: Implications for higher education*. New York, NY: Higher Education Academy.

Jones, N., Blackey, H., Fitzgibbon, K., & Chew, E. (2010). Get out of MySpace! *Computers & Education, 54*, 776–782. doi:10.1016/j.compedu.2009.07.008

Jones, S., Johnson-Yale, C., Millermaier, S., & Seoane-Perez, F. (2009, October 5). Everyday life, online: U.S. college students' use of the internet. *First Monday, 14*(10).

Junco, R. (2010). The effect of twitter on college student engagement and grades. *Journal of Computer Assisted Learning, 27*(2), 1-14. doi:10.1111/j.1365- 2729.2010.00387.x

Junco, R. (2011). The relationship between frequency of Facebook use, participation in Facebook activities, and student engagement. *Computers & Education, 58*(1). doi:doi:10.1016/j.compedu.2011.08.004

Junco, R., & Cole-Avent, G. A. (2008). An introduction to technologies commonly used by college students. *New Directions for Student Services, 124*, 3–17. doi:10.1002/ss.292

Junco, R., Heiberger, G., & Loken, E. (2011). The effect of Twitter on college student engagement and grades. *Journal of Computer Assisted Learning, 27*(2), 119–132. doi:10.1111/j.1365-2729.2010.00387.x

Kamenetz, A. (2009). *DIY U: Edupunks, edupreneurs and the coming transformation of higher education.* Vermont: Chelsea Green Publishing.

Kang, I., Bonk, C. J., & Kim, M.-C. (2011). A case study of blog-based learning in Korea: Technology becomes pedagogy. *Journal of Internet and Higher Education, 14*, 227–235. doi:10.1016/j.iheduc.2011.05.002

Kaplan, A. M., & Haenlein, M. (2010). Users of the world, unite! The challenges and opportunities of social media. *Business Horizons, 53*, 59–68. doi:10.1016/j.bushor.2009.09.003

Karlin, S. (2007). Examining how youths interact online. *School Board News, 73*(4), 6–9.

Karl, K. A., & Peluchette, J. V. (2011). "Friending" professors, parents and bosses: A Facebook connection conundrum. *Journal of Education for Business, 86*(4), 214–222. doi:10.1080/08832323.2010.507638

Karppinen, P. (2005). Meaningful learning with digital and online videos: Theoretical perspectives. *AACE Journal on Information Technology in Education, 13*(3), 233–250.

Kato, H., & Tan, K. T. (2005). 2D barcodes for mobile phones. *Proceedings of 2nd International Conference on Mobile Technology, Applications and Systems*, (p. 8).

Kato, H., Tachibana, K., Tanabe, M., Nakajima, T., & Fukuda, Y. (2003). A city-planning system based on augmented reality with a tangible interface. *Proceedings of the Second IEEE and ACM International Symposium on Mixed and Augmented Reality* (ISMAR'03), (pp. 340-341).

Katz, R. N. (2010). Scholars, scholarship, and the scholarly enterprise in the digital age. *EDUCAUSE Review, 45*(2), 44-56. Retrieved July 20, 2011, from http://www.educause.edu/EDUCAUSE+Review/EDUCAUSEReviewMagazineVolume45/ScholarsScholarshipandtheSchol/202341

Kaufer, D. G. (2011). Bringing social media to the writing classroom: Classroom salon. *Journal of Business and Technical Communication, 25*(3), 299–321. doi:10.1177/1050651911400703

Kaufmann, H., & Meyer, B. (2008). Simulating educational physical experiments in augmented reality. In *ACM SIGGRAPH ASIA 2008 Educators Programme on - SIGGRAPH Asia '08*. New York, NY: ACM Press. doi:10.1145/1507713.1507717

Kawachi, P. (2003). Initiating intrinsic motivation in online education: Review of the current state of the art. *Interactive Learning Environments, 11*(1), 59–81. doi:10.1076/ilee.11.1.59.13685

Kay, D., McGonigle, B., Tabbiner, B., & Patterson, W. (2008). *Next generation users skills*. Retrieved from www.digital2010.org

Kear, K., Woodthorpe, J., Robertson, S., & Hutchison, M. (2010). From forums to wikis: Perspectives on tools for collaboration. *Journal of Internet and Higher Education, 13*, 218–225. doi:10.1016/j.iheduc.2010.05.004

Kearney, M., & Schuck, S. (2006). Spotlight on authentic learning: Student developed digital video projects. *Australasian Journal of Educational Technology, 22*(2), 189–208.

Keengwe, J., & Kidd, T. T. (2010). Towards best practices in online learning and teaching in higher education. *Journal of Online Teaching and Learning, 6*(2), 533–541.

Keim, N., & Clark, J. (2009 October). *Public media 2.0 field report: building social media infrastructure to engage publics: Twitter vote report and inauguration report '09*. Retrieved on December 18, 2011, from http://www.centerforsocialmedia.org/sites/default/files/documents/pages/TVR_Inaug09_Oct.pdf

Kelly, D. (2003). *Adult learners: Characteristics, theories, motivations, learning environment*. Retrieved October 4, 2003, from www.dit.ie/DIT/lifelong/adult/adlearn_chars.pdf

Kent, M. L., Carr, B. J., Husted, R. A., & Pop, R. A. (2011). Learning web analytics: A tool for strategic communication. *Public Relations Review, 37*, 536–543. doi:10.1016/j.pubrev.2011.09.011

Keskin, N., & Matcalf, D. (2011). The current perspectives, theories and practices of mobile learning. *Turkish Online Journal of Educational Technology, 10*(2).

Khaizuran, A. J. (2010). *Social media and the practice of public relations in Malaysia: Where do we stand?* Paper presented at the International Conference on Communication & Media 2010, Melaka.

Kienle, A., & Ritterskamp, C. (2007). Facilitating asynchronous discussions in learning communities: The impact of moderation strategies. *Behaviour & Information Technology, 26*(1), 73–80. doi:10.1080/01449290600811594

Kiili, K., Multisilta, J., Suominen, M., & Ketamo, H. (2010). Learning experiences on mobile social media. *International Journal of Mobile Learning and Organisation, 4*(4), 346–359. doi:10.1504/IJMLO.2010.037533

Kim, D., & King, P. (2011). Implementing podcasts and blogs with ESOL teacher candidates' preparation: Interpretations and implications. *International Forum of Teaching and Studies, 7*(2), 5-19).

Kim, E., & Gilber, S. (2009). *Detecting sadness in 140 characters*. Web Ecology Project. Pub. 03. Retrieved from http://www.webecologyproject.org/2009/08/detecting-sadness-in-140-characters/

Kim, H. N. (2008). The phenomenon of blogs and theoretical model of blog use in educational contexts. *Computers & Education, 51*, 1342–1352. doi:10.1016/j.compedu.2007.12.005

Kim, K., & Bonk, C. J. (2006). The future of online teaching and learning in Higher education: The survey says…. *EDUCAUSE Quarterly, 29*(4), 22–30.

Kim, S., & Lee, Y.-J. (2012). The complex attribution process of CSR motives. *Public Relations Review, 38*(1), 168–170. doi:10.1016/j.pubrev.2011.09.024

Kim, W., Jeong, O.-R., & Lee, S.-W. (2010). On social websites. *Information Systems, 35*, 215–236. doi:10.1016/j.is.2009.08.003

Kindervatter, S. (1979). *Nonformal education as an empowering process*. Amherst, MA: Center for International Education.

King, A. (1993). From sage on the stage to guide on the side. *College Teaching, 41*(1), 30–35. doi:10.1080/87567555.1993.9926781

King, K., & Gura, M. (2007). *Podcasting for teachers: Using a new technology to revolutionize teaching and learning*. Charlotte, NC: Information Age Publishing.

Kirschner, P. A., & Lai, K.-W. (2007). Online communities of practice in education. *Technology, Pedagogy and Education, 16*(2), 127–131. doi:10.1080/14759390701406737

Kirschner, P., & Karpinski, A. (2010, November). Facebook and academic performance. *Computers in Human Behavior, 26*(6), 1237–1245. doi:10.1016/j.chb.2010.03.024

Klopfer, E., Squire, K., & Jenkins, H. (2002). Environmental detectives: PDAs as a window into a virtual simulated world. *Proceedings of the IEEE International Workshop on Wireless and Mobile Technologies in Education*. IEEE. Retrieved March 6, 2012, from http://140.115.126.240/mediawiki/images/9/93/Environment_Detective.pdf

Knight, J. (2010). Distinguishing the learning approaches adopted by undergraduates in their use of online resources. *Journal of Active Learning in Higher Education, 11*(1), 67–78. doi:10.1177/1469787409355873

Knight, R. A. (2010). Sounds for study: Speech and language therapy students' use and perception of exercise podcasts for phonetics. *International Journal of Teaching and Learning in Higher Education, 22*(3), 269–276.

Knox, S., Sharpe, G., Oldham, E., Weber, S., Soloway, E., & Jennings, K. (2010). Towards the use of smartphones for the contextualized teaching of mathematics. In E. Brown (Ed.), *Education in the wild: contextual and location-based mobile learning in action* (pp. 13–16). A report from the STELLAR Alpine Rendez-Vous workshop series. Retrieved March 7, 2012, from http://www.lsri.nottingham.ac.uk/ejb/preprints/ARV_Education_in_the_wild.pdf

Koch, M., & Richter, A. (2008). *Enterprise 2.0: Planung, Einführung und erfolgreicher Einsatz von Social Software in Unternehmen. München*. Germany: Oldenbourg.

Kohyama, K. (1968). *Introduction to information society theory*. Tokyo, Japan: Chuo Koron.

Kolek, E. A., & Saunders, D. (2008). Online disclosure: An empirical examination of undergraduate Facebook profiles. *NASPA Journal, 45*(1), 1–25.

Kolowich, S. (2010, September 7). Wikipedia for credit. *Inside Higher Ed*. Retrieved from http://www.insidehighered.com/news/2010/09/07/wikipedia

Konrad, M.-H., & Ally, M. (2009). Mobile learning. Transforming the delivery of education and training. In Ally, M. (Ed.), *Der anaesthesist (Vol. 58)*. AU Press.

Kress, G. (2003). *Literacy in the new media age*. London, UK: Routledge. doi:10.4324/9780203164754

Kress, G., & Van Leeuwen, T. (2010). *Multimodal discourse. The modes and media of contemporary communication* (2nd ed.). London, UK: Bloomsbury Academic.

Kress, G., & van Leeuwen, Th. (2006). *Reading images. The grammar of visual design*. London, UK: Routledge. doi:10.1016/S8755-4615(01)00042-1

Kruckeberg, D. (1998). The future of PR education: Some recommendations. *Public Relations Review, 24*(2), 235–248. doi:10.1016/S0363-8111(99)80053-8

Krüger-Ross, M., & Holcomb, L. (2011). Towards a theoretical best practices of Web 2.0 and web-based technologies. *Meridian, 13*(2). Retrieved on February 27, 2012, from http://www.ncsu.edu/meridian/winter2011/Krugerross/index.htm

Krüger-Ross, M., Farwell, T., & Waters, R. D. (2012in press). (2012). Everyone's all a-Twitter about Twitter: Three operational perspectives on using Twitter in the classroom. In Seo, K. (Ed.), *Using social media effectively in the classroom: Blogs, wikis, twitter and more*.

Kukulska-Hulme, A., Pettit, J., Bradley, L., Carvalho, A. A., Herrington, A., Kennedy, D. M., & Walker, A. (2011). Mature students using mobile devices in life and learning. *International Journal of Mobile and Blended Learning, 3*(1), 18–52. doi:10.4018/jmbl.2011010102

Kukulska-Hulme, A., Sharples, M., Milrad, M., Arnedillo-Sánchez, I., & Vavoula, G. (2009). Innovation in mobile learning: A European perspective. *International Journal of Mobile and Blended Learning, 1*(1), 13–35. doi:10.4018/jmbl.2009010102

Kukulska-Hulme, A., Sharples, M., Milrad, M., Arnedillo-Sánchez, I., & Vavoula, G. (2010). The genesis and development of mobile learning in Europe. In Parsons, D. (Ed.), *Combining e-learning and m-learning: New applications of blended educational resources* (pp. 151–177). Hershey, PA: Information Science Reference (an imprint of IGI Global). doi:10.4018/978-1-60960-481-3.ch010

Kukulska-Hulme, A., & Traxler, J. (2005). *Mobile learning: A handbook for educators and trainers*. London, UK: Routledge.

Kurosawa, K., Miyamoto, K., Nagase, Y., Ikegami, H., Sato, K., & Otsubo, M. (2003). *Mobile phones application LSI design using c based design methodology*. Tech. Report 4, NEC Corporation.

Kwak, H., Lee, C., Park, H., & Moon, S. (2010). *What is Twitter, a social network or a news media?* In WWW 2010, April 26–30, 2010, Raleigh, North Carolina, USA.

L'Etang, J. (1999). Public relations education in Britain: An historical review in the context of professionalisation. *Public Relations Review, 25*(3), 261–289. doi:10.1016/S0363-8111(99)00019-3

Lampe, C., Ellison, N., & Steinfeld, C. (2007). A familiar Face(book): Profile elements as signals in an online social network. *Proceedings of Conference on Human Factors in Computing Systems* (pp. 435-444). New York, NY: ACM Press.

Lane, C. (2006). *Podcasting at the UW: An evaluation of current use*. Retrieved June 5 from www.washington.edu/lst/research/papers/2006/podcasting_report.pdf

Lankshear, C., Gee, J. P., Knobel, M., & Searle, C. (1997). *Changing literacies*. Buckingham, UK: Open University Press.

Lankshear, C., & Knobel, M. (2008). Digital literacies: Concepts, policies and practices. In Allan, M. (Ed.), *Digital literacy and the "digital society"*. New York, NY: Peter Lang Publishing.

Latiffah, P., Samsudin, A. R., & Fauziah, A. (2009). Media consumption among young adults: A look at labels and norms in everyday life. [Malaysian Journal of Communication]. *Jurnal Komunikasi, 25*, 21–31.

Laurillard, D. (2006). E-learning in higher education. In Ashwin, P. (Ed.), *Changing higher education: The development of learning and teaching* (pp. 71–84). London, UK: Routledge Falmer.

Laurillard, D., & Pachler, N. (Eds.). (2007). *Pedagogical forms of mobile learning: Framing research questions. Mobile learning: Towards a research agenda* (pp. 33–54). London, UK: WLE Centre, Institute of Education.

Lave, J., & Wenger, E. (1991). *Situated learning: Legitimate peripheral participation*. Cambridge, UK: University of Cambridge Press. doi:10.1017/CBO9780511815355

Lawless, K. A., & Pellegrino, J. W. (2007). Professional development in integrating technology into teaching and learning: Knowns, unknowns, and ways to pursue better questions and answers. *Review of Educational Research, 77*(4), 575–614. doi:10.3102/0034654307309921

Lazzari, M. (2008). Creative use of podcasting in higher education and its effect on competitive agency. *Computers & Education, 52*(1), 27–34. doi:10.1016/j.compedu.2008.06.002

Lebel, J. (2010, March 5). *5 examples of how schools are using social media to enhance learning* [Web log post]. Retrieved on April 18, 2010, from http://blog.thekbuzz.com/2010/03/5-examples-of-using-social-media-to-enhance-learning.html

Ledgerwood, N. (2001). Evolving support for online learning: An action research model. In M. Wallace, A. Ellis, & D. Newton (Eds.), *Moving Online II Conference*, Gold Coast, Australia, 2 - 4 September, Southern Cross University, (pp. 18-29).

Lee, J., & Young, C. (2011). Building wikis and blogs: Pre-service teacher experiences with web-based collaborative technologies in an interdisciplinary methods course. *Journal of Technology, Humanities. Education and Narrative, 8*, 8–37.

Lee, M., & Chan, A. (2007). Pervasive, lifestyle-integrated mobile learning for distance learners: An analysis and unexpected results from a podcasting study. *Open Learning: The Journal of Open and Distance Learning, 22*(3), 201–218.

Lee, M., McLoughlin, C., & Chan, A. (2008). Talk the talk: Learner-generated podcasts as catalysts for knowledge creation. *British Journal of Educational Technology, 39*(3), 501–521. doi:10.1111/j.1467-8535.2007.00746.x

Lee, Y., & Choi, J. (2010). A review of online course dropout research: Implications for practice and future research. *Educational Technology Research and Development, 59*(5), 593–618. doi:10.1007/s11423-010-9177-y

Lemeul, J. (2006). Why I registered on Facebook. *The Chronicle of Higher Education, 53*(2), C1.

Lenhart, A., & Fox, S. (2006). *Bloggers: A portrait of the Internet's new storytellers*. Pew Internet & American Life Project. Retrieved February 27, 2012, from http://www.pewinternet.org/Reports/2006/Bloggers.aspx

Lenhart, A., Purcell, K., Smith, A., & Zickuhr, K. (2010). *Social media and mobile Internet use among teens and young adults*. Retrieved on February 27, 2012 from http://pewinternet.org/Reports/2010/Social-Media and-Young-Adults.aspx

Lenhart, A. P. (2010). *Social media and mobile internet use among teens and young adults*. Washington, DC: Pew Research Center.

Lenhart, A., Purcell, K., Smith, A., & Zickuhr, K. (2010). *Social media and mobile Internet use among teens and young adults*. Washington, DC: Pew Research Centre.

Lerman, K. (2008). *Social browsing & information filtering in social media*. Retrieved March 6, 2012, from http://arxiv.org/abs/0710.5697

Lester, R. K. (2005). *Universities, innovation, and the competitiveness of local economies: Summary report from the local innovation project.* Retrieved March 20, 2010, from http://ekstranett.innovasjonnorge.no/Arena_fs/Local%20nnovation%20Project_MIT.pdf

Lester, D. (2012). Social media: Changing advertising education. *Online Journal of Communication and Media Technologies, 2*(1), 116–125.

Letierce, J., Passant, A., Decker, S., & Breslin, J. G. (2010). *Understanding how Twitter is used to spread scientific messages*. In Web Science Conf. 2010, April 26-27, 2010, Raleigh, NC, USA.

Levin, D., Araheh, S., Lenhart, A., & Rainie, L. (2002). *The digital disconnect: The widening gap between internet-savvy students and their schools*. Retrieved January 5, 2006, from http://www.pewinternet.org/report_display.asp?r=67

Li, C., & Bernoff, J. (2011). *Groundswell, expanded and revised edition: Winning in a world transformed by social technologies.* Cambridge, MA: Harvard Business Review Press.

Liaw, S. S., Hatala, M., & Huang, H. M. (2010). Investigating acceptance toward mobile learning to assist individual knowledge management: Based on activity theory approach. *Computers & Education, 54*(2), 446–454. doi:10.1016/j.compedu.2009.08.029

Lieber, P. S. (2008). Moral development in public relations: Measuring duty to society in strategic communication. *Public Relations Review, 34*(3), 244–251. doi:10.1016/j.pubrev.2008.03.028

Liedka, J. (1999). Linking competitive advantage with communities of practice. *Journal of Management Inquiry, 8*(1), 5–16. doi:10.1177/105649269981002

Li, L., & Pitts, J. P. (2009). Does IT really matter? Using virtual office hours to enhance student-faculty interaction. *Journal of Information Systems Education, 20*(2), 175–185.

Lilleker, D. G., & Jackson, N. (2008). *Politicians and Web 2.0: The current bandwagon or changing the mindset?* Paper presented at the Politics: Web 2.0 International Conference, April 17-18, 2008. London, UK: Royal Holloway, University of London.

Lilleker, D. G., Michalska, K. K., Schweitzer, E., Jacunski, M., Jackson, N., & Vedel, T. (2011). Informing, engaging, mobilising or interacting: Searching for a European model of web campaigning. *European Journal of Communication, 26*(3), 195–213. doi:10.1177/0267323111416182

Lindquist, D., Denning, T., Kelly, M., Malani, R., Griswold, W. G., & Simon, B. (2007). Exploring the potential of mobile phones for active learning in the classroom. *ACM SIGCSE Bulletin, Session: Emerging Instructional Technologies, 39*(1). Retrieved March 6, 2012, from http://cseweb.ucsd.edu/~wgg/Abstracts/fp142-lindquist.pdf

Lipka, S. (2007, December 8). For professors, "friending" can be fraught. *The Chronicle of Higher Education, 54*(15).

Liu, T.-Y., Tan, Y.-H., & Chu, Y.-L. (2007). 2D barcode and augmented reality supported English learning system. *Proceedings 6th IEEE/ACIS International Conference on Computer and Information Science* (ICIS 2007), Melburne, Australia, (pp. 5-10).

Livingstone, S. (2010). *Youthful participation: What have we learned, what shall we ask next?* Paper presented at the 2010 Digital Media and Learning Conference. Retrieved March 5, 2010, from http://www.scribd.com/doc/27906764/Sonia-Livingstone-2010-Digital-Media-and-Learning-Conference-Keynote

Livingstone, S., Haddon, L., Görzig, A., & Ólafsson, K. (2011). *Risks and safety on the Internet.* Retrieved 25 June, 2012, from http://www2.lse.ac.uk/media@lse/research/eukidsonline/eukidsii%20(2009-11)/eukidsonlineiireports/d4fullfindings.pdf

LLIDA. (Learning Literacies for the Digital Age) framework wiki. (2009). *JISC Project.* Retrieved April 15, 2011, from http://caledonianacademy.net/spaces/LLiDA/index.php?n=Main.FrameworkOfFrameworks

Loh, T. (April 12, 2011). *Stop, drop and roll out Yammer.* Blog post. Retrieved March 2, 2012, from http://blog.yammer.com/blog/2011/04/emergency-preparedness-with-yammer.html

Lopes, L., & Ribeiro, B. (2010). GPUMLib: An efficient open-source GPU machine learning library. *International Journal of Computer Information Systems and Industrial Management Applications, 3,* 355–362.

Lovett, J., & Owyang, J. (2011). *Social marketing analytics: A new framework for measuring results in social media.* Retrieved January 12, 2012, from http://www.slideshare.net/jlovett/social-marketing-analytics-7985404

Lowenthal, P. R. (2010). The evolution and influence of social presence theory on online learning. In Kidd, T. T. (Ed.), *Online education and adult learning: New frontiers for teaching practices* (pp. 124–139). Hershey, PA: IGI Global.

LSE Public Policy Group. (2011). *Maximising the impacts of your research: A handbook for social scientists,* [Consultation draft 3 online]. Retrieved July 7, 2011, from http://blogs.lse.ac.uk/impactofsocialsciences/2011/04/14/maximizing-the-impacts-of-your-research-a-handbook-for-social-scientists-now-available-to-download-as-a-pdf/

Lubbers, C. A. (2002). Using alternative teaching techniques to enhance student performance in the traditional introductory public relations course. *Public Relations Review, 28*(2), 157–166. doi:10.1016/S0363-8111(02)00122-4

Luke, C. (2003). Pedagogy, connectivity, multimodality, and interdisciplinarity. *Reading Research Quarterly, 38*(3), 397–403.

Lynch, K. (1966). *La imagen de la ciudad*. Buenos Aires, Argentina: Infinito.

Maag, M. (2006). Podcasting and mp3 players: Emerging education technologies. *Computers, Informatics, Nursing*, *24*(1), 9–12. doi:10.1097/00024665-200601000-00005

Mack, D., Behler, A., Roberts, B., & Rimland, E. (2007). Reaching students with Facebook: Data and best practices. *Electronic Journal of Academic and Special Librarianship, 8*(2).

Madge, C., Meek, J., Wellens, J., & Hooley, T. (2009). Facebook, social integration and informal learning at university: 'It is more for socialising and talking to friends about work than for actually doing work'. *Learning, Media and Technology*, *34*(2), 141–155. doi:10.1080/17439880902923606

Malaysian Communications and Multimedia Commissions. (2010). *National broadband initiatives*. Retrieved from http://www.skmm.gov.my/index.php?c=public&v=art_view&art_id=36

Malinowski, B. (1922). *Argonauts of the Western Pacific*. New York, NY: E.P. Dutton & Co. Inc.

Malkawi, A., & Srinivasan, R. (2004). Building performance visualization using augmented reality. *Proceedings of the Fourteenth International Conference on Computer Graphics and Vision*, (pp. 122-127).

Maloney, E. J. (2007). What Web 2.0 can teach us about learning. *The Chronicle of Higher Education*, *53*(18), B26.

Marambio, A., Corso, J., Lucena, J., & Roca, J. (2010). Nuevas formas de accesibilidad a través de aplicaciones con realidad virtual y aumentada en el museo marítimo de Barcelona: Proyecto PATRAC. *Architecture. City and Environment*, *13*, 145–160.

Marktest. (2011). *Os Portugueses e as redes sociais*. Retrieved 25th November, 2011, from http://www.marktest.com/wap/a/n/id~1891.aspx\

Marquis, J. (March 12, 2012). *Is Twitter the driving force behind upcoming educational challenge?* Blog post. Retrieved March 12, 2012, from http://www.onlineuniversities.com/blog/2012/03/is-twitter-the-driving-force-behind-upcoming-educational-change/

Martin A. (2005). DigEuLit- A European framework for digital literacy: A progress report. *Journal of eLiteracy, 2.*

Martindale, T., & Wiley, D. A. (2005). Using weblogs in scholarship and teaching. *TechTrends*, *49*(2), 55–61. doi:10.1007/BF02773972

Martin, J., & Normann, A. R. D. (1970). *The computerized society*. Bethesda, MD: World Future Society.

Martin, R. A. (2006). *The psychology of humor: An integrative approach*. Burlington, MA: Elsevier Academic Press.

Mashable. (2011). *ComScore says you don't got mail: Web email usage declines, 59% among teens*. Retrieved November 2, 2011, from http://techcrunch.com/2011/02/07/comscore-says-you-dont-got-mail-web-email-usage-declines-59-among-teens/

Mason, R. (2006). Learning technologies for adult continuing education. *Studies in Continuing Education*, *28*(2), 121–133. doi:10.1080/01580370600751039

Mattson, E., & Barnes, N. G. (2009). *Social media and college admissions: The first longitudinal study*. Retrieved January 12, 2012, from http://www.umassd.edu/cmr/studiesresearch/mediaandadmissions.cfm

Mayer, J. P. (2006). *Legal education podcasting project – End of semester survey results*. Retrieved June 5, 2012, from http:// caliopolis.classcaster.org/blog/legal_education_podcasting_project/2006/07/05/leppsurvey

Mayernik, M., & Pepe, A. (2009). *Microblogging from the field: Capturing contextual information in highly mobile research*. Retrieved from http://research.cens.ucla.edu/events/?event_id=231

Mayfield, A. (2008). *What is social media?* Retrieved December 18, 2011, from http://www.iCrossing.com/ebooks

Mazer, J. P., Murphy, R. E., & Simonds, C. J. (2007). I'll see you on Facebook: The effects of computer-mediated teacher self-disclosure on student motivation, affective learning, and classroom climate. *Communication Education*, *56*(1), 1–17. doi:10.1080/03634520601009710

Mazer, J. P., Murphy, R. E., & Simonds, C. J. (2009). The effects of teacher self-disclosure via Facebook on teacher credibility. *Learning, Media and Technology*, *34*(2), 175–183. doi:10.1080/17439880902923655

Maznevski, M. C. (2000). Bridging space over time: Global virtual team dynamics and effectiveness. *Organization Science*, *11*(5), 473–492. doi:10.1287/orsc.11.5.473.15200

McAfee, A. (2009). *Enterprise 2.0: New collaborative tools for your organization's toughest challenges*. Boston, MA: Harvard Business Press.

McCarthy, J. (2010). Blended learning environments: Using social networking sites to enhance the first year experience. *Australasian Journal of Educational Technology*, *26*(6), 729–740.

McCrae, R. R., & Costa, P. T. (1997). Personality trait structure as a human universal. *The American Psychologist*, *52*, 509–516. doi:10.1037/0003-066X.52.5.509

McCroskey, J. C. (1992). *An introduction to communication in the classroom*. Edina, MN: Burgess International Group.

McCroskey, J. C., & Teven, J. J. (1999). Goodwill: A reexamination of the construct and its measurement. *Communication Monographs*, *66*, 90–103. doi:10.1080/03637759909376464

McCroskey, J. C., Valencic, K. M., & Richmond, V. P. (2004). Toward a general model of instructional communication. *Communication Quarterly*, *52*, 197–210. doi:10.1080/01463370409370192

McFedries, P. (2007). All a-Twitter. *IEEE Spectrum*, *84*. doi:doi:10.1109/MSPEC.2007.4337670

McGann, M. (2010). *Communications audit: Why and how to do it*. Retrieved January 8, 2012, from http://2mcommunications.wordpress.com/2010/07/05/communications-audit-why-and-how-to-do-it/

McGarr, O. (2009). A review of podcasting in higher education: Its influence on the traditional lecture. *Australasian Journal of Educational Technology*, *25*(3), 309–321.

McGonigal, J. (2011). *Reality is broken: Why games make us better and how they can change the world*. New York, NY: The Penguin Press.

McKinney, D. E. (2005). Annual community reports. In Heath, R. L. (Ed.), *Encyclopedia of public relations* (*Vol. 2*, pp. 27–28). Thousand Oaks, CA: Sage Publications.

McLoughlin, C. L. (2007). Social software and participatory learning: Pedagogical choices with technology affordances in the web 2.0 era. *Proceedings ASCILITE* (pp. 664-675). Singapore: ASCILITE.

McLuhan, M. (1964). *Understanding media: The extensions of man*. London, UK: Routledge & Kegan Paul.

McNely, B. (2009). *Backchannel persistance and collaborative meaning-making*. In SIGDOC'09, October 5-7 2009. Bloomington, IN: ACM.

Meadows, D. (2003). Digital storytelling: Research-based practice in new media. *Visual Communication*, *2*(2), 189–193. doi:10.1177/1470357203002002004

Meehan, J. (2006). Toward an archival concept of evidence. *Archivaria*, *61*, 127–146.

Melville, D., et al. (2009). Higher education in a web 2.0 world. *Committee of Inquiry into the Changing Learner Experience*. Retrieved from http://www.jisc.ac.uk/media/documents/publications/heweb20rptv1.pdf

Mendoza, M., Poblete, B., & Castillo, C. (2010). *Twitter under crisis: Can we trust what we RT?* In 1st Workshop on Social Media Analytics (SOMA 10), KDD '10 Workshops, ACM, Washington, USA (July 25, 2010).

Merzenich, M. (2008, August 11). Going Googly. *On the Brain with Dr. Mike Merzenich*. [Web log post]. Retrieved December 30, 2011, from http://merzenich.positscience.com/?p=177

Meyer, K. A. (2010). Web 2.0 Research. Introduction to the special issue. *Journal of Internet and Higher Education*, *13*(4), 177–178. doi:10.1016/j.iheduc.2010.07.004

Milgram, P., & Takemura, H. (1994). *Augmented reality: A class of displays on the reality-virtuality continuum*. Presented at Telemanipulator and Telepresence Technologies. doi:10.1117/12.197321

Millan, N., & Bromage, A. (2011). An initial approach to the integration of Web 2.0 technologies in the research environment. *Interactive Technology and Smart Education*, *8*(3), 148–160. doi:10.1108/17415651111165384

Minocha, S. (2009). *A study on the effective use of social software by further and higher education in the UK to support student learning and engagement.* JISC. Retrieved from http://www.jisc.ac.uk/media/documents/projects/effective-use-of-social-software-in-education-finalreport.pdf

Minocha, S. (2009). A case study-based investigation of students' experiences with social software tools. *New Review of Hypermedia and Multimedia, 15*(3), 245–265. doi:10.1080/13614560903494320

Minocha, S., & Roberts, D. (2008). Social, usability, and pedagogical factors influencing students' learning experiences with wikis and blogs. *Pragmatics & Cognition, 16*(2), 272–306.

Mitchell, O. (2009). *How to present with Twitter (and other backchannels).* Retrieved from http://www.speakingaboutpresenting.com/wp-content/uploads/Twitter.pdf

Moeglin, P. (Ed.). (2003). *Industriile educaţiei şi noile media.* Iaşi, Romania: Polirom.

Mokhtari, K., Reichard, C., & Gardner, A. (2011). The impact of Internet and television use on the reading habits and practices of college students. *Journal of Adolescent & Adult Literacy, 52*(7), 609–619. doi:10.1598/JAAL.52.7.6

Moran, M., Seaman, J., & Tinti-Kane, H. (2011). *Teaching, learning and sharing: How today's higher education faculty use social media.* Pearson Learning Solution and Babson Survey Research Group. Retrieved from http://www.pearsonlearningsolutions.com/educators/pearson-social-media-survey-2011-bw.pdf

Moran, M., Seaman, J., & Tinti-Kane, H. (2011). *Teaching, learning, and sharing: How today's higher education faculty use social media.* Boston, MA: Pearson Learning Solutions.

Moscovici, S., & Buschini, F. (Eds.). [2003]. (2007). *Metodologia ştiinţelor socioumane.* Iaşi, Romania: Polirom.

Motiwalla, L. F. (2007). Mobile learning: A framework and evaluation. *Computers & Education, 49*(3), 581–596. doi:10.1016/j.compedu.2005.10.011

Motschnig-Pitrik, R., & Holzinger, A. (2002). Student-centered teaching meets new media: Concept and case study. *Journal of Educational Technology & Society, 5*(4), 160–172.

Moulton, J. (2007). *Formal and nonformal education and empowered behavior: A review of the research literature. Prepared for the support and analysis in Africa (SARA) project, USAID.* Washington, DC: Academy for Educational Development, manuscript.

Mousten, B. M. (2010). Learning localization through trans-atlantic collaboration: Bridging the gap between professionsetween professions. *IEEE Transactions on Professional Communication, 53*(4), 401–411. doi:10.1109/TPC.2010.2077481

Mühlburger, H., Ebner, M., & Taraghi, B. (2010). @ twitter try out #Grabeeter to export, archive and search your tweets. *Research 2.0 Approaches to TEL* (2010), (pp. 76–85).

Mumby, D. K., & Clair, R. P. (1997). Organizational discourse. In van Dijk, T. A. (Ed.), *Discourse as social interaction (Discourse studies: A multidisciplinary introduction)* (Vol. 2, pp. 181–205). London, UK: Sage Publications.

Muñoz, C. L., & Towner, T. L. (2009). *Opening Facebook: How to use Facebook in the college classroom.* Paper presented at the Society for Information Technology and Teacher Education Conference, Charleston, South Carolina, USA.

Munoz, C., & Towner, T. (2011). Back to the wall: Facebook in the college classroom. *First Monday, 16*(12).

Murphy, S. (2011, July 6). Tech withdrawal similar to giving up drinking, smoking. *Tech News Daily.* Retrieved December 30, 2011, from http://www.technewsdaily.com/2937-internet-addictions-similar-to-tobacco-addictions.html

Murray, J. (2011, November 21). Do students know more about technology than their teachers? We ask education experts for their verdicts. *The Guardian.* Retrieved from http://www.guardian.co.uk/education/2011/nov/21/multiple-choice-students-teachers-technology?newsfeed=true

Mwanza-Simwami, D. (2007). Concepts and methods for investigating learner activities with mobile devices: An activity theory perspective. In I. Arnedillo-Sánchez, M. Sharples, G. Vavoula G. (Eds.), *Beyond Mobile Learning Workshop* (pp. 24–25). Trinity College Dublin Press.

Myers, S., & Bryant, L. (2004). College Students' perception of how instructors convey credibility. *Qualitative Research Reports in Communication, 5*, 22–27.

Nagel, D. (2011). Online learning set for explosive growth as traditional classrooms decline. *Campus Technology.* Retrieved May 20, 2012, from http://campustechnology.com/articles/2011/01/26/online-learning-set-for-explosive-growth-as-traditional-classrooms-decline.aspx

Naismith, L. (2004). *Literature review in mobile technologies and learning. NESTA Futurelab series, report 11.* Bristol, UK: NESTA Futurelab.

Nardi, B. A., Schiano, D. J., Gumbrecht, M., & Swartz, L. (2004). Why we blog. *Communications of the ACM, 47*(12), 41–46. doi:10.1145/1035134.1035163

Nardi, B., & O'Day, V. (1999). *Information ecologies: Using technology with heart.* Cambridge, MA: MIT Press.

Narkhede, P., Rajesh, P., & Kumar, S. (2010). Analysis on general profile of Plurk users. In *Rev Systems*, Bangalore. Retrieved from http://www.slideshare.net/bexdeep/plurk-analysis-4136802

National Archives and Records Administration (NARA). (2010). *Implications of recent web technologies for NARA web guidance.* Retrieved from http://www.archives.gov/recordsmgmt/initiatives/web-tech.html

National Research Council. (1999). *How people learn: Brain, mind, experience, and school.* Washington, DC: National Academy Press.

National Schools Board Association (NSBA). (2007). *Creating and connecting: Research and guidelines on online social and education-networking.* Retrieved 12th November, 2011, from http://www.nsba.org/site/docs/41400/41340.pdf.

Naughtie, J. (2011). *Will Bahrain's Arab Spring bear fruit?* Retrieved January 13, 2012, from http://news.bbc.co.uk/today/hi/today/newsid_9499000/9499462.stm

Navarro, I. (2011). *Learning 3.0: Mobile-learning, augmented reality...in architecture.* Tech Architecture La Salle Blogging. Retrieved October 15, from http://blogs.salleurl.edu/tech-architecture/2011/05/19/hola-mundo/

Nelson, T., & Fernheimer, J. (n.d.). *Welcome to the blogosphere: Using weblogs to create classroom community.* Retrieved from http://www.cwrl.utexas.edu/whitepapers/030822-1

Nevas, B. (2010). *Inquiry through action research: Effects of the Edmodo microblog on student engagement and performance.* Retrieved from http://www.scribd.com/doc/27372047/Edmodo-Research

New Media Consortium & the EDUCAUSE Learning Initiative. (2007). *The horizon report.* Retrieved on February 27, 2012 from http://www.nmc.org/horizon/2007/report

New Media Consortium (NMC) & EDUCAUSE Learning Initiative. (ELI). (2002). *The horizon reports.* Retrieved 12th November, 2011, from http://www.nmc.org/horizon-project/horizon-reports

Newman, D. (1992). Technology as support for school structure and school restructuring. *Phi Delta Kappan, 74*(4), 308–315.

Nguyen, J. (2010). *The state of social networks* [Electronic Version]. Retrieved 1st November, 2010, from http://www.comscore.com/content/search?SearchText=social+media

Nikirk, M. (2009). Today's millennial generation: A look ahead to the future they create. *Techniques: Connecting Education and Careers, 84*(5), 20–23.

NMC Horizon Report Project. (2012). *Short list, higher education edition.* Retrieved from http://horizon.wiki.nmc.org/file/view/2012-Horizon.HE-Shortlist.pdf

Noor, M. N. M., & Saabar, S. (2008). *Blogsphere: Ruang kontra hegemoni? Analisis terhadap blog politik Malaysia terpilih dalam PRU 2008.* Paper presented at the Seminar Politik Malaysia.

Norberg-Schulz, C. (1971). *Existence, space and architecture.* London, UK: Praeger Publishers.

Novak, E., Razzouk, R., & Johnson, T. E. (2012). The educational use of social annotation tools in higher education: A literature review. *The Internet and Higher Education, 15*(1), 39–49. doi:10.1016/j.iheduc.2011.09.002

NTSE. (2007). *National educational technology standards.* USA: International Society for Technology in Education.

Nussbaum, J. F., Comadena, M. E., & Holladay, S. J. (1987). Classroom verbal behaviors of highly effective teachers. *Journal of Thought*, *22*, 73–80.

Nworie, J., & Haughton, N. (2008). Good intentions and unanticipated effects: The unintended consequences of the application of technology in teaching and learning environments. *TechTrends*, *52*(5), 52–58. doi:10.1007/s11528-008-0197-y

O'Hare, M. (1982). Copyright and the protection of economic rights. *Journal of Cultural Economics*, *6*(1), 33–48. doi:10.1007/BF00162292

O'Malley, C., Vavoula, G., Glew, J. P., Taylor, J., Sharples, M., & Lefrere, P. (2003). *Guidelines for learning/teaching/tutoring in a mobile environment*. Mobilearn Project. Open University. Retrieved February 17, 2012, from http://www.mobilearn.org/download/results/guidelines.pdf

O'Reilly, T. (2007). What is web 2.0: Design patterns and business models for the next generation of software. *Communications & Strategies*, *65*(1), 17-37. Retrieved December 20, 2012, from http://ssrn.com/abstract=1008839

O'Reilly, T., & Battelle, J. (2009). *Web squared: Web 2.0 five years on*. Special report, Web 2.0 Summit. Retrieved December 20, 2012, from http://assets.en.oreilly.com/1/event/28/web2009_websquaredwhitepaper

O'Sullivan, P. B., Hunt, S. K., & Lippert, L. R. (2004). Mediated immediacy: A language of affiliation in a technological age. *Journal of Language and Social Psychology*, *23*, 464–490. doi:10.1177/0261927X04269588

O'Connor, E. (2012). A survival guide from an early adopter: How Web 2.0 and the right attitude can enable learning and expansive course design. *Journal of Educational Technology Systems*, *40*(2).

Office of the Information and Privacy Commissioner of British Columbia (OIPCBC). (2012). *Cloud computing guidelines for public bodies*. OIPBC.

Ohbuchi, E., Hanaizumi, H., & Hock, L. A. (2004). Barcode readers using the camera device in mobile phones. *Proceedings of the 2004 International Conference on Cyberworlds* (CW'04), (pp. 260-265).

Olaniran, B. A. (2008). Cultural implications of collaborative information technologies (CITs) in international online collaborations and global virtual teams. In Zemliansky, P., & St.Amant, K. (Eds.), *The handbook of research on virtual workplaces and the new nature of business practices* (pp. 120–129). Hershey, PA: IGI Global. doi:10.4018/978-1-59904-893-2.ch010

Oldfather, P., West, J., White, J., & Wilmarth, J. (1999). *Learning through children's eyes: Social constructivism and the desire to learn*. Washington, DC: American Psychological Association. doi:10.1037/10328-000

Onlineuniversities.com. (in press). How higher education uses social media. *mashable.com*. Retrieved February 5, 2012, from http://mashable.com/2012/02/03/higher-education-social-media/

Oprea, L. (2005). *Responsabilitate socială corporatistă*. Bucureşti, Romania: Tritonic.

Oradini, F., & Saunders, G. (2008). *The use of social networking by students and staff in higher education*. iLearning Forum, European Institute of E-Learning, Paris, France. Retrieved on February 29, 2012, from http://www.eife-l.org/publications/proceedings/ilf08/contributions/improving-quality-of-learning-with-technologies/Oradini_Saunders.pdf

Orihuela, J. (9 June 2011). *Enseñar aprendiendo con medios sociales*. Retrieved October 24, 2011, from http://www.newmedia.ufm.edu/gsm/index.php/Orihuel-aensenaraprendiendo

Ormrod, J. E. (2004). *Human learning* (4th ed.). Upper Saddle River, NJ: Pearson Educational Inc.

Ovadia, S. (2009). Exploring the potential of Twitter as a research tool. *Behavioral & Social Sciences Librarian*, *28*(4), 202–205. doi:10.1080/01639260903280888

Owyang, J. (2009). The importance of social media audits. Retrieved January 13, 2012, from http://www.web-strategist.com/blog/2009/07/28/the-importance-of-a-social-media-audits/

Owyang, J., & Toll, M. (2007). *Tracking the influence of conversations: A roundtable discussion on social media metrics and measurement*. New York, NY: Dow Jones Inc.

Oztok, M., & Brett, C. (2011). Social presence and on-line learning: A review of research. *Journal of Distance Education, 25*(3), 1–16.

Paas, L. (2008). *How information and communications technologies can support education for sustainable development current uses and trends.* Canada: International Institute for Sustainable Development. Retrieved February 10, 2011, from http://www.iisd.org/pdf/2008/ict_education_sd_trends.pdf

Pachler, N., Cook, J., & Bachmair, B. (2010). Appropriation of mobile cultural resources for learning. *International Journal of Mobile and Blended Learning, 2*(1), 1–21. doi:10.4018/jmbl.2010010101

Paisley, W. J. (2001). Public communication campaign: The American experience. In Rice, R. E., & Atkin, C. K. (Eds.), *Public communication campaigns* (3rd ed., pp. 3–21). Thousand Oaks, CA: Sage Publications.

Palloff, R. M., & Pratt, K. (2001). *Lessons from the cyberspace classroom.* San Francisco, CA: Jossey-Bass.

Palloff, R., & Pratt, K. (1999). *Building learning communities in cyberspace: Effective strategies for the online classroom.* San Francisco, CA: Jossey-bass.

Papert, S. (1993). *The children's machine: Rethinking school in the age of the computer.* New York, NY: Basic Books, Inc.

Papert, S. (1997). Why school reform is impossible. *Journal of the Learning Sciences, 6*(4), 417–427. doi:10.1207/s15327809jls0604_5

Parra-López, E., Bulchand-Gidumal, J., Gutiérrez-Taño, D., & Díaz-Armas, R. (2011). Intentions to use social media in organizing and taking vacation trips. *Computers in Human Behavior, 27*(2), 640–654. doi:10.1016/j.chb.2010.05.022

Parry, D. (2008). *Twitter for academia.* Blog post. Retrieved from http://academhack.outsidethetext.com/home/2008/twitter-for-academia

Pasadeos, Y., Berger, B., & Renfro, R. B. (2010). Public relations as a maturing discipline: An update on research networks. *Journal of Public Relations Research, 22*(2), 136–158. doi:10.1080/10627261003601390

Pascarella, E. T., & Terenzini, P. T. (1991). *How college affects students: Findings and insights from twenty years of research.* San Francisco, CA: Jossey-Bass.

Pask, A. G. S. (1976). *Conversation theory: Applications in education and epistemology.* Amsterdam, The Netherlands: Elsevier.

Passant, A., Hastrup, T., Bojars, U., & Breslin, J. (2008). Microblogging: A semantic and distributed approach. In *Proceedings of the 4th Workshop on Scripting for the Semantic Web*, Tenerife, Spain, June 02, 2008.

Pătruţ, M., & Cmeciu, C. (2011). Blogs – A means of consolidating the National Liberal Party identity. In G. Drulă, L. Roşca, & R. Boicu (Eds.), *The Role of New Media in Journalism: International Conference, NM-JUR-2011* (pp. 23-40). Bucureşti, Romania: Editura Universităţii din Bucureşti.

Patten, B., Sanchez, A., & Tangney, B. (2006). Designing collaborative, constructionist and contextual applications for handheld devices. *Computers & Education, 46*, 294–308. doi:10.1016/j.compedu.2005.11.011

Pearce, N., Weller, M., Scanlon, E., & Kinsley, S. (2010). Digital scholarship considered: How new technologies could transform academic work. *Education, 16*(1). University of Regina. Retrieved May 15, 2011, from http://www.ineducation.ca/article/digital-scholarship-considered-how-new-technologies-could-transform-academic-work

Pedersen, M. E. (1995). Storytelling and the art of teaching. *FORUM, 33*(1), 2–5. Retrieved March 14, 2012, from http://eca.state.gov/forum/vols/vol33/no1/P2.htm

Pedró, F. (2011). La tecnología y la educación: Una dosis de realismo. *El País.* Retrieved December 20, 2011, from ww.elpais.com/articulo/educacion/tecnologia/educacion/dosis/realismo/elpepusocedu/20111121elpepiedu_1/Tes

Peluchette, J., & Karl, K. (2010). Examining students' intended image on facebook: "What were they thinking?! *Journal of Education for Business, 85*, 30–37. doi:10.1080/08832320903217606

Phillips, F. L., Baird, D. E., & Fogg, B. J. (2011). *Facebook for educators.* Retrieved January 25, 2012, from http://facebookforeducators.org/educators-guide.

Phillips, D. (2002). *On-line public relations*. London, UK: Kogan Page.

Phillips, D., & Young, P. (2009). *Online public relations: A practical guide to developing an online strategy in the world of social media*. London, UK: Kogan Page.

Phillips-Fogg, L., Baird, D., & Fogg, B. J. (2011). *Facebook for educators*. Retrieved May 15, 2011, from http://facebookforeducators.org/educators-guide

Phippen, A., Sheppard, L., & Furnell, S. (2004). A practical evaluation of Web analytics. *Internet Research, 14*(4), 284–293. doi:10.1108/10662240410555306

Piekarski, W., & Thomas, B. (2001). Tinmith-Metro: New outdoor techniques for creating city models with an augmented reality wearable computer. *First International Symposium on Wearable Computers* (ISWC '01), (pp. 31-38).

Pigliapoco, E., & Bogliolo, A. (2008). The effects of psychological sense of community in online and face-to-face academic courses. *International Journal of Emerging Technologies in Learning, 3*(4), 60–69.

Pimmer, C., Pachler, N., & Attwell, G. (2010). Towards work-based mobile learning: What can we learn from the fields of work-based learning and mobile learning. *International Journal of Mobile and Blended Learning, 2*(4), 1–18. doi:10.4018/jmbl.2010100101

Plowman, K. D. (1998). Power in conflict for public relations. *Journal of Public Relations Research, 10*, 237–261. doi:10.1207/s1532754xjprr1004_02

Poldrack, R. (2011, October 12). May I have your attention: The brain, multitasking, and information overload. *Project Information Literacy Smart Talk, 9*. Retrieved from http://projectinfolit.org/st/poldrack.asp

Popescu, E. (2010). Students' acceptance of Web 2.0 technologies in higher education: Findings from a survey in a Romanian university. *Proceedings of DEXA 2010 Workshops*, (pp. 92–96). IEEE Computer Society Press.

Prabowol, R., & Thelwall, M. (2009) Sentiment analysis: A combined approach. *Journal of Infometrics, 3*(2), 143-157. Retrieved from www.cyberemotions.eu/rudy-sentiment-preprint.pdf on January 12, 2012.

Preece, J. (2000). *Online communities: Designing usability, supporting sociability*. Chichester, UK: John Wiley & Sons. Retrieved from www.ifsm.umbc.edu/onlinecommunities

Preece, J. S. (2009). The reader to leader framework: Motivating technology-mediated social participation. *Transactions on Human-Computer Interactions, 1*(1), 13–32.

Preece, J., & Shneiderman, B. (2009). The reader-to-leader framework: Motivating technology-mediated social participation. *Transactions on Human-Computer Interaction, 1*(1), 13–32.

Prensky, M. (2001). Digital natives, digital immigrants: Part 1. *On the Horizon, 9*(5), 1-6. Retrieved February 10, 2011, from http://www.emeraldinsight.com/journals.htm?articleid=1532742

Press, O. T. R. (2011). Los hombres son los principales usuarios de iPad. *Diario de Sevilla*. Retrieved December 16, 2011, from http://www.diariodesevilla.es/article/tecnologia/964075/los/hombres/principales/usuarios/ipad.html

Procter, R., Williams, R., & Stewart, J. (2010). *If you build it, will they come? How researchers perceive and use Web 2.0*. Research Information Network. Retrieved February 20, 2011, from http://www.rin.ac.uk/system/files/attachments/web_2.0_screen.pdf

Pumarola, F. (15th November, 2011). *De la Sociedad de la información a la sociedad de la conversación*. Retrieved February 20, 2012, from http://gugleandoporlared.com/blog/2011/11/de-la-sociedad-de-la-informacion-a-la-sociedad-de-la-conversacion/

Punie, Y., & Ala-Mutka, K. (2007). Future learning spaces: New ways of learning and new digital spaces to learn. *Digital Kompetanse, 2*(4), 210–225.

Qualman, E. [2009]. (2011). *Socialnomics: How social media transforms the way we live and do business*. Hoboken, NJ: John Wiley & Sons Inc.

Qualman, E. (2010). *Socialnomics: How social media transforms the way we live and do business*. Hoboken, NJ: John Wiley & Sons.

Quinn, C. (2000). mLearning: Mobile, wireless, in your pocket learning. *LineZine, Fall 2000.* Retrieved February 16, 2012, from http://www.linezine.com/2.1/features/cqmmwiyp.htm

Raacke, J., & Bonds-Raacke, J. (2008). MySpace and Facebook: Applying the uses and gratifications theory to exploring friend-networking sites. *Cyberpsychology & Behavior, 11,* 169–174. doi:10.1089/cpb.2007.0056

Ramsden, A. (2011). *The potential of QR codes in education.* JISC Emerge User & Innovation Programme Meeting. Retrieved August 15, 2011, from http:77www.slideshare.net/andyramsden/potential-qr-codes-education-emerge-20098-presentation

Ras, E., & Rech, J. (2009). Using Wikis to support the Net Generation in improving knowledge acquisition in capstone projects. *Journal of Systems and Software, 82*(4), 553–562. doi:10.1016/j.jss.2008.12.039

Rawlins, B. L. (2005). Corporate social responsibility. In Heath, R. L. (Ed.), *Encyclopedia of public relations* (pp. 210–214). Thousand Oaks, CA: Sage Publications.

Read, B., & Young, J. R. (2006, August 4). Facebook and other social-networking sites raise questions for administrators. *The Chronicle of Higher Education, 52*(48), 37.

Redecker, C., Ala-Mutka, K., & Punie, Y. (2010). *Learning 2.0 – The impact of social media on learning in Europe.* Luxembourg: European Commission Joint Research Centre. Retrieved February 20, 2012, from http://ftp.jrc.es/EURdoc/JRC56958.pdf

Redondo, E., Fonseca, D., Sánchez, A., & Navarro, I. (2012). Augmented reality in architecture degree new approaches in scene illumination and user evaluation. *Journal of Information Technology and Application in Education, 1*(1), 19–27.

Redondo, E., Navarro, I., Sánchez, A., & Fonseca, D. (2011). Visual interfaces and user experience: augmented reality for architectural education: One study case and work in progress. *Communications in Computer and Informatic Science, 166*(3), 355–367. doi:10.1007/978-3-642-21984-9_31

Regalado, O. (20th November 2011). *¿Cómo deberían usar las universidades las redes sociales?* Retrieved February 20, 2012, from http://www.dosensocial.com/2011/11/20/como-deberian-usar-las-universidades-las-redes-sociales/

Reinhardt, W. (2009) Visualizing the dynamics of communication of communities of practice on Twitter. In *Proceedings of the 3rd International Workshop on Building Technology Enhanced Learning solutions for Communities of Practice.*

Reinhardt, W. (2009). *Tracking the dynamics of social communities - Visualising altering word clouds of twitter groups.* Special Track on MashUps for Learning, ICL2009.

Reinhardt, W., Ebner, M., Beham, G., & Costa, C. (2009). How people are using Twitter during conferences. In V. Hornung-Prahauser & M. Luckmann (Eds.), *Creativity and Innovation Competencies on the Web, Proceeding of 5 EduMedia Conference* (pp. 145-146). Salzburg.

Renegade. (2010). *Social media audit.* Retrieved January 9, 2012, from http://www.slideshare.net/RenegadeSMAudit/renegade-social-media-audit-4411127

Rennie, L. J., & McClafferty, T. P. (1996). Science centres and science learning. *Studies in Science Education, 27*(1), 53–98. doi:10.1080/03057269608560078

Resta, P., & Laferriere, T. (2007). Technology in support of collaborative learning. *Educational Psychology Review, 19*(1), 65–83. doi:10.1007/s10648-007-9042-7

Reviglio, M. C. (2010). La mediatizacion del discurso academico en los decires delos ingresantes a la Universidad. *Revista Latinoamericana de Comunicacion, 11,* 33–37.

Rheingold, H. (2011). *Exploring social media literacies in teaching and learning: Howard Rheingold's keynote at CHI 2011.* Interactive Multimedia Technology Blog. Retrieved January 10, 2012, from http://interactivemultimediatechnology.blogspot.com/2011/05/exploring-social-media-literacies-in.html

Ribble, M. S., Bailey, G. D., & Ross, T. W. (2004, September). *Digital citizenship – Addressing appropriate technology behaviour, learning & leading with technology.* ISTE-International Society for Technology in Education, USA.

Richardson, J., & Swan, K. (2011). *Examining social presence in online courses in relation to students' perceived learning and satisfaction*. Retrieved May 23, 2012, from http://hdl.handle.net/2142/18713

Richardson, J. C., & Swan, K. (2003). Examining social presences in online courses in relation to students' perceived learning and satisfaction. *Journal of Asynchronous Learning Networks, 7*(1), 68–88.

Rick, S., & Weber, R. A. (2010). Meaningful learning and transfer of learning in games played repeatedly without feedback. *Games and Economic Behavior, 68*(2), 716–730. doi:10.1016/j.geb.2009.10.004

Robbins-Bell, S. (2008). Higher education as virtual conversation. *EDUCAUSE Review, 43*(5), 24-34. Retrieved January 19, 2012, from http://net.educause.edu/ir/library/pdf/ERM0851.pdf

Robin, B. R. (2005). *The educational uses of digital storytelling*. Retrieved March 13, 2012, from http://faculty.coe.uh.edu/brobin/homepage/Educational-Uses-DS.pdf

Robin, B., & Pierson, M. (2005). *A multilevel approach to using digital storytelling in the classroom*. Digital Storytelling Workshop, SITE 2005, University of Houston. http://www.coe.uh.edu/digital-storytelling/course/SITE2005.

Robin, B. R. (2008). Digital storytelling: A powerful technology tool for the 21st century classroom. *Theory into Practice, 47*(3), 220–228. doi:10.1080/00405840802153916

Roblyer, M. D., & Wiencke, W. R. (2003). *Validation and uses of a rubric to assess and encourage interaction in distance learning*. Paper presented at the annual meeting of the American Educational Research Association, Chicago.

Robyler, M. D., McDaniel, M., Webb, M., Herman, J., & Witty, J. (2010). Findings on Facebook in higher education: A comparison of college faculty and student uses and perceptions of social networking sites. *The Internet and Higher Education, 13*, 134–140. doi:10.1016/j.iheduc.2010.03.002

Rogers, E. M. (1995). *Diffusion of innovations* (4th ed.). New York, NY: Free Press.

Rogers, Y., Price, S., Randell, C., Stanton-Fraser, D., Weal, M., & Fitzpatrick, G. (2005). Ubi-learning: Integrating outdoor and indoor learning experiences. *Communications of the ACM, 48*(1), 55–59. doi:10.1145/1039539.1039570

Roschelle, J., Pea, R., Hoadley, C., Gordin, D., & Means, B. (2001). Changing how and what children learn in school with computer-based technologies. *The Future of Children, 10*(2), 76–101. doi:10.2307/1602690

Rosenbloom, A. (2004). The blogosphere. *Communications of the ACM, 47*(12), 31–33.

Rothman, S., & Mosmann, C. (1972). *Computers and society*. Chicago, IL: Science Research Associates, Inc.

Rovai, A. P. (2003). Strategies for grading online discussion: Effects on discussions and classroom community in internet-based university courses. *Journal of Computing in Higher Education, 15*(1), 89–107. doi:10.1007/BF02940854

Rovai, A. P. (2004). A constructivist approach to online college learning. *The Internet and Higher Education, 7*(2), 79–93. doi:10.1016/j.iheduc.2003.10.002

Rúas, X., & Dapena, B. (2011). Los diputados del parlamento gallego en Facebook. *Revista Redmarka: Revista digital de marketing aplicado*. Retrieved February 23, 2012, from http://www.cienciared.com.ar/ra/usr/39/1254/redmarkan7v1pp77_106.pdf

Rushton, K. (2011, February 28) Texting too distracting? Using cell phones creates problems for students. *The Oracle: West Springfield High School Newspaper*. Retrieved from http://www.theoracleonline.org/news/2011/02/28/texting-too-distractingusing-cell-phones-creates-problems-for-students/

Russo, C. J., Squelch, J., & Varnham, S. (2010). Teachers and social networking sites: Think before you post. *Journal of Law and Social Justice, 5*(5), 1–15.

Russo, T., & Benson, S. (2005). Learning with invisible others: Perceptions of online presence and their relationship to cognitive and affective learning. *Journal of Educational Technology & Society, 8*(1), 54–62.

Ruyters, M., Douglas, K., & Law, S. F. (2011). Blended learning using role-plays, wikis and blogs. *Journal of Learning Design, 4*(4), 45–55.

Sacks, I. (2009). Student, professor Facebook friendships bring communication, risks. *The Maneater*. Retrieved January 14, 2012, from http://www.themaneater.com/stories/2009/2/23/student-professor-facebook-friendships-bring-commu/

Sadik, A. (2008). Digital storytelling: A meaningful technology-integrated approach for engaged student learning. *Educational Technology Research and Development*, *56*(4), 487–506. doi:10.1007/s11423-008-9091-8

Saeed, N., Yang, Y., & Sinnappan, S. (2009). Emerging Web technologies in higher education: A case of incorporating blogs, podcasts and social bookmarks in a web programming course based on students learning styles and technology preferences. *Journal of Educational Technology & Society*, *12*(4), 98–109.

Safurah Abd, J., Khairuzan Abd, J., & Azmi Abdul, L. (2010). *Social media and our youths today: Exploring the impact of social media on Malaysian youths.* Paper presented at the International Conference on Communication and Media, Melaka.

Salamanca, F. D. (2008). *Galería de fcomsalamanca.* Retrieved February 24, 2012, from http://www.flickr.com/people/orionmedialab/

Säljö, R. (2004). Learning and technologies, people and tools in co-ordinated activities. *International Journal of Educational Research*, *41*(6), 489–494. doi:10.1016/j.ijer.2005.08.013

Säljö, R. (2010). Digital tools and challenges to institutional traditions of learning: Technologies, social memory and the performative nature of learning. *Journal of Computer Assisted Learning*, *26*(1), 53–64. doi:10.1111/j.1365-2729.2009.00341.x

Salmon, G. (2005). *E-moderating: The key to teaching and learning online.* New York, NY: Routledge Falmer.

Sanna, R., Pintus, A., Giroux, S., & Moulin, C. (2002). Mobile lessons: Lessons based on geo-referenced information. In M. Driscoll & T. Reeves (Eds.), *Proceedings of World Conference on E-Learning in Corporate, Government, Healthcare, and Higher Education*, (pp. 331-338).

Saravani, S. J., & Cayton, J. (2009). A conceptual model for the education deployement of QR codes. *Proceedings ASCILITE*, Auckland, (pp. 919-922).

Saunders, N., Beltrão, P., Jensen, L., Jurczak, D., Krause, R., Kuhn, M., & Wu, S. (2009). Microblogging the ISMB: A new approach to conference reporting. *PLoS Computational Biology*, *5*(1), e1000263. doi:10.1371/journal.pcbi.1000263

Scardamalia, M., & Bereiter, C. (1991). Higher levels of agency for children in knowledge-building: A challenge for the design of new knowledge media. *Journal of the Learning Sciences*, *1*(1), 37–68. doi:10.1207/s15327809jls0101_3

Scardamalia, M., & Bereiter, C. (1994). Computer support for knowledge-building communities. *Journal of the Learning Sciences*, *3*(3), 265–283. doi:10.1207/s15327809jls0303_3

Schmidt, J. (2006). Social software: Onlinegestütztes Informations-, Identitäts- und Beziehungsmanagement. *Neue Soziale Bewegungen*, *19*(2), 37–47.

Schonfeld, R. C., & Housewright, R. (2010). *Faculty survey 2009: Key strategic insights for libraries, publishers, and societies.* Ithaka Report. Retrieved July 25, 2010, from http://www.ithaka.org/ithaka-s-r/research/faculty-surveys-2000-2009/faculty-survey-2009

Schoop, E., Bukvova, H., & Lieske, C. (2006). *Blended learning arrangements for higher education in the changing knowledge society.* Retrieved from www.qucosa.de/.../2009_Riga_Schoop.pdf

Schroeder, J., & Greenbowe, T. J. (2009). The chemistry of Facebook: Using social networking to create an online community for the organic chemistry. *Innovate: Journal of Online Education*, *5*(4).

Schuck, S., & Kearney, M. (2004). *Students in the director's seat. Teaching and learning across the school curriculum with student-generated video.* Faculty of Education, University of Technology, Sydney. Retrieved from http://www.ed-dev.uts.edu.au/teachered/research/dvproject/home.html

Schwartz, H. (2009). Facebook: The new classroom commons? *The Chronicle of Higher Education*, 1–5.

Searson, M., Dawley, L., Field, W., Owens, C., & Penny, C. (2011). *There's an app for that! The role of mobile learning in education.* Panel presentation at the Society for Information Technology & Teacher Education Annual Conference, Nashville, Tennessee.

Seichter, H., & Schnabel, M. A. (2005). Digital and tangible sensation: An augmented reality urban design studio. *Proceedings of the 10th International Conference on Computer Aided Architectural Design Research in Asia* (CAADRIA 2005), Vol. 2, (pp. 193-202).

Selwyn, N. (2007, November). *'Screw Blackboard... do it on Facebook!': An investigation of students' educational use of Facebook*. Paper presented at the 'Poke 1.0 - Facebook social research symposium', University of London, UK. Retrieved January 13, 2012, from http://www.scribd.com/doc/513958/Facebook-seminar-paper-Selwyn

Selwyn, N. (2010). *The educational significance of social media: A critical perspective*. Key note talk at the ED-MEDIA 2010 Conference, Toronto. Retrieved August 20, 2010, from http://www.scribd.com/doc/33693537/The-educational-significance-of-social-media-a-critical-perspective

Selwyn, N. (2011). Social media in higher education. *The Europa World of Learning 2012*, 62nd ed. Retrieved December 20, 2011, from http://www.educationarena.com/pdf/sample/sample-essay-selwyn.pdf

Selwyn, N. (2000). Creating a "connected" community? Teachers' use of an electronic discussion group. *Teachers College Record*, *102*, 750–778. doi:10.1111/0161-4681.00076

Selwyn, N. (2008). *Education 2.0? Designing the web for teaching and learning. A commentary by the technology enhanced learning phase of the teaching and learning research programme*. London, UK: TLRO-TEL Institute of Education.

Selwyn, N. (2009). Faceworking: Exploring students' education-related use of Facebook. *Learning, Media and Technology*, *34*(2), 157–174. doi:10.1080/17439880902923622

Selwyn, N. (2011). Finding an appropriate fit for me: Examining the (in)flexibilities of international distance learning. *International Journal of Lifelong Education*, *30*(3), 367–383. doi:10.1080/02601370.2011.570873

Selwyn, N. (2012). *Social media in higher education. The Europa World of Learning 2012*. Routledge.

Șerbu, V. M. (2011). *Paradigma învățământului centrat pe student. Abordarea etnografică a unei comunități profesionale*. Unpublished doctoral dissertation, University of Bucharest, Bucharest.

Seufert, S. (2002, May). *Design and management of online learning communities*. 2002 European Academy of Management Conference.

Shaheen, M. A. (2008). Use of social networks and information seeking behavior of students during political crises in Pakistan: A case study. *The International Information & Library Review*, *40*, 142–147. doi:10.1016/j.iilr.2008.07.006

Shamma, D., Kennedy, L., & Churchill, E. (2009). *Tweet the debates*. Paper presented at WSM'09 October 23, 2009, Beijing, China.

Shamma, D., Kennedy, L., & Churchill, E. (2010). *Twetgeist: Can the Twitter timeline reveal the structure of broadcast events?* Paper presented at CSCW 2010, February 610, 2010, Savannah, Georgia, USA.

Sharp, C., Pocklington, K., & Weindling, D. (2002). Study support and the development of the self-regulated learner. *Educational Research*, *44*(1), 29–41. doi:10.1080/00131880110107333

Sharpe, R., Beetham, H., & de Freitas, M. (2010). *Rethinking learning for a digital age: How learners are shaping their own experiences*. London, UK: Routledge.

Sharples, M. (2010). Foreword. In E. Brown (Ed.), *Education in the wild: Contextual and location-based mobile learning in action* (pp. 4–6). A report from the STELLAR Alpine Rendez-Vous workshop series. Retrieved March 7, 2012, from http://www.lsri.nottingham.ac.uk/ejb/preprints/ARV_Education_in_the_wild.pdf

Sharples, M., Taylor, J., & Vavoula, G. (2005). Towards a theory of mobile learning. *Proceedings of mLearn 2005 Conference*, Cape Town, South Africa.

Sharples, M. (2000). The design of personal mobile technologies for lifelong learning. *Computers & Education*, *34*, 177–193. doi:10.1016/S0360-1315(99)00044-5

Sharples, M., Milrad, M., Arnedillo Sánchez, I., & Vavoula, G. (2009). Mobile learning: Small devices, big issues. In Balacheff, N., Ludvigsen, S., de Jong, T., Lazonder, A., & Barnes, S. (Eds.), *Technology enhanced learning: Principles and products* (pp. 233–249). Berlin, Germany: Springer.

Sharples, M., Taylor, J., & Vavoula, G. (2007). A theory of learning for the mobile age. In Andrews, R., & Haythornthwaite, C. (Eds.), *The SAGE handbook of e-learning research* (pp. 221–224). London, UK: Sage. doi:10.4135/9781848607859.n10

Shawkath, A. (2010, November 12). 7.5 juta pemilik akaun Facebook. *KOSMO.*

Shen, T. W. (2010). *Plurk intervention on artificial intelligent learning for higher education.* Paper presented at 2010 Conference on Teaching Excellence, 29-30 Nov. 2010. Retrieved from http://tec.tcu.edu.tw/et2010/paper/27.pdf

Shen, H., & Toth, E. L. (2008). An ideal public relations master's curriculum: Expectations and status quo. *Public Relations Review, 34,* 309–311. doi:10.1016/j.pubrev.2008.03.030

Shepherd, A. (2010). *Social media audit: Understanding and implementation.* Retrieved January 11, 2012, from http://ashshepherd.com/blog/5-planning-and-process/24-social-media-audit-understanding-and-implementation

Shepherd, E., & Yeo, G. (2003). *Managing records: A handbook of principles and practice.* London, UK: Facet Publishing. doi:10.1108/00220410310506349

Shiratuddin, N., & Zaibon, S.-B. (2010). Mobile game-based learning with local content and appealing characters. *International Journal of Mobile Learning and Organisation, 4*(1), 55–82. doi:10.1504/IJMLO.2010.029954

Siciliano, P., Jenks, M., Dana, M., & Talbert, B. (2011). The impact of audio technology on undergraduate instruction in a study abroad course on English gardens. *NACTA Journal, 55*(1), 46–53.

Siemens, G. (2005). Connectivism: A learning theory for the digital age. *International Journal of Instructional Technology & Distance Learning, 2*(1). Retrieved February 10, 2011, from http://www.itdl.org/Journal/Jan_05/article01.htm

Siemens, G., & Tittenberg, P. (2009). *Handbook of emerging technologies for learning.* University of Manitoba.

Sievert, H. (2009, September). *Some ideas for new systematics.* Input to the Round Table "PR practices and qualifications. EUPRERA 2009, Bucharest.

Simanowski, R. (2009). Teaching digital literature didactic and institutional aspects. In Simanowski, R., Schäfer, J., & Gendolla, P. (Eds.), *Reading moving letters: Digital literature in research and teaching: A handbook* (pp. 15–28). Bielefeld, Germany: Transcript Verlag.

Simoes, l., & Borges Gouveia, L. (2008). Web 2.0 and higher education: Pedagogical implications. IN *Proceedings of the 4th International Barcelona Conference on Higher Education Vol. 2 Knowledge technologies for social transformation.* Barcelona, Spain: GUNI. Retrieved February 13, 2012, from Http://www.guni-rmies.net

Simon, M., Graziano, M., & Lenhart, A. (2001). *The internet and education.* Pew Internet & American Life Project Report. Retrieved 12th November, 2011, from http://www.pewinternet.org/Reports/2001/The-Internet-and-Education.aspx

Simonson, M., Smaldino, S., Albright, M., & Zvacek, S. (2003). *Teaching and learning at a distance.* Upper Saddle River, NJ: Prentice Hall.

Singh, N., Kwon, I., & Pereira, A. (2003). Cross-cultural consumer socialization: An exploratory study of socialization influences across three ethnic groups. *Psychology and Marketing, 20*(10), 867–881. doi:10.1002/mar.10100

Sloan Consortium. (2010). *Class differences: Online education in the United States.* Retrieved on February 27, 2012, from http://sloanconsortium.org/publications/survey/class_differences

Smith, A. (2011, September 9). *Americans and text messaging.* Pew Internet & American Life Project website. Retrieved November 18, 2011, from http://www.pewinternet.org/Reports/2011/Cell-Phone-Texting-2011.aspx

Smith, A., & Brenner, J. (2012). *Twitter use 2012.* A report by Pew Research Center. Retrieved from http://pewinternet.org/~/media//Files/Reports/2012/PIP_Twitter_Use_2012.pdf

Social Bakers. (2012). *Spain Facebook statistics.* Retrieved February 24, 2012, from http://www.socialbakers.com/facebook-statistics/spain

Soder, C. (2009). Social media extend search for prospective students; Universities build relationships, canvass recruits with Facebook, other online tools. *Crain's Cleveland Business,* 0012.

So, H. J., & Brush, T. A. (2008). Student perceptions of collaborative learning, social presence and satisfaction in a blended learning environment: Relationships and critical factors. *Computers & Education, 51*(1), 318–336. doi:10.1016/j.compedu.2007.05.009

Solis, B. (2012, 27 February). *The state of Twitterverse 2012*. Blog post. Retrieved March 1, 2012, from http://socialmediatoday.com/node/457621

Song, L., Singleton, E. S., Hill, J. R., & Koh, M. H. (2004). Improving online learning: Student perceptions of useful and challenging characteristics. *The Internet and Higher Education, 7*, 59–70. doi:10.1016/j.iheduc.2003.11.003

Spitzer, K. L., Eisenberg, M. B., & Lowe, C. A. (1998). *Information literacy- Essential skills for the information age*. Syracuse, NY: ERIC Clearinghouse on Information and Technology.

Squire, K., & Johnson, C. (2000). Supporting distributed communities of practice with interactive television. *Educational Technology Research and Development, 48*(1), 23–43. doi:10.1007/BF02313484

Sriramesh, K., & Hornaman, L. B. (2006). Public relations as a profession: An analysis of curricular content in the United States. *Journal of Creative Communications, 1*(2), 155–172. doi:10.1177/097325860600100202

Sriramesh, K., & Vercic, D. (2007). The impact of globalization on public relations: A special section from the BledCom 2007 Conference. *Public Relations Review, 33*, 355–444. doi:10.1016/j.pubrev.2007.09.002

St.Amant, K. (2005). A prototype theory approach to international website analysis and design. *Technical Communication Quarterly, 14*(1), 73–91. doi:10.1207/s15427625tcq1401_6

Standley, M. (2003). *Digital storytelling using new technology and the power of stories to help our students learn—and teach*. Cable in the Classroom. Retrieved from http://www.ciconline.org/home.

Starke-Meyerring, D. A. (2006). Building a shared virtual learning culture: An international classroom partnership. *Business Communication Quarterly, 69*(1), 25–49. doi:10.1177/1080569905285543

Starr, P. (1996). Computing our way to educational reform. *The American Prospect, 27*, 50–59.

Starr, R. H., & Murray, T. (2005, October). Education goes digital- The evolution of online learning and the revolution in higher education. *Communications of the ACM, 48*(10), 59–64.

Stevens, B. (2005). What communication skills do employers want? Silicon Valley recruiters respond. *Journal of Employment Counseling, 42*(1), 2–10. doi:10.1002/j.2161-1920.2005.tb00893.x

strengthen a scientific. *Workshop Science 2.0 for TEL*, ECTEL 2009

Sturgeon, C. M., & Walker, C. (2009). *Faculty on Facebook: Confirm or deny?* The 14th Annual Instructional Technology Conference. Middle Tennessee State University Murfreesboro, Tennessee, US.

Stutzman, F. (2009). *Information seeking during a life transition*. AOIR 2009 Doctoral Colloquium, Milwaukee. Retrieved from http://fredstutzman.com/papers/AOIRDC2009_Stutzman.pdf

Sundara Rajan, M. (2004). Moral rights in information technology: A new kind of personal right? *International Journal of Law & Information Technology, 12*(1), 32–54. doi:10.1093/ijlit/12.1.32

Susono, H., & Shimomura, S. (2006). Using mobile phones and QR codes for formative class assessment. In Mendez-Vilas, A., Solano, A., & Mesa, J. A. (Eds.), *Current developments in technology-assisted education*. Badajoz, Spain.

Suster, M. (29 December 2010). *The power of Twitter in information discovery*. Retrieved March 1, 2012, from http://www.aonetwork.com/AOStory/Power-Twitter-Information-Discovery-0

Suter, V., Alexander, B., & Kaplan, P. (2005). Social software and the future of conferences—Right now. *EDUCAUSE Review, 40*(1), 46–59.

Sutton, J. (2010). Twittering Tennessee: Distributed networks and collaboration following a technological disaster. In *Proceedings of the 7th International ISCRAM Conference* – Seattle, USA, May 2010.

Swan, K. (2005). A constructivist model for thinking about learning online. In Bourne, J., & Moore, J. C. (Eds.), *Elements of quality online education: Engaging communities* (pp. 13–30). Needham, MA: Sloan-C.

Swanson, D. J. (2011). The student-run public relations firm in an undergraduate program: Reaching learning and professional development goals through 'real world' experience. *Public Relations Review, 37*(5), 499–505. doi:10.1016/j.pubrev.2011.09.012

Tallinn, Estonia. boyd, d. m., & Ellison, N. B. (2007). Social network sites: Definitions, history, and scholarship. *Journal of Computer-Mediated Communication, 13*(1), 210–230.

Tapscott, D., & Williams, A. (2007). *Wikinomics*. New York, NY: Atlantic.

Tavares, D. M., & De Paula-Caurin, G. A. (2010). *Proposal for the use of QR code in supply chain management*. Production Online Magazine.

Taylor, M., & Kent, M. L. (2010). Anticipatory socialization in the use of social media in public relations: A content analysis of PRSA's Public relations tactics. *Public Relations Review, 36*, 207–214. doi:10.1016/j.pubrev.2010.04.012

Tello, S. F. (2007). An analysis of student persistence in online education. *International Journal of Information and Communication Technology Education, 3*(3), 47–62. doi:10.4018/jicte.2007070105

Templeton, M. (2008). *Microblogging defined*. Retrieved from http://microblink.com/2008/11/11/microblogging-defined/

Tench, R., & Yoemans, L. (2009). *Exploring public relations*, 2nd ed. London, UK: Financial Times/ Prentice Hall.

Tengku Faekah, T. A. (2010). *A structural model of the relationships between personality factors, perceptions of the school as a learning organization, workplace learning and job performance of teachers*. Unpublished doctoral thesis, College of Arts and Sciences, Universiti Utara Malaysia.

Thomas, D., & Brown, J. S. (2011). *A new culture of learning: Cultivating the imagination for a world of constant change*. Createspace.

Thonhauser, P., Selver, S., & Ebner, M. (2012). Thought bubbles - A conceptual prototype for a Twitter based recommender system for research 2.0. *iKnow 2012, Proceedings of the 12th International Confrerence on Knowledge Management and Knowledge Technologies*.

Thorne, S., Black, R., & Sykes, J. (2009). Second language use, socialization, and learning in internet interest communities and online gaming. *Modern Language Journal, 93*(S1), 802–821. doi:10.1111/j.1540-4781.2009.00974.x

Tinoca, L. (2011). *Assessment 2.0*. Retrieved from http://www.slideshare.net/luistinoca/assessment-20-10291238

Tonn, C., Petzold, F., & Bimber, O., Grundhö, Fer, A., & Donath, D. (2008). Spatial augmented reality for architecture designing and planning with and within existing buildings. *International Journal of Architectural Computing, 6*(1), 41–58. doi:10.1260/147807708784640126

Towner, T., VanHorn, A., & Parker, S. (2007). Facebook: Classroom tool for a classroom community? *Midwestern Political Science Association Conference*, (pp. 1-18). Retrieved January 28, 2012, from http://citation.allacademlc.com/meta/p_mla_apa_research_citation/1/9/7/1/3/pages197133/p197133-1.php

Trilling, B., & Hood, P. (1999). Learning, technology, and education reform in the knowledge age or we're wired, webbed, and windowed, now what? *Educational Technology, 39*(3), 5–18.

Tsou, W., Wang, W., & Tzeng, Y. (2006). Applying a multimedia storytelling website in foreign language learning. *Computers & Education, 47*, 17–28. doi:10.1016/j.compedu.2004.08.013

Tsvetozar, G., Evgenia, G., & Smrikarov, A. (2004). *M-learning - A new stage of e-learning*. International Conference on Computer Systems and Technologies, CompSysTech.

Tu, B.-M., et al. (2011). Applying the perspective of technology sensemaking to Plurk user behaviors: An exploratory study. In *HICSS '11 Proceedings of the 2011 44th Hawaii International Conference on System Sciences*.

Tuenti. (2012). *Blog English version*. Retrieved February 28, 2012, from http://blog.tuenti.com/en/

Túñez, M., & Sixto, J. (2011). Redes sociales, política y Compromiso 2.0: La comunicación de los diputados españoles en Facebook. *Revista Latina de Comunicación Social*, 210-246. Retrieved February 23, 2012, from http://www.revistalatinacs.org/11/art/930_Santiago/09_Tunez.html

Tuomi, P., & Multisilta, J. (2010). MoViE: Experiences and attitudes—Learning with a mobile social video application. *Digital Culture & Education, 2*(2), 127–151.

Tuomi, P., & Multisilta, J. (2012). Comparative study on use of mobile videos in elementary and middle school. *International Journal of Computer Information Systems and Industrial Management Applications*, *4*, 255–266. http://www.mirlabs.org/ijcisim/regular_papers_2012/Paper28.pdf Retrieved March 6, 2012

Turkle, S. (2009). Interview Sherry Turkle [Television series episode]. *Frontline*. Los Angeles, CA: PBS. Retrieved from http://www.pbs.org/wgbh/pages/frontline/digitalnation/interview/turkle.html

Turkle, S. (1995). *Life on the screen: Identity in the age of the internet*. New York, NY: Simon & Schuster Paperbacks.

Turkle, S. (2011). *Alone together: Why we expect more from technology and less from each other*. New York, NY: Basic Books.

Turner, C. S. M., Robinson, D., Lee, M., & Soutar, A. (2009). Using technology to direct learning in higher education. The way forward? *Journal of Active Learning in Higher Education*, *10*(1).

Twitter. (2011). *#numbers: Official Weblog of Twitter*. Retrieved from http://blog.twitter.com/2011/03/numbers.html

Tyner, K. R. (1998). *Literacy in a digital world-Teaching and learning in the age of information* (pp. 18–20). Lawrence Erlbaum Associates, Inc.

U.S. Department of Education, National Center for Education Statistics. (1999). *Distance education at postsecondary education institutions: 1997-98*. NCES 2000-013, by Laurie Lewis, Kyle Snow, Elizabeth Farris, Douglas Levin. Bernie Greene, project officer.

U.S. Department of Education, National Center for Education Statistics. (2008). *Distance education at degree-granting postsecondary institutions: 2006–07* (NCES 2009-044).

Udrea, C., & Ionescu, A.-C. (2007). *CSR and competitiveness European SMEs' good practice – National report Romania*.

Uehara Henrikson, J. (2011). *The growth of social media: An infographic*. Retrieved September 1, 2011, from http://www.searchenginejournal.com/the-growth-of-social-media-an-infographic/32788/

University of Minnesota. (2008, June 21). Educational benefits of social networking sites. *ScienceDaily*. Retrieved January 20, 2009, from http://www.sciencedaily.com/releases/2008/06/080620133907.htm

UPV. C. G. (10th February 2012). *La Universitat al teu centre: IES Veles e Vents (Grao de Gandía)*. Retrieved February 25, 2012, from http://www.youtube.com/watch?v=csBUC19ZxeY

US Department of Education. (2010). *Evaluation of evidence-based practices in online learning: A meta-analysis and review of online learning studies*. Retrieved January 13, 2012, from http://www.ed.gov/about/offices/list/opepd/ppss/reports.html

Uso-Juan, E. (2006). The compensatory nature of discipline-related knowledge and English-language proficiency in reading for academic purposes. *Modern Language Journal*, *90*(2), 210–227. doi:10.1111/j.1540-4781.2006.00393.x

Uys, D. P. (2010). Blended learning in the ICT-enabled learning and teaching community of practice at Charles Sturt University. In *Proceedings of World Conference on Educational Multimedia, Hypermedia and Telecommunications 2010* (pp. 258-267). Chesapeake, VA: AACE. Retrieved from http://www.editlib.org/p/34647

Vaira, M. (2004). Globalization and higher education organizational change: A framework for analysis. *Higher Education*, *48*, 483–510. doi:10.1023/B:HIGH.0000046711.31908.e5

Van Buskirk, E. (2009, August 10). Open source 'Twitter' could fend off the next twitpocalypse. Wired. Retrieved from http://www.wired.com/epicenter/2009/08/twitpocalypse

Van Dijk, J. (2005). *The network society: Social aspects of new media* (2nd ed.). London, UK: Sage. (Original work published 1999)

van Dijk, T. A. (2000). *Ideology – A multidisciplinary approach*. London, UK: Sage.

Van Leuven, J. (1999). Four new course competencies for majors. *Public Relations Review*, *25*(1), 77–85. doi:10.1016/S0363-8111(99)80129-5

Van Ruler, B. (2005). Commentary: Professionals are from Venus, scholars are from Mars. *Public Relations Review, 31*, 159–173. doi:10.1016/j.pubrev.2005.02.022

Vartiainen, H., & Enkenberg, J. (2011). Enlargement of educational innovation: An instructional model of the case forest pedagogy. In H. Ruokamo, M. Eriksson, L. Pekkala, H. Vuojärvi (Eds.), *Social media in the middle of nowhere – Proceedings of the NBE 2011 Conference* (pp. 76–86). Rovaniemi, Finland: Lapland University Press.

Veletsianos, G. (2010). Participatory scholars and 21st century scholarship. *George Veletsianos's blog.* Retrieved July 18, 2010, from http://www.veletsianos.com/2010/04/06/participatory-scholars-scholarshi/

Veletsianos, G., & Kimmons, R. (2012). Networked participatory scholarship: Emergent techno-cultural pressures towards open and digital scholarship in online networks. *Computers & Education, 58*(2), 766-774. Retrieved November 6, 2011, from http://www.veletsianos.com/2011/11/06/networked-participatory-scholarship/

Violino, B. (2009). The buzz on campus: Social networking takes hold. *Community College Journal, 79*(6), 28–30.

Visser, W. (2010). The age of responsibility. CSR 2.0 and the new DNA for business. *Journal of Business Systems. Governance and Ethics, 5*(3), 7–22.

Vlachopoulas, P., & Cowan, J. (2010). Choices of approaches in e-moderation: Conclusions from a grounded theory study. *Journal of Active Learning in Higher Education, 11*(3), 213–224. doi:10.1177/1469787410379684

Vonderwell, S. (2003). An examination of asynchronous communication experiences and perspectives of students in an online course: A case study. *The Internet and Higher Education, 6*, 77–90. doi:10.1016/S1096-7516(02)00164-1

Voogt De, J., & Knezek, G. A. (2008). *International handbook of information technology in primary and secondary education*, (p. 18). Springer Science+ Business Media.

Vrasidas, C., & Stock-McIssac, M. (1999). Factors influencing interaction in an online course. *American Journal of Distance Education, 13*(3), 22–35. doi:10.1080/08923649909527033

Vuojärvi, H., Eriksson, M. J., & Ruokamo, H. (in press). Designing pedagogical models for tourism education: Focus on work-based mobile learning. *International Journal of Mobile and Blended Learning.*

Vygotsky, S. L. (1978). *Mind in society*. Cambridge: Harvard University Press.

Wagner, D., & Schmalstieg, D. (2007). ARToolKitPlus for pose tracking on mobile devices. *Proceedings of the 12th Computer Vision Winter Workshop* (CVWW'07), (pp. 6-8).

Wagner, R. (2011). Educational technology: Social media tools for teaching and learning. *Athletic Train Education Journal, 6*(1), 51–52.

Waldeck, J. H., Kearney, P., & Plax, T. G. (2001). Teacher email message strategies and students' willingness to communicate online. *Journal of Applied Communication Research, 29*, 5470. doi:10.1080/00909880128099

Walker, B. K. (2007). *Bridging the distance: How social interaction, presence, social presence, and sense of community influence student learning experiences in an online virtual learning environment.* Unpublished doctoral dissertation, The University of North Carolina at Greensboro, Greensboro, North Carolina.

Wallace, L. (1996). Changes in the demographics and motivations of distance education students. *Journal of Distance Education, 11*(1), 1-31. Retrieved December 2, 2003, from http://cade.athabascau.ca/vol11.1/wallace.html

Wallis, C. (2010). *The impacts of media multitasking on children's learning and development: Report from a research seminar.* New York, NY: The Joan Ganz Cooney Center as Sesame Workshop.

Walsh, A. (2010). QR codes-using mobile phones to deliver library instruction and help at the point of need. *Journal of Information Literacy, 4*(1), 55–64.

Wankel, C. (2009). Management education using social media. *Organization Management Journal, 6*(4), 251–262. doi:10.1057/omj.2009.34

Watkins, S. C. (2009, August 24). Interview by M. Beja: How students, professors, and colleges are, and should be, using social media. *Wired Campus*. Retrieved on December 30, 2011 from http://chronicle.com/blogs/wiredcampus/how-students-professorscolleges-areshould-be-using-social-media/7787

Watters, A. (6 March 2012). *Edmodo makes the move from Social network to Educational platform*. Blog post. Retrieved March 12, 2012, from http://hackeducation.com/2012/03/06/edmodo-makes-the-move-from-social-network-to-education-platform/

Wecker, M. (2011, October 24). Yammer trumps Facebook for some graduate students. *US News Education*. Retrieved from http://www.usnews.com/education/best-graduate-schools/articles/2011/10/24/yammer-trumps-facebook-for-some-graduate-students

Weller, M. (2011). Digital resilience. In *The digital scholar*. Bloomsbury Academic. Retrieved September 16, 2011, from http://www.bloomsburyacademic.com/view/DigitalScholar_9781849666275/chapter-ba-9781849666275-chapter-014.xml;jsessionid=466C69AA7FAE21941D713D8324F68744

Weller, M. (2011). Digital, networked and open. In *The digital scholar*. Bloomsbury Academic. Retrieved September 16, 2011, from http://www.bloomsburyacademic.com/view/DigitalScholar_9781849666275/chapter-ba-9781849666275-chapter-001.xml;jsessionid=466C69AA7FAE21941D713D8324F68744

Weller, M. (2011). The digital scholar: How technology is transforming scholarly practice. London, UK: Bloomsbury Academic. Retrieved September 16, 2011, from http://www.bloomsburyacademic.com/view/DigitalScholar_9781849666275/book-ba-9781849666275.xml

Weller, M. (2011). The nature of scholarship. *The digital scholar*. Bloomsbury. Retrieved September 16, 2011, from http://www.bloomsburyacademic.com/view/DigitalScholar_9781849666275/chapter-ba-9781849666275-chapter-004.xml;jsessionid=13C1CCC4B35C0F37EDE362F5B7718D5D

Wellman, B. (1999). The network community: An introduction to networks in the global village. In *Networks in the global village* (pp. 1–48). Boulder, CO: Westview Press.

Wellman, B., & Gulia, M. (1999). Net surfers don't ride alone. In Wellman, B. (Ed.), *Networks in the global village* (pp. 331–366). Boulder, CO: Westview Press.

Wenger, E. (1998). *Communities of practice: Learning, meaning, and identity*. New York, NY: Cambridge University Press.

Wenger, E., McDermott, R., & Snyder, W. (2002). *Cultivating communities of practice. A guide to managing knowledge*. Cambridge, MA: Harvard Business School Press.

Wesch, M. (10th October 2007). *A vision of students today*. Retrieved February 27, 2012, from http://www.youtube.com/watch?v=dGCJ46vyR9o

West, A., Lewis, J., & Currie, P. (2009). Students' Facebook 'friends': public and private spheres. *Journal of Youth Studies, 12*(6), 615–627. doi:10.1080/13676260902960752

White, D. (2011, 30th September). The learning black market. *TALL Blog: Online education with the University of Oxford*. Retrieved February 10, 2012, from http://tallblog.conted.ox.ac.uk/index.php/2011/09/30/the-learning-black-market/

White, D., & Le Cornu, A. (2011). Visitors and residents: A new typology for online engagement. *First Monday, 16*(9). Retrieved September 15, 2011, from http://firstmonday.org/htbin/cgiwrap/bin/ojs/index.php/fm/article/view/3171/3049

Wijers, M., & Jonker, V. (2010). MobileMath: A location-aware game for mathematics. In E. Brown (Ed.), *Education in the wild: Contextual and location-based mobile learning in action* (pp. 20–22). A report from the STELLAR Alpine Rendez-Vous workshop series. Retrieved March 7, 2012, from http://www.lsri.nottingham.ac.uk/ejb/preprints/ARV_Education_in_the_wild.pdf

Wilcox, D. L. (2009). Preserving reputation in the internet age. In A. Rogojinaru, & S. Wolstenholme (Eds.), *Current trends in international public relations* (pp. 13-27). București, Romania: Tritonic.

William, R. (2011). *Edmodo*. Blog note. Retrieved from http://richardeducate.blogspot.com/2011/07/2nd-project-edmodo.html

Williams, B. J., & Jacobs, J. (2004). Exploring the use of blogs as learning spaces in the higher education sector. *Australasian Journal of Educational technology, 20*(2), 232-247.

Williams, J., & Fardon, M. (2007). Perpetual connectivity: Lecture recordings and portable media players. In R. J. Atkinson & C. McBeath (Eds.), *Proceedings of ASCILITE,* (pp. 1084-1092).

Williams, R., Karousou, R., & Mackness, J. (2011). Emergent learning and learning ecologies in Web 2.0. *The International Review of Resaerch in Open and Distance Learning, 12*(3). Retrieved January 20, 2012, from http://www.irrodl.org/index.php/irrodl/article/view/883

Williams, J. B., & Jacobs, J. (2004). Exploring the use of blogs as learning spaces in the higher education sector. *Australasian Journal of Educational Technology, 20*(2), 232–247.

Wilson, L. (2009). *Practical teaching: A guide to PTLLS & DTLLS*. Andover, MD: Cengage Learning EMEA.

Winer, D. (September 22, 2009). *What is the real time web?* Retrieved from on March 14, 2012, from http://scripting.com/stories/2009/09/22/whatIsTheRealtimeWeb.html

Wingkvist, A., & Ericsson, M. (2010). Extracting and expressing experience with mobile learning: Lessons learned. *International Journal of Mobile Learning and Organisation, 4*(4), 428–439. doi:10.1504/IJMLO.2010.037538

Wise, A., Chang, J., Duffy, T., & Del Valle, R. (2004). The effects of teacher social presence on student satisfaction engagement, and learning. *Journal of Educational Computing Research, 31*(3), 247–271. doi:10.2190/V0LB-1M37-RNR8-Y2U1

Wodzick, K., Schwämmlein, E., & Moskaliuk, J. (2012). "Actually, I wanted to learn": Study-related knowledge exchange on social networking sites. *The Internet and Higher Education, 15*(1), 9–14. doi:10.1016/j.iheduc.2011.05.008

Wolfe, K. (2009). *Facebook: Not just for students. What started as a college networking site now has university faculty jumping on the bandwagon.* Retrieved January 13, 2012, from http://www.mndaily.com/2009/02/25/facebook-not-just-students

Woods, R. H. (2002). How much communication is enough in online courses? Exploring the relationship between frequency of instructor-initiated personal email and learners' perceptions of and participation in online learning. *International Journal of Instructional Media, 29*(4), 377–394.

Worthen, B. R., Borg, W. R., & White, K. R. (1993). *Measurement and evaluation in the schools*. White Plains, NY: Longman.

Wu Horng-Jyh, P. (2010). Towards the preservation of web records: A case study of the capture, arrangement and description of a professional seminar eLearning space. *Archivi, 4*(1), 65–93.

WWF. (n.d.). *WWF international communications department. Programme/project communications strategy template.* Retrieved January 9, 2012, from http://assets.panda.org/.../wwf_communications_strategy_template__t_.doc

Xiang, Z., & Gretzel, U. (2010). Role of social media in online travel information search. *Tourism Management, 31*, 179–188. doi:10.1016/j.tourman.2009.02.016

Yang, S.-H. (2009). Using blogs to enhance critical reflection and community of practice. *Journal of Educational Technology & Society, 12*(2), 11–21.

Yin, R. K. [1984](2005). *Studiul de caz. Designul, colectarea şi analiza datelor*. Iaşi: Polirom.

Yin, R. K. (1994). *Case study research: Design and methods*. Thousand Oaks, CA: Sage Publications.

Yoo, K.-H., & Gretzel, U. (2010). Influence of personality on travel-related consumer-generated media creation. *Computers in Human Behavior, 27*(2), 609–621. doi:10.1016/j.chb.2010.05.002

Young, J. (2008, August 18). When professors create social networks for classes, some students see a "creepy treehouse". *The Chronicle of Higher Education*. Retrieved January 10, 2012, from http://chronicle.com/wiredcampus/article/3251/when-professors-create-social-networks-for-classes-some-students-see-a-creepy-treehouse

Young, J. R. (2008). When professors create social network for classes, some students see creepy treehouse. *The Chronicle of Higher Education*.

Yuh-Shyan, C., Tai-Chien, K., & Jang-Ping, S. (2005). Realizing outdoor independent learning with a butterfly-watching mobile learning system. *Journal of Internet Technology*, *6*(1), 77–87.

Yuksel, P., Robin, B. R., & McNeil, S. (2011). *Educational uses of digital storytelling around the world*. Retrieved from http://digitalstorytelling.coe.uh.edu/survey/SITE_DigitalStorytelling.pdf

Zaman, M. (2010). Doctoral programs in the age of research 2.0. In Anandarajan, M. (Ed.), *E-research collaboration: Theory, techniques and challenges* (pp. 233–245). Springer. doi:10.1007/978-3-642-12257-6_14

Zanariah, J., Siti Rohana, O., & Norun Najjah, A. (2008). *Political discourse in Malaysian blogs*. Paper presented at the Seminar Politik Malaysia.

Zappavigna, M. (2011). Ambient affiliation: A linguistic perspective on Twitter. *New Society and Media*, *13*(5), 788–806. doi:10.1177/1461444810385097

Zerfass, A., Tench, R., Verhoeven, P., Vercic, D., & Moreno, A. (2009). *European Communication Monitor 2008. Trends in communication management and public relations – Results and implications.* Brussels, Belgium: EUPRERA. Retrieved 12th October, 2009, from www.communicationmonitor.eu

Zerfass, A., Verhoeven, P., Tench, R., Moreno, A., & Verčič, D. (2011). *European Communication Monitor 2011: Empirical insights into strategic communication in Europe- Results of an empirical survey in 43 countries (Chart Version).* Brussels, Belgium: EACD, EUPRERA. Retrieved December 10, 2011 from www.communicationmonitor.eu

Ziegler, S. (2007). The (mis)education of Generation M. *Learning, Media and Technology*, *32*(1), 69–81. doi:10.1080/17439880601141302

Zoch, L. M., Collins, E. L., Sisco, H. F., & Supa, D. H. (2008). Empowering the activist: Using framing devices on activist organizations' web sites. *Public Relations Review*, *34*(4), 351–358. doi:10.1016/j.pubrev.2008.07.005

About the Contributors

Bogdan Pătruț is Associate Professor in Computer Science at Vasile Alecsandri University of Bacău, Romania, with a Ph D in Computer Science and a Ph D in Accounting. His domains of interest/ research are multi-agent systems and computer science applied in social and political sciences. He published and edited more than 25 books on programming, algorithms, artificial intelligence, and interactive education. He is also the editor-in-chief of *BRAIN: Broad Research in Artificial Intelligence and Neuroscience*, and software developer in EduSoft company.

Monica Pătruț is Senior Lecturer in Political Science at Vasile Alecsandri University of Bacău, Romania. Her domains of research are political communication and computer science applied in social and political sciences. She is member of the editorial advisory board of *BRAND: Broad Research in Accounting, Negotiation, and Distribution*. She published several academic books on applying computer science in educational, social and political topics, and papers in international journals like *Public Relations Review, Journal of Media Research*.

Camelia Cmeciu is an Associate Professor in the Department of Communication Studies at the Danubius University of Galați, Romania. Her research interests cover semiotics, organizational, and political communication, advertising discourse, and linguistics. Camelia is the author of *Strategii persuasive în discursul politic (Persuasive Strategies in Political Discourse*, 2005, Universitas XXI, Iași, Romania) and *Semiotici textuale (Textual Semiotics*, 2011, Institutul European, Iași, Romania). She is the editor-in-chief of the journal *Styles of Communication*. Her work on social semiotics, organizational discourse and political discourse appears in academic journals like *Semiotica, Public Relations Review, International Journal of Humanities and Social Science, European Legacy: Towards New Paradigms*, and *Journal of Media Studies*.

* * *

Ana Adi is a Lecturer in Marketing and Corporate Communications in the Media School of Bournemouth University where she delivers courses related to emerging media and digital communication. Before joining BU she worked in Romania, Belgium, USA, and Bahrain. Ana has a background in Public Relations, Strategic Communication, Management and Business Communication. She obtained her degrees from in Romania, the United States and Scotland. Ana is also a Public Relations Consultant specialising in social media strategies and training for small and medium companies. She has served American and European clients, both from the profit and the non-profit sector including Netlog from

Belgium, Help Our World from Brazil, Coca-Cola in Romania, and Deloitte in the USA. She is also an Advisory Board member of the Social Media Global Education Connection Project (SMGECP), an education initiative of the Social Media Club (founded by Chris Heuer) focused on improving the quality of Social Media education in universities and empowering its community of Social Media professors.

Derek E. Baird, M.A., B.A. Brigham Young University, M.A. Pepperdine University, is an Educational Technologist and Digital Media Strategist specializing in the design of multi-platform experiences focused on kids, learning, and digital media. He is currently Director, Consumer Product Management at Disney Interactive. Recently he partnered with Facebook to co-author, Facebook for Educators (http://facebookforeducators.org/educators-guide), the official guide to help teachers learn how to integrate Facebook into their classroom. Derek has published articles on education technology, social media and online communities in several publications, including: *Campus-Wide Information Systems, The Journal of Education Technology Systems, Ypulse.com,* and *Didactics World*. He has also presented at educational technology events including the National Science Digital Library (NSDL) Conference, Anti-Defamation League (ADL) Conference on Cyberbullying and American Federation of Teachers (AFT) Technology Conference. Derek received his M.A. in Education Technology from the Graduate School of Education and Psychology (GSEP) at Pepperdine University and holds Masters Certificates in both Project Management (University of Utah) & Online Digital Strategies (University of San Francisco).

Mihai Deac has been an Assistant Teacher at the department of Communication, Public Relations, and Advertising, Babes-Bolyai University, Cluj-Napoca, ever since 2007, when he graduated with a Master's Degree from the Advertising program. In 2012, he obtained his PhD title in Sociology, with a thesis on the social representations of families in Romanian advertising. His research interests include: the use and effects of product placements, advertising and culture, social representations in advertising, online communication and the use of ITC in academic settings. His interest in the use of ITC in the educational process stems from the fact that Mihai has created and used an academic blog for the past two years. He is the creator and administrator of blogdeseminar.wordpress.com and co-creator of crpedia.com.

Maria-Jesus Diaz-Gonzalez holds a PhD in Communication (University of Navarra) and a Master Degree in Education and New Technologies e-Learning (Universitat Oberta de Catalunya UOC). She is now a Lecturer at the School of Communication Sciences at the Universidad A Coruña. She had previously taught at the School of Communication at several Spanish universities, Universidad de Navarra and IE University, among others. Her main teaching subjects are Media Economics and Management of Cultural Industries. From 2008 she has been using Internet and e-Learning methodologies in her teaching. She is part of a research group at Instituto de la Comunicación, at Universidad Autónoma de Barcelona (InComm UAB) and she has a long standing research experience in university-business collaboration projects developed at Universidad de Navarra and IE University.

Luciana Duranti is Chair of the Archival Studies Master's and Doctoral programs at the School of Library, Archival and Information Studies of the University of British Columbia, and a Professor of archival theory, diplomatics, and the management of digital records. She is also Affiliate Full Professor of the iSchool of the University of Washington. Dr. Duranti is Project-Director of InterPARES, the largest research project on the long-term preservation of authentic electronic records; Principal Investigator in three other related projects: "Digital Records Forensics," "Universities Institutional Repositories: Copyright and Preservation," and "Records in the Cloud," and Co-investigator in the "The Law of Evidence in the Digital Environment" project. She is a member of the UNESCO International Advisory Committee of the Memory of the World Program; and has been honored with several research prizes, such as the Emmett Leahy Award, the Government of British Columbia Innovation Council Award; the Killam Research Prize; the Jacob Biely Research Prize, and the ARMA Foundation Award for Academic Excellence.

Martin Ebner is currently head of the Department for Social Learning at Graz University of Technology and therefore responsible for all university wide e-learning activities. He is an Associate Professor of Media Informatics and works also at the Institute for Information System Computer Media as Senior Researcher. His research focuses strongly on e-learning, mobile learning, learning analytics, social media, and the usage of Web 2.0 technologies for teaching and learning. Martin gives a number of lectures in this area as well as workshops and talks at international conferences.

Manuela Epure is a Professor at the Faculty of Marketing and International Business, Spiru Haret University, Romania, with 22 years of academic career. She has become in 2007 a full member of Chartered Institute of Marketing, UK, and a full member of Academy of Marketing, UK and elected in 2009 as Vice-president of the Alliance of Central-Eastern European Universities. Author and co-author of 11 textbooks, 6 distance learning course materials and more than 32 articles in Romanian and foreign scientific journals, getting involved in two EU COST research networks, being rewarded in 2004 with the second prize for special merits in education by the Romanian President.

Miikka Eriksson is a Post-Doctoral researcher in the Centre for Media Pedagogy at University of Lapland (Finland). He received his MS and PhD degrees in Biology from the University of Joensuu (Finland) in 2003 and 2007, respectively. Since his graduation he has also been working as a teacher in comprehensive and secondary school and as a researcher at the Finnish Forest Research Institute. In the educational context he has previously studied the use of laptops in higher education. His current research interests include the use of mobile technologies and social media tools in educational context.

Antonella Esposito has been an e-learning practitioner since 1996. She led the CTU (E-learning university center) of the University of Milan for seven years. Currently she is a PhD candidate in the E-learning program, Open University of Catalonia (UOC), working on a project focusing on doctoral e-researchers and new forms of research apprenticeship. In 2011 she was awarded the MRes in Educational and Social Research (Institute of Education, University of London), by submitting a dissertation on the interplay of digital scholarship and open scholarship practices of researchers in an Italian university. Her main research interests refer to social media in higher education, research ethics in online settings, issues related to emerging forms of academic scholarship and innovation in doctoral pedagogy. Among the most recent and forthcoming publications there are book chapters such as "Social media e didattica universitaria: tensioni e casi studio nel panorama internazionale."

Mercedes Fisher, PhD, is currently Associate Dean Business and Information Technology at Milwaukee Area Technical College. Her expertise lies in the intelligent use of technology for learning and development, designing collaborative learning models in Web-based environments, and project-based learning. In March 2002, Fisher was named Fulbright Senior Specialist Scholar by the Council for International Exchange of Scholars, a position she held for five years. Recently, she has worked with grants from the Bureau of Justice Assistance, Office of Justice Programs, U.S. Department of Justice, Microsoft Corporation, the U.S. Department of Education, Technology Literacy Challenge, and the Wisconsin Department of Public Instruction. In 1997, she was selected as an International Group Study Exchange Team Member to study the development of online teaching and learning resources in Denmark and Germany. In January 2004 she published "Designing Courses and Teaching on the Web: A 'How to' Guide to Proven, Innovative Strategies."

Nadia Florea has been a Lecturer at the Department of Teacher Training, *Spiru Haret* University in Bucharest, since 2000, with a PhD in Education (2006). Published works: "Pedagogy. Initial training for the teaching career" (Eds., 2008), "Teaching specialty. Applications to economic school disciplines" (2010), "Recovery assessments of educational achievement to improve teaching" (2010). Also, she signed articles in the press for improvement specialist teachers (e.g., *Tribune Education*, *Journal of Science Education*) and the volumes of recognized national and international scientific ("Science and Technology in the Context of Sustainable Development", 2008; The 4th International Conference EduWorld 2010, "Education Facing Contemporary World Issues"; The 7th International Scientific Conference "eLearning and Software for Education", 2011).

David Fonseca was born in Barcelona, Spain, 21/08/1973. He has earned Technical Telecommunication Engineer (Ramon LLull University -URL-, Barcelona, Spain, 1998), Degree of Audiovisual Communication (Open University of Catalonia –UOC-, Spain, 2006), Master's of Science (URL, Barcelona, Spain, 2007), and finally, he presented his PhD Thesis title: "User's Emotional Evaluation of the Architectural Imagery Experience according to the Visual Environment" (URL, Barcelona, Spain 2011). As a member of the research group Media Technologies Department (DTM) of La Salle (2005-2011), He has focused his research on HCI projects. He is a Main Educational Tutor of Architecture Degree La Salle (Barcelona, Spain), and with publications in: User Experiences and differences in viewing architectural images with various interfaces in *International Journal of Creative Interfaces and Computer Graphics* (IJCICG, 2011); book chapter: Multimedia Edutainment: Designing Professional Profiles, in Multimedia in Education, Adaptative Learning and Testing (Singapore, World Scientific Publishing, 2010); and other international Latin journals as well as chapter books.

Almudena González Del Valle Brena has been teaching in the field of Marketing, Communications, and Media regulation in several Spanish and British universities for the past decade. She is now teaching online for Universidad Internacional de la Rioja (UNIR), Instituto de Posgrado (IEP) and Bureau Veritas (BVBS), in Spain. She holds a Ph. D. in Communications (University of Westminster), a M.A. in Communications (The Annenberg School for Communication, U. of Pennsylvania) and is a Business Administration graduate from ICADE (Universidad Pontificia Comillas). She worked in media marketing both in Spain and in Italy, at Publiespaña S. A. Other professional experience includes free-lance research for the Advertising Association in the UK, which resulted in the publication of a report on children's advertising regulation in the EU. Her research focuses on social media and mass media, CSR communication and European media policy and advertising laws for television.

Olena Goroshko is Professor of Linguistics and Sociology of Communication, chairperson of Cross-Cultural Communication and Modern Languages Department at National technical University "Kharkiv Polytechnic Institute" (Ukraine). Goroshko's professional interests cover psycho-sociolinguistics, gender and Internet studies, CMC, e-learning 2.0. She is the author of many articles and four books on sociolinguistics, gender and Computer-Mediated Communication. Goroshko's works appeared in *The Handbook of Research on Virtual Workplaces and the New Nature of Business Practices, Russian Cyberspace Journal,* Yezyk@multimedia, *Linguistica Computizionale, Gendered Transformations in New Media* and *the Wiener Slawistischer Almanach,* among others. She teaches MA courses in Sociology of Internet, Sociology of Mass Communication, Gender Studies. She participates in a number of international projects as Oxford Colleges Hospitality Scheme, Joint Russian - German Project "Russian Cyberspace" (Developer of Distance Learning Module and Researcher on Gendered Facets of RuNet) sponsored by Volksvagen Foundation (Germany), etc.

Gabriela Grosseck is Associate Professor in the Department of Psychology at the West University of Timisoara, Romania. She received her PhD in 2006 with a thesis on marketing on Internet. She has particular expertise in ICT in education (teaching, learning and researching), a solid experience in students'/teachers' training both f2f and online environments. Her research interests cover main aspects of Web 2.0 tools and technologies in education, collaborative aspects and proper use of social media (by teachers, students, researchers, policy makers and other educational actors). She is also an editor-in-chief of *Romanian Journal of Social Informatics,* an author of many articles in the field of e-learning 2.0, a speaker at different international events, a workshop organizer and a member of editorial committees (journals and conferences).

Norsiah Abdul Hamid is a Senior Lecturer at the Department of Multimedia Technology, School of Multimedia Technology and Communication, Universiti Utara Malaysia (UUM). She holds a PhD in Information Science from Universiti Kebangsaan Malaysia, a Master of Science in Communications Studies from the University of Leeds, United Kingdom and a Bachelor of Information Technology from UUM. Her focus areas of teaching, supervision, research, and publications are the impact of ICT and media on society, information society and knowledge, and studies on women and gender. Her current research projects include the development of social media model for young women and girls, as well as publication of books related to social media in ASEAN member countries.

Lori B. Holcomb is an Assistant Professor of Instructional Technology in the department of Curriculum, Instruction, and Counselor Education at North Carolina University. Dr. Holcomb earned her doctoral degree from the University of Connecticut in Cognition and Instruction with an emphasis in Learning Technologies. Her research emphasis is governed by the integration of technology into teaching and learning. Dr. Holcomb has focused her research on distance education and emerging technologies. Her research in these areas provides empirical support that expands our understanding of emerging technologies and how they can be utilized to support learning and communication in distance education courses.

Charlotte Holland is Chair of Undergraduate Studies in the School of Education Studies at Dublin City University. She actively lectures, undertakes research and publishes at national and European levels in the areas of Information and Communications Technologies, Education for Sustainability, curriculum development and values-based learning. She is principal investigator within an EU-level project that is currently re-orienting University curricula across the EU and Middle East to address sustainability. She has also contributed to the development of an online Master's in ICT-enabled Education for Sustainable Development, in partnership with six European universities, that will be launched in 2012 as part of an Erasmus initiative.

Carmen Holotescu teaches for the Computer Science Department of Politehnica University of Timisoara, Romania, having a large experience in using Social Media / Web2.0 technologies in education and collaboration. She has participated in many European projects, and has written papers and books/ebooks related to eLearning, Web2.0 technologies, teacher training. Carmen is also the Director of Timsoft, a company specialized in eLearning and mobile applications, and a certified online instructor for University of Maryland University College, USA since 2001.

Ioan Hosu has been a Lecturer at the department of Communication, Public Relations, and Advertising, Babes-Bolyai University, Cluj-Napoca, ever since 2004. In 2012, he became director of the department. He has obtained a PhD title in Sociology, with a thesis on the mobilization of resources for collective action. His vast field research experience includes doing work as a community facilitator, a regional development strategy builder, as well as an active researcher in image and client satisfaction studies. Academically, his interests cover the areas of sociology of the media, internal communication in institutions, political communication, research methodology, and others. He is currently the project manager for a joint French-Romanian research team for the study of the use of ITC in organizations.

Mohd Sobhi Ishak received his Bachelor's in Information Technology (Hons.) in 1996 from Universiti Utara Malaysia (UUM, Northern University of Malaysia), his Master's of Science in Communication Technology in 2004, and his Ph.D degree in Mass Communication from Putra University, Malaysia in 2012. He is currently a Senior Lecturer in the Department of Multimedia Technology, School of Multimedia Technology and Communication, College of Arts and Sciences, UUM. Dr. Mohd Sobhi has been involved in a few fundamental grant and long-term research grants at national level. His research focus is on credibility and social media. His main research interests are the relatedness of media with Islam, society, and politic. He is also interested in construct development from an Islamic perspective, and applying statistical analysis of Structural Equation Modeling (SEM) in developing new theory.

Syamsul Anuar Ismail is a Senior Lecturer at the Department of Multimedia Technology, School of Multimedia Technology and Communication, Northern University of Malaysia Universiti Utara Malaysia (UUM). He holds a Master of Science in Communication Technology from Putra University, Malaysia (2003), and a Bachelor's of Information Technology from Universiti Utara Malaysia (1999). He has been involved in various research projects and publications in university and national levels. His current research focuses on credibility and social media. His main research interests are media and politics, and computer-mediated communication.

Miriam Judge is Program Chair of the BSc in Multimedia Studies in the School of Communications at Dublin City University (DCU), Ireland. In addition to lecturing on both the Masters and undergraduate programmes in multimedia Dr Judge regularly undertakes research in the area of ICT in Education. She has managed a number of national research and evaluation projects in this field on behalf of the National

Centre for Technology in Education, the Department of Education and Science and IBM Ireland. These include the Wired for Learning Project (2001-2003), the Dundalk Learning Network (2003- 2004), the Interactive Whiteboard Project (2005-2007) and the Hermes Thin Client Project (2004-2009). More recently, Dr. Judge has become active in the area of Education for Sustainable Development (ESD) and is currently involved in two EU projects in this area along with partner universities in Europe and the Middle East.

Matthew J. Kruger-Ross completed his BS in Middle Grades Education from NC State University in May 2005. Matthew stepped into the classroom at an independent Quaker school called Carolina Friends School in Durham, North Carolina where he taught math, music, and technology in the middle school. In May 2009, he chose to leave CFS and pursue advanced degrees in Educational Technology, Philosophy, and Critical Studies. In May 2012, Matthew completed his Masters of Science in Instructional Technology at NC State University in Raleigh, North Carolina. He is currently a Doctoral student in the Curriculum Theory & Implementation: Philosophy of Education program in the Faculty of Education at Simon Fraser University. His research interests include educational technology, Web-based tools and learning, educational philosophy, transformative learning, and critical studies.

Isidro Navarro was born in Barcelona, Spain, 05/05/1971. He is an Architect by the ETSAB-UPC, Barcelona Tech. Univ. 1999. He teaches Architectural Representation and Visual Communication in the ETSAB-UPC. He is a Doctoral student in application of new technologies in representation of architecture projects for disabled people. He has organized several courses in the field of augmented reality and has focused his research on teaching methodologies with users with disabilities experience. He is Assistant Professor in the Department of Architectural Graphic Expression II, ETAB-UPC and Assistant Professor in the Architectural department and Main Educational Tutor of Architecture Degree La Salle (Barcelona, Spain). Also he is Director of Master in Sustainable Architecture and Efficiency Energy and Coordinator in Postgraduate Course in Environment and Architecture and Sustainable Urbanism in Business Engineering School of La Salle, Barcelona. He is Coordinator of the Master of Integral Management of Building in the School of Architecture La Salle, Barcelona.

Laura Păuleț-Crăiniceanu is a PhD candidate in Education Sciences at "Alexandru Ioan Cuza" University of Iaşi, Romania. She holds a MSc degree in Social Psychology and a BA degree in Journalism and Communication Sciences. She works as a Teaching Assistant at the Department of Journalism and Communication Sciences at the same university, where she delivers courses and seminars in Media Techniques, Current Trends in Print and Online Media, Interactive Media and Management of Media Institutions. She is the director of a students' magazine where she coordinates a team of journalism students in writing and editing press articles and designing newspaper pages. Her research interests address the impact of new technologies and of Social Media communication tools on education and media.

Francesc Pumarola is an expert in Internet issues with over 14 years of work experience in the field. He is Director at *Gugleando* (agency specializing in digital marketing) and academic director of the Master Degree in Social Media and Digital Marketing at IFFE Business School (http://www.iffe. es). He also writes a blog about these issues: *Gugleando por la red* (http://www.gugleando.com/blog/). From 2006 to November 2011 he was Head of Internet Area at *La Voz de Galicia* (newspaper) where he managed Internet and developed corporate websites. He also implemented social media strategy. From May 2001 to 2006 he was responsible of the digital editions at *Corporación Voz de Galicia: La Voz de Galicia, Diario de León,* and *Diario 16*. He was then commissioned to establish the digital department team and structure.

Natalia Quintas-Froufe is Advertising and Public Relations graduate and holds a Ph.D from Universidad de Vigo. She was Junior Lecturer at Universidad de Alicante from 2008 to 2010, lecturing "The Language of Advertising." She has been Lecturer at Universidad da Coruña since 2010, teaching Audiovisual Advertising and Audience Analysis. At present, her teaching methods integrate social media and Internet technology.

Ernesto Redondo was born in Girona, Spain 15/05/1957. He is Architect by the ETSAB-UPC, Barcelona Tech Univ. 1981. He earned Dr. Arch 1992., Ph.D. Thesis Award extraordinary UPC 1994, Professor TU 1993. He teaches Architectural Representation in ETSAB-UPC. He is Former Director Dept., EGAI (1994-2000), Vice Dean ETSAB, Director Research Group MSVA - Modeling and Visual Simulation in Architecture, and Doctorate Program. Coord. Visual Communication in Architecture and Design. (2009-2012). He has focused his research in educational research in architectural representation. He is co-author: Delgado, M. Redondo E. Freehand Drawing for Architects an Interior Designers, NY, USA. WW Norton & C., 2005 (translated 8 edi.) and two book chapters in Digital Information and Communication Technology and Its Applications. *Communications in Computer and Information Science, 2011, 166, 3.* Dr. Redondo is member of the scientific committee of SIGRADI: 2010-2011, IEEE2011 International Conference on Multimedia. DICTAP2011 International Conference on Digital Information and Communication Technology and its Applications. Editorial member of the Journal: *Arquitetura Revista* (ISSN 1808-5741).

Albert Sánchez was born in Barcelona, Spain, 14/01/1973. He has been or earned Architect by the ETSAV-UPC, Barcelona Tech. Univ. 1999, Postgraduate Course in project execution, (U.P.C-Sert School, Barcelona 2001), Postgraduate Course in Urban Management, (U.A.B-APCE, Barcelona, 2005), Official Master in Urban Management and Valuation, by Center of Land Policy and Valuations (UPC Barcelona Tech, Barcelona, 2010). He is a Doctoral student in mobile augmented reality, focused on applications in the field of architecture, urbanism, and building construction. He is Assistant Professor in the Building Construction School in Barcelona (EPSEB), UPC Barcelona Tech, since 2007. He is member of the research group of building and heritage in the Department of Architectural Graphic Expression II, and has organized several courses and teaching experiences in the field of augmented reality.

Sónia Pedro Sebastião is Assistant Professor at the Institute of Social and Political Science (ISCSP - UTL), teaching Cultural Studies, Media Studies and Public Relations courses since the year 2001. She has published her Master thesis about the Swiss Political System (2005) in Portugal, her PhD thesis about the Portuguese identity and mythology (forthcoming); a textbook of Public Relations theory and practice (*Comunicação Estratégica – As Relações Públicas* - 2009), and a book about Contemporary Culture, contributes to cultural, media, and digital studies (2012). Her main interests are related with cultural identities and the influence of culture in political constructions and speeches, intercultural business practices and the relation between tradition and technology in cultural sociology, politics, and public relations.

Violeta Maria Şerbu is currently working as a Preparatory Teacher of Pedagogy at the Teachers Training Department of The Bucharest Academy of Economic Studies. Her ten years professional experience consists mainly in Education and Training. Her main professional project (since 2008) is that of developing an alternative model of higher education. She studied Educational Sciences, followed by a Bachelor's in Pedagogy, a Master's in Educational Management and Evaluation, and a PhD in Educational at The University of Bucharest. Her main research interests cover learning theories and educational models, sociology of higher education, the use of IT&C in education, et cetera.

Elizabeth Shaffer is a Doctoral student at the School of Library, Archival, and Information Studies of the University of British Columbia from which she received a Master's of Archival Studies degree in 2009. She is a researcher on the InterPARES (International Research on Permanent Authentic Records in Electronic Systems) 3, the "University Institutional Repositories Copyright and Long-Term Preservation," "Records Management and Peer-Reviewed Journals: An Assessment," and "Tweeting the Government: e-Government" research projects. Her dissertation research focuses on record creation in social media/networking environments and its implications for archival theory, recordkeeping and information policy. She has presented at national and international conferences on issues related to digital preservation and copyright, web 2.0, social networking, and policy development.

Laurenţiu Şoitu, PhD, is Professor at the Faculty of Psychology and Education Sciences, "Alexandru Ioan Cuza" University of Iaşi, Romania. He is teaching special courses in the organization of scientific research and performs teaching activity with undergraduate, MA, and Doctoral students. Laurenţiu Şoitu is involved in: coordination of training activities for teachers in higher institutions; coordination of work of first degree teacher candidates, coordination of assessment activities of skills acquired through formal, non-formal, and informal education. Among his areas of competences are educational communication, strategies of communication in adult education, mass-media and cultural integration, and conflict mediation.

Pauliina Tuomi, Master of Arts, is a PhD student in Digital Culture at the University of Turku and works currently as a researcher at the Tampere University of Technology. Her Doctoral thesis concentrates on interactive TV and it is set to define the different characteristic elements of participatory and intermedial TV culture in the 21st century. Her research interests include iTV-entertainment, participatory media culture, and iTV-hosting & mediated communication.

Ruxandra Vasilescu is Associate Professor PhD, Faculty of Letters, Spiru Haret University, Romania, PhD in Education. Scientific publications: author of 3 books and academic courses, 2 explanatory dictionaries, 2 novels, and an essay translated and published by Romanian publishing houses, over 20 articles in Romanian and international reviews, including ISI Thomsons Journals. She is Co-author of a chapter, *E-learning challenges in the European knowledge-based society,* in vol. *Developing and Utilizing E-Learning Applications*, published by IGI Global USA in 2010. Research competency includes: education (testing and evaluation, in particular), applied linguistics (semiotics, ESP), and translation studies.

Hanna Vuojärvi is a researcher in the Centre for Media Pedagogy at the University of Lapland (Finland), where she also received her Master's degree in Education in 2003. Since graduation, she has worked as a Lecturer of Information Technology, Project Manager, and Researcher at the same university. Her PhD studies and recent research interests include the use of mobile technologies in vocational tourism education and in the creation of and learning in personal learning environments in higher education.

Theresa Renee White is an Assistant Professor in the Pan African Studies Department at California State University, Northridge. Her research interests include Film Criticism; Media Representations; New Media; Black Sexuality/Masculinity; Obesity and Health Disparities for Minority Populations. Her publications include Missy "Misdemeanor" Elliot and Nicki Minaj: Fashionistin' Black Female Sexuality in Hip Hop Culture---Girl Power of Overpowered? *Journal of Black Studies: Special Issue--Popular Culture* (forthcoming) and Visual Literacy and Cultural Production: Examining Black Masculinity through Community Engagement, *Journal of Visual Literacy* (forthcoming). She has co-authored Deconstructing ideological notions of otherness in *Far from Heaven. Interactions: Studies in Communication and culture, 1(3),* 391-409 and *Parental Support and Psychological Control in Relation to African* American College Students' Self-Esteem. *Journal of Black Studies* (forthcoming). She holds a PhD from UCLA in Education, Cultural Studies; MA in African American Studies/Critical Studies in Film & Television; B.A. in Communications and Public Relations at the University of Southern California (USC).

Siti Syamsul Nurin Mohmad Yazam is a Lecturer at the School of Multimedia Technology and Communication, College of Arts and Sciences, Universiti Utara Malaysia. She holds a Bachelor Degree in Information Technology from Universiti Utara Malaysia and Master of Arts (MA) in Advertising from RMIT University, Melbourne, Australia. At present, she teaches advertising courses for undergraduate programs. Her fields of interest are advertising, culture and media.

Pavel Zemliansky is an Associate Professor in the Department of Writing and Rhetoric at the University of Central Florida where he also directs UCF's Writing across the Curriculum Program. His research focuses on professional writing and rhetoric in international contexts and on writing across the curriculum. His work has appeared in the journals *IEEE Transactions on Professional Communication, Kairos, Programmatic Perspectives*, and others. He has also published books and book chapters on the theory and pedagogy of writing instruction, technical communication, and on digital media. Dr. Zemliansky recently co-edited, with Constance Kampf of the University of Aarhus, Denmark, a special issue of *IEEE Transactions on Professional Communication* dedicated to the practice of technical communication outside of the US. He regularly collaborates on research and teaching projects with colleagues in other countries.

Index